MEDICAL PROOF

OF

SOCIAL SECURITY DISABILITY

By

DAVID A. MORTON III, M.D.

Little Rock, Arkansas

ST. PAUL, MINN.

WEST PUBLISHING CO.

1983

610 Opperman Drive
P.O. Box 64526
St. Paul, MN 55164-0526

Printed in the United States of America

Library of Congress Cataloging in Publication Data

Morton, David A., 1945-
Medical proof of Social Security disability

Includes index.
1. Insurance, Disability—Law and legislation—United States. 2. Social security—Law and legislation—United States. 3. Medical jurisprudence—United States.
I. Title. [DNLM: 1. Disability evaluation. 2. Social security—United States. W 925 M889m]
KF3649.M67 1983 344.73'023 83-16800
347.30423

ISBN 0-314-72082-0

Morton—Med.Proof of Soc.Sec.Disab.
2nd Reprint—1992

TO MY DARLIN' LYDIA

*

INTRODUCTION

Each year, millions of people apply for S.S. Disability benefits, and the amounts paid total many billions of dollars annually. At the present time, about thirty percent of the applications result in allowance of benefits, although this number may change from year to year. Of course, this means that about seventy percent of applications are denied.

Despite the enormous size and expense of the S.S. Disability system, very few applicants really understand how decisions are reached in their particular cases. Such people often turn to their treating doctors for help, asking that the doctor explain to S.S. Disability why they are disabled. Unfortunately, only a relative handful of doctors in the U.S. know anything helpful about the complex medical and administrative regulations that control S.S. Disability. In the opinion of the author, this is also true of attorneys that the applicant may hire to argue his case.

This book hopes to render a social service to potential applicants, by offering some practical insight into the S.S. Disability system. It could also be of great benefit to physicians and attorneys who are attempting to help their patients or clients obtain disability benefits. The medical explanations have been necessarily simplified to help the reader who is not a doctor. Additionally, medical terms are explained as they occur in the text. If the reader is a physician, he can still learn a great deal about *how* medical information is evaluated by S.S. Disability. Without this knowledge, the most learned doctor in the country is at a very great disadvantage in trying to help his patients obtain disability benefits. Attorneys face the same disadvantage. What is academic knowledge in a book of regulations, and at least somewhat a matter of opinion, is of little use when facing the everyday practical operations of the giant S.S. Disability system. Such operations are *interpretations* of regulations in many instances, and can only be found in federal documents within S.S. Disability itself. In fact, there are so many such policies that it is highly doubtful that they have all been written down. This is not to deceive the public—it is because the S.S. Disability system is so vast and complex.

This book is for reference, in some ways like an encyclopedia. It is not meant to be read straight through, from cover to cover, like a novel (see the section on "How To Use This Book"). Some readers might find that the material is a little difficult to understand at first glance; they may need to read the parts that interest them several times, but their effort will be well repaid. This book is meant to be a practical tool for anyone interested in S.S. Disability, and too great an oversimplification would ruin its practical value.

Amazingly few people are even aware of the definition of disability under Social Security. The definition of S.S. Disability as defined in law is as follows:

> "The inability to engage in any substantial gainful activity by reason of any medically determinable physical or mental impairment which can be expected to result in death or which has lasted or can be expected to last for a continuous period of not less than 12 months."

It is this core definition of disability that is the basis for all further law, interpretations, or policies concerning disability cases. It should be read carefully, several times if necessary, until it is fully understood. Probably the most important part of the definition is that which deals with the *duration* of a medical impairment. S.S. Disability is meant for people with severe, chronic diseases that are not expected to improve much with time. No illness or injury that can be effectively treated in less than a year can qualify for disability. The only exception to the duration requirement is in certain cases of legal blindness. For everyone else, it is impossible to get disability benefits without an impairment that has lasted or is expected to last 12 months. For example, pregnancy never lasts 12 months, and applications for disability because of pregnancy are doomed to be denied, as is other illness or injury that won't last 12 months.

The most important *medical* rules that S.S. Disability uses in evaluating impairments are called *Listings.* By means of the Listings, all claimants get as equal a treatment under the law as possible. Everyone working in S.S. Disability is bound to stay within the rules of the Listings, despite any particular feelings or prejudices that they may have as individuals. Every attempt is made to base decisions on medical information that is fact, rather than opinion. There are stringent controls, to ensure that this is true. Decisions regarding particular cases are reviewed at the level of the State agency making them. They are also reviewed at several other levels of government. There are too many cases for each one to be reviewed for accuracy, but a certain percentage is picked at random. In short, no-one working in S.S. Disability is permitted to allow or deny a case, based only on their personal feelings or opinions.

It should be noted that attempts to "apply pressure" on S.S. Disability are useless. S.S. Disability does not make decisions based on what a claimant's lawyer, family members, doctors, or politicians demand. If S.S. Disability did respond to such pressure, equal treatment under the law would not be possible. Some successful applicants may think that they were awarded benefits, because of the influence of people they think are important and powerful. Nothing could be farther from the truth, as least in the experience of the author. If disability benefits are given, it is only because the applicant is legally qualified to receive them.

It was stated above that this book was written to fulfill a social service to potential disability applicants. That is true, but this book was *not* written to "take sides", either with potential applicants or with the S. S. Disability system. Every attempt has been made to be as accurate as possible without distortion of the facts, in the available space of this book. On the other hand, nothing has been intentionally withheld which might benefit a potential applicant. It has been said that the Social Security system is the largest and most expensive bureacracy in the history of the world. Therefore, it is certainly worthy of attention—especially for those potential disability applicants who have paid money into Social Security, but who are no longer able to work and need financial assistance.

It should be pointed out that in the last several years there has been considerable public outcry against medical and administrative requirements of Social Security Disability that are perceived as too harsh. This has entangled doctors, lawyers, claimants, politicians, states, courts, and Social Security in numerous conflicts, both personal and legal. Even the Executive, Judicial, and Legislative branches of the federal government have different perspectives on Social Security Disability. Congress has held extensive hearings and investigations of Social Security Disability, in an attempt to provide a body of regulatory law that will soften perceived injustices. In addition, the Social Security Administration is internally reviewing its regulatory policies regarding disability evaluations and requirements. However, since the final outcome of this upheaval is yet unknown, it cannot be reflected in the present work. Since Social Security administers its disability program through state governments, some states have taken actions to resist the federal government's disability policies at the level of the State Agencies, attempting to impose their own policies to at least some degree. The aim of the states has been to make it easier for their citizens to obtain and keep disability benefits. This book does not reflect the many variations of state involvement in the disability program policies. In some instances, it is too early to know what the reaction of the federal government will be to attempts by states to make it easier to qualify for benefits. Also, different states are approaching the problem in different ways. It would be impossible for the author to include these differences in all of their ramifications in the following book, but the reader should be aware that they exist and may modify the way the information in this book applies to actual cases in some circumstances.

Ideally, the same regulations and policies should be applied to claimants in all states and at all levels of appeal within the federal government, from the level of the State Agency to the administrative law judge to the Appeals Council to the federal courts. That is not the case at the present time, and that is why some state governments have found it necessary to take special actions attempting to protect the rights of their respective citizens. Only if Congress, the Social Security Administration, and the federal courts find reasonable and mutually consistent solutions to the difficult problems they face will the outcome be harmonious and just.

In summary, it must be emphasized that any interpretation or understanding of the content or meaning of what is written in this book is the sole responsibility of the reader.

DAVID A. MORTON III, M.D.

Little Rock, Arkansas
September, 1983

HOW TO USE THIS BOOK

1. Read the Introduction and Chapter 1. These sections contain general background information, definitions, and concepts necessary to use the rest of the book effectively.
2. Once the above important background information is obtained, the reader should follow the same sequence of reasoning that Social Security (S.S.) Disability itself uses, as follows:

   (a) What are the impairments that need to be investigated (arthritis, heart disease, lung disorders, etc.).

   (b) Determine whether each impairment Meets or Equals any Listing. This is done by referring to Chapter 2 or Chapter 3, which contain the Listings for adults and children. These are organized by categories of disease, and each Listing contains the exact wording of the federal documents from which they were obtained. Following each Listing, there is a discussion and explanation of the Listing, to help the reader understand both the medical terms used and the way S.S. Disability interprets and uses the Listing in question. This discussion in *not* taken word for word from federal documents; it is based both on federal documents controlling policy, as well as the author's experience with such policies.

   (c) In the case of children, failure to Meet or Equal will usually terminate evaluation of the case, and benefits will be denied. However, adults may still be allowed benefits for an impairment for vocational reasons. This based on age, education, work experience, and residual functional capacity ratings. To make this evaluation, the reader should first refer to Chapter 4 for a general introduction to the vocational disability rules. The reader should then try to determine if his impairment fits one of the common residual functional capacity ratings in Chapter 5. Once this is done, the vocational rule tables in Chapter 4 can be used to determine if the impairment in question would result in allowance of benefits on a vocational basis.

   (d) Finally, there are a number of Appendices that not only contain samples of the most important forms used by S.S. Disability, but also discussions of special subjects that might be of interest to the reader.

The more that the reader understands about the actual medical data related to his own impairment, the closer he can come to a reasonable opinion about his chances of obtaining disability benefits. How much access the reader can have to his own medical records from his treating doctor, or how much help that treating doctor would give the reader in understanding such records, is clearly a matter in which the author can offer little assistance in individual cases.

SUMMARY OF CONTENTS

*

TABLE OF CONTENTS

TABLE OF CONTENTS

APPENDICES

TABLE OF CONTENTS

MEDICAL PROOF

OF

SOCIAL SECURITY DISABILITY

*

CHAPTER 1

GENERAL FACTS ABOUT SOCIAL SECURITY DISABILITY

Table of Sections

---

§ 1.1 What Is Social Security Disability?

Social Security Disability was originally created to provide financial help to people with illnesses or injuries that prevent them from holding gainful employment. Social Security (S. S.) Disability benefits are given to people falling into one of two major legal categories. The first is the Social Security Disability Program. These are called *Title II* cases. The second category is the Supplemental Security Income Disability Program.

These are called *SSI* cases, *Title XVI* cases, or Welfare Disability. They all mean the same thing. The major difference is that Title II applicants are people who have worked and paid Social Security taxes, while Title XVI applicants are people who can receive disability benefits without ever having worked or paid Social Security taxes. Some people are qualified to receive both Title XVI and Title II benefits, though most are not. These are called *concurrent* claims. In other words, the fact that someone has paid Social Security taxes doesn't necessarily mean he can't get Title XVI benefits. On the other hand, people who have never paid such taxes can never get Title II benefits.

Benefits Payable to Children

Children can qualify for disability benefits, under either Title II or Title XVI laws. However, there is a difference in the privileges given. Children under Title XVI can apply for benefits at any age less than 18 years. Children under Title II can also receive benefits related to impairments they may have as a child, but they cannot actually apply for or receive such benefits, until they are 18 years old. In addition, children of a disabled parent can receive benefits, although they are not themselves disabled. Such benefits can be received up to age 18.

"Impairment" and "Disability" Distinguished

An important distinction must be made between the word *impairment* and the word *disability.* To S. S. Disability, an impairment only refers to the type of medical problems a person has. Two people might have exactly the same *impairment,* yet only one of them qualify for *disability. Disability* is a legal term, meaning that someone cannot engage in meaningful work with the impairment that he has. If an impairment Meets or Equals a Listing (see below), then the difference between the meaning of the two words is not very important—two different people with the same impairment that Meets or Equals a Listing will always both qualify for disability benefits. The difference becomes important, when a case is being evaluated for possible allowance for vocational reasons; then the same impairment in two different people could result in allowance of benefits for one and denial of benefits for the other. For example, a bank president following a heart attack that doesn't Meet or Equal a Listing might be able to go back to his desk job, while a man who has known only heavy labor might not be able to return to his work after a heart attack. A more detailed discussion of this difference can be found in Chapter 4 of this book, which deals with vocational disability.

Disability Duration Requirement

Under both Title II and Title XVI programs, the definitions of adult disability and blindness are essentially the same. As noted previously, the legal definition of disability means that a person cannot work, because of a physical or mental impairment that has lasted or is expected to last at least 12 months, or which is expected to result in death. The disability need not be permanent, but it *must* last a minimum of 12 months. The only exceptions are Title XVI blind applicants, who do not have to fulfill the duration requirement.

Income Requirement

In order to be eligible for benefits under Title II, the applicant's income must be less than $300 per month. Further details about the income requirement can be found in Appendix VIII. Title XVI applicants are eligible, if they meet certain "income & resources" requirements, which must not be too high. Other special rules determine which applicants are eligible to apply under both Title II and Title XVI.

Claim Procedure—Generally

Application for disability benefits is usually made at a Social Security District Office, where a determination is made concerning the person's eligibility to apply. If the applicant is eligible to apply, his case is then sent to a State agency (DDS) for further development and evaluation. (See "The Organization of Social Security Disability").

S. S. Disability refers to applicants as *claimants.* After leaving the District Office, the claimant's case goes to the DDS, where it is assigned to a *disability examiner.* The examiner has the major responsibility of developing the claimant's case, and in making the decision regarding disability benefits. The examiner must gather all important evidence in a case, both medical and administrative. This evidence must then be interpreted in terms of the laws and policies controlling disability decisions. Every DDS has a number of medical doctors who provide medical advice concerning impairments, in the more difficult cases. These doctors are called *medical consultants,* and they do *not* examine applicants. There are also other physicians who do examine applicants for S. S. Disability during what is called a "consultative examination", which may be either physical or mental. These doctors are also sometimes called medical consultants, but it is important to know that they are *not* the same as a DDS medical consultant and do *not* give advice to examiners. Unlike DDS medical consultants, they are neither asked nor trained to give such advice. Examiners use their own judgment, regarding when to ask for medical advice from a DDS medical consultant. Technically, DDS medical consultants offer advice only concerning impairments (medical data), and how such medical information fits with policies and regulations that involve medical data. The final decision regarding disability is a legal one, falling to examiners and their administrative superiors. Examiners and administrators can accept or reject the advice given by a DDS medical consultant. If such advice doesn't fit the medical policies of S. S. Disability, the examiner will not use it. DDS medical consultants must stick to the legal framework they work in, and avoid personal opinions and prejudices that would result in bad advice affecting the ultimate case decision.

Listings of Impairments

The first thing that an examiner tries to determine, after collecting adequate information, is whether or not a claimant's impairment fulfills one of the *Listings* of impairments. Listings are rules showing the necessary medical data required to qualify for disability benefits. There are separate Listings for children and adults, and they cover most common illnesses or injuries. In Chapters 2 and 3 of this book, the Listings are given, exactly as written in federal documents that examiners and DDS medical consultants must use. The rules set forth by the Listings cannot be violated by anyone working in a DDS, or at least they are not supposed to be. If an impairment *exactly* fulfills one of the Listings, then the impairment is said to *Meet* that Listing. Disability benefits would then be allowed. If the claimant has an impairment or impairments that do not Meet a Listing, he can still qualify by means of what is called an *Equal*. There are three ways an impairment can be said to qualify as an Equal:

1. There are actually a combination of impairments, none of which alone Meet any Listing, but which *taken together* are of equivalent severity to the intent of the Listings.

2. There is an impairment just as severe as one in a Listing, but the medical data proving that severity is different from that required by the Listing—although it shows the same thing. For example, the Listing for heart attacks requires abnormal EKG's (tracings of the heart's electrical activity) that show a heart attack has taken place. However, enzyme studies or special radioactive studies could be used to

prove that a heart attack occurred, even though the Listing doesn't mention them.

3. There is an impairment that isn't mentioned in any Listing, but which is just as severe as impairments given in the Listings. The Listings were designed to merely cover the most common impairments; they are by no means the only ones by which disability benefits can be obtained.

Equal decisions are made much less often by the DDS than Meet decisions. They require a great deal more judgment, and are more subjective.

If the claimant's impairment does not Meet or Equal any Listing, it is not necessarily denied. At this point, the examiner tries to determine what is called a *residual functional capacity* (RFC). This is S. S. Disability's best guess concerning what a particular claimant is still capable of doing physically and/or mentally. Once the RFC is determined, it is then analyzed in terms of the claimant's age, education, and work experience. If it appears unlikely that the claimant can return to work, then an allowance of disability benefits will be made. This is called a *vocational* allowance. Otherwise, the case will be denied. Vocational allowances usually only apply to adults (18 years or older). Children do not usually qualify for vocational allowances; they can obtain benefits in most cases only if they Meet or Equal a Listing.

Medically Determinable Impairment

To qualify for benefits under either Title II or Title XVI, an individual must have a medically determinable impairment. This means an impairment that can be demonstrated by a physical or mental examination, and/or by X-rays, laboratory tests, etc. Such abnormalities that can be objectively identified are called *signs*. *Symptoms* are a person's own private experience and may or may not be caused by a real physical or mental illness. A brain tumor can produce abnormalities which can be identified (e.g. abnormal reflexes), and are therefore signs. But a headache is a symptom that may or may not be caused by a brain tumor, so it can't be taken as proof of a brain tumor. It is more likely to be a tension headache. Symptoms cannot be accepted by S. S. Disability as proof of any impairment, unless those symptoms are backed up by signs that can be identified, or other objective evidence such as X-rays and laboratory tests. To do otherwise would allow everyone to establish their own qualifications for disability. Obviously, that won't work. Statements by the claimant (or anyone else), including his own description of his impairment, are insufficient to establish disability, unless such statements are backed up by objective data.

Medical Evidence

Under both Title II and Title XVI disability programs, medical evidence forms the backbone for the determination of disability. The existence of a disabling condition must be supported by a medical report, signed by a duly licensed physician. Such a report must contain the claimant's medical history, relating to the impairment or impairments that prevent him from working. The report must contain a description of a physical examination and such supporting tests and X-rays needed to determine the nature and severity of the claimant's physical problem, or a full psychiatric examination for impairments involving mental illness, including relevant psychological tests.

Just as S. S. Disability cannot accept only the subjective opinions of applicants, it also cannot accept only the subjective opinions of the doctors who treat them. For example, a treating physician might state his opinion that a claimant is "totally and permanently disabled". This is a subjective opinion, which by itself has no value as medical evidence. Such opinions must be backed up by facts, or they will be ignored by S. S. Disability. Claimant's treating doctors are not asked to make a decision concerning the presence or absence of disability. As noted previously, that is a legal decision designed to maintain equal consistency and fairness for all claimants. Such treating doctors are asked to submit objective information from physical examinations, X-rays, and other laboratory tests. In the case of mental illness, psychiatric examination would replace a physical exam. The opinions of treating doctors are valued, only if supported by adequate medical data.

Consultative Examinations

If a claimant has no treating doctor, or information from that doctor is not sufficient, or the treating doctor refuses to provide the needed data, then S. S. Disability will send the claimant for an examination by a doctor. This exam would be paid for by S. S. Disability. It is called a *consultative examination*, and is necessary for S. S. Disability to obtain medical information, in such cases. Some claimants prefer to choose their own doctor, and this is acceptable, provided that S. S. Disability gets the information that it needs. However, S. S. Disability will not pay doctors chosen by claimants; that is the claimant's personal choice and expense.

Reference Source

For comprehensive coverage of all aspects of social security disability claims, see McCormick, Social Security Claims and Procedures, 3rd (West 1983).

§ 1.2 Who Can Apply for Social Security Disability?

Under Title II, there are three basic categories of individuals who can apply for disability benefits. They are as follows:

(1) *Disabled workers under 65 years of age, if the worker has paid sufficient Social Security taxes.* To have disability protection, most workers need Social Security credits for at least five of the ten years preceding the alleged onset of disability. A minimum of $370.00 a quarter (every 3 months) will produce the needed credits. Some older workers may need additional credits, depending on their age at the time they become disabled. For the worker who becomes disabled before the age of 31 years, the requirement can drop to as little as 1½ years of work. Social Security District Offices in every State can help answer questions about such credits. This category of claimant can get benefits by Meeting a Listing, Equalling a Listing, or be allowed benefits on a vocational basis.

(2) *A person continuously disabled since childhood (under age 22), if one of the parents who is covered under Social Security retires at age 62 or older, becomes disabled, or dies.* These childhood disability benefits can continue for as long as the individual continues to be disabled. Such a person need not have worked and paid Social Security taxes himself. In this category, benefits can be allowed by Meeting or Equalling a Listing, or by vocational factors. Application for benefits can be made at any time after age 17½. The person does not have to be found disabled at the time of application, but the impairment must have ended no earlier than 14 months prior to application. No payment is given for the years before age 17½.

(3) *A disabled widow or widower, age 50 to 60 years, if the deceased spouse was covered under Social Security.* This also applies to certain disabled surviving divorced wives, age 50 to 60 years. Widows and widowers need not have worked and paid Social Security taxes themselves to apply for benefits. But they can only be eligible if their disability occurs no later than 7 years after their spouse's death. There are no allowances of benefits vocationally in this cate-

gory; to obtain benefits, the impairment must Meet or Equal a Listing.

Under Title XVI (Welfare Disability), there are four basic categories of disability claims, as follows:

(1) *An adult (age 18 and over) who meets the income and resources requirement.* The definition of disability for the disabled adult under Title XVI is essentially the same as that for Title II cases. However, eligibility to be considered for benefits is different, since Title XVI applicants are not required to have paid Social Security taxes. Instead of previous payment of Social Security taxes, there is the requirement that the applicant's income and resources do not exceed a certain level. Since "resources" can mean all sorts of things besides money, no detailed explanation is possible here. However, a District Office can make the necessary calculations for anyone who wants to find out if they are eligible to apply under Title XVI. Allowance of benefits in this category can be made by Meeting a Listing, Equalling a Listing, or because of vocational factors.

(2) *An adult who meets the definition of statutory blindness.* Under Title XVI law, a claimant who fulfills the income and resources requirement to be eligible, and who is statutorily (legally) *blind,* does not have to fulfill the duration requirement. In other words, a person who is legally blind does not have to be disabled for 12 consecutive months—they can receive benefit payments for blindness lasting less than 12 months. This is in contrast to blind claimants under Title II, who must be blind for at least 12 months. Also, regulations allowing a blind claimant under Title XVI to work while receiving benefits are more liberal than for other types of claimants.

(3) *A child (under age 18) whose parents meet the income and resources requirements.* The requirements for childhood disability are such that there must be an impairment of comparable severity to that which is considered disabling for an adult. However, since a child is not normally considered able to engage in work activity, vocational factors are usually not considered, and the impairment must Meet or Equal a Listing, in order for benefits to be obtained. Interference with normal growth and development is an important factor in the childhood Listings. Title XVI children can start receiving benefits at any age.

(4) *A blind child who meets the definition of statutory blindness.* As with adults filing under Title XVI, there is no duration requirement for children who meet the definition of statutory blindness. Unlike Title II blind children, Title XVI blind children do not have to wait until they are age 18 to apply for benefits. No allowances are made vocationally. Benefits are received only if the child Meets or Equals a childhood Listing for statutory blindness.

Sometimes, a claimant can be eligible for both Title II and Title XVI benefits, if they are insured under Title II and meet the income and resources requirements for Title XVI (Welfare Disability).

§ 1.3 How to Apply for Disability Benefits—Form 3368 (Disability Report)

To apply for Title II or Title XVI benefits, the applicant should go to a Social Security District Office, Branch Office, or Contact Station near their home. District Offices or Branch Offices will usually be located in larger towns and cities. Contact Stations are usually set up in some of the smaller towns. A Social Security representative comes to the Contact Station from time to time, in order to answer questions and to take claim applications. Applicants who have a question or want to file a disability claim, and who are unable to go to their nearest District Office, Branch Office, or Contact Station can solve their problem by telephone. All that is needed is to call the Social Security office "Collect", and they will accept the call. To find the address and telephone number of one of these Social Security offices, reference can be made to a telephone book under "Government Offices—United States". Or the telephone company's "Directory Assistance" can help.

No matter what kind of medical condition a person has, the District Office, Branch Office, or Contact Station must take the claim, *if* the applicant is eligible. Such eligibility is established for Title II, if the person is insured under Social Security, by having paid Social Security taxes. Title XVI (Welfare Disability) applicants are eligible, if they fulfill the income and resources requirements for Title XVI. The personnel at such offices *cannot* reject a claim, because they don't think an applicant's medical illness is important enough. Nor would they try. The DDS determines the meaning of the claimant's medical impairment.

It is usually best not to be working when applying for disability benefits; however, it is possible to work at a reduced level and still qualify. The District Office can evaluate the claimant's work and tell him if it affects his ability to apply for benefits. If the claimant is involved in what is called *Substantial Gainful Activity,* then he usually will not be eligible to have his claim processed further. Some Title XVI blind applicants might be an exception. Substantial Gainful Activity (SGA) is S. S. Disability's definition of economically meaningful work, and a detailed explanation can be found in Appendix VIII.

When applying for disability benefits, the District Office will have the claimant complete a Form 3368, which is a Disability Report containing some general background information about the claimant and his impairment. A sample of this form can be found in Appendix II. For claims filed by telephone, the form is mailed to the claimant. If an applicant goes personally to a District Office, a claims representative will ask him questions and complete the form for him.

Many of the questions on the 3368 Form are easy to answer, but this should be done carefully. Such documents are *not* mere bureaucratic formalities—S. S. Disability pays serious attention to them. Although completing this form the best way possible will not in itself get anyone disability benefits, it sometimes does push a decision toward an allowance or denial, in borderline cases.

What follows are some general suggestions about answering the questions on Form 3368:

A. *"Name of applicant."* Only the claimant's name should be placed in this space.

B. *"Social Security number."* Only the claimant's Social Security Number should be put in this space, and care should be taken to make sure that it is accurate.

C. *"Telephone number."* The claimant should write down a telephone number where he can be reached between 8 A.M. and 5 P.M. If the claimant doesn't have a telephone, he may use the number of a relative or friend who can pass messages to him. In that case, "Message Telephone" should be written in the blank, along with the telephone number.

D. *"What is your disabling condition?"* In this blank, the claimant should list every illness or injury which he feels is disabling. This is extremely important, and the claimant should be as specific as possible about his impairments.

S. S. Disability is required to find out how each given im pairment affects the claimant's ability to work. However, the more complaints that are listed by the claimant, the longer it will take to process the claim. It does little good to list relatively minor illnesses, such as gallstones or sinusitis. No-one has ever received benefits by a DDS for such minor disorders, that the author is aware of. Appendix I contains some examples of disorders for which disability is rarely or never given. Also, it does no good for a claimant to list impairments that he does not have, because S. S. Disability will verify each complaint in detail before accepting it as valid.

"Part I. Information About Your Condition"

1. *"When did your condition first bother you?"* The claimant should write in this space the earliest date that he became aware of an impairment.

2A. *"Did you work after the date shown in item 1?"* This simply requires a "Yes" or "No" answer.

2B. *"If you did work since the date in Item 1, did your condition cause you to change?" This question simply requires "Yes" or "No" answers about whether job duties, hours of work, attendance at work, or other factors were affected by the claimant's impairments.*

2C. *"If you answered "Yes" to any item in 2B, explain . . ."* This blank is for more detailed explanations of any "Yes" answers given to the question in item 2B above. The claimant should be as specific as possible, and explain all "Yes" answers from item 2B.

3A. *"When did your condition finally make you stop working?"* The claimant should write in this blank the date on which he feels that he became unable to work, because of his impairment.

3B. *"Explain how your condition now keeps you from working."* The claimant should explain in his own words how he thinks his condition prevents him from working. Simple, straightforward explanations are best. Applicants sometimes point out that they are disabled, because they are receiving benefits from some other State or federal agency. S. S. Disability is not impressed by such statements; it has its own criteria for disability.

"Part II. Information About Your Medical Records"

4. *"List the name, address and telephone number of the doctor who has the latest medical records about your disabling condition."* The claimant should be as specific as possible in providing the requested information about who has his current medical records. Problems obtaining medical records slow case processing more than any other single factor.

5A. *"Have you seen any other doctors since your illness or injury began?"* Complete in the same way as item 4.

5B. *"Identify below any other doctor you have seen since your illness or injury began."* Complete in the same way as item 4.

6A. *"Have you been hospitalized or treated at a clinic for your disabling condition?"* This question requests specific information about hospitals or clinics that may have treated the claimant, rather than individual doctors. The more accurate this information is, the faster the claim can be processed.

6B. *"If you have been in other hospital or clinic for your illness or injury, identify it below."* Complete in the same way as item 6A.

7. *"Have you been seen by other agencies for your disabling condition?"* S. S. Disability is interested in medical records that might be available from other State or federal agencies. However, S. S. Disability is not the least interested in whether such agencies found the claimant disabled.

8. *"Have you had any of the following tests in the last year?"* This question asks about certain tests the claimant may have had. It is important to fill out this item as completely as possible, because it will help the disability examiner get an idea of what tests were done regarding the claimant's impairments. This helps S. S. Disability process the claim more quickly, rather than having to repeat tests that have already been done.

9. *"If you have a medicaid card, what is your number?"* If the claimant has a medicaid card number, it should be written here.

"Part III. Information About Your Activities"

10. *"Has any doctor told you to cut back or limit your activities in any way?"* If "Yes", the claimant should give the name of the doctor, and what that doctor told him about cutting back or limiting his activities. The claimant should be as accurate as possible, and write down only what he was actually told.

11. *"Describe your daily activities in the following areas and state what and how much you do of each and how often you do it:"* The claimant should describe his normal daily activities involving "household maintenance", "recreational activities and hobbies", "social contacts", and "other" miscellaneous activities. How these blanks are filled out is extremely important, because it gives S. S. Disability practical examples of what the claimant is really capable of doing physically and mentally. In cases where decisions are difficult or "borderline", this information can make the difference between allowance and denial of the claim. Some claimants just don't fill out these blanks at all, or write "None" in each blank. However, S. S. Disability is well aware that everyone does *something*, even if they only sit and stare at a wall all day. So it's not very believable, if a claimant says he does absolutely nothing. That is an impossibility. Furthermore, a statement by a claimant that he does nothing at all makes it more likely that the disability examiner will call the claimant and ask him specific and detailed questions about what he does with his time. Also, the examiner may ask family members, or the treating doctor about the claimant's activities, if appropriate. On the other hand, the claimant should make sure that he does not leave the impression that he can do things that he isn't really capable of doing. For example, if the claimant goes shopping but must have someone else to go with him, he should say that he cannot do this alone and why he must have help. If the claimant has any type of social contacts or recreational activities, he should note how often this occurs and how such activities are restricted by his impairment. This includes relationships with family members.

"Part IV. Information About Your Education"

12. *"What is the highest grade of school that you completed and when?"* S. S. Disability is interested in the

claimant's education, because the higher his education the more likely it is that he could find some type of work. On the other hand, lower education restricts job opportunities and makes it more likely that disability benefits can be given on a vocational basis. S. S. Disability does not usually check to verify that the claimant is telling the truth. In fact, it would be rare for such a check to be made. However, it would not be very believable for a college professor to say that he only has a high school education.

13. *"Have you gone to trade or vocational school or had any type of special training?"* Like regular education, S. S. Disability is interested in any special training that the claimant may have had, because it increases the chances that he could find some type of work using those skills. S. S. Disability does not usually check to verify that the answer is correct, but it is best to be truthful.

"Part V. Information About the Work You Did"

14. *"List all jobs you have had in the last 15 years before you stopped working . . ."* Job title, type of business, dates worked, and rate of pay are requested here. It is important to be accurate, since this information may affect the final disability decision. This is more to the advantage of claimants with a history of heavy and unskilled labor.

15A. *"Provide the following information . . ."* This item asks about supervisory experience, paperwork experience, experience with tools and machines, and technical knowledge. Abilities in any of these areas increases the likelihood that the claimant could perform some type of work. Only "Yes" or "No" answers are requested.

15B. *"Describe your basic duties . . . below."* This space is for a more detailed description of the claimant's job duties. If an older claimant does not Meet or Equal a Listing, he is more likely to be allowed benefits vocationally, if he did only heavy types of work, had no supervisory duties, and did not use special tools or have special skills. S. S. Disability usually does not check on the accuracy of the claimant's answers, but it is still best to be truthful. If S. S. Disability wants still more details, it will request that the claimant complete Vocational Report Form 3369, which will be discussed in another section of this book. A sample of that Form can be found in Appendix III.

15C. *"Describe the kind and amount of physical activity this job involved . . ."* This question seeks still further information about the claimant's past job in terms of the physical exertion required—the amount of weight that had to be lifted, and the amount of walking, standing, sitting, bending, and reaching required. The more strenuous the physical exertion required, the less likely that S. S. Disability would expect the claimant to return to such work, if he has an impairment affecting his ability to do physical work. That is, the advantage goes to the claimants with a history of the heaviest type of physical work.

"Part VI. Remarks"

This is a blank section of the form that the claimant can use to make any additional comments he may feel are important to his application. The claimant should try to confine his statements to things that are actually related to his impairments, and which he feels affect his ability to work. Emotional statements expressing anger, threats, or the fact that the claimant needs money have little influence on what decision will be made in the case.

Following the final remarks, there is a space for the claimant's signature and the date. Above the place for the signature, there is a warning that it is a federal crime to provide false information on this document.

"Part VII. For SSA Use Only. Do Not Write Below This Line"

The following sections of the form are filled out by Social Security representatives. However, a brief explanation of these parts of the form will be given.

16. *"Presumptive disability consideration."* In order to speed up the processing of claims, some applicants are presumed to be disabled if they fall under one of the Items A–K. A person under one of these categories has a high likelihood of qualifying for benefits, even before their medical data has been evaluated. This allows the claimant to start receiving benefits early, before a final decision is made. That final decision is made only after all important medical data has been reviewed. The final decision can either uphold the decision for presumptive disability or reverse it. Benefits will last 3 months, even if the final decision goes against the claimant.

The privilege of presumptive disability payments only extends to Title XVI (Welfare Disability) applicants; Title II applicants cannot have presumptive disability.

17A. *"Does the claimant speak English?"* The inability to speak English increases the chances of being allowed vocationally, since it makes finding a job more difficult.

17B. *"Does the claimant need assistance in prosecuting his or her claim?"*

If the claimant appears too physically or mentally ill to carry out his own application, S. S. Disability will try to find help for him. Usually, this is a family member or friend who knows something about his condition.

17C. *"Can the claimant (or his representative) be readily reached by telephone . . ."* S. S. Disability wants to know whether telephone contact with the claimant might be hampered by language, speech, or hearing difficulties. This is important, because much information may be sought from a claimant over the telephone, during the development of his claim. If this cannot be done, other methods have to be worked out.

18A. *"Check each item to indicate if any difficulty was observed."*

These are a series of general observations that Social Security representatives make about the claimant if he goes personally to a Social Security office to make his application. It assists S. S. Disability in picking up problem areas that might need evaluation.

18B. *"If any of the above items were checked . . . describe the exact difficulty involved."*

This question asks the Social Security representative to provide more details about any problems they might have noticed about the claimant.

18C. *"Describe the claimant fully . . ."*

Further details about the claimant that the Social Security representative might think important are recorded in this space. Observations that Social Security representatives might make about a claimant are very important, and in "borderline" cases they can make the difference between allowance and denial of benefits. Although, this is not generally true, such observations should not be in obvious conflict with what the treating doctor says about the claimant. For example, if the treating doctor says the claimant's hands are so severely deformed from arthritis as to be virtually useless, yet he uses his hands perfectly normally at a District Office then S. S. Disability would be likely to send the claimant to another doctor for a different opinion.

19. *"Does the claimant speak English?"* The inability to speak English increases the chances of being allowed vocationally, since it makes finding a job more difficult.

21. *"Is capability development by the DDS necessary?"* If the Social Security representative has reason to think the claimant is mentally unable to handle his benefits, this question will be marked "Yes". The DDS will then try to make a formal determination about the claimant's ability to handle benefits. If he cannot, his benefit checks will be controlled by another person—often a relative.

22. *"Is development of work activity necessary?"* If the claimant is working at the time of application, this will be noted. If his income is too high as a result of working, his application will be rejected—unless he is a blind applicant filing under Title XVI. These people can engage in substantial gainful activity and still be eligible, as long as they don't exceed income and resources requirements for such Title XVI cases. This privilege does not extend to blind applicants under Title II. For further information about what S. S. Disability considers meaning work, the reader should refer to Appendix VIII, "Substantial Gainful Activity."

The remaining items on the form would be of little interest to the reader (items 20, 23, 24).

§ 1.4 Organizational Levels for Considering Disability Claims

After a claim is filed at the Social Security District Office (DO), it is sent to a State government agency called Disability Determination Services for Social Security (DDS). Each State has a DDS, usually located in the State capitol. The DDS's are managed by State governments, but are actually monitored and controlled by the federal Social Security system. All money used in running the DDS's and all money given out in disability benefits comes from the federal government. A DDS must obey whatever regulations and policies that are handed down from the federal government.

The federal government wants tight control over the State agencies, so that all disability cases will be evaluated the same way in each State. Without this consistency, equal treatment under the law would not be possible. On the other hand, it means increased bureaucracy and inefficiency.

Above the level of the State agencies (DDS's), there are a number of what are called "Regional Offices". These are federal agencies with federal employees, and each one has the responsibility of over-seeing a group of State agencies. A Regional Office reviews a certain number of disability cases evaluated by State agencies in their region. If the Regional Office does not agree with the way a DDS has evaluated a case, then the case will be returned to the DDS with some attached suggestions. Actually, these are not suggestions at all, but orders concerning the case in question. Generally, these orders take one of two forms. First, there are orders to obtain more information about the case in question, before a decision is made. This happens, if the Regional Office feels that there is not enough information about the claimant or his impairment to make a fair decision under the law. Secondly, there are orders stating that the DDS has made an incorrect decision, and the demand will be made that the decision be changed from an allowance to a denial, or vice versa. The DDS can argue with such an order to a certain extent, but ultimately the Regional Office can force the DDS to do what it wants. It might be weeks before the Regional Office sends back a case it disagrees with.

There is another level of power above that of the Regional Office. This is called various things, including the "Bureau of Disability Insurance" (BDI), the "Central Office", or the "Office of Disability Operations". BDI operates out of a gigantic administrative complex in Baltimore, Maryland. It is the highest federal authority in S. S. Disability, controlling both the Regional Offices and DDS's. BDI also reviews a certain number of disability cases coming from each DDS, and can return them to the DDS for further development, or reversal of the decision. A DDS can argue with BDI, and in some cases might succeed in getting BDI to change its position. In the end, however, the DDS must do exactly what BDI tells it to do. The Regional Offices must also obey BDI. DDS's are not required to argue a decision reversal with either BDI or the Regional Offices. Such arguments are done, only when the DDS feels that it is clearly correct and that it has some reasonable chance of winning. Also, the federal government keeps performance statistics on the work of the DDS's, coding an error each time a DDS decision is reversed. This is an incentive for DDS's to argue reversals, though this is not done in all cases.

BDI makes the ultimate policies concerning the interpretation of the laws governing disability. Although the laws themselves are enacted by Congress, laws are written in words and all words are open to interpretation. Because of this, BDI has enormous power in controlling disability decisions. This is not necessarily a bad thing, because that responsibility must fall to someone. Without such centralized control, the federal government could not assure everyone of equal treatment under the disability laws. Even so, errors are made due to the size of the disability system. This is an unavoidable effect of large bureaucracies, though this can be minimized by having thoroughly competent people at all levels.

There are other power structures which can influence S. S. Disability decisions, and which do not answer to BDI. These are Administrative Law Judges and courts of law to which a claimant can appeal his case, if he is not allowed benefits. These are discussed in more detail in another section of this book (see § 1.11, "What to Do if Benefits are Terminated or Denied", infra).

§ 1.5 Presumptive Disability

Presumptive disability means that a temporary decision is made to allow a claim, before full development of the case is done. It is not a permanent decision, and might be reversed to a denial when a final decision is made. However, presumptive disability is only given to those claimants who seem to have such severe impairments that S. S. Disability is pretty sure they will be allowed anyway, when full analysis of the case is done. (See Item 16 on Form 3368 for a few examples of impairments that are likely to rate presumptive disability. There may be others, besides those listed.)

Applicants under Title II *cannot* have presumptive disability, no matter how sick they appear to be. Presumptive disability is only for Title XVI (Welfare Disability) applicants. The reasoning behind this is that a Title II applicant supposedly has enough money to live on, until a final decision is made in his case. Title XVI applicants are felt to need money more quickly, since they have not had productive jobs allowing them to save money.

If a claimant is found presumptively disabled, he will receive money for up to 3 months, while a final decision is being made concerning his case. If the final decision is an allowance, then benefits will continue. Otherwise, payments will stop. If the final decision is a denial, the money does not have to be repaid.

§ 1.6 Closed Periods

Sometimes allowance of benefits is made under what is called a *closed period.* This simply means that the claimant was considered disabled during some limited time in the past. That time interval must cover at least 12 months. Although a claimant may not be considered disabled at the time of his application, he can still qualify for a closed period and be paid benefits for past disability. However, a closed period cannot be given, unless the interval of time considered ended no more than 14 months before the application for disability. A closed period can be obtained by both Title II and Title XVI applicants, but Title XVI applicants can get a closed period only if the last month of disability was the month of application or later.

§ 1.7 Waiting Period Before Receiving Benefits

Most disability cases involve neither presumptive disability nor closed periods. The majority of claimants are given benefits based on the fact that they are disabled at the time of application. They still must have already fulfilled the minimum 12 month duration requirement, or have an impairment that is expected to last that long. Only Title XVI blind applicants are allowed to violate the 12 month duration requirement.

For Title II applicants, the waiting period means they will not receive any money for 5 months from the date their disability starts. Of course, that starting date can be any length of time before the actual date of application, so some claimants have their 5 months finished by the time they apply for benefits, and don't have to wait any longer. But a Title II applicant who becomes disabled near his application date will have to wait the full 5 months, unless he had previously received benefits sometime in the 5 years before his current disability began. Title XVI applicants (Welfare Disability) do not have the waiting period requirement. They can receive money, as soon as an allowance decision is made, the payments usually starting from the month of application.

The amount of money that a claimant can receive depends on a number of factors, such as the claimant's age and the amount of money paid in Social Security taxes. Of course, the amount paid in taxes only applies to Title II applicants; Title XVI applicants can qualify without this requirement, though they must not exceed certain income and resource levels. In general, younger claimants receive more money monthly than older people. This is supposedly because older claimants are closer to retirement age, and have thus saved more money. This age difference applies only to Title II cases. Income and resource levels determine the amount of monthly benefits payable to Title XVI claimants.

§ 1.8 Medicare and Medicaid Benefits

There are other benefits attached to S. S. Disability. If the claimant is receiving benefits under Title II, he will become eligible for Medicare on the 25th month of payments. This means 24 months must pass, *after* the 5 month waiting period. Medicare is an insurance program which helps Title II disabled people pay their medical bills. If the claimant is receiving benefits under Title XVI, he can become eligible for Medicaid, which is a similar insurance program designed to help Welfare Disability claimants pay their medical expenses. However, unlike Title II claimants, Title XVI claimants become eligible for Medicaid during the very first month of their disability, rather than on the 25th month after the waiting period.

§ 1.9 Vocational Rehabilitation Services

Under both the Title II and Title XVI disability programs, some people will qualify for what is called vocational rehabilitation. Every State has these services. Vocational rehabilitation attempts to help disabled people overcome their handicaps, so that they can find gainful employment. Referral to vocational rehabilitation is done only in those cases in which re-training is reasonably possible. If someone receiving S. S. Disability benefits is referred for such services, he does *not* have the free choice to accept or reject such a re-training effort. However, refusal of such services is acceptable if:

(1) The refusal is for legitimate health reasons, including mental incapacity.

(2) The refusal is based on the fact that the required absence from the home will adversely affect the welfare of the person's family.

(3) The person refuses, because he is working or being rehabilitated under some other type of plan.

(4) The person refuses, because he is a student.

(5) The person refuses, because of religious reasons.

(6) The person refuses, because after completing rehabilitation training, he still would not receive adequate pay for the type of work he would be trained to do.

If someone refuses rehabilitation without an acceptable reason as given above, his disability benefits will be stopped.

In some cases, claimants who are denied disability benefits can still receive rehabilitation, if they wish to undergo such training. This is possible, if the claimant has some impairment that prevents him from returning to the usual type of work that he has done during the past 15 years. Of course, the fact that someone undergoes vocational rehabilitation is no guarantee that he will be able to find a satisfactory job, but it is a step in the right direction.

§ 1.10 Termination of Benefits

A. Case Re-evaluation

If a claimant is found to be disabled, the examiner handling his case will try to decide if his condition is likely to improve enough to allow him to return to work, at some time in the future. In that event, he will place an order on the case that it be re-examined at some future date. This is called a *medical re-exam diary.* In every State agency (DDS), there are examiners who do nothing but re-evaluate the cases of people who were previously considered disabled. This is called a *continuing disability investigation.*

The re-examination of a claimant's file, except possibly in Title XVI blind cases, is never done earlier than 12 months from the date he is first found to be disabled. Note that the date a claimant is found to be disabled may be earlier than the application date, so a case in some instances may be re-examined sooner than 12 months after application. A re-exam diary can be set for much longer than 12 months, but rarely would it be longer than 3 years from the application date. In the past, cases that were not diaried for re-examination when they were first allowed might never face re-examination. In other cases, though not many, the re-examination was over-looked for years, through errors in the Social Security system itself. At the present time, all adult Title II and Title XVI cases will be re-evaluated no longer than every 3 years for claimants with *nonpermanent* impairments, with the exception of claimants who are at least 62 years old, or widows and widowers who are at least 60 years old.

If a claimant undergoing periodic review has a *permanent impairment*, and there is no report of work activity or medical improvement, development of the case will not be done again after the initial decision resulting in benefits. Such claims will be automatically continued by S. S. Disability. These are impairments that have previously been determined to *Meet* a Listing, and simply come up in periodic review. This does not apply to cases falling into what is called a *medical re-exam diary.* These are cases in which a special re-examination date had been set at the original time of allowance, because it was unclear if meet level severity would continue indefinitely. A list of the permanent impairments in which re-evaluation will not be done are as follows:

1. Arthritis of one major joint in each upper extremity (Listing 1.04).

2. Disorders of the spine (arthritis manifested by ankylosis or fixation at 30° or more (Listing 1.05A).

3. Amputation or permanent loss of use of two limbs (Listing 1.09).

4. Amputation of leg at hip (Listing 1.10A).

5. Amputation of leg or foot because of diabetes or peripheral vascular disease (Listing 1.10B).

6. Statutory blindness, except if due to cataracts or detached retina—markedly reduced ability to see objects—not correctable by surgery, other treatment, or glasses (Listings 2.02, 2.03).

7. Loss of visual efficiency (visual efficiency of better eye after best correction 20 percent or less) (Listing 2.04).

8. Hearing impairments (hearing not restorable by a hearing aid) (Listings 2.08A, 2.08B).

9. Chronic obstructive airway disease (Listing 3.02).

10. Ischemic heart disease with chest pain of cardiac origin (Listings 4.04A, 4.04B).

11. Arteriosclerosis obliterans or thromboangiitis (Listing 4.13).

12. Chronic liver disease with esophageal varices resulting in massive hemorrhage or requiring shunt operation (Listings 5.05A, 5.05B).

13. Impaired renal function due to chronic progressive disease, incurable kidney disease (documented by persistent

adverse objective findings) resulting in severely reduced function which may require dialysis or transplant (Listing 6.02).

14. Diabetes mellitus with manifestations as required by the applicable Listing (9.08).

15. Central nervous system vascular accident, with manifestations as required by the applicable Listing more than 3 months postvascular accident (Listing 11.04).

16. Parkinsonian syndrome, with disturbance of movement, gait, or station as required by the applicable Listing (11.06).

17. Cerebral palsy, with manifestations as required by the applicable Listing (11.07).

18. Spinal cord or nerve root lesion resulting in paraplegia or quadriplegia, damage to the spinal cord or major branches resulting in markedly reduced function in two or more extremities (Listing 11.08).

19. Multiple sclerosis, damage to the nervous system due to areas of inflammation which recur and may progress to interference with function of the nervous system, including severe weakness or paralysis (Listing 11.09).

20. Amyotrophic lateral sclerosis (Listing 11.10).

21. Anterior poliomyelitis, with interference in swallowing, breathing, speech or motor function as described in the applicable Listing (11.11).

22. Muscular dystrophy, a chronic progressive disease causing irreversible wasting of the muscles with a significant effect on the ability to use the arms and/or legs (Listing 11.13).

23. Degenerative disease, such as Huntington's chorea, Friedreich's ataxia, and spinocerebellar degeneration, with manifestations as required by the applicable Listing (11.17).

24. Chronic brain syndrome (organic brain syndrome) with manifestations as required by the applicable Listing (12.02).

25. Functional psychotic disorders if institutionalized in a licensed mental hospital for the past 12 months without releases that would indicate improvement (Listing 12.03).

26. Functional non-psychotic disorders if institutionalized in a licensed mental hospital for the past 12 months

without releases that would indicate improvement (Listing 12.04).

27. Severe mental retardation, with manifestations as required by the applicable Listings (12.05A, 12.05B, 12.05C).

28. Age 55 and over with the following condition that Meets a Listing:

(a) Arthritis of a major weight-bearing joint (Listing 1.03A).

(b) Organic loss of speech (Listing 2.09).

(c) Diffuse pulmonary fibrosis (Listing 3.04).

(d) Other restrictive ventilatory disorders (Listing 3.05).

(e) Chronic venous insufficiency (Listing 4.12).

(f) Scleroderma or progressive systemic sclerosis (Listings 10.05A, 10.05B).

(g) Tabes dorsalis (Listing 11.15).

(h) Subacute combined cord degeneration (Listing 11.16).

(i) Syringomyelia (Listing 11.19).

(j) Ischemic heart disease (chest pain of cardiac origin) (Listings 4.04C, 4.04D).

Note: All impairments listed above are applicable only to cases originally allowed as Meeting the Listings. The impairments listed below do not have a specific Listing equivalent.

29. Amputation of a limb, current age 55 or older.

30. Age 55 and over with two substantiated myocardial infarctions.

In addition to the above permanent impairments in which reevaluation will not be done, special policy rules are currently in effect regarding impairments due to mental illness. Claims previously allowed with a primary or secondary diagnosis of functional psychotic disorder, functional psychosis, involutional psychosis, manic-depressive illness, psychotic reaction, schizophrenias, or paranoid states will continue to receive disability benefits regardless of whether the relevant Listing 12.03 was fulfilled in the past or present. Currently, this applies only to cases already receiving benefits with these types of mental disorders. New claims still have to fulfill the requirements of Listing 12.03.

There are certain disorders that the examiner in most cases *must* ask to be re-examined (diaried) at some point in the future. Such re-examination is usually done 12–18 months later. The following list of disorders to be re-examined is verbatim from federal documents:

(1) Respiratory disease based on frequency of acute episodes (e.g., asthma, bronchiectasis).

(2) Functional nonpsychotic disorders.

(3) Active rheumatoid arthritis, or other inflammatory arthritis, without residual structural deformity.

(4) Any case in which corrective surgery is planned or where adjudication takes place during the postsurgical convalescent period and recovery can be anticipated. This includes cases involving cardiovascular and renal surgery, laryngectomy, peripheral vascular surgery, laminectomy, and lumbar (lumbosacral) fusion.

(5) *Obesity.* In and of itself producing manifestations limiting work capacity.

(6) Fracture(s) of any bone(s) without severe residual functional loss or structural deformity which is by itself disabling.

(7) All infections (e.g., tuberculosis, mycosis, leprosy, osteomyelitis) without severe, irreversible structural damage.

(8) Peripheral neuropathies.

(9) Sarcoidosis without severe organ damage, e.g., pulmonary, ocular, renal, etc.

(10) Progressive neoplastic disease is highly probable but full medical work-up falls short of a definite diagnosis.

(11) Neoplastic disease which has been treated and incapacitating residuals exist, but improvement of those residuals is probable.

(12) Epilepsy.

(13) *Acute leukemia.* Onset within 2½ years of determination.

(14) Central nervous system trauma, where progressive improvement of function is evident, but the impairment is expected to be disabling at 12 months from onset.

(15) All back conditions amenable to treatment, where permanently incapacitating residuals are not established.

The above list applies to both adults and children. The following list applies only to children:

(1) Mental deficiency, where testing is performed under the age of 16.

(2) *Growth impairments.* All cases allowed under Listing 100ff. (author's note: 100ff refers to any of the Listings dealing with growth impairments.)

(3) *Endocrine disorders.* All cases allowed under Listing 109ff, except those Meeting Listing 109.05A or 109.08D.

(4) Lymphoreticular malignant neoplasms.

(5) Malignant solid tumors.

A case might be re-examined sooner than planned, if a claimant goes back to work. This can come about if the claimant honestly informs S. S. Disability that he is trying to work, or if S. S. Disability finds out in some other way. In most cases, when a claimant who has an impairment that has *not improved* returns to work (if it is substantial gainful activity—see Appendix VIII), then he may still continue working and receive benefits for what is called a *trial work period,* lasting up to 24 months. He can engage in substantial gainful activity during those 24 months, without losing his benefits. Trial work periods can apply to both Title II and Title XVI cases, with the exception that Title XVI blind claimants are not eligible.

A case might also be re-examined earlier than planned, if someone who knows a claimant provides information that he is not nearly as sick as he is supposed to be. This happens most frequently, when someone tells S. S. Disability that a claimant is working and not reporting this fact. *Any* kind of work is supposed to be reported by a claimant receiving disability benefits.

Another way for a claimant to get his case re-evaluated early is to insist that the onset date of his disability wasn't set back far enough, and that he should therefore get more money. Sometimes, claimants support their argument by sending in more medical information for S. S. Disability to look at. If the claimant is right, then S. S. Disability will correct the error and give him the money. But when such a claimant brings attention to his case, he also runs the risk that S. S. Disability will reach the conclusion that it made a mistake and change the onset date, so that the claimant will get less money, instead of more. S. S. Disability might even find out that it made a mistake in allowing the claim to begin with, and terminate benefits completely. That is not an unusual event. There is nothing mean about S. S. Disability doing this, but if it finds a mistake that error will be corrected. It should not stop claimants from asking for an earlier onset date, if they think they really deserve that change, and feel confident that re-evaluation of their cases will hold up.

People who know a claimant may write S. S. Disability with information that he is engaging in work, or other types of activity that he shouldn't be able to do with the impairment that he has. This doesn't happen very often. It is more likely that someone close to the claimant reveals that perhaps he isn't as sick as he is supposed to be. This usually happens when a disability examiner calls a claimant's home to get information of some kind, and a family member answers the telephone. S. S. Disability finds it very interesting if a claimant's spouse or children say he isn't home, because he's out working. Even if the claimant is not making money, he might be doing something that shows he is not as physically or mentally ill as he is supposed to be. That would make anyone curious, including disability examiners. Pursuing this line of questions can lead to some very revealing answers. S. S. Disability doesn't try to trick claimants or their family members into providing such information, but if it comes up it won't be ignored.

Despite the above possibilities, the great majority of claimants who have their benefits terminated, find that this is done through a routine re-evaluation of their cases. This continuing disability investigation can cause termination of benefits in one of five ways:

(1) The claimant has returned to productive work, other than in a trial work period.

(2) S. S. Disability finds out that it made a mistake in allowing the case.

(3) The claimant refuses to cooperate in helping S. S. Disability obtain current medical or other important information necessary to process his claim.

(4) The claimant's condition has improved to the point that he is no longer qualified to receive benefits.

(5) The claimant's case was originally allowed under prior law, and when evaluation under current law is done, he is

found to no longer be disabled, even though his impairment has not changed.

B. Case Re-evaluation—Form 454 BK

When a claimant who is already receiving disability benefits has his claim come up for routine review, he will be asked to complete a form called "Report of Continuing Disability Interview" (454 BK). This can be done over the telephone, or by personal interview with a Social Security representative. A sample copy of this form can be found in Appendix IV, infra, but a few comments about it may be helpful:

"Part I. Information About Your Condition"

1.a *"What is your disabling condition?"* S. S. Disability wants to know what illness the claimant feels he has that prevents him from working and why. Many claimants write brief, general statements such as, "My doctor said to stay off my feet as much as possible," or "I am unable to stand or walk for any length of time." More detailed answers might be better, assuming the claimant feels he can write a logical argument, in terms of his own impairment. For example, suppose a claimant has severe chest pain from heart disease, when he does even a little physical exertion. Such a person might say, "I still have severe chest pain, even when I try to walk a block." This is a logical and meaningful answer. [As an aside, it is extremely important to realize that many claimants receiving benefits have heart disease and the type of chest pain they have often determines whether benefits are continued or stopped, in the final analysis. It is critical that claimants with heart disease and chest pain make sure that their treating doctor really knows what kind of symptoms they are having, because S. S. Disability will put great weight on what the treating doctor says, in most instances.] A claimant with a broken hip might say, "I still can't walk without the help of crutches." Of course, S. S. Disability cannot simply take the claimant's word for these statements; the truth of such comments would still be checked against what the claimant's treating doctor, or other examining physician, says about him. Also, emotional pleas are of no value. For example, S. S. Disability often sees such pleas based on the need of money, or the fact that the claimant can't work because he has to take care of a sick relative, etc. Emotional pleas won't hurt the claimant's case; S. S. Disability is used to them. But they certainly won't help, and are not nearly as good as a logical argument. The disability examiner must work cases based on Social Security regulations, and cannot continue a claim based on sympathy, even if he really feels sorry for the claimant.

2.a *"Do you feel you are able to return to work?"* This is simply an expansion of question 1.a above. Ample space is given under "Part VI–Remarks", for any detailed comments the claimant wishes to make.

2.b *"Has your doctor told you that you are able to return to work?"* This question must be answered "Yes" or "No" or "Did not say." The answer to this question can and probably will be checked by S. S. Disability. However, it should be pointed out that the treating doctor's opinion that the claimant could return to work would not necessarily mean termination of benefits. That would put the treating doctor in the position of making the actual disability decision, and that is not permitted—it would not allow equal treatment under Social Security regulations. The opposite is also true—a statement by the treating doctor that the claimant cannot work will not in and of itself result in continuing benefits, for the same reason benefits will not be terminated on the basis of the treating doctor's opinion alone. Still, S. S. Disability is interested in any medical records supporting the treating doctor's opinion that the claimant can or cannot work and subsequent sections of Form 454 BK asks for such data about treating doctors, hospitals, and medical studies that may have been done. (See "Part II—Information About Your Medical Records").

"Part III. Information About Your Activities"

7. *"Has any doctor told you to cut back or limit your activities in any way . . .?"* This question is simply seeking the names of doctors who may have information helpful in showing ways the claimant is limited in what he can do.

8. *"Describe your daily activities . . ."* Often, the treating doctor does not know very much about what the claimant actually does in the way of daily activities. Yet this information can be critical in determining what the claimant is actually capable of doing, both physically and mentally. That is why this question wants very specific information about "Personal Mobility", "Personal Needs and Grooming", "Household Maintenance", "Recreational Activities", and any

other relevant data about what the claimant does with his time. By means of such questions, S. S. Disability can obtain actual information about what the claimant is capable of doing in spite of his impairment. It should be noted that S. S. Disability may give great weight to the answers in these questions, especially when it is unclear exactly how much restriction their impairment would cause. Nor is it likely that a claimant will have no activities in any of these areas, unless he is suffering from a very profound mental or physical impairment. Therefore, S. S. Disability will not necessarily take the claimant's statements at face value, if he simply writes "None" in all of the blanks, unless the medical records show such extreme incapacity to be likely. If the claimant does not perform some of the activities listed as examples, it is important that he explain the reason, because S. S. Disability wants to know about things the claimant *cannot* do because of his impairment vs. things the claimant is simply not interested in doing. If the claimant feels he cannot perform a given activity, it is important to say why. If he does things not listed in the examples, these should be noted. It is not the intent of S. S. Disability to invade the privacy of the claimant's personal life, but information about activities can assist in making a more accurate decision about the claimant's ability to work.

9. *"Have you attended . . .?"*

10. *"Are you attending school?"* These questions are designed to find out if the claimant has improved his educational skills since the time he was placed on disability. This may indicate the ability to return to work, by virtue of the new training.

"Part VIII. For SSA Use Only—"

This section of the form requests observations Social Security representative may make about the claimant during an interview, and is similar to that on Form 3368. For more information about this section, the reader should refer to the discussion of Form 3368.

C. Termination Effective Date; Appeal Rights Generally

If the claimant is found to no longer be disabled, after a continuing disability investigation of his case, then benefits will be stopped 2 months after the date he is *notified* by the DDS that he is able to engage in some type of meaningful work (substantial gainful activity). Although the claimant may not actually be working, S. S. Disability may consider him capable of working, even though it may not be the kind of work that the claimant previously engaged in. If the claimant feels it is not true that he has recovered enough to return to work, then he can file an application for reconsideration of his claim by the DDS. This only applies to Title II cases. Title XVI cases have the privilege of appealing their cases directly to an Administrative Law Judge, which is the level of appeal just above the DDS. Appeal before an Administrative Law Judge is discussed in more detail elsewhere in this book. Title II claimants who have benefits cut off can appeal to such a judge, after they have a reconsideration claim denied by the DDS. However, it is important to know that recent laws permit both Title II and Title XVI claimants to continue receiving their benefit checks, even after a DDS terminates their disability status, provided that the claimant files a formal appeal for his case to be heard before an Administrative Law Judge. Benefit checks will continue until the claimant's case is heard by the judge. But if such appeal is lost by the claimant the federal government will expect repayment of the benefits received between the time of termination by the DDS and hearing by the judge. Currently, this continuation of payment rule extends only to January 1984, unless Congress renews the legislation.

§ 1.11 What to Do if Benefits Are Terminated or Denied

A. Initial Reconsideration Procedure

The first application for disability filed by a claimant is called an *initial* claim. Usually, it takes about 50 days for the DDS to make a decision on such a claim. This is only an average time. If the District Office where the application is made has difficulty verifying some important information, it could take weeks or even months for the case to be sent to the DDS where its real evaluation begins. Further weeks, or even months, can pass within the DDS itself, depending on their workload, the type of impairments the claimant has, and the ease with which his medical records can be obtained. After the DDS reaches a decision on a claim, it takes about a month for the claimant to receive a letter telling him that his case has either been allowed or denied.

If a claimant calls the DDS examiner to see if his claim has been allowed or denied, the examiner handling the case will usually not reveal what the decision is. The reason for this is that the examiner does not have the last word concerning the decision. Any case written by an examiner might be picked at random and reviewed by a Quality Assurance Unit within the DDS itself. This can result in decision reversal from allowance to denial, or vice versa. The case might also be returned to the examiner for further development, if Quality Assurance thinks there is insufficient information for a good decision. In at least some DDS's performance statistics are kept on the work of examiners, and serious errors picked up by Quality Assurance might affect the examiner's ability to get salary increases or promotions. However, this is probably different for different DDS's. Every case picked in the Quality Assurance daily sample is reviewed by a Quality Assurance examiner, and sometimes also by a medical doctor. Cases may also be reviewed after leaving the DDS, either at a Regional Office or at BDI.

If an initial claim is denied, then the claimant has 65 days from the date of the denial letter to file for *reconsideration* of his case. If more than 65 days passes, then the claimant cannot file a reconsideration claim (unless he has a good reason). But he could still file another initial claim, if he wanted his case reevaluated. But a reconsideration claim will usually be processed much faster than an initial claim, because current information is already in the file, and the file is easier for the DDS to find. The same examiner who evaluated the initial claim does not handle the reconsideration claim.

B. Form 3441—Reconsideration Disability Report

For reconsideration of a disability claim, a Reconsideration Disability Report Form 3441 must be completed. A sample copy of this form can be found in Appendix V. Also, some of the following suggestions about filling out this form may be helpful as follows:

"Part I. Information About Your Condition"

1. *"Has there been any change . . . in your illness or injury since you filed your claim?"* Check "Yes" or "No". If "Yes", describe changes in symptoms in the space provided. The claimant should provide a brief description of how his symptoms or medical findings have changed, without resorting to emotional arguments.

2. *"Describe any physical or mental limitations you have as a result of your condition."* This question asks the

claimant what he can or cannot do, because of his impairment. The answer should be logical, brief, and to the point.

3. *"Have any restrictions been placed on you by a physician?"* If "Yes", describe the restrictions. Also, give the name, address, and telephone number of the doctor in the spaces provided on page 2 of the form. Failure to write down the requested information can slow the processing of the case, while S. S. Disability tries to find the answers.

4. *"Do you have any additional illness or injury that isn't recorded in the file?"* If the claimant forgot to mention a significant impairment which he thinks isn't already recorded in his file, he should write it here. He should not write down things that S. S. Disability already knows about. It is always a temptation for claimants to write down some trivial illness or injury here, after they have already been turned down for their main complaints. This simply creates more work for everyone, including the claimant, and slows down processing of the claim. If the claimant knows that a certain problem isn't really very important, it is pretty certain that S. S. Disability won't find it important either. Wishful thinking does not work in disability claims.

"Part II. Information About Your Medical Records"

Items 5 through 8 simply request specific information about any additional sources of medical data that the claimant wishes S. S. Disability to obtain. Note that S. S. Disability is *only* interested in *new* information that is not already in the claimant's file. It is useless to refer S. S. Disability to information it already has; that can only slow up the decision.

"Part III. Information About Work"

Item 9 asks if the claimant has worked, since filing his initial disability claim. If the answer is "Yes", the details will be required on a separate document.

"Part IV. Information About Your Activities"

10. *"How does your illness or injury affect your ability to care for your personal needs?"* Personal needs are such things as bathing, shaving, combing hair, dressing, etc.

11. *"What changes have occurred in your daily activities since your filed your claim?"* Some claimants indicate that their daily activities have further decreased, since they first filed their initial claim. If this is true, the claimant should give specific examples of the things he cannot do.

"Part V. Remarks And Authorizations"

12(a) This is an agreement by the claimant that S. S. Disability can have access to additional medical records. If the claimant objects to this, he should clearly state his objections and the reasons for them. However, it should be pointed out that it is difficult for S. S. Disability to evaluate data that it does not have.

12(b) (See page 4 of form) *"Use this section to continue information . . . ."* This is a section for any remarks that the claimant may wish to add to his reconsideration application. Comments should confine themselves to the impairments that the claimant has. S. S. Disability will not be impressed by emotional pleas, threats, insults, or the fact that the claimant has been found disabled by some other State or federal agency. On the other hand, reasonable comments relating to the claimant's impairments will get attention.

"Part VI. For SSA Use Only—Do Not Write Below This Line"

Items 13–18 involve observations made about the claimant by Social Security representatives, concerning the way the claimant acts, moves, and thinks.

There is a signature blank on the last page of the form. Note that there is the usual warning about falsifying information on this document.

C. Face to Face Interview After Reconsideration

Currently, the first level of appeal after being turned down by the Reconsideration level of the DDS is a hearing before an Administrative Law Judge. However, new congressional legislation will create another level of appeal between Reconsideration and the Administrative Law Judge. The implementation date is officially January, 1984. This level of appeal will consist of a face to face interview between the claimant and a *federal hearing officer*, and applies to claimants who have already been receiving benefits, but who have been terminated by the DDS. The law regarding the federal hearing level specifies Title II claims which have had benefits ceased, but the Social Security Administration has expressed the intent to extend this to Title XVI claims as well.

The face to face interview will be held at Disability Hearing Offices, if the claimant has to travel no more than 75 miles. Otherwise, the hearing officer will have to go to the claimant.

Federal hearing officers will have the power to overrule decisions made by the DDS by allowing cases denied by the DDS. They may discuss cases with physicians working for a Regional Office, but not those working for a DDS. They may request further information as they think necessary. Claimants will be notified of the hearing officer's decision by mail.

Further detail or modifications will undoubtedly arise as this level of appeal is actually implemented.

D. Appeal Before Administrative Law Judge

If a reconsideration claim is denied, then the claimant has 65 days from the date of the denial letter to file an appeal with an Administrative Law Judge. Missing this 65 day limit for appeal will force the claimant to start all over again with another initial claim. Like initial and reconsideration claims, application for appeal before an Administrative Law Judge can be done by telephone. However, unlike initial and reconsideration claims, the District Office does not send the file to the DDS. Instead, it will go to the Administrative Law Judge hearing the case. The DDS has nothing to do with the decision by such a judge, except to help him acquire additional information, if the judge requests it. Every State has at least several Administrative Law Judges. A sample form for requesting a hearing before an Administrative Law Judge can be found in Appendix X.

At the level of the Administrative Law Judge, cases are handled much differently than claims evaluated by the DDS. Such judges rely much more heavily on the claimant's subjective complaints, such as those involving pain that cannot be objectively measured. A claimant does not necessarily have to personally appear before an Administrative Law Judge; he can send his lawyer instead. But if a claimant does go to the hearing himself, the judge will certainly be observing him for signs of physical or mental impairment. The judge could call one or more of the claimant's doctors to personally testify, but most doctors are very busy and don't like this. They would rather mail in written reports. With a few exceptions, the claimant can count on his doctor saying that he is "totally and permanently disabled". Unlike DDS's, an Administrative Law Judge may pay a great deal of attention to such statements.

While a DDS must abide by stringent regulations and policies with very little deviation, an Administrative Law Judge has much more latitude interpreting the laws relating to S. S. Disability. In illustration of how great this difference can be, an Administrative Law Judge may find a claimant disabled under S. S. Disability although the DDS found the same individual to have no significant disability.

Most doctors are too afraid of legal entanglements with their patients, or of having their doctor-patient relationships damaged to do anything but say what the claimant wants in regard to whether or not he is disabled. A few are more truthful about what they really think, but such physicians are very rare. In this regard, it should be noted that claimants have the right to review their file at the level of the Administrative Law Judge, or at any other level. Although treating doctors know more about the claimant's illness [pure medical impairment] than anyone else, they usually know very little about an individual claimant's ability to work. To know that requires more than knowledge about the claimant's medical impairment; it requires specialized knowledge of Social Security Disability regulations, as well as the age, education, and work experience of the claimant. Still, opinions from treating doctors are important to Administrative Law Judges, although certainly not the only factor influencing their decisions. The judge will also make his own evaluation of the objective medical evidence (physical examinations & laboratory studies such as X-rays), and may solicit medical examinations and opinions from various medical specialists in private practice.

Based on the above considerations, a claimant has not lost all hope, if turned down on the initial and reconsideration levels, because he still may have a very good chance of obtaining benefits through an Administrative Law Judge. Of course, a favorable decision by such a judge is still not a certainty, and such a decision favoring the claimant certainly doesn't last forever. The judge himself might ask that the claimant's condition be re-evaluated, after a certain amount of time. Also, the claimant's case might be re-evaluated at some future date by a DDS, even in the absence of such a request by the judge. If cases allowed originally by an Administrative Law Judge are re-evaluated at some future time, it is never done by the judge himself, and the DDS is not particularly interested in whether the judge gave the claimant benefits or not. Such a judge *cannot* prevent a DDS from re-evaluating a case that the judge allowed, nor can such a judge exert any influence over the decision reached by the DDS. In other words, the DDS can terminate benefits allowed by an Administrative Law Judge, if that case is re-evaluated at some future time. Of course, if this happens, the claimant can appeal his case back to an Administrative Law Judge again. A claimant who is just starting his application for disability benefits *cannot* go directly to an Administrative Law Judge; his case *must* go through the initial and reconsideration levels first.

E. Appeal to Appeals Council

If an Administrative Law Judge turns down a claimant's appeal for benefits, the claimant has 65 days to appeal his case to the next, higher level. If the 65 day limit is missed, he would have to start all over again by filing an initial claim with the DDS. The next level is the *Appeals Council.* The Appeals Council may refuse to review the claimant's case, uphold the Administrative Law Judge's decision, request that more information be obtained, or actually reverse the judge's decision and allow benefits. Sometimes, the Appeals Council will review a case denied by an Administrative Law Judge, even though this was not requested by the claimant. To get his case before the Appeals Council, the claimant has to complete a form requesting it. A sample of this form can be found in Appendix XI.

F. Appeal to U.S. District Court

Failure to get benefits through the Appeals Council is still not the end of the claimant's rights to appeal his case. The next level is to file for a hearing before a United States District Court judge. Most claimants don't go on to the District Court level, although it is still possible that they could be allowed benefits, after being turned down by all prior levels of appeal. But this is much less likely. In such cases, the Secretary of H.H.S. is the defendant and represented by the Department of Justice. The claimant would have to have the help of an attorney, with the accompanying legal expenses. Also, it can take many months for the claimant's case to come before the federal District Court, which has a heavy schedule of cases besides disability claims. Theoretically, disability cases can be appealed all the way to the U.S. Supreme Court. The author doesn't know if any case has made its way to the U.S. Supreme Court; if so, it would be a very rare occurrence.

G. Refiling of Claim

Actually getting benefits allowed above the District Court level are probably exceedingly small, but the claimant can start all over again, by filing another initial claim at the level of the DDS. Some claimants do this, filing over and over again, sometimes for years. This is pretty much a waste of time, unless the claimant's condition has gotten considerably worse by the time he starts over again. These "professional filers" can use up many thousands of dollars in government time and money, but it is their legal right to file as many times as they want. There are even rare cases in which the DDS allows cases originally turned down by both the DDS and an Administrative Law Judge. This could because of a worsening in the claimant's condition, new medical information, or the fact that the DDS decides that both it and the Administrative Law Judge made a mistake in denying benefits the first time the claimant tried to get them. Medical data isn't usually considered current enough by a DDS, if it is more than 6 months old. Rapid changes in the claimant's condition might outdate medical data even faster. Therefore, someone who chronically files for disability, even though turned down many times, can get some very expensive physical examinations and laboratory tests done over and over at government expense, sometimes several times a year. The average cost of processing a claim, whether allowed or denied, is several hundred dollars and steadily rising. That is just the DDS's and District Office's work. A claimant can file for the most trivial illness, and get a free medical evaluation at government expense even if he is not allowed benefits.

H. Reversal Rates

Lastly, it should be pointed out that Administrative Law Judges are currently reversing about 50% of cases denied by DDS's, and changing them into allowances. In some areas, this reversal rate is higher. Many claimants are unaware of this fact, and give up after being turned down by a DDS when appeal before an Administrative Law Judge would greatly increase their chances of getting benefits.

CHAPTER 2

LISTINGS OF IMPAIRMENTS FOR ADULTS

Table of Sections

---

§ 2.1 Introduction

These Listings apply to adults. Adult claimants are those who are at least 18 years old. Technically, a claimant is legally 18 years old when the age 17½ has been reached. These adult Listings may also be applied to childhood disability cases in those instances in which they are more appropriate for a particular childhood case that the childhood Listings.

The Listings of impairments are "lists" of rules used by S. S. Disability in evaluating all disability cases.

The Listings are divided into sections dealing with the various parts of the body. Each Listing is numbered and sets forth the medical requirements that must be met to fulfill that Listing. If a Listing is fulfilled, then the claimant is considered to have an impairment severe enough to qualify for disability benefits.

The Listings were not meant to be read in their entirety. They are to be used for reference, depending on what kind of impairment the reader is interested in.

The Listings themselves are virtually word for word as they appear in federal documents used by S. S. Disability. Following each Listing, there is a detailed explanation of the Listing. This explanation is divided into "General Considerations" and "Specific Requirements". Unlike the Listings themselves, the explanations that follow each one are based on the author's experience, and do not represent any federal document word for word. These explanations are meant to help the reader understand what the Listings mean, and how they are interpreted and used by S. S. Disability. Without these explanations of how S. S. Disability interprets the Listings for its own use, the reader would gain very little insight about how decisions are really reached. Although these explanations are felt to be accurate and based on the extensive experience of the author, they are not equivalent to written law; they reflect the author's understanding of the complex policies S. S. Disability uses in interpreting the Listings for actual disability decisions. Such policies can change over time. Furthermore, the author offers no guarantee that the federal government won't disagree with certain elements of these explanations of the Listings, in the present or future.

Each Listing the reader refers to should be read very carefully, as well as the explanation that follows. Every attempt has been made to define and explain medical terms that might not be familiar to the reader. However, too much simplification would have destroyed the practical usefulness of this book. On the other hand, it has been necessary to avoid complex medical concepts that could only be understood by a medical doctor. Hopefully, a reasonable middle-ground has been reached.

§ 2.2 Musculoskeletal System (Bones and Joints)

Listing 1.02

Active rheumatoid arthritis and other inflammatory arthritis. With both A and B:

A. Persistent joint pain, swelling, and tenderness involving multiple joints with signs of joint inflammation (heat, swelling, tenderness) despite therapy for at least 3 months, and activity expected to last over 12 months; AND

B. Corroboration of diagnosis at some point in time by either:

1. Positive serologic test for rheumatoid factor; OR
2. Antinuclear antibodies; OR
3. Elevated sedimentation rate.

I. General Considerations

A. This Listing deals with *inflammation* of the soft tissues around joints. *Only* those kinds of arthritis that produce inflammation are evaluated under this Listing.

B. The most common form of inflammatory arthritis is rheumatoid arthritis. However, any disease that produces joint inflammation could qualify. For example, very severe arthritis can be associated with the skin condition known as psoriasis.

C. The most common form of arthritis is osteoarthritis, also known as "degenerative arthritis". This form of arthritis does not produce inflammation, and is not evaluated under this Listing. Arthritis that has caused actual damage to the bones in joints is considered under other Listings (such as 1.03 and 1.04). Osteoarthritis would fall into this second category. Listing 1.02 only considers the degree of impairment caused by the inflammatory part of the arthritic disease. Exactly what "inflammation" means medically will be considered a little later.

D. If a claimant has inflammatory arthritis that is severe enough to have caused bone damage, then the impairment could be evaluated under this Listing *and* those Listings dealing with actual damage to bones in a joint.

E. A claimant may be allowed under this Listing without any bone damage at all. But if that is the case, S. S. Disability will evaluate the case again in 12 months, to see if treatment has caused any improvement in the inflammation. On the other hand, the claimant might have severe bone damage, in addition to the inflammation. In these cases, it is unlikely that re-evaluation at some future date will result in benefits being cut off, since such bone damage is permanent.

F. Since no bone damage has to be present to qualify under this Listing, X-rays are *not* necessary. The claimant should not be led to believe that there must be X-rays showing bone damage.

G. The claimant does not have to show that there is a loss of normal motion in the inflamed joints. Also, the inflammation only has to be severe enough to be clearly present under examination by a medical doctor.

H. For purposes of this Listing, a hand and wrist together are considered as only one joint.

I. *Both* Part A and Part B must be fulfilled to qualify under this Listing.

II. Specific Requirements

A. Part A

1. There must be a history of almost continuous joint pain, swelling, and tenderness. The history of these symptoms must come from a treating doctor.

2. "Inflammation" refers to hot, swollen, and tender joints found on physical examination of the claimant by a medical doctor. "Hot" means that the joints are warmer to the touch than normal skin. No special device is used to measure the temperature of the joints involved; this is a matter of judgment by the doctor. It is important to know that joints can be swollen and tender without being inflamed—no heat would be present. So the doctor must be careful in his examination. If joints are inflamed, then erythema (redness of the skin) is also often present. The Listing does not require this, however.

3. Part A states that symptoms and physical findings of inflammation *must* have been present at least 3 months, at the time of application for S. S. Disability. This is an absolute minimum time. S. S. Disability must also feel that the inflammation is likely to last a full 12 months. If inflammation hasn't been present for 3 months at the time of application, S. S. Disability will hold the case to see if treatment will be effective. More information will then be sought from the treating doctor, after inflammation has been present for at least 3 months.

4. It is absolutely necessary that the claimant be under treatment for their arthritis at the time they apply for S. S. Disability. And the treatment being given must be failing to control the inflammation caused by the arthritis.

5. More than one joint must be involved with inflammation.

B. Part B

1. Part B demands abnormal laboratory test results to help support the diagnosis of inflammatory arthritis. Three such tests are listed. Only *one* of these tests has to be abnormal. It does not matter when the test was done—it could have been done years before the claimant applied for disability.

2. All of the tests are based on the analysis of blood. S. S. Disability often orders one or more of these tests and pays for them, when the treating doctor has not done them or will not provide the information.

3. Which test is likely to be abnormal depends on the type of arthritis present. Usually, all three have already been done by the treating doctor when the claimant applies for disability.

4. Part B.1 refers to a positive test for "rheumatoid factor". Rheumatoid factor is an antibody often present in people with rheumatoid arthritis. On the other hand, some people with very severe rheumatoid arthritis don't have a postive test. S. S. Disability is well aware of this, and would not penalize such a claimant. It is also possible for people to have a positive test for rheumatoid factor without having rheumatoid arthritis. Therefore, such a positive test without findings of arthritis on physical examination does not mean anything important.

5. Part B.1 only requires that there be a positive test for rheumatoid factor. If there is any rheumatoid factor antibody present at all in the claimant's bloodstream, that is acceptable. This is very important for the claimant to know, because some tests for rheumatoid factor just measure whether or not it is present, while others also measure how much is present. No matter how small an amount is present, the claimant can still qualify.

6. Part B.2 is a test for "antinuclear antibodies". In some diseases associated with arthritis, these antibodies are present. This applies especially to the so-called "auto-immune" diseases, in which the victim forms antibodies against parts of his own cells.

7. Part B.3 refers to an "elevated sedimentation rate" (ESR). This is simply a test which measures how fast red blood cells fall to the bottom of a tube. Normally, they should not fall faster than 10 millimeters/hour in a male or 20 millimeters/hour in a female. The ESR isn't a test for any specific disease. It is abnormal in many diseases, not just inflammatory arthritis. A common cold can elevate the ESR. A claimant with rheumatoid arthritis and actively inflamed joints should also have an elevated ESR; if not, S. S. Disability would be suspicious that inflammation was not really present.

Listing 1.03

Arthritis of a major weight-bearing joint (due to any cause): With limitation of motion and enlargement or effusion in the affected joint, as well as a history of joint pain and stiffness. With:

A. Gross anatomical deformity such as subluxation, contracture, bony or fibrous ankylosis, or instability; OR

B. Ankylosis of the hip outside of the position of function (i.e., at less than 20° or more than 30° of flexion measured from the neutral position) and X-ray evidence of either joint space narrowing with osteophytosis or bony destruction (with erosions or cysts); OR

C. Reconstructive surgery or surgical arthrodesis of a major weight-bearing joint and return to full weight-bearing status did not occur, or is not expected to occur, within 12 months of onset.

I. General Considerations

A. This Listing deals with any kind of arthritis that has produced bone damage.

B. Application of this Listing is restricted to arthritis of the "weight-bearing" joints. Specifically, this means the joints of the ankles, knees, and hips.

C. The claimant must have a history of complaints about stiffness and pain in the joints involved.

D. Usually, there must be a current and thorough physical examination with special attention to the damaged joints. If possible, this is obtained from the treating doctor. Otherwise, S. S. Disability will have one of their consultative doctors perform the examination.

E. Often, it is too difficult for S. S. Disability to make a decision using only the physical examination of the diseased joints. therefore, all kinds of data showing how much the claimant is impaired in moving about is also sought:

1. Does the claimant have a limp? How severe does the examining doctor say it is?

2. Can the claimant squat down and get back up without any help?

3. Did the claimant have any trouble getting on and off of the examining table?

4. Does the claimant have to use a cane, crutch, brace, or other kind of device to walk? S. S. Disability is not the least interested in whether or not a claimant states that he has to use an assistive like those mentioned. This is true,

even if the claimant has a medical specialist swearing that it is necessary. S. S. Disability makes up its own mind, using all of the available facts.

5. Some examining doctors are very observant and will watch the claimant when he is not aware of it. For example, does the claimant squat down to get his shoes after stating he couldn't squat at all during his physical exam? Does he show a severe limp during his exam, only to walk quickly to his car after leaving the doctor's office?

6. The claimant is being carefully observed, even when he goes to the District Office to file his application. Some of these observations deal with the impression of the officials about how well he walks, gets out of a chair, etc. This information is not as important as a doctor's exam or opinion, but it shouldn't be too far out of line.

F. The arthritis must be severe enough to have caused a decrease from the normal range of motion of the joint. There is no exact rule for how much decrease must be present.

G. The joint should either be enlarged, or have some evidence of excess fluid in it (effusion). This is indicative of more advanced arthritis.

H. Only *one* joint has to be involved.

I. Part A, B, or C must be fulfilled, but not all three.

II. Specific Requirements

A. Part A

1. Part A is fulfilled if there is "gross anatomical deformity". Examples of such deformity are:

(a) "*Subluxation*". The bones of the joint are no longer lined up correctly. They are out of normal position.

(b) "*Contracture*". This may develop when arthritis is so severe that the joint cannot be used very much, if at all. The tissues around the joint—muscles, tendons, and ligaments—may undergo fibrotic degeneration from not being used. This adds to the severity of the arthritis, making it even more difficult for the claimant to use the arthritic joint.

(c) "*Ankylosis*". This means the fixation of a joint, so that it cannot be moved. Advanced arthritis can cause such destruction of bone that the joint is literally "fused" with abnormal bone or fibrous tissue, so that it cannot be moved.

(d) "*Instability*". This can be caused by either the damage to the bones of the joint and/or the ligaments that hold the bones in the correct position. An example would be the so-called "trick-knee" that gives way. (A trick-knee is an example of instability, but it is a long way from qualifying under this Listing.)

2. X-rays are *not* required, but they are often helpful to S. S. Disability in making an accurate decision.

3. Sometimes, a surgeon fuses a knee-joint, because it is so unstable that his patient can't walk on it. This is really an artificial ankylosis or fixation of the knee. Even so, this does not qualify as the ankylosis mentioned in Part A. Such people can often walk fairly well. The ankylosis in Part A must be due to arthritis. Such a knee is much worse than one which has been surgically fused.

B. Part B

1. Part B deals *only* with arthritis of the hip.

2. The arthritis must be so severe that ankylosis (fixation) has taken place. This fixation must be such that the hip is "outside the position of function". This means the hip is fixed at an angle, so that the claimant can't really walk on it effectively, or even sit down normally. Such an abnormal angle of fixation would be anything in which the hip is fixed at a flexed angle of less than 20° or more than 30°. An examining doctor would not be able to move it. A flexed position is one in which the hip is raised up toward the front of the body. When standing, or lying with the legs straight out, the hip is at zero degrees.

3. Unlike Part A, there must be X-rays to fulfill Part B. These X-rays should show the expected severe changes of advanced arthritis.

4. "Joint space narrowing with osteophytosis" refers to the X-ray changes seen with osteoarthritis. Osteophytes are abnormal bony outgrowths caused by overreaction of the bone trying to heal itself.

5. "Bony destruction with erosions or cysts" would be X-ray findings expected in severe rheumatoid arthritis.

C. Part C

1. "Reconstructive surgery" means major surgery on the bone structures of a joint, in an attempt to make it function more normally. It also includes the placing of artificial joints.

2. "Surgical arthrodesis" literally means the surgical fixation (ankylosis) of a joint.

3. Such major surgery often has complications associated with it. Many of these complications are minor, but if they were so serious that the claimant were unable to walk on the joint a

year after surgery, then Part C would be fulfilled. S. S. Disability won't grant benefits just because there might be complications. They must be present at the time of application for disability.

4. "Full weight-bearing status" means that the claimant should be able to walk without a cane, brace, crutch, or other assistive device to help.

Listing 1.04

Arthritis of one major joint in each of the upper extremities (due to any cause): With limitation of motion and enlargement or effusion in the affected joints as well as a history of joint pain and stiffness and X-ray evidence of either joint space narrowing with osteophytosis or bony destruction (with erosions or cysts). With:

A. Abduction of both arms at the shoulders, including scapular motion, restricted to less than 90 degrees; OR

B. Gross anatomical deformity such as subluxation, contracture, bony or fibrous ankylosis, joint instability, or ulnar deviation.

I. General Considerations

A. This Listing deals *only* with arthritis in the "upper extremities". Specifically, that means arthritis of the hands, wrists, elbows, and shoulders.

B. Both upper extremities must be involved.

C. Note that there must be X-rays showing the expected severe changes of arthritis.

D. *Any* kind of arthritis can qualify.

E. Arthritis in a hand and wrist count as only one joint.

F. Although not specifically stated in this Listing, S. S. Disability may use other types of information to help it reach a decision, such as observations by Social Security officials, the claimant's hobbies and activities, and observations by examining doctors. For example, suppose a claimant has arthritis in both shoulders, and insists that he can't lift his arms over his head when examined by a doctor. If the claimant were then seen by the doctor to stick his arms straight up in the air in putting on a sweater, it would be obvious that the claimant has more motion in his shoulders than he will admit. S. S. Disability does not ignore such facts.

II. Specific Requirements

A. Part A

1. Part A deals only with arthritis in the shoulders.

2. Arthritis in the shoulders should be severe enough that when the claimant sticks his arms straight out from his body sideways and tries to lift them he cannot get them higher than a level position (90°).

3. "Abduction" simply means to move a limb away from the body.

B. Part B

1. "Ulnar deviation" refers to a sideways pointing of the fingers, caused by such severe arthritis that they can no longer be held in a normal position. It is most frequently seen in severe rheumatoid arthritis.

2. For an explanation of "subluxation, contracture" etc., see the discussion of these words given under Listing 1.03.

Listing 1.05

Disorders of the spine:

A. Arthritis manifested by ankylosis or fixation of the cervical or dorsolumbar spine at 30° or more of flexion measured from the neutral position,with X-ray evidence of:

1. Calcification of the anterior and lateral ligaments; OR

2. Bilateral ankylosis of the sacroiliac joints with abnormal apophyseal articulations; OR

B. Osteoporosis, generalized (established by X-ray) manifested by pain and limitation of back motion and paravertebral muscle spasm with X-ray evidence of either:

1. Compression fracture of a vertebral body with loss of at least 50 percent of the estimated height of the vertebral body prior to the compression fracture, with no intervening direct traumatic episode; OR

2. Multiple fractures of vertebrae with no intervening direct traumatic episode; OR

C. Other vertebrogenic disorders (e.g., herniated nucleus pulposus, spinal stenosis) with the following persisting for at least 3 months despite prescribed therapy and expected to last 12 months. With both 1 and 2:

1. Pain, muscle spasm, and significant limitation of motion in the spine; AND

2. Appropriate radicular distribution of significant motor loss with muscle weakness and sensory and reflex loss.

I. General Considerations

A. Any kind of arthritis involving the spine can qualify under this Listing.

B. Part A, B, or C must be fulfilled, but not all three.

II. Specific Requirements

A. Part A

1. Part A is really concerned with the findings in a specific disease called ankylosing spondylitis. This is a disease of unknown cause in which the entire spine eventually becomes fixed and fused, in some cases. It is also called Marie-Strumpell Disease.

2. "Ankylosis" refers to fixation or fusion of the spine, so that it can't move.

3. "Cervical spine" refers to the part of the spine in the neck. "Dorsolumbar spine" means the rest of the spine.

4. The spine must be fixed in a bent-forward position (flexed) of at least 30°.

5. X-rays are required and must show one of the following:

(a) Calcium in the ligaments that run up and down the spine, OR

(b) Ankylosis (fusion) of the sacroiliac joints. These are thin joints most people aren't even aware of, between the sacrum and iliac bones of the pelvis. In addition the X-rays must show arthritis in the little apophyseal joints between the vertebral bodies of the spine.

B. Part B

1. "Osteoporosis" refers to the general thinning of the substance of bone, so that it is weaker and tends to break more easily than normal bone.

2. Part B does not refer to the thinning of bone in the spine that some elderly women have after menopause. (There are exceptions, of course).

3. The osteoporosis must be proven by X-ray. It cannot exist only in the spine. X-rays must show that the osteoporosis is actually affecting all of the bones in the body. That is the meaning of the word "generalized".

4. "Paravertebral muscle spasm" means tightening of the muscles in the back near the spine. Such spasm is usually present when pain is severe.

5. There must be less than a normal range of motion in the spine, caused by damage to the spine.

6. In addition to the above findings, one of the following must be present:

(a) Part B.1 requires a compression fracture of a vertebral body. This is something seen on X-ray. If the compression of the vertebral body is no more than half its normal height, then it usually doesn't cause any real problem. The compression of one of the vertebral bodies which make up the spine must be *more* than half of the normal height. Note that there must be "no intervening direct traumatic episode". This is to make sure that the collapse of the vertebral body is due to the weakness caused by osteoporosis, and not some kind of accident.

(b) Part B.2 is the same as B.1, except that many compression fractures of less than 50% can be used.

7. There are many hormonal diseases that can produce the generalized thinning of bone required by Part B. Also, people who are on long term therapy for diseases which require the use of steroid drugs sometimes develop this problem.

C. Part C.

1. Parts A and B above deal with bony disease of the spine. Part C is concerned with damage to the spinal cord itself, or the nerves which leave the spinal cord—in other words, neurological impairment rather than bony impairment.

2. Several examples of diseases that will do this are given by the Listing. "Spinal stenosis" refers to narrowing of the hole in the spine that the spinal cord runs through. This can squeeze down on the nerve pathways of the spinal cord. But the most common application of this Listing is for "herniated nucleus pulposus". See below.

3. The bony spine protects the delicate spinal cord that runs up and down the length of the body. Separate little bones called vertebral bodies make up the bony spine, and are separated from each other by cushions called intervertebral disks. These disks allow the spine to be flexible, so that it can bend. Inside

of each intervertebral disk, there is a harder little piece of tissue called a "nucleus pulposus". Sometimes the nucleus pulposus will push its way out of the intervertebral disk, and then it is called a *herniated* nucleus pulposus, or HNP. The importance of an HNP (sometimes also called a "herniated disk") is that it might press on the nerve roots leaving the spinal cord and produce neurological damage. Arthritic bone pressing up against a nerve root can do the same thing.

4. The claimant must be under treatment by a medical doctor. The abnormal findings must be present for at least 3 months *and* expected to last a full 12 months.

5. Abnormal findings on physical examination must be present as follows:

(a) Part C.1 demands that there be complaints of pain, spasms of the muscles near the spine, and loss of normal motion in the spine.

(b) Part C.2 must be fulfilled, as well as Part C.1. For Part C.2, there must be "appropriate radicular distribution of significant motor loss . . ." etc. What all of this means is that the findings on physical examination must indicate that abnormal pressure on a nerve root exists, as shown by changes in sensation and reflexes. Also, there must be "significant" muscle weakness. This means weakness in some of the larger muscles in the legs.

6. In actual practice, very few claimants are allowed disability under Part C. There are several reasons for this. First, few people have the abnormalities long enough to qualify. They either have surgery, or get better without surgery. If they *don't* get better, S. S. Disability demands so much muscle weakness that it is very difficult to qualify (the claimant would have to show a clear problem in walking normally). It is very unusual to allow a claimant disability under Part C.

7. Before leaving discussion of Part C of the Listing, several final and very important points should be made. These relate to how S. S. Disability determines how much weakness of muscles a claimant has. As noted previously, people with a HNP who have to undergo surgery have had an operation to relieve the pressure that is being placed on nerve roots leaving the spinal cord. Some of these nerve roots supply the muscles of the legs, and if such a nerve root is damaged, then the claimant may have weakness in one or more leg muscles. Sometimes this damage is present, even after surgery. S. S. Disability sees many cases in which the claimant states he has weakness after

surgery, remaining in the muscles of his legs. The problem for S. S. Disability is how to tell the claimants with real weakness from those who exaggerate when examined by a doctor. There are two general ways in which this is done:

(a) The examining doctor may be asked how well the claimant walks, puts on his clothes, steps up on the examining table, or how strongly he can push against the doctor's hand. Observations at the District Office by the officials that take the claimant's application add further information. What kinds of interests and activities that the claimant writes on various forms adds even more data.

(b) The most important thing that S. S. Disability uses in evaluating weakness of muscles is whether or not there is atrophy of the muscles. Atrophy is a shrinkage of muscle fibers. This can be measured by wrapping a tape measure around the muscle concerned. Atrophy sets in very rapidly, and if a claimant doesn't walk for even a couple of weeks it may be detectable. So if a claimant says his right leg is weaker than his left leg to any great degree, then the right leg should be smaller than the left leg. There is absolutely no way to fake atrophy of muscles. It is not uncommon at all for a claimant to go to a S. S. Disability examination using a cane or crutches after back surgery, stating that one of his legs is too weak to support his weight without help. S. S. Disability is not going to believe a word of this, unless the weak leg shows atrophy by actually being smaller than the normal leg. On the other hand, it is not easy for S. S. Disability to get the examining doctor to make the necessary measurements, although they are easy to do. The examining doctor must be very careful, or he might miss atrophy that is present. Difference in leg sizes of less than about 1/2 inch are not very impressive, since it is difficult to measure much more accurately than this.

Listing 1.08

Osteomyelitis (established by X-ray):

A. Located in the pelvis, vertebra, femur, tibia, or a major joint of an upper or lower extremity, with persistent activity or occurrence of at least two episodes of acute activity within a 5-month period prior to adjudication, manifested by local inflammatory, and systemic signs and laboratory findings (e.g., heat, redness, swelling, drainage, leucocytosis, or increased sedimentation rate); OR

B. Multiple localizations and systemic manifestations as in A above.

I. General Considerations

A. This Listing deals *only* with osteomyelitis.

B. Contrary to popular opinion, bone is not dead. It is a living tissue. For this reason it can become infected, and that's what osteomyelitis is—infection of bone.

C. One of the most frequent causes of osteomyelitis results from broken bones due to accidents, in which the wound is severe enough to let contamination and bacteria into the body.

D. Some osteomyelitis is "acute". That is, it occurs once and is cured with antibiotics. But sometimes the infection is extremely difficult to cure, and the claimant develops "chronic" osteomyelitis. If the chronic infection of bone is severe enough, it can result in substantial impairment to the claimant. This Listing deals only with *chronic* osteomyelitis.

E. X-rays are required.

F. Part A or B must be fulfilled, but not both.

II. Specific Requirements

A. Part A

1. To qualify under Part A, the infection must be in a bone of the pelvis, vertebra of the spine, femur (thigh bone), tibia (shin-bone), or a major joint of the arms or legs (such as the hip joint, knee joint, ankle joint, elbow joint, or shoulder joint).

2. Chronic osteomyelitis may be present as flare-ups of acute infection at unpredictable times, or it might be continuously present. For Part A, it must be either continuously present, or there must be evidence of at least 2 acute flare-ups within the 5 months before the application for disability.

3. There must be certain medical evidence that the osteomyelitis is continuously active, or that there is an acute flare-up:

(a) ". . . local inflammatory signs . . ." refers to the area of skin and soft tissue over the place where the bone is infected. Because of its closeness to the infected bone, there should be inflammation of the skin and other tissues in this area. This would be seen as warmth of the skin, as well as redness and swelling. If the infected bone is close to the surface of the skin (such as the tibia) then pus may drain out through the skin. These things can be seen by a doctor on physical examination.

(b) ". . . systemic signs . . ." refers to the fact that the infected bone can let bacteria out into the bloodstream, resulting in general infection. This will sometimes make the claimant even more ill with fever and weakness. Laboratory tests indicating that this is happening are "leucocytosis" and an increased "sedimentation rate". Leucocytosis is simply a term for an increase above normal of the number of white blood cells. This is a general reaction to the body's attempt to fight infection. The "sedimentation rate" refers to a more general test (see discussion of Listing 1.02).

B. Part B

The requirements for Part B are the same as those for Part A, except that many smaller areas of infection are present.

Listing 1.09

Amputation or anatomical deformity of (i.e. loss of major function due to degenerative changes associated with vascular or neurological deficits, traumatic loss of muscle mass or tendons and X-ray evidence of bony ankylosis at an unfavorable angle, joint subluxation or instability):

A. Both hands; OR

B. Both feet; OR

C. One hand and one foot.

I. General Considerations

A. This Listing deals with multiple amputations of limbs, though it could also refer to extremely severe deformity of arms or legs, if they were more or less useless.

B. Many cases qualifying under this Listing have suffered very extensive injuries from accidents. "Vascular or neurological damage" refers to damage to blood vessels and nerves. Tendons and muscles may also be torn away by a severe accident, so that a limb has to be amputated or becomes useless.

C. In cases involving severe deformity on an arm or leg, rather than actual amputation, X-rays of involved joints may be needed. These X-rays should show ankylosis, subluxation, or instability of the joint. These terms are discussed in more detail under Listing 1.03.

D. Part A, B, or C must be fulfilled, but not all three.

II. Specific Requirements

A. Part A

Part A is fulfilled, if there has been amputation of both hands, regardless of the reason.

B. Part B

Part B is fulfilled, if both feet have been amputated, regardless of the reason.

C. Part C

Part C is fulfilled, if a hand and foot have been amputated, regardless of the reason.

D. Part A, B, or C may also be fulfilled, if there is severe deformity of the hands or feet. The deformity must be severe enough to produce very substantial subluxation, ankylosis, or instability of a major joint. The cause of the deformity does not matter.

Listing 1.10

Amputation of one lower extremity (at or above the tarsal region):

A. Hemipelvectomy or hip disarticulation; OR

B. Amputation at or above the tarsal region due to peripheral vascular disease or diabetes mellitus; OR

C. Inability to use a prosthesis effectively, without obligatory assistive devices, due to one of the following:

1. Vascular disease; OR

2. Neurological complications (e.g., loss of position sense); OR

3. Stump too short or stump complications persistent, or are expected to persist, for at least 12 months from onset; OR

4. Disorder of contralateral lower extremity causing mobility restrictions.

I. General Considerations

A. This Listing deals *only* with amputation involving a leg. However, there are additional requirements, since only one leg need be involved.

B. The Listing states that the amputation must be "above the tarsal region". This means that at least the entire foot, including the ankle, must be removed.

C. Part A, B, or C must be fulfilled, but not all three.

II. Specific Requirements

A. Part A

1. If the amputation is so high up that even part of the pelvic bones must be cut away with the leg, then a "hemipelvectomy" has been done.

2. If the place of amputation is a little lower—through the hip joint—then there has been an amputation with hip "disarticulation". This also qualifies.

B. Part B

1. Part B simply states that amputation (above the tarsal region) will qualify *if* the amputation was necessary because of "peripheral vascular disease" "diabetes mellitus".

2. Peripheral vascular disease refers to the gradual blockage of arteries supplying blood to the arms or legs. It is more common in the legs, and involves the fatty build-up of fatty deposits in the blood vessels. The cause is unknown. The blood flow may eventually drop to such a low level that the foot or leg can no longer survive and must be amputated. There are other types of peripheral vascular disease besides blockage by fatty deposits, but they are not common enough causes of amputation to be discussed here. Sometimes, a claimant has undergone surgery to restore the blood flow to the part of the leg involved. If this is successful, the claimant could be saved from the need of amputation.

3. "Diabetes mellitus" refers to the kind of diabetes most people talk about—so-called "sugar" diabetes, in which the blood sugar is abnormally high. Diabetes is worse than just having a high blood sugar. It has very destructive effects on muscles, nerves, and bloodvessels. It also makes the claimant less able to fight infection, for reasons that are far too complex to discuss here. By infection that is difficult to cure, disease of the bloodvessels to the legs, or both together, amputation may be necessary. And infection is more common than in normal people, because the damage diabetes does to the nerves in the legs and feet may make the claimant unaware that an injury has taken place. Because of the decreased blood flow and decreased resistance to infection, even a little injury can sometimes lead to the loss of a foot or leg in very severe diabetics. Even such a minor

thing as not cutting the toenails correctly can lead to infection and eventual amputation.

4. The reader may wonder why only one amputation is required, instead of two as in the previous Listing 1.09. The reason is that diabetes and peripheral vascular diseases are not cured by the amputation; they still exist and are expected to get worse, not better.

C. Part C

1. Part C is for claimants who can't walk on their artificial leg (prosthesis) without also using "obligatory assistive devices". This means that in *addition* to an artificial leg, they also must use something else to help them walk, such as a cane or crutch, etc.

2. It is not enough for a claimant to just say that he can't use an artificial leg. There must be a good reason, based on one of the following problems:

(a) "*Vascular disease* . . . ." If the claimant clearly has such poor blood supply in the place their leg was amputated (stump) that an artificial leg can't be worn, then Part C. 1 is fulfilled. The reason behind this is that the weight of the body pushing the amputated stump down against the artificial leg would decrease the blood flow even more, and lead to increased damage to the part of the leg that is left. This problem is most frequently seen in claimant with severe diabetes.

(b) "*Neurological complications* . . . ." There are special nerve pathways in normal people that involve a "position sense". These special nerves allow a person to tell where their arms or legs are, even with their eyes closed. Some diseases cause so much damage to these nerves that the claimant loses this "position sense". It can be an unpleasant complication of diabetes. Claimants with this problem would have a difficult time walking on a normal leg, much less an artificial one. They would qualify under Part C.1 of the Listing.

(c) "*Stump too short* . . . *etc.*" Part C.3 can be fulfilled if so much of the leg was amputated that an artificial leg can't be fitted to what is left. Other types of medical problems resulting in inability to use an artificial leg could also be considered here, such as an infection on the end of the stump that won't heal. Note that the complication must have lasted at least 12 months, or be so severe that S. S. Disability thinks it will last that long.

(d) "*Disorder of contralateral lower extremity* . . . ." Part C.4 can be fulfilled, if the *non*amputated leg has something wrong with it that keeps the claimant from using an artificial leg on the amputated side. For example, suppose that the claimant had an amputated right leg, and could be fitted with an artificial leg without any problem. But suppose that the left leg had severe arthritis in the knee joint. Then it might be too difficult to walk on the arthritic left leg and artificial right leg at the same time. Of course, other problems in the left leg could also do this, such as arthritis in the hip or ankle, loose ligaments, or nerve problems in the left leg which affect the ability to use it normally.

3. S. S. Disability often sees a claimant who says that he can't walk on his artificial leg, because of the pain it causes in his amputated stump. S. S. Disability will not accept this as valid excuse, unless there is a good medical reason for it. S. S. Disability will not make an allowance under Part C, if the complaint of pain is the only thing that can be found wrong. This is often simply due to poor fitting of the artificial leg. If there is that much pain present, S. S. Disability feels that there should be some reason for it that a doctor can find.

Listing 1.11

Fracture of the femur, tibia, tarsal bone, or pelvis: With solid union not evident on X-ray and not clinically solid, when such determination is feasible, and return to full weight-bearing status did not occur or is not expected to occur within 12 months of onset.

I. General Considerations

A. This Listing deals *only* with fractures of bones. Arthritis is *not* considered under this Listing.

B. Note that only certain bones can qualify.

II. Specific Requirements

A. The bones that qualify are the femur (thigh-bone), tibia (shin-bone), tarsal bone (at least one of the ankle bones), or one of the bones of the pelvis (ischium, ilium, pubis).

B. There must be X-ray evidence that the fracture has not healed. That is what "non-union" means—the two sides of the break have not mended together.

C. The unhealed fracture must not be "clinically solid". This means that an examining doctor should be able to tell by physical examination that the fracture has not healed. This does not apply if the broken leg is in a cast or other device where such examination cannot be made.

D. It is extremely important to note that the fracture must be unhealed by the above criteria for at least 12 months. Most fractures heal long before 12 months, and such cases would *not* qualify. Many claimants apply for disability right after they break a bone in a motorcycle or automobile wreck. But, after getting the treatment data, S. S. Disability will usually decide that the fracture is likely to heal within 12 months, and the claim will be denied. S. S. Disability will not assume that complications are going to occur. That doesn't mean that the claimant would necessarily have to wait a whole year with an unhealed fracture, before being granted disability. If the fracture has shown little evidence of healing for 6 months, S. S. Disability will start considering the possibility of allowing the case. But every case is different, and no general rule can be given. That is because the possible medical problems in any case are very numerous.

E. The phrase "full weight-bearing status did not occur . . ." is very important. It is critical that the potential claimant understand this to protect his rights. Before S. S. Disability should consider the fracture healed, there should be evidence that the claimant can walk without any special devices to help. This includes cane, crutches, and braces. It is not uncommon for a claimant to have a fracture that has healed enough at 12 months, so that he can walk a little with the help of a crutch, but *full* weight cannot be put on the broken leg. Or there might be a brace to keep full weight off of the fractured leg. This claimant would still qualify for disability, because "full weight-bearing status did not occur". On the other hand, the need of a cane, crutch, or other device to walk *must* be due to the incompletely healed fracture. Some claimants use a cane or crutch, although their fracture has healed. They would not qualify. This is true, even if the claimant's treating doctor says that, for example, a crutch is needed to walk. S. S. Disability will use its own judgment. Finally, some people with fractures (especially of the tibia) may also do some nerve damage to certain leg muscles. This could mean that even after the fracture itself is healed, the claimant has to wear a short brace, due to muscle weakness. This would *not* qualify. The use of canes, crutches, braces, etc. *must* be due to unhealed bone.

Listing 1.12

Fractures of an upper extremity: With non-union of a fracture of the shaft of the humerus, redius, or ulna under continuing surgical management directed toward restoration of functional use of the extremity and such function was not restored or expected to be restored within 12 months after onset.

I. General Considerations

A. This Listing deals *only* with fractures.

B. Only fractures of certain bones in the arms qualify.

II. Specific Requirements

A. There must be lack of healing of the fracture (non-union).

B. The bones involved must be the humerus (bone in the upper arm between the shoulder and elbow), radius, or ulna. These latter two bones are in the forearm, between the elbow and wrist.

C. The claimant must be under treatment by a surgeon who has made definite efforts to heal the arm and make it usable again.

D. Although not stated by the Listing, X-rays clearly are necessary to evaluate such cases.

E. The unhealed fracture must have been present for at least 12 months, or have lasted long enough that S. S. Disability thinks it will still be unhealed in 12 months. It is impossible to say exactly how long a claimant must have an unhealed fracture, before S. S. Disability decides that it will probably last 12 months. The reason for this is that all cases are different and involve different kinds of medical problems. All of this is taken into account. As a general rule of thumb only, a claimant is extremely unlikely to qualify without an unhealed fracture at least 6 months old despite treatment.

Listing 1.13

Soft tissue injuries of an upper or lower extremity: Requiring a series of staged surgical procedures within 12 months after onset for salvage and/or restoration of major function of the extremity, and such major function was not restored or expected to be restored within 12 months after onset.

I. General Considerations

A. This Listing deals with injuries to the tissues of the legs or arms other than bones. Fractures are not considered under this Listing.

B. Note that there must be an injury to an arm or leg. Injury to other parts of the body are not considered under this Listing.

II. Specific Requirements

A. Soft tissue refers to everything but bone, such as muscles, nerves, ligaments, blood vessels, and tendons.

B. There must be a series of surgical procedures directed toward restoring the usefulness of the arm or leg.

C. The surgical treatment must take up to at least 12 months, or be expected to last that long. It is not enough for the claimant or his treating surgeon to simply say that more surgery is planned in the "near future". The treating surgeon must tell S. S. Disability that there is a definite plan for further surgery, with the date it is to be done. The surgeon must also specify the nature of the surgery and why it is being done. Definite dates for planned hospitalization and surgery should be available to S. S. Disability, as noted above. This cannot be emphasized too strongly.

D. Claimants allowed disability under this Listing may have their cases reviewed again in the future, to determine how successful the surgery was in restoring function to the damaged limb.

§ 2.3 Special Senses and Speech

Listing 2.02

Impairment of central visual acuity. Remaining vision in the better eye after best correction is 20/200 or less.

I. General Considerations

A. This Listing deals only with what is called "central visual acuity". Central acuity is that part of vision that allows the seeing of detail, such as small objects or reading.

B. Central acuity is what most people have checked when they go to an eye specialist (ophthalmologist), and this is why glasses are worn—to correct defective central acuity. For example, being "near-sighted" is a defect in central acuity due to an abnormal shape of the eyeball. When central acuity is impaired, vision is blurry instead of clear. Most visual problems are defects in the acuity of vision.

C. Central acuity is measured by numbers such as "20/20", a term which everyone has heard about. If a person has 20/20 acuity, then their acuity is normal. The larger the second number, the worse the acuity is. For example, 20/50 represents worse vision than 20/20. Likewise, 20/100 is worse than 20/50. On the other hand, 20/15 represents better than normal acuity.

D. Measuring central acuity obviously requires the cooperation of the claimant. When tested, some claimants simply say they can't see anything—that they can't see any of the letters on the eye-chart. If this were true, the claimant would qualify for disability, since "blindness" would be present. However, S. S. Disability requires that there be some kind of eye injury or disease present, which could explain such "blindness". If a doctor can't find anything wrong on examining the claimant's eyes, S. S. Disability is not going to believe that the claimant has serious visual problems, no matter what the claimant says about his vision. Also the eye disease, if any, must be severe enough to reasonably cause the amount of visual loss that the claimant states is present. In some cases, S. S. Disability has gone so far as to obtain computerized brainwave analysis to help prove the presence of vision in claimants who continued to insist they couldn't see, even though eye specialists could find nothing wrong with them. Such tests cannot be faked. On the other hand, a claimant that *did* have a fairly severe eye disease might be able to pretend that it was somewhat worse than it really is, and not be caught. For example, suppose a claimant had a real visual acuity of 20/150, which is not quite severe enough to qualify under this Listing. If on testing his vision seemed to be no better than 20/200, which is bad enough to fulfill this Listing, it would be very difficult to say that the claimant was lying and he would probably get benefits. Such dishonest behavior is certainly not condoned by the author.

E. *Any* disease or injury to the eyes could qualify under this Listing. S. S. Disability is not so much interested in the desease, as it is in the degree that the disease has affected the claimant's vision.

F. S. S. Disability may use other data, besides examination by a doctor. For example, if a claimant acts like he is totally blind when examined by a doctor, but appears to see very well when doing other things, then S. S. Disability is going to be suspicious. No matter what eye tests seem to show, how blind could a claimant be who reads and writes well, drives, and goes hunting?

G. S. S. Disability often purchases examinations by eye specialists when a claimant alleges difficulty seeing. These specialists are medical doctors (M.D.'s) called *ophthalmologists*. Information about a claimant's blindness may be acceptable from medical doctors who are not eye specialists, but it would be unlikely that a claimant who provides "proof" of his blindness based on an exam by a non-medical doctor would be accepted.

II. Specific Requirements

A. Note that evaluation under this Listing is based on the eye with the *best* vision. For example, if a claimant were totally blind in one eye, but could see normally out of the other eye, there would be no chance of qualifying under this Listing.

B. Note the phrase ". . . after best correction . . . ." This means that vision must be poor *even with glasses or contact lenses*. Whether the vision can be made better does *not* depend on the claimant using his own glasses. The claimant might simply need a new pair of glasses. Claimants sometimes go to examinations set up by S. S. Disability and leave their glasses at home, perhaps hoping that this will make their eyesight appear worse than it really is. S. S. Disability cannot be so easily fooled.

C. The *best* eye after best correction, *must* have a central acuity of 20/200 or worse. Vision of 20/200 is not total blindness, but it is statutory (legal) blindness. "Best correction" means that an eye specialist uses his own special equipment to determine how well the claimant's vision could be improved with glasses; it does not mean how well the claimant sees with the glasses that he happens to have. As noted above, the claimant's glasses might not be as good as they could be.

D. Sometimes a claimant has so little vision remaining that they cannot even be tested in the normal way (reading a chart with letters on it). Such a claimant might only be able to see a little light, or the doctor's hand moving close to their face. These people would clearly have an acuity worse than 20/200, even though it can't be exactly measured, and would still qualify under this Listing. Also, there are special ways to test vision in people who never learned to read.

E. Unless the cause of blindness is clearly something that has been present from birth, S. S. Disability will not usually set the onset date of allowance much earlier than the actual date of medical records which first show the blindness to be present. Thus, it is important that medical records be available.

Listing 2.03

Contraction of peripheral visual fields in the better eye.

A. To 10° or less from the point of fixation; OR

B. So the widest diameter subtends an angle no greater than 20°; OR

C. To 20 percent or less visual field efficiency.

I. General Considerations

A. This Listing deals only with what are called *peripheral* visual defects. (Unlike the previous Listing 2.02, which deals only with defects in *central* vision.)

B. Peripheral vision does not involve detail such as reading or seeing things at a distance. It is peripheral vision that allows people to see things "out of the corner of the eye". For example, if the reader looks straight ahead without moving his eyes or head and wiggles his finger out to the side of his head, he will see the finger, although not clearly. This is peripheral vision, where things can be seen even though the eyes are not focusing on them.

C. Note that only the eye with the *best* vision is used in S. S. Disability's evaluation.

D. Many people aren't even aware of their peripheral vision, until they start to lose it. Then they realize how important it is. In the worst form, there is so-called "tunnel-vision", in which vision is constricted to a small area like looking down a tube or tunnel. Diseases which affect large areas of the retina, optic nerves, or brain can cause defective peripheral fields.

E. It is not uncommon for a claimant to say that nothing can be seen on testing of their peripheral visual fields. They may have terrible "tunnel-vision". S. S. Disability is not going to believe this, unless there is some kind of disease present that could be responsible.

F. A doctor may very crudely test a claimant's peripheral fields by having the claimant focus on a spot straight ahead without moving their eyes or head. Then the doctor moves his finger around the sides of the face toward the front, until the claimant can see it. This is sometimes done by doctors on routine physical examinations, but it is not accurate enough for S. S. Disability to make a decision.

G. Special testing is required to determine how much of a claimant's peripheral field is missing due to some eye disease. Special charts are used for this testing. The size and shape of the claimant's peripheral fields are plotted on these charts by an eye specialist, one chart for each eye. Figure No. 1 gives an idea of what these charts look like. Referring to Figure 1, it can be seen that the peripheral field in the right eye is normal in size. But in the left eye the visual field is squeezed down (contracted), and vision is possible only in a much smaller area. Notice that the charts are marked off in circles from 10° to at least 90°.

H. Peripheral field testing is done *without* glasses, because the frames of the glasses would interfere with the measurements. Contact lenses are left on.

I. Part A, B, or C must be fulfilled, but not all three.

II. Specific Requirements

A. Part A

1. The "point of fixation" refers to the point where the examining doctor asks the claimant to look, while his peripheral fields are being tested. The claimant must focus on this point and not move his eyes during the testing. In Figure 1, the point of fixation that the claimant focuses on during the test is right in the center of the chart for whichever eye is being tested.

2. The first little circle on the peripheral field chart for each eye is the 10° circle. If the claimant can't see anything outside of that little circle going in any direction from the center point of fixation, then Part A is fulfilled. In the example given in Figure 1, there is contraction of the visual field in the *left* eye, but it is not severe enough to qualify under Part A. This is because some of the claimant's vision goes out beyond the 10° circle.

B. Part B

Part B says the same thing as Part A, but just in a different way.

C. Part C

1. Part C deals with what is called *visual field efficiency.* It is important to note that this is different from *visual efficiency,* which is considered in the next Listing, 2.04.

2. The percent of visual field efficiency is obtained by adding the number of degrees of the eight principal meridians of the contracted field and dividing by 500. For example, Figure No. 1 shows the visual field in the left eye contracted to 30° in the temporal and down and out meridians and to 20° in the remaining six meridians. The percent of visual field efficiency in the left eye is: $6 \times 20 + 2 \times 30 = 180 \div 500 = 0.36$ or 36 percent remaining visual field efficiency, or 64 percent loss. Since a 20 percent or less visual field efficiency is required, the above example with 36 percent would not qualify.

3. It should be noted that there are tests which measure only the central most part of the visual peripheral field, and these are called *tangent screen visual fields.* They are also called *central visual fields,* and are not accepted by S. S. Disability for its purposes. To qualify under Part C, the requisite peripheral contraction of 20 percent or less must be present using a method of measurement called *arc perimetry.* Peripheral fields plotted by a machine (auto-plot devices) are not acceptable to S. S. Disability.

Figure 1. Visual Field Charts For Right and Left Eyes

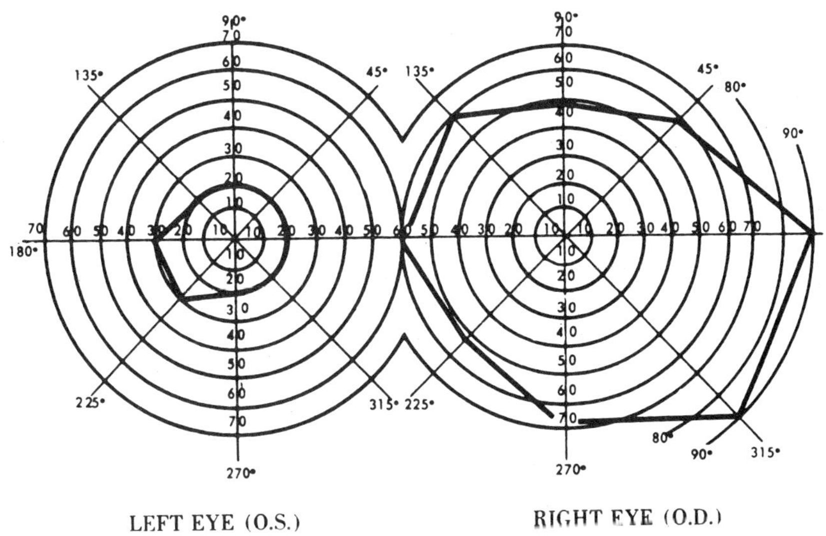

Listing 2.04

Loss of visual efficiency. Visual efficiency of better eye after best correction 20 percent or less. (The percent of remaining visual efficiency=the product of the percent of remaining central visual efficiency and the percent of remaining visual field efficiency.)

I. General Considerations

A. This Listing deals with what is called *visual efficiency.* Note that this is something different from *visual field* efficiency, as discussed above in Listing 2.03.

B. The general concept behind visual efficiency is really very simple. A claimant may have defective vision, because their central visual acuity involved in things like reading is impaired. This was considered in Listing 2.02. Also, a claimant may have defective vision, because their peripheral vision is impaired. This was considered in Listing 2.03. However, some people have defects in *both* their central acuity of vision *and* their peripheral visual fields. Neither defect alone might be severe enough to get a claimant disability benefits, but combining both types *together* might be. That is what visual efficiency rating does—it combines the degree of impairment from both types of defect to produce an "over-all" rating of the degree of visual impairment.

II. Specific Requirements

A. The calculations are done using only the claimant's *best* eye.

B. The claimant's acuity of vision and peripheral fields are both used for the calculations. The visual acuity is based on how well an eye specialist can correct the vision with contact lenses or glasses.

C. The final number representing the visual efficiency must not be higher than 20 percent. To make the calculation of visual efficiency, the determination of visual *field* efficiency is first made, as in Listing 2.03C. The percent *central* visual efficiency is then determined from Table 1 using the central visual acuity. The visual efficiency is obtained by simply multiplying the percent visual field efficiency by the percent central visual efficiency.

D. The first two columns in Table 1 are merely two different ways of expressing visual acuity. Which column is used simply depends on whether the acuity is expressed in the "English" or the "Metric" system. The percent central visual efficiency is then determined from the "Phakic", "Aphakic Monocular", or "Aphakic Binocular" columns by the instructions given under "Column and Use". These instructions should be read very carefully, before attempting to use Table 1. "Phakic" means the eye still has its lens, and "Aphakic" means that the lens has been removed.

Table 1

Percentage of central visual efficiency corresponding to central visual acuity notations for distance in the phakic and aphakic eye (using better eye).

Snellen		Percent Central Visual Efficiency		
English	Metric	Phakic 1/	Aphakic Monocular 2/	Aphakic Binocular 3/
20/16	6/5	100	50	75
20/20	6/6	100	50	75
20/25	6/7.5	95	47	71
20/32	6/10	90	45	67
20/40	6/12	85	42	64
20/50	6/15	75	37	56
20/64	6/20	65	32	49
20/80	6/24	60	30	45
20/100	6/30	50	25	37
20/125	6/38	40	20	30
20/160	6/48	30	—	22
20/200	6/60	20	—	—

Column Use:

1/ Phakic—1. A lens is present in both eyes.
2. A lens is present in the better eye and absent in the poorer eye.
3. A lens is present in one eye and the other eye is enucleated.

2/ Monocular—1. A lens is absent in the better eye and present in the poorer eye.
2. The lenses are absent in both eyes; however, the central visual acuity in the poorer eye after best correction is 20/200 or less.
3. A lens is absent from one eye and the other eye is enucleated.

3/ Binocular—1. The lenses are absent from both eyes and the central visual acuity in the poorer eye after best correction is greater than 20/200.

Listing 2.05

Complete homonymous hemianopsia (with or without macular sparing). Evaluate under Listing 2.04.

I. General Considerations

A. This Listing refers to a special kind of visual field defect called homonymous hemianopsia, in which the peripheral visual field is half missing in each eye. People with this kind of defect in their peripheral fields have problems with the optic nerve pathways from the eyes to the brain, or within the brain itself. A common cause is a large pituitary tumor pressing on the optic nerves.

B. The statement "with or without macular sparing" is simply a reminder to the person reviewing the case not to take into account whether or not a special area of the retina of the eye called the macula is involved in the visual field defect. The macula contains the retinal cones necessary for color vision and is also responsible for the sharpest vision (central visual acuity).

C. More explanation about the nature of peripheral visual field defects can be found in the discussions of Listings 2.03 and 2.04.

II. Specific Requirements

If the claimant has homonymous hemianopsia, no special evaluation is done under this Listing. The actual evaluation is done under Listing 2.04. The only reason this Listing exists is to remind the person reviewing the case that a defect in peripheral visual fields called homonymous hemianopsia should only be evaluated under Listing 2.04.

Listing 2.06

Total bilateral ophthalmoplegia.

I. General Considerations

A. This Listing simply says "total bilateral ophthalmoplegia". "Ophthalmoplegia" means paralysis of the little muscles attached to the eye, which allow it to move. There are six such muscles for each eye, called "extraocular muscles".

B. When *all* of the muscles controlling the eye are paralyzed, then the ophthalmoplegia is *total*.

II. Specific Requirements

A. The ophthalmoplegia *must* be total. This not only requires that the six extraocular muscles be paralyzed, but also special little muscles inside the eye which control the size of the pupil and the shape of the lens of the eye.

B. Special testing would be necessary for any claimant to qualify under this Listing. It is not enough for even an eye specialist to simply say that the claimant cannot move his eyes. Actual measurements must be done, concerning the claimant's ability to move his eyes.

C. *Both* eyes must be involved.

D. A claimant who has the severity required by this Listing would have absolutely no ability to move either eye. The pupils of his eyes would be wide and not respond to light; the eye could not protect itself by becoming smaller in bright light. Since the little muscles controlling the shape of the lenses in the eyes must also be paralyzed, the claimant would have trouble focusing on anything clearly.

E. The author, in his experience, has not seen a single claimant qualify under this Listing. Perhaps there are claimants who have this degree of severity and qualify under this Listing, but they must be very rare.

Listing 2.07

Disturbance of labyrinthine-vestibular function (including Meniere's Disease), characterized by a history of frequent attacks of balance disturbance, tinnitus, and progressive loss of hearing. With both A and B:

A. Disturbed function of vestibular labyrinth demonstrated by caloric or other vestibular tests; AND

B. Hearing loss established by audiometry.

I. General Considerations

A. The terms "labyrinthine" and "vestibular" refer to little bony spaces and tubes in the inner ear. Nerve impulses from these little organs constantly tell a person the position of the head. This is important in maintaining balance of the body while walking, or even just standing in one place.

B. An example is given as Meniere's Disease. Actually, many claimants have a diagnosis of Meniere's Disease from their treating doctors, because of symptoms of "dizziness". If "dizziness" is the only complaint, S. S. Disability will *not* accept the diagnosis of Meniere's Disease.

C. The claimant must have a history of illness showing frequent episodes of difficulty with balance, "ringing" in the ears (tinnitus), and *increasing* deafness. Exactly how often these attacks must occur is not spelled out by S. S. Disability. It would partly depend on how severe the individual attacks are, but there is no definite rule; it is a matter of judgment by the person reviewing the case. However, it is probably pretty unlikely that anyone having attacks less than once a month would qualify.

D. It is not enough that the claimant have complaints of trouble keeping his balance, dizziness, ringing in the ears, or deafness. There must be special tests showing that this is true. See below. *Both* Part A and Part B must be fulfilled.

II. Specific Requirements

A. Part A

1. The Listing mentions tests which prove that the claimant should have difficulty with balance and "dizziness".

2. "Caloric" testing is one such method. Warm fluid is placed in the ears; following this, special measurements allow a doctor to determine if there is a problem in balance from problems with the "inner ear".

B. Part B

1. The claimant must have defective hearing. Hearing is measured by special testing call "audiometry", which will be discussed in more detail under Listing 2.08.

2. *How much* hearing loss there is doesn't matter as much as the fact that some amount of deafness is present and is *getting worse. One* test of hearing loss is not enough to show that hearing is getting worse. This requires several tests over a period of time, which shows increasing deafness.

Listing 2.08

Hearing impairments (not restorable by a hearing aid) manifested by:

A. Average hearing threshold sensitivity for air conduction of 90 decibels or greater, and for bone conduction to corresponding maximal levels, in the better ear, determined by the simple average of hearing threshold levels at 500, 1000, and 2000 hz.; OR

B. Speech discrimination scores of 40 percent or less in the better ear.

I. General Considerations

A. This Listing deals with impairment of hearing. This is done by special testing called audiometry.

B. People hear both by sounds conducted through the air *and* sound conducted through bones in the ear and skull. Audiometry tests *both* types of hearing.

C. If hearing can be improved with a hearing aid, the claimant may no longer qualify under this Listing.

D. It is not uncommon for people to apply for disability, stating that they are "totally deaf". Testing involves asking the claimant if he can hear certain kinds of sounds. The claimant could, of course, just state that he can't hear anything at all. Unfortunately, it is not rare for a claimant to try to fake more deafness than is actually present. But there are all kinds of ways that this can be detected:

1. A claimant acts like he is totally deaf, but the doctor calls out his name when he's walking out of the doctor's office. If the claimant turns around, then he heard the doctor's voice. Officials at the District Office where the application is filed, may try similar things. Incredibly, a claimant faking a hearing loss may go through a complete exam by a doctor without slipping up only to give himself away by falling for this old test.

2. During the testing of the claimant's hearing, he will be given sounds with different amounts of loudness. The persons giving the test can change this loudness any way they want. If the claimant says he can hear a weak sound and then says he can't hear a louder one, this will produce suspicion of faking hearing loss.

3. There are special tests which no claimant can fake, no matter how smart or knowledgeable he is. If the claimant *persists* in stating that he is totally deaf when observation and testing indicate he should not be, then S. S. Disability has more than once ordered computorized brainwave analysis to prove that the claimant's brain is receiving signals from their ears.

E. While "total" deafness is difficult to fake for reasons given above, a claimant with a reasonable amount of genuine deafness might be able to exaggerate enough to get disability benefits without being detected. However, attempts at such dishonesty is certainly not recommended, because the whole test would be considered invalid by S. S. Disability and make it impossible to accurately rate the claimant's hearing impairment. Benefits certainly would not be granted if a claimant attempted to do this and was caught.

F. Before S. S. Disability will purchase testing of a claimant's hearing, there should be some significant problem in that area. If the claimant appears to only have a mild hearing loss, S. S. Disability will not spend money on audiometric testing, the test would not be expected to result in allowance of benefits. If the claimant is able to talk fairly well with his treating doctor, or with the officials at the District Office where he makes application for disability, or over the telephone to officials representing S. S. Disability, then he is not going to be considered very deaf. Special testing of the claimant's hearing defect would not be done.

G. Few people are really deaf enough to qualify under this Listing. The claimant has to be *extremely* deaf.

H. Part A or Part B must be fulfilled, but not both.

II. Specific Requirements

A. Part A

1. As noted above, people can hear sound conducted either through the air, or through the bones of their skull. *Both* types of hearing are tested by audiometry.

2. The *loudness* of sound is measured in units called *decibels.*

3. The specialist who tests the claimant's hearing gradually turns up the loudness (decibel level), until the claimant states that he can hear it. This is the "threshold sensitivity" of loudness for the claimant to even be aware that there is a sound.

4. S. S. Disability doesn't consider all frequencies of sound that are a normal part of hearing. It only considers the impor-

tant frequencies that are needed to understand and use speech. These frequencies are 500, 1000 and 2000 cycles per second ("Hertz"). Only these frequencies are used for calculation.

5. S. S. Disability averages together the loudness of sound necessary to hear at each of the above frequencies. This average is calculated for hearing through air and through bone. The final average must not be lower than 90 decibels of "loudness" necessary for the claimant to hear sounds in the air, and not lower than a "corresponding level" of "loudness" necessary to hear sounds through bone. This would be about 65 decibels for sounds through bone.

6. S. S. Disability will do its evaluation based on how much hearing defect there is in the *best* ear. In other words, a claimant could be "stone deaf" in one ear and he would still have to be deaf enough in the other ear to qualify under the Listing.

B. Part B

1. *Speech discrimination* is the ability to identify spoken words.

2. Speech discrimination is a standard part of audiometry.

3. The speech discrimination in the *best* ear is used to decide if disability benefits will be awarded.

4. To qualify, the claimant must not be able to identify more than 40% of the words spoken to him from a special list of words.

5. A claimant who has poor speech discrimination should have at least some degree of deafness also. A claimant who could hear all frequencies of sound normally, but who claimed he couldn't hear speech might not be completely honest.

Listing 2.09

Organic loss of speech due to any cause with inability to produce by any means speech which can be heard, understood, and sustained.

I. General Considerations

A. This Listing deals with the ability to speak effectively.

B. The word "organic" means that the loss of speech must be due to actual physical disease, and not some type of mental illness.

C. The Listing states that *any* cause of loss of speech can be considered. However, this is not entirely true. The Listing applies to damage to the tongue, throat, voice-box (larynx), etc. It does *not* apply to claimants who can't speak due to some kind of brain damage, such as a cerebrovascular accident (CVA, "stroke"). Those claimants are evaluated under a special Listing dealing with strokes (Listing 11.04).

D. Claimants most often evaluated under this Listing are those who have had surgical removal of part of the larynx (voice-box), tongue, or mouth because of cancer.

II. Specific Requirements

A. It is not enough for the claimant to be unable to speak. The claimant must also be unable to *learn* to speak. For example, a claimant who has had his larynx removed for cancer might be able to learn what is called *esophageal speech.* Some claimants can learn this, some cannot. Even if a claimant can't learn esophageal speech, if he can use special devices to help him speak, he *still* might not qualify under this Listing. For example, there are devices that can be held against the outside of the throat that may help the claimant speak. If one of these devices can be used effectively, the claimant might not qualify under this Listing.

B. A claimant with a problem speaking won't necessarily be denied benefits, simply because he can produce a little speech. Before he can be denied benefits, a claimant must be able to produce speech that can be *heard* with reasonable ease by other people. Also, before a claimant is denied benefits under this Listing, he should be able to produce speech that other people can *understand.* Lastly, a claimant should not be denied benefits under this Listing, unless he can produce *sustained* speech—in other words, carry on a conversation for a reasonable length of time.

§ 2.4 Respiratory System

Listing 3.02

Chronic obstructive airway disease (due to any cause). With:

Spirometric evidence of airway obstruction demonstrated by MVV and FEV_1, both equal to, or less than, the values specified in Table I, corresponding to the person's height.

Table I

Height (Inches)	MVV (MBC) Equal to or Less Than	AND	FEV_1 Equal to or Less Than
	Liters/Min.		Liters
57 or less	32		1.0
58 or less	33		1.0
59 or less	34		1.0
60 or less	35		1.1
61 or less	36		1.1
62 or less	37		1.1
63 or less	38		1.1
64 or less	39		1.2
65 or less	40		1.2
66 or less	41		1.2
67 or less	42		1.3
68 or less	43		1.3
69 or less	44		1.3
70 or less	45		1.4
71 or less	46		1.4
72 or less	47		1.4
73 or more	48		1.4

I. General Considerations

A. This Listing deals *only* with lung disease that is of the *obstructive* type. The most common examples of this type of lung disease are emphysema and asthma. In emphysema, the lung tissue itself is destroyed. By far, the most common cause is cigarette smoking. Most claimants allowed under this Listing have emphysema. In asthma, the bronchial tubes leading to the lungs constrict making it difficult for air to get in and out of the lungs.

B. Before any claimant is allowed disability under this Listing, they must undergo special tests called *pulmonary function studies* (P.F.S.). P.F.S. measure the ability of the claimant to move air in and out of the lungs. The claimant breathes through a tube into a machine which plots out curves representing the flow of air on graph paper. These graphs are then analyzed and the final results reported as numbers. Sometimes, this analysis is done by a human being and sometimes it is done by a computer.

C. Often, a claimant has had P.F.S. done before he applies for S. S. Disability But these are almost never acceptable to S. S. Disability. The reason for this is that in order to maintain consistency and quality, S. S. Disability will only accept P.F.S. done under very exact standards. This means that S. S. Disability has to buy P.F.S. testing on a large number of claimants with lung disease, so that the tests will be done the way S. S. Disability desires.

D. S. S. Disability *never* trusts anyone to interpret the graphs produced by a P.F.S. This includes treating doctors, lung specialists, and computers. The actual graphic tracings are *always* required for S. S. Disability to analyze. S. S. Disability will go over these graphs in extreme detail. If there is anything wrong with the test, S. S. Disability may either deny the claimant benefits or insist that the P.F.S. be done again.

E. S. S. Disability insists that the person who gives a P.F.S. test to a claimant state how *cooperative* the claimant was in taking the test. If that person (usually a respiratory technician, sometimes a doctor) says that the claimant wasn't cooperative, then S. S. Disability is likely to reject the results of the test. In fact, S. S. Disability doesn't even trust the person who gives the test. The reason for this is that the respiratory technician or doctor who gives the test often says that the claimant was cooperative when in fact the graphs clearly show that the claimant was not doing the test in the right way. S. S. Disability makes up its own mind about how cooperative the claimant was during the test.

F. Many claimants allege that they are "short of breath" when they apply for disability. But S. S. Disability will not buy P.F.S. unless there is some legitimate reason, based on physical examination by a doctor, to believe that some significant lung disease may be present.

G. In evaluating the results of P.F.S., S. S. Disability will always take the highest numbers for rating. That is, the final decision will be based on the *best* performance by the claimant, not the worst (each part of the test is done several times to increase reliability).

II. Specific Requirements

A. "Spirometry" is another word for P.F.S. testing.

B. S. S. Disability looks for two measurements plotted out on graphs: the "MVV" and "FEV_1". "MVV" stands for "Maximum Voluntary Ventilation", and simply refers to the maximum amount of air that a person can breathe in and out of their lungs in one minute. The person taking the test must try as hard as he can to make it valid. "FEV_1" stands for "Forced Expiratory Volume in One Second". This means the amount of air that a person can breathe out in one second, after taking a deep breath and blowing as hard as he can.

C. If the person giving the test doesn't think the claimant tried as hard as he could have, that may be noted on the test report. This could make the test invalid, though if the curves show that the claimant did in fact do his best what the person giving the test says might be ignored.

D. First, the FEV_1 is done three times and the MVV is done once. This is recorded on graph paper. Then a special drug is given, called a "bronchodilator". This drug makes the bronchial tubes leading to the lungs open wider. The FEV_1 is then done three more times, and the MVV once again. The reason for giving bronchodilator drugs is to see if the claimant can breath better by using them. This is especially important in people with asthma, whose major breathing problem is that their bronchial tubes constrict, making them smaller and thus more difficult to move air in and out of the lungs. But if this is present and can be reversed by bronchodilator drugs, S. S. Disability wants to know more about it. Such claimants could be treated by doctors and breathe much better. S. S. Disability only wants to allow benefits to those claimants with lung disease that can't be effectively treated.

E. Sometimes a claimant will refuse to have their breathing tested with bronchodilator drugs. The most common reason for this is that they are "allergic" to these drugs. S. S. Disability would never insist in that against the claimant's wishes, but it might deny benefits to one who couldn't show reasonable evidence from a doctor that they are in fact allergic to bronchodilator drugs. Although such drugs are used on millions of people routinely in medical practice for P.F.S. testing without ill effect, people with certain kinds of heart disease might be at increased risk for ill effects from bronchodilators. These individuals can be exempted from the requirement, as well as those who truly are allergic to such drugs. S. S. Disability does not want to harm anyone during its testing procedures.

F. A claimant's "normal" FEV_1 and "normal" MVV depend on how tall he is and how old he is. These numbers are also different for men and women. S. S. Disability only takes into account the height of the claimant, however.

G. Table I shows how low the FEV_1 and MVV have to be in order to qualify under this Listing, for different heights. These heights are without shoes.

H. In evaluating cases under this Listing, S. S. Disability takes the very *highest* FEV_1 it can find in the test of the 6 total done. It also takes the *highest* of the 2 MVV's done. It doesn't matter whether the FEV_1 was done before or after the bronchodilator drug; the highest value is *always* used. The same thing applies to the MVV.

I. In addition to the highest FEV_1 and MVV values being used to evaluate the claimant's case, *neither* of them can be higher than the values given in Table I. For example, suppose a claimant is 57 inches tall with an MVV of 32 or less, and an FEV_1 of 1.0 or less. If these are the *best* that the claimant can do, he would qualify under this Listing. But if the MVV were 33, instead of 32, the claimant would *not* qualify. To re-emphasize this point, S. S. Disability always makes its decision using the highest numbers it can find, whether they are an MVV or FEV_1 and whether or not they are obtained before or after bronchodilator. In addition both the FEV_1 and MVV must be no higher than the values in Table I, for a given height of the claimant.

J. Being "close" to the numbers in Table I isn't good enough. The numbers in the table *cannot* be violated.

K. It is very difficult for a claimant to "fake" a pulmonary function study. A claimant who is really sick and trying as hard as he can will produce graphs that all look reasonably similar. A claimant who is trying to control his breathing to fake the results will probably produce graphs that look too different from each other for each test run. Graphs of the FEV_1 that are more than 10% different from each other make S. S. Disability suspicious that the claimant's performance is too uneven to give reliable results. This can be intentional on the part of the claimant, or it can be due to the claimant not understanding the instructions very well. But either way the results are less reliable than S. S. Disability wants. However, a few clever claimants have learned to raise up their tongue in the front of their mouth just a little bit, so that it is always in the same place during each test run. This can block down the air flow during the breathing tests, but all of the curves will look similar just like S. S. Disability wants. In the author's opinion, this is easier said than done, even though many doctors and respiratory technicians giving P.F.S. don't even know about this trick. Also, S. S. Disability will have a great deal of trouble believing a breathing test, if the claimant doesn't have any evidence of lung disease after a physical exam and chest X-ray by a doctor. Perhaps a claimant who has lung disease which is not quite severe enough to qualify under this Listing could exaggerate his breathing difficulty and fool S. S. Disability into thinking he is worse than he really is. Although it might be possible for a few claimants to cheat on P.F.S., the author strongly recommends that no such dishonest attempts be made. The claimant is much more likely to mess up the test and be denied benefits. S. S. Disability would not deny benefits as punishment, but a messy test cannot be read accurately and cannot be used for a decision. This can mean that a claimant who would have qualified had he been cooperative and honest in his attempts to perform the test is denied benefits because his attempts to fake the results make the test unusable.

Listing 3.03

Asthma. With:

A. *Chronic asthmatic bronchitis.* Evaluate under the criteria for chronic obstructive airway disease in 3.02; OR

B. Episodes of severe attacks, in spite of prescribed treatment, occurring at least once every 2 months, or on an average of at least 6 times a year and prolonged expiration with wheezing or rhonchi between attacks.

I. General Considerations

A. Asthma is a disease which causes narrowing of the bronchial tubes leading to the lungs. This makes it difficult to move air in and out of the lungs, and causes symptoms of "shortness of breath".

B. Treatment usually consists of giving "bronchodilator" drugs that keep the bronchial tubes open. In some cases, steroid drugs are necessary.

C. If a doctor listens to a claimant's lungs, he will often hear "wheezing" sounds if the bronchial tubes are too narrow.

D. Often, the narrowing of the bronchial tubes is not continuous, but occurs in "attacks" of asthma. Asthmatic attacks may be very mild or very severe. In the worst cases, they have resulted in death.

E. Asthma is a type of *obstructive* lung disease. It is called this because normal air flow is *obstructed* (partly blocked) by the narrowed bronchial tubes.

F. If the bronchial tubes can be kept open by treatment with bronchodilator drugs, breathing is often fairly normal.

G. S. S. Disability is interested in the cases in which treatment is not effective in keeping the bronchial tubes open.

H. Part A or Part B must be fulfilled, but not both.

II. Specific Requirements

A. Part A

1. Part A refers to "asthmatic bronchitis" which is "chronic". These are the claimants who *continuously* have some narrowing of their bronchial tubes.

2. The actual evaluation is done under Listing 3.02 for *obstructive* lung disease. That means that for a claimant to be allowed disability under Part A, pulmonary function testing must be done to actually measure how severe the breathing problem is. Further comments about this testing can be found in the discussion of Listing 3.02.

3. It should be noted that the pulmonary function testing will include giving bronchodilator drugs to the claimant to see if the bronchial narrowing can be reversed.

4. S. S. Disability does not give pulmonary function testing to every claimant with asthma. This is done only if there is medical evidence that the asthma is severe enough to justify these tests.

B. Part B

1. Part B is for evaluation of claimants who have attacks of asthma, but are fairly normal in between attacks.

2. Pulmonary function testing does *not* have to be done to qualify under Part B.

3. Part B is meant to allow disability to claimants who have attacks of asthma which are so *frequent* and *severe* that they cannot work.

4. The claimant must be under treatment by a doctor (so that S. S. Disability will know treatment does not work).

5. Attacks must occur at least "once every 2 months", or average at least 6 times per year. It should be noted, however, that if attacks were bunched up (say 6 in one month) with no other attacks over a year's time, the claimant might not qualify.

6. In between attacks, there must be medical data from treating doctors which shows "prolonged expiration" (increased

time to breathe out air), "wheezing", or other abnormal lung sounds on examination that indicate that at least some degree of problem is *continuously* present in addition to the more severe attacks of asthma.

7. The difficult thing about Part B lies in the definition of "severe" attacks. Many asthmatics have attacks which can be treated by shots of epinephrine under the skin. This is often done in the emergency rooms of hospitals, and sometimes a doctor's office. Epinephrine is a drug that is too dangerous to use continuously, but is used in an emergency situation. However, the injection of epinephrine under the skin to control an attack of asthma is not enough for S. S. Disability—it is not an indication that the asthma is *severe* for S. S. Disability. To S. S. Disability, "severe" means that the asthmatic attack is so intense and life-threatening that *intravenous* drugs have to be given. Or drugs have to be given by *inhalation* (breathing the drug into the lungs). Treatment for such attacks is almost never given anywhere but in a hospital (including emergency room), and an attack must last "several hours".

8. In summary, only the very worst cases of asthma which can't be controlled by medical treatment can qualify under Part B.

Listing 3.04

Diffuse pulmonary fibrosis (sarcoidosis, Hamman-Rich syndrome, idiopathic intestitial fibrosis, and similar diffuse fibroses substantiated by chest X-ray or tissue diagnosis. This category does not include cases of bronchitis or emphysema with incidental scarring or scattered parenchymal fibrosis on X-ray). With

A. Total vital capacity equal to, or less than, values specified in Table II corresponding to the person's height.

Table II

Height (Inches)	V.C. Equal to or Less Than (L)
57 or less	1.2
58 or less	1.3
59 or less	1.3
60 or less	1.4
61 or less	1.4
62 or less	1.5

Table II—Continued

Height (Inches)—Continued	**V.C. Equal to or Less Than (L)**—Continued
63 or less	1.5
64 or less	1.6
65 or less	1.6
66 or less	1.7
67 or less	1.7
68 or less	1.8
69 or less	1.8
70 or less	1.9
71 or less	1.9
72 or less	2.0
73 or less	2.0

B. Diffusing capacity of the lungs for carbon monoxide less than 6 ml./mm. Hg./min. (steady-state methods) or less than 9 ml./mm. Hg./min. (single-breath methods) or less than 30 percent of predicted normal. (All methods, actual values and predicted normal values for the method used should be reported); OR

C. Arterial oxygen tension (pO_2) at rest and simultaneously determined arterial carbon dioxide tension (pCO_2) equal to, or less than, the values specified in Table III.

Table III

Arterial pCO_2 (mm. Hg.)	**AND**	**Arterial pO_2 Equal to or Less Than (mm. Hg.)**
30 or below		65
31 or below		64
32 or below		63
33 or below		62
34 or below		61
35 or below		60
36 or below		59
37 or below		58
38 or below		57
39 or below		56
40 or below		55

I. General Considerations

A. This Listing is used in evaluating any case in which there is a disease which has caused "fibrosis" of lung tissue. The Listing gives several examples, but any disease which causes fibrosis of lung tissue can qualify for evaluation under this Listing.

B. Previously, asthma and emphysema were mentioned as being "obstructive" lung diseases, because in these diseases air cannot be moved in and out of the lung normally—there is some "blockage" of air flow. But in diseases that cause *fibrosis* of lung tissue that is not the problem. Fibrosis destroys normal lung tissue, and decreases the amount of lung tissue into which air can flow. The *volume* of the lungs is decreased, and this can be measured by special tests. In other cases, the fibrosis blocks the transfer of oxygen across the little air sacs in the lung to the blood.

C. Claimants who have a little fibrosis in their lungs are not evaluated under this Listing. This Listing applies *only* to those diseases which cause fibrosis in a large amount of lung tissue.

D. Part A, B, or C must be fulfilled, but not all three.

E. The diseases under this Listing are called *restrictive* lung diseases.

II. Specific Requirements

A. Part A

1. The "total vital capacity" refers to the amount of air a claimant can blow out of his lungs, after taking as deep a breath as possible. It doesn't matter how long it takes to blow out the air. This detects the decrease in volume of air that lung tissue can hold in some cases of lung disease that cause fibrosis.

2. The "total vital capacity" is measured by special testing called a "pulmonary function study". More information about pulmonary function testing can be found in the discussion of Listing 3.02. However, it should be noted that bronchodilator drugs are not required to measure the vital capacity.

3. The "normal" vital capacity that a claimant should have depends partly on how tall he is. Age and sex also influence it, but are not taken into account for this Listing.

4. When S. S. Disability evaluates the case under Part A, it will take the very *best* vital capacity measured on testing. Then the claimant's height is noted and the test results compared to the numbers in Table II. For example, if a claimant is 64 inches

tall, he will qualify under Part A *only* if the best result is 1.6 or less.

B. Part B

1. The "fibrotic" lung disease in some people interferes with the movement of oxygen from the air to the bloodstream. This can be detected by measuring what is called the "diffusing capacity" of the lungs.

2. The "diffusing capacity" is not actually measured with oxygen, since there is already oxygen in the air which would interfere with the test. The actual measurements are done with carbon monoxide gas.

3. The testing can be done with either a "steady-state" or "single breath" method. Part B gives the required abnormal numbers for either kind of test. Also, if the test gives numbers less than 30% of normal, the claimant will qualify.

4. S. S. Disability does not usually order tests of "diffusing capacity", unless review of the medical data indicates that it should be done. So most claimants allowed disability under Part B have that test already in their file at the time they apply.

C. Part C

1. Part C deals with what are called "arterial blood gases". This simply means the amount of oxygen and carbon dioxide in *arterial* blood, as well as the acidity of the blood, along with other measurements.

2. These tests give a crude idea of how well oxygen is passing from the lungs into the bloodstream, and how well "wastes" (carbon dioxide) are being removed from the blood through the lungs.

3. These tests are made completely invalid by the claimant having pneumonia, or other lung infection. S. S. Disability will *not* use the results, if such infection was present at the time the test was done.

4. The value of carbon dioxide in the blood and the value of oxygen measurements are evaluated under Table III. If the carbon dioxide is 30 or less, then the value of oxygen in the blood must not be higher than 65, etc.

5. S. S. Disability may sometimes order this test, but not in most cases. S. S. Disability must think there is a fairly good chance of the test being abnormal, before purchasing it. Of course, it will use results reported by the treating doctor or hospital.

Listing 3.05

Other restrictive ventilatory disorders (e.g., Kyphoscoliosis, thoracoplasty, pulmonary resection). With:

Total vital capacity equal to, or less than, values specified in Table IV corresponding to the person's height.

Table IV

Height (Inches)	V.C. Equal to or Less Than (L)
59 or less	1.0
60 or less	1.1
61 or less	1.1
62 or less	1.1
63 or less	1.1
64 or less	1.2
65 or less	1.2
66 or less	1.2
67 or less	1.3
68 or less	1.3
69 or less	1.3
70 or less	1.4

I. General Considerations

A. The previous Listing deals with diseases which cause fibrosis of the lung tissue itself, and thereby decreases the amount of air the lung can hold. However, there are things that are not diseases of lung tissue, but still cause restriction of the amount of air the lungs can hold.

B. Several examples are given by the Listing, of the kind of things that can qualify. "Kyphoscoliosis" literally refers to a twisted, "hunched-over" shape to the spine. This decreases the amount of air the claimant can move in and out of the lungs, because the shape of the chest is abnormal, so that it can't expand with breathing the way it should. Other serious deformities of the spine can do the same thing.

C. "Thoracoplasty" refers to any kind of surgery involving the chest which alters the shape of the chest. This can have the same effect on breathing as a crooked spine.

D. "Pulmonary resection" refers to surgery which removes part of a lung. (This would include pneumonectomy, in which an entire right or left lung is removed.) In this case, the amount of air that can be used for breathing is decreased by the lowered volume of the lung tissue that is left. Most pulmonary resections seen by S. S. Disability were done because of surgery attempting to remove a lung cancer.

II. Specific Requirements

A. S. S. Disability evaluates the degree of severity by testing of breathing no different from that discussed under Listing 3.04 A. However, this Listing is more difficult to qualify under than Listing 3.04 A, because the vital capacity values must be lower.

B. The vital capacity measurements are evaluated under "Table IV" in the same way as for Listing 3.04 A. Different values are required for claimants of different heights.

Listing 3.06

Pneumoconiosis (demonstrated by X-ray evidence). With:

A. Nodular or focal fibrosis (non-conglomerative). Evaluate under the criteria for chronic obstructive airway disease in Listing 3.02; OR

B. Interstitial or disseminated fibrosis or conglomerative disease. Evaluate under the criteria for pulmonary fibrosis in Listing 3.04; OR

C. Where A and B are mixed or cannot be differentiated—evaluate under the criteria in Listing 3.02 or 3.04.

I. General Considerations

A. "Pneumoconiosis" is a general term, supposedly caused by the repeated breathing of small, dust-like particles such as coal-dust, asbestos, silicon, and beryllium. Clearly, miners and industrial workers are at the highest risk. The degree of lung damage depends on how much is inhaled and how long.

B. There must be X-ray evidence that pneumoconiosis is present.

C. Pneumoconiosis comes in several forms, as evaluated under specific parts of the Listing. Part A, B, or C must be fulfilled, but not all three. *Which* type is present depends on what the chest X-ray looks like.

II. Specific Requirements

A. Part A

1. Part A deals with the "nodular or focal fibrosis" pattern of lung damage. This is also called "non-conglomerative".

2. This type of pheumoconiosis produces *obstructive* lung disease. That means it has an effect on breathing similar to emphysema.

3. The actual evaluation of the case would be done under Listing 3.02, and the reader should refer to the discussion of that Listing for details.

B. Part B

1. Part B deals with the form of pneumoconiosis in which the volume of air that can be held by the lungs is decreased, as well as the ability for oxygen to get through the abnormal lung tissue to the bloodstream. This is a type of *restrictive* lung disease.

2. The actual evaluation of the case would be done under Listing 3.04, which deals with restrictive lung disease caused by "pulmonary fibrosis". The reader should refer to the discussion of that Listing for details.

C. Part C

1. Sometimes the chest X-ray will show that *both* of the above types of pneumoconiosis are present in a claimant.

2. Since both types are present, the case will be evaluated under *both* Listing 3.02 for obstructive lung disease *and* Listing 3.04 for restrictive lung disease. This doesn't mean that the claimant has to qualify under both of those Listings. It only means that S. S. Disability owes it to the claimant to make sure that he doesn't fulfill either one before denying benefits.

Listing 3.07

Bronchietasis (demonstrated by radio-opaque material). With:

A. Episodes of acute bronchitis or pneumonia or hemoptysis (more than blood-streaked sputum) occurring at least once every 2 months; OR

B. Impairment of pulmonary function due to extensive disease should be evaluated under the criteria for chronic obstructive airway disease in Listing 3.02 or where extensive fibrosis is evident on chest film, under the criteria for pulmonary fibrosis in Listing 3.04.

I. General Considerations

A. "Bronchiectasis" is a serious lung disease in which some of the bronchial tubes in the lungs are severely damaged from infection which is difficult to cure. The infection causes increasing amounts of damage to the lungs.

B. The diagnosis of bronchiectasis is *not* likely to be accepted by S. S. Disability, unless there are special X-ray studies showing it to be present. An ordinary chest X-ray is *not* enough. S. S. Disability will *not* usually accept the word of even a lung specialist unless these X-ray studies have been done. Furthermore, S. S. Disability does not order such studies, because they are not completely safe. They must have already been done, and available to S. S. Disability to review.

C. Part A or Part B must be fulfilled, but not both.

II. Specific Requirements

A. Part A

1. If the infection from the bronchiectasis causes further infections in episodes involving the larger bronchial tubes, then "acute bronchitis" is present. This can qualify under Part A, if such episodes are documented in medical records to happen at least as frequently as once every 2 months.

2. If the infection from the bronchiectasis is severe enough to cause episodes of pneumonia at least once every 2 months, then Part A is fulfilled. It is not likely that S. S. Disability will accept the diagnosis of such pneumonia without chest X-ray showing it to be present.

3. "Hemoptysis" means the coughing up of blood. Note that this means blood from the lungs, *not* the stomach! "Blood-streaked sputum" means that there is just a little blood coloring the material that the claimant coughs up. This is very frequent, especially among cigarette smokers, and *not* enough to qualify under Part A. The medical records must show that the claimant with bronchiectasis coughs up more blood than that. There is no exact number for how much, but it must be more than just blood-streaked sputum. ("Sputum" means anything that someone coughs up out of the lungs.) Note that there must be records showing that the claimant has hemoptysis at least once every 2 months.

B. Part B

1. If the bronchiectasis is severe enough and has been present long enough, it may cause a type of "obstructive" lung disease. This has the same effect on breathing as emphysema. If it is present in a claimant with bronchiectasis, the actual evaluation is done under Listing 3.02, which deals with all kinds of obstructive lung disease. Special breathing tests are necessary. For further information, the reader should refer to the discussion of Listing 3.02.

2. If the bronchiectasis is severe enough, it may cause fibrosis of lung tissue—a type of "restrictive" lung disease. If this is severe enough to be visible on a chest X-ray, then the case will be evaluated under Listing 3.04 which deals with various kinds of restrictive lung disease. Special tests of breathing, as well as other tests, might be used in the evaluation. The reader should refer to the discussion of Listing 3.04 for more details.

Listing 3.08

Pulmonary tuberculosis (caused by M. tuberculosis or pathogenic atypical mycobacteria).

Impairment of pulmonary function due to extensive disease should be evaluated under criteria in Listing 3.02, 3.04 or 3.05.

I. General Considerations

A. This Listing deals *only* with lung disease caused by tuberculosis.

B. "M. tuberculosis" simply refers to the usual bacterium that causes tuberculosis. ". . . pathogenic atypical mycobacteria" refers to other types of bacteria similar to the usual kind which also produce tuberculosis.

C. There must be sufficient data to convince S. S. Disability that tuberculosis is present. This often means X-ray, physical examination data, and symptoms. Most importantly, S. S. Disability will look for cultures of the sputum showing the tuberculosis bacterium to be present. (Sputum is anything someome coughs up from their lungs. When sputum is cultered, it is put on special medium that bacteria likes to grow on. If enough bacteria grow to be identified, then the diagnosis can be made with certainty. Tuberculosis organisms are slow growing and take about a month to grow in cultures.)

C. Most cases of tuberculosis in this country which are discovered early enough respond very well to treatment with special drugs. In cases where there are no serious complications and the claimant is responding to treatment well, S. S. Disability is likely to conclude that total cure will take place long before the minimum 12 month duration requirement is fulfilled.

E. Sometimes the tuberculosis, for a variety of reasons, causes more damage to the lungs than usual. It is these claimants that are most likely to qualify under this Listing.

F. If the tuberculosis involves other parts of the body besides the lungs, the evaluation might include Listings dealing with those parts of the body.

II. Specific Requirements

A. If the destruction of lung tissue produces enough damage, the case may be evaluated under Listing 3.02, which deals with "obstructive" lung disease. If the damage is of so-called "restrictive" type, then evaluation will be done under Listing 3.04. If surgery had to be performed to remove part of a lung, the case would be evaluated under Listing 3.05.

B. The reader should refer to the discussion of the above Listings for details.

C. The claimant has the right to qualify under *any* of the Listings 3.02, 3.04, or 3.05. Some claimants qualify under more than one of them. The claimant does *not* have to qualify under more than one.

Listing 3.09

Mycotic infection of lung. With:

A. Culture of specific organisms from sputa and serial X-ray evidence of increasing or decreasing extent of lesion, both persisting for at least 3 months despite prescribed therapy; OR

B. Culture of specific organisms from sputa and current X-ray evidence of a lesion and episodes of hemoptysis occurring at least once every 2 months; OR

C. Impairment of pulmonary function due to extensive disease should be evaluated under the criteria in Listings 3.02, 3.04, or 3.05.

I. General Considerations

A. This Listing deals only with infections of the lung by fungus. These are called "mycotic" infections. A fungus is a plant, not the usual type of bacterium.

B. Fungus infections are not as often seen in healthy people. They occur most often in people with other serious diseases who have very low resistance to this type of infection.

C. Part A, B or C must be fulfilled, but not all three.

II. Specific Requirements

A. Part A

1. Certain tests are required by S. S. Disability to be sure not only that a fungus infection of lung is present, but also to evaluate whether or not it is getting better with treatment.

2. First of all, the organism must be identified as a fungus by growth in cultures of the sputum the claimant has coughed up.

3. Secondly, there must be a series of X-rays showing whether or not the fungal infection is getting better, staying the same, or getting worse.

4. The X-rays have to show that the fungal infection of lung has been present for a minimum of 3 months.

5. The claimant *must* be under the treatment of a medical doctor.

B. Part B

1. There must be culture of the claimant's sputum showing the presence of fungus in the lung.

2. Past X-rays are not required, but there must be X-rays at the time of application (or close to the time of application) showing the disease in the lung.

3. There must be evidence from past medical records that the claimant has been coughing up blood (hemoptysis) at least every 2 months.

C. Part C

1. If the fungus infection is severe enough and has been present long enough, extensive damage may be done to lung tissue.

2. If such extensive damage is present, the impairment is evaluated under Listings 3.02, 3.04, or 3.05. These Listings deal with "obstructive" and "restrictive" lung diseases. A claimant only has to qualify under *one* of these Listings. Special testing

of the claimant's breathing is involved, and the reader should refer to the discussion of those Listings for more details.

3. Part C is not *necessarily* used to evaluate fungal infections of lung. It applies only to those cases severe enough to warrant special testing done in Listings 3.02, 3.04, or 3.05.

Listing 3.11

Cor pulmonale. Evaluate under the criteria for Listing 4.02D.

I. General Considerations

A. "Cor pulmonale" is a special kind of heart disease which is related to lung disease.

B. No actual evaluation is ever done under this Listing.

II. Specific Requirements

A. If "cor pulmonale" is present, the actual evaluation is done under Listing 4.02D, which specifically deals with this type of heart disease.

B. For more information, the reader should refer to the discussion of Listing 4.02D.

Listing 3.12

Pleurocutaneous fistula. With persistent purulent drainage.

I. General Considerations

A. A "pleurocutaneous fistula" is an abnormal opening between the inside of the chest and the outside skin. This results from infection that has affected the chest wall.

B. No special breathing tests are required under this Listing.

II. Specific Requirements

A. Infected material must drain out from the fistula. This has to be substantiated by medical records. This drainage must be more or less present *continuously.* "Purulent" literally means pus. The presence of pus indicates the presence of active infection.

B. Drainage of clear or straw-colored fluid from the fistula does *not* indicate the presence of infection and does *not* qualify under this Listing.

§ 2.5 Cardiovascular System

Listing 4.02

Congestive heart failure (manifested by evidence of vascular congestion such as hepatomegaly, peripheral or pulmonary edema). With:

A. Persistent congestive heart failure on clinical examination despite prescribed therapy; OR

B. Persistent left ventricular enlargement and hypertrophy documented by both:

1. Extension of the cardiac shadow (left ventricle) to the vertebral column on a left lateral chest roentgenogram; AND

2. ECG showing QRS duration less than 0.12 second with S_{V1} plus R_{V5} (or R_{V6}) of 35 mm. or greater *and* ST segment depressed more than 0.5 mm. and low, diphasic or inverted T waves in leads with tall R waves; OR

C. Persistent "mitral" type heart involvement documented by left atrial enlargement shown by double shadow on PA chest roentgenogram (or characteristic distortion of barium-filled esophagus) and either:

1. ECG showing QRS duration less than 0.12 seconds with S_{V1} plus R_{V5} (or R_{V6}) of 35 mm. or greater *and* ST segment depressed more than 0.5 mm. and low, diphasic or inverted T waves in leads with tall R waves; OR

2. ECG evidence of right ventricular hypertrophy with R wave of 5.0 mm. or greater in lead V_1 *and* progressive decrease in R/S amplitude from lead V_1 to V_5 or V_6; OR

D. Cor pulmonale (non-acute) documented by both:

1. Right ventricular enlargement (or prominence of the right outflow tract) on chest roentgenogram or fluoroscopy; AND

2. ECG evidence of right ventricular hypertrophy with R wave of 5.0 mm. or greater in lead V_1 *and* pro-

gressive decrease in R/S amplitude from lead V_1 to V_5 or V_6.

I. General Considerations

A. This Listing deals with what is called "congestive heart failure". The abbreviation "CHF" is commonly used by doctors.

B. The heart is complex, but basically it is nothing but a muscular pump. It receives blood from the rest of the body, after the tissues have taken out the nutrients and oxygen they need. The heart then pumps this "used" blood through the lungs, where waste carbon dioxide gas is given off the fresh oxygen is picked up by the red blood cells. Coming from the lungs, the blood goes back into the heart, from where it is pumped again to the body's tissues. This whole cycle repeats itself continuously.

As the heart pumps blood, it takes part of this blood to supply its own need for energy. This blood flows to the heart muscle through special bloodvessels called *coronary arteries.*

C. Like most pumps, the heart has valves which control the one-way flow of blood through the heart chambers. The heart is stimulated to pump blood (contract) by electrical signals coming from a small piece of special tissue within the heart itself. If the heart needs to beat faster, this little piece of tissue sends out more electrical signals. It's called the *sino-atrial node.*

D. In congestive heart failure (CHF) the heart is "weakened"—it can no longer pump out the amount of blood needed by the body. There are a very large number of diseases that can cause CHF, but basically it is usually caused by one of three general things: disease damaging the heart muscle itself, disease damaging the valves in the heart, or disease causing blockage of the blood flow through the coronary arteries that supply the heart.

E. When the heart "fails" in CHF, it can no longer pump out blood as fast as it receives blood. This increases the pressure in the chambers of the heart, causing the heart to increase in size. CHF is one of the causes of *cardiomegaly,* a word which simply means an enlarged heart.

F. But when a weakened heart "fails", it also affects other parts of the body. (Of course, if it *totally* fails then the patient will die!). Blood builds up in the liver, causing it to get larger. This is one of the causes of *hepatomegaly,* which means an enlarged liver. Fluid collects in the legs and feet; this is called *edema.* Fluid can also build up in the lungs. This is called *pul-*

monary edema. Pulmonary edema can be heard by a doctor listening to the claimant's chest with a stethoscope; it can also be seen on an X-ray of the chest. The edema of the feet can be found by a doctor on physical examination. The doctor can also feel an enlarged liver, if it is present. In addition, the heart is likely to produce abnormal sounds, which can be heard by a doctor, if CHF is present.

G. CHF may be very mild, or it may be very severe. It must be severe enough for S. S. Disability to definitely know that it is present. This requires a complete examination of the patient, as well as a chest X-ray. The chest X-ray should show an enlarged heart (cardiomegaly) and signs of pulmonary edema, in most cases.

H. Doctors usually treat CHF by giving two drugs. One drug would be some kind of *diuretic.* A diuretic drug is one that acts on the kidneys to cause more fluid to be lost through urination. This decreases the total amount of fluid in the body, and takes some of the strain off of the weakened heart. There are many kinds of diuretics. The second important drug used in treating CHF is *digitalis.* Actually, digitalis is not a specific drug. There are a whole group of drugs that qualify as "digitalis", but all do more or less the same thing. The effect of digitalis on the heart is extremely complicated, but basically what it does is to make the heart contract more efficiently. In a very simple way, one might say that digitalis "strengthens" the heart muscles.

I. There are a few types of CHF caused by diseases that might eventually go away. In these cases, the heart might return to "normal" and not require any more treatment. For example, this is sometimes true when the heart is infected with a virus. But most people with CHF have to take digitalis and diuretics for the rest of their lives. If they stop taking the drugs, their heart failure will come back. On the other hand, CHF might be due to a defective heart valve (such as may occur in rheumatic fever), and this might be totally and permanently curable with surgery that puts a new valve in the heart. If such surgery were done, S. S. Disability would evaluate the claimant's condition *after* the surgery is done.

J. Parts of this Listing refer to an "ECG". "ECG" stands for *electrocardiogram;* it is just as frequently called an "EKG". EKG's are a very basic part of medicine, and most doctors' offices have a machine to do them. Little electrodes are attached to the arms, legs, and chest. These electrodes pick up the electrical impulses given off by the heart when it beats, and are traced out on a piece of paper for the doctor to look at. In fact, it would be very negligent for a doctor not to run an EKG on a person suspected of having significant heart disease.

K. An EKG can tell a doctor some important things about the heart, but not everything. It is only one way heart disease is diagnosed. In certain parts of this Listing, the abnormality looked for is called *hypertrophy.* Hypertrophy simply means enlargement of an organ, and cardiac hypertrophy means that the heart has increased the size of its muscle, in an attempt to compensate for some type of abnormal strain put on it. When the heart muscle is bigger, then larger electrical signals are produced and this can be seen on an EKG.

L. It is important for the reader to understand that *before* a claimant can be allowed benefits under Part A, B, C, or D of the Listing, there is the general requirement that CHF happened at least once in the past. It doesn't matter how long ago this happened, but there must be good evidence that it did happen. S. S. Disability must be able to get those records to prove it. *Then* the claimant's case is evaluated under Part A, B, C, or D.

M. Part A, B, C, or D must be fulfilled, but not all four.

II. Specific Requirements

A. Part A

1. Part A is *only* fulfilled in cases where the CHF has not gone away with treatment. For a claimant to have had CHF at some time in the past is *not* enough. CHF *must* also be present at the time the claimant applies for disability.

2. If a claimant applies for disability during an episode of CHF which has *just happened,* then S. S. Disability will *wait* to see if the CHF gets better with treatment. This requires a minimum of several months, in most cases.

3. "Clinical examination" just means a physical examination by a doctor. This must show convincing evidence that CHF is present. The opinion of the examining doctor that CHF is present is not enough, even if the doctor is a heart specialist. S. S. Disability will make up its own mind whether CHF is present, based on the requirements of the Listing.

4. Although not stated under Part A as a requirement, it is sometimes too difficult to decide if CHF is present by using only a physical examination. Because valuable information about whether CHF is present can be obtained with a chest X-ray, this is very often used also. As noted previously, two things are looked for on the chest X-ray to determine if CHF is present. One is enlargement of the heart (cardiomegaly). The other is

pulmonary edema (fluid in the lung tissues). It is not likely that S. S. Disability will consider the heart enlarged, unless it is at least 55% as wide as the chest cavity on X-ray. This would be called a *C/T ratio* of 55%. (If the heart were 1/3 as wide as the chest cavity, the C/T ratio would be 33%.)

B. Part B

1. Part B is fulfilled if there are certain abnormal findings on an EKG *and* chest X-ray at the time the claimant applies for disability.

2. The abnormal findings needed require enlargement of the main pumping chamber of the heart (left ventricle), and hypertrophy (muscular enlargement or thickening) of the left ventricle. Parts B.1 *and* B.2 must be fulfilled, as follows:

(a) Part B.1 of the Listing states that a chest X-ray taken through the left side of the chest must show the left ventricle of the heart so enlarged that it goes all the way back to the spinal column.

(b) Part B.2 of the Listing states that the EKG must show that the muscle in the wall of the left ventricle is thickened from the strain put on it (hypertrophied). The exact details that the EKG must show are given by the Listing, but such interpretation requires special training and would be of little interest to most readers.

C. Part C

1. Part C is fulfilled if there are certain abnormal findings on EKG and chest X-ray. These abnormalities involve the right side of the heart. (Part B involved the left side of the heart.)

2. To begin with, there must be a chest X-ray showing enlargement of the heart chamber called the "left atrium". This can be verified by either the way the heart looks ("double shadow"), or by special additional X-rays done with the chest X-ray showing the esophagus pushed out of the way by the enlarged heart chamber.

3. Then Part C.1 or Part C.2 must be fulfilled, but not both:

(a) Part C.1 is an EKG showing hypertrophy (thickening of the heart muscle) of the left side of the heart.

(b) Part C.2 is an EKG showing hypertrophy of the right side of the heart.

D. Part D

1. Part D is fulfilled if *cor pulmonale* exists.

2. Cor pulmonale is a form of heart disease caused by lung disease. Cor pulmonale does damage to the right side of the heart.

3. Part D.1 *and* Part D.2 must be fulfilled to qualify under Part D:

(a) Part D.1 requires that the main pumping chamber on the right side of the heart (right ventricle) be enlarged either on a chest X-ray or other special studies.

(b) Part D.2 requires that the EKG show evidence that the heart muscle on the right side of the heart is thickened (hypertrophy).

Listing 4.03

Hypertensive vascular disease. Evaluate under Listing 4.02 or 4.04 or under the criteria for the affected body system.

I. General Considerations

A. This Listing deals with hypertension ("high blood pressure").

B. Hypertension can damage just about any organ in the body, but the kidney, brain, eyes, and heart are the most frequently affected.

C. Blood pressure measurements are given with 2 numbers. The first number stands for the *systolic* pressure. This is the pressure in the artery concerned when the heart contracts. The second number is the *diastolic* pressure. This is the pressure in the artery concerned when the heart is *not* contracting and is *always* a lower number than the systolic pressure. Blood pressure is usually measured in the brachial artery of the arm, by wrapping a blood pressure cuff around the arm. Blood pressure in the arm of adults which is greater than 140/90 is generally considered "high blood pressure", and should be treated. (140 is the systolic pressure and 90 is the diastolic pressure.) Blood pressure in arteries other than the arm may have different normal values, but by far most blood pressure is measured in the arm.

D. More than 90% of cases of high blood pressure come from causes which are unknown. This is called *essential* hypertension. The other 10% may be due to a variety of diseases—frequently hormonal diseases, or diseases of the kidneys. Unlike essential hypertension, cure of one of these diseases might lead to permanent cure of the hypertension. But since essential hypertension has no known cause, permanent cure is not possible; in many cases, drugs must be continuously used to keep it under control. Unfortunately, most people with essential hypertension obviously fall in this category; if they stop taking their drugs, their hypertension will come back.

E. Almost all high blood pressure can be treated with drugs, so that the readings return to normal or at least significantly improve. If the claimant is not getting treatment, S. S. Disability will almost always take the position that the claimant could obtain treatment if he wanted to do so. Exceptions to this attitude might be the mentally ill or mentally retarded; these people could have difficulty seeking out adequate treatment and/or taking their drugs correctly.

F. Even if the claimant has high blood pressure that is *not* controlled with treatment, they will *not* qualify under this Listing. The Listing is for claimants who have severe damage to their body because of the hypertension. For example, such damage might occur in the eyes, brain, kidneys, or heart as mentioned above. There is also general damage to the bloodvessels.

G. There is a form of high blood pressure called "malignant hypertension" that causes very rapid damage to organs in the body. But it takes many years for most people to suffer damaged organs from high blood pressure, and S. S. Disability does not take into account what might happen many years in the future. This is not to say that people don't suffer damage from hypertension from not being treated adequately, or not taking their drugs as prescribed by a doctor; hypertension is a major cause of damage to multiple body organs, and S. S. Disability sees such cases frequently. But until hypertension does such damage, S. S. Disability will not give great weight to it. The author strongly advises anyone with uncontrolled hypertension to find adequate treatment; failure to do so often leads to future tragedy.

II. Specific Requirements

A. As noted above, a claimant cannot qualify under any Listing for having high blood pressure itself; there must be damage to some important part of the body as a result of the hypertension. For example, hypertension is a major contributing cause of heart disease.

B. No actual evaluation is done under this Listing. If the high blood pressure has damaged some organ of the body, the case is evaluated under whatever Listing deals with that organ.

Listing 4.04

Ischemic heart disease with chest pain of cardiac origin . . . . With:

A. Treadmill exercise test . . . demonstrating one of the following at an exercise level of 5 METS or less:

1. Horizontal or down-sloping ischemic depression of the ST segment to 1.0 mm. or greater, clearly discernible in at least two consecutive complexes which are on a level baseline in any lead; OR

2. Premature ventricular systoles which are multiform or bidirectional or are sequentially inscribed (3 or more); OR

3. ST segment elevation to 3 mm. or greater; OR

4. Development of second or third degree heart block; OR

B. In the absence of a report of an acceptable treadmill exercise test . . . one of the following:

1. Transmural myocardial infarction exhibiting a QS pattern or a Q wave with amplitude at least 1/3 of R wave and with a duration of 0.04 seconds or more. (If these are present in leads III and AVF only, the requisite Q wave findings must be shown, by labelled tracing, to persist on deep inspiration); OR

2. Resting ECG findings showing ischemic-type depression of ST segment to more than 0.5 mm. in either (a) leads I and AVL and V_6 or (b) leads II and III and AVF or (c) leads V_3 through V_6; OR

3. Resting ECG findings showing an ischemic configuration or current of injury with ST segment elevation to 2 mm. or more in either (a) leads I and AVL and V_6 or (b) leads II and III and AVF or (c) leads V_3 through V_6; OR

4. Resting ECG findings showing symmetrical inversion of T waves to 5.0 mm. or more in any two leads except leads II or AVR or V_1 or V_2; OR

5. Inversion of T wave to 1.0 mm. or more in any of leads I, II, AVL, V_2 to V_6 *and* R wave of 5.0 mm. or more

in lead AVL *and* R wave greater than S wave in lead AVF; OR

6. "Double" Master Two-Step test demonstrating one of the following:

a. Ischemic depression of ST segment to more than 0.5 mm. lasting for at least 0.08 seconds beyond the J junction and clearly discernible in at least two consecutive complexes which are on a level baseline in any lead; OR

b. Development of a second or third degree heart block; OR

7. Angiographic evidence (obtained independent of social security disability evaluation) showing one of the following:

a. 50 percent or more narrowing of the left main coronary artery; OR

b. 70 percent or more narrowing of a proximal coronary artery (excluding the left main coronary artery); OR

c. 50 percent or more narrowing involving a long (greater than 1 cm.) segment of a proximal coronary artery or multiple proximal coronary arteries; OR

C. Resting ECG findings showing left bundle branch block as evidenced by QRS duration of 0.12 seconds or more in leads I, II, or III *and* R peak duration of 0.06 seconds or more in leads I, AVL, V_5, or V_6, unless there is a coronary angiogram of record which is negative; OR

D. Left ventricular ejection fraction of 30 percent or less measured at cardiac catheterization or by echocardiography.

I. General Considerations

A. Most claimants with heart disease are evaluated under this Listing. Furthermore, heart disease is the most frequent cause of disability. Therefore, it is very important for the reader to have a good understanding of what is involved, if he applies for benefits on the basis of heart disease.

B. This Listing deals with extremely complicated medical data, in many cases. There is a very large amount of medical and administrative "policy" which controls how the Listing is to be interpreted. Many critical points controlling whether a claim will be allowed or denied will be discussed under this Listing. The following discussion of this Listing should be read with *very great care.*

C. Before a claimant is even considered under this Listing, there must be "chest pain of cardiac origin". That simply means chest pain caused by heart disease. First, S. S. Disability determines if the claimant has chest pain that *might* be due to heart disease. If so, further evaluation is done under Part A, B, C, or D. What the claimant says about his chest pain is *subjective.* Parts A, B, C, and D require *objective* evidence that the chest pain is in fact due to heart disease. Parts A, B, C, and D are necessary because what someone says about their chest pain is not a reliable way of telling whether the pain is due to heart disease.

D. Everyone has chest pain of some kind or another at some time in their lives. This can be due to many things besides heart disease. For example, disease of the esophagus, bronchitis, lung disease, muscular strain, pneumonia, and arthritis of the rib joints can cause chest pain. And there are other causes. It is a very difficult problem in medicine to tell if chest pain is due to heart disease.

E. Chest pain caused by heart disease is called *angina pectoris.* Basically, a person feels angina when the heart is not getting enough blood (therefore, not enough oxygen) to supply the heart's needs. This could be due to a narrowed valve in the heart. It could also be due to disease of the heart muscle (myocarditis). But usually it is due to *coronary artery disease* in which one or more of the arteries supplying the heart itself become blocked from fatty deposits. The coronary arteries which are involved don't have to be totally blocked; they only have to be blocked enough to prevent the heart muscle from getting as much blood as it needs. This is called *cardiac ischemia.* A person at rest with a partially blocked coronary artery might get as much blood to his heart as it needs, but if he gets excited or especially if he does physical exercise the heart might not get as much blood as it needs, and this will result in cardiac ischemia. Cardiac ischemia can produce the type of chest pain known as angina pectoris. This chest pain can be of all degrees of severity, depending on how bad the coronary artery disease is; in some people a little exercise will cause angina, and in others angina will not appear except on heavy exertion.

F. It is a difficult problem for S. S. Disability to decide if a claimant has chest pain that might reasonably be angina pectoris. In the author's opinion, the evaluation of chest pain is the most difficult problem that S. S. Disability has in analyzing cases of heart disease. If a claimant has angina, S. S. Disability doesn't want to deny benefits that are deserved. On the other hand, *everyone* has some kind of chest pain, as noted above; most of this chest pain is *not* caused by heart disease. Even many people with heart disease have chest pain that is not angina. The number of claimants stating that they have chest pain is incredibly high, and each complaint of chest pain must be carefully checked out. Since chest pain of cardiac origin (angina) is necessary to be allowed under any part of this Listing, and since so many cases are evaluated under this Listing, its importance cannot be overestimated. Here are a few specific problems that arise when S. S. Disability tries to get an accurate description of a claimant's chest pain:

1. S. S. Disability considers the claimant's treating doctor to know more about his chest pain than anyone else, since that doctor usually knows the claimant better. So if a claimant states that he has chest pain, an effort is usually made to contact the treating doctor first. *Most* doctors are cooperative about this, *but*:

(a) A few treating doctors won't talk to S. S. Disability at all. When this happens, the claimant is rarely aware of it.

(b) Although a treating doctor's office or hospital records may be adequate for him to treat the claimant, they rarely have enough description for someone else reading the records to know if angina is present or not. This doesn't mean the treating doctor is incompetent. It does mean the written records often aren't complete enough to be used by S. S. Disability.

(c) A small minority of treating doctors will tell S. S. Disability that the claimant has angina, but will get very offended if asked for the detailed description of the pain. Apparently, they consider this an insult to their professional ability. Such a physician might have very nasty things to say to a disability examiner who calls him on the telephone. This might be a good emotional outlet for the doctor, but it doesn't help the claimant at all.

2. For whatever reason, if an adequate description of the claimant's chest pain is not available from the treating doctor, S. S. Disability will be forced to send the claimant to another doctor, who will provide the necessary description. Al-

though this costs S. S. Disability money, the claimant's rights to adequate evaluation are protected.

3. Some doctors are better at taking chest pain descriptions than others. Also, some claimants are better at describing what they feel than others.

4. S. S. Disability has to deal with unbelievable volumes of medical records daily. This vast experience (in the author's opinion) has revealed a very disturbing fact about chest pain in claimants. Many times, a claimant will have seen more than one doctor. It is not at all unusual for each doctor to get a *different* description of the claimant's chest pain. Whether the fault lies with claimants or doctors is open to argument, but it still leaves S. S. Disability with the very difficult problem of deciding what to believe.

G. Most chest pain due to angina pectoris has certain characteristics that S. S. Disability will look for. This involves a *minimum* of 5 things that *must* be included in the description:

1. *"Location"*. Where in the chest is the pain? Most true angina is in the center of the chest, feeling as if it is beneath the sternum (breastbone). That is, the pain is *substernal.* Sometimes the pain also goes out into one of the arms, or up into the neck.

2. *"Quality"*. What does the pain feel like? Many claimants, especially those who do not have a great deal of education, have difficulty describing what the pain feels like. Most angina feels like an "ache", "dull", "heavy", "pressure", "weight", "tight", or even "burning". Angina does not tend to be "sharp", "knifelike", "stabbing", "jabbing", "needlelike", "electric shock", or "throbbing". Unfortunately, many claimants use the word "sharp", because they can't think of a better word.

3. *"Precipitating factors"*. What kinds of things cause the claimant to have chest pain? Although angina can occur at rest with anxiety or other emotions, it usually occurs with physical exertion. This is because the heart can't get enough blood for the work it is being asked to do. Some examples would be walking, lifting heavy objects, vacuuming, or any other kind of physical activity—especially things involving the arms, since this puts greater strain on the heart. If the chest pain does not tend to be produced by physical exertion, S. S. Disability will *not* consider the pain to be angina in most instances.

4. *"Mode of relief"*. Angina tends to be relieved with rest. That is, if the claimant has chest pain produced by some kind of exercise, stopping to rest should cause the pain to go away. Also, most people being treated for angina by their doctors are given a little white pill to put under their tongue when they have chest pain. This is a drug called *nitroglycerin*, and opens up the coronary arteries so that more blood can get to the heart muscle. Nitroglycerin tends to help relieve chest pain that is due to angina. There are also other drugs available, but nitroglycerin and drugs similar to it are the most frequently used.

5. *"Duration"*. How long does the pain last after the claimant stops to rest and/or takes nitroglycerin? Most angina will go away in several minutes, if the claimant stops physical exercise and rests. It will tend to go away even faster, if nitroglycerin is also taken. Most claimants will stop having pain in 3–5 minutes, after they start to rest. But there is a lot of variability between people, depending on how severe the angina is. Since most people don't actually time their chest pain, they may be mistaken as to how long it lasts. True angina is rarely as short as seconds, or as long as hours. The longer the chest pain lasts, the less likely the chances of it being angina. Recognizing the difficulties involved in getting an accurate estimate of a claimant's chest pain, S. S. Disability is pretty lenient in accepting durations less than 30 minutes. This is not official policy, but based on the author's experience. Durations over 30 minutes are a strong argument against chest pain being angina, except in cases of extremely severe heart disease. Such long durations are acceptable only in *rare* cases, supported by a tremendous amount of accurate and detailed medical information that proves the exception.

H. S. S. Disability recognizes exceptions to the chest pain description given in "G" above, but not very often. The closer the chest pain is to the above description, the more likely that S. S. Disability will consider it angina.

I. If S. S. Disability gets a chest pain description that might be angina, then the case is further evaluated under Part A, B, C, or D of the Listing. Only one of these has to be fulfilled. Of course, the order of evaluation could be just the opposite. S. S. Disability often sees cases which fulfill Part A, B, C, or D and then has to find out if angina is present.

J. One of the greatest flaws in Listing 4.04 is that a claimant can say anything he wants about chest pain. For example, fulfilling Part A, B, C, or D doesn't necessarily mean a person has angina. But if a claimant does fulfill one of these Parts of the Listing, and then says he has chest pain that might be angina the result would be allowance of disability benefits. This is certainly no recommendation that such dishonesty be carried out by any claimant, but the only way it could be blocked would be by the treating doctor signing a statement that the claimant does not have angina, since it is the treating doctor who will be asked about the claimant's chest pain instead of the claimant himself. If the claimant doesn't tell the truth to his treating doctor, or if the doctor himself is not completely truthful, there is little S. S. Disability can do to prove the contrary. In evaluating chest pain complaints that might be angina, S. S. Disability is very much at the mercy of both the claimant and his treating doctor in many instances. However, it should be pointed out that S. S. Disability is most likely to believe a claimant has angina if this is verified by the actual records from his treating doctor. If the treating doctor provides S. S. Disability with a perfect description of anginal chest pain, but his medical records show that the claimant has not complained of chest pain then S. S. Disability is not going to accept the chest pain description as truthful. Unfortunately, such instances are not rare.

II. Specific Requirements

A. Part A

1. A "treadmill exercise test" is a special test designed to find out if a person's chest pain symptoms are likely to be caused by heart disease. There are other uses of such exercise tests in medicine, but S. S. Disability uses them mainly for diagnostic purposes in trying to determine if ischemic heart disease is present. Exercise tests to diagnose heart disease aren't perfect; they may look positive for abnormalities that aren't really present, and they may look negative for abnormalities of the heart which really are present. But the test is far better than nothing at all, and all claimants equally face the possibility that it might not be completely accurate in any individual case. Treadmill cardiac stress testing is widely used in medicine, both in and outside of S. S. Disability. To perform the test, the claimant walks on a moving platform. If he successfully completes the first stages, then the speed and upward tilt of the platform are gradually increased every 2–3 minutes. Electrodes are attached to the claimant as he walks, which are connected to an EKG machine so that the electrical activity of the heart can be continuously watched for abnormalities. Blood pressure is also carefully watched, as well as any abnormal symptoms that

the claimant might have. If the claimant has heart disease causing poor blood flow to the heart muscle, then certain abnormalities may appear in the EKG tracings. It is these tracings that are the most important, and it should be emphasized that no claimant has to have chest pain during such a test to qualify for benefits because of heart disease.

2. If the claimant shows any signs that may endanger him, the test should be stopped immediately by the doctor who is present, and such a test should *never* be done without a medical doctor present. While it is very rare for anyone to be harmed by a treadmill stress test, it sometimes does happen. The worst thing that can happen is a "heart attack", or even death. The author is not aware of anyone even dying while undergoing cardiac stress testing for S. S. Disability, but rare "heart attacks" have occurred. The odds of being seriously hurt by such testing are much less than 1% in most people.

3. If a treadmill exercise test has already been done before the claimant applies for S. S. Disability, an attempt will be made to get the results from the treating doctor or hospital where the test was done. Although a treadmill type of test is desirable, S. S. Disability will also accept other types. For example, there is a cardiac stress test which involves the claimant riding a bicycle that doesn't move ("bicycle ergometry"). The 750 KPM level of work on a bicycle ergometer is arbitrarily considered equivalent to 5 METS on a treadmill.)

4. S. S. Disability is mainly interested in the actual EKG *tracings* done during the test, and how far in the test the claimant is able to go, before these EKG tracings become abnormal (if they do become abnormal at all). S. S. Disability is *not* supposed to take anyone's word about whether the test is abnormal or normal. The test results are reported on an "interpretation" sheet. This includes a doctor's opinion about whether or not the test was abnormal, and other data about blood pressure, the patient's symptoms, speed and tilt of the treadmill, etc. This interpretation sheet is *not* enough for S. S. Disability to use in evaluating a case. To use the same standards for all claimants, S. S. Disability *must* have the actual EKG tracings and make up its own mind about what those tracings show. Unfortunately, some hospitals and treating doctors throw the actual EKG tracings away, lose them, or even refuse to send them to S. S. Disability. But S. S. Disability will pay no attention to the interpretation of a cardiac stress test by a claimant's treating doctor, unless the actual EKG tracings are sent as well. This can be unfortunate for the claimant, but S. S. Disability really has no

choice in this rule due to the fact that private doctors interpret the tests many different ways. One will read a test as positive and another negative. The only way S. S. Disability can be fair to all claimants is to evaluate the tracings, using the same rules for everyone. Without the actual EKG tracings, S. S. Disability is *never* supposed to use the interpretation of a cardiac stress test. If for some reason another stress test cannot be done, this may be a serious disadvantage to the claimant and result in denial of benefits if that test is the only objective evidence that the claimant has heart disease. In other cases, the failure of S. S. Disability to obtain the EKG tracings from the test could result in allowance of benefits, when they would be denied if S. S. Disability had the tracings to analyze (see #9 below about the priority given to stress testing in the evaluation of heart disease).

5. To qualify under Part A, the EKG tracings must clearly show abnormalities as given in Parts A.1, A.2, A.3, A.4, or A.5 of the Listing. Only one of these need be fulfilled. These abnormalities all indicate serious heart disease, but more detailed discussion would be of little value to the reader due to the experience needed in interpreting EKG tracings. The tracings must show one of the required abnormalities at less than 5 METS exertion by the claimant. A MET is a method of measuring how much exertion a person does; the more exertion a person does, the higher the MET level achieved. (For technically minded readers 1 MET=3.5 ml oxygen/minute/kilogram of body weight.) If the EKG tracings show abnormalities which only appear at *more* than 5 METS of exertion, then the claimant *cannot* qualify under Part A—such a claimant may have heart disease, but it won't be severe enough to qualify under this Listing. It should be noted that Part A.1 requires 1 mm depression of the ST segment compared to the baseline EKG tracing before exercise. However, if the ST segment is *upsloping* or the claimant is taking a form of the drug digitalis, then a 2 mm change in the ST segment is required. That is because the diagnosis of cardiac ischemia is less reliable in such cases.

6. If the treating doctor has not done a cardiac stress test, *S. S. Disability* may ask that the claimant undergo such a test. However, precautions are taken to make sure that this test presents as little danger to the claimant as possible:

(a) If the claimant can be allowed disability benefits by any other means, S. S. Disability is not supposed to request such a test. Although the risk is very small, such a test should not be done when it is not needed.

(b) If the claimant has some kind of heart disease which would significantly increase the danger of the test, it is *not* supposed to be requested by S. S. Disability. Also, the test should not be performed if the claimant's blood pressure is too high.

(c) If the treating doctor states that it is too dangerous for the claimant to have the test, S. S. Disability will often not request the claimant to undergo such a test. This may be true, even though the treating doctor is wrong about there being any danger to a particular claimant.

(d) The claimant is supposed to get a complete physical examination before being asked to take the test, and a medical doctor is *always* supposed to be present during the test to watch over the claimant's welfare. If S. S. Disability requests that the claimant undergo cardiac stress testing, this is usually done by consulting doctors in private medical practice paid by S. S. Disability to do them. Of course, that doctor must feel comfortable that the test is not contraindicated in a particular claimant. It is acceptable to S. S. Disability that the claimant's treating doctor perform such testing, assuming that such doctor is willing to do this and accept the fee offered by S. S. Disability.

(e) The claimant is supposed to be fully informed of the nature and possible dangers of the test, by the physician giving it to him. This is standard medical practice for all possibly hazardous procedures, whether they have anything to do with S. S. Disability or not.

7. If a cardiac stress test is the only way S. S. Disability can determine if the claimant has heart disease but the test cannot be done, S. S. Disability will *not* assume that heart disease is present. This will result in denial of benefits, because S. S. Disability would not attempt to obtain the test if there were any other way to allow a claimant's case. It is extremely important to fully understand the underlying reasoning behind such denials. It is necessary *by law* for there to be objective evidence of an impairment, before benefits can be allowed. *If for whatever reason a cardiac stress test is necessary for allowance of benefits but cannot be performed then S. S. Disability will have insufficient evidence. Without such evidence it is legally impossible to allow a case.* Such a case will be denied, due to lack of such evidence. That is, an impairment that *might* exist is treated by S. S. Disability as unproven; a possible impairment is not acceptable as one that has been demonstrated. S. S. Disa-

bility really has no choice in this, because to do otherwise would open the doors to speculation in disability cases rather than evaluation based on objective evidence. There are several ways in which a claimant with heart disease finds himself in a position in which he can't prove it:

(a) The treating doctor says that cardiac stress testing is contraindicated, whether he is right or wrong. It is legally hazardous for S. S. Disability to ask a claimant to take a cardiac stress test against the wishes of the treating doctor.

(b) A claimant's blood pressure might be too high to allow him to safely undergo cardiac stress testing. At some future time, when his blood pressure is controlled, he could undergo such testing—but if this takes too long, S. S. Disability won't be able to hold the case. This will result in denial.

(c) The claimant may have some impairment that prevents him from doing a cardiac stress test, such as a broken leg or severe arthritis.

(d) The claimant refuses to take the test. This is certainly the claimant's right, but it prevents S. S. Disability from getting the information it needs to allow the claim.

8. The drug *digitalis,* used widely by doctors, produces changes on EKG tracings that are difficult to distinguish from true ischemic heart disease. This can make the EKG's from cardiac stress testing unreliable. If a claimant is taking digitalis during a cardiac stress test, that will be taken into account and the abnormalities will have to be much worse to be convincing.

9. *A cardiac stress test takes priority over other Parts of the Listing.* That means that even if the claimant has anginal type chest pain and fulfills Part B, C, or D he *might* not be allowed benefits *if* S. S. Disability can get the EKG tracings from a cardiac stress test, and the results don't fulfill Part A of the Listing. So some claimants are lucky that S. S. Disability can't get their cardiac stress tests. (The opposite might also be true, depending on circumstances. See #4 above.)

10. Many claimants simply get tired taking a cardiac stress test, or decide to impress the observing doctor that they are very sick by dropping out of the test before they go very far. Unless the EKG tracings are abnormal, S. S. Disability will not be very impressed (assuming also that no other serious abnormalities appear). Poor physical conditioning or theatrical exaggeration of symptoms are not substitutable for objective evidence, and don't fool the examining doctor or S. S. Disability.

B. Part B

1. As noted previously, the claimant can qualify under Part B, C, or D only if S. S. Disability does not have the EKG tracings and other important data from an *acceptable* cardiac stress test.

2. Even if the treating doctor has done a cardiac stress test on the claimant, it may not be acceptable. Some things that make such a test unacceptable to S. S. Disability are:

(a) Inability of S. S. Disability to tell what kind of "protocol" was used. There are many protocols, and each one subjects the claimant to different amounts of physical exertion.

(b) Inability of S. S. Disability to get the actual EKG tracings done during the test.

(c) Poor quality tracings that make them impossible to read.

(d) The claimant didn't go far enough in the test to make it mean anything.

(e) The test is too old. This is a matter of judgement by the person reviewing the case, but as a rule of thumb tests are considered out of date if more than a year old.

(f) The test is no longer valid for other reasons. For example, the claimant has had heart surgery since the stress test was done.

If any of these things are true, then the stress test is *not* supposed to be used in evaluation of the claimant's case, and the claimant has a right to be evaluated under Part B of the Listing.

3. If a claimant has EKG's showing any of the abnormalities given under Part B.1–7, *then S. S. Disability is not supposed to demand that the claimant undergo a cardiac stress test.* (This also applies to Part C and Part D of the Listing.) However, if a claimant's treating doctor has done such a test, S. S. Disability can and will attempt to obtain and use it for evaluation of the case, and the test results will have priority over Part B, C, or D. This was noted previously, and is re-emphasized here. Such tests from the treating doctor are considered "evidence of record" and can be used, but if S. S. Disability tries to purchase a cardiac stress test on a claimant who already qualifies for benefits under Part B, C, or D then this is an intentional attempt to turn an allowance into a possible denial. This is definitely not acceptable, and any such attempt is not officially permissible by S. S. Disability.

4. Part B.1 describes abnormal findings on a resting EKG (not done during a stress test) which indicate that the claimant has had a "heart attack". Further important points are as follows:

(a) "Transmural myocardial infarction" means that the claimant has had a heart attack in which part of the muscle of the heart was completely killed, and which extends through the full thickness of the heart's muscular wall in the area involved. This happens when the blood supply to part of the heart is completely cut off by total blockage of one of the coronary arteries supplying the heart. (Myocardial *infarction* differs from myocardial *ischemia* in that myocardial infarctions by definition kill part of the heart muscle, whereas ischemia means the heart muscle isn't getting enough blood but still receives a sufficient amount to stay alive.)

(b) it is totally irrelevant to S. S. Disability how long ago the myocardial infarction occurred. A myocardial infarction is usually abbreviated by the term "MI".

(c) S. S. Disability is not interested in whether or not the treating doctor thinks the EKG shows an MI; the requirements of Part B must be fulfilled.

(d) If S. S. Disability decides that the claimant had an MI, then it will not make a decision until at *least* 3 months have passed after the heart attack. This is to see how well the claimant recovers. If angina pectoris is present 3 months after the MI, then the claimant Meets the Listing under Part B.1. (There is one exception to this that was previously mentioned, but is very important: If the claimant's treating doctor did a cardiac stress test following the MI, then this test may take priority over Part B.1 and the claimant would have to qualify under Part A.1. S. S. Disability denies quite a few cases after an MI that would have been allowed, if they had not had a cardiac stress test that S. S. Disability obtained for review.

5. Part B.2 describes abnormal findings on a resting tracing necessary to qualify as evidence of cardiac *ischemia*, or decreased blood flow to a part of the heart muscle. The blood flow has not dropped off enough to actually kill part of the heart (as in an MI), but it still indicates severe disease.

(a) The previous discussion of cardiac stress tests also applies to Part B.2.

(b) The required abnormalities are given in B.2(a), B.2(b), or B.2(c). Only one of these has to be present on a resting EKG.

(c) It doesn't matter, unless the claimant has had heart surgery, how many EKG's have been done or how old they are. Nor does the most recent EKG have to be the one showing the abnormalities, because ischemia comes and goes; it may show on one tracing but not another one done at a different time. If even *one* tracing shows the needed abnormalities, the claimant can Meet the Listing under Part B.2 (provided, of course that he also has angina).

(d) Certain chemical abnormalities in the body (such as low blood potassium) and certain drugs (especially digitalis) can make EKG tracings appear abnormal when they are really normal. S. S. Disability will take that into account.

6. Part B.3 is evaluated just like Part B.2, except for the fact that it allows for different types of resting EKG abnormalities. There is just one important difference. If the abnormality reflects what is called a "current of injury", this implies that a myocardial infarction (MI, "heart attack") has occurred. Although the Listing doesn't say so, these cases would be held 3 months to see how well the claimant recovers. Of course, if 3 months have already passed when the claimant applies for disability then the case could be evaluated right away. Part B.3(a), B.3(b), or B.3(c) must be fulfilled, but not all three. (Of course, angina must also be present to Meet the Listing.)

7. Part B.4 is evaluated just like B.2 and B.3. It just takes into account different kinds of resting EKG abnormalities which indicate cardiac ischemia.

8. Part B.5 is like B.2, B.3, and B.4. It simply lists more acceptable kinds of resting EKG abnormalities indicating cardiac ischemia.

9. Part B.6 deals with an older kind of cardiac stress test called a "Double Master's Two Step". Some doctors still perform these. If such a test exists, then S. S. Disability is supposed to obtain it. S. S. Disability treats this differently from other types of cardiac stress tests. If it is *abnormal*, benefits can be allowed, but if it is *normal* it cannot be used to evaluate the case—that is, a negative result cannot be used for denial of benefits. Unlike the other types of cardiac stress test, such as a treadmill, the Master's test does *not* take priority over any other part of Listing 4.04. Part B.6(a) and B.6(b) give the required

abnormalities on a resting EKG. Only one of these has to be fulfilled.

10. Part B.7 does not deal with EKG tracings at all, but with what is called *coronary angiography*. This is a special type of X-ray study that involves injecting a special "contrast" material into the coronary arteries supplying the heart. Many people erroneously call the contrast material a "dye", but that is not correct. The contrast material allows the coronary arteries supplying the heart to be seen on X-ray. This permits the treating doctor to calculate how much blockage there may be in the coronary arteries. If there is enough blockage, then the heart probably isn't getting as much blood as it needs. Blockages of less than 50% are generally not thought to have much influence on the flow of blood through a coronary artery. Some important points about Part B.7 are as follows:

(a) S. S. Disability *never* orders this test on claimants because of the risk involved in inducing a heart attack or even death. This is true, although the risk is not great if done by an experienced doctor. But S. S. Disability does try to get the results of the test, if it has been done by the treating doctor because it can help the claimant prove he has heart disease.

(b) Very frequently, a claimant with severe coronary artery disease will undergo heart surgery called "coronary bypass surgery". Sections of veins are taken from the legs and sewed around the blocked parts of the coronary arteries to restore normal blood flow to the heart muscle. If a claimant has this type of surgery, S. S. Disability will find out how well the surgery worked. *If the claimant is better and his chest pain is completely gone after the surgery, then he will no longer qualify under Part B.7.* S. S. Disability waits at least 3 months after such surgery, before making a decision. The treating doctor is then asked if the claimant still has anginal chest pain. If the answer is "Yes", and S. S. Disability is convinced that the chest pain still sounds like angina, then it will be assumed that the surgery didn't work very well and the claimant would still qualify under Part B.7.

(c) Some claimants undergo coronary bypass surgery, and then get better (in fact, many get better). Some even return to work, but at some point after their surgery (perhaps years) they get angina again. If this is true, the claimant can be allowed disability benefits, beginning at the time his chest pain starts again. No further proof that his chest pain is due to heart disease is required, if there was enough blockage in his coronary arteries at the time of surgery. Of course, the new chest pain must be described completely by the treating doctor and it must sound like angina to S. S. Disability. If this is true, S. S. Disability is *not* supposed to ask that the claimant undergo a cardiac stress test.

(d) Often the treating doctor *will* do a cardiac stress test on a claimant that has coronary artery blockage proven by angiography. This test will take priority over Part B.7 and the case will be evaluated under Part A. This also applies to stress tests done *after* coronary bypass surgery. Such a case will be evaluated under Part A. But if a stress test were done *before* such surgery, then S. S. Disability can no longer use it to deny a case, but only to help establish the onset date in allowance cases. *Many cases that otherwise have qualified for benefits are denied because S. S. Disability got cardiac stress test tracings from the claimant's treating doctor or hospital.* However, it has already been pointed out that S. S. Disability cannot use the "reported" results of such a test, unless it is done properly *and* the actual EKG tracings can be obtained for review.

(e) Parts 7.a, 7.b, and 7.c tell the exact amount of blockage that must be present to qualify under Part B.7. Only one of these must be fulfilled. (If the reader is a physician, note that the word "proximal" means before the take-off of the first septal perforator in the left anterior descending vessel, or before the acute marginal branch of the right coronary artery, or before the first obtuse marginal branch of the circumflex coronary artery.)

C. Part C

1. Part C refers to a certain kind of abnormality present on some people's EKG tracings called a "left bundle branch block". This occurs when one of the important nerves in the heart itself is "blocked"—that is, when it doesn't carry nerve impulses.

2. A left bundle branch block might be due to disease of the coronary arteries (in which case it is serious), or it might not mean anything serious at all. If the treating doctor has done coronary angiography studies of the claimant's heart which show that there is no disease of those arteries, then the claimant *cannot* qualify under Part C.

3. If the treating doctor has not done coronary angiography, or S. S. Disability can't get the results, then it is *assumed*

that the claimant's left bundle branch block is due to coronary artery disease—S. S. Disability *must* give the claimant the benefit of the doubt. The reason for this is that S. S. Disability can't do any tests to find out the truth. It just so happens that cardiac stress tests cannot be interpreted, if a left bundle branch block is present.

4. It should be remembered that chest pain which has the characteristics of angina must also be present, just as for the other parts of this Listing.

D. Part D

1. Part D deals with what is called the "left ventricular ejection fraction". This just means the percentage of blood that the main pumping chamber of the heart (the left ventricle) can pump out with each beat. A "sick" heart often can't pump out as much with each beat as a healthy one. A normal ejection fraction is about 55%.

2. Part D mentions two ways that an ejection fraction can be calculated. One of these is "cardiac catheterization". As previously discussed, this is a special X-ray procedure involving injecting the coronary arteries and ventricles (chambers) of the heart so that they can be seen with X-rays. A special substance called "contrast material" is used for the injection; it does not harm the heart. When the contrast material outlines the ventricles, their size can be calculated both between beats and during contraction of the heart muscle. This allows calculation of the ejection fraction.

3. Another way to measure the ejection fraction is by what is called "echocardiography". This involves bouncing a sound wave off of the structures of the heart. This method of measuring the ejection fraction is not as accurate as one done by cardiac catheterization. Echocardiography of a claimant's heart is sometimes purchased by S. S. Disability, because it can provide valuable information and is completely harmless. But, as stated previously, cardiac catheterization carries some risks (although such risk is small if done by an experienced doctor), and is never purchased by S. S. Disability.

4. Another way an ejection fraction can be measured is by injecting special radioactive materials into the bloodstream, which are then taken to the heart. These tests are acceptable, although not purchased by S. S. Disability. The level of radiation is essentially harmless. These are various types of "radionuclide" studies.

5. The ejection fraction must be 30% or less for the claimant to qualify under Part D. It should be pointed out that if the claimant has an ejection fraction which has been measured more than once over a period of time, the most recent value is the one that will be used in evaluation of the case. Also, claimants who have an episode of congestive heart failure (see Listing 4.02) may have a very low ejection fraction which improves after treatment of the heart failure; this would not qualify under Part D.

6. Like the other parts of this Listing, it should be remembered that chest pain with the characteristics of angina pectoris must also be present.

7. Since echocardiograms are not as accurate in measuring the ejection fraction as cardiac catheterization or radionuclide studies, they are given the least weight in analyzing the data, if more than one type of study has been done in a particular case.

Listing 4.05

Recurrent arrhythmias (not due to digitalis toxicity) resulting in uncontrolled repeated episodes of cardiac syncope and documented by resting or ambulatory (Holter) electrocardiography.

I. General Considerations

A. This Listing deals with what are called cardiac *arrhythmias*. Arrhythmias are abnormalities in the *pattern* or *rate* in which the heart beats.

B. Arrhythmias result when the electrical impulses travelling through the heart are abnormal. There are many types, and they can be *very* complicated.

C. Some arrhythmias are harmful, and some do no harm at all. It is sometimes difficult even for a heart specialist to tell which is the case.

D. Serious arrhythmias cause the heart to beat at the wrong time, and this can decrease the amount of blood that the heart pumps out to the rest of the body. If severe enough, almost no blood is pumped by the heart, and the victim will die very quickly. Arrhythmias are a major cause of "sudden death", especially after a "heart attack" (myocardial infarction).

E. Arrhythmias caused by the drug *digitalis* do not qualify under this Listing, no matter how serious they are. The reason for this is that the arrhythmia can be stopped by decreasing the drug. This should not be interpreted by the reader to mean that a claimant who takes digitalis cannot qualify under this Listing; digitalis would have to be the cause of the arrhythmia for that to be true, by being at abnormally high ("toxic") levels in the claimant's bloodstream. Although digitalis can be used to treat some types of arrhythmias, it will cause arrhythmias if too much of the drug is taken. But it is still one of the most important drugs in the history of medicine, having been used for thousands of years.

F. If the claimant had a serious arrhythmia in the past, but his treating doctor brought it under control with therapy, then he would no longer qualify under this Listing.

G. Angina pectoris does not have to be present, in order to qualify under this Listing.

II. Specific Requirements

A. As mentioned above, the arrhythmia cannot be caused by the drug digitalis.

B. The arrhythmia must happen frequently enough to be a problem to the claimant. These episodes *must* be recorded on EKG tracings that S. S. Disability can evaluate.

C. The episodes of arrhythmia must be severe enough to cause "cardiac syncope". This is loss of consciousness caused by decreased blood flow to the brain.

D. ". . . ambulatory (Holter) electrocardiography . . ." refers to a special procedure used to detect arrhythmias. Most EKG's are run for only about a minute in the doctor's office or hospital. They can totally miss very serious arrhythmias, because the EKG tracings are not run continuously for a long enough period of time. In people suspected of having serious arrhythmias, *Holter* monitors get around this problem by recording the claimant's heart beats for a long time, usually as long as 24 hours. The claimant simply wears a small device similar to a tape recorder, except electrodes connect it to the claimant's chest to pick up the electrical impulses from the heart. While wearing the Holter monitor, the claimant goes about his everyday life. If he has some kind of symptoms, he writes down what they feel like, what he is doing when they happen, and what time it is. After the 24 hours is up, he goes back to his doctor to turn in the long recording. Of course, this can also be done on people in a hospital. The number of abnormal heart beats is analyzed by the doctor, especially in relation to the claimant's symptoms. If the claimant's symptoms are due to arrhythmias of the heart, then the tracings should be abnormal at the same time. It is not uncommon for people to have symptoms that sound like they may be due to an arrhythmia, to show no abnormalities on their Holter monitor tracing. People who excessively worry about their heart are most likely to be in this situation. Of course, some claimants really are sick and the abnormalities are present on the Holter EKG tracings.

E. How often "repeated episodes" means in the Listing is not clearly defined. This is up to the judgment of person reviewing the claimant's case, and would have to take into account the type of arrhythmia and the circumstances involved in syncopal episodes in a particular claimant.

F. It should be pointed out that this is a very *difficult* Listing to qualify under. It is not enough for a claimant to have symptoms from an arrhythmia. He actually has to lose consciousness. The loss of consciousness from a cardiac arrhythmia can be extremely dangerous for someone who suffers it, especially if they have an arrhythmia involving the large ventricular chambers of the heart which do most of the work in pumping blood. With such ventricular arrhythmias (the major cause of sudden death from heart disease), the person involved is coming very close to death and has a good chance of not surviving at all. Yet one such episode of cardiac syncope is not enough; they must occur over and over again, according to the Listing. Also, if the claimant is not wearing a Holter monitor, or in their doctor's office, or in a hospital, it becomes very difficult to prove that their loss of consciousness is due to cardiac arrhythmia.

Listing 4.09

Myocardiopathies, rheumatic or syphilitic heart disease. Evaluate under the criteria in Listing 4.02, 4.04, 4.05, or 11.04.

I. General Considerations

A. "Myocardiopathies" are diseases which affect the heart muscle itself, rather than the coronary arteries that supply it blood. Myocardiopathy can be caused by alcohol, drugs, and viruses among other things. Many times, the cause is unknown. The disease may get better with treatment, or it may not. If severe enough, heart failure and arrhythmias of the heart may result.

B. Heart disease caused by rheumatic fever and syphilis mainly damage the heart valves. This can lead to further damage to other parts of the heart, causing heart failure or arrhythmias.

C. Angina is not required to fulfill this Listing, *unless* the actual evaluation is done under Listing 4.04.

II. Specific Requirements

A. No actual evaluation is done under this Listing.

B. Evaluation is done under whichever other Listing most accurately applies to the type of heart damage that the claimant has.

Listing 4.11

Aneurysm of aorta or major branches (demonstrated by roentgenographic evidence). With:

A. Acute or chronic dissection not controlled by prescribed medical or surgical treatment; OR

B. Congestive heart failure as described under the criteria in Listing 4.02; OR

C. Renal failure as described under the criteria in Listing 6.02; OR

D. Repeated syncopal episodes.

I. General Considerations

A. An "aneurysm" is an abnormal swelling in a blood-vessel, usually an artery. This may happen when the wall of an artery is weakened by disease. The pressure inside the artery can then cause it to "balloon up" at the weakened place.

B. The danger of having an aneurysm is that it might eventually break open (rupture) and cause serious bleeding.

C. The "aorta" is the largest artery in the body; coming directly from the main pumping chamber of the heart (left ventricle), it gives off all of the other major arteries in the body. If a large aortic aneurysm ruptures, the massive bleeding may cause death very quickly.

D. Whether a claimant has an aneurysm cannot be a matter of guesswork. X-rays must be available to S. S. Disability, showing such an aneurysm to exist. S. S. Disability does not purchase such tests; they must be available from the treating doctor or hospital.

II. Specific Requirements

A. Part A

1. "Dissection" of the aorta means that the high pressure blood inside the aorta has forced its way through a weak spot *into* the wall of that large artery. This produces even more weakness in the wall, and more rapid development of an aneurysm. So it means that the aorta is even more likely to rupture. Aneurysms never get smaller; they tend to get larger and larger.

2. Sometimes the growth in size of the aneurysm can be stopped by medical therapy, such as lowering the blood pressure.

3. But some aneurysms cannot be stopped by medical therapy. In that case, surgery might be done to remove the damaged part of the aorta and replace it with an artificial tube (such as a dacron graft).

4. Some people with aortic aneurysms are too sick for surgery (or the surgery didn't work), and medical treatment doesn't work either. It is *these* claimants who would qualify under Part A. They are at high risk for death. But note that the aneurysm must be a dissecting type. It can be acute or chronic.

B. Part B

1. An aortic aneurysm can be associated with congestive heart failure.

2. No actual evaluation is done under Part B. If heart failure exists, the case is then developed under the Listings that deals with heart failure (4.02).

C. Part C

1. Aneurysms may be associated with kidney failure.

2. If there is kidney failure, it is evaluated under the Listing that deals with the problem (6.02). No actual evaluation is done under Part C.

D. Part D

1. A large aneurysm of the aorta (especially of the upper part) can cause loss of consciousness (syncope).

2. One such episode is not enough. Part B requires "repeated" episodes of syncope. Exactly how often "repeated" means is a matter of judgment by the person evaluating the claimant's case and is based on the circumstances involved in that particular case. It must be an ongoing problem at the time the claimant applies for disability.

Listing 4.12

Chronic venous insufficiency of the lower extremity with incompetency or obstruction of the deep venous return, associated with superficial varicosities, extensive brawny edema, stasis dermatitis, and recurrent or persistent ulceration which has not healed following at least 3 months of prescribed medical or surgical therapy.

I. General Observations

A. This Listing deals with disease affecting veins.

B. "Chronic venous insufficiency" means that the claimant has an *incurable* problem with veins that no longer carry blood properly; veins are very weak and easily damaged by diseases which affect them.

C. Problems with veins occur more frequently in the legs than anywhere else. This is at least partly because of the higher pressure in veins of the legs. The blood must fight the force of gravity in getting back up to the heart. (Venous blood is "used" blood that must get back to the heart and lungs to pick up more oxygen again.)

D. If the venous blood cannot get back from the legs very well, certain kinds of damage can be done to the legs. The nature of this damage in order to qualify under this Listing is discussed below.

II. Specific Requirements

A. As noted above *only* venous disease of the legs is considered under this Listing. (Arterial disease in the legs is considered in Listing 4.13.)

B. Only *one* leg has to be involved.

C. "Incompetency" simply means that the vein is too weak to carry blood the way it should.

D. The veins in the legs consist of *two* systems. One of these is "superficial", and the other is a "deep" system of veins in the legs. The superficial system consists of veins everyone can see under their skin on the outer part of their legs. If the superficial veins are damaged, they can swell up into superficial "varicosities". These are the "varicose veins" that people talk about. The other system consists of veins deeper down in the legs.

E. If *only* the superficial system is involved, the claimant cannot qualify under this Listing. This applies to most people with "varicose veins". But disease in the deep system is much more serious. The deep system *must* be involved.

F. Disease of the deep vein system of the legs can lead to severe damage to the other tissues of the leg. It is this damage that S. S. Disability is interested in, and which must be present to qualify under this Listing:

1. There must be "extensive" (involving most of the leg) "brawny edema". *Brawny edema* is a very severe kind of firm swelling of the leg caused by disease of deep veins.

2. There must be "stasis dermatitis", which is a kind of skin damage from the venous disease.

3. There must be at least one ulcer on the leg involved. An ulcer is an open sore caused by tissue damage. When the leg is swollen up with venous blood that can't get out because of incompetent veins, there may be this severe form of tissue damage. There has to be a history of these ulcers being present over and over again, or present at the time of application for disability. In addition there has to be evidence that the ulcers can't be healed even with at least 3 months of treatment.

4. In addition to the damage done by disease in the deep veins, the Listing requires that superficial varicose veins also be present.

Listing 4.13

Arteriosclerosis obliterans or thromboangiitis. With:

A. Intermittent claudication with failure to visualize (on arteriogram obtained independent of social security disability evaluation) the common femoral or deep femoral artery in one extremity; OR

B. Intermittent claudication and absence of peripheral arterial pulsations in the femoral, popliteal, dorsalis pedis, and posterior tibial arteries by Doppler or plethysmography, in one extremity; OR

C. Amputation at or above the tarsal region due to peripheral vascular disease.

I. General Considerations

A. This Listing deals with what is called "peripheral vascular disease".

B. Only arterial disease in the legs can qualify under this Listing.

C. Two different types of peripheral vascular disease can qualify. One is "thrombo-angiitis". It is sometimes called Buerger's Disease. This is an interesting disease of arteries which decreases blood flow. It mainly affects men who smoke tobacco. It usually stops, if smoking is stopped. However, such people rarely stop smoking even if the disease leads to amputation. Buerger's Disease is relatively uncommon. The most frequently seen type of peripheral vascular disease is caused by "arteriosclerosis obliterans". In this disease, fatty deposits build up in the arteries and decrease the amount of blood flow that the tissues supplied by that artery can get. The general disease process is no different from that which causes blockage of coronary arteries, except this is occurring in the legs.

D. Although Buerger's Disease can affect the hands, as well as the legs, arteriosclerosis obliterans is much more common and more likely to affect the arteries supplying the legs. Therefore, this Listing focuses on arterial disease in the legs. Sometimes, surgery can be done in which the blood supply is restored by sewing artificial tubes (such as dacron grafts) around the blocked parts of arteries in the legs. If this is successful, S. S. Disability would evaluate the claimant's condition *after* surgery.

II. Specific Requirements

A. Part A

1. "Intermittent claudication" must be present. This is a pain in the legs caused by the muscles not getting enough blood. It usually affects the calf muscles, but can also involve pain in the thighs or hip muscles—depending on which artery is partly or completely blocked. When a person with intermittent claudication is not doing anything, there may be no pain present at all because the leg is getting all the blood flow it needs. But if the person tries to get out and walk there may not be enough blood flow to satisfy the muscles with the increased work they have to do. This can produce what is usually called an "aching" or "cramping" pain which is intermittent claudication and will go away in a few minutes with rest.

2. Only *one* leg need be involved to qualify under this Listing.

3. Part A requires a special X-ray procedure called an arteriogram, in order to prove that there are occlusions in the arteries to the legs. This involves injecting a "contrast material" into

the arteries to make them visible on X-ray. Since this test carries some risk, S. S. Disability *never* purchases it though the risk is small when done by an experienced doctor. Therefore, to qualify under this Listing, arteriography must have already been done by the claimant's treating doctor, and the results available to S. S. Disability.

4. If a claimant has the symptoms of intermittent claudication but no evidence of vascular disease, then he will *not* qualify under Part A.

5. The arteriography must show complete blockage of one of two major arteries called the "common femoral" and "deep femoral" arteries.

B. Part B

1. Symptoms compatible with intermittent claudication must be present. Symptoms like those of intermittent claudication without evidence of peripheral vascular disease cannot qualify under Part B.

2. Only one leg need be involved.

3. When doing a physical examination, a careful physician attempts to palpate (feel) the major arterial pulses in the legs and feet. Decreased pulses may indicate decreased blood flow to the lower extremities. Other evidence of such decreased flow is also searched for—for example, cool feet, hair loss, changes in the toenails. Combined with symptoms and other findings on the history and rest of the physical examination, he may make a judgment whether a given patient has significant peripheral vascular disease. However, this is often not exact enough to judge the severity of disease. Given two doctors, one may not be able to feel any pulses in the feet while another will report that he can feel all of them.

4. A helpful tool in determining blood flow in the arteries of the legs and feet involves the use of a device called a Doppler. This harmless instrument allows blood pressure readings to be taken by placing it over the artery in question.

5. Normally, the *systolic* blood pressure in an artery at the ankle should be higher than the systolic pressure in the arm ("brachial" artery systolic B.P.). Therefore, in a normal person, the ankle/brachial systolic blood pressure ratio should always be higher than 1.0. This ratio is called the Doppler Index, and if less than 1.0 it indicates decreased blood flow in the ankle artery. (For more information about blood pressure in general see the discussion of Listing 4.03.)

6. While Doppler measurements have their value, S. S. Disability realizes that they may fail to reveal the true severity in some particular types of peripheral vascular disease, such as calcific (Monckeberg's) sclerosis or small vessel disease in people with diabetes mellitus. In diabetes, for example, there may be widespread severe disease in blood vessels too small for pressure measurement by Doppler.

7. It is of critical importance in the use of this Listing to note that Part B requires the *absence* of blood flow measurable by Doppler in *all* of the major arteries of one leg. This is completely unreasonable medically, and in real case evaluation S. S. Disability does not make this requirement. Part B is considered to be fulfilled if there is a Doppler Index of 0.5 or less in the ankle artery (posterior tibial artery) of one leg.

8. The above Doppler studies are done with the claimant at rest. However, *exercise Dopplers* are sometimes purchased by S. S. Disability, to evaluate adequacy of blood flow to the legs during physical work in the form of walking on a treadmill. If blood flow is significantly impaired at low levels of exercise, allowance under Part B might be made through use of an Equal code. This would not be done if Part B were already fulfilled with resting Doppler measurements.

C. Part C

1. If peripheral vascular disease is severe enough and cannot be treated by surgery or drugs, then the tissues supplied by the blocked arteries may die for lack of blood. This is called *gangrene.*

2. Gangrene can necessitate the amputation of a foot or part of a leg. (Gangrene cannot be ignored, because it would cause infection of the entire body from bacteria that would start to grow in the damaged tissues. This would result in death.)

3. The amputation need involve only one leg to qualify.

4. Amputation of a toe or part of a foot is not enough to qualify under Part C. The amputation must be above the ankle bones or higher (". . . at or above the tarsal region . . .").

5. Note that the amputation *must* be due to peripheral vascular disease (arterial). A leg which is amputated secondary to an accident would *not* qualify.

§ 2.6 Digestive System

Listing 5.02

Recurrent upper gastrointestinal hemorrhage from undetermined cause. With anemia manifested by hematocrit of 30 percent or less on repeated examinations.

I. General Considerations

A. This Listing deals only with bleeding from the *upper* gastrointestinal tract. Such locations of bleeding would include the esophagus, stomach, and small intestine.

B. The Listing involves cases of such bleeding in which the cause is not known.

II. Specific Requirements

A. "Recurrent" is not exactly defined by the Listing. How often the bleeding has to occur is a matter of judgment by the person in S. S. Disability reviewing the claimant's case. It would at least partly depend on how severe each bleeding episode was, how long it takes the claimant to recover from an episode, and other complications that might exist in an individual case.

B. The Listing refers to chronic problems with upper gastrointestinal bleeding which are present at the time of application for disability—not something that has happened only in the past and no longer of concern.

C. "Anemia" means a decrease in the number of red blood cells, which carry oxygen to the tissues of the body. One way to measure the severity of anemia is by what it called a "hematocrit". This is simply the percentage of a volume of blood that is made up by red cells. Therefore, the hematocrit will fall to abnormally low levels, if there is enough blood lost.

D. To qualify under this Listing, the hematocrit must not be above 30 percent on *repeated* testing. The hematocrit must be at least that low over a reasonable period of time, so that S. S. Disability will feel sure that the bleeding problem is chronic. As in all Listings, the 12 month minimum duration requirement must be fulfilled. At the very minimum, S. S. Disability must have hematocrit values over a period of several months, before it will be believed that the problem will be likely to last at least 12 months. If S. S. Disability is not sure about this, it may hold the claimant's case for months (up to 5 months), and ask for more hematocrit tests to be done.

E. The anemia shown by the low hematocrit values *must* be due to bleeding from the upper gastrointestinal tract. The reason for this is that there are many causes of anemia; most frequently, it is a deficiency of iron. For example, a claimant might have just a little bleeding from somewhere in his upper gastrointestinal tract (such as the stomach), but not enough bleeding to cause anemia. That same claimant might have a hematocrit of 30% or less from some other disease. In that case, the claimant would *not* qualify under this Listing.

F. Most claimants qualifying under this Listing have been hospitalized by their treating doctors, in an attempt to find a cause and a cure.

Listing 5.03

Stricture, stenosis, or obstruction of the esophagus (demonstrated by X-ray or endoscopy). With weight loss as described under Listing 5.08.

I. General Considerations

A. This Listing deals *only* with diseases of the esophagus.

B. What kind of disease causes the problem is not as important as the effect it has on the claimant in terms of his ability to eat enough food to remain healthy.

II. Specific Requirements

A. Whatever disease of the esophagus is present, it must be severe enough to cause "stricture, stenosis, or obstruction" of the esophagus. Put in plain language, that means that the esophagus must be narrowed, so that it is difficult for swallowed food to get to the stomach.

B. If the narrowing of the esophagus is severe enough, the claimant will not be able to take in enough food to supply the body with the nutrients it needs. This will result in a loss of weight.

C. Narrowing of the esophagus must be proven to exist by special X-ray studies or by "endoscopy". Endoscopy is a method by which a doctor can look into some area of the body through a flexible tube. If the esophagus is being examined, the patient swallows the tube.

D. No actual evaluation is done under this Listing, other than to prove that narrowing of the esophagus exists in the claimant to more than just a mild degree. Then the amount of weight loss is compared to the requirements of Listing 5.08, which deals with weight loss.

Listing 5.04

Peptic ulcer disease (demonstrated by X-ray or endoscopy). With:

A. Recurrent ulceration after definitive surgery persistent despite therapy; OR

B. Inoperable fistula formation; OR

C. Recurrent obstruction demonstrated by X-ray or endoscopy; OR

D. Weight loss as described under Listing 5.08.

I. General Considerations

A. This Listing deals *only* with "peptic ulcer disease". These are ulcers, or damaged areas of the small intestine close to the stomach. Often, they occur in the duodenum which is the name of the first part of the small intestine coming from the stomach.

B. Millions of people have peptic ulcer disease (PUD) and most are cured either by medical treatment or by surgery.

C. In order for S. S. Disability to be sure that a peptic ulcer exists, there must be special X-rays showing it. It can also be proven by what is called "endoscopy". In this case, the patient would swallow a long flexible tube through which the examining doctor can "look around" in the esophagus, stomach, and finally the small intestine where the ulcer is usually located. It would be unusual for S. S. Disability to order this test on a claimant. It must have already been done by the treating doctor and the results available to S. S. Disability to review.

D. Part A, B, C, or D must be fulfilled, but not all four.

II. Specific Requirements

A. Part A

1. Part A requires that "definitive surgery" has already been done on the claimant. This means surgery that would normally be expected to cure the ulcer in most people. It could involve many types of surgery, but usually consists of cutting out

part of the stomach (partial gastrectomy), operating on the small intestine, and cutting certain nerves to the stomach.

2. The above surgery must have *failed* to cure the claimant of his ulcer. In other words, the ulcer disease has to come back, even though surgery has been done. Of course, if the ulcer comes back it has to be proven *again* to exist by X-rays or endoscopy.

3. The new ulcer that has come back after surgery has to be "persistent". That is, S. S. Disability must feel that the new ulcer is not going to be cured. So the claimant must have this new ulcer after surgery at the time he applies for disability, or reasonably close to the time of application.

4. It is not uncommon for S. S. Disability to see claimants who have had surgery years before, and recently developed another ulcer. S. S. Disability must have enough information to believe that the new ulcer will not be cured. If necessary, the claimant's case will be held until this can be determined.

B. Part B

1. An ulcer can be very damaging to the intestine; it might break through the wall of the intestine and create an abnormal connection between the intestine and some other organ. This would be called a "fistula".

2. The fistula must be serious enough that surgery cannot be done to cure it ("inoperable").

C. Part C

1. Scarring from an ulcer or previous surgery can block off or "obstruct" the small intestine by fibrous tissues called "adhesions".

2. The obstruction has to be proven by X-rays or endoscopy.

3. The obstruction must be "recurrent". How often "recurrent" means depends on the problems of an individual claimant and the judgement of the person in S. S. Disability reviewing the case. It has to be often enough that S. S. Disability feels it is a current problem that is not likely to be cured within a 12 months period.

D. Part D

1. Peptic ulcer disease involves an important part of the small intestine. Recurrent ulcers, fistula formation, or obstruction as discussed above can make it impossible for a claimant to eat enough to keep his weight normal. Such people will have considerable pain and loss of appetite, and other problems associated with eating. If the weight loss is serious enough, the claimant could qualify under Part D. Note, however, that the

weight loss *must* be due to the peptic ulcer disease or its complications, not the fact that the claimant simply chooses not to eat much; there must be *physical* reasons the claimant can't keep normal weight, not mental ones.

2. The degree of weight loss needed is not considered under Part D. That is actually evaluated under the Listing dealing with weight loss (5.08), after it has been determined that the weight loss is due to complications of peptic ulcer disease.

Listing 5.05

Chronic liver disease (e.g. portal, postnecrotic, or biliary cirrhosis; chronic active hepatitis; Wilson's disease). With:

A. Esophageal varices (demonstrated by X-ray or endoscopy) with a documented history of massive hemorrhage attributable to these varices; OR

B. Performance of a shunt operation for esophageal varices; OR

C. Serum bilirubin of 2.5 mg. per deciliter (100 ml.) or greater persisting on repeated examinations for at least 5 months; OR

D. Hepatic encephalopathy. Evaluate under the criteria in Listing 12.02; OR

E. Confirmation of chronic liver disease by liver biopsy (obtained independent of social security disability evaluation) and one of the following:

1. Ascites not attributable to other causes, recurrent or persisting for at least 3 months, demonstrated by abdominal paracentesis or associated with persistent hypoalbuminemia of 3.0 gm. per deciliter (100 ml.) or less.

2. Serum bilirubin of 2.5 mg. per deciliter (100 ml.) or greater on repeated examinations for at least 3 months.

3. Hepatic cell necrosis or inflammation, persisting for at least 3 months, documented by repeated abnormalities of prothrombin time and enzymes indicative of hepatic dysfunction.

I. General Considerations

A. This Listing deals with *liver* disease. Some examples are given by the Listing, but *any* type of liver disease could potentially qualify. The most frequent type of liver disease seen by S. S. Disability is cirrhosis of the liver caused by the abuse of alcohol.

B. Note that this Listing requires *chronic* liver disease (not likely to improve).

C. Part A, B, C, D, or E must be fulfilled, but not all four.

II. Specific Requirements

A. Part A

1. Part A deals only with "esophageal varices" caused by liver disease.

2. Esophageal varices are weak little "ballooned-out" areas in the veins running through the esophagus. In very severe liver disease, these are sometimes created by abnormally high pressures inside the veins. The increased pressure is directly related to the liver disease.

3. Because the walls of veins are very weak, the esophageal varices can break open and bleed. If they bleed enough, the person will obviously die from the shock of massive blood loss unless medical treatment can be given in time.

4. The varices must be proven to exist either by endoscopy (in which a doctor looks down into the esophagus through a flexible tube), or by special X-rays. It does not matter when these tests were done, but S. S. Disability must be able to obtain the results. Having the varices alone is not enough—there must be reasonable evidence that they are the source of the bleeding.

5. There must be at least one "massive hemorrhage". Exactly how much bleeding this means is not exactly defined by the Listing. But this is usually interpreted to mean that the claimant had to be hospitalized for emergency treatment to prevent death from blood loss.

6. A claimant who has bled even once from esophageal varices will have a tendency to bleed again. So one massive episode of bleeding is enough to convince S. S. Disability that the problem is not going to be cured, and it does not matter when the episode happened. The development of esophageal varices and bleeding from them due to liver disease is an indication that the liver disease is very advanced.

B. Part B

1. A "shunt operation" is a special type of surgery done to decrease the blood pressure inside of esophageal varices, so that they will be less likely to break open and bleed.

2. Such shunt operations are "last ditch" efforts and do not work well in every case. The fact that such an operation was

performed at all indicates advanced liver disease. If a claimant has had even one such operation, no matter when it was, he can qualify under Part B.

C. Part C

1. If liver disease is severe enough, a chemical called "bilirubin" may increase in the bloodstream.

2. The bilirubin must be elevated in the blood to at least 2.5, and must stay at least that high for a minimum of 5 months.

3. If not enough time has passed, S. S. Disability may hold the claimant's case to see what will happen. Normal levels are not much higher than 1.

If the bilirubin level has stayed at a level of 2.5 or higher for at least 5 months, S. S. Disability will assume that the liver disease is not going to improve much, and Part C can be fulfilled.

D. Part D

1. Part D takes into consideration what is called "hepatic encephalopathy". This means the liver disease is so advanced that the liver has almost completely failed to work, and very abnormal mental changes happen as a result. These mental changes are like those of a severe mental illness; the claimant cannot act or think normally. In some cases, it can be reversed; in others the hepatic encephalopathy deepens into coma and death.

2. No actual evaluation is done under Part D. The severity of the hepatic encephalopathy must fulfill the requirements of Listing 12.02, which is a Listing specifically created to evaluate certain kinds of mental disorders called "organic brain syndromes" which are caused by damage to the brain from disease or accidents.

E. Part E

1. Part E requires that liver disease has been proven to exist by what is called a "liver biopsy". This involves cutting out a small piece of liver tissue to examine under a microscope. A liver biopsy allows a more exact diagnosis to be made. (Note that a liver biopsy is *not* required for Parts A, B, C, or D of the Listing.).

2. S. S. Disability does *not* order liver biopsies on claimants, because the procedure can be hazardous. Such a biopsy must have been done by the treating doctor and the results available to S. S. Disability.

3. Parts E.1, E.2 or E.3 of the Listing must be fulfilled, but not all three. Of course, these are not even considered by S. S. Disability, unless the necessary liver biopsy has been done.

4. Part E.1 refers to "ascites". This is a sign of very serious liver disease, and means a build-up of fluid in the abdomen. If the ascites is bad enough, a doctor can feel it in the claimant's abdomen on a physical examination. But sometimes this is not really certain. So if the only evidence of ascites is by physical examination, a laboratory test is also required. This test must show "hypo-albuminemia"—a decrease in the amount of a protein called albumin in the bloodstream. On the other hand, if *paracentesis* has been done, this blood test is not required. The reason for this is that paracentesis can actually *prove* that ascites is present, so that the blood test is not needed. Paracentesis is a procedure by which the treating doctor sticks a needle into the abdomen and tries to suck out some of the ascitis fluid. S. S. Disability *never* orders this test on a claimant, because it can be hazardous. To qualify under Part E.1, the claimant must have ascites present at least most of the time over a 3 month period. If it lasts that long, S. S. Disability will assume that it is not likely to improve very much; this would certainly indicate very severe liver disease.

5. Part E.2 only requires that a blood test called the "serum bilirubin" be at least 2.5 or greater over a 3 month period. This abnormal increase in bilirubin in the bloodstream is associated with severe liver disease.

6. Part E.3 is fulfilled by certain kinds of laboratory tests which indicate that the liver disease is very severe. "Hepatic cells" refers to cells that make up the liver tissue. These cells may be either "inflammed" or some of them may actually be dead ("necrosis"). There are certain kinds of chemicals present in the liver which help it work, called liver "enzymes". If the liver is diseased, these enzymes are abnormally increased. Examples of such enzymes are "LDH, SGOT, and SGPT". Part E.3 also requires that a test called the "prothrombin time" be abnormally increased. This also is a sign of severe liver disease. Prothrombin is a protein made by the liver, which is important in blood coagulation; a highly diseased liver can lead to decreased prothrombin production which can then be measured by a blood test showing an abnormal "prothrombin time". The above laboratory tests must be abnormal over a period of at least 3 months, for S. S. Disability to feel that there will probably be no improvement in the liver disease. (No "normal" or "abnormal" numbers are given here for these tests, because what is normal or abnormal depends on how the tests are done by a given laboratory doing them.)

Listing 5.06

Chronic ulcerative or granulomatous colitis (demonstrated by endoscopy, barium enema, biopsy, or operative findings). With:

A. Recurrent bloody stools documented on repeated examinations and anemia manifested by hematocrit of 30 percent or less on repeated examinations; OR

B. Persistent or recurrent systemic manifestations, such as arthritis, iritis, fever, or liver dysfunction, not attributable to other causes; OR

C. Intermittent obstruction due to intractable abscess, fistula formation, or stenosis; OR

D. Recurrences of findings of A, B, or C above after total colectomy; OR

E. Weight loss as described under Listing 5.08.

I. General Considerations

A. This Listing deals with either of two very serious diseases that can affect the large intestine (colon), called "ulcerative" colitis and "granulomatous" colitis. Although the diseases are different, they have very similar effects. "Colitis" simply means inflammation of the colon.

B. The cause of these diseases is not known, but they can lead to tremendous inflammation and damage of the large intestine.

C. How these disease affect any individual person is different. There may be "flare-ups" occurring only rarely, with the claimant feeling pretty good between them. Or such "flare-ups" may be very frequent. S. S. Disability is interested in the cases which are *chronic.* Those are the cases in which the disease severely impairs the claimant (in one way or another) almost continuously.

D. The diagnosis *must* be reasonably proven, before the claimant can fulfill the Listing. There are several ways this can be done:

1. *Endoscopy.* This is a method by which the treating doctor inserts a long flexible tube up into the large intestine through the rectum. He can look through the other end of the tube and examine the intestine; in fact, the entire large intestine can be examined this way. Small pieces of tissue can even be snipped out for more detailed examination. This

is called a "biopsy". S. S. Disability does not order endoscopy on claimants.

2. *Barium enema.* This is a special X-ray technique. S. S. Disability doesn't usually order this test, but might do so under unusual circumstances.

3. *Biopsy.* As noted above, this simply means taking a small piece of tissue for analysis. It might be done during endoscopy or during surgery.

4. *Operative findings.* This simply means that if there has been abdominal surgery, the doctor might have noted the presence of the disease, or even biopsied a small piece of tissue from the intestine for analysis.

E. After the disease has been proven to exist in the claimant, Part A, B, C, D, or E must be fulfilled, but not all three.

II. Specific Requirements

A. Part A

1. Because the large intestine is inflammed, the claimant may bleed from his colon. This is what is meant by "bloody stools". If this is severe, it is quite obvious.

2. The term "recurrent" blood stools is not exactly defined by the Listing, because individual cases are too complicated to make an exact rule. S. S. Disability decides how severe these bleeding episodes are, by considering how *anemic* the claimant is. Anemia means a decrease in the number of red blood cells for some reason. In this case, it would be from loss of blood. One test used to show the degree of anemia is called the "hematocrit", which is simply the percentage of red cells in a volume of blood. The hematocrit must not be higher than 30 percent on *repeated* testing. That means at *least* several months of laboratory tests for S. S. Disability to review. The anemia must be present long enough to convince S. S. Disability that it probably isn't going to improve much. If necessary, S. S. Disability may have to hold such a case for months, while the necessary tests are done. Of course, the anemia must be due to bleeding caused by the colitis, and not from some other cause.

B. Part B

1. Part B takes into account that these diseases don't just affect the large intestine. They can affect the entire body by producing arthritis, severe fever, liver damage, or iritis (inflammation of part of the eye). Note that these effects *must* be due to the colitis.

2. The above effects must be more or less continuously present, or "flare-ups" so frequent that the claimant is more or less continuously impaired. There must be enough information to convince S. S. Disability that the claimant's condition isn't likely to improve much.

C. Part C

1. Part C takes into account that either of these diseases can cause blockage of the large intestine. Scar tissue from the disease itself can cause the intestine to become "stenosed", or narrowed down so that the normal passage of feces through it is blocked. Or a large abscess full of pus might block the intestine.

2. Another way the intestine can be blocked by these diseases is the production of a "fistula". This is caused by the disease destroying part of the wall of the intestine, so that there is an abnormal opening into another part of the body.

3. If any of the above complications is cured by surgery, the claimant will *not* qualify under Part C. They must happen frequently enough to convince S. S. Disability that they are a *chronic* problem that isn't likely to improve.

D. Part D

1. Sometimes ulcerative colitis or granulomatous colitis are so severe that the entire large intestine must be surgically removed ("total colectomy").

2. If a total colectomy has been done, and any of the problems in Part A, B, or C come back then Part D is fulfilled. If such problems come back even *once*, Part D is fulfilled.

E. Part E

1. Severe disease of the large intestine can cause considerable weight loss, due to the inability to maintain proper nutrition.

2. If the weight loss is great enough, Part E can be fulfilled. *But* no actual evaluation for this is done under Listing 5.08, which deals with weight loss due to intestinal disease. The reader should refer to the discussion of Listing 5.08, for more information about the requirements of that Listing.

Listing 5.07

Regional enteritis (demonstrated by operative findings, biopsy, or endoscopy). With:

A. Persistent or recurrent intestinal obstruction evidenced by abdominal pain, distention, nausea, and vomiting and accompanied by stenotic areas of small bowel with proximal intestinal dilation; OR

B. Persistent or recurrent systemic manifestations such as arthritis, iritis, fever, or liver dysfunction, not attributable to other causes; OR

C. Intermittent obstruction due to intractable abscess or fistula formation; OR

D. Weight loss as described under Listing 5.08.

I. General Considerations

A. This Listing deals with a disease of unknown cause called "regional enteritis" (Crohn's Disease).

B. Regional enteritis is a disease which causes inflammation of the *small* intestine.

C. Certain special tests must be done to prove the diagnosis. These tests are essentially the same as those needed in Listing 5.06, except that they are done on the small intestine rather than the large intestine. For further details about these tests, the reader should refer to the discussion of Listing 5.06.

D. Part A, B, C, or D must be fulfilled, but not all four.

II. Specific Requirements

A. Part A

1. Regional enteritis can damage the small intestine enough so that it gets narrower (stenosed) and at least partially blocked (obstructed). This obstruction of the small intestine can cause the abdominal pain, distention (swelling of the abdomen), nausea, and vomiting that Part A refers to. These findings must be documented in the claimant's medical records. *One* episode is not enough; S. S. Disability must be convinced that the disease is severe enough that it probably won't get much better.

2. "Proximal intestinal dilation" means that the part of the intestine right before the blocked area will get larger, due to the increased pressure inside. This can be demonstrated by X rays, which can also show the narrowing (stenosis) which is necessary to fulfill Part A.

B. Part B

1. Regional enteritis is a disease that can affect more than just the small intestine; it can affect many parts of the body.

2. The requirements under Part B are the same as those for Part B of Listing 5.06. The reader should refer to the discussion of Part B of Listing 5.06 for more information.

C. Part C

1. Regional enteritis can cause blockage of the small intestine from abscesses (infected areas filled with pus) or a fistula.

2. The specific requirements are the same as those for Listing 5.06 C; the reader should refer to that discussion for more details.

D. Part D

1. The inflammation of the small intestine caused by regional enteritis can cause weight loss.

2. If weight loss is the problem, the actual evaluation is done under Listing 5.08, which deals with weight loss due to gastrointestinal disease.

Listing 5.08

Weight loss (due to any gastrointestinal disorder). With:

A. Weight equal to or less than the values specified in table I or II; OR

B. Weight equal to or less than the values specified in table III or IV and one of the following abnormal findings on repeated examinations:

1. Serum albumin of 3.0 gm. per deciliter (100 ml.) or less; OR

2. Hematocrit of 30 percent or less; OR

3. Serum calcium of 8.0 mg. per deciliter (100 ml.) (4.0 meq/l) or less; OR

4. Uncontrolled diabetes mellitus due to pancreatic dysfunction with repeated hyperglycemia, hypoglycemia, or ketosis; OR

5. Fat in stool of 7 gm. or greater per 24-hour specimen; OR

6. Nitrogen in stool of 3 gm. or greater per 24-hour specimen; OR

7. Persistent or recurrent ascites or edema not attributable to other causes.

[*Tables of weight reflecting malnutrition scaled according to height and sex. To be used only in connection with Listing 5.08.*]

Table I. Men

Height (Inches)[1]	Weight (Pounds)
61	90
62	92
63	94
64	97
65	99
66	102
67	106
68	109
69	112
70	115
71	118
72	122
73	125
74	128
75	131
76	134

1. Height measured without shoes.

Table II. Women

Height (Inches)[1]	Weight (Pounds)
58	77
59	79
60	82
61	84
62	86
63	89
64	91
65	94
66	98
67	101
68	104
69	107
70	110
71	114
72	117
73	120

1. Height measured without shoes.

Table III. Men

Height (Inches)[1]	Weight (Pounds)
61	95
62	98
63	100
64	103
65	106
66	109
67	112
68	116
69	119
70	122
71	126
72	129
73	133
74	136
75	139
76	143

1. Height measured without shoes.

Table IV. Women

Height (Inches)[1]	Weight (Pounds)
58	82
59	84
60	87
61	89
62	92
63	94
64	97
65	100
66	104
67	107
68	111
69	114
70	117
71	121
72	124
73	128

1. Height measured without shoes.

I. General Considerations

A. This Listing deals with claimants who have a severe impairment due to weight loss.

B. It is important to note that the weight loss *must* be due to "gastrointestinal" disease. That means disease of the mouth, esophagus, stomach, small intestine, or large intestine.

C. There *must* be proof that some type of gastrointestinal disease is present (findings at surgery, X-rays, etc.)

D. The gastrointestinal disease *must* be the cause of the weight loss. Some examples of disease which can do this are given in previous Listings. If the gastrointestinal disease it not severe enough, or was only present in the past, S. S. Disability may not be convinced that it is the cause of the weight loss.

E. Part A or Part B must be fulfilled, but not both.

II. Specific Requirements

A. Part A

1. Part A refers to Table I or Table II. Table I is for men and Table II is for women. These tables also take into account the height of the claimant, since weight is normally greater for men and people who are taller.

2. The heights given in the tables are without shoes on.

3. *One* weight is almost never enough to convince S. S. Disability that it will remain low. There have to be enough weight measurements over a long enough period of time to be convincing that they will stay that way. This depends somewhat on the individual claimant's problems, but *at least* three months of low weights would be needed to argue that the minimum 12 month duration requirement (necessary for any Listing) would be fulfilled.

4. Nothing else is required to fulfill Part A.

B. Part B

1. Part B uses tables III and IV. These don't require as much weight loss as needed to fulfill Part A, but additional special tests must be added to the evaluation.

2. The additional laboratory tests needed are given in Part B.1 through B.7, and must be abnormal over and over again—long enough to convince S. S. Disability that they are not going to get better. This means such tests must cover a period of time of *at least* three months, in order to argue that the minimum duration requirement of 12 months (necessary for any Listing) would be fulfilled. Only *one* of these tests has to be abnormal.

3. Specific tests are as follows:

(a) Part B.1 refers to a blood test showing the amount of a protein called "albumin" in the blood. It must not be higher than 3.0 on most, if not all of the tests.

(b) Part B.2 deals with anemia, or an inadequate number of red blood cells. This can be measured by a test called a "hematocrit", which must not be higher than 30% on most if not all of the tests.

(c) Part B.3 refers to an abnormally low serum calcium level. This must not go above the values given (8.0 or 4.0, depending on the way the test results are reported).

(d) Part B.4 refers to weight loss due to uncontrolled diabetes. There must be abnormally high blood sugars (*hyper*glycemia), abnormally low blood sugars (*hypo*glycemia), or "ketosis". Ketosis refers to an abnormal acidity of the blood that indicates severe uncontrolled diabetes. *How* abnormal these tests have to be is not given; that is a matter of judgment by the person in S. S. Disability reviewing the case. The problems of an individual claimant are too complicated for a general rule covering everyone to be made.

(e) Part B.5 refers to abnormally high levels of fat in the stool. This indicates poor absorption of fat by the intestine, associated with disease.

(f) Part B.6 shows that "nitrogen" is not being properly absorbed by the intestine. This means the poor absorption of protein from food, and indicates intestinal disease. The nitrogen in a sample of stool collected over a 24 hour period must be at least 3 grams or higher.

(g) Part B.7 refers to fluid in the abdomen (ascites) or swelling of the arms or legs from fluid (edema) which is caused by a gastrointestinal disease.

4. It should be emphasized that the abnormal laboratory tests in Part B.1 through B.7 *must* be due to gastrointestinal disease. A claimant could be underweight, but have an abnormal laboratory test from some different kind of disease. That would *not* qualify under Part B.

§ 2.7 Genito-Uninary System

Listing 6.02

Impairment of renal function, due to any chronic renal disease expected to last 12 months (e.g., hypertensive vascular disease, chronic nephritis, nephrolithiasis, polycystic disease, bilateral hydronephrosis, etc.). With:

A. Chronic hemdialysis or peritoneal dialysis necessitated by irreversible renal failure; OR

B. Kidney transplant. Consider under a disability for 12 months following surgery; thereafter, evaluate the residual impairment; OR

C. Persistent elevation of serum creatinine to 4 mg. per deciliter (100 ml.) or greater or reduction of creatinine clearance to 20 ml. per minute (29 liters/24 hours) or less, over at least 3 months, with one of the following:

1. Renal osteodystrophy manifested by severe bone pain and appropriate radiographic abnormalities (e.g., osteitis fibrosa, severe osteoporosis, pathologic fractures); OR

2. A clinical episode of pericarditis; OR

3. Persistent motor or sensory neuropathy; OR

4. Intractable pruritus; OR

5. Persistent fluid overload syndrome resulting in diastolic hypertension (110 mm. or above) or signs of vascular congestion; OR

6. Persistent anorexia with recent weight loss and current weight meeting the values in Listing 5.08, Table II or IV; OR

7. Persistent hematocrits of 30 percent or less.

I. General Considerations

A. This Listing deals with kidney disease (renal disease).

B. The kidneys must be *permanently* damaged. That is, the disease must be *chronic* (incurable).

C. A person can have a great deal of kidney damage from some disease, before it really begins to cause problems. This Listing deals only with claimants who have very advanced kidney disease.

D. It does not matter what disease caused the kidney failure. There are many diseases that can damage the kidneys. The Listing gives a few examples, but other causes can also qualify.

E. Some of the common causes of kidney disease are given as follows:

1. "Hypertensive vascular disease". High blood pressure can damage the tiny blood vessels in the kidneys.

2. "Chronic nephritis" is not a specific disease; it refers to several different diseases, the causes of which are unknown or only partially understood.

3. "Nephrolithiasis" means "kidney stones" within the kidney itself. These can cause severe damage. They are formed when certain chemicals are deposited out of the blood stream into the kidney.

4. "Polycystic disease" is inherited and involves parts of the kidney being replaced with cysts or cavities.

5. "Hydronephrosis" refers to damage to the kidneys by urine that they form not being excreted. For example, there are tubes called "ureters" coming from each kidney. The ureters drain the urine formed by the kidney as it filters the blood. The ureters normally carry urine down to the bladder, where it is stored until eliminated from the body. If a ureter gets blocked (such as by a kidney stone getting stuck in it), the drainage of urine to the bladder is stopped. That makes the urine "back-up" into the kidney.

F. Part A, B, C, or D must be fulfilled, but not all three.

II. Specific Requirements

A. Part A

1. When the kidneys fail to function, they can no longer filter "waste" products from the blood. "Dialysis" is a method by which machines artificially filter the blood, and is necessary to maintain life if the kidneys have been completely destroyed by disease.

2. There are two types of dialysis. One is *hemo*dialysis, in which the blood is filtered directly. By surgery, special connections are made to some blood vessels in the person's arm. The blood is then filtered through a machine and circulated back to the body. In *peritoneal* dialysis, special fluids are put into the abdominal cavity. There is a smooth membrane which lines everyone's abdominal cavity, called the peritoneum. Waste materials from the blood will cross the peritoneum and be picked up by the fluids that have been put into the abdomen. Then the fluids are taken back out and discarded.

3. If the kidney failure is total and cannot be reversed by treatment ("irreversible"), then dialysis will be necessary for the

rest of the claimant's life (unless a kidney transplant is done). The procedure is usually required several times a week.

4. Some people have *temporary* kidney failure, for which they must have dialysis. When their kidneys recover, dialysis is no longer necessary. Such a claimant *cannot* qualify under Part A; the kidney failure must be *permanent.*

B. Part B

1. Part B is only for claimants who have a kidney transplant.

2. Since it takes a long time to tell if the transplant will work, S. S. Disability will grant benefits for one full year from the time of the surgery.

3. After a year has passed, the claimant's case will be re-evaluated, to determine if the transplanted kidney is working normally. If it is, the claimant's disability benefits will be stopped. In fact, after a year, the claimant will have to qualify under Part A or Part C to remain on disability. A second transplanted kidney would result in another year of benefits under Part B, starting from the date of the transplant.

C. Part C

1. "Serum creatinine" refers to the level of a chemical called creatinine that is normally present in the bloodstream. It is normally filtered out by the kidneys, so if there is severe kidney disease the amount of creatinine in the blood will increase. This laboratory test gives doctors an idea of how severe kidney disease is. Normal values don't go higher than about 1.5. Part C requires that the value be at least 4.0 or higher. This must be true on repeated blood tests for *at least* 3 months.

2. Another blood test for the severity of kidney disease is called a "creatinine clearance". A creatinine clearance is the amount of blood that is cleansed of creatinine in one minute's time. The worse the kidney disease, the *lower* the creatinine clearance will be, since less blood will be cleansed of creatinine in one minute. Normal values are about 85–100 ml. of blood cleansed in one minute. To qualify under Part C, this value must not be higher than 20 ml./minute over *at least* a period of 3 months. To do the test, both blood and urine samples must be taken. *Either* the serum creatinine or the creatinine clearance can be used to qualify under Part C. They are just different tests for showing severe kidney disease.

3. The serum creatinine and creatinine clearance tests discussed above indicate very severe kidney disease, if they are as low as Part C requires. *But* S. S. requires other information

that shows that the kidney failure has actually caused damage to other parts of the body. These additional requirements are given in Part C.1 through C.7. Only one of these needs to be fulfilled, as follows:

(a) Part C.1 requires what is called "renal osteodystrophy". This means bone disease caused by kidney failure. First, there must be symptoms of *severe* bone pain in the claimant's medical records. In addition, there must be abnormal X-rays of bones showing what would be expected if kidney failure were damaging them. In simple terms, "osteitis fibrosa" is a fibrous degeneration of bone with cysts (cavities). "Osteoporosis" is a thinning of bone, making it weaker. "Pathologic fractures" are broken bones caused by some disease which has weakened them.

(b) Part C.2 requires at least one episode of what is called "pericarditis". Pericarditis means inflammation of the pericardium, which is a thin membrane surrounding the heart like a sack. A "clinical episode" means that the claimant has had symptoms which are likely due to pericarditis.

(c) Part C.3 refers to "persistent motor or sensory neuropathy". Nerves which allow a person to move his muscles (motor nerves) and nerves which allow a person to "feel" (sensory nerves) can be damaged by severe kidney disease. The reason for this is not completely known. If motor or sensory neuropathy is present, the claimant can qualify under Part C.3. However it must be *persistent.*

(d) Part C.4 requires "intractable pruritis". This is a severe itching sensation that some people with advanced kidney disease have. If it is present, Part C.4 is fulfilled. The problem must be chronic.

(e) Severely diseased kidneys can no longer filter out extra water from the body efficiently. Increased fluid in the blood stream can then cause the blood pressure to go up. If what is called the *diastolic* blood pressure is 110 or higher, then Part C.5 can be fulfilled. (See the short discussion of "systolic" and "diastolic" blood pressure discussed under Listing 4.03, for a better understanding of these terms). It should be emphasized that the high diastolic blood pressure of 110 *must* be due to fluid overload from kidney disease. High blood pressure for some other reason would *not* qualify. Another way to fulfill Part C.5 is by "signs of vascular congestion". This means signs of abnormal fluid accumulation on physical examination by a doctor, such as swelling of the feet, arms, or face or other findings that excess fluid is present in the body.

(f) Part C.6 refers to "anorexia", or loss of appetite. This can be an effect of severe kidney disease, and cause loss of weight. If so, the claimant's weight must qualify under Table III or IV given with Listing 5.08 (Table III is for men and Table IV for women.) Note that the other requirements of Listing 5.08 do *not* have to be fulfilled.

(g) Part C.7 requires that there be anemia caused by the kidney disease. Anemia is a decrease in the amount of red blood cells in the bloodstream. Normal kidneys release a special "hormone" which helps keep the number of red blood cells normal. Severely diseased kidneys no longer do this and the claimant may develop anemia. One way to measure the amount of anemia is by way of a test called a "hematocrit". This is the percentage of red cells in a volume of blood. The hematocrit must not be higher than 30% to qualify under Part C.7. One low hematocrit would certainly not be enough. There must be readings over a long enough period of time to convince S. S. Disability that the anemia is not going to get better. The hematocrit would have to be abnormal over a period of *at least* several months. It must also be clear that the anemia is caused by the kidney disease, and not some other disorder.

Listing 6.06

Nephrotic syndrome, with severe anasarca, persistent for at least 3 months despite prescribed therapy. With:

A. Serum albumin of 3.0 gm. per deciliter (100 ml.) or less and proteinuria of 3.5 gm. per 24 hours or greater; OR

B. Proteinuria of 10.0 gm. per 24 hours or greater.

I. General Considerations

A. This Listing deals with what is called the "nephrotic syndrome". The nephrotic syndrome may or may not be present with the findings discussed above for Listing 6.02, and is also an indication of severe kidney disease.

B. The nephrotic syndrome develops when the damaged kidneys let too much protein in the bloodstream "spill" through them. This causes an abnormal loss of protein from the body, which in turn can cause swelling in the feet, hands, or face.

("Edema" is the medical term for such swelling.) If enough protein in lost, the entire body can show this swelling, and is called *anasarca*. It is this total body swelling (anasarca) that the Listing requires. Even this isn't enough. The anasarca must be very severe, and be present at least 3 months, even with medical treatment. Part A and Part B of the Listing require laboratory tests to show that the anasarca is caused by severe kidney disease and resultant protein loss from the body.

C. Part A or Part B must be fulfilled, but not both.

II. Specific Requirements

A. Part A

1. The protein that is lost through diseased kidneys in the greatest amount is one called *albumin*. If the amount of albumin in the bloodstream is abnormally low, that would support the fact that it is being lost through the damaged kidneys. It must not be higher than 3.0.

2. The albumin that is being lost through the kidneys should also show up in the urine. So Part A also requires that the abnormally high value of at least 3.5 grams of protein be found in a urine sample collected over a 24 hour period. This proves that the low amount of protein found in the bloodstream are actually being lost through damaged kidneys.

B. Part B

1. Part B only requires that abnormally large amounts of protein be found in a sample of urine collected over a 24 hour period. Unlike Part A, it is not necessary to know the amount of protein in the bloodstream. The reason for that is that Part B requires so much protein to show up in the urine sample that kidney disease must be the cause of the anasarca.

2. At least 10 grams of protein must be measured in the claimant's sample of urine collected over a 24 hour period. This is a very large amount of protein to lose in 24 hours.

§ 2.8 Hemic and Lymphatic System

Listing 7.02

Chronic anemia (hematocrit persisting at 30 percent or less due to any cause).

A. Evaluate the resulting impairment under criteria for the affected body system; OR

B. Requiring one or more blood transfusions on an average of at least once every 2 months.

I. General Considerations

A. This Listing deals with *anemia*. Anemia is a decrease in the number of red blood cells in the bloodstream. One laboratory test indicating the severity of anemia is called a *hematocrit*. It involves taking a small sample of blood from a vein, and is one of the most frequent tests performed by doctors. The hematocrit is simply the percentage of red cells in a volume of blood. For example, if 50% of the volume of a sample of blood is made up of red cells, then the hematocrit is 50%.

B. A normal hematocrit is different for men and women. For a man, a normal hematocrit is about 42–48%. For a woman, the value is about 38–44%. These are only general ranges. But the Listing doesn't take the sex of the claimant into account, or other things which can influence the hematocrit—such as the altitude at which the claimant lives. The Listing simply requires that the hematocrit not be higher than 30%.

C. The Listing deals with *chronic* anemia that supposedly isn't going to get better. In order to convince S. S. Disability of this, the low hematocrits must cover a period of *at least* 3 months, in order to indicate that the minimum 12 month duration requirement (necessary for all Listings) is likely to be fulfilled.

D. There are many medical diseases that cause anemia. The most common is a deficiency of iron in the diet, but this is easily treated by taking pills with iron in them.

E. There should be medical records with tests showing S. S. Disability what kind of anemia the claimant has.

F. Part A or Part B must be fulfilled, but not both.

II. Specific Requirements

A. Part A

1 Anemia itself doesn't necessarily mean that a claimant is severely impaired. That depends on the type of anemia, and what it does to the claimant. For example, a person with lung disease may have trouble getting enough oxygen into his bloodstream. Oxygen is carried by red blood cells, and anemia means there are an abnormally low number of red blood cells. So if that person has anemia along with his lung disease, his condition will be even more severe. There are also many other ways that anemia can harm a claimant, but it is not the anemia itself that

S. S. Disability looks at—it is the harm that the anemia has caused, if any.

2. If the anemia has had some severe effect on a claimant, then the actual evaluation is done under whatever Listing that deals with the disorder the anemia is causing. So no actual evaluation is done under Part A. For example, if a claimant with heart disease also had anemia that was making his heart disease even worse, evaluation would actually be done under one of the Listings dealing with heart disease, and the requirements of that Listing would have to be fulfilled.

B. Part B

1. Some claimants *are* so sick from anemia itself, that they are severely impaired. Such people can be very weak and fatigue easily, if the anemia is bad enough.

2. Part B deals with anemia so severe that blood transfusions are required. These transfusions must not raise the hematocrit above 30% (at least not very long), or the claimant will not qualify under Part B.

3. The transfusions must be necessary on an average of at least once every 2 months.

Listing 7.05

Sickle cell disease, or one of its variants. With:

A. Documented painful (thrombotic) crises occurring at least three times during the 5 months prior to adjudication; OR

B. Requiring extended hospitalization (beyond emergency care) at least three times during the 12 months prior to adjudication; OR

C. Evaluate the resulting impairment under the criteria for the affected body system.

I. General Considerations

A. This Listing is specifically designed for those claimants who have sickle cell anemia. This is a hereditary disorder occurring most frequently in black people. In sickle cell anemia, the red blood cells are abnormal and do not last as long as normal red blood cells. This can result in a decreased number of red cells, with the result being *anemia*. It is called *sickle* cell anemia, because the abnormal red cells may have a sickle shape.

B. There is a type of anemia called sickle cell *trait;* this is not as severe as sickle cell anemia in most cases. True sickle cell anemia must be proven to exist by special tests of the blood that S. S. Disability will accept. These tests have usually already been done by the claimant's treating doctor, since they are a standard part of the diagnosis. There are blood diseases similar to sickle cell anemia and are the "variants" mentioned by the Listing. These are also acceptable, but most cases by far have pure sickle cell anemia.

C. Part A, B, or C must be fulfilled, but not all three.

II. Specific Requirements

A. Part A

1. Because the red cells in sickle cell anemia are not normal and have a sickle shape, they don't move through the bloodstream as easily as normal red blood cells. In fact, they sometimes tend to "clog up" blood vessels. This can happen anywhere in the body, and can cause a great deal of pain. Such episodes are the "painful (thrombotic) crises" that Part A refers to. The amount of damage done by blockage of such a blood vessel depends on how large the vessel is and where in the body it is located.

2. If the claimant has one of these painful crises at least 3 times in the 5 month period before he applies for disability, then Part A is fulfilled.

3. The word "documented" means that the treating doctor must provide medical records showing that the episodes happened. These episodes do not necessarily mean that the claimant had to be hospitalized.

B. Part B

1. Part B is a different way a claimant with sickle cell anemia can qualify under the Listing. Part B *requires* that the claimant had to be hospitalized for treatment.

2. Being treated only in a hospital emergency room does *not* qualify as the "extended hospitalization" mentioned in Part B.

3. Such hospitalization must have happened at least 3 times in the year before the claimant applies for disability, and the medical records must be available for S. S. Disability to review.

4. If a claimant has to go into the hospital for some other disease, this would *not* qualify.

5. The hospital data must show that the sickle cell crisis caused major damage to some part of the body—for example, the heart, brain, bones, lungs, or kidneys.

C. Part C

1. Part C takes into account that a claimant with sickle cell anemia may have had episodes that caused severe damage to the body which can't be cured. If the claimant has such permanent damage, then *when* that damage occurred is not important since it cannot be reversed.

2. If the claimant has some kind of permanent damage from sickle cell anemia, it is not actually evaluated under Part C. The evaluation would be done under whatever Listing that deals with that kind of damage. For example, if the claimant had damage to the brain, his case would be evaluated under a Listing that deals with such brain disorders, and would have to fulfill the requirements of that Listing.

Listing 7.06

Chronic thrombocytopenia (due to any cause), with platelet counts repeatedly below 40,000/cubic millimeter. With:

A. At least one spontaneous hemorrhage, requiring transfusion, within 5 months prior to adjudication; OR

B. Intracranial bleeding within 12 months prior to adjudication.

I. General Considerations

A. This Listing deals with "thrombocytopenia". This means that there are a decreased number of thrombocytes in the bloodstream. Thrombocytes are also called "platelets", and they play an important role in preventing abnormal bleeding.

B. The normal platelet "count" in a sample of blood is somewhere between 150,000 to 300,000 in a cubic millimeter (a small drop) of blood. The Listing requires that this count be *less* than 40,000 on *repeated* tests, over a period of at least 3 months.

C. There are many causes of thrombocytopenia, but the Listing is not so much interested in the cause as what harm it does to the claimant.

D. Part A or Part B must be fulfilled, but not both.

II. Specific Requirements

A. Part A

1. Part A requires a "spontaneous hemorrhage". Claimants who have thrombocytopenia with platelet counts below 40,000 are in constant danger of bleeding internally into some part of their body. They could also bleed externally—for example, from the nose or intestine. But the bleeding must be *spontaneous*. That is, it must not be caused by some kind of trauma or accident to the body which would cause bleeding in anyone.

2. If the bleeding is so severe that a transfusion must be given at least 3 times in the 5 months before the claimant applies for disability, then Part A is fulfilled.

B. Part B

1. "Intracranial bleeding" means bleeding inside the head, and would probably be inside the brain itself. Either way, it is a very serious thing and would have the same effect as a "stroke".

2. If this happens even once in the year before the claimant applies for disability, then Part B is fulfilled.

3. It should be noted that if the claimant bled very seriously into his brain longer than a year before application for disability, he might still qualify under one of the Listings dealing with disorders of the brain (mental or physical), if there has been no improvement. (See Listings 11.04 or 12.02)

Listing 7.07

Hereditary telangiectasia. With hemorrhage requiring transfusion at least three times during the 5 months prior to adjudication.

I. General Considerations

A. This Listing deals with a hereditary disorder called "hereditary telangiectasia". Abnormal "clumps" of blood vessels may grow in any part of the body.

B. This Listing is only concerned with the severe bleeding that can occur from the abnormal blood vessels.

II. Specific Requirements

A. The bleeding must be so severe that blood transfusions are necessary.

B. S. S. Disability must be able to obtain medical records showing that the telangiectasia caused bleeding requiring transfusion at least 3 times during the 5 months period before the application for disability.

Listing 7.08

Coagulation defects (hemophilia or a similar disorder). With spontaneous hemorrhage requiring transfusion at least three times during the 5 months prior to adjudication.

I. General Considerations

A. This Listing deals with "coagulation defects" of blood. Put into simple terms, this means diseases that cause trouble with the "clotting" of blood. The formation of blood clots is extremely important in the body's ability to stop abnormal bleeding.

B. An example given is hemophilia, which is an inherited disease. Actually, there are many types of hemophilia of all degrees of severity.

II. Specific Requirements

A. Note that a "spontaneous hemorrhage" is required. This means that the abnormal bleeding must not be caused by some type of accident or trauma that would cause even a normal person to bleed. The bleeding must be caused by the hemophilia itself.

B. The abnormal bleeding episodes must occur at least 3 times in the 5 months before the claimant applies for disability. S. S. Disability must be able to obtain the medical records proving this, and the bleeding must have been severe enough to have required transfusions of blood.

Listing 7.09

Polycythemia vera (with erythrocytosis, splenomegaly, and leukocytosis or thrombocytosis). Evaluate the resulting impairment under the criteria for the affected body system.

I. General Considerations

A. This Listing deals with a disease called "polycythemia vera". Other Listings have dealt with anemia, in which there are not enough red blood cells in the bloodstream. Polycythemia means that there are *too many* red cells.

B. Polycythemia can damage the body, because the greatly increased number of red blood cells can "clog up" or block important arteries anywhere in the body. One might say the blood gets "too thick".

II. Specific Requirements

A. It should be noted that the Listing says polycythemia *vera.* This is a special kind of polycythemia, and the worst that a claimant could have. Other kinds of polycythemia do *not* qualify. For example, a claimant with lung disease might have increased numbers of red blood cells (secondary polycythemia), because the body is trying to put out more red blood cells to carry oxygen. But this is not nearly as serious a disease as polycythemia *vera* and does not qualify.

B. If the claimant has polycythemia vera, then there should be other abnormalities of the blood. Proof of these abnormalities is required by the Listing as follows:

1. "Erythrocytosis" simply means the increased number of red blood cells expected with polycythemia.

2. "Splenomegaly" means an enlarged spleen.

3. "Leucocytosis" means an increased number of white blood cells.

4. "Thrombocytosis" means an increase in the number of thrombocytes (platelets) in the blood.

C. No actual evaluation is done under this Listing in terms of the final decision by S. S. Disability. Depending on what type of damage the polycythemia has done to the claimant, the case would be evaluated under whatever Listing that deals with the problem involved. For example, if the polycythemia caused blockage to one of the arteries of the brain, the case would be considered under a Listing dealing with brain damage and would have to fulfill the requirements of that Listing.

Listing 7.10

Myelofibrosis (myeloproliferative syndrome). With:

A. *Chronic anemia.* Evaluated according to the criteria of Listing 7.02; OR

B. Documented recurrent systemic bacterial infections occurring at least 3 times during the 5 months prior to adjudication; OR

C. Intractable bone pain with radiologic evidence of osteosclerosis.

I. General Considerations

A. This Listing deals with "myelofibrosis", which is a very serious disease affecting the blood-forming organs, especially the marrow of bones where most blood cells are produced.

B. The marrow inside of bones must continuously produce new blood cells to make up for the ones that are too old and disappearing. The bone marrow makes most of the types of cells that appear in the bloodstream (red blood cells, white blood cells etc.). The cause of myelofibrosis is not exactly known, but it causes replacement of the bone marrow with fibrous tissue that can't make the needed blood cells.

C. Part A, B or C must be fulfilled, but not all three.

D. S. S. Disability must have reasonable evidence that the claimant suffers from myelofibrosis. That usually requires that a piece of bone and bone marrow be removed for analysis. S. S. Disability does not order this test. If the treating doctor diagnoses myelofibrosis, he should already have done this test, and S. S. Disability must be able to obtain the results.

II. Specific Requirements

A. Part A

1. "Anemia" is simply a decreased number of red blood cells in the bloodstream. As discussed above, myelofibrosis produces anemia by damaging the bone marrow, so that less red cells are produced.

2. No actual evaluation is done under Part A. If a claimant with myelofibrosis is anemic, evaluation is done according to the requirements of Listing 7.02 which deals with all types of anemia.

B. Part B

1. Part B takes into account that when myelofibrosis damages the bone marrow, less white cells than normal will be produced. White blood cells play a very important part in the body's ability to resist infection, so if there are too few of them, the claimant will have more infections than a normal person. In

fact, serious infection is a major cause of death in people with myelofibrosis.

2. The infections must be due to bacteria, not viruses.

3. The infections must be *systemic.* This means they have to be serious enough to affect the whole body. An infection affecting a small part of the body would not qualify (such as an infected cut on the arm).

4. The infections must be *documented.* That means S. S. Disability must be able to obtain the medical records concerned.

5. At least 3 such bacterial infections must have occurred in the 5 months period before the claimant applies for disability.

C. Part C

1. Part C can be fulfilled if the claimant has *intractable* bone pain. This means severe bone pain that is continuously present.

2. There must be X-ray showing the kind of bone damage that would be expected if the myelofibrosis were causing bone pain (findings on X-ray of "osteosclerosis" which means abnormal "hardening" or "denseness" of bone).

Listing 7.11

Acute leukemia. Consider under a disability for 2½ years from the time of initial diagnosis.

I. General Considerations

A. This Listing deals with leukemia, which is a form of cancer affecting white blood cells. The type of leukemia depends on what type of white blood cells is involved.

B. The leukemia must be of the *acute* form. That means it is a more serious form of leukemia, because the abnormal white blood cells are more malignant (cancerous) than some other form of leukemia called *chronic* leukemia. Claimants with acute leukemia are more difficult to treat and do not live as long as those with chronic leukemia. Whether a leukemia is classified as "acute" or "chronic" depends on how malignant the cells look under a microscope.

II. Specific Requirements

A. Because *acute* leukemia is so serious, S. S. Disability does not require any evidence except proving the claimant has the disease. S. S. Disability must be able to obtain the claimant's medical records proving this. It is not sufficient for the treating doctor to simply tell S. S. Disability that the claimant has acute leukemia.

B. If *acute* leukemia is proven, the claimant automatically fulfills the Listing for a period of 2½ years. S. S. Disability will then evaluate the case again, to see if the claimant has improved. 2½ years is automatically given, because of the serious nature of the disease. The diagnosis alone is evidence of severe disability.

Listing 7.12

Chronic leukemia. Evaluate according to the criteria of Listing 7.02, 7.06, 7.10B, or 13.06A.

I. General Considerations

A. Like Listing 7.11, this Listing also deals with leukemia, but this Listing considers leukemias of the *chronic* form.

B. As noted above, *chronic* leukemias, while they are extremely serious disease, do not tend to be quite as severe as the acute form of leukemias considered under Listing 7.11. For that reason, the claimant is *not* automatically allowed under this Listing simply because he has the disease. Some people with chronic leukemia live for years with treatment.

II. Specific Requirements

A. S. S. Disability must have medical records proving that the claimant has chronic leukemia of some kind.

B. Other than requiring that the claimant proves he has leukemia, no actual evaluation is done under this Listing. Actual evaluation would be done under Listings 7.02, 7.06, 7.10B, or 10.06A. These Listings deal with the major serious effects of having chronic leukemia, and for more information, references should be made to the discussions of those Listings. However, if the claimant should have some other kind of problems due to the leukemia, the case could also be evaluated under whatever Listing that would most accurately deal with the problem. For example, if the leukemia caused a "stroke", it could be evaluated under Listing 11.04.

C. Sometimes a chronic form of leukemia begins to transform itself into something that looks like an acute leukemia. This is a very serious turn of events, and is called a "blast crisis" or "blastic transformation." If that happens in a case of chronic leukemia, allowance should be made by use of an Equal code to Listing 7.11 for acute leukemia.

Listing 7.13

Lymphomas. Evaluate under the criteria in Listing 13.06A.

I. General Considerations

A. This Listing only deals with a type of cancer called "lymphoma".

B. There are many types of lymphoma, which is a form of cancer affecting lymph nodes.

II. Specific Requirements

A. S. S. Disability must be able to obtain medical records showing that the claimant has some kind of lymphoma. Usually, the diagnosis is made by taking a small piece of tissue from a lymph node and looking at the cells under a microscope.

B. Other than proving the claimant has lymphoma, no actual evaluation is done under this Listing. The case would really be considered under Listing 13.06A, and would have to fulfill the requirements of that Listing.

Listing 7.14

Macroglobulinemia or heavy chain disease, confirmed by serum or urine protein electrophoresis or immunoelectrophoresis. Evaluate impairment under criteria for affected body system or under Listings 7.02, 7.06, or 7.08.

I. General Considerations

A. This Listing deals with a special disorder of blood called "macroglobulinemia" or "heavy chain disease".

B. Macroglobulinemia is a disorder of the "immune" system of the body. Part of the immune system deals with the production of antibodies to defend against disease. For example, without antibodies, the body cannot protect itself against bacteria that produce infections. Without enough of the right kind of antibodies, a person may become the victim of serious infections. In macroglobulinemia, abnormal antibodies are produced.

II. Specific Requirements

A. Special tests are required to prove that the claimant has macroglobulinemia. The tests needed are "protein electrophoresis" or "immunoelectrophoresis", which allow the abnormal antibodies to be detected. S. S. Disability must be able to obtain the results of these tests from the claimant's medical records. The tests are acceptable, if done on samples of either blood or urine.

B. Other than proving the diagnosis, no actual evaluation is done under this Listing. It is not the macroglobulinemia itself that S. S. Disability is looking for; it is the other severe problems that can be associated with the disease. So actual evaluation is done under Listing 7.02, 7.06, or 7.08 and the requirements of one of those Listings must be fulfilled. For further information, reference should be made to the discussion of those Listings.

Listing 7.15

Chronic granulocytopenia (due to any cause). With both A and B:

A. Absolute neutrophil counts repeatedly below 1,000 cells/cubic millimeter; AND

B. Documented recurrent systemic bacterial infections occurring at least 3 times during the 5 months prior to adjudication.

I. General Considerations

A. This Listing deals with "granulocytopenia", which means an abnormal decrease in the number of white blood cells. It can be caused by several different diseases, but often the cause is unknown. Granulocytopenia can also be a side effect of certain kinds of drugs.

B. It is not the granulocytopenia itself that is impairing, but white blood cells are necessary to help the body fight infection, and repeated serious infections can be very severely impairing.

C. Part A *and* Part B must be fulfilled.

II. Specific Requirements

A. Part A

1. Part A allows S. S. Disability to determine that the claimant has granulocytopenia, by measuring the number of

white cells called "neutrophils" in the bloodstream. This only involves a simple blood test.

2. A normal neutrophil "count" is about 5,000 10,000 per cubic millimeter of blood (a small drop). Part A requires that the count be *lower* than 1,000. At this low level, the claimant is at great risk of developing severe infections.

3. It would probably require at least 3 months of blood tests showing a neutrophil count this low to convince S. S. Disability that the disease is chronic and not likely to improve.

B. Part B

1. Part A establishes that the claimant does have granulocytopenia, but that in itself is not harmful; as noted above, it is the resultant infections that do the harm. Part B requires that such infections be proven.

2. The infections must be *systemic*. In other words, the infections must be severe enough to affect the whole body—such as pneumonia. Local infections, such as an infected cut on the skin, would not qualify.

3. The infections must be bacterial infections (not viral).

4. S. S. Disability must be able to obtain medical records showing at least 3 such infections in the 5 month period before the claimant applies for disability.

Listing 7.16

Myeloma (confirmed by appropriate serum or urine protein electrophoresis and bone marrow findings). With:

A. Radiologic evidence of bony involvement with intractable bone pain or pathological fracture; OR

B. Evidence of renal impairment as described in Listing 6.02; OR

C. Hypercalcemia with serum calcium levels persistently greater than 11 mg. per deciliter (100 ml.) for at least one month despite prescribed therapy; OR

D. Plasma cells (100 or more cells/cubic millimeter) in the peripheral blood.

I. General Considerations

A. This Listing deals with a form of cancer called "multiple myeloma".

B. Multiple myeloma involves malignant plasma cells. These cells normally play an important role in the immune system of the body through antibodies which are necessary for fighting disease.

C. To fulfill the Listing, the diagnosis of multiple myeloma must first be proven. This requires special tests on the claimant's blood or urine called "protein electrophoresis". The treating doctor will have done this test, in most instances. In addition, a sample of bone marrow (where plasma cells are made) must show the presence of the disease, and the results available to S. S. Disability.

D. Part A, B, C, or D must be fulfilled, but not all four.

II. Specific Requirements

A. Part A

1. Multiple myeloma can damage bones. If this is true, S. S. Disability requires X-ray reports showing the damage.

2. If the X-rays show that the bones are being damaged by the myeloma, it is then also required that there be either "intractable bone pain" (severe, persistent bone pain), or "pathological fractures" of bone. A pathological fracture is one in which bone breaks, because of the disease affecting it. A broken bone caused by an accident would *not* qualify, even in a claimant with multiple myeloma.

B. Part B

1. Multiple myeloma can damage the kidneys, and Part B takes this possibility into account.

2. No actual evaluation is done under Part B. If the myeloma has caused kidney damage, the case would be evaluated under Listing 6.02, which deals with kidney disease, and the requirements of that Listing would have to be fulfilled.

C. Part C

1. Myeloma may increase the level of calcium in the blood, and this is called "hypercalcemia". Too much calcium in the bloodstream can be very damaging to the kidneys, eyes, heart and other organs.

2. The calcium levels must be *higher* than 11 to satisfy Part C. One blood test is not enough to do this. At least a month of repeated laboratory tests must show values this high.

3 The abnormally high calcium in the blood must be present, even if the claimant is under treatment for the myeloma. If the claimant is *not* under treatment, he *cannot* qualify under Part C.

D. Part D

1. If a great number of the cancerous plasma cells have made their way from the bone marrow to the bloodstream ("peripheral blood"), then the myeloma is not being well controlled and severe impairment is likely.

2. If a blood count of plasma cells is at least 100, then Part D is fulfilled. Since this indicates that the disease is out of control, nothing else is required.

§ 2.9 Skin

Listing 8.02

Exfoliative dermatitis, ichthyosis, ichthyosiform erythroderma. With extensive lesions not responding to prescribed treatment.

I. General Considerations

A. This Listing deals with three skin diseases called "exfoliative dermatitis", "ichthyosis", and "ichthyosiform erythroderma".

B. These are damaging, inflammatory diseases of the skin often of unknown cause. They are different diseases, which are put together under this Listing, because of the similar effects they can produce.

C. Such diseases are usually diagnosed and treated by a skin specialist (dermatologist). S. S. Disability must be able to obtain detailed data from the treating doctor.

II. Specific Requirements

A. *Extensive* skin lesions are required. "Lesions" are the abnormal areas of skin caused by the disease, and must affect enough area of skin to be impairing. The most important areas of skin to be involved are the hands and feet, because the claimant must be able to use these to do any meaningful work. The groin and armpit areas are also important.

B. The claimant must be under medical treatment for the skin lesions. This is the only way S. S. Disability can know that it is unlikely to improve.

Listing 8.03

Pemphigus, erythema multiforme bullosum, bullous pemphigoid, dermatitis herpetiformis. With extensive lesions not responding to prescribed treatment.

I. General Considerations

A. This Listing deals with four skin diseases called "pemphigus, erythema multiforme bullosum, bullous pemphigoid and dermatitis herpetiformis". These are diseases tending to cause severe "blistering of the skin", and are often of unknown origin.

B. Other "General Considerations" are the same as for Listing 8.02.

II. Specific Requirements

These are exactly the same as discussed for Listing 8.02.

Listing 8.04

Deep mycotic infections. With extensive fungating, ulcerating lesions not responding to prescribed treatment.

I. General Considerations

A. This Listing deals with "deep mycotic infection". The word "mycotic" refers to infections by a fungus. Mild fungal infections of the skin are common, and do qualify. This Listing only applies to very serious fungal infections that go deeply into the skin and tissues beneath.

B. Other "General Considerations" are the same as given in Listing 8.02.

II. Specific Requirements

These are the same as those discussed for Listing 8.02.

Listing 8.05

Psoriasis, atopic dermatitis, dyshidrosis. With extensive lesions, including involvement of the hands or feet which impose a severe limitation of function and which are not responding to prescribed treatment.

I. General Considerations

A. This Listing deals with "psoriasis", "atopic dermatitis", and "dyshidrosis".

B. Psoriasis is a disease of unknown cause that produces scaly, inflamed, reddened lesions of the skin. (It can also produce a serious form of arthritis, but that would be evaluated under a Listing concerning arthritis.) Many people have psoriasis, but for this Listing the psoriasis must involve the hands or feet to a severe degree—enough to make it difficult for the claimant to stand or walk very long, or to use his hands very well.

C. Atopic dermatitis is an allergic skin disease. There must be severe involvement of the hands or feet.

D. Dyshidrosis is a defect in the ability of the skin to form sweat normally. The hands or feet must be severely affected.

II. Specific Requirements

A. As noted above, the hands or feet must be so severely involved that it is difficult for the claimant to use them.

B. The claimant *must* be under treatment, and still have the degree of severity required by the Listing.

Listing 8.06

Hydradenitis suppurative, acne conglobata. With extensive lesions involving the axillae or perineum not responding to prescribed medical treatment and not amenable to surgical treatment.

I. General Considerations

A. This Listing deals with "hydradenitis suppurative" and "acne conglobata".

B. Both of the above diseases involve bacterial infection of skin.

C. Acne conglobata is an uncommon and severe form of acne. Hydradenitis suppurative is a severe, chronic, and painful infection of sweat glands.

II. Specific Requirements

A. The lesions must involve a large area of the axillae (armpits) or perineum (area around the genitalia).

B. The claimant must be under treatment by a doctor, and the disease must be incurable either by medical treatment such as drugs *and* be incurable by surgery.

§ 2.10 Endocrine System

Listing 9.02

Thyroid disorders. With:

A. Progressive exophthalmos as measured by exophthalmometry; OR

B. Evaluate the resulting impairment under the criteria for the affected body system.

I. General Considerations

A. This Listing deals with disorders of the thyroid gland.

B. Disease of the thyroid gland (which produces thyroid hormone) is quite common and can usually be completely controlled with treatment. This Listing is interested in the severe cases that can't be treated effectively.

C. S. S. Disability must be able to obtain medical records from the treating doctor or hospital showing the claimant has thyroid disease.

D. Part A or Part B must be fulfilled, but not both.

II. Specific Requirements

A. Part A

1. Part A deals with "exophthalmos". Exophthalmos is a bulging outward of the eyes, caused by fibrous and fatty tissue building up behind the eyeballs. No-one really knows why, but this tends to occur in some cases of severe *hyper*thyroidism, in which the thyroid gland produces too much thyroid hormone.

2. S. S. Disability doesn't consider a claimant disabled just because his eyes abnormally protrude. The claimant would be considered disabled, because severe exophthalmos might indicate that the thyroid disease is not being well controlled with treatment. It is important to note that the Listing says *progressive* exophthalmos. It is not enough that the claimant simply have exophthalmos; it must be getting worse, even under treatment.

4. The amount of bulging of the eyes is measured by "exophthalmometry". It is insufficient for the claimant's doctor to say that the exophthalmos is continuing to get worse. S. S. Disability must have the medical records showing exophthalmometry measurements proving that this is true. Usually, only medical specialists in treating hormonal diseases have the instrument necessary to make such measurements.

B. Part B

1. *Hyper*thyroidism involves the thyroid gland producing too much thyroid hormone. *Hypo*thyroidism involves its producing too little of that hormone. In either case, the diseases can cause severe abnormalities in most organs of the body, although different for the two diseases.

2. Because there are so many possible abnormal effects that can be produced by either hyperthyroidism or hypothyroidism, it is not practical to list them here. They can also be of all degrees of severity. Therefore, no actual evaluation is done under Part B. Cases involving severe complications from either disease would be evaluated under whatever Listing that deals with the specific type of problem being produced. For example, a claimant with hyperthyroidism affecting his heart would have his case evaluated under a Listing dealing with that kind of heart disease.

Listing 9.03

Hyperparathyroidism. With:

A. Generalized decalcification of bone on X-ray study and elevation of plasma calcium to 11 mg. per deciliter (100 ml.) or greater; OR

B. Evaluate the resulting impairment according to the Listing under the affected body system.

I. General Considerations

A. There is a set of hormone-producing glands very close to or even within the thyroid gland, but are entirely different from the thyroid gland. These are the *parathyroid* glands with which this Listing is concerned, and in most people there are four of them.

B. The parathyroid glands produce a hormone called *parathormone,* or parathyroid hormone.

C. Parathormone plays a very important role in the way the body uses calcium.

D. This Listing deals only with *hyper*parathyroidism, in which too much parathormone is produced.

E. Part A or Part B must be fulfilled, but not both.

II. Specific Requirements

A. Part A

1. Too much parathyroid hormone in the blood causes excess calcium to be taken away from bones. This can be seen on X-rays as the "generalized decalcification of bone" required by Part A. Note that such X-rays are necessary to qualify under Part A.

2. If the loss of calcium from bones seen on X-rays is really due to hyperparathyroidism, then the amount of calcium in the bloodstream should be abnormally high. Part A requires that the level must be at least 11.0 to qualify. One such abnormal blood test would not be very convincing. Probably at least 3 months of such tests would be required to convince S. S. Disability that the condition isn't likely to improve.

B. Part B

1. Hyperparathyroidism affects the whole body, and many different problems can arise in an individual claimant. There are too many possibilities to list under Part B.

2. Actual evaluation would be done under whatever Listing most accurately matches a claimant's individual problems. For example, if the hyperparathyroidism caused kidney damage, the case would be evaluated under one of the Listings dealing with kidney disease.

Listing 9.04

Hypoparathyroidism. With:

A. Severe recurrent tetany; OR

B. Recurrent generalized convulsions; OR

C. Evaluate lenticular cataracts under the criteria in 2.00ff. (Author's note: 2.00ff refers to the group of Listings dealing with visual problems.)

I. General Considerations

A. This Listing deals with *hypo*parathyroidism—a disease in which the parathyroid glands do not produce enough parathyroid hormone.

B. S. S. Disability must be able to obtain medical records showing that the claimant has hypoparathyroidism.

C. Part A, B, or C must be fulfilled, but not all three.

II. Specific Requirements

A. Part A

1. When there is not enough parathyroid hormone in the blood, then levels of calcium in the bloodstream will fall below normal.

2. Abnormally low calcium levels in the blood can cause muscles to undergo severe, uncontrolled spasms called "tetany"—which is similar to having a muscle cramp, only much worse.

3. Small amounts of tetany involving a few small muscles is not sufficient. The tetany must be severe enough to involve the larger muscles in the body, to such an extent that the claimant is obviously severely affected by it.

4. The episodes of tetany must be *recurrent.* That is, they must occur over and over again, and S. S. Disability must be able to obtain medical records proving that this is true. There is no exact rule for how often "recurrent" means. This partly involves how severe each individual episode is for a given claimant.

B. Part B

1. Low serum calcium from hypoparathyroidism can cause convulsions (seizures).

2. Note that Part B requires that the convulsions be "generalized". That means affecting the entire body.

3. The convulsions must be *recurrent*—they must happen repeatedly. S. S. Disability must be able to obtain medical records proving this is true, as well as a detailed description of these "convulsions". How frequent "recurrent" means is a matter of judgment by the person in S. S. Disability evaluating the case. It would partly depend on how severe each convulsion was, and how it affected a particular claimant.

C. Part C

1. Hypoparathyroidism can cause "lenticular cataracts". This is a form of degeneration of the lens of the eye, and if severe enough would interfere with clear vision.

2. If a claimant with hypoparathyroidism has cataracts, no actual evaluation would be done under Part C. The case would be evaluated under one of the Listings dealing with impairment of vision, and would have to fulfill the requirements of one of those Listings.

Listing 9.05

Neurohypophyseal insufficiency (diabetes insipidus). With urine specific gravity of 1.005 or below, persistent for at least 3 months and recurrent dehydration.

I. General Considerations

A. This Listing deals with "neurohypophyseal insufficiency", or "diabetes insipidus". "Hypophysis" is the medical word for pituitary gland, and the *neuro*hypophysis is simply the posterior part (backside) of the pituitary gland. It produces different hormones than the anterior (front-side) of the pituitary gland. (The pituitary gland is popularly called the "master-gland" of the body, because it produces so many important hormones. It hangs down on a stalk from the bottom of the brain.)

B. Diabetes insipidus occurs when the back part of the pituitary gland doesn't produce enough of a hormone called *vasopressin,* which is also called *anti-diuretic hormone* (ADH).

C. Diabetes insipidus is not the same as "sugar" diabetes that most people think about when they talk about someone diabetic. Antidiuretic hormone acts on the kidneys, to prevent too much water from being lost through urination. Many people experience a mild form of diabetes insipidus when they drink alcoholic beverages. The alcohol interferes with the release of antidiuretic hormone from the pituitary gland, and increased fluid is lost through the kidneys. This causes a need to urinate more frequently.

II. Specific Requirements

A. Since abnormally large amounts of water are being lost from the body, the urine should be more dilute than it normally is in a person with diabetes insipidus. This can be measured by a test of the "specific gravity" of a sample of urine. The number must be 1.005 or less to qualify.

B. One specific gravity test is not enough. The test must be abnormal over a period of at least 3 months to convince S. S. Disability that the diabetes insipidus isn't likely to improve.

C. The claimant must be *dehydrated,* which means that he cannot keep the amount of water in his body at normal levels, even if he drinks fluids in an attempt to do so. This dehydration can be detected on examination by a medical doctor. One episode of dehydration is not enough. There must be evidence that such episodes happen over and over again—that they are *recur-*

rent. Of course, if a claimant suffered continuous dehydration, that would also qualify.

Listing 9.06

Hyperfunction of the adrenal cortex. Evaluate the resulting impairment under the criteria for the affected body system.

I. General Considerations

A. This Listing deals with disease that affects the outer part of the adrenal glands. There is one adrenal gland sitting on top of each kidney, and the cells in the outer part are called the "adrenal cortex".

B. The adrenal cortex produces a group of hormones called "steroids". These steroids are extremely important in helping the body adjust to any kind of "stress". Such stress could be anything from fear to physical injury. (If there were a complete lack of such steroid, life would be impossible, unless they were replaced with artificial hormones.)

II. Specific Requirements

A. S. S. Disability must be able to obtain medical records showing that the claimant does have disease of the adrenal cortex.

B. This Listing deals only with *hyper*function of the adrenal cortex—that is, the production of *too much* steroid hormones. This can be caused by disease in the adrenal glands themselves, or other diseases which affect the adrenal glands.

C. Overproduction of hormones by the adrenal cortex can cause many different kinds of physical illness, and it can also lead to abnormal mental changes. Because of the numerous possibilities involved, actual evaluation is not done under this Listing. The case would be considered under whatever Listing most accurately fits a particular claimant's problems, and the requirements of the Listing would have to be fulfilled.

Listing 9.08

Diabetes mellitus. With:

A. Neuropathy demonstrated by significant and persistent disorganization of motor function in two extremities resulting in sustained disturbance of gross and dexterous movements, or gait and station; OR

B. Acidosis occurring at least on the average of once every 2 months documented by appropriate blood chemical tests (pH or pCO_2 or bicarbonate levels); OR

C. Amputation at, or above, the tarsal region due to diabetic necrosis or peripheral vascular disease; OR

D. Retinitis proliferans. Evaluate the visual impairment under the criteria in Listing 2.02, 2.03, or 2.04.

I. General Considerations

A. This Listing deals with *diabetes mellitus*, popularly called "sugar" diabetes. It is the type of diabetes most people are familiar with, and the most frequent hormone disorder for which claimants allege disability.

B. The cells of the body need a form of sugar called "glucose". But glucose cannot get inside the cells where it is needed, unless the hormone insulin is also present. If the pancreas suffers disease that prevents it from producing enough insulin, then diabetes mellitus will develop. The level of "sugar" (glucose) in the bloodstream will become abnormally high. Sometimes injections of insulin must be taken to correct the problem. These comments are very much of a simplification. Diabetes mellitus is a fantastically complicated disease and although it has been studied for centuries, there is no *complete* agreement among doctors about the cause or even the best treatment.

C. Diabetes mellitus affects the entire body, and may exist in any degree of severity. This Listing takes into account the most common problem caused by diabetes mellitus.

D. Part A, B, C, or D must be fulfilled, but not all four.

II. Specific Requirements

A. Part A

1. One possible effect of diabetes mellitus is "neuropathy". Neuropathy means that the disease is having an abnormal effect on nerves.

2. Diabetes mellitus can cause both *motor* neuropathy and *sensory* neuropathy. *Motor* neuropathy means that motor nerves are affected. These nerves allow a person to move their muscles, and without them no movement would be possible. *Sensory* neuropathy means that sensory nerves are affected. These nerves allow a person to "feel" such things as pain, temperature, and touch. Part A deals *only* with motor neuropathy,

though in reality sensory neuropathy could play a role in evaluation if very severe.

3. The most serious motor neuropathy caused by diabetes mellitus is that which affects the ability to use the arms, hands, or legs. So S. S. Disability is most interested in how the neuropathy affects the claimant's ability to grasp with the hands and to walk.

4. Use of the legs is evaluated by "gait and station". Gait means walking, and station refers to the posture used in standing and walking.

5. Use of the arms and hands is evaluated by "gross and dextrous movements". Gross movements involves the ability to grasp large sized objects with normal or abnormal coordination and speed. Dexterous movements are fine movements, such as picking up small objects or writing.

6. "Two extremities" means that the neuropathy can affect both legs, both arms, or one arm and one leg. But one arm or one leg alone would not qualify.

7. The impairment caused by neuropathy must be *sustained.* It must be severe enough to be present continuously. S. S. Disability must have enough information over a long enough period of time to be convinced that the neuropathy isn't likely to improve. This usually requires at least several months of medical records, showing the severe neuropathy to be present.

B. Part B

1. If diabetes mellitus is severe enough and cannot be controlled with treatment, it can produce "acidosis" or abnormally increased acidity of the blood. (Such diabetics that are difficult to control with treatment are called "brittle" diabetics.)

2. If the acidosis is severe enough, the claimant is very sick and needs very careful medical attention—usually in a hospital.

3. The episodes of acidosis must occur on an *average* of at least once every 2 months, and S. S. Disability must be able to obtain medical records showing that this is true. These records must contain "appropriate blood chemical tests" to prove that acidosis has occurred. Such tests involve taking samples of arterial blood, and any physician treating someone for diabetic acidosis would have done these tests.

4. It should be noted that if a claimant could avoid developing episodes of acidosis by following his doctor's instructions, but refuses to do so, he may not qualify under this Listing. Ex-

ceptions would be the mentally ill, or mentally retarded. Such people may have difficulty following treatment instructions.

C. Part C

1. One of the worst problems with having severe diabetes mellitus comes from its tendency in some people to damage bloodvessels. This can interfere with tissues getting as much blood as they need to stay healthy. This is what happens in diabetic peripheral vascular disease, which is especially common in the legs and feet. If the blood flow drops low enough, then the tissues receiving blood from that bloodvessel will die. This would be diabetic *gangrene*, and the dead tissue would have to be surgically removed (amputated).

2. In addition to interfering with blood flow to tissues, diabetes can also produce a decreased ability to fight infection. This is because white blood cells important in fighting infection don't function normally in diabetics. Even a minor infection in a diabetic can be much more serious than in a normal person.

3. These problems with poor circulation and infection occur most often in the feet and legs. The inability to feel things very well (sensory neuropathy) makes conditions even worse, because the person might not even be aware of an injury, or might ignore it due to the fact it doesn't hurt very much. For example, a person with severe diabetes could get a small cut on his foot. This could happen just by clipping the toenails in the wrong way. Because he is a diabetic with poor immunity and poor circulation, an infection could very easily develop in the cut. Due to the sensory neuropathy preventing feelings of pain, the person is less likely to seek medical help until the infection is advanced. By then, amputation of a toe, foot, or even a leg might be required to remove the dead tissue.

4. To qualify under Part C, such amputation must be "above the tarsal level". This means that the entire foot, including the bones in the ankle, must be amputated. Of course, an amputation higher up on the leg would also qualify.

D. Part D

1. As noted under the discussion of Part C, diabetes mellitus can damage bloodvessels. Damage to the bloodvessels of the eyes is commonly caused by severe diabetes. In its worse form, this is called "retinitis proliferans", and can be easily seen by a doctor examining the claimant's eyes.

2. If retinitis proliferans is present, the actual evaluation is not done under Part D. It would be done under the Listings dealing with visual impairments—2.02, 2.03, or 2.04. The reader

should refer to discussions of those Listings for more information.

§ 2.11 Multiple Body Systems

Listing 10.02

Hansen's disease (leprosy). As active disease or consider as "under a disability" while hospitalized.

I. General Considerations

A. This Listing deals only with leprosy (Hansen's disease).

B. Leprosy is a disease caused by the organism Mycobacterium leprae, which can lead to destruction of tissues anywhere in the body. The disease is fairly rare in this country.

II. Specific Requirements

A. The Listing is fulfilled, if the leprosy is "active"—that is, actively destroying tissue.

B. The Listing is also fulfilled, if the claimant is hospitalized for treatment of leprosy.

Listing 10.03

Polyarteritis or periarteritis nodosa (established by biopsy). With signs of generalized arterial involvement.

I. General Considerations

A. This Listing deals with a disease called "polyarteritis", or "periarteritis nodosa". They are the same disease.

B. Polyarteritis literally means inflammation of many arteries. The cause is unknown. It tends to occur in medium-sized arteries, and inflammation of these arteries can cause damage to any organ in the body.

II. Specific Requirements

A. S. S. Disability must be able to obtain data showing that the claimant does have polyarteritis. This must be in the form of a "biopsy", which means surgically taking a small piece of tissue for study under a microscope. The disease would then be identifiable, if present. S. S. Disability does *not* order biopsies. A biopsy must have been done by the treating doctor, and the results available to S. S. Disability.

B. There must be signs that the periarteritis shows "generalized arterial involvement". This means that S. S. Disability must have enough information to show that the inflammation of arteries is widespread throughout the arteries of the body.

Listing 10.04

Disseminated lupus erythematosus (established by a positive LE preparation or biopsy or positive ANA test). With frequent exacerbations demonstrating involvement of renal or cardiac or pulmonary or gastrointestinal or central nervous systems.

I. General Considerations

A. This Listing deals with a disease of unknown cause named lupus erythematosus. Often, it is just called "lupus". Lupus can have complicated destructive effects on the tissues of any organ in the body. The most important areas that can be involved are the kidneys, lungs, heart, intestine, and nervous system.

B. The Listing requires that the lupus be of "disseminated" kind. This means the disease is affecting major organs in the body. There is a form of lupus called *discoid* lupus, which principally affects the skin. Discoid lupus does *not* qualify under this Listing.

II. Specific Requirements

A. S. S. Disability must have one of three different tests to reasonably believe that lupus is present, as follows:

1. *"Positive LE preparation"*. Lupus tends to form special cells that can be seen under a microscope. This test is done with a sample of blood.

2. *"Biopsy"*. A biopsy is the surgical removal of a piece of tissue. This is then studied under a microscope. Such a biopsy may show the abnormal changes in tissues which are expected from lupus. Biopsies are *not* ordered by S. S. Disability. If this has been done, it must come from the treating doctor.

3. *"Positive ANA test"*. People with lupus may form antibodies against parts of their own cells, and this can be detected in a sample of blood.

B. As noted above, the worse damage done by lupus is usually to the kidneys, heart, lungs, central nervous system, and gastrointestinal tract. At least one of these areas must be involved to qualify under the Listing. Note that if the nervous system is involved, it must be the *central* nervous system. This means the brain or spinal cord. *Peripheral* nerves, such as run down the arms and legs, do not qualify. The gastrointestinal tract refers to the esophagus, stomach, small intestine, and large intestine. Only one of these parts of the gastrointestinal tract would need to be involved.

C. Lupus is a disease that may be of any degree of severity, with "flare-ups" that make the disease worse at certain times. These flare-ups are called "exacerbations" by the Listing, and they must occur frequently enough to have a severe effect on the claimant. There are no exact rules concerning how often "frequent" means, or how severe each flare-up must be. This is a matter of judgment on the part of the person in S. S. Disability evaluating the case. The way the disease can affect individual claimants is too complicated to make simple rules that apply to everyone. In general, it is safe to say that S. S. Disability must have medical records clearly showing that substantial damage is being done to the claimant by the disease. Flare-ups that are serious would usually result in the claimant having been hospitalized on at least some occasions.

Listing 10.05

Scleroderma or progressive systemic sclerosis (the diffuse or generalized form). With:

A. Advanced limitation of use of hands due to sclerodactylia or limitation in other joints; OR

B. Significant visceral manifestations of digestive, cardiac, or pulmonary impairment.

I. General Considerations

A. This Listing deals with a disease of unknown cause, called scleroderma. Another name for it is "progressive systemic sclerosis".

B. Scleroderma attacks the "connective tissues" of the body, and the damage it does depends on which organ is the victim.

II. Specific Requirements

A. Part A

1. When scleroderma affects the connective tissue of skin, then the skin becomes hardened and stiff. Part A is mainly concerned with the effect of scleroderma on the hands; since the

hands are necessary for grasping and manipulating objects, scleroderma affecting the hands can be very severely impairing. Unfortunately, the hands are often involved. "Sclerodactylia" means scleroderma of the fingers.

2. There must be "advanced limitation of use of hands". This means things like being able to make a fist, grasp objects, push, pull, etc. Severe scleroderma of the hands can make them essentially useless.

3. Although the hands are frequently affected, Part A can also be fulfilled if scleroderma severely affects the skin around other joints, so that the joints can't move normally. For example, if it severely affected the skin around the elbow joints, then there would be difficulty in bending the arms.

B. Part B

1. Part B deals with "visceral manifestations" of scleroderma. This means cases where the scleroderma affects internal organs.

2. The heart, digestive tract, and lungs are most frequently involved. The esophagus, stomach, and intestines (both large and small) would qualify under the term "digestive tract".

3. Note that there must be "significant" visceral manifestations to qualify. This is somewhat a matter of judgment by the person in S. S. Disability evaluating the case. For example, if the lungs were involved, S. S. Disability would probably ask the claimant to undergo special breathing tests, to determine how severely the lungs are damaged. If the heart were involved, S. S. Disability would require medical records showing a significant problem to be present. This could be heart failure, abnormal rhythms of the heart, etc. If the digestive tract were involved, S. S. Disability would require data showing the type and degree of damage—X-rays, biopsies, etc.

Listing 10.10

Obesity. Weight equal to or greater than the values specified in Table I for males, Table II for females (100 percent above desired level) and one of the following:

A. History of pain and limitation of motion in any weight bearing joint or spine (on physical examination) associated with X-ray evidence of arthritis in a weight bearing joint or spine; OR

B. Hypertension with diastolic blood pressure persistently in excess of 100 mm HG measured with appropriate size cuff; OR

C. History of congestive heart failure manifested by past evidence of vascular congestion such as hepatomegaly, peripheral or pulmonary edema; OR

D. Chronic venous insufficiency with superficial varicosities in a lower extremity with pain on weight bearing and persistent edema; OR

E. Respiratory disease with total forced vital capacity equal to or less than 2.0 L. or a level of hypoxemia at rest equal to or less than the values in the following table:

Arterial pCO_2 (mm Hg.)	AND	Arterial pCO_2 Equal to or Less Than (mm Hg.)
30 or below		65
31 or below		64
32 or below		63
33 or below		62
34 or below		61
35 or below		60
36 or below		59
37 or below		58
38 or below		57
39 or below		56
40 or above		55

Table I. Men

Height (Inches)	Weight (Pounds)
60	246
61	252
62	258
63	264
64	270
65	276
66	284
67	294
68	302
69	310
70	318

Table I. Men—Continued

Height (Inches)—Continued	**Weight (Pounds)**—Continued
71	328
72	336
73	346
74	356
75	364
76	374

Table II. Women

Height (Inches)	**Weight (Pounds)**
56	208
57	212
58	218
59	224
60	230
61	236
62	242
63	250
64	258
65	266
66	274
67	282
68	290
69	298
70	306
71	314
72	322

I. General Considerations

A. This Listing deals with obesity.

B. The first thing that must be demonstrated is that the weight of the claimant is sufficiently great to qualify. This is determined by Table I (Men) and Table II (Women). These tables are adjusted for the height of the claimant, since a taller person will normally weigh more, and this has to be taken into account. Also, men normally weigh more than women, so the tables require greater weight for men to qualify. The height measurements are without shoes. If the height of the claimant is between one of these numbers, further calculations may be needed, but this is rarely necessary

C. The weight tables represent weights that are twice what would be expected of a normal person. Since S. S. Disability expects all claimants to be disabled for at least a year, one weight is not enough. S. S. must be able to obtain medical records showing that the claimant tends to stay above the weight values given in the tables.

D. Most obesity is voluntary over-eating. However, S. S. Disability does not hold this against the claimant in any way. The *cause* of the obesity is not important.

E. Obesity itself that qualifies under the values of Table I or Table II is not sufficient to qualify under the Listing. There must be some other additional impairment, as in Part A, B, C, or D. Only one of these has to be fulfilled.

II. Specific Requirements

A. Part A

1. Part A deals with arthritis. What kind of arthritis is not important.

2. There must be a history of painful joints. This means that the claimant must have complained of painful joints to his doctor.

3. There must be limitation of normal motion in the joint involved with arthritis. This is determined by a doctor examining the claimant. It is important to note, however, that very obese people have a limitation of normal motion in their joints, simply because of the fat present. If that is the only problem, it does *not* qualify. The limitation of motion must at least partly be caused by the arthritis. And the decrease in normal motion of the joint due to the arthritis must be enough to reasonably have an impairing effect on the claimant.

4. The arthritis *must* be in a "weight bearing" joint. This means a hip joint, knee joint, or ankle joint. The spine is also included.

5. There must be X-rays of the joints involved with the arthritis, or spine of the back is involved. These X-rays must show enough arthritic change to justify the claimant's complaints.

B. Part B

1. Part B deals with "hypertension" (high blood pressure).

2. Every blood pressure reading consists of a "systolic" and a "diastolic" measurement. The *diastolic* pressure is what Part B is interested in. The diastolic pressure is always lower than the systolic pressure, and is the second number in a blood pressure reading. For example, a blood pressure reading of 140/90 means that the systolic pressure is 140 and the diastolic pressure is 90. In this example, the diastolic pressure is too low to qualify under Part B. But if the blood pressure were 140/110, then the diastolic pressure is greater than 100 and it does qualify.

3. Note that the diastolic pressure must "persistently" be over 100. High blood pressure cannot be diagnosed by just one reading. S. S. Disability must have enough readings over a long enough period of time to be convinced that the claimant's diastolic blood pressure is always (or almost always) over 100. This would require *at least* several months of blood pressure readings from the treating doctor. S. S. Disability would not accept blood pressure readings that the claimant does on himself.

4. Blood pressure is usually measured by a cloth "cuff" wrapped around the upper arm with a gauge attached to it. Part B requires that the cuff be of "appropriate size". The reason for this is that obese people have large arms, so that if a normal sized cuff is used the pressure will appear higher than it really is. To get accurate readings in an obese person, a larger than normal blood pressure cuff must be used. S. S. Disability must be assured by the treating doctor that he used a cuff that was large enough. If he used only a normal size cuff, S. S. Disability will *not* accept the blood pressure readings. Nor will the readings be accepted, if S. S. Disability can't find out what size cuff was used.

5. A claimant who had diastolic pressures over 100 in the past, but who has a normal blood pressure because of treatment, would *not* qualify.

C. Part C

1. Part C deals with "congestive heart failure". The reader should refer to the discussion of Listing 4.02 for more information about heart failure, and the terms "vascular congestion", "hepatomegaly", and "peripheral or pulmonary edema".

2. It is important to note that the obese claimant does *not* have to show heart failure at the time of application for disability. It is only necessary to show that heart failure happened

even once, at any time in the past. But S. S. Disability must be able to get enough information to show that this really happened.

D. Part D

1. Part D deals with "chronic venous insufficiency". Discussion of this can be found under Listing 4.12. However, the venous insufficiency does *not* have to be as severe as that required by Listing 4.12.

2. To fulfill Part D, the venous insufficiency must only show:

(a) "*Superficial varicosities*". These are the swollen veins just under the skin that people call "varicose veins".

(b) The varicose veins must be in at least one leg, and the claimant must complain of pain in the leg while standing.

(c) There must be *persistent* swelling in the leg involved. Swelling (edema) that comes and goes would not qualify.

E. Part E

1. Part E deals with "respiratory disease". It is extremely important to know that obesity itself can cause difficulty breathing and can be called a respiratory disease. There does *not* have to be disease in the lungs themselves.

2. Special breathing tests can show how much the claimant's breathing is affected by their obesity. If a measurement called the "total forced vital capacity" is equal to or less than 2.0 Liters, then Part E is fulfilled. The vital capacity is simply the amount of air that a person can blow out, after taking as deep a breath as he can. If a claimant is obese enough to exceed the values in the weight tables and complains of shortness of breath, then his breathing will be tested, to see if he qualifies under Part E.

3. Another way to qualify under Part E is to have "hypoxemia", which is decreased oxygen in the bloodstream. This is measured by taking a small sample of blood from an artery. The amount of oxygen is called the "arterial pO_2". The amount of carbon dioxide is also important and is called the "arterial pCO_2". The two numbers must match up to one of the places in table of values given with Part E. For example, if the oxygen (pO_2) is 62, then the carbon dioxide (pCO_2) must be 33 or less for the claimant to qualify. S. S. Disability will *not* use such numbers, if the test was done while the claimant had some kind of lung infection, such as pneumonia. That would make the numbers appear lower than they normally are.

4. If a claimant wants to qualify under Part E, he must *complain* of shortness of breath when he applies for disability. Otherwise, S. S. Disability might not know that the claimant has a problem breathing, and the necessary tests might not be done.

§ 2.12 Neurological

Listing 11.02

Epilepsy—Major motor seizures (grand mal or psychomotor), documented by EEG and by detailed description of a typical seizure pattern, including all associated phenomena; occurring more frequently than once a month, in spite of at least 3 months of prescribed treatment. With:

A. Diurnal episodes (loss of consciousness and convulsive seizures); OR

B. Nocturnal episodes manifesting residuals which interfere significantly with activity during the day.

I. General Considerations

A. This Listing deals with any form of *major* motor epilepsy. These are seizures (convulsions) that affect most of the body. The two types of epilepsy that may qualify are "grand mal" epilepsy and "psychomotor epilepsy".

B. There should be a report of an EEG in the file. An EEG is an "*E*lectro*e*ncephalo*g*ram". An EEG is made by attaching small electrodes to the head, and recording the tiny electrical impulses from the brain on a piece of paper. Epilepsy is related to abnormal electrical activity in the brain, and sometimes this will show up on an EEG. However, it is important to note that the claimant can qualify under this Listing whether the EEG is abnormal or normal. The reason for this is that epilepsy can still be present with a normal EEG, as well as an abnormal one. But if the EEG is abnormal, this more strongly suggests that epilepsy is present. That is the only reason it is obtained.

C. There must be a detailed description of the claimant's seizures, preferably by a medical doctor. Generally, this should fit the pattern of either grand mal epilepsy or psychomotor epilepsy. Also, supplemental information may be obtained by sending the claimant forms to fill out, in which a variety of questions are asked about his seizures. These are called *lay statements*. The claimant fills one out himself, and gives the others to members of his family, friends, or others who have seen him have a seizure. Or S. S. Disability may send the claimant to a consulting doctor to get more information about his seizures. This is especially true, if there is evidence that the seizures may be more hysterical than real, and the claimant may be asked to undergo neuropsychiatric examination in such instances. However, it should be emphasized that the greatest weight is generally given to information provided by the treating doctor. Unfortunately, this is often not very detailed.

D. In a typical grand mal seizure, the claimant may feel the seizure coming. This is called an *aura*, in which many types of strange sensations may be felt, depending on the person. When the seizure actually comes, the claimant stiffens throughout his body, loses consciousness and falls. Jerking movements then follow. There may be biting of the tongue, urination, or loss of control of the bowels. The claimant would not be aware of any of this. When the seizure is over, sleep may follow or the claimant could wake up. Often, there is confusion and weakness when coming out of the seizure state. How long this is depends on the person, and is called the *postictal* state.

E. Temporal lobe epilepsy is different from grand mal epilepsy; a different area of the brain is involved. In temporal lobe epilepsy, the claimant may not fall down, but he will lose conscious awareness of what he is doing. He may engage in acts not knowing what he is doing, experience strange emotions, see things that are not there (hallucinate), or have a feeling of unreality. There are many possibilities.

F. The seizures that the claimant experiences *must* occur more often than once a month. Claimants with epilepsy often apply for disability, stating that they have an incredible number of seizures—sometimes hundreds per month. This is extremely unlikely, and S. S. Disability will *not* take the claimant's word for how many seizures he is having. This information will be sought from the treating doctor, or from the claimant's hospital records. However, it sometimes happens that the treating doctor won't give S. S. Disability any information at all, and often they have not made an exact record over time concerning exactly how many seizures the claimant is having. If that happens, S. S. Disability is under no obligation to believe whatever the claimant says about the number of seizures he is having, nor must S. S. Disability necessarily accept at face value comments by family, friends, neighbors, employers, teachers, etc., that the claimant is having a certain number of seizures. Therefore, it is important that the treating doctor have good medical records concerning the claimant's seizures *and* be willing to release these to S. S. Disability.

G. S. S. Disability will not allow any claimant under this Listing, unless they are under treatment for their epilepsy. The treatment must have been going on for *at least* 3 months, to convince S. S. Disability that the seizures can't be controlled with treatment. The claimant must be under *active* treatment. That means the claimant must be making a reasonable effort with his treating doctor to control his seizures. For example, if a claimant said he was having seizures despite being under treatment, this would not be very convincing if he had not seen his doctor for a year or longer. The point is that if the claimant doesn't seek medical help for his uncontrolled seizures, then his story isn't very convincing at all for being under prescribed treatment. The claimant *must* be under therapy, unless he is too mentally retarded or mentally ill to have rational judgment.

H. Almost all epilepsy can be controlled with the proper treatment. If the claimant is not getting proper treatment from his doctor, S. S. Disability does not enter into this matter at all, and does *not* hold that against the claimant. S. S. Disability also does not express any opinion to the claimant that he is getting improper treatment, because that is interference with the relationship between a claimant and his doctor. If such a claimant feels dissatisfied with the treatment he is receiving, then it is up to him to seek advice from another doctor. If there is any evidence in medical records, or from the treating doctor, that the claimant is not following medical advice in taking their drugs, then the claimant will *not* qualify under this Listing, since failure to follow medical advice means that the claimant is not under prescribed treatment as required by the Listing.

I. It should be noted that if a claimant does not see his doctor, but simply goes to the drug store year after year to refill his prescriptions, that does *not* qualify as being under prescribed treatment—a doctor cannot really treat someone who he does not see for such long periods. In fact, it is illegal in many if not all states for pharmacists to refill prescriptions for some anti–epileptic drugs beyond a certain amount of time without a new prescription from the treating doctor. The drug phenobarbital is the most common example, and laws controlling prescriptions for it are based on its high drug-abuse potential. It is also one of the most frequently used drugs to treat epilepsy.

J. In order for a drug to work in controlling seizures, there must be enough of it in the bloodstream to do some good. If a claimant has fulfilled all other criteria to be allowed under this

Listing, then S. S. Disability will order blood levels of the claimant's antiepileptic drugs to be measured. If *any* of the drug levels are *zero* or so close to zero that the laboratory can't measure them, S. S. Disability will make the reasonable assumption that the claimant is not taking the drugs as prescribed by his doctor. In such a case, the claimant would *not* qualify under the Listing. If any of the drug blood levels are higher than zero, but lower than necessary to have a beneficial effect on the seizures, then there are several possibilities: (1) The claimant is not taking the drugs as prescribed by his doctor, or (2) The claimant is having poor absorption of the drugs from his intestinal tract, or abnormal metabolism of the drug after it is absorbed. If poor absorption or abnormal metabolism is the reason for the low blood levels, then the claimant can still qualify under the Listing. Otherwise, it will be assumed that the claimant is not cooperating with treatment and will *not* qualify. S. S. Disability will make a judgment about which choice to believe, based on all available medical information. Low blood levels are far more often due to the claimant not taking his drugs properly than anything else, and it is not sufficient for the treating doctor to merely express the opinion that poor absorption or abnormal metabolism is at fault, unless there is some objective medical reason for that to be true.

Sometimes, claimants are taking very high doses of antiepileptic drugs to control their seizures and such doses may be producing *toxic effects* that decrease the claimant's ability to work. If so, S. S. Disability will take this fact into account when evaluating the claimant's over-all impairment. However, S. S. Disability will also take into account medical records which show that the claimant is using excessive alcohol or other drugs which affect his ability to stay on prescribed treatment, interfere with the action of his antiepileptic drugs, or actually play a part in the precipitation of seizures. For example, if a claimant is using illegal street drugs which could produce or even worsen his seizure condition, he certainly would not qualify under this Listing, even if he fulfilled all of the other requirements of the Listing. He would not be considered compliant with prescribed therapy.

II. Specific Requirements

A. Part A

1. Part A deals with "diurnal" seizures. These are seizures that occur during the daytime.

2. As noted previously, there must be loss of consciousness and convulsions.

B. Part B

1. Part B deals with nocturnal seizures, which are those occurring at night.

2. Nocturnal seizures are treated a little differently by the Listing, because they might not interfere with work during the daytime.

3. In order for a claimant to qualify due to nighttime seizures, there must be evidence that it interferes *substantially* with his daytime activities. As noted previously, someone coming out of a seizure may feel weak and confused, or even have temporary paralysis of part of their body. This *postictal* phase after a seizure, and how severe and long-lasting it is depends on the individual claimant. If these abnormal effects last into the daytime to such a degree that normal activities cannot be carried out, then Part B may be fulfilled. Also, some claimants have so many seizures during the night that they are too exhausted to do much of anything the next day. Others may have seizures during sleep without knowing it, and wake up feeling fine. S. S. Disability will rely on what the claimant's treating doctor says about his nighttime seizures and whether they interfere with his activities the next day. If inadequate information is available from the treating doctor, then much less weight will be given to what the claimant himself says about his seizures.

Listing 11.03

Epilepsy—minor motor seizures (petit mal, psychomotor, or focal), documented by EEG and by detailed description of a typical seizure pattern, including all associated phenomena; occurring more frequently than once weekly in spite of at least 3 months of prescribed treatment. With alteration of awareness or loss of consciousness and transient postictal manifestations of unconventional behavior or significant interference with activity during the day.

I. General Considerations

A. Some requirements of this Listing are the same as those of Listing 11.02. The reader should refer to some part of the discussion of that Listing for more information, namely "B, C, F, G, H, I and J" under "General Considerations". Note that the "monthly" frequency of seizures in "F" would be "weekly".

B. This Listing deals with epilepsy which is in the form of "minor motor" seizures, of which there are several common examples given:

1. "Petit mal epilepsy" involves a very brief loss of awareness by the claimant, often lasting only a few seconds. Sometimes, the person having one and even others present at the same time will be unaware of anything happening.

2. "Psychomotor epilepsy" was discussed under Listing 11.02. The only difference is that psychomotor epilepsy considered under Listing 11.03 is not as severe. Which Listing a case of psychomotor epilepsy would be evaluated under is a matter of judgment by the person in S. S. Disability reviewing the case. If the psychomotor seizures are very short, they would be evaluated under Listing 11.03 as minor motor seizures.

3. "Focal motor seizures" are small seizures that only affect a part of the body.

II. Specific Requirements

A. Since minor motor seizures are not as severe as major motor seizures, they must occur *more* often than once a week.

B. The claimant must have been under treatment for at least 3 months.

C. Complete loss of consciousness is not necessary, but there should at least be some decrease in the claimant's awareness of what is going on around him during one of these seizures.

D. The *postictal* phase refers to the time after a seizure in which a person has not yet become fully normal again. The Listing requires that during this postictal phase that there be "unconventional behavior". This means behavior that is not normally done by the claimant. If there is no "unconventional behavior", then there should be interference with the claimant's normal daily activities by the seizures. In other words, no matter how many seizures a claimant has, this will not necessarily interfere with work if they are very brief and without after-effects (such as confusion) that linger after the seizure is over. The seizure activity must have *significant* effects on the claimant's daily activities, to the extent that they interfere with normal life and the reasonable ability to work. This is a matter of judgment on the part of the person in S. S. Disability reviewing the claimant's case.

Listing 11.04

Central nervous system vascular accident. With one of the following more than 3 months post-vascular accident:

A. Sensory or motor aphasia resulting in ineffective speech or communication; OR

B. Significant and persistent disorganization of motor function in two extremities, resulting in sustained disturbance of gross and dexterous movements, or gait and station.

I. General Considerations

A. This Listing deals with impairment due to a cerebrovascular accident, more commonly known as a stroke. It is often called "CVA", and refers either to a blood vessel bleeding into the brain, or a blood vessel supplying part of the brain having its blood flow blocked (thrombosis). Either way, brain tissue is damaged.

B. CVA's can be of all degrees of severity, and the type of damage they do depends on where in the brain they occur. Some CVA's immediately kill the person who has it, while others may cause little damage. There might be good recovery, or very little.

C. Evidence that a CVA has occurred can come from either a physical exam and/or laboratory studies that have been done. These are usually some form of special X-ray of the brain that the treating doctor has ordered.

D. Any claimant who is alleging disability because of a CVA will not have his case evaluated, until at least 3 months have passed since the CVA occurred. It takes at least this long to find out how much recovery will take place.

E. Part A or Part B has to be fulfilled, but not both.

II. Specific Requirements

A. Part A

1. Part A deals with impairments from CVA's that affect the mind, by producing either *sensory* or *motor aphasia.*

2. In sensory aphasia, the claimant may be unable to understand written or spoken words. There are other types of sensory aphasia, but these are the most important for S. S. Disability.

3. In motor aphasia, the claimant may know what he wishes to say, but is unable to find the needed words to speak them.

4. There are all degrees of sensory or motor aphasia possible, but to fulfill Part A, it must be so severe that communica-

tion with other people is "ineffective". "Ineffective" is defined by S. S. Disability to mean that "useful verbal communication is not possible".

B. Part B

1. Part B deals with physical impairments caused by a CVA. These could be almost anything, but S. S. is mainly interested in the ability to walk ("gait and station") and to use the arms and hands ("disturbance of gross and dexterous movements").

2. *Two* extremities must be involved. This means both legs, both arms, or one arm and one leg.

3. In evaluating how well a claimant stands and walks, S. S. Disability requires a detailed description from a medical doctor. This involves things like how weak the claimant's legs are, how much difficulty there is in keeping balance, how fast the claimant walks, how much help must be given to the claimant in walking, etc. It is *not* necessary that the claimant have to use a cane, crutch, brace, walker, or other assistive device to get about. Of course, if such devices were necessary, it would indicate a very severe impairment. On the other hand, it is important to note that S. S. Disability is not impressed just because a claimant uses an assistive device such as a cane or crutch, or even a wheelchair, *unless* it were obvious that the claimant really needed it. This is true, even if the treating doctor says such a device is needed. S. S. Disability will reach its own conclusions.

4. The use of the arms and hands is evaluated by looking at "gross and dexterous movements". Dexterous movements are things like writing, picking up small objects, or other types of fine movements. Gross movements involve larger motions with the arms and hands. These can be influenced by weakness, or loss of control over the way an arm or hand moves, such as tremors.

5. Many claimants are impaired after a CVA, because the area of their brain controlling a certain part of their body has been destroyed or severely damaged. This can lead to paralysis of an arm or leg, so that they are too weak to use normally. Such weakness is a frequent complaint in the application for disability. An arm or leg that has become useless or extremely weak from a CVA might show *atrophy*. Atrophy is the decrease in size of a muscle that is not being used. If a claimant goes to a doctor 3 months after a CVA, and states that there is severe weakness in an arm or leg, then S. S. Disability is going to ask if atrophy is present. This can be determined by simply wrapping a tape measure around the "bad" arm or leg and comparing that measurement with the "good" arm or leg. Unfortu-

nately, the degree of muscle atrophy after a CVA is not a completely reliable way to confirm muscle weakness. But if it is present, it argues in favor of the claimant's complaint of weakness.

Listing 11.05

Brain tumors:

A. Malignant gliomas (astrocytoma—grades III and IV, glioblastoma multiforme), medulloblastoma, ependymoblastoma, or primary sarcoma; OR

B. Astrocytoma (grades I and II), meningioma, pituitary tumors, oligodendroglioma, ependymoma, clivus chordoma, and benign tumors. Evaluate under Listings 11.02, 11.03, 11.04A or B, or 12.02.

I. General Considerations

A. This Listing deals with brain tumors.

B. Part A or Part B must be fulfilled, but not both.

II. Specific Requirements

A. Part A

1. Part A deals with brain tumors that are usually malignant (cancerous), and often result in death no matter what kind of treatment is given.

2. "Malignant gliomas" refers to what is called a glioblastoma multiforme. This is also called a grade III or IV astrocytoma. They are called astrocytomas, because they come from cells in the brain called astrocytes. It is important to understand what is meant by "grade III or IV". Astrocytomas can have cells that are only a "little" cancerous, or cells that are very cancerous. This is determined by studying the cells under a microscope, after a piece of the tumor has been removed during brain surgery. The least malignant types of astrocytomas are called "grade I" and the most malignant are called "grade IV". To qualify under Part A, the tumor must be either grade III or grade IV.

3. Other types of tumors that can qualify under Part A are given as "primary sarcoma", "medulloblastoma", "ependymoblastoma". These do not have to be graded on a scale of I–IV like the malignant gliomas discussed above. The diagnosis is made by studying a piece of the tumor removed during brain surgery.

4. If the claimant is not seen by a doctor, until the brain tumor is so advanced that brain surgery would do no good at all, there is not a piece of brain tumor to prove exactly what kind it is. Such a claimant would not be denied benefits, if all of the medical data argued very strongly that a malignant brain tumor were present.

5. If the claimant has any of the types of brain tumor listed, then he qualifies under Part A. No other information is required.

B. Part B

1. Part B deals with brain tumors that are either not as cancerous as those in Part A, or which are not cancerous at all. Note that grade I and grade II astrocytomas must be considered under Part B.

2. Part B lists several types of brain tumors, but any type will qualify, even if it is not listed. A "meningioma" is a tumor coming from the meninges, which is a protective covering over the brain. Although it is not in the brain itself, a meningioma can push into the brain as it grows. "Pituitary tumors" come from the pituitary gland at the base of the brain. "Oligodengrogliomas" are tumors that start in the brain itself from cells called oligodendrocytes. "Ependymomas" are tumors that start in the fluid-filled cavities of the brain called ventricles. Note that *ependymomas* are not malignant, whereas *ependymoblastomas* are cancerous and qualify under Part A. "Clivus chordomas" are very rare tumors arising from the back of the skull.

3. Because the tumors given under Part B are not as cancerous as those under Part A of the Listing, it is not sufficient simply to have such a tumor. So further evaluation is necessary. Depending on what kind of impairment is being caused by the brain tumor, the case would be further evaluated under Listings 11.02, 11.03, 11.04, or 12.02. The specific requirements of one of these other Listings must be fulfilled.

Listing 11.06

Parkinsonian syndrome. With the following signs: Significant rigidity, bradykinesia, or tremor in two extremities, which, singly or in combination, result in sustained disturbance of gross and dexterous movements, or gait and station.

I. General Considerations

A. This Listing deals with a disease of the brain which produces what is called the Parkinsonian syndrome, or Parkinson's Disease.

B. Parkinson's Disease is caused by a certain area of the brain ceasing to produce enough of a chemical called "dopamine" that is normally there. This impairs the ability of the claimant to control his muscles normally. Sometimes it can be effectively treated by giving artificial dopamine-like drugs.

C. If the Parkinsonism is being effectively treated with drugs, the claimant would *not* qualify under this Listing.

II. Specific Requirements

A. "Rigidity" is one thing that impairs claimants with Parkinsonism. This is an uncontrollable "tenseness" of muscles that makes them difficult to control. There is also a tendency to have tremors, especially of the arms and hands. These can interfere with the ability to use the hands. "Bradykinesia" refers to an abnormal slowness of movements.

B. If rigidity, tremors, or bradykinesia (or combination of all three) cause substantial impairment of the claimant's ability to walk, stand, or use the arms or hands, then the Listing can be fulfilled. *Two* extremities must be affected—both legs, both arms, or an arm and a leg. Whether the amount of impairment that any particular claimant has qualifies under the Listing is a matter of judgment on the part of the person in S. S. Disability reviewing the case, but it certainly has to be more than a slight amount. It does *not* have to be so severe that the claimant can't walk at all, or so severe that his arms and hands are totally useless.

Listing 11.07

Cerebral palsy. With:

A. IQ of 69 or less; OR

B. Abnormal behavior patterns, such as destructiveness or emotional instability; OR

C. Disorganization of motor function as described in Listing 11.04B.

I. General Considerations

A. This Listing deals with "Cerebral palsy".

B. Cerebral palsy is not really a specific disease, but refers to various degrees and types of brain damage present from a very early age, often from the time of birth.

II. Specific Requirements

A. Part A

1. Part A deals with mental retardation in claimants with cerebral palsy. It should be noted, however, that not everyone with cerebral palsy is mentally retarded.

2. To qualify under Part A, the claimant must have an I.Q. score that is no higher than 69. Not all types of I.Q. tests are acceptable to S. S. Disability. The one most often used is called the W.A.I.S., or "Wechsler Adult Intelligence Scale".

3. Some I.Q. tests, such as the W.A.I.S. have more than one score. S. S. Disability must use the *lowest* score from the test.

B. Part B

1. Part B deals with mental impairment that is supposedly related to some cases of cerebral palsy.

2. There must be "abnormal" behavior, such as "destructiveness" or "emotional instability". This requires a great deal of judgment by the person in S. S. Disability who is evaluating the claimant's file. Usually, all possible information is sought that might help in the decision. This includes medical reports, reports from psychologists, teachers, friends, employers, or anything else of that type that might be helpful.

C. Part C

1. Part C deals with impairment of seeing, hearing, or speaking caused by cerebral palsy.

2. Part C requires that the impairment "significantly" interfere with the claimant's communication with other people. The Listing does not give rules for how severe "significant" has to be. This leaves room for a great deal of judgment on the part of the person in S. S. Disability evaluating the case. The claimant would certainly have to show more than minor difficulty in communicating with others—enough that it interferes with normal activities

D. Part D

1. Part D deals with abnormalities in the ability to walk or use the arms and hands, caused by cerebral palsy.

2. No actual evaluation is done under Part D. The same requirements as for Listing 11.04, Part B would have to be fulfilled.

Listing 11.08

Spinal cord or nerve root lesions, due to any cause. With disorganization of motor function as described in Listing 11.04B.

I. General Considerations

A. This Listing deals with impairment from disease of the spinal cord or nerve roots.

B. The spinal cord is about the size of a pencil, running from the base of the skull to the lower back area. It is protected by the bony structure of the spine.

C. The spinal cord gives off pairs of nerves along it's length called "nerve roots". These nerves go to most areas of the body. Impulses travel down the spinal cord from the brain and out these nerves to allow movement of the body. Other impulses related to cold, touch, heat, pain, and body position travel through these nerves, up the spinal cord, and back to the brain.

D. Defects in the spinal cord itself, or the nerve roots, can clearly impair the ability of a claimant to move about. For example, there might be inability to feel anything in a leg or to move it. Certain kinds of diseases, trauma, bleeding in the spinal cord, or tumors can cause this kind of problem.

II. Specific Requirements

A. No actual evaluation of the severity of the impairment is done under this Listing. The impairment must qualify under the same criteria as given in Listing 11.04B.

B. See the discussion of Listing 11.04, Part B for more details.

Listing 11.09

Multiple sclerosis. With:

A. Disorganization of motor function as described in Listing 11.04B; OR

B. Visual or mental impairment as described under criteria in Listings 2.02, 2.03, 2.04, or 12.02.

I. General Considerations

A. This Listing deals with "multiple sclerosis".

B. Multiple sclerosis is a disease of the nervous system, the cause of which is not known.

C. What multiple sclerosis does to the person concerned depends on what part of their nervous system is involved at any particular time. It is an unpredictable disease, which tends to "flare-up", and then quiet down, leaving more damage each time. Sometimes it takes years to cause any severe impairment, and in other cases, it affects the claimant much more quickly and severely.

D. Part A or B must be fulfilled, but not both.

II. Specific Requirements

A. Part A

1. Part A deals with "disorganization of motor function", which means impairment of the claimant's ability to walk, or use their arms and hands effectively.

2. The actual evaluation is not done under Part A. The requirements are the same as those for Listing 11.04, Part B. More details can be found under the discussion of that Listing.

B. Part B

1. Part B deals with visual or mental impairments caused by multiple sclerosis.

2. Multiple sclerosis tends to damage the optic nerves to the eyes. If this is the problem, the impairment would be evaluated under Listings 2.03, 2.04, or 2.02, all of which deal with visual impairment. Further details are given in the discussion of those Listings. Their specific requirements must be fulfilled.

3. If the multiple sclerosis has caused some type of mental impairment, the case would be evaluated under Listing 12.02. The specific requirements of Listing 12.02 would have to be fulfilled.

Listing 11.10

Amyotrophic lateral sclerosis. With:

A. Significant bulbar signs; OR

B. Disorganization of motor function as described in Listing 11.04B.

I. General Considerations

A. This Listing deals with "amyotrophic lateral sclerosis", which is a rare disease of the nervous system, usually starting after age 50.

B. Impairment is caused by the gradual death of cells in the spinal cord. Increasing weakness gradually destroys even the ability to breathe, and it is always fatal.

C. Part A or B must be fulfilled, but not both.

II. Specific Requirements

A. Part A

1. Part A requires "significant bulbar signs".

2. Example of bulbar signs would be difficulty in speaking, swallowing or breathing.

B. Part B

1. Part B deals with "disorganization of motor function", which is the inability to walk, or use the arms and hands normally.

2. No actual evaluation is done under Part B. The impairment must fulfill the requirements for disorganization of motor function given under Listing 11.04, Part B. Further details can be found under the discussion of that Listing.

Listing 11.11

Anterior poliomyelitis. With:

A. Persistent difficulty with swallowing or breathing; OR

B. Unintelligible speech; OR

C. Disorganization of motor function as described in Listing 11.04B.

I. General Considerations

A. This Listing deals with "anterior poliomyelitis", more commonly known as "polio".

B. This nervous system disease is caused by a virus, and is fortunately rare in this country, because of vaccinations.

C. Most claimants applying for disability because of "polio" do not have the active disease. They usually have damage caused from having the disease in their childhood, before vaccines were available.

D. Parts A, B, or C must be fulfilled, but not all three.

II. Specific Requirements

A. Part A

1. Part A can be fulfilled, if there is significant difficulty with swallowing or breathing.

2. Note that the difficulty with swallowing or breathing has to be *persistent*, it cannot be a problem that comes and goes.

B. Part B

1. Part B is fulfilled if there is "unintelligible speech".

2. Note that "unintelligible" means other people must be unable to understand the claimant during normal conversation. The fact that friends or family might be able to understand the claimant after long practice would not prevent qualification under Part B.

C. Part C

1. "Disorganization of motor function" means impairment of the ability to walk normally, or to use the arms and hands normally.

2. No actual evaluation is done under Part C. The impairment must fulfill the specific requirements of Listing 11.04, Part B. Further details can be found under the discussion of that Listing.

Listing 11.12

Myasthenia gravis. With:

A. Significant difficulty with speaking, swallowing or breathing while on prescribed therapy; OR

B. Significant motor weakness of muscles of extremities on repetitive activity against resistance while on prescribed therapy.

I. General Considerations

A. This Listing deals with a disease of the nervous system called "myasthenia gravis".

B. When nerves activate muscles to move, the end of the nerve gives off a special chemical that is decreased in myasthenia gravis. Therefore, its main sign is weakness, which can affect any muscle in the body.

C. Sometimes, myasthenia gravis can be effectively treated with drugs.

D. Part A or Part B must be fulfilled, but not both.

II. Specific Requirements

A. Part A

1. Part A is fulfilled if there is significant difficulty in breathing, swallowing, or speaking.

2. The claimant *must* be under treatment to qualify.

B. Part B

1. Part B is fulfilled if there is significant weakness of the extremities—that is, arms or legs.

2. Note that this must be present on "repetitive activity against resistance". For example, if a doctor pulled against a claimant's arm, the claimant would get weaker and weaker the longer the claimant had to use the muscles in his arm.

3. Note that Part B *cannot* be fulfilled unless the claimant is under treatment by a medical doctor.

Listing 11.13

Muscular dystrophy. With disorganization of motor function as described in Listing 11.04B.

I. General Considerations

A. This Listing deals with "muscular dystrophy".

B. Muscular dystrophy is not one disease, but really refers to a whole group of diseases, which are often inherited.

C. All of the types of muscular dystrophy have in common the increasing weakness of muscles. Some tend to involve all the muscles in the body, while others tend to involve a certain group of muscles.

D. There is no known effective treatment.

II. Specific Requirements

A. "Disorganization of motor function" is required. In other words, there must be significant difficulty in walking, or using the arms and hands.

B. No actual evaluation is done under this Listing. The specific requirements are the same as those of Listing 11.04, Part B. Further details can be found in the discussion of that Listing.

Listing 11.14

Peripheral neuropathies. With disorganization of motor function as described in Listing 11.04B, in spite of prescribed treatment.

I. General Considerations

A. This Listing deals with "peripheral neuropathies". This simply means disease of the peripheral nerves.

B. The peripheral nerves are the nerves that the spinal cord gives off to the legs and arms. (Actually there are other nerves the spinal cord gives off which go to the internal organs, but this Listing is concerned with those that control the arms and legs.)

C. Many diseases can cause damage to the peripheral nerves, but one of the most common is diabetes mellitus. However, *any* such disease can qualify. Of course, the neuropathy must be more or less permanent. For example, a peripheral neuropathy caused by vitamin deficiency might be treatable with vitamins, and not be present long enough to qualify.

II. Specific Requirements

A. If there is any treatment that can be given for the type of peripheral neuropathy that the claimant has, he *must* be under treatment for it.

B. No actual evaluation is done under this Listing. The requirements are the same as the specific requirements given in Listing 11.04, Part B. Further details can be found in the discussion of that Listing.

Listing 11.15

Tabes dorsalis. With:

A. Tabetic crises occurring more frequently than once monthly; OR

B. Unsteady, broad-based or ataxic gait causing significant restriction of mobility substantiated by appropriate posterior column signs.

I. General Considerations

A. This Listing deals with "tabes dorsalis", which is syphilis of the spinal cord.

B. Since the spinal cord links the brain to the rest of the body, damage to the nerves in the spinal cord can cause substantial impairment.

C. Tabes dorsalis is not a common disease in this country. It usually doesn't occur, until untreated syphilis has been present many years.

D. Part A or B must be fulfilled, but not both.

II. Specific Requirements

A. Part A

1. A "tabetic crisis" is a painful episode of symptoms that may occur in a person with syphilis of the spinal cord.

2. Loss of coordination, difficulty in walking normally, pain in the arms, legs, or abdomen, vomiting, and visual difficulties are some of the more common symptoms.

3. Medical records must show that the claimant has episodes of tabetic crisis *more frequently* than once a month.

B. Part B

1. Part B deals with problems walking caused by tabes dorsalis.

2. "Ataxia" is a general term referring to unsteady, clumsy walking (gait). There is more than one form of ataxia, but one frequently seen in tabes dorsalis is an "unsteady, broad-based" gait. "Broad-based" simply means that the claimant walks with his feet wide apart to keep from falling.

3. "Appropriate posterior column signs" refers to special abnormalities of the nervous system that a doctor should be able to find on physical examination of the claimant, if tabes dorsalis is present. These abnormalities are far too complicated to discuss here in any detail, but S. S. Disability will look for them when reviewing the claimant's case. One such abnormality is loss of the ability to tell where the feet and legs are, without looking at them. A normal person can close their eyes and still know what position their feet or legs are in, and even walk with their eyes closed by means of this "position sense". But spinal cord damage from tabes dorsalis may result in loss of the "position sense". In that case, the claimant could only walk with his eyes open, to watch where his feet are going, and only clumsily at that. There might be difficulty in even standing still in one position with the eyes closed, so that the claimant would fall down if not caught by someone else.

Listing 11.16

Subacute combined cord degeneration (pernicious anemia). With disorganization of motor function as described in Listing 11.04B or 11.15B, not significantly improved by prescribed treatment.

I. General Considerations

A. "Subacute combined cord degeneration" refers to damage to the nerve pathways in the spinal cord, due to a deficiency of Vitamin B_{12}. Since the spinal cord carries nerve impulses back and forth between the brain and the rest of the body, this may cause difficulties in walking, or using the arms and hands.

B. The Listing also mentions "pernicious anemia". This is just one disease associated with a deficiency of Vitamin B_{12}. The Listing is not interested in anemia (deficiency of red blood cells); the important consideration is whether or not there has been spinal cord damage from not having enough Vitamin B_{12}. If the claimant also had severe anemia from the Vitamin B_{12} deficiency, the anemia would be evaluated under Listing 7.02, which deals with anemia.

II. Specific Requirements

A. "Disorganization of motor function" means difficulty in walking or using the arms and hands caused by spinal cord damage from Vitamin B_{12} deficiency. The actual evaluation is done under either Listing 11.04, Part B or under Listing 11.15, Part B. The specific requirements of Part B of one of these other Listings must be fulfilled. Further details can be found in the discussion of those Listings.

B. Since the spinal cord damage caused by a deficiency of Vitamin B_{12} can sometimes be improved by giving the claimant Vitamin B_{12}, the claimant *must* be under such treatment by a medical doctor. Only in this way can S. S. Disability be sure that the damage is permanent.

Listing 11.17

Degenerative disease not listed elsewhere, such as Huntington's chorea, Friedreich's ataxia, and spinocerebellar degeneration. With:

A. Disorganization of motor function as described in Listing 11.04B or 11.15B; OR

B. Chronic brain syndrome. Evaluate under Listing 12.02.

I. General Considerations

A. This Listing deals with "degenerative diseases" of the spinal cord or brain. Examples are given as "Huntington's chorea", "Friedreich's ataxia", and "spinocerebellar degeneration", but other kinds could qualify.

B. All of these diseases are at least partly inherited and cause degeneration (death) of nerve cells in the spinal cord or brain. There is no treatment for any of them.

C. In addition to having one of these diseases, either Part A or Part B must be fulfilled.

II. Specific Requirements

A. Part A

1. Part A deals with "disorganization of motor function". This simply means difficulty in walking or using the arms and hands.

2. No actual evaluation is done under Part A. The impairment must fulfill the same specific requirements as those given under Listing 11.04, Part B or under Listing 11.15, Part B. Further details can be found in the discussion of those Listings.

B. Part B

1. Part B deals with "chronic brain syndrome" caused by one of these diseases. This simply means physical damage to the brain producing mental impairment.

2. No actual evaluation is done under Part B. If a chronic brain syndrome is present, it is evaluated under Listing 12.02 and must fulfill the requirements of that Listing. Further details can be found under the discussion of Listing 12.02.

Listing 11.18

Cerebral trauma. Evaluate under the provisions of Listings 11.02, 11.03, 11.04, and 12.02, as applicable.

I. General Considerations

A. Brain trauma is the subject of this Listing.

B. Some of the most frequent causes of brain trauma are accidents in motorcycles or automobiles, when seat harnesses are not being worn. But S. S. Disability is more interested in the result than the cause.

II. Specific Requirements

Depending on what type of brain damage occurs, the case would be evaluated under Listing 11.02, 11.03, 11.04, or 12.02. The requirements of one of those Listings must be fulfilled.

Listing 11.19

Syringomyelia. With:

A. Significant bulbar signs; OR

B. Disorganization of motor function as described in Listing 11.04B.

I. General Considerations

A. This Listing deals with a disease of the nervous system called "syringomyelia", the cause of which is not known. There is no effective treatment.

B. In syringomyelia, fluid-filled cavities start forming and growing in the spinal cord or lower part of the brain. These cavities destroy nerve tissue as they grow.

C. Part A or Part B must be fulfilled, but not both.

II. Specific Requirements

A. Part A

1. Part A is fulfilled if there are "significant bulbar signs". Examples of significant bulbar signs would be difficulty in swallowing, breathing, or speaking.

2. Note that "significant" means that more than just a minor problem must be present.

B. Part B

1. Part B deals with "disorganization of motor function". This means difficulty in walking, or using the arms and hands.

2. No actual evaluation is done under Part B. The impairment must fulfill the specific requirements given under Listing 11.04, Part B. Further details can be found under the discussion of that Listing.

§ 2.13 Mental Disorders

Author's Note:

Before beginning a discussion of the Listings on mental disorders, it is important to know that special policy rules apply to all psychotic disorders involving Listing 12.03. All claimants already receiving benefits which were placed on disability for meeting Listing 12.03 will automatically continue receiving benefits regardless of their current mental condition, and regardless of whether they truly fulfilled Listing 12.03 at the time of original allowance. Under current policy, no such case should be terminated from the disability rolls. How long this policy will last or in what way it may be modified in the future by the Social Security Administration is unknown. This is a "stop-gap" measure to protect claimants from disability termination, while S. S. Disability re-evaluates the appropriateness of the mental impairment Listings in general.

Listing 12.02

Chronic brain syndromes (organic brain syndromes). With both A and B:

A. Demonstrated deterioration in intellectual functioning, manifested by persistence of one or more of the following clinical signs:

1. Marked memory defect for recent events; OR
2. Impoverished, slowed, perseverative thinking, with confusion or disorientation; OR
3. Labile, shallow, or coarse affect;

B. Resulting persistence of marked restriction of daily activities and constriction of interests and deterioration in personal habits and seriously impaired ability to relate to other people.

I. General Considerations

A. This Listing deals with "chronic brain syndromes". These are also known as "organic brain syndromes".

B. An organic brain syndrome can result from any disease affecting the brain *physically* which is severe enough to produce mental effects. Damage done to the brain because of trauma (accidents, acts of violence such as gunshot wounds to the brain, etc.) can also cause an organic brain syndrome, as well as infection and other diseases.

C. Although it is possible to have a temporary organic brain syndrome, S. S. Disability is interested in the cases in which permanent damage has been done to the brain.

D. Note that this Listing deals with *mental* problems caused by brain damage, not physical problems such as paralysis which would be considered under Listing 11.18.

E. A claimant cannot fulfill this Listing simply by being in a hospital or nursing home.

F. *Both* Part A and Part B must be fulfilled.

II. Specific Requirements

A. Part A

1. Part A deals with decrease in intelligence caused by an organic brain syndrome.

2. S. S. Disability may use or order I.Q. testing to evaluate a particular case, but this is not absolutely necessary. What is definitely needed are "clinical signs" of severe problems in thinking on the part of the claimant. This means abnormalities noted by a medical doctor. Sometimes this is the treating doctor, and in other cases S. S. Disability may send the claimant to a psychiatrist for evaluation. The psychiatrist would then do what is called a "mental status" examination which involves the claimant's ability to think normally. Several things looked for would be memory impairment, emotional problems, etc. Specifically, A.1, A.2, or A.3 must be fulfilled as follows:

(a) Part A.1 requires that the claimant have a severe memory loss, even for recent events. For example, does the claimant know any recent news? Does he remember how he got to the doctor's office? Can he remember things he did earlier in the day? Can he remember even for a few minutes things that the doctor asks him to remember?

(b) Part A.2 can be fulfilled if several things are present. "Impoverished" thinking means that the claimant doesn't think as much as a normal person, and thoughts are much simpler. Thinking may also be slowed down, so that it takes the claimant much longer than normal to even answer a simple question. "Perseverative thinking" is thinking in which the claimant repeats the same thoughts over and over. "Confusion and disorientation" refers to whether or not the claimant knows what is going on around him, or even who he is, where he is, and the date.

(c) Part A.3 requires "labile, shallow, or coarse affect". "Labile" emotions are emotions that are abnormal because they change more quickly than a normal person's, and may not have any real relation to what is going on around them. "Shallow and coarse affect" refers to emotions that are more simple and child-like than would be expected of an adult.

B. Part B

1. Part A of the Listing considered what the claimant's *thinking* is supposedly like, and this leaves a lot of room for error. Part B tries to make the evaluation more accurate by considering what a claimant *does*. If the claimant is really as "bad off" as Part A would suggest, then his behavior should also be abnormal.

2. S. S. Disability uses various ways to find out about the claimant's behavior. Information is sought from the treating doctor. If the claimant applied for disability in person at the District Office, the officials there would also make notes about how the claimant acted. S. S. Disability may call the wife or husband, the claimant, or other people who know the claimant well. In addition, when the claimant fills out his application for disability there are blanks on the form asking him what kinds of things he does and what interests him. This information is also used.

3. Specifically, things that S. S. Disability looks for in regard to Part B are as follows:

(a) "Marked restriction of daily activities . . ."—if the claimant has a severe organic brain syndrome, he will only be able to do simple things. If he does things that a normal person would do, then his impairment may not really be very severe. Questions asked would be things like: "Does the claimant do this?" "Does he go shopping or to other places without needing anyone with him?" "Does he do repair works around the house, and if so, how complicated is it?" "Does the claimant take care of children, if there are any?" "Does the claimant do housework, such as cooking and cleaning?" These are only a few examples of the questions that might be asked, and would of course be different for different claimants and for men and women. A person with a severe organic brain syndrome doesn't do much of anything, and that is what S. S. Disability wants to find out. Simple things not requiring much thinking like watching television would not keep the claimant from qualifying under Part B.

(b) "Constriction of interests" should be present. Questions asked would be things like: "What kind of hobbies or other special interests did the claimant have in the past? Is he still capable of doing any of these things?" For example, if the claimant had a hobby of repairing radios or television sets and could still do that, S. S. Disability might conclude that the claimant is still capable to do quite a lot. Such things are much more complicated for someone with a severe organic brain syndrome. A claimant with a severe organic brain syndrome is not interested in anything very complicated. Such a claimant has lost the ability to be interested in very many things.

(c) "Deterioration in personal habits" is frequently seen in claimants with severe organic brain syndromes. This involves the loss of abilities that relate to personal cleanliness, such as bathing, changing dirty clothes, etc.

(d) "Seriously impaired ability to relate to other people" means that a claimant with a severe organic brain syndrome has lost social abilities such as talking to other people meaningfully, interested in other people, or the ability to get along with other people in socially acceptable ways.

Listing 12.03

Functional psychotic disorders (mood disorders, schizophrenias, paranoid states). With both A and B:

A. Manifested persistence of one or more of the following clinical signs:

1. Depression (or elation); OR
2. Agitation; OR
3. Psychomotor disturbances; OR
4. Hallucinations or delusions; OR
5. Autistic or other regressive behavior; OR
6. Inappropriateness of affect; OR
7. Illogical association of ideas;

B. Resulting persistence of marked restriction of daily activities and constriction of interests and seriously impaired ability to relate to other people.

I. General Considerations

A. This Listing deals with *psychotic* disorders of the mind. Schizophrenia is the most frequent type seen by S. S. Disability.

Actually, there many types of psychotic disorders, and any of them may qualify.

B. Many claimants allege disability because their "nerves" bother them. Most of these claimants do not have the serious mental illness that this Listing requires.

C. A psychosis is a very serious mental disorder, but regardless of the type a claimant has, they all show certain things in common which are necessary to qualify under this Listing. It is important to note that it is *not* enough for a claimant's treating doctor (even if he is a psychiatrist) to merely say that the claimant is too mentally ill to work. S. S. Disability requires hard facts to back up such an allegation.

D. Specific abnormalities must be present which fulfill *both* Part A and Part B.

II. Specific Requirements

A. Part A

1. Part A deals with abnormalities in the claimant's *thinking* that would indicate a severe psychosis to be present. This requires evaluation by a psychologist or psychiatrist called a *mental status examination.* This can come from a treating psychologist or psychiatrist, or S. S. Disability may send the claimant to see one. Note that the abnormalities must be *persistent.* That is, the abnormality considered must be present more or less continously.

2. If the mental status examination shows any *one* of the following abnormalities, then Part A can be fulfilled:

(a) Part A.1 requires "depression" or "elation". In simple terms, depression means feeling "hopeless", "worthless", "down and out", "blue", etc. Even if the word is hard to define, most people know what it means to be depressed. But feeling abnormally "elated" and "high" can also be the result of psychosis. It should be noted, that the little bit of depression and elation that normal people feel does not qualify here. The abnormalities must be severe.

(b) Part A.2 requires "agitation". This means very severe anxiety in which the claimant cannot control the anxiousness that he feels. The minor nervousness that normal people feel would not qualify here.

(c) Part A.3 requires "psychomotor disturbances". A claimant with a severe psychotic depression will think and move very slowly. One with severe elation will be jumpy and have thoughts that "run away from them".

(d) Part A.4 requires "hallucinations" *or* "delusions". A hallucination is a mental abnormality involving sensing something that is not real. For example, if a claimant sees an animal that is not really present then he has had a visual hallucination. But hallucinations can involve any sense. For example, hearing voices from people who are not real is auditory hallucination. This is common in schizophrenia. Hallucinations can also involve smelling, tasting, and touch. A "delusion" is a false belief. For example, if a claimant believes that certain people, organizations are out to get him, and all this is really not true, then he suffers from a delusion. This is common in people with paranoia, such as the paranoid form of schizophrenia. However, any type of false belief is a delusion. Even normal people have delusions, but the ones considered here are very severe.

(e) Part A.5 deals with "autistic or other regressive behavior". Autistic behavior involves the claimant cutting himself off from the world and other people around him. For example, he may stay to himself, and not talk to anyone. Regressive behavior means going back to more childlike level of behavior, instead of that of an adult.

(f) Part A.6 requires "inappropriateness of affect". This means experiencing emotions that a normal person wouldn't feel in the same situation. For example, if a claimant felt sad about something that would normally make someone feel happy, then that would be inappropriate affect, or an abnormal emotion.

(g) Part A.7 deals with "illogical association of ideas". This means difficulty in thinking logically. Of course, all normal people have trouble thinking logically at times, but Part A.7 requires that this be very severe. Such thinking would not "make any sense" to normal people.

B. Part B

1. While Part A deals with how a claimant *thinks*, Part B looks at what kinds of things the claimant *does*. If the claimant's thinking is abnormal from severe mental illness, then his behavior should also be abnormal.

2. Except for "deterioration in personal habits", Part B requires the same kind of information as Part B of Listing 12.02. Further details can be found in the discussion of Part B of Listing 12.02.

Listing 12.04

Functional nonpsychotic disorders (psychophysiologic, neurotic, and personality disorders; addictive dependence on alcohol or drugs). With both A and B:

A. Manifested persistence of one or more of the following clinical signs:

1. Demonstrable and persistent structural changes mediated through psychophysiological channels (e.g., duodenal ulcer); OR

2. Recurrent and persistent periods of anxiety, with tension, apprehension, and interference with concentration and memory; OR

3. Persistent depressive affect with insomnia, loss of weight, and suicidal preoccupation; OR

4. Persistent phobic or obsessive ruminations with inappropriate, bizarre, or disruptive behavior; OR

5. Persistent compulsive, ritualistic behavior; OR

6. Persistent functional disturbance of vision, speech, hearing, or use of a limb with demonstrable structural or trophic changes; OR

7. Persistent, deeply ingrained, maladaptive patterns of behavior manifested by either:

a. Seclusiveness or autistic thinking; OR

b. Pathologically inappropriated suspiciousness or hostility;

B. Resulting persistence of marked restriction of daily activities and constriction of interests and deterioration in personal habits and seriously impaired ability to relate to other people.

I. General Considerations

A. This Listing deals with mental disorder which do not involve psychosis. These disorders do not involve as much confusion concerning what is real and unreal, as the psychotic disorders evaluated under Listing 12.03. But they can still cause severe impairments.

B. Whatever kind of mental disorder is involved, it must be *persistent*. That is, it must produce an impairment that is more or less continously present.

C. Specific requirements are given under Part A and Part B, *both* of which must be fulfilled.

II. Specific Requirements

A. Part A

1. Part A can be fulfilled by a variety of abnormalities, numbered A.1 through A.7. These abnormalities must be observed by a doctor or other professionals trained in evaluating mental illness. Part A.1 and A.6 involve physical illness also, and informations regarding these would have to come from a doctor.

2. If any *one* of the following abnormalities is present, then Part A can be fulfilled:

(a) Part A.1 deals with "psychophysiologic disorders". This means disorders to the body caused by the mind. Actually, all illness is "psychophysiologic" to some degree, in which the mind and body are both involved. But A.2 deals with serious physical problems that supposedly would not exist, without a mental problem to cause them. A common example is a claimant who keeps developing ulcers of the small intestine that can reasonably be related to a mental disorder such as excessive nervousness. Note that the claimant would need a "persistent" (continuous) problem.

(b) Part A.2 is fulfilled if there is such persistent nervousness of such severe degree that the ability to concentrate and remember things is significantly impaired.

(c) Part A.3 deals with persistent depression. The depression must be severe enough to cause loss of sleep ("insomnia"), weight loss (due to decreased appetite), and thoughts of suicide that the claimant takes seriously. S. S. Disability takes suicidal potential in claimants very seriously, since there have been a few cases of suicide by claimants following termination of benefits. The unfortunate fact is that even physicians treating patients who are depressed have a difficult time predicting whether they will or will not commit suicide. S. S. Disability tries to study all relevant data regarding a claimant's suicide potential, although it is subject to great uncertainty. Variables such as age, sex, employment status, marital status, and previous suicide attempts are important. A suicide threat alone, in the absence of evidence of significant mental illness is not likely to be carried out, and S. S. Disability cannot be placed in a position where that threat alone means the granting of disability benefits.

(d) Part A.4 refers to persistent abnormal fears (phobias), obsessions (abnormal concerns with just about anything), or extremely abnormal behavior. Note that it wouldn't be enough for a claimant merely to take illegal drugs, or alcohol, or pick fights with other people, *unless* these things were due to mental illness.

(e) Part A.5 is fulfilled by persistent "compulsive, ritualistic behavior". This means doing things over and over again without any good reason, as if "compelled" by the mental illness. An example would be a claimant continuously worried about keeping his hands clean, and washes them fifty times a day.

(f) Part A.6 refers to persistent difficulty in seeing, hearing, or speaking which is "functional". This means that there is no physical reason for difficulty in doing one of these things. For example, a claimant who states that he is blind, but who has nothing wrong with his eyes or brain, would fall into this category. Note that it is not enough for a claimant to say that he can't see, or hear, or talk. Anyone can say that. The problem must be caused by mental illness. Part A.6 can also be fulfilled if there is difficulty in using an arm or leg, if this is not due to physical illness. It is easy to tell if a claimant really hasn't been using an arm or leg due to mental illness. The muscles in even a normal arm or leg will get smaller if they are not being used. Changes will also occur in the skin, tendons, and ligaments that will prevent normal movement. In other words, not using an arm or leg because of mental illness will eventually produce physical damage to that limb. These abnormalities can be seen on examination by a doctor.

(g) Part A.7 requires persistent and very abnormal behavior shown by one of the two different ways:

(1) "Seclusiveness or autistic thinking. . .". This means a very abnormal lack of interest in things happening around the claimant, and thoughts that don't involve the real world or other people. Such a claimant would live continously in a state of "withdrawal into himself", and would have difficulty in even communicating with another person in any normal way.

(2) "Pathologically inappropriate suspiciousness or hostility" refers to extremely abnormal anger and suspicion of other people—in other words, "paranoia".

B. Part B

1. While Part A deals with some of the abnormalities that must be fulfilled to qualify under this Listing, the specific requirements of Part B must also be present.

2. Part B of this Listing has exactly the same requirements as Part B of Listing 12.02. Further details can be found in the discussion of Part B of Listing 12.02.

Listing 12.05

Mental retardation. As manifested by:

A. Severe mental and social incapacity as evidenced by marked dependence upon others for personal needs (e.g., bathing, washing, dressing, etc.) and inability to understand the spoken word and inability to avoid physical danger (fire, cars, etc.) and inability to follow simple directions and inability to read, write, and perform simple calculations; OR

B. I.Q. of 59 or less;

C. I.Q. of 60 to 69 inclusive and a physical or other mental impairment imposing additional and significant work related limitation of function.

I. General Considerations

A. This Listing deals with mental retardation, or abnormally low intelligence.

B. The cause of the mental retardation is not important. It could be caused by some accident to the brain, a disease affecting the brain, or present from birth.

C. Part A or Part B must be fulfilled, but not both.

II. Specific Requirements

A. Part A

1. Part A refers to claimants who are so severely mentally retarded that testing of their I.Q. could not even be done accurately.

2. A claimant who is that retarded must be unable to take care of even their basic personal needs, such as bathing, dressing, etc. The claimant must be unable to understand things said to him by other people, unable to follow even simple directions (such as "put on your shoes, open the door, and go outside."), and even unable to avoid physical danger such as cars, etc. In

addition, the claimant must be unable to read, write, or do simple calculations such as adding two small numbers together.

3. From the above, it should be clear that the claimant must have very severe mental retardation to fulfill Part A. Most such claimants are in mental institutions where someone can take care of them. A few live with their families. It should be noted that just because a claimant is in an institution for the mentally retarded, this is not enough in itself to qualify under Part A. S. S. Disability would still get details about the claimant's life from the treating doctor, nurses, etc.

B. Part B

1. Part B deals with claimants that are not quite as retarded as those in Part A. For that reason, S. S. Disability expects to be able to measure the claimant's I.Q. accurately with I.Q. testing.

2. Not any kind of I.Q. test is acceptable. It must be a well recognized I.Q. test, such as the W.A.I.S. (Wechsler Adult Intelligence Scale).

3. The I.Q. tests must be someone qualified to give such tests, such as a psychologist or psychiatrist.

4. The claimant must make a reasonable effect to do his best in the I.Q. test. If not, the test would be considered as not accurate. In addition, if an I.Q. test was given during a severe mental illness, it would not be considered accurate.

5. If the I.Q. test has more than one score, then S. S. Disability will require all of the scores. For example, the W.A.I.S. has a "performance" score, a "verbal" score, and a "full-scale" score.

6. If there is more than one score on a test, S. S. Disability must take the *lowest* score.

7. If the lowest I.Q. score is not higher than 59, then the claimant qualifies under Part B.

C. Part C

1. Comments about I.Q. tests discussed under Part B also apply to Part C.

2. Part C only requires that the lowest I.Q. score not be higher than 69, but there is the additional requirement that the claimant also have some mental or physical illness that would also decrease his ability to work. This additional impairment can be just about anything, as long as it is severe enough to significantly affect the claimant's ability to work. For example, a claimant with an I.Q. of 63 and arthritis in one of his knees

might qualify, if the arthritis is more than minor. There are many possibilities.

§ 2.14 Neoplastic Disease—Malignant

Author's Note:

* All of the following Listings deal with cancer. With rare exceptions, cancer is diagnosed by biopsy. That is, a piece of the suspected abnormal tissue is taken and carefully examined, especially under a microscope. This is done by specialists in medicine called *pathologists*. A biopsy and examination by a pathologist is the only really reliable way to tell if a piece of tissue is cancerous, or what kind of cancer is present. It is very important that S. S. Disability be able to get the pathology report showing that cancer is present. ** In the Listings that follow, it is emphasized that certain Parts cannot be fulfilled longer than 3 years without evidence of persistent or recurrent cancer. Actually, this general rule applies to *all* forms of cancer under *all* conditions: a claimant who has been without any evidence of cancer for 3 years or longer cannot qualify under any of the Listings dealing with cancer. This is the *longest* period that can be given without evidence of recurrent cancer. If there is recurrence, the assumed period of disability would again be 3 years, starting from the date the cancer re-appeared. In some instances, where allowance is based on lack of control by prescribed therapy, the impairment may cease to be an allowance as soon as control is achieved by treatment. This could be much less than 3 years. Of course, if a claimant has had no evidence of cancer for 3 years, it would be useless to apply for disability on the basis of cancer, although residual remaining impairment from the cancer and/or treatment might be of some importance in obtaining benefits.

Listings in which the claimant qualifies for benefits for 3 years from the time of onset in cases of cancer are as follows: 11.05A, 13.02D, 13.03A, 13.05B, 13.07, 13.09A, 13.09B, 13.09C, 13.09D, 13.09E, 13.10B, 13.11A, 13.11B, 13.11C, 13.11D, 13.11E, 13.11F, 13.12A, 13.13A, 13.13B, 13.13C, 13.13D, 13.13E, 13.14A, 13.14B, 13.15A, 13.15C, 13.16A, 13.16B, 13.16C, 13.16E, 13.16F, 13.17A, 13.17B, 13.18A, 13.18B, 13.18C, 13.19A, 13.19B, 13.19C, 13.20A, 13.20B, 13.21A, 13.21B, 13.22A, 13.22B, 13.22C, 13.22D, 13.24A, 13.25A, 13.25B, 13.25C, 13.26A, 13.26B, 13.26C, 13.26D, 13.28. Medical policy regarding exactly which cases fall under this "3 year rule" is not completely clear. This is the author's best estimation of its meaning.

Listing 13.02

Head and neck (except salivary glands—Listing 13.07, thyroid glands—Listing 13.08, and mandible, maxilla, orbit, or temporal fossa—Listing 13.11):

A. Inoperable; OR

B. Not controlled by prescribed therapy; OR

C. Recurrent after radical surgery or irradiation; OR

D. With distant metastasis; OR

E. Epidermoid carcinoma occurring in the pyriform sinus or posterior third of the tongue.

I. General Considerations

A. This Listing deals with cancer of the head and neck areas.

B. There are several forms of cancer of the head and neck that are *not* evaluated under this Listing. Cancer of the salivary glands is evaluated under Listing 13.07. Cancer of the thyroid gland is evaluated under Listing 13.08. Cancer involving certain bones of the skull is evaluated under Listing 13.11.

C. For this Listing, it does not matter exactly what type of cancer of the head or neck is present.

D. Part A, B, C, D, or E must be fulfilled, but not all five.

II. Specific Requirements

A. Part A

1. Part A can be fulfilled if the cancer is "inoperable". This means cancer which cannot be removed by surgery.

2. A further important fact should be noted in regard to surgery. "Inoperable" means that a reasonable chance of curing the cancer is not to be expected by surgery. So if a particular doctor does surgery, but the surgery is not likely to help much, then the cancer would still be considered "inoperable" and the claimant could still qualify under Part A. For example, some cancer surgery is done just to make the claimant feel better (palliative surgery), not to cure the cancer.

B. Part B

1. Part B requires cancer "not controlled by prescribed therapy". What type of therapy is used for any given cancer depends on the type of cancer, exactly where it is, and how far it has spread. Other illnesses and the individual desires of the patient must also be taken into account.

2. In trying to determine whether the cancer is controlled by prescribed therapy, S. S. Disability gets all the information that is available and then reaches what is considered a reasonable decision. Treatment might be radiation, drugs, surgery or all three.

C. Part C

1. Part C refers to cancer that comes back, after it has already been treated.

2. The previous treatment must have been either radiation, or "radical surgery". Radical Surgery is very extensive surgery.

3. The claimant can still qualify under Part C, even if the cancer that comes back is successfully treated a second time.

D. Part D

1. Part D is fulfilled, if there is "distant metastasis" of the cancer. Metastasis means spread of the cancer from where it started to somewhere else in the body. Distant metastasis means that it has spread so far that it cannot be removed by surgery.

2. The Listing assumes that if distant metastasis of the cancer is present, then the claimant's chances of living very long are not good. However, this is not always true, and some claimants with distant metastasis might actually be cured. If that happens, and it has been at least 3 years since there was any evidence of cancer, the claimant would *not* qualify under this Listing.

E. Part E

1. Part E deals with a particular kind of cancer called "epidermoid carcinoma", a frequent kind of cancer occurring in the head and neck areas. It is also called "squamous cell carcinoma".

2. If such cancer occurs in a place called the pyriform sinus, or in the back 1/3 of the tongue, then the claimant automatically qualifies under Part E. It does not matter what kind of treatment has been given.

Listing 13.03

Sarcoma of skin:

A. Angiosarcoma with metastasis to regional lymph nodes or beyond; OR

B. Mycosis fungoides with lymph node or visceral involvement.

I. General Considerations

A. This Listing deals with certain types of cancer involving the skin called "sarcomas".

B. It should be emphasized that most skin cancer does not fall into this category. Most skin cancer is of a type that affects probably 50% of people at some time in their lives, but can be easily cured if medical treatment is sought early enough. These occur in later life, after excessive exposure to sunlight in many cases. The sarcomas considered by this Listing are much more serious.

C. Part A or B must be fulfilled, but not both.

D. There must be a pathology report showing the cancer to be present.

II. Specific Requirements

A. Part A

1 Part A deals with a type of sarcoma called "angiosarcoma", which is a type of cancerous growth involving blood vessels in the skin.

2. "Regional lymph nodes" refers to a local group of lymph nodes that drain lymphatic fluid from the area concerned. If the cancer is found in even one of these lymph nodes, the claimant qualifies under Part A. Of course, this also applies if the cancer has spread anywhere in the body farther away than the regional lymph nodes.

3. There is one possible exception to the Listing. If the claimant has been free of cancer of at least 3 years before applying for disability, he would probably be considered cured and *not* qualify under Part A.

B. Part B

1. Part B deals with a rare and cancerous skin disease called "mycosis fungoides".

2. Part B is fulfilled if the disease has spread to any lymph nodes (even one), or to any other organs in the body.

3. But, if by some stroke of uncommonly good luck, the claimant had no evidence of the disease for 3 years, S. S. Disability would consider him cured, and he would not qualify under Part B. This is not very likely.

Listing 13.04

Sarcoma of soft parts: Not controlled by prescribed therapy.

I. General Considerations

A. "Sarcoma" is not a specific form of cancer. It is a word referring to any one of a large group of possible cancer called sarcoma. Usually, these are malignancies of muscle, blood vessels, bone, or connective tissue. For example, rhabdomyosarcoma is a form of muscle cancer, angiosarcoma is a blood vessel cancer, osteosarcoma is a form of bone cancer, and chondrosarcoma is cancer of the cartilages.

B. S. S. Disability must be able to obtain a pathology report showing the type of sarcoma present.

II. Specific Requirements

A. "Soft parts" means anything other than bone.

B. The claimant must be under treatment, and medical records must show that the therapy is not controlling the cancer.

Listing 13.05

Malignant melanoma:

A. recurrent after wide excision; OR

B. With metastasis to adjacent skin (satellite lesions) or elsewhere.

I. General Considerations

A. This Listing deals with a very malignant form of cancer that usually starts in the skin, called "malignant melanoma". (More rarely, it can start in the eye or pineal gland of the brain.)

B. Malignant melanoma is a very dangerous form of cancer that is often fatal. It is extremely difficult to treat, unless caught so early that it is completely removed by surgery. Otherwise, it can rapidly spread from a small place on the skin to every area of the body.

C. There must be a pathology report showing the diagnosis of malignant melanoma to be correct.

D. Part A or B must be fulfilled, but not both.

II. Specific Requirements

A. Part A

1. If a surgeon thinks the melanoma has been found early enough, surgery may be attempted, if it is thought that all of the cancer can be removed. In this case, a wide area of skin is removed around the cancer in the hope that it can be eliminated. This is what is meant by "wide excision", and the hope is that it will actually cure the cancer.

2. After a wide excision is done, if the cancer comes back anywhere in the body, then the surgery didn't cure the cancer and Part A is fulfilled.

B. Part B

1. If the malignancy has spread anywhere at all to other places in the body, then Part B is fulfilled. This is true, even if the cancer is detected only in other areas of skin where the original cancer started ("satellite lesions").

2. But if by some chance a claimant with malignant melanoma was so effectively treated that there was no evidence of cancer for at least 3 years, S. S. Disability would consider a cure to have taken place, and the claimant would not qualify under Part B.

Listing 13.06

Lymph nodes:

A. Hodgkin's disease or non-Hodgkin's lymphoma with progressive disease not controlled by prescribed therapy; OR

B. Metastatic carcinoma in a lymph node (except for epidermoid carcinoma in a lymph node in the neck) where the primary site is not determined after adequate search; OR

C. Epidermoid carcinoma in a lymph node in the neck not responding to prescribed therapy.

I. General Considerations

A. This Listing deals with cancer in the lymph nodes. Lymph nodes are small pieces of tissue throughout the body which play an important part in the immune system necessary for combating infection.

B. Some forms of cancer start in the lymph nodes themselves, while in other cases the lymph nodes pick up malignant cells from somewhere else in the body. Usually, it is not easy to even feel lymph nodes on a physical examination. But those that are involved with cancer may get quite large and hard.

C. S. S. Disability must be able to get a pathology report showing the kind of cancer present.

D. Part A, B, or C must be fulfilled, but not all three.

II. Specific Requirements

A. Part A

1. Part A deals with any of several possible cancers that begin in lymph nodes called "lymphomas". One particular type is called "Hodgkin's disease".

2. The malignant lymphoma must be getting *worse* at the time the claimant applies for disability.

3. The claimant must be getting worse, even though treatment is being received.

B. Part B

1. Part B deals with "metastatic carcinoma in a lymph node". This means malignant carcinoma cells have been caught in lymph nodes, rather than starting there. There are several types of cancer which would fall into the category of "carcinoma".

2. Note that the origin of the cancer must be *unknown,* even after a reasonable search has been made to find it. Not being able to find the origin of the cancer makes it very difficult to treat. The one exception is if the lymph node with cancer is in the neck, and the cancer is a type called epidermoid carcinoma. In this case, the origin of the cancer will be easier to find because it will have to be somewhere in the head and neck area.

3. Also, if a claimant has been so successfully treated that there has been no evidence of cancer for 3 years, before applying for disability, the claimant will not qualify under this Listing. This is not likely to happen, if the origin of the cancer cannot be found.

C. Part C

1. Part C deals with a form of cancer called "epidermoid carcinoma" found in a lymph node in the neck. (This form of cancer doesn't start in lymph nodes, but must come from somewhere else.)

2. The cancer must not respond to treatment.

3. If a claimant were so successfully treated that there was no evidence of cancer for at least 3 years before applying for disability, it would be assumed that cure has taken place and the claimant would no longer qualify under this Listing.

Listing 13.07

Salivary glands. Carcinoma or sarcoma with metastasis beyond the regional lymph nodes.

I. General Considerations

A. This Listing deals with cancer of the salivary glands.

B. S. S. Disability must be able to get a pathology report to show the type of cancer present.

II. Specific Requirements

A. The cancer must be of a "carcinoma" or "sarcoma" type that starts in the salivary glands (one of the glands in the mouth that produces saliva).

B. "Metastasis beyond the regional lymph nodes" means that the cancer has spread far enough to other parts of the body that it cannot all be removed with surgery.

C. However, if a claimant has gone as long as 3 years without evidence of the cancer (treated successfully), then he would be considered cured and not qualify under this Listing.

Listing 13.08

Thyroid gland. Carcinoma with metastasis beyond the regional lymph nodes, not controlled by prescribed therapy.

I. General Considerations

A. This Listing deals with cancer of the thyroid gland, which is located in the front of the neck.

B. Thyroid cancer can often be controlled with treatment, but there are exceptions.

C. S. S. Disability must be able to get a pathology report showing some type of thyroid cancer is present.

II. Specific Requirements

A. There must be "metastasis beyond the regional lymph nodes". In other words there must be evidence that the cancer has spread far enough to other parts of the body that it cannot be removed completely with surgery.

B. The claimant must have the cancer, even though he is under treatment. That is, the treatment must be failing. If the claimant is not under treatment, S. S. Disability has no way of knowing whether the cancer can be controlled or not.

Listing 13.09

Breast:

A. Inoperable carcinoma; OR

B. Inflammatory carcinoma; OR

C. Recurrent carcinoma, except local recurrence controlled by prescribed therapy; OR

D. Distant metastasis from breast carcinoma (bilateral breast carcinoma, synchronous or metachronous, is usually primary in each breast); OR

E. Sarcoma with metastasis anywhere.

I. General Considerations

A. This Listing deals with cancer of the breast. Although this occurs principally in women, it can also sometimes be found in men.

B. There are several types of breast cancer, and they can all qualify under this Listing.

C. S. S. Disability must be able to obtain a pathology report showing that breast cancer is present.

D. Part A, B, C, D, or E must be fulfilled, but not all five.

II. Specific Requirements

A. Part A

1. Part A is fulfilled if the breast cancer is "inoperable".

2. It is important to note that "inoperable" means that there is no reasonable chance that the claimant can be completely cured with surgery. Sometimes a surgeon may operate on breast cancer, to remove *some* of the cancer under special circumstances. This would only be "palliative" surgery and would not keep the claimant from qualifying under Part A.

B. Part B

1. Part B is fulfilled if "inflammatory carcinoma" is present. Inflammatory carcinoma refers to some of the most dan-

gerous forms of breast cancer, which are so aggressive and malignant that a great deal of the breast is inflamed on physical examination.

2. The mere existence of inflammatory carcinoma is enough to fulfill Part B. Nothing else is required.

C. Part C

1. Part C is fulfilled if the breast cancer comes back after surgery.

2. The one exception is cancer that only comes back in the area where the breast was originally removed. This would be "local recurrence", and if treatment can control it, the claimant would not qualify under Part C.

D. Part D

1. Part D is fulfilled if there is "distant metastasis" of the breast cancer. That is, if the cancer has spread so far from the breast that removal of the cancer with surgery is impossible.

2. It is important to note that if cancer occurs in *both* breasts, whether at the same time or at different times, S. S. Disability will consider them different cancers in each breast. So cancer involving both breasts does not count as "distant metastasis", and does *not* qualify under Part D, unless of course other areas of the body are also involved.

3. It should also be noted that if the claimant were fortunate enough to have such successful medical treatment that all evidence of the breast cancer disappeared for at least 3 years, S. S. Disability would probably consider her cured, although there would always be a small chance of it returning even many years later.

4. It should also be pointed out that breast cancer has often spread into the axilla (armpit), by the time surgery is done. This is *not* considered "distant metastasis".

E. Part E

1. Part E refers to breast cancer of a "sarcoma" type.

2. If the sarcoma has spread anywhere at all beyond where it started, Part E is fulfilled. It does *not* have to spread to distant places in the body. For example, spread of the breast cancer even as far as the armpit (axilla) would qualify.

3. But if the claimant was so successfully treated that there had been no evidence of cancer for more than 3 years, S. S. Disability would assume that cure has taken place.

Listing 13.10

Skeletal system (exclusive of the jaw):

A. Malignant primary tumors with evidence of metastases and not controlled by prescribed therapy; OR

B. Metastatic carcinoma to bone where the primary site is not determined after adequate search.

I. General Considerations

A. This Listing deals with cancer of any bones, with the exception of the jaw-bone.

B. The type of cancer does not matter, but S. S. Disability must be able to obtain a pathology report showing that cancer is present.

C. Part A or B must be fulfilled, but not both.

II. Specific Requirements

A. Part A

1. Part A deals with cancer that *starts* in a bone.

2. There must be evidence that the cancer has spread to other places.

3. The cancer must be uncontrolled, even by treatment.

B. Part B

1. Part B deals with cancer that started somewhere else in the body, but which spread to a bone.

2. Where the cancer started must be unknown, even after a reasonably thorough effort to find it by the treating doctor. If the place where the cancer started cannot be found, it would be much more difficult to cure it.

Listing 13.11

Mandible, maxilla, orbit, or temporal fossa:

A. Sarcoma of any type with metastasis; OR

B. Carcinoma of the antrum with extension into the orbit or ethmoid or sphenoid sinus, or with regional or distant metastasis; OR

C. Orbital tumors with intracranial extension; OR

D. Tumors of the temporal fossa with perforation of skull and meningeal involvement; OR

E. Adamantinoma with orbital or intracranial infiltration; OR

F. Tumors of Rathke's pouch with infiltration of the base of the skull or metastasis.

I. General Considerations

A. This Listing deals with cancer in certain bones. Included are the "mandible" (jaw-bone), "maxilla" (a facial bone), "orbit" (the bone of the eye-socket), and "temporal fossa" (a bone of the side of the skull).

B. S. S. Disability must be able to obtain a pathology report showing cancer to be present.

C. Part A, B, C, D, E, or F must be fulfilled, but not all six.

II. Specific Requirements

A. Part A

1. Part A deals with any type of "sarcoma" cancer starting in one of the listed bones.

2. If the cancer has spread anywhere outside of the bone where it started, Part A is fulfilled.

3. However, if the claimant were treated so that there had been no evidence of cancer for at least 3 years, he would probably be considered cured.

B. Part B

1. Part B refers to a cancer starting in a certain area of the facial bone called the "antrum".

2. If the cancer has spread into either of the bones surrounding the eyes (orbits), or one of the cavities in the facial bones called the ethmoid or sphenoid sinuses, then Part B is fulfilled. Part B is also fulfilled if the cancer has spread to the neck or other parts of the body.

3. However, if the claimant was treated successfully enough that no evidence of cancer was present for at least 3 years, S. S. Disability would consider the claimant cured, and he would not qualify under Part B.

C. Part C

1. Part C deals with tumors starting in the bones around the eyes (orbit).

2. If the tumor has spread into the skull cavity ("intracranial extension") then Part C is fulfilled.

D. Part D

1. Part D deals with tumors starting in the temporal bone on the side of the skull.

2. If the tumor has spread through this bone to the inside of the skull ("intracranial extension"), *and* also involves the meninges, then Part D is fulfilled. (The meninges is a protective membrane that covers the brain.)

E. Part E

1. Part E deals with a type of tumor called an "adamantinoma".

2. If the tumor has spread either to the orbital bones surrounding the eye, or has spread inside the skull ("intracranial infiltration"), then Part E is fulfilled.

F. Part F

1. Part F deals with tumors starting in "Rathke's pouch", which is another way of saying tumors starting near the pituitary gland at the bottom of the brain.

2. If the tumor has spread into the base of the skull-bones or anywhere else, then Part F is fulfilled.

Listing 13.12

Brain or spinal cord:

A. Metastatic carcinoma to brain or spinal cord.

B. Evaluate other tumors under the criteria described in Listings 11.05 and 11.08.

I. General Considerations

A. This Listing deals with any type of tumor involving the brain or spinal cord.

B. S. S. Disability must be able to obtain a pathology report showing the tumor to be present.

II. Specific Requirements

A. Part A

1. Part A deals with tumors that started somewhere else in the body, besides the brain or spinal cord.

2. If there is evidence that the tumor has spread to the brain or spinal cord (metastasized), then Part A is fulfilled.

B. Part B

1. Part B deals with tumors that start in the brain or spinal cord.

2. No actual evaluation is done under Part B. It is simply a reminder to evaluate such cases under Listing 11.05 (which deals specifically with brain tumors), or Listing 11.08 (which deals with spinal cord tumors or disease). More details can be found in the discussion of those Listings.

Listing 13.13

Lungs:

A. Unresectable; OR

B. With metastases; OR

C. Recurrent after resection; OR

D. Incomplete excision; OR

E. Oat cell carcinoma.

I. General Considerations

A. This Listing deals with any type of lung cancer.

B. S. S. Disability must be able to obtain a pathology report showing that lung cancer is present.

C. Part A, B, C, D, or E must be fulfilled, but not all five.

II. Specific Requirements

A. Part A

1. Part A is fulfilled if the lung cancer is "unresectable". That means that there is no reasonable chance of curing the cancer by removing it surgically.

2. It is important to note that just because a claimant undergoes surgery, it does not necessarily disqualify him from fulfilling Part A. For example, sometimes it is unknown whether the cancer can be removed by surgery until the surgeon actually operates and gets a closer look at the cancer. If the findings at surgery show that the cancer cannot all be removed, it would still be called "unresectable". Also, a particular surgeon might operate on a lung cancer that most other doctors would consider incurable by surgery. If this happens, S. S. Disability will still consider the cancer unresectable.

B. Part B

1. Part B is fulfilled if the cancer has spread from where it started in the lung to other parts of the body ("metastases")

2. However, if a claimant were fortunate enough to be free of the cancer for at least 3 years as a result of successful treatment, the S. S. Disability would assume the claimant is cured, and he would *not* qualify under Part B.

C. Part C

1. Part C deals with lung cancer that is "recurrent after resection". This simply means that the cancer comes back, after surgery has been done to remove it.

2. It does not matter how long it has been since the original surgery, when the cancer comes back. It might be many years. The claimant can still qualify under this Listing, even if he is being treated for cancer that has returned.

D. Part D

1. Part D is fulfilled if there is "incomplete excision" of the lung cancer. In other words, Part D is fulfilled if there is any evidence that the surgeon did not remove all of the cancer.

2. Often, surgery appears to remove all of the cancer but some hidden malignant cells are still present somewhere that can grow into another tumor at some time in the future. Part D does not take this into account. There must be evidence that some of the tumor cells were not removed with surgery at the time the surgery was done. Incomplete excision might be determined from material removed at surgery, what the surgeon sees at surgery, or special laboratory tests.

E. Part E

1. Part E deals with an especially dangerous form of lung cancer called "oat cell carcinoma" (also called "small cell carcinoma").

2. Oat cell carcinoma is so lethal, that the claimant qualifies under Part E if he has it at all. It doesn't matter what kind of treatment is being given, or how well the claimant is responding to that treatment. The reason for this is that this form of lung cancer usually won't respond to treatment very long, even if the treatment seems to be successful at first.

3. But if there were a rare case that had been treated 3 years or more without evidence of cancer, then S. S. Disability would consider the claimant cured, and he would *not* qualify under Part E. This would be very unusual.

Listing 13.14

Pleura or mediastinum:

A. Malignant mesothelioma of pleura; OR

B. Malignant tumors, metastatic to pleura; OR

C. Malignant primary tumor of the mediastinum not controlled by prescribed therapy.

I. General Considerations

A. This Listing deals with cancer of the "pleura or mediastinum".

B. The pleura is a smooth, thin membrane lining the inside of the chest, and outside of the lung. The "mediastinum" is the space in the center of the chest, between the lungs. The heart is in the mediastinum, as well as lymph nodes, blood vessels, nerves, and parts of the trachea and esophagus.

C. S. S. Disability must have a pathology report showing cancer to be present. Any type of cancer affecting the pleura or mediastinum can qualify.

D. Part A, B, or C must be fulfilled, but not all three.

II. Specific Requirements

A. Part A

1. Part A deals with a cancer of the pleura membrane called "malignant mesothelioma".

2. If the cancer is present, nothing else by the claimant has to be proven, merely the existence of this cancer is enough to qualify under Part A. This is true, even if the claimant is receiving treatment. However, if the claimant had been successfully treated, so that no evidence of cancer had been present for at least 3 years, S. S. Disability would probably assume that cure has taken place. In that case, the claimant would not qualify under Part A.

B. Part B

1. Part B refers to any cancer that has spread to the pleura membrane. Any cancer, starting anywhere in the body, that sends malignant cells to the pleura qualifies.

2. However, it should be noted that if a claimant had been so successfully treated that there was no evidence of cancer anywhere in the body for at least 3 years, S. S. Disability would consider a cure to have taken place, and the claimant would *not* qualify under Part B.

C. Part C

1. Part C deals with any kind of cancer starting anywhere in the mediastinum.

2. The cancer must be uncontrolled despite treatment.

Listing 13.15

Abdomen:

A. Generalized carcinomatosis; OR

B. Retroperitoneal cellular sarcoma not controlled by prescribed therapy; OR

C. Ascites with demonstrated malignant cells.

I. General Considerations

A. This Listing deals with some forms of abdominal cancer.

B. S. S. Disability must be able to obtain a pathology report showing the cancer to be present.

C. Part A, B, or C must be fulfilled, but not all three.

II. Specific Requirements

A. Part A

1. Part A is fulfilled if there is "generalized carcinomatosis". This simply means that the cancer is widespread throughout the abdomen, and is usually detected during exploratory surgery in the abdomen. Such widespread cancer cannot be removed surgically. Examples of cancer that could do this are cancer of the intestine or ovary spreading throughout the abdominal cavity.

2. If the claimant has generalized carcinomatosis of the abdomen, then he qualifies under Part A, even if treatment is being given, since such treatment is not likely to be successful for very long.

B. Part B

1. A smooth membrane called the peritoneum lines the abdominal cavity.

2. Any "sarcoma" type of cancer involving the *retro*peritoneum can qualify under Part B. The retroperitoneum is the space behind the abdominal cavity.

3. The cancer must be uncontrolled, despite the claimant receiving treatment.

C. Part C

1. "Ascites" refers to any abnormal fluid collection in the abdomen.

2. There must be malignant (cancerous) cells floating in this fluid. If so, the cancer has probably spread widely throughout the abdomen. A common example of this is a malignant tumor of the ovary that ruptures, spilling out cancerous cells and fluid.

Listing 13.16

Esophagus or stomach:

A. Carcinoma or sarcoma of the upper two-thirds of the esophagus; OR

B. Carcinoma or sarcoma of the distal one-third of the esophagus with metastasis to the regional lymph nodes or extension to surrounding structures; OR

C. Carcinoma of the stomach with metastasis to the regional lymph nodes or extension to surrounding structures; OR

D. Sarcoma of stomach not controlled by prescribed therapy; OR

E. Inoperable carcinoma; OR

F. Recurrence or metastasis after resection.

I. General Considerations

A. This Listing deals with cancer of the esophagus or stomach.

B. S. S. Disability must be able to obtain a pathology report showing that cancer is present.

C. Part A, B, C, D, E, or F must be fulfilled, but not all six.

II. Specific Requirements

A. Part A

1. Part A is fulfilled if the cancer involves the *upper* 2/3 of the esophagus. Nothing else is required.

2. Part A can be fulfilled, even if treatment is being given, since such treatment is not likely to be successful for very long.

B. Part B

1. Part B deals with cancer starting in the *lower* 1/3 of the esophagus.

2. The cancer must have spread to the lymph nodes nearby, or involve other organs besides the esophagus.

C. Part C

1. Part C deals with cancer of the stomach.

2. The cancer must have spread to the lymph nodes nearby, or involve other organs besides the stomach.

3. It is important to note that Part C deals with a form of cancer called *carcinoma* only.

D. Part D

1. Part D deals with a type of cancer called *sarcoma.*

2. If sarcoma starting in the stomach is not controlled by treatment, then Part D is fulfilled. The cancer doesn't necessarily have to have spread anywhere else in the body.

E. Part E

1. Part E is fulfilled if the cancer is "inoperable". This simply means that the cancer is so advanced that it cannot be removed by surgery.

2. It is important to note that it might not be known whether the cancer is inoperable, until surgery is actually attempted. In that case, the claimant would still qualify under Part E, even though some surgery was done.

F. Part F

1. Part F is fulfilled if either cancer of the stomach or esophagus returns, after surgery has been done.

2. It doesn't matter how much time has passed since the surgery was done and the cancer reappears. It could be years, and the claimant still qualify if the cancer comes back.

3. Part F is also fulfilled if, after surgery, it is then found that the cancer had also spread to other parts of the body.

Listing 13.17

Small intestine.

A. Carcinoma, sarcoma, or carcinoid tumor with metastasis beyond the regional lymph nodes; OR

B. Recurrence of carcinoma, sarcoma, or carcinoid tumor after resection; OR

C. Sarcoma, not controlled by prescribed therapy.

I. General Considerations

A. This Listing deals with any type of cancer of the small intestine.

B. S. S. Disability must be able to obtain a pathology report showing the cancer to be present.

C. Part A, B, or C must be fulfilled, but not all three.

II. Specific Requirements

A. Part A

1. Part A specifically refers to the three major types of cancer occurring in the small intestine: "carcinoma", "sarcoma", and "carcinoid".

2. There must be evidence that the cancer has spread "beyond the regional lymph nodes". In practical terms, this means the cancer has spread far enough that removal by surgery is impossible.

3. It should be noted that if a claimant were treated and fortunate enough to not have any evidence of cancer for at least 3 years, S. S. Disability would consider him cured, and he would *not* qualify under Part A.

B. Part B

1. Part B is fulfilled if the carcinoma, sarcoma, or carcinoid cancer returns after surgery was done to remove it ("resection").

2. It does not matter how long it has been since the original surgery and the time when the cancer returns. Also, the claimant can still qualify under Part B, if receiving treatment for the cancer that has come back.

C. Part C

1. Part C deals *only* with a "sarcoma" form of cancer.

2. If treatment is not controlling the growth of the cancer, then Part C is automatically fulfilled. Nothing else is required.

Listing 13.18

Large intestine (from ileocecal valve to and including anal canal)—carcinoma or sarcoma:

A. Unresectable; OR

B. Metastasis beyond the regional lymph nodes; OR

C. Recurrence or metastasis after resection.

I. General Considerations

A. This Listing deals with "sarcoma" or "carcinoma" type cancers of the large intestine, which are the most common.

B. The statement "from the ileocecal valve to and including anal canal" means that cancer anywhere in the large intestine can qualify.

C. S. S. Disability must be able to obtain a pathology report showing that the cancer is present.

D. Part A, B, or C must be fulfilled, but not all three.

Specific Requirements

A. Part A

1. Part A is fulfilled if the cancer is "unresectable". This simply means that the cancer cannot be removed with surgery, because it has spread too far.

2. Sometimes it is not known whether the cancer is unresectable or not, until surgery is actually done to take a closer look at the cancer. Unless the surgeon actually succeeds in apparently removing all of the cancer, it is still unresectable and the claimant still qualifies under Part A.

B. Part B

1. Part B is fulfilled if there is evidence that the cancer has spread to lymph nodes farther away than those closest to the cancer.

2. Lymph nodes are often taken out during cancer surgery, to see which ones may or may not have cancer. If only the lymph nodes near the main cancer are involved ("regional" lymph nodes), then by removing those also, the cancer might be completely removed. But if it has gone farther away to more distant lymph nodes, even if they were also removed at surgery, the odds are that some hidden cancer was missed and remained in the body. In practical terms, Part B really means the same thing as Part A: There is still cancer present that could not be removed.

3. However, if a claimant was lucky enough that successful treatment had left him free of any evidence of cancer for at least 3 years, then S. S. Disability would consider him cured, and he would *not* qualify under Part B.

C. Part C

1. Part C is fulfilled if there is return of the cancer anywhere in the body after surgery has been done to remove it.

2. It should be noted that it doesn't matter how much time has passed from the time of the original surgery and when the

cancer comes back. It could be years and the claimant would still qualify under Part C, even if he is undergoing treatment for the cancer that has returned.

Listing 13.19

Liver or gallbladder:

A. Primary or metastasic malignant tumors of the liver; OR

B. Carcinoma of the gallbladder; OR

C. Carcinoma of the bile ducts, unresectable or with metastases.

I. General Considerations

A. Cancer of the liver or gallbladder is considered by this Listing.

B. S. S. Disability must be able to obtain a pathology report showing that cancer is present.

C. Part A, B, or C must be fulfilled, but not all three.

II. Specific Requirements

1. Part A is fulfilled if there is a "primary" liver cancer. This means a cancer that starts in the liver.

2. Part A is also fulfilled if cancer starting somewhere else in the body has spread to the liver.

3. Any type of cancer fulfilling these requirements may qualify.

B. Part B

1. Part B is fulfilled if there is a "carcinoma" type of cancer of the gallbladder.

2. Nothing else is required, even if the claimant is under treatment. Having the cancer itself is sufficient to qualify under Part B.

C. Part C

1. Part C deals with "carcinoma" type cancer of the bile ducts. The bile ducts are little tubes that carry bile from liver and gallbladder to the small intestine.

2. The main tumor must be too advanced to remove by surgery (unresectable), or there must be evidence that the cancer

has spread to other parts of the body, which means that it can't be removed by surgery.

Listing 13.20

Pancreas:

A. Carcinoma except islet cell carcinoma; OR

B. Islet cell carcinoma which is unresectable and physiologically active.

I. General Considerations

A. This Listing deals with cancer of the pancreas.

B. S. S. Disability must be able to obtain a pathology report showing that cancer is present.

C. Part A or B must be fulfilled, but not both.

II. Specific Requirements

A. Part A

1. Part A is fulfilled if there is evidence that the claimant has "carcinoma" type cancer of the pancreas. This is true, even if the claimant is undergoing treatment. Nothing but proof of the cancer is required.

2. The one *exception* to Part A is "islet cell carcinoma" of the pancreas. It must be evaluated under Part B.

B. Part B

1. Part B deals with only "islet cell carcinoma" of the pancreas.

2. The cancer must be "unresectable". That is, complete removal of the cancer by surgery is impossible.

3. The cancer must also be "physiologically active". Islet cells in the pancreas normally produce insulin, and the cancer arises in these cells. If the cancer is physiologically active, it will produce abnormally large amounts of insulin which can be measured in the bloodstream.

4. These tumors are also called "insulinomas", and they may be either benign, or malignant (cancerous). Only the malignant forms qualify under Part B.

Listing 13.21

Kidneys, adrenal glands, or ureters—carcinoma:

A. Unresectable; OR

B. With metastasis.

I. General Considerations

A. This Listing deals with "carcinoma" types of cancer involving the kidneys, adrenal glands, or ureters. The adrenal glands sit on top of the kidneys. The ureters are tubes that carry urine from the kidneys to the bladder.

B. S. S. Disability must be able to obtain a pathology report showing that cancer is present.

C. Part A or B must be fulfilled, but not both.

II. Specific Requirements

A. Part A

1. Part A is fulfilled if the cancer is "unresectable". This means that the cancer cannot be removed by surgery.

2. It should be noted that the claimant might still qualify under Part A, if during surgery or after surgery it were discovered that some of the cancer was left behind. In that case, the cancer would still be considered unresectable, even though the claimant had surgery.

B. Part B

1. Part B is fulfilled if the cancer has spread anywhere else in the body, besides where it started. This is true, even if the claimant received surgery or other kind of treatment.

2. However, if the claimant were fortunate enough to have been treated with no evidence of cancer anywhere in the body for at least 3 years, then S. S. Disability would consider him cured, and he would *not* qualify under Part B.

Listing 13.22

Urinary bladder-carcinoma. With:

A. Infiltration beyond the bladder wall; OR

B. Metastasis; OR

C. Unresectable; OR

D. Recurrence after total cystectomy; OR

E. Evaluate urinary division after cystectomy under the criteria in Listing 6.02.

I. General Considerations

A. This Listing deals with "carcinoma" type cancer of the bladder.

B. S. S. Disability must be able to obtain a pathology report showing that cancer is present.

C. Part A, B, C, D, or E must be fulfilled, but not all five.

II. Specific Requirements

A. Part A

1. Part A is fulfilled if there is evidence that the cancer has spread through the wall of the bladder.

2. Nothing else is required, the claimant still qualifies even if under treatment.

B. Part B

1. Part B is fulfilled if the cancer has spread to other parts of the body (metastasis).

2. Nothing else is required, the claimant still qualifies, even if under treatment. However, if the claimant were fortunate enough to have such successful treatment that there was no evidence of cancer anywhere in the body for at least 3 years, S. S. Disability would consider him cured, and he would *not* qualify under Part B.

C. Part C

1. Part C is fulfilled if the bladder cancer is "unresectable". This means that the cancer cannot be removed by surgery.

2. A claimant would still qualify under Part C, even if surgery was done, if there is any evidence that some cancer remains in the body.

D. Part D

1. Part D is fulfilled if the cancer returns after surgery that removed the whole bladder ("total cystectomy").

2. It does not matter how much time has passed from the time of the original surgery, to the time the cancer comes back. It could be years. Nor does it matter if the claimant is receiving treatment for the cancer that has returned.

E. Part E

1. Part E deals with what is called "urinary diversion". If the bladder has been removed, the urine draining from the kid-

neys must be diverted somewhere else. Sometimes the ureters carrying the urine from the kidneys are sewed into the intestine. Other procedures may also be done.

2. Urinary diversion itself is not enough to qualify under Part E. The problem is that there may be complications leading to kidney damage (for example, damage due to repeated kidney infections). Therefore, if urinary diversion has been done, the impairment would be evaluated under Listing 6.02, which deals with kidney disease. The specific requirements of Listing 6.02 must be fulfilled. Further details can be found in the discussion of that Listing.

Listing 13.23

Prostate gland. Carcinoma not controlled by prescribed therapy.

I. General Considerations

A. This Listing deals with cancer of the prostate gland.

B. S. S. Disability must be able to obtain a pathology report showing that cancer is present.

II. Specific Requirements

A. Sometimes prostatic cancer can be completely cured, if caught early enough.

B. The Listing cannot be fulfilled, unless the cancer cannot be brought under control by some form of treatment. Even if the cancer has spread throughout the body, there must be evidence that it is not responding to treatment.

Listing 13.24

Testicles:

A. Choriocarcinoma; OR

B. Other malignant primary tumors with progressive disease not controlled by prescribed therapy.

I. General Considerations

A. This Listing deals with cancer of the testicles.

B. S. S. Disability must be able to obtain a pathology report showing that cancer is present.

C. Part A, or B must be fulfilled, but not both.

II. Specific Requirements

A. Part A

1. Part is fulfilled if the claimant has a form of testicular cancer called "choriocarcinoma".

2. Nothing else is required. The claimant can still qualify under Part A, even if treatment is being received.

B. Part B

1. Part B deals with all other forms of cancer starting in the testicles.

2. There must be evidence that the cancer is getting worse, even under treatment.

3. If the cancer has metastasized (spread to other places in the body), this would qualify as evidence that it is not controlled.

Listing 13.25

Uterus. Carcinoma or sarcoma (corpus or cervix):

A. Inoperable and not controlled by prescribed therapy; OR

B. Recurrent after total hysterectomy; OR

C. Total pelvic exenteration.

I. General Considerations

A. This Listing deals with cancer of the uterus. It applies to all uterine cancer, involving either the body of the uterus (corpus) or the cervix leading to the vagina.

B. Both "carcinoma" and "sarcoma" types of cancer may qualify.

C. S. S. Disability must be able to obtain a pathology report showing that cancer is present.

D. Part A, B, or C must be fulfilled, but not all three.

II. Specific Requirements

A. Part A

1. Part A is fulfilled if the cancer is "inoperable". The cancer is still considered inoperable, even if surgery is done, if there is any evidence that cancer was left behind.

2. In addition to being inoperable, the cancer must be uncontrolled by whatever treatment is being given (radiation or drugs).

B. Part B

1. "Total hysterectomy" means complete removal of the uterus.

2. If the cancer returns after such surgery is done, then Part B is fulfilled.

3. It does not matter how much time has passed since the hysterectomy was done and the return of the cancer. It could be years. The claimant still qualifies, even if under treatment for the cancer that has come back.

C. Part C

1. Part C is fulfilled if "total pelvic exenteration" has been done. This is extremely extensive surgery, involving the removal of a large amount of tissue from the abdomen.

2. Nothing else is required, except for the fact that this surgery has been done. It is only performed in very advanced disease.

3. However, if the claimant were fortunate enough to have remained free of any cancer for at least 3 years, S. S. Disability would probably consider her cured. In that case, the claimant would *not* qualify under Part C.

Listing 13.26

Ovaries. All malignant primary or recurrent tumors. With:

A. Ascites with demonstrated malignant cells; OR

B. Unresectable infiltration; OR

C. Unresectable metastasis to omentum or elsewhere in the peritoneal cavity; OR

D. Distant metastasis.

I. General Considerations

A. This Listing deals with any type of cancer starting in the ovaries. It applies for cancer starting in the ovaries for the first time, or cancer that has returned after previous treatment.

B. S. S. Disability must be able to obtain a pathology report showing that cancer is present.

C. Part A, B, C, or D must be fulfilled, but not all four.

II. Specific Requirements

A. Part A

1. "Ascites" refers to any abnormal collection of fluid in the abdominal cavity. This can happen when a cancerous ovarian tumor ruptures, spilling fluid and tumor cells into the abdominal cavity.

2. Since there are other diseases that can cause ascites (for example, liver disease), there must be evidence that it is caused by the ovarian cancer. This proof is supplied by finding cancerous cells floating in the fluid. Since these cancerous cells can come into contact with any of the other organs in the abdomen, finding them in the ascitic fluid is a poor sign.

B. Part B

1. Part B is fulfilled if there is "unresectable infiltration" of the ovarian cancer. This simply means the cancer has spread too far to be removed by surgery.

2. Merely having surgery does not disqualify the claimant under Part B, if there is evidence that any cancer was left behind.

C. Part C

1. The "omentum" is a sheet of fatty connective tissue that hangs down in the front part of the abdomen.

2. If during surgery on the abdomen, the ovarian cancer is found in the omentum or anywhere else in the abdominal cavity (besides the ovary), *and* it cannot be surgically removed, then Part C is fulfilled.

D. Part D

1. Part D is fulfilled if there is "distant metastasis" of the ovarian cancer. This means that the cancer has spread so far from the ovary that it would be impossible to remove it with surgery.

2. However, if a claimant had been successfully treated so that she had no evidence of cancer anywhere in the body for at least 3 years, S. S. Disability would consider her cured of the cancer, and she would *not* qualify under Part D.

Listing 13.27

Leukemia. Evaluate under the criteria of the Hemic and Lymphatic System.

I. General Considerations

A. This Listing refers to any form of leukemia.

B. S. S. Disability must be able to obtain a pathology report showing that cancer is present.

II. Specific Requirements

A. No actual evaluation is done under this Listing.

B. If leukemia is present, the case is evaluated under the Listings dealing with blood disorders—"Hemic and Lymphatic System". Further discussion can be found under the discussion of those Listings.

Listing 13.28

Uterine (Fallopian) tubes. Carcinoma or sarcoma, unresectable or with metastasis.

I. General Considerations

A. This Listing deals with either "carcinoma" or "sarcoma" types of cancer involving the fallopian tubes, which connect the uterus to the ovaries.

B. S. S. Disability must be able to obtain a pathology report showing that cancer is present.

II. Specific Requirements

A. This Listing is fulfilled if the cancer is "unresectable". This means that it is too advanced to be removed with surgery. Merely having surgery does not disqualify the claimant under this Listing, if there is evidence that any cancer was left behind.

B. This Listing is also fulfilled, if there is evidence that the cancer has spread to other parts of the body.

C. However, if a claimant were so successfully treated that there had been no evidence of cancer anywhere in the body for at least 3 years, S. S. Disability would consider her cured, and she would *not* qualify under this Listing.

CHAPTER 3

LISTINGS OF IMPAIRMENTS FOR CHILDREN

Table of Sections

Sec.

---

§ 3.1 Introduction

The Listings of impairments for children applies to claimants under age 18. Other than this difference, they are used in the same way as the Listings of impairments for adults (see the introductory comments to Chapter 2 Listings Of Impairments For Adults).

§ 3.2 Growth Impairment

Listing 100.02

Growth impairment, considered to be related to an additional specific medically determinable impairment, and ONE of the following:

(a) Fall of greater than 15 percentiles in height which is sustained; OR

(b) Fall to, or persistence of, height below the third percentile.

I. General Considerations

A. This Listing deals with impairments of growth.

B. In this Listing, the decrease in normal growth *must* be due to an identifiable medical illness. For example, an intestinal disease causing poor absorption of nutrients from food might impair growth.

C. The height of a child is generally thought to be better indicator of growth impairment than weight, and only height is considered in this Listing.

D. What would be considered a normal height for any particular child depends on how old he is. It is also different for boys and girls. In addition, children have different heights at the same age and sex, because they are individuals and have different "normal" heights.

E. This Listing deals with children that are so abnormal in their growth that they clearly have a problem. There are standard "growth charts" used widely in medicine which allow calculation of how a particular child's growth compares to other children of the same age and sex. S. S. Disability uses these charts in evaluating growth impairments under this Listing.

F. In evaluating a child's growth with "growth charts", a number called a "percentile" is used in the calculations.

G. Part (a) or Part (b) must be fulfilled, but not both.

II. Specific Requirements

A. Part (a)

1. Part (a) requires a fall in the claimant's height of *more* than 15 percentiles. To determine this, at least several different heights at different ages is required. Unless there are heights over a period of at least 6 months, it is difficult to get an accurate answer.

2. The abnormality of the claimant's height must be *sustained;* it must *stay* low.

B. Part (b)

1. Part (b) requires that the claimant's height either fall to the "third percentile", or stay that low and not improve.

2. Unless there are heights over a period of at least 6 months, it is difficult to show that this is true.

Listing 100.03

Growth impairment, not identified as being related to an additional, specific medically determinable impairment. With:

(a) Fall of greater than 25 percentiles in height which is sustained; AND

(b) Bone age greater than two standard deviations (2 SD) below the mean for chronological age.

I. General Considerations

A. This Listing deals with impairments of growth.

B. Unlike Listing 100.01, this Listing deals with impairments of growth for which the cause is unknown.

C. Other "General Considerations" are the same as for Listing 100.01.

II. Specific Requirements

A. Part (a)

1. Part (a) requires a fall in the claimant's height of *more* than 25 percentiles.

2. The fall in height must be *sustained;* that is, it must not improve. To determine this, at least several different heights at different ages is required. Unless there are heights over a period of at least 6 months, it is difficult to show this to be true.

B. Part (b)

1. Part (b) requires that the "bone age" of the claimant be determined.

2. Bones in children with growth impairments should be abnormally slow in their growth, and this can be detected with special X-rays of certain bones. X-rays of the bones of the left hand and wrist are taken. If the claimant is an older child, or one past puberty, X-rays are also taken of the knee and ankle.

3. The results of the bone age X-rays must be more than "two standard deviations below the mean for chronological age". This is simply a way of calculating the degree of abnormal bone growth.

§ 3.3 Musculoskeletal System

Listing 101.02

Juvenile rheumatoid arthritis. With:

(a) Persistence or recurrence of joint inflammation despite six months of medical treatment and ONE of the following:

(1) Limitation of motion of two major joints of 50 percent or greater; OR

(2) Fixed deformity of two major weight-bearing joints of 30 degrees or more; OR

(3) Radiographic changes of joint narrowing, erosion, or subluxation; OR

(4) Persistent or recurrent systemic involvement, such as iridocyclitis or pericarditis; OR

(b) Steroid dependence.

I. General Considerations

A. This Listing deals with the type of rheumatoid arthritis that affects children.

B. Part (a) or (b) must be fulfilled, but not both.

II. Specific Requirements

A. Part (a)

1. There must be persistent or frequently recurrent *inflammation* of the affected joints. Inflammation means tissues around the joint are swollen, red, and warm to the touch. This indicates that the arthritis is "active".

2. The inflammation must be present over at least a 6-month period, *and* the claimant must be receiving treatment.

3. If one of the above requirements of Part (a) are fulfilled, one of the following must also be present:

(a) Part (a)(1) requires that there must be at least a 50% loss of motion in at least 2 major joints. Major joints are hand and wrist (together), elbow, shoulder, knee, hip, and ankle. A finger joint is *not* a major joint.

(b) Part (a)(2) requires several things. First, there must be a "fixed deformity". This means that the arthritis has destroyed a joint so much that it cannot move at all. Secondly, at least 2 joints must be involved. Thirdly, the 2 involved joints must be "weight-bearing" joints. This means the hip, knee, or ankle. Lastly, the abnormal joint must be fixed at an abnormal angle of at least "30 degrees" from normal.

(c) Part (a)(3) requires X-rays that show the abnormal changes caused by severe rheumatoid arthritis. These can be narrowing of the joint space, destruction of bone ("erosion"), or bones in a joint that have slipped out of their normal relation to each other ("subluxation").

(d) Part (a)(4) is fulfilled if there is significant "systemic" effects caused by the rheumatoid arthritis. This is because rheumatoid arthritis is not a disease that affects only joints; it can also damage other parts of the body. Common examples are "iridocyclitis" (inflammation of part of the eye), and "pericarditis" (inflammation of the pericardium—the thin sack that surrounds the heart).

B. Part (b)

1. Part (b) refers to claimants who have to take steroid type drugs for their rheumatoid arthritis.

2. Note that the claimant must be *steroid dependent.* This means that the steroid drugs are necessary on a continuous basis, not just part of the time.

Listing 101.03

Deficit of musculoskeletal function due to deformity or musculoskeletal disease and ONE of the following:

(a) Walking is markedly reduced in speed or distance despite orthotic or prosthetic devices; OR

(b) Ambulation is possible only with obligatory bilateral upper limb assistance (e.g., with walker, crutches); OR

(c) Inability to perform age-related personal self-care activities involving feeding, dressing, and personal hygiene.

I. General Considerations

A. This Listing deals with impairments that involve "musculoskeletal disease". This means *any* impairment affecting the use of muscles and joints, such as walking or using the hands and arms. Examples would be congenital (dating from birth) disease of bones or joints, arthritis, and damage caused by accidents.

B. Part (a), (b), or (c) must be fulfilled, but not all three.

II. Specific Requirements

A. Part (a)

1. Part (a) deals with problems walking.

2. A "prosthesis" is an artificial limb, such as an artificial leg. An "orthotic" device would be something like a cane or crutch.

3. Walking must be "markedly reduced" in speed or distance, even though prosthetic or orthotic devices are used; the case is evaluated with the claimant using such devices.

4. Whether speed or distance of walking is "markedly reduced" or not is a matter judgment by the person in S. S. Disability evaluating the case. It partly depends on the age of the claimant, because children are capable of different things at different ages, and that must be taken into account.

B. Part (b)

1. Part (b) also deals with problems walking.

2. If walking ("ambulation") is possible only with devices which require use of the arms, then Part (b) is fulfilled. Having to use crutches to walk is an example, because the arms must grasp the crutches.

C. Part (c)

1. Part (c) deals with inability of the claimant to do personal self-care activities, such as feeding, dressing, and personal hygiene.

2. Since the ability of a particular child to do self-care activities depends on his age, this must be taken into account. The claimant's abilities is compared to what a normal child could be expected to do at the same age.

Listing 101.05

Disorders of the spine.

(a) Fracture of a vertebra with cord involvement (substantiated by appropriate sensory and motor loss).

(b) Scoliosis (congenital idiopathic or neuromyopathic).

With:

(1) Major spinal curve measuring 60 degrees or greater; OR

(2) Spinal fusion of six or more levels. Consider under a disability for one year from the time of surgery; thereafter, evaluate the residual impairment; OR

(3) FEV (vital capacity) of 50 percent or less of predicted normal values for the individual's measured (actual) height.

(c) Kyphosis or lordosis measuring 90 degrees or greater.

I. General Considerations

A. This Listing deals with impairments caused by disorders of the spine.

B. Part (a), (b), or (c) must be fulfilled, but not all three.

II. Specific Requirements

A. Part (a)

1. Part (a) deals with a fracture of at least one of the bony vertebral bodies that make up the spine.

2. The spinal cord carries nerves to the body and is normally protected by the bony spine. A serious fracture of one of the vertebral bodies of the spine can damage the spinal cord. Depending on where the damage is, a doctor examining the claimant should find abnormalities relating to that area of damage. These abnormalities involve "motor loss" (some degree of paralysis), and "sensory loss" (the ability to "feel" things such as touch, heat, cold, etc.). The motor loss and/or sensory loss must be of more than a minor degree; it must substantially affect the claimant's ability to use his legs or arms. For example, paralysis of a leg which greatly interferes with normal walking (considering the child's age) could qualify

3. It should be remembered that the problem has to last, or be expected to last, at least 12 months. A temporary injury to the spinal cord would not qualify.

B. Part (b)

1. Part (b) deals with impairments caused by "scoliosis", which is an abnormal "sideways" curve to the spine. The cause of the scoliosis doesn't matter. The cause could be unknown and be present from birth ("congenital idiopathic"), or the scolio-

sis could be the result of some disease appearing later in the child's life ("neuromyopathic").

2. To fulfill Part (b), *one* of three things is required:

(a) Part (b)(1) requires that the largest abnormal curve caused by the scoliosis be at *least* 60°.

(b) Part (b)(2) deals with spinal fusion. This is a surgical procedure that attempts to straighten the abnormally curved spine. "Six or more levels" means that at least 6 vertebral bodies have to be surgically fused together. The claimant is automatically given disability for one year from the time of surgery. After that amount of time, the case would be re-evaluated to see how well the surgery worked.

(c) Part (c)(3) deals with decreased ability to breathe normally. This can occur, because the abnormal curve of the spine in scoliosis can produce such an abnormal shape of the chest that normal breathing movements are difficult. The degree of breathing impairment is measured by a special breathing test which shows what the "vital capacity" is. The vital capacity is also called the "FEV" (forced expiratory volume). The FEV represents the amount of air that a claimant can breathe out as fast as he can, after taking in as deep a breath as possible. To qualify under Part (c)(3), the FEV must not be more than 50% of what would be expected of a normal child of the same height. It should be noted that the claimant must really try when given this test. Otherwise, S. S. Disability will not consider the results as valid.

C. Part (c)

1. Part (c) deals with "kyphosis" or "lordosis". Kyphosis is an abnormal curve to the spine, so that it is curved too far forward. Lordosis is an abnormality in which the spine is curved too far backwards. Either may qualify, if severe enough.

2. The abnormal curve due to kyphosis or lordosis must be at *least* 90°. This is essentially a right-angle and is extremely abnormal.

Listing 101.08

Chronic osteomyelitis, with persistence or recurrence of inflammatory signs of drainage for at least six months despite prescribed therapy, and consistent radiographic findings.

I. General Considerations

A. This Listing deals with "osteomyelitis", which means an infection of bone.

B. The osteomyelitis must be "chronic". That is, it must be an infection that cannot be cured.

II. Specific Requirements

A. "Inflammatory signs" must be present either continuously, or at least very frequently. Inflammatory means tenderness, swelling, redness, and warmth of the tissues over the area of infected bone. Sometimes, the infection in the bone can make its way to the surface of the skin and drain pus to the outside of the body. Either inflammation or drainage indicates that the infection is active (not under control).

B. In addition, the inflammation or drainage must be present for at *least* 6 months, and the claimant must be under treatment. Otherwise, S. S. Disability cannot know if treatment would be effective.

C. Also, there must be "consistent radiographic findings". This means X-rays must show the kind of bone damage expected if osteomyelitis is present.

§ 3.4 Special Sense Organs

Listing 102.02

Impairment of central visual acuity:

(a) Remaining vision in the better eye after best correction is 20/200 or less.

(b) For children below three years of age at time of adjudication:

(1) Absence of accommodative reflex; OR

(2) Retrolental fibroplasia with macular scarring or neovascularization; OR

(3) Bilateral congenital cataracts with visualization of retinal red reflex only or when associated with other ocular pathology.

I. General Considerations

A. This Listing deals with visual problems.

B. The degree of impairment of vision is measured by the "central visual acuity", which simply involves the ability to see clearly. This is reported by two numbers measured by an eye specialist (ophthalmologist). For example, a normal person's vision is usually 20/20. Acuity of 20/50 would be worse, and one of 20/200 would mean blindness for S. S. Disability purposes.

C. The testing of visual acuity requires the cooperation of the claimant, in telling the doctor what he can and cannot see. But no matter what the claimant says, there must be an identifiable eye disease which the doctor can find to explain the poor vision. Unless there is a severe enough eye disease to explain the results of the testing, S. S. Disability will not believe that an eye impairment is present.

D. The eye specialist who diagnoses disease in the claimant's eyes *must* be a medical doctor (ophthalmologist).

E. Part (a) or (b) must be fulfilled, but not both.

II. Specific Requirements

A. Part (a)

1. S. S. Disability will evaluate the vision in the *best* eye.

2. The vision in the *best* eye is measured after an eye specialist has tried to improve it as much as possible with lenses (glasses or contact lenses).

3. The vision in the best eye (after correction with contact lenses or glasses) must be no better than 20/200.

4. Part (a) is only used for evaluation of children under 3 years of age, or older.

B. Part (b)

1. Part (b) is used only for children less than 3 years old. Such children are too young to cooperate in testing their vision as required in Part (a).

2. The age of the child refers to the age at time of application for disability.

3. One of the following abnormalities must be present:

(a) Part (b)(1) requires the absence of what is called the "accommodative reflex" in the eye. This is evidence that the eye is impaired. Note that this test cannot be used, if the claimant is less than 6 months old, since not even normal children have an accommodative reflex until that time.

(b) Part (b)(2) is fulfilled if "retrolental fibroplasia" is present in the retina of the claimant's eyes. This is damage caused by too much oxygen having been given after birth. There must be scarring of the macular, which is the area of the retina of the eye allowing clear vision. Also, there must be "neovascularization" of the retina of the eyes. This means an abnormal growth of blood vessels.

(c) Part (b)(3) requires cataracts in both eyes. Cataracts are damaged areas in the lens of the eye, which can prevent clear vision. In addition, there must be absence of what is called the "retinal red reflex" (absent because the retina in the back of the eye cannot be seen through the cataracts), or some other type of eye damage associated with the cataracts.

Listing 102.08

Hearing impairments:

(a) For children below five years of age at time of adjudication, inability to hear air conduction thresholds at an average of 40 decibels (db) hearing level or greater in the better ear.

(b) For children five years of age and above at the time of adjudication:

(1) Inability to hear air conduction thresholds at an average of 70 decibels (db) or greater in the better ear; OR

(2) Speech discrimination scores at 40 percent or less; OR

(3) Inability to hear air conduction thresholds at an average of 40 decibels (db) or greater in the better ear, and a speech and language disorder which significantly affects the clarity and content of the speech and is attributable to the hearing impairment.

I. General Considerations

A. This Listing deals with hearing impairments.

B. The cause of the hearing impairment is not important, but it must be a long term problem not one that lasts a short while and gets better.

C. Testing of the hearing is done by a special procedure called audiometry. This tests hearing of sounds through the air. Hearing is tested at several different frequencies (500, 1000, 2000, and 3000 cycles per second are frequencies important to S. S. Disability). How loud a sound has to be for the claimant to hear it is determined for each separate frequency. Such loudness is measured in "decibels".

D. Audiometry also involves a test concerning how well the claimant can understand words.

E. S. S. Disability will not consider the results of a hearing test accurate, unless the claimant cooperates in taking the test. The test results also will not be accepted, unless there is some evidence of disease that would cause a hearing impairment. For example, if the claimant could hear perfectly well in talking to other people, but couldn't hear at all on the audiometry, it would be difficult to believe that the test results were valid.

F. Part (a) or (b) must be fulfilled, but not both.

II. Specific Requirements

A. Part (a)

1. Part (a) only applies to children less than 5 years old, at the time they apply for disability.

2. For children this young, only sound conducted through the air is used for testing.

3. The hearing in the *best* ear is always used by S. S. Disability.

4. The loudness of sound necessary for the child to hear in the best ear at each of the required frequencies is measured. These numbers are then averaged. This average loudness must be at least 40 decibels or more to qualify under Part (a).

B. Part (b)

1. Part (b) deals with children 5 or more years old.

2. One of the following must be fulfilled:

(a) Part (b)(1) requires that the *average* loudness of the four required frequencies of sound be heard only at 70 decibels or more. Note that this applies to the *best* ear.

(b) Part (b)(2) measures the ability of the claimant to understand spoken words ("speech discrimination"). The child must be able to hear 40% or less of the words given in the test.

(c) Part (b)(3) requires that the *average* loudness of the four required frequencies of sound be heard only at 40 decibels or more. Note that this applies to the *best* ear. *In addition,* there must be a problem in speaking effectively in a way that can be understood by other people. This problem speaking effectively must be due to the hearing impairment.

§ 3.5 Respiratory System

Listing 103.03

Bronchial asthma. With evidence of progression of the disease despite therapy and documented by ONE of the following:

(a) Recent, recurrent intense asthmatic attacks requiring parenteral medication; OR

(b) Persistent prolonged expiration with wheezing between acute attacks and radiographic findings of peribronchial disease.

I. General Considerations

A. This Listing deals with asthma.

B. Asthma is a disorder of the bronchial tubes, causing them to "constrict down" to an abnormally narrowed condition. This decreases the ability of the claimant to get air in and out of the lungs. Often, this constriction of the bronchial tubes it not continuously present, but occurs during "attacks" of asthma. These attacks may be mild or severe. They may occur frequently or very rarely. Or there may be such severe asthma that the bronchial tubes are partly constricted all of the time.

C. The claimant *must* be receiving treatment, and the asthma must be getting worse even though such treatment is being given.

D. Part (a) or (b) must be fulfilled, but not both.

II. Specific Requirements

A. Part (a)

1. Part (a) requires "recent" asthmatic attacks. This means these attacks must be a problem about the time the claimant applies for disability; attacks years in the past would not qualify.

2. The attacks must be "recurrent". That is, they must occur often enough to cause the claimant to have a severe problem with them. An attack every 2 months would probably be sufficient, but it partly depends on the particular case considered.

3. The attacks must be so severe that "parenteral" drugs are necessary. Parenteral drugs are ones that are given beneath the skin (subcutaneously), injected into a muscle (intramuscularly), injected into a vein (intravenously), or breathed in (inhalation). Attacks which can be treated by drugs that are swallowed do not qualify. An "intense" attack is one so severe

that it lasts several hours, and requires treatment in a hospital or hospital emergency room.

B. Part (b)

1. Part (b) can be fulfilled if there is "prolonged expiration" (taking an abnormally long time to breathe air out of the lungs), and "wheezing" sounds. These are things observed on physical examination, and must be noted in the treating doctor's records. These abnormal findings must be present on a "repeated" basis. That is, they must be present more or less every time the treating doctor examines the claimant.

2. In addition, there must be X-rays of the lungs which show "peribronchial disease". This refers to damage to areas of the lung outside of the bronchial tubes, and indicates that very severe asthma has been present for a long time.

Listing 103.13

Pulmonary manifestations of cystic fibrosis. With:

(a) FEV_1 equal to or less than the values specified in Table I; OR

(b) For children where ventilatory function testing cannot be performed;

(1) History of dyspnea on mild exertion or chronic frequent productive cough; AND

(2) Persistent or recurrent abnormal breath sounds, bilateral rales or rhonchi; AND

(3) Radiographic findings of extensive disease with hyperaeration and bilateral peribronchial infiltration.

Table I

Height (cm.)	$F.E.V._1$ Equal to or Less Than (Liters)
110 or less	0.6
120	0.7
130	0.9
140	1.1
150	1.3
160	1.5
170 or more	1.6

I. General Considerations

A. This Listing deals with the disease called cystic fibrosis.

B. Note that *only* the effect of cystic fibrosis on the *lungs* is considered under this Listing. Lung damage is a direct or indirect effect of excessive mucus secretion in the bronchial tubes of the lungs.

C. In addition to a history and physical examination indicating that the claimant has cystic fibrosis, the results of tests done on the child's sweat *must* be available to S. S. Disability. These tests should show an abnormal increase of sodium or chloride in the sweat. Such tests are standard medical practice in making the diagnosis of cystic fibrosis, and S. S. Disability should be able to obtain the results.

D. Part (a) or (b) must be fulfilled, but not both.

II. Specific Requirements

A. Part (a)

1. Part (a) deals with the fact that mucus secretions in the bronchial tubes of claimants with cystic fibrosis will slow down the ability to breathe air in and out of the lungs.

2. To determine how severe this is, the claimant must undergo pulmonary function testing. During this test of breathing, a number called the "FEV_1" will be calculated. This stands for the "forced expiratory volume in one second". It means the maximum amount of air that a person can breathe out of his lungs in one second after taking as deep a breath as possible, then blowing it all out as fast as he can. Required values depend on the claimant's height as shown in Table I.

3. There must be a statement by the person giving the test that the child understood and cooperated during the test. Otherwise, the results would not be considered accurate. Children under 5 or 6 years old are usually too young to test, and so could not be evaluated under Part (a).

B. Part (b)

1 Part (b) is for claimants on whom pulmonary function testing as in Part (a) cannot be performed. This could be because the child is too young to do such testing, or mentally ill, or mentally retarded.

2. *All* three of the following must be fulfilled to qualify under Part (b):

(a) Part (b)(1) requires that the claimant's medical records show a history of difficulty breathing on mild exertion ("dyspnea"), or a frequent problem of coughing up mucus secretions ("productive" cough).

(b) Part (b)(2) requires that the claimant's medical records show frequent or continuously abnormal "breath sounds". These abnormal sounds are heard in the claimant's lungs when examined by the treating doctor, and are called "rales or rhonchi". There must be repeated examinations by the treating doctor showing these abnormal lung sounds to be present.

(c) Part (b)(3) requires abnormal X-rays of the lung showing changes expected with severe and persistent cystic fibrosis. The abnormalities are called "hyperaeration" and "bilateral peribronchial infiltration".

§ 3.6 Cardiovascular System

Listing 104.02

Chronic congestive failure. With TWO or MORE of the following signs:

(a) Tachycardia (see Table I).

(b) Tachypnea (see Table I).

(c) Cardiomegaly on chest roentgenogram.

(d) Hepatomegaly (more than 2 cm. below the right costal margin in the right mid-clavicular line).

(e) Evidence of pulmonary edema, such as rales or orthopnea.

(f) Dependent edema.

(g) Exercise intolerance manifested as labored respiration on mild exertion (e.g., in an infant, feeding).

Table I. Tachycardia at Rest

Age	Apical Heart
Under 1 year	150 beats/min.
1 through 3 years	130 beats/min.
4 through 9 years	120 beats/min.
10 through 15 years	110 beats/min.
Over 15 years	100 beats/min.

Table II. Tachypnea at Rest

Age	Respiratory Rate Over
Under 1 year	40/min.
1 through 5 years	35/min.
6 through 9 years	30/min.
Over 9 years	25/min.

I. General Considerations

A. This Listing deals with "congestive heart failure". Heart failure results when the heart becomes too "weakened" to pump as much blood as the rest of the body needs. This could be due to any disease that produces enough damage to the heart's internal valves, the heart muscle, the coronary arteries supplying blood to the heart, or the nerves in the heart necessary to activate it to beat properly. In children, a major cause of heart failure is congenital heart disease (dating from birth). In these cases, the heart did not grow normally before birth. There are many types of congenital heart disease, which can affect any of the parts of the heart.

B. Note that the Listing requires *chronic* congestive heart failure. This means that the claimant has heart failure so severe that it can't be completely reversed by surgery or other medical therapy.

C. At the time of application for disability, the claimant must have heart failure and fulfill at *least* two of the requirements given in Parts (a) through (g).

II. Specific Requirements

A. Part (a) can be fulfilled in the presence of "tachycardia". Tachycardia means an abnormally fast heart rate. In an adult, any heart rate over 100 beats per minute is classified as tachycardia. But in children this depends on the age of the child. To determine whether any particular child has tachycardia, his heart rate must be compared to the values given in Table I for different ages.

B. Part (b) can be fulfilled if the claimant has "tachypnea". Tachypnea means an abnormally fast breathing rate. This is different for children of different ages, and the requirements of Table II must be fulfilled.

C. Part (c) can be fulfilled if the claimant has "cardiomegaly" on a chest X-ray. Cardiomegaly means an enlarged heart. (The chest X-ray must be a standard one taken 6 feet away from the claimant, and most X-rays are taken this way.) The size of the heart on a chest X-ray is determined by measuring what is called the "C/T" ratio (cardiothoracic ratio). This means the width of the heart compared to the width of the chest (on X-ray). For example, if a claimant has a C/T ratio of 50%, then the heart is half as wide as the chest. If the claimant is one year old or less, the C/T ratio must be at *least* 55%. S. S. Disability will also consider cardiomegaly to exist if the heart size on a chest X-ray is 15% larger than it was on a previous X-ray.

D. Part (d) can be fulfilled if there is an enlarged liver ("hepatomegaly"). The liver is in the right side of the abdomen, up under the rib cage. If on physical examination by a doctor, the liver is felt below the rib cage, then it may be enlarged. The "right costal margin" refers to the front, bottom edge of the rib cage on the right side. The liver must be felt in this area by the examining doctor. It must come down below the rib cage at least 2 centimeters (a little less than an inch), to qualify under part (d).

E. Part (e) requires evidence of "pulmonary edema". Pulmonary edema is an abnormal accumulation of fluid in the lungs, due to severe heart failure. "Rales" are abnormal sounds heard in the chest by a doctor when pulmonary edema is present. "Orthopnea" means that the claimant gets short of breath when lying down. This can also be a sign of heart failure. It should be pointed out that pulmonary edema can sometimes also be seen on a chest X-ray when heart failure is present. This would also qualify under Part (e).

F. Part (f) can be fulfilled if there is "dependent edema". This refers to swelling in the feet or legs from fluid accumulation due to heart failure. It can be detected on physical examination by a doctor.

G. Part (g) is fulfilled if there is inability of the claimant to do much physical exercise, because of heart failure being present. This would be evaluated in terms of the age of the claimant and what types of activities he could not do. For example, in the case of an infant with heart failure, shortness of breath might occur even in the mild exertion of feeding.

Listing 104.03

Hypertensive cardiovascular disease. With persistently elevated blood pressure for age (see Table III) and ONE of the following:

(a) Impaired renal function as described under the criteria in Listing 106.02; OR

(b) Cerebrovascular damage as described under the criteria in Listing 111.06; OR

(c) Congestive heart failure as described under the criteria in Listing 104.02.

Table III. Elevated Blood Pressure

Age	Systolic (Over) in mm. Hg.	Diastolic (Over) in mm. Hg.
Under 6 months	95	60
6 months to 1 year	110	70
1 through 8 years	115	80
9 through 11 years	120	80
12 through 15 years	130	80
Over 15 years	140	80

I. General Considerations

A. This Listing deals with high blood pressure ("hypertension").

B. What would be considered high blood pressure for any particular child depends on his age, and this is determined by looking at Table III. Note that for each age in Table III, there are *two* blood pressures (taken in the arm). One is the "systolic" blood pressure, which is the pressure while the heart is actually contracting. The other is the "diastolic" pressure, or the pressure between beats of the heart. If the pressure is over *either* of these numbers, then the claimant fulfills Table III.

C. It should be pointed out that high blood pressure cannot be diagnosed from a single reading in a child or an adult. The Listing requires "persistently" high blood pressure over a period of at least 3 months to be convincing.

D. High blood pressure in itself is not an impairment. In order to qualify under this Listing, the increased blood pressure must have done damage to some part of the body. To demonstrate this, Part (a), (b), or (c) must be fulfilled, but not all three.

II. Specific Requirements

A. Part (a)

1. Part (a) deals with damage to the kidneys caused by high blood pressure.

2. No actual evaluation is done under Part (a). If the kidney damage has occurred, the impairment must fulfill the requirements of Listing 106.02, which deals with kidney disease.

3. Further details can be found in the discussion of Listing 106.02.

B. Part (b)

1. Part (b) deals with damage to the brain caused by high blood pressure.

2. No actual evaluation is done under Part (b). If brain damage has occurred, the impairment must fulfill the requirements of Listing 111.06, which deals with that type of disorder.

C. Part (c)

1. Part (c) deals with damage to the heart by high blood pressure.

2. No actual evaluation is done under Part (c). If there is heart failure caused by high blood pressure, then the impairment must fulfill the requirements of Listing 104.02, which deals with heart failure. Further details can be found under the discussion of Listing 104.02.

Listing 104.04

Cyanotic congenital heart disease. With ONE of the following:

(a) Surgery is limited to palliative measures; OR

(b) Characteristic squatting, hemoptysis, syncope, or hypercyanotic spells; OR

(c) Chronic hematocrit of 55 percent or greater or arterial 0_2 saturation of less than 90 percent at rest, or arterial oxygen tension of less than 60 Torr at rest.

I. General Considerations

A. This Listing deals with congenital heart disease, or heart disease caused by abnormal growth of the heart before birth.

These abnormalities can include any part of the heart not developing normally.

B. A particular type of congenital heart disease of a *cyanotic* type must be present. Cyanotic heart disease refers to types in which the heart doesn't pump blood through the lungs normally. Such blood doesn't pick up enough oxygen.

C. If the claimant has cyanotic type of congenital heart disease, then Part (a), (b), or (c) must be fulfilled, but not all three.

II. Specific Requirements

A. Part (a)

1. Part (a) is fulfilled if open heart surgery has been done but is limited to "palliative measures". This means that although heart surgery was done, it will only temporarily improve the claimant's health at best.

2. Of course, if claimants were so sick that not even "palliative" surgery would do any good, he would still qualify under this Listing. (Naturally, this doesn't apply to claimants who don't even need surgery.)

B. Part (b)

1. Part (b) refers to certain things seen in children with severe cyanotic congenital heart disease, especially one called the "Tetralogy of Fallot".

2. Such children may be observed to get in "squatting" positions, in order to breathe better. Or the claimant may cough up blood ("hemoptysis"). There may be "syncope" (loss of consciousness), or "hypercyanotic" spells in which the claimant turns blue, because of not having enough oxygen.

C. Part (c)

1. Part (c) deals with blood studies which indicate that severe cyanotic congenital heart disease is present. These studies may show that there is inadequate oxygen in the blood.

2. One study that will fulfill part (c) is a "chronic hematocrit of 55%" or more. An hematocrit is the percentage of the volume of blood that red blood cells make up. Red blood cells carry oxygen. For example, a hematocrit of 55% means that 55% of the volume of the claimant's blood is made up of red blood cells. This is an abnormally high number, and indicates that the claimant's body is making more red blood cells in order to attempt to carry more oxygen to the tissues. Note the word "chronic". One abnormal hemotocrit is not enough. There must be multiple hematocrits over 55%, for a long enough period

of time to show that the condition isn't likely to improve. This would be at *least* several months.

3. Another way of fulfilling Part (c) is by measuring the "saturation" of oxygen in the blood. If this number is less than 90%, there is inadequate oxygen in the blood stream. More than one abnormal value over a period of at *least* a few months would be necessary.

4. Part (c) can also be fulfilled by a blood test showing abnormally decreased oxygen. This test must show that the "oxygen tension" in arterial blood is less than "60 Torr". This might be considered the "pressure" of oxygen in blood. More than one abnormal reading is required. Abnormal readings over at *least* several months would be necessary. Note that this test must be done with the claimant *resting*. The reason for this is that physical exercise will lower the results of the test, and it would not be considered valid if done on a claimant who was doing some type of physical exertion at the same time.

Listing 104.05

Cardiac arrhythmia, such as persistent or recurrent heart block or A–V dissociation (with or without therapy). And ONE of the following:

(a) Cardiac syncope; OR

(b) Congestive heart failure as described under the criteria in Listing 104.02; OR

(c) Exercise intolerance with labored respirations on mild exertion (e.g., in infants, feeding).

I. General Considerations

A. This Listing deals with abnormal rhythms of the heart—abnormalities in the "timing" of heart beats. Examples would be abnormally fast or slow heart rates. Other examples are "heart blocks" and "A–V dissociation", in which the electrical impulses activating the heart to beat are "blocked" from going down the correct nerve fibers in the heart. These are all abnormalities that can be seen on tracings which record the electrical impulses coming from the heart. These tracings are called *electrocardiograms* (EKG's or ECG's), and are frequently used in medicine to diagnose and treat heart disease. There are many types of abnormalities that can be seen on EKG's, but they are far too complicated to consider in any detail here.

B. It does not matter whether the claimant is receiving treatment for his abnormal heart rhythm or not—either way, the claimant can qualify under this Listing. However, if the abnormality were being controlled with treatment, the claimant would *not* qualify.

C. S. S. Disability *must* be able to obtain EKG's from the treating doctor or hospital showing the particular type of abnormal heart rhythm that is supposed to be present.

D. Part (a), (b), or (c) must be fulfilled, but not all three.

II. Specific Requirements

A. Part (a)

1. Part (a) requires that the claimant have "cardiac syncope", as a result of the abnormal heart rhythm. This means loss of consciousness caused by heart disease. Consciousness may be lost, because the heart does not pump enough blood to the brain during episodes when the abnormal rhythm is especially severe.

2. One episode of syncope would certainly not be enough. Medical records must show that these episodes are severe enough and frequent enough to substantially impair the claimant. Exactly how frequent this has to be is not defined in the Listing. This is a matter of judgement on the part of the person in S. S. Disability reviewing the claimant's case, and all important facts about a particular claimant's disease must be taken into account. However, a claimant who suffered such episodes only once or twice a year would not qualify.

B. Part (b)

1. Part (b) is fulfilled if the claimant suffers from congestive heart failure.

2. No actual evaluation is done under Part (b). If the claimant has heart failure, the case is evaluated under Listing 104.02, which deals with heart failure, and the requirements of that Listing must be fulfilled. Further details can be found under the discussion of Listing 104.02.

C. Part (c)

1. Part (c) is fulfilled if there is inability of the claimant to do much physical exercise, because of his heart disease.

2. The claimant should be unable to do even "mild" exercise without getting short of breath ("labored respirations"). Of course, this must be evaluated in terms of the age of the child, and what he would normally be expected to be able to do at his age. For example, in an infant, merely feeding might be enough

to produce shortness of breath. This could be seen by an abnormally increased breathing rate.

Listing 104.07

Cardiac syncope. With at least one documented syncopal episode characteristic of specific cardiac disease (e.g., aortic stenosis).

I. General Considerations

A. This Listing deals specifically with "cardiac syncope". This means loss of consciousness, due to heart disease.

B. Any type of heart disease can cause syncope, or temporary loss of consciousness, by not pumping enough blood to the brain.

II. Specific Requirements

A. At least one "documented" episode must have occurred. This means there must be medical records by a physician showing that it happened.

B. The "syncopal episode" must be due to a heart disease. Unless it were caused by heart disease, the claimant would not qualify under this Listing. Also, if the claimant has heart disease, it must be severe enough to reasonably cause a syncopal episode. An example is given as "aortic stensis", which means a narrowing of the aortic valve in the heart. This could keep adequate blood from getting to the brain, but if the claimant only has mild aortic stensis and has a syncopal episode, it is not reasonable to blame it on the heart disease.

Listing 104.08

Recurrent hemoptysis. Associated with either pulmonary hypertension or extensive bronchial collaterals due to documented chronic cardiovascular disease.

I. General Considerations

A. This Listing deals with "recurrent hemoptysis", which means recurrent episodes of coughing up blood from the lungs.

B. Recurrent hemoptysis can be a sign of severe heart disease, in some cases.

II. Specific Requirements

A. The recurrent hemoptysis *must* be due to heart disease.

B. The Listing is fulfilled if there is "pulmonary hypertension". This means high blood pressure in the blood vessels of the lungs. This occurs in some types of severe heart disease, when the abnormal heart pumps too much blood through the lungs. This damages the delicate blood vessels in the lungs and increases the pressure in them. Special X-ray studies are needed to detect pulmonary hypertension. S. S. Disability does not order these studies, but must be able to obtain the reports of what they show. If there is a good reason to think that pulmonary hypertension might be present, these studies should have been done by the treating doctor.

C. Medical records showing "extensive bronchial collaterals" indicate abnormal blood flow through bronchial arteries due to heart disease. This will also fulfill the Listing.

Listing 104.09

Chronic rheumatic fever or rheumatic heart disease. With:

(a) Persistence of rheumatic fever activity for six months or more, with significant murmur(s), cardiomegaly, and other abnormal laboratory findings (such as elevated sedimentation rate or electrocardiographic findings); OR

(b) Congestive heart failure as described under the criteria in Listing 104.02.

I. General Considerations

A. This Listing deals with "rheumatic heart disease", which is caused by "rheumatic fever". Rheumatic fever is a disease that sometimes develops after a sore throat caused by a certain kind of bacteria. It may affect the heart, joints, and skin, among other things. It can be especially damaging to the valves in the heart, which decreases the heart's ability to efficiently pump blood.

B. Part (a) or (b) must be fulfilled, but not both.

II. Specific Requirements

A. Part (a)

1. Part (a) requires evidence of rheumatic fever for at *least* a 6 month period.

2. Such evidence may include several things. "Murmurs" are abnormal heart sounds, heard by a doctor listening to the claimant's heart. They are caused by blood flowing through abnormal valves. "Cardiomegaly" means an enlarged heart. How

large the heart must be depends on the age of the child. If the claimant is one year old or less, the heart must be at least 60% as wide as the chest cavity on a chest X-ray. For claimants more than one year old, it must be at least 55%. Cardiomegaly will also be said to exist, if the heart is 15% larger on a chest X-ray than it was on the previous X-ray.

3. Electrocardiograms (electrical tracings of the heart) may be abnormal, as well as certain kinds of laboratory tests, such as the "erythrocyte sedimentation rate". This is a measure of how fast red blood cells from a sample of blood fall ("sediment") in the tube. In rheumatic fever they will fall faster than normal. (This test can also be abnormal in many other diseases, and does not by itself prove that rheumatic fever is present.)

B. Part (b)

1. Part (b) is fulfilled if the rheumatic fever is severe enough to cause heart failure.

2. No actual evaluation is done under this Listing, but under Listing 104.02 which deals with heart failure. The requirements of that Listing must be fulfilled. Further details can be found in the discussion of Listing 104.02.

§ 3.7 Digestive System

Listing 105.03

Esophageal obstruction, caused by atresia, stricture, or stenosis. With malnutrition as described under the criteria in Listing 105.08.

I. General Considerations

A. This Listing deals with obstruction (blockage) of the esophagus, from any disease. The blockage doesn't have to be complete.

B. "Atresia" refers to partial or complete blockage of a part of the esophagus at birth, due to its failure to develop normally. "Stricture" and "stenosis" refer to narrowing of the esophagus. This could be due to atresia dating from the time of birth, or to some disease developing later which damages the esophagus.

II. Specific Requirements

A. The narrowing of the esophagus must be severe enough to cause malnutrition—adequate food cannot get through an esophagus that is too narrow, and the claimant could become malnourished and lose weight.

B. The claimant must show weight loss which fulfills the requirements of Listing 105.08, which deals with malnutrition. Further details can be found in the discussion of Listing 105.08.

Listing 105.05

Chronic liver disease. With ONE of the following:

(a) Inoperable biliary atresia demonstrated by X-ray or surgery; OR

(b) Intractable ascites not attributable to other causes, with serum albumin of 3.0 gm./100 ml. or less; OR

(c) Esophageal varices (demonstrated by angiography, barium swallow, or endoscopy or by prior performance of a specific shunt or plication procedure); OR

(d) Hepatic coma, documented by findings from hospital records; OR

(e) Hepatic encephalopathy. Evaluate under the criteria under Listing 112.02; OR

(f) Chronic active inflammation or necrosis documented by SGOT persistently more than 100 units or serum bilirubin of 2.5 mg. percent or greater.

I. General Considerations

A. This Listing deals with diseases of the liver which are long-lasting and difficult, if not impossible, to cure. Any type of liver disease which is severe enough can qualify (except for Part (a), which requires a specific type of disease).

B. Part (a), (b), (c), (d), (e), or (f) must be fulfilled, but not all six.

II. Specific Requirements

A. Part (a)

1. Part (a) deals with "biliary atresia". This is a disease in which the bile ducts inside or outside of the liver fail to develop normally.

2. That the biliary atresia must be proven by observation at the time of surgery, or by special X-ray studies. S. S. Disability does not order either surgery or X-ray studies. These must be available from the treating doctor or hospital.

3. The biliary atresia must be "inoperable". This means that it cannot reasonably be corrected by surgery. The mere

fact that the claimant may have had surgery would not keep him from qualifying under Part (a), if the surgery was not reasonably successful in correcting the biliary atresia.

B. Part (b)

1. Part (b) requires to have abnormal fluid accumulation in the abdomen ("ascites"), which is an indication of severe liver disease (although other diseases can also cause ascites).

2. If the ascites is really due to severe liver disease, then there should also be an abnormally low level of a protein called "albumin" in the blood stream. Blood tests showing the albumin level to be no higher than 3.0 are necessary.

3. It should be noted that the ascites must be present all the time, this abnormal fluid in the abdomen cannot be something that was present in the past, but improved with therapy. Also, the abnormally low albumin in the blood must stay low on *repeated* tests of the blood. Medical records covering a period of at *least* several months would be required to show this.

C. Part (c)

1. Part (c) is fulfilled if esophageal varices are present. These are literally varicose veins in the esophagus, which are often associated with severe liver disease.

2. The presence of esophageal varices can be shown by a variety of methods. "Angiography" and "barium swallow" are special X-ray procedures. "Endoscopy" involves looking down into the esophagus through a flexible tube. S. S. Disability doesn't order these tests; they must be available from the treating doctor or hospital.

3. "Performance of a specific shunt or plication procedure" will also fulfill part (c). These are special types of surgery sometimes done in claimants with severe liver disease and esophageal varices, which hopefully decrease the chance of bleeding from the esophageal varices. Whether the surgery is successful or not is not important; the mere fact that this surgery is done (at any time) is sufficient to qualify under part (c).

D. Part (d)

1. Part (d) is fulfilled if the claimant has suffered "hepatic coma", as a result of severe liver disease.

2. S. S. Disability must be able to obtain hospital records clearly showing that the claimant became comatose, because of liver disease.

E. Part (e)

1. Part (e) is fulfilled if there is evidence that the claimant developed "hepatic encephalopathy", as a result of severe liver disease. This refers to profound mental changes, due to the effects on the brain caused by advanced liver failure.

2. No actual evaluation is done under Part (e). The mental impairment caused by hepatic encephalopathy is evaluated under Listing 112.02, which deals with mental impairments caused by brain damage. The requirements of that Listing must be fulfilled. Further details can be found under the discussion of Listing 112.02.

F. Part (f)

1. Part (f) can be fulfilled if there is evidence that there is "active", ongoing destruction of liver tissue.

2. If there is active liver inflammation, an enzyme in the liver called "SGOT" must be increased. This can be measured in the blood stream. Also, a chemical called "bilirubin" may also be increased during active liver inflammation, and it must be increased in the blood stream to at least 2.5.

3. Note that the word "chronic" requires that the liver inflammation be continuously present. To show this, *repeated* blood tests showing elevated SGOT and bilirubin are necessary. This would require at *least* several months of lab tests recorded in medical records and available to S. S. Disability.

Listing 105.07

Chronic inflammatory bowel disease (such as ulcerative colitis, regional enteritis). With ONE of the following:

(a) Intestinal manifestations or complications, such as obstruction, abscess, or fistula formation which has lasted or is expected to last 12 months; OR

(b) Malnutrition as described under the criteria in Listing 105.08; OR

(c) Growth impairment as described under the criteria in Listing 100.03.

I. General Considerations

A. This Listing deals with diseases which produce severe inflammation of the large or small intestine. "Ulcerative colitis" involves the large intestine, and "regional enteritis" ("Crohn's Disease") involves the small intestine.

B. There must be evidence that the intestinal disease exists. This can be done by information obtained from surgery, a small piece of tissue (biopsy) which shows the disease to be present, or special X-ray studies. There is also a method called "endoscopy" by which a doctor can look into the intestine through a flexible tube and see the abnormalities. This also is sufficient. S. S. Disability does not order these studies, they must be available from the treating doctor or hospital.

C. Part (a), (b), or (c) must be fulfilled, but not all three.

II. Specific Requirements

A. Part (a)

1. Part (a) can be fulfilled if medical records show complications such as "obstruction" (intestinal blockage), "abscess" (intestinal infection), or "fistula" formation (abnormal openings to another part of the body caused by the inflammation breaking through the wall of the intestine).

2. Any of these problems must be *chronic*; that is, the problem must have already lasted 12 months, or reasonably be expected to last that long. For example, a claimant who had an intestinal blockage cured by surgery would not qualify.

B. Part (b)

1. Part (b) deals with malnutrition caused by inflammatory disease of the intestine. Such disease, if severe enough, can affect the ability to eat normally and to absorb nutrients from food normally. This can lead to weight loss.

2. No actual evaluation is done under Part (b). If the claimant is malnourished, the evaluation is done under Listing 105.08, and the requirements of that Listing must be fulfilled. Further details can be found under the discussion of Listing 105.08.

C. Part (c)

1. Part (c) deals with "growth impairment" caused by inflammatory disease of the intestine. This refers to decreased growth in *height,* not weight.

2. No evaluation is done under Part (c). If there is such a growth impairment, it is evaluated under Listing 100.03, the requirements of which must be fulfilled. Further details can be found under the discussion of Listing 100.03.

Listing 105.08

Malnutrition, due to demonstrable gastrointestinal disease causing either a fall of 15 percentiles of weight which persists or the persistence of weight which is less than the 3 percentile (on standard growth charts). And ONE of the following:

(a) Stool fat excretion per 24 hours:

(1) More than 15 percent in infants less than 6 months.

(2) More than 10 percent in infants 6–18 months.

(3) More than 6 percent in children more than 18 months; OR

(b) Persistent hematocrit of 30 percent or less despite prescribed therapy; OR

(c) Serum carotene of 40 mcg./100 ml. or less; OR

(d) Serum albumin of 3.0 gm./100 ml. or less.

I. General Considerations

A. This Listing deals with malnutrition, due to any disease of the gastrointestinal tract. This would include the esophagus, stomach, large intestine, or small intestine. Such malnutrition is evaluated in terms of weight loss, and such weight loss *must* be due to a demonstrated gastrointestinal problem of some kind.

B. The normal weight of any child depends on age and sex. There are also variations. To determine whether any particular claimant is abnormally underweight, special "growth charts" must be used. The claimant's weight over a period of time (at *least* several months) is plotted on these charts, and a number called a "percentile" is calculated. There must be either a *persistent* fall of at least 15 percentiles in weight, or a persistently low weight that doesn't get above the third percentile.

C. Once it is established that the claimant's weight is low enough to qualify, then Part (a), (b), (c), or (d) must be fulfilled, but not all four.

II. Specific Requirements

A. Part (a)

1. Some intestinal disease prevent adequate absorption of fats from food. If that is true, then a sample of the claimant's stool collected over a 24 hour period will show an abnormally high percentage of fat that wasn't absorbed.

2. The amount of fat normally absorbed depends on age. Part (a)(1), (a)(2), and (a)(3) give the percentages of fat in the stool necessary at given ages to qualify under Part (a).

B. Part (b)

1. Part (b) deals with claimants who are anemic, because of malnutrition. Anemic means a decrease in the normal number of red blood cells in the blood stream. One way of measuring the number of red blood cells is by a blood test called "hematocrit". This is the percentage of the volume of blood taken up by red blood cells. For example, a hematocrit of 50% means that half of the volume of a sample of blood is made up of red blood cells.

2. To qualify under Part (b), the hematocrit (despite treatment) must be no higher than 30%. *Repeated* blood tests are required over a period of time (at *least* several months), to demonstrate that the anemia is not likely to improve.

C. Part (c)

1. Part (c) requires a low serum "carotene" in the blood. Carotene is a substance that may be poorly absorbed from food in the presence of intestinal disease.

2. The carotene level in the blood must not be higher than 40. This would have to be shown on *repeated* blood tests (over at *least* a several month period), to demonstrate that the condition is not likely to improve.

D. Part (d)

1. Part (d) can be fulfilled by having an abnormally low level of albumin in the blood. Albumin is a very important protein that should be low in the blood, if intestinal disease prevents adequate absorption of nutrients from food.

2. The albumin level in the blood must not be higher than 3.0. This must be shown on *repeated* tests (over at *least* a several month period), to demonstrate that the condition is not likely to improve.

§ 3.8 Genito-Urinary System

Listing 106.02

Chronic renal disease. With:

(a) BUN of 30 mg./100 ml., or greater; OR

(b) Serum creatinine of 3.0 mg./100 ml. or greater; OR

(c) Creatinine clearance equal to or less than 42 ml./min./1.73m^2; OR

(d) Chronic renal dialysis program for irreversible renal failure; OR

(e) *Renal transplant.* Consider under a disability for 12 months following surgery; thereafter, evaluate the residual impairment.

I. General Considerations

A. This Listing deals with chronic kidney disease. That means kidney disease that cannot be reversed with treatment.

B. There are many diseases that cause kidney damage, and any of these may qualify. One of the most frequent causes of kidney failure is diabetes.

C. Part (a), (b), (c), (d), or (e) must be fulfilled, but not all five.

II. Specific Requirements

A. Part (a)

1. Part (a) requires an abnormally high "BUN". This stands for "blood urea nitrogen". The BUN tends to be elevated in kidney disease, because the damaged kidneys cannot adequately filter it out of the blood stream.

2. Blood tests must show the BUN to be at *least* 30 or higher. Such abnormally high values must be present on *repeated* blood tests (over a period of at *least* several months) to show that improvement is not likely.

3. There is one very interesting and important thing about Part (a). It is by far the easiest way to qualify under this Listing. The reason for this is that a BUN of 30 can be produced by only relatively mild kidney disease, so it is to the advantage of the claimant if this type of blood test has been done.

B. Part (b)

1. Part (b) is fulfilled if there is an abnormally elevated creatinine in the blood, to a level of at *least* 3.0. The creatinine rises, because the damaged kidneys cannot adequately filter it from the blood stream.

2. The creatinine level must be increased on *repeated* blood tests (over a period of at *least* several months), to show that improvement is not likely.

C. Part (c)

1. Part (c) is fulfilled, if there is a sufficiently abnormal test called a "creatinine clearance". This is simply another way of measuring kidney function, and means the amount of blood that is "cleansed" of creatinine every minute. The worse the kidney disease is, the less blood can be cleansed of creatinine every min-

ute. Samples of both blood and urine are used to perform this test.

2. The creatinine clearance must not be higher than 42 (somewhat less than half normal value). The test must be abnormal on *repeated* testing (at *least* a period of several months), to show that it is not likely to improve.

3. In giving the required value for the creatinine clearance, Part (c) mentions the number "1.73m^2". This is a correction factor for the size of the claimant, and is not usually important. But in some instances, involving very small or very large claimants, this correction factor can alter the value of the required creatinine clearance value from 42 to something else, higher or lower.

D. Part (d)

1. Part (d) can be fulfilled, if there is "chronic renal dialysis". If kidney failure becomes nearly complete, then the blood must be "cleansed" by artificial methods called "dialysis" to prevent death. There are two major kinds of dialysis. One is "hemodialysis", in which the claimant's blood is gradually circulated out of the body through a machine that removes waste material (an artificial kidney machine). The other method is called "peritoneal dialysis", in which fluids are put into the abdominal cavity. "Waste" materials from the blood stream then move across the membrane lining the abdominal cavity (the peritoneal membrane), and are taken up by the fluid, which is then removed. Either type of dialysis may qualify.

2. Note that the dialysis cannot be a temporary requirement. The claimant must have kidney disease so severe that *permanent* dialysis is required.

E. Part (e)

1. Part (e) can be fulfilled if the claimant has received a transplanted kidney from someone else.

2. Since it takes a fair amount of time to find out if a transplant is going to work, the claimant automatically qualifies under Part (e) for a period of one year from the time of the surgery.

3. After one year has passed from the time of surgery, S. S. Disability will then evaluate the claimant again, to see how effective the transplant was. If the transplant surgery was effective, the claimant's disability benefits will be stopped. In order to show that the transplant surgery was *not* effective, the claim-

ant would have to fulfill one of the *other* Parts of this Listing a year after surgery was done.

Listing 106.06

Nephrotic syndrome, with edema not controlled by prescribed therapy. AND:

(a) Serum albumin less than 2 gm./100 ml.; OR

(b) Proteinuria more than 2.5 gm./1.73m^2/day.

I. General Considerations

A. This Listing deals with what is called the "nephrotic syndrome". Essentially what happens in the nephrotic syndrome is that the damaged kidneys from some type of kidney disease allow important proteins in the blood to escape in the urine. One might say these proteins "fall through" damaged areas in the kidneys that normally would not allow this to happen.

B. Claimants with nephrotic syndrome tend to have swelling ("edema") in some part of the body (usually the feet, hands, and face). Such swelling is required, but any amount may qualify. It must be seen on physical examination by a doctor.

C. Part (a) or (b) must be fulfilled, but not both.

D. The claimant must be under treatment. Most cases respond to treatment.

II. Specific Requirements

A. Part (a)

1. The protein most frequently lost from the blood stream due to kidney disease is one called "albumin".

2. If the blood albumin falls to *less* than 2.0, then Part (a) is fulfilled.

3. The albumin level must be low on *repeated* tests (over a period of at *least* several months), to show that improvement is not likely. S. S. Disability must be convinced that the impairment will last at least a year.

B. Part (b)

1. Part (b) can be fulfilled, if there are abnormally large amounts of protein in the urine. This is called "proteinuria". The test is done by taking a sample of urine collected over a 24 hour period and measuring the amount of protein present.

2. The urine must contain *more* than 2.5 grams of protein in a 24 hour period. This must be demonstrated on *repeated* tests

(over a period of at *least* several months), to show that improvement is not likely. S. S. Disability must be convinced that the impairment will last at least a year.

3. In giving the required value for the proteinuria, Part (b) mentions the number "$1.73m^2$". This is a correction factor for the size of the claimant, and is not usually important. But in some instances, involving very small and very large claimants, this correction factor can alter the required value of higher than 2.5 grams to something else, higher or lower.

§ 3.9 Hemic and Lymphatic System

Listing 107.03

Hemolytic anemia (due to any cause). Manifested by persistence of hematocrit of 26 percent or less despite prescribed therapy, and reticulocyte count of 4 percent or greater.

I. General Considerations

A. This Listing deals with "hemolytic anemia". Anemia is any blood disease in which there is a decrease in the normal number of red cells in the blood stream. There are many types of anemia, and any may qualify, as long as they are of the "hemolytic" variety. Hemolytic anemias are ones in which red blood cells undergo an abnormally high rate of destruction after they are formed. Other types of anemia may be caused by an abnormally low rate of production of red blood cells, but they would not qualify under this Listing. Sickle cell anemia is a type of hemolytic anemia, but there are many others.

B. Once there is sufficient evidence to show that the claimant has some type of hemolytic anemia, several other specific requirements must be fulfilled.

II. Specific Requirements

A. The claimant must be undergoing treatment, because many cases of hemolytic anemia can be improved with treatment.

B. A blood test called "hematocrit" must be 26% or less. This test is one way of judging the severity of anemia. It simply refers to the percentage of a volume of blood that is taken up by red blood cells. A hematocrit of 26% indicates that only 26% of the volume of blood is taken up by red cells, and this is an abnormally low number indicating severe anemia.

C. There must also be a "reticulocyte count" of at least 4%. This blood test measures what percent of red blood cells are of a special kind called reticulocytes. The marrow inside of bone makes red blood cells. When the cells have grown to maturity, the bone marrow releases them into the blood stream. But when hemolytic anemia is present, the bone marrow attempts to correct the anemia by turning out more red blood cells, earlier than they would normally be released into the blood stream. These more immature red cells are called reticulocytes. Normally, reticulocytes make up only about 1% of the red cells in the blood stream, but more of them appear in severe hemolytic anemia.

D. Both the hematocrit and the reticulocyte count must be abnormal on *repeated* blood tests (over a period of at *least* several months), to show that the anemia is not likely to improve. This is necessary to convince S. S. Disability that the condition is going to last a minimum of 12 months.

Listing 107.05

Sickle cell disease. With:

(a) Recent, recurrent, severe vaso-occlusive crises (musculoskeletal, vertebral, abdominal); OR

(b) A major visceral complication in the 12 months prior to application; OR

(c) A hyperhemolytic or aplastic crisis within 12 months prior to application; OR

(d) Chronic, severe anemia with persistence of hematocrit of 26 percent or less; OR

(e) Congestive heart failure, cerebrovascular damage, or emotional disorder as described under the criteria in Listing 104.02.

I. General Considerations

A. This Listing deals *only* with sickle cell anemia.

B. Sickle cell anemia is an inherited disease, caused by abnormal hemoglobin inside red blood cells. Hemoglobin is the chemical inside red blood cells that carries oxygen. Most sickle cell anemia occurs in black people.

C. In sickle cell anemia, the red blood cells are abnormal, and do not last as long as normal red blood cells. This can result in a decreased number of red blood cells, and the claimant becomes more anemic. It is called "sickle" cell anemia, because these abnormal red cells may have a sickle shape.

D. There is a type of anemia called sickle cell *trait*; this is usually not as severe as sickle anemia. True sickle cell anemia must be proven to exist by special tests of the blood that S. S. Disability will accept. These tests have usually already been done by the claimant's treating doctor.

E. Sickle cell anemia is a type of *hemolytic* anemia, and a claimant with this disease might also qualify under Listing 107.03, which deals with all types of hemolytic anemia.

F. Part (a), (b), (c), (d), or (e) must be fulfilled, but not all five.

II. Specific Requirements

A. Part (a)

1. Part (a) is fulfilled if there are "vaso-occlusive crises" documented.

2. Because the red blood cells in sickle cell anemia are not normal and have a sickle shape, they don't move through the blood stream as easily as normal red cells. In fact, they sometimes tend to clog up blood vessels. This can happen anywhere in the body, and can cause a great deal of pain. Episodes in which this happens are the "vaso-occlusive crises" that Part (a) refers to.

3. The amount of damage done by a vaso-occlusive crisis depends on how large the blocked blood vessel is, and what part of the body is concerned.

4. There must be medical records from a doctor documenting that such episodes are an ongoing problem at the time of application for disability (not something that happened years in the past), that such episodes happen over and over again, and that they are severe. Painful episodes involving the abdomen, muscles, bones, or spine may qualify.

5. A "severe" crisis is one requiring treatment in a hospital emergency room. In general, "recurrent" means at least an average of one episode per month over a period of 6 months.

B. Part (b)

1. Part (b) requires a "major visceral complication" in the 12 months before application for disability. Only *one* is required.

2. A major visceral complication is more serious than a vaso-occlusive crisis. It means that a vaso-occlusive crisis actually damages a major organ in the body.

3. There are several types of major visceral episodes that will fulfill Part (b), as follows:

(a) Part (b) can be fulfilled by "meningitis". This is infection of the meninges, which is a protective membrane covering the brain and spinal cord.

(b) Part (b) can be fulfilled by "osteomyelitis", which is an infection of bone.

(c) Part (b) can be fulfilled by "pulmonary infections or infarctions". Pulmonary infection means some type of pneumonia. Pulmonary infarction refers to the actual death of some part of the lung tissue, because the blood supply has been cut off by a vaso-occlusive crisis.

(d) Part (b) can be fulfilled by "cerebrovascular accidents", or strokes which damage the brain.

(e) Part (b) can be fulfilled by "congestive heart failure", caused by a vaso-occlusive crisis blocking part of the heart's blood supply.

(f) Part (b) can be fulfilled by kidney damage, caused by a vaso-occlusive crisis.

(g) The above complications are given only as examples. Other major organs which are significantly damaged by a vaso-occlusive crisis might also qualify as a major "visceral complication" as required by Part (b).

C. Part (c)

1. Part (c) is fulfilled, if there was a "hyperhemolytic" or "aplastic" crisis in the 12 months before application for disability. Only *one* such episode is required.

2. A "Hyperhemolytic" crisis means an episode in which a claimant with sickle cell anemia suddenly starts destroying red blood cells even faster than he usually does. The number of red cells drops so low (severe anemia), that blood transfusions are often necessary. However, Part (c) doesn't require that the claimant had to receive blood transfusions.

3. An "aplastic" crisis is similar to a hyperhemolytic crisis, except that there is a decreased ability of the bone marrow (which produces cells for the blood stream) to make red blood cells or white blood cells in sufficient amounts.

D. Part (d)

1. Part (d) can be fulfilled, if there is "chronic, severe anemia". anemia means a decreased number of red cells in the blood stream.

2. One way to measure the degree of anemia is by what is called a "hematocrit", which is simply the percentage of a volume of blood taken up by red blood cells.

3. If the claimant has a hematocrit of 26% as required by Part (d), then red cells take up only 26% of the volume of a sample of blood. This is an abnormally low number which indicates severe anemia.

4. There must be *repeated* blood tests showing a hematocrit of no higher than 26%, to convince S. S. Disability that improvement is not likely. This means abnormal tests of over a period of at *least* several months.

E. Part (e)

1. Part (e) can be fulfilled, if the sickle cell anemia has led to heart failure, "cerebrovascular damage" (strokes), or mental illness caused by brain damage.

2. No actual evaluation is done under Part (e). Heart failure would be evaluated under Listing 104.02, and would have to fulfill the requirements of that Listing. Cerebrovascular damage would be evaluated under one of the Listings in the "Neurological System" (whichever applies), and would have to fulfill the requirements of the Listing concerned. Emotional disorders would be evaluated under one of the Listings dealing with "Mental and Emotional Disorders", and would have to fulfill the requirements of the Listing concerned. Further details can be found under the discussion of the Listing which applies.

Listing 107.06

Chronic idiopathic thrombocytopenic purpura of childhood. With purpura and thrombocytopenia of 40,000 platelets/cu.mm. or less despite prescribed therapy or recurrent upon withdrawal of treatment.

I. General Considerations

A. This Listing deals with a disease called "idiopathic" (of known cause) "chronic" (incurable) "thrombocytopenic" (decreased platelets in the blood) "purpura" (areas of bleeding into the skin).

B. Platelets are necessary to prevent abnormal bleedings. The normal platelet "count" in the blood is 150,000–300,000. If the value drops too low, there is increased danger of bleeding into the internal organs.

II. Specific Requirements

A. "Purpura" must be present, and the platelet blood count must not be higher than 40,000. At this level of platelets, there is very great danger of serious bleeding.

B. These abnormalities must persist long enough to show that the disease isn't likely to improve. This requires abnormal blood tests and physical findings over at *least* a several month period, even though treatment is being received.

C. The Listing can also be fulfilled, if the above abnormalities reappear when treatment is withdrawn. In such circumstances, the claimant wouldn't have to show such abnormalities while under treatment. Sometimes physicians gradually withdraw treatment (decrease drug dosages gradually), to see if the disease has been cured. If this has been attempted by the treating doctor, and the low blood platelet count and purpura come back, then the claimant qualifies under this Listing, even if these abnormalities weren't present during treatment. S. S. Disability does *not* ever recommend to the claimant or the treating doctor that this experiment is tried. But in a claimant being effectively treated, S. S. Disability will *not* assume that the abnormalities would return if treatment were stopped, unless that has already been documented by the treating doctor.

Listing 107.08

Inherited coagulation disorder. With:

(a) Repeated spontaneous or inappropriate bleeding; OR

(b) Hemarthrosis with joint deformity.

I. General Considerations

A. This Listing deals with "inherited coagulation disorder". There are several types of specific disease that would qualify, but they all have in common a poor ability of the blood to clot normally. A complicated group of proteins must work together to produce blood clotting. If even one of these is abnormal or missing, the whole process of forming a blood clot may not function correctly. And the ability of the body for forming blood clots is extremely important in preventing abnormal amounts of bleeding. It is a clot that "plugs up" the hole in a bleeding vessel. The most well-known disorder of this kind is "hemophilia", in which there is deficiency in one of the proteins necessary for the clotting of blood. Actually, there is more than one type of hemophilia.

B. Part (a) or (b) must be fulfilled, but not both.

II. Specific Requirements

A. Part (a)

1. Part (a) is fulfilled, if there is "spontaneous" bleeding. This means bleeding (inside or outside the body) that just starts for no apparent reason. For example, even a normal person might bleed in their lungs if they were involved in an automobile accident that damaged their chest. That would not qualify under Part (a), even if the person involved had a disorder like hemophilia. Such bleeding is not abnormal—it is something that might be expected. On the other hand, if a person with hemophilia started bleeding in his lungs for no apparent reason, this would be a spontaneous episode of bleeding and would qualify under Part (a).

2. Part (a) can also be fulfilled, if there is "inappropriate bleeding". For example, if a person with hemophilia damaged his lungs in an automobile accident, and bled much *more* than a normal person would, then Part (a) would be fulfilled.

3. As noted above, Part (a) can be fulfilled if there is bleeding for no apparent reason, or if bleeding (from anything) is much more than normal. However, one such episode is not enough. The Listing requires "repeated" episodes. How often "repeated" has to be is not given. This is a matter of judgement on the part of the person in S. S. Disability evaluating the claimant's case. It partly depends on the particular claimant's problems—the circumstances associated with the bleeding episodes, how often they occur, and how severe they are, what damage they do to the body, how long it takes to recover, etc. All of these things must be taken into account in reaching a reasonable decision.

B. Part (b)

1. Part (b) is fulfilled if there is "hemarthrosis with joint deformity". Hemarthrosis means bleeding inside of a joint. Blood is extremely irritating to the tissues inside a joint, and can cause great damage.

2. Any important body joint can qualify (for example, ankles, knees, hips, elbows and shoulders).

3. It doesn't matter what causes the bleeding into a joint.

Listing 107.11

Acute leukemia. Consider under a disability:

(a) For $2^1/_2$ years from the time of initial diagnosis; OR

(b) For $2^1/_2$ years from the time of recurrence of active disease.

I. General Considerations

A. This Listing deals with leukemia. Leukemia is a cancer of the white blood cells. There are different types of leukemia, depending on what type of white blood cell is involved. Leukemias involving any particular type of cell are also divided into *acute* and *chronic* types. If the leukemia is an *acute* type, the cells involved are usually "more cancerous" and the disease more severe than in the *chronic* types of leukemia. This Listing deals *only* with *acute* types of leukemia. A chronic leukemia might turn into an acute leukemia and this would also qualify.

B. S. S. Disability must be able to obtain a pathology report proving that the claimant has leukemia. A pathology report is based on an analysis of tissue by a specialist called pathologist. In the case of leukemia, the tissue would be a sample of bone marrow.

C. Part (a) or (b) must be fulfilled, but not both.

II. Specific Requirements

A. Part (a)

1. For *any* type of acute leukemia, Part (a) is automatically fufilled for $2^1/_2$ years, from the time the diagnosis is first proven. No other evidence is necessary.

2. A claimant still qualifies under Part (a) for $2^1/_2$ years from the time of diagnosis, even if he is under treatment and even if the treatment appears to be working. For example, a claimant with acute leukemia might receive treatment that makes him improve to a temporarily "normal" condition (this is called "remission"), but it doesn't necessarily mean that he is permanently cured. If at any time within $2^1/_2$ years of the time of diagnosis he applies for disability, then the claimant will automatically be given benefits for the time remaining.

3. After $2^1/_2$ years from the time of diagnosis, S. S. Disability will evaluate the claimant's case again. If there has been no return of the leukemia for a period of at least $2^1/_2$ years, it will be assumed that complete cure has taken place, and disability benefits will be terminated.

B. Part (b)

1. Part (b) deals with acute leukemia that comes back again, after there has been a temporary cure (remission). If this happens, the claimant qualifies under Part (b) for 2½ years from the time the leukemia comes back.

2. It doesn't matter how long it has been since the original diagnosis of leukemia, or how effective previous treatment has been. If the leukemia comes back, 2½ years of benefits are automatically given. In other ways, Part (b) is exactly like Part (a), as discussed above.

§ 3.10 Endocrine System

Listing 109.02

Thyroid disorders:

(a) *Hyperthyroidism.* With clinical manifestations despite prescribed therapy, and ONE of the following:

(1) Elevated serum thyroxine (T_4) and either elevated free T_4 or resin T_3 uptake; OR

(2) Elevated thyroid uptake of radioiodine; OR

(3) Elevated serum triiodothyronine (T_3).

(b) *Hypothyroidism.* With ONE of the following, despite prescribed therapy:

(1) I.Q. of 69 or less; OR

(2) Growth impairment as described under the criteria in Listing 100.02A and B; OR

(3) Precocious puberty.

I. General Considerations

A. This Listing deals with disorders of the thyroid gland. This means disorders in which there is too much secretion of thyroid hormone (*hyper*thyroidism), or too little secretion of thyroid hormone (*hypo*thyroidism).

B. Part (a) deals with cases of hyperthyroidism, and Part (b) with cases of hypothyroidism. Of course, only one of these has to be fulfilled.

II. Specific Requirements

A. Part (a)

1. Part (a) deals *only* with hyperthyroidism.

2. Medical records should reasonably show that the claimant has hyperthyroidism, based on physical examination and abnormal laboratory tests showing abnormally elevated thyroid hormone in the blood stream.

3. The claimant *must* be under treatment, and have at least one of the following:

(a) Part (a)(1) is fulfilled if one of the mentioned laboratory tests shows an abnormally active thyroid gland.

(b) Part (a)(2) is fulfilled if the laboratory test mentioned is abnormal.

(c) Part (a)(3) is fulfilled, if the laboratory test mentioned is abnormal.

B. Part (b)

1. Part (b) deals *only* with hypothyroidism.

2. Medical records should reasonably show that the claimant has hypothyroidism, based on physical examination and laboratory tests showing abnormally low thyroid hormone in the blood.

3. The claimant *must* be under treatment, and have at least one of the following:

(a) Part (b)(1) is fulfilled, if the claimant has a measured I.Q. of 69 or less. It should be noted that if the I.Q. test has more than one score, S. S. Disability is supposed to use the *lowest* score.

(b) Part (b)(2) is fulfilled, if the hypothyroidism has caused sufficient decrease in normal growth. No actual evaluation is done under Part (b)(2). If there is a growth impairment due to hypothyroidism, then the case would be evaluated under Listing 100.02, which deals with growth impairments. The requirements of Listing 100.02 must be fulfilled. Further details concerning Listing 100.02 can be found under the discussion of that Listing.

(c) Part (b)(3) is fulfilled, if the hypothyroidism is associated with "precocious puberty", or the development of adult sexual characteristics at an abnormally young age.

Listing 109.03

Hyperparathyroidism. With:

(a) Repeated elevated total or ionized serum calcium; OR

(b) Elevated serum parathyroid hormone.

I. General Considerations

A. This Listing deals with *hyper*parathyroidism. This means a disorder, in which there is an overproduction of parathyroid hormone by the parathyroid glands.

B. Medical records should show that the claimant has hyperparathyroidism, based on physical examination and laboratory tests associated with that disease.

C. Part (a) or (b) must be fulfilled, but not both.

II. Specific Requirements

A. Part (a)

1. Part (a) can be fulfilled, if there are tests showing abnormally elevated calcium in the blood stream. The reason for this is that the abnormal amounts of parathyroid hormone in the blood associated with hyperparathyroidism causes abnormally large amounts of calcium to be released from bones.

2. The word "repeated" means there must be more than one test, over a period of at *least* several months to show that the condition is not likely to improve.

B. Part (b)

1. Part (b) is fulfilled, if there is an elevated level of parathyroid hormone in the blood.

2. Part (b) does not say anything about repeated blood tests being necessary, but there would have to be reasonable evidence that the parathyroid hormone level in the blood was elevated at the time of application for disability.

Listing 109.04

Hypoparathyroidism or pseudohypoparathyroidism. With:

(a) Severe recurrent tetany or convulsions which are unresponsive to prescribed therapy; OR

(b) Growth retardation as described under the criteria in Listing 100.02A and B.

I. General Considerations

A. This Listing deals with hypoparathyroidism, or production of too little parathyroid hormone. (A similar disease called pseudohypoparathyroidism can also qualify under this Listing.)

B. Medical records must first show that the claimant has the disease, based on physical examination and laboratory tests.

C. Part (a) or (b) must be fulfilled, but not both.

II. Specific Requirements

A. Part (a)

1. Part (a) is fulfilled if there are severe, repeated episodes of "tetany" (uncontrollable muscle contractions) or actual convulsions.

2. The required abnormalities must be present, even though the claimant is under treatment.

B. Part (b)

1. Part (b) is fulfilled, if there is an abnormal decrease in growth, caused by the hypoparathyroidism.

2. No actual evaluation is done under Part (b). Evaluation would be done under Listing 100.02, which deals with growth impairments. The requirements of that Listing must be fulfilled. Further details can be found under the discussion of Listing 100.02.

Listing 109.05

Diabetes insipidus, documented by pathologic hypertonic saline or water deprivation test. And ONE of the following:

(a) Intracranial space-occupying lesion, before or after surgery; OR

(b) Unresponsiveness to Pitressin; OR

(c) Growth retardation as described under the criteria in Listing 100.02A and B; OR

(d) Unresponsive hypothalamic thirst center, with chronic or recurrent hypernatremia, OR

(e) Decreased visual fields attributable to a pituitary lesion.

I. General Considerations

A. This Listing deals with diabetes *insipidus*. This is not the form of diabetes that most people mean when they say "diabetes". That is "sugar" diabetes, or diabetes *mellitus.* Unlike diabetes mellitus, diabetes *insipidus* has nothing to do with lack of insulin or high blood sugar. This form of diabetes is caused by a deficiency of a special hormone called *anti-diuretic hormone,* or ADH. ADH is produced by the pituitary gland, acts on the kidneys, and helps the body save water that it would otherwise lose through the kidneys. A good example of this is the increased frequency of urination many people have, after drinking alcoholic beverages. The alcohol inhibits the release of ADH from the pituitary gland, and increased fluid is lost through the kidneys. So alcohol produces in many people a kind of "artificial" and temporary diabetes insipidus.

B. "Hypertonic saline" and "water deprivation" are special tests used in the diagnosis of diabetes insipidus. S. S. Disability does not order these tests; they must be done in a hospital.

C. Part (a), (b), (c), (d), or (e) must be fulfilled, but not all five.

II. Specific Requirements

A. Part (a)

1. Diabetes insipidus is often caused by a tumor of the pituitary gland ("intracranial space-occupying lesion"), and if medical records show this to be true, the claimant qualifies under Part (a).

2. Surgery is sometimes done to remove such tumors, but the claimant can still qualify under Part (a) whether or not surgery has been done.

B. Part (b)

1. Part (b) is fulfilled, if there is "unresponsiveness to Pitressin". Pitressin is another word for ADH. Vasopressin also means the same thing.

2. If there is no response to ADH, it means that the diabetes insipidus can't be reversed by giving the claimant the missing hormone that he lacks.

C. Part (c)

1. Part (c) can be fulfilled if there is sufficient growth retardation. For example, a tumor of the pituitary gland causing diabetes insipidus could also damage other areas of the pituitary gland which release growth hormone.

2. No actual evaluation is done under Part (c). The evaluation would be done under Listing 100.02, which deals with

growth impairments. The requirements of that Listing must be fulfilled. Further details can be found under the discussion of Listing 100.02.

D. Part (d)

1. Part (d) can be fulfilled, if the claimant has an "unresponsive hypothalamic thirst center". There is an area at the bottom of the brain, near the pituitary gland, called the hypothalamus, and there is a little group of cells in one part of the hypothalamus called the "thirst center", because it controls how thirsty a person feels.

2. If the claimant has diabetes insipidus which can't be helped by treatment, then he will lose an abnormally large amount of water through the kidneys (increased urine flow), and this will cause the chemicals in the blood to become more concentrated. For example, the amount of sodium in the blood will abnormally increase, and this is called "hypernatremia". Normally, if a person loses too much water from the body for whatever reason, the increased sodium in the blood will trigger the thirst center to cause the person to become more thirsty, so that he will drink more water and make up for the amount lost. But some claimants have such severe diabetes insipidus that when too much water is lost through the kidneys, the thirst center is not triggered like it should be. If this is true, then Part (d) is fulfilled.

E. Part (e)

1. Part (e) is fulfilled, if there are "decreased visual fields attributable to a pituitary lesion". If the claimant has diabetes insipidus caused by a pituitary tumor, then this tumor might press on the optic nerves, which are close to the pituitary gland.

2. The optic nerves carry visual information from the eyes to the brain, and pressure on them from a pituitary tumor can decrease the ability to see normally. This impairment in seeing can be detected through testing by an eye specialist, and would show up as a "decreased visual field". Visual fields refer to that part of vision in which a person can see things he is not looking at directly (for example, things seen "out of the corner of the eye"). Without visual fields, a person would have pinpoint or tunnel vision, like looking through a tube.

Listing 109.06

Hyperfunction of the adrenal cortex (primary or secondary). With:

(a) Elevated urinary 17-hydroxycorticosteroids (or 17-ketogenic steroids); AND

(b) Unresponsiveness to low-dose dexamethasone suppression.

I. General Considerations

A. This Listing deals with "hyperfunction of the adrenal cortex". There are two adrenal glands, one sitting on top of each kidney. The outer layer of cells in the adrenal glands is called the adrenal cortex, and produces special kinds of hormones called steroids. Hyperfunction simply means that the adrenal cortex cells are producing too much steroid hormones. This can be caused by several different diseases (for example, a tumor of the adrenal gland), but any type can qualify under this Listing.

B. Part (a) *and* (b) must be fulfilled.

II. Specific Requirements

A. Part (a)

1. If there is hyperfunction of the adrenal cortex, as required by the Listing, there should be increased amounts of steroid hormones in the urine.

2. If tests done on the claimant's urine show that there is an increased amount of "17-hydroxycorticosteroids" or "17-ketosteroid", then Part (a) is fulfilled. The results of these tests must be available to S. S. Disability.

B. Part (b)

1. Part (b) requires an abnormal test called a "low-dose dexamethasone suppression" test.

2. S. S. Disability does not order this test. It must have been done by the treating doctor, and the results available to S. S. Disability.

Listing 109.07

Adrenal cortical insufficiency. With recent, recurrent episodes of circulatory collapse.

I. General Considerations

A. This Listing deals with "adrenal cortical insufficiency", or too little steroid hormones produced by what are called the cortical cells of the adrenal glands.

B. There must be medical records with physical examinations and laboratory tests showing the disease to be present. The laboratory tests would be ones showing abnormally low levels of certain steroid hormones in the blood stream or urine.

C. Sometimes adrenal insufficiency can be treated by giving artificial steroid drugs. Claimants receiving effective treatment would not qualify under this Listing.

II. Specific Requirements

A. There must be medical records showing episodes of "circulatory collapse". Circulatory collapse means a very severe, life-threatening fall in the blood pressure (severe shock). This can come about when there are insufficient steroid hormones in the blood stream, because they play an important part in keeping blood pressure normal.

B. These episodes must be "recent" enough to really apply to the claimant's current condition. How much time has passed since the last episode and the application for disability is taken into account by S. S. Disability, but there is no exact time for how short this must be. This depends on the problems of the individual claimant, considering all of the important facts in the case. If the last episode occurred years in the past, it certainly would not qualify.

C. "Recurrent" means that more than one episode must be documented in medical records. There is no exact number for how often "recurrent" means. That depends on the individual claimant's problems—such as how severe the episodes were, the effectiveness of treatment, etc. Since circulatory collapse from adrenal insufficiency is very serious, several episodes in a year would probably be sufficient to qualify under this Listing.

Listing 109.08

Juvenile diabetes mellitus requiring parenteral insulin. And ONE of the following, despite prescribed therapy:

(a) Recent, recurrent hospitalizations with acidosis; OR

(b) Recent, recurrent episodes of hypoglycemia; OR

(c) Growth retardation as described under the criteria in Listing 100.02A and B; OR

(d) Impaired renal function as described under the criteria in Listing 106.02 or Listing 106.06.

I. General Considerations

A. This Listing deals with diabetes mellitus in children (more commonly known as "sugar" diabetes). This type of diabetes is caused by a deficiency of insulin from the pancreas. Without insulin, the cells of the body cannot use a type of blood sugar called glucose that they need.

B. The diabetes must be severe enough that the claimant has to take insulin injections.

C. The claimant must be under treatment by a medical doctor.

D. Part (a), (b), (c), or (d) must be fulfilled, but not all four.

II. Specific Requirements

A. Part (a)

1. Part (a) requires "recent" and "recurrent" hospitalizations with "acidosis".

2. "Acidosis" refers to abnormal changes in the acidity of blood, due to diabetes that is out of control. Special blood tests must have been done to show that this is true. It should be noted that a Diabetic that intentionally ignores the treatment prescribed by the doctor might not qualify under this Listing.

3. At least 3 episodes of documented acidosis requiring hospitalization in the year prior to the application for disability would probably be sufficient to qualify under this Listing.

B. Part (b)

1. Part (b) requires "recent" and "recurrent" episodes of "hypoglycemia".

2. Hypoglycemia refers to an abnormally low blood sugar (glucose). This isn't caused by the diabetes, which causes abnormally high blood sugar. But diabetics which are difficult to treat are in constant danger of taking too much insulin, with too great a lowering of their blood sugar.

3. At least 3 episodes of documented hypoglycemia must occur in the year prior to application for disability. These episodes must be severe enough to cause significant symptoms.

C. Part (c)

1. Part (c) deals with decreased growth caused by diabetes.

2. No actual evaluation is done under Part (c). If there is impairment of growth, this would be evaluated under Listing

100.02, the requirements of which must be fulfilled. Further details can be found under the discussion of Listing 100.02.

D. Part (d)

1. Diabetes frequently damages the kidneys, and if this is severe enough, then Part (d) can be fulfilled.

2. No actual evaluation is done under Part (d). If kidney damage has been done, the requirements of Listing 106.02 or 106.06 must be fulfilled. These Listings are used for the evaluation of all types of kidney disease. Further details can be found under the discussion of Listings 106.02 or 106.06.

Listing 109.09

Iatrogenic hypercorticoid state. With chronic glucocorticoid therapy resulting in ONE of the following:

(a) Osteoporosis; OR

(b) Growth retardation as described under the criteria in Listing 100.02A or B; OR

(c) Diabetes mellitus as described under the criteria in Listing 109.08; OR

(d) Myopathy as described under the criteria in Listing 111.06; OR

(e) Emotional disorder as described under the criteria in Listings 112.03 or 112.04.

I. General Considerations

A. This Listing deals with what is called an "iatrogenic hypercorticoid state". In other words, this Listing deals with the problems that can arise from the side-effects of taking steroid drugs for the treatment of some diseases. There are many diseases that require steroid drugs for treatment (for example, adrenal cortical insufficiency as in Listing 109.07), but that is not important for this Listing. Steroids are extremely potent drugs, and can in themselves cause medical problems.

B. "Chronic glucocorticoid therapy" means that the claimant is receiving some kind of steroid drug for the treatment of a disease that requires such drugs.

C. Part (a), (b), (c), (d), or (e) must be fulfilled, but not all five.

II. Specific Requirements

A. Part (a)

1. Part (a) is fulfilled, if there is "osteoporosis".

2. Osteoporosis refers to an abnormal "thinning" of bone which can be seen on X-rays. It is one of the possible side-effects of steroid drugs.

B. Part (b)

1. Growth retardation caused by the side-effect of steroid drugs is required to fulfill Part (b).

2. No actual evaluation is done under Part (b). If the steroid drugs are responsible for a decrease in normal growth, the case would be evaluated under Listing 100.02. The requirements of that Listing must be fulfilled. Further details can be found under the discussion of Listing 100.02.

C. Part (c)

1. One possible side-effect of steroid drugs is the development of diabetes, and this is required to fulfill Part (c).

2. No actual evaluation is done under Part (c). If diabetes has developed, because of taking steroid drugs, the case would be evaluated under Listing 109.08, which deals with diabetes mellitus. The requirements of that Listing must be fulfilled. Further details can be found under the discussion of Listing 109.08.

D. Part (d)

1. Part (d) can be fulfilled, if steroid drugs have caused "myopathy". This simply means damage to muscle tissue, which can cause weakness, if severe enough.

2. No actual evaluation is done under Part (d). The case would be evaluated under Listing 111.06, which deals with muscle weakness. The requirements of that Listing must be fulfilled. Further details can be found under the discussion of Listing 111.06.

E. Part (e)

1. Steroid drugs can have abnormal effects on the mind. If an emotional disorder is caused by such drugs, then Part (e) may be fulfilled.

2. No actual evaluation is done under Part (e). That would be done under Listing 112.03 or 112.04, which deal with mental disorders, and the requirements of which must be fulfilled. Further details can be found under the discussion of those Listings.

Listing 109.10

Pituitary dwarfism (with documented growth hormone deficiency). And growth impairment as described under the criteria in Listing 100.02(b).

I. General Considerations

A. This Listing deals with "pituitary dwarfism".

B. Pituitary dwarfism refers to a decrease in normal growth, caused by disease of the pituitary gland, in which not enough "growth hormone" is produced. What type of pituitary disease does this is not important, but S. S. Disability must be able to obtain records of laboratory tests showing an abnormally low amount of growth hormone in the claimant's bloodstream.

II. Specific Requirements

A. No actual evaluation is done under this Listing, except to prove that the claimant has pituitary dwarfism.

B. Pituitary dwarfism can be of all degrees of severity, but in order to fulfill this Listing, it must be severe enough to qualify under Listing 100.02(b). Further details can be found under the discussion of Listing 100.02(b).

Listing 109.11

Adrenogenital syndrome. With:

(a) Recent, recurrent salt-losing episodes despite prescribed therapy; OR

(b) Inadequate replacement therapy manifested by accelerated bone age and virilization; OR

(c) Growth impairment as described under the criteria in Listing 100.02A or B.

I. General Considerations

A. This Listing deals with what is called the "adrenogenital syndrome".

B. The adrenogenital syndrome refers to one of several possible diseases producing abnormalities in the genitalia and adrenal glands. All of them are based on the deficiency of one of the enzymes normally present in the adrenal glands. The exact disease caused depends on which enzyme is missing, but all produce generally similar effects.

II. Specific Requirements

A. Part (a)

1. Some types of adrenogenital syndrome cause abnormal loss of sodium from the blood ("salt-losing"). If this is severe enough, then low blood pressure, dizziness and even loss of consciousness may result.

2. If severe salt-losing episodes are occurring repeatedly, then Part (a) may be fulfilled.

3. The claimant *must* be under prescribed therapy; otherwise, S. S. Disability would not know if the condition is treatable.

4. The word "recent" means that salt-losing episodes must be a current problem at the time of application for disability, not simply a past problem that no longer affects the claimant.

B. Part (b)

1. "Inadequate replacement therapy" means that treatment with artificial hormones is not working.

2. The bone structure of a child with adrenogenital syndrome may mature too quickly ("accelerated bone age"). Also, sexual characteristics may develop earlier in life than they normally would, with male sexual characteristics showing up in the female child ("virilization"). Accelerated bone age and virilization indicate that treatment is not effective, and are necessary to fulfill Part (b). Bone age is determined by special X-rays.

C. Part (c)

1. Part (c) can be fulfilled, if the adrenogenital syndrome produces growth retardation.

2. No actual evaluation is done under Part (c). If growth retardation is present, the case would be evaluated under Listing 100.02A or B, which deals with all types of growth impairments. The requirements of Listing 100.02 must be fulfilled, and further details can be found in the discussion of that Listing.

Listing 109.12

Hypoglycemia. With recent, recurrent hypoglycemic episodes producing convulsion or coma.

I. General Considerations

A. This Listing deals with any disease that produces "hypoglycemia".

B. Hypoglycemia means an abnormally low blood sugar (glucose). Diabetics who develop hypoglycemia from over-reaction to insulin could also qualify under this Listing [as well as Listing 109.08(b)].

C. S. S. Disability must be able to obtain medical records that clearly show hypoglycemia to be present. Hypoglycemia itself is not enough to qualify under this Listing, because blood sugar (glucose) can drop extremely low even in normal people, without producing any ill effects.

II. Specific Requirements

A. The hypoglycemia episodes must be "recent" and "recurrent". Three such episodes in the year prior to application for disability would probably be enough.

B. The episodes of hypoglycemia must be severe enough to produce coma or convulsions.

Listing 109.13

Gonadal Dysgenesis (Turner's Syndrome), chromosomally proven. Evaluate the resulting impairment under the criteria for the appropriate body system.

I. General Considerations

A. This Listing deals with a hereditary disease called "Gonadal Dysgenesis" or "Turner's Syndrome".

B. Since this disease is caused by abnormal genes, it must be proven by studies which show such abnormal genes to be present ("chromosomally proven").

II. Specific Requirements

A. No actual evaluation is done under this Listing.

B. Depending on the particular claimant with Turner's Syndrome, there are many types of mental and physical disorders that might be present. Evaluation of the case would be done under whatever Listing most accurately applies to the claimant's problems. For example, if mental retardation is present, this would be evaluated under Listing 112.05.

§ 3.11 Multiple Body Systems

Listing 110.08

Catastrophic congenital abnormalities or disease. With:

(a) A positive diagnosis (such as anencephaly, trisomy D or E, cyclopia, etc.), generally regarded as being incompatible with extrauterine life; OR

(b) A positive diagnosis (such as cri du chat, Tay-Sachs Disease) wherein attainment of the growth and development level of 2 years is not expected to occur.

I. General Considerations

A. This Listing deals with "catastrophic congenital abnormalities". This refers to extremely abnormal physical disorders dating from the time of birth. Such disorders usually result from some type of genetic abnormality.

B. Part (a) or Part (b) must be fulfilled, but not both.

II. Specific Requirements

A. Part (a)

1. Part (a) is fulfilled, if there is a disease so severe that life after birth is impossible ("incompatible with extrauterine life").

2. There must be a "positive diagnosis". In other words, it must be very clear that such severe disease is present. This might only require information from physical examination of the claimant, but special studies of the claimant's chromosomes might also be necessary to prove abnormal genes are present.

3. Several examples are given by the Listing, but other disorders can also qualify. "Anencephaly" is a disorder in which most of the brain is missing at birth. "Cyclopia" means the presence of only one eye, but other severe abnormalities go along with it. "Trisomy D or E" refers to several types of severe genetic abnormalities which can be diagnosed by studies of the claimant's chromosomes.

B. Part (b)

1. Part (b) deals with abnormalities in which the claimant would be expected to live longer than those in Part (a), but which are still so severe that physical and mental development would not be expected to progress beyond the level of a 2 year old child.

2. There must be enough information to make a positive diagnosis that such a disease is present. Examples of such genetic diseases as "cri du chat" syndrome or "Tay-Sachs Disease" are given, but other genetic abnormalities could also qualify.

Listing 110.09

Immune deficiency disease:

(a) *Hypogammaglobulinemia or dysgammaglobulinemia.* With:

(1) Recent, recurrent severe infections; OR

(2) A complication such as growth retardation, chronic lung disease, collagen disorder, or tumors.

(b) Thymic dysplastic syndromes (such as Swiss, diGeorge).

I. General Considerations

A. This Listing deals with disease of the immune system of the body, in which there is inadequate production of antibodies needed to fight infection.

B. Part (a) or Part (b) must be fulfilled, but not both.

II. Specific Requirements

A. Part (a)

1. Part (a) requires decreased gammaglobulin antibodies ("hypogammaglobulinemia"), or abnormal gammaglobulin antibodies that don't work correctly ("dysgammaglobulinemia"). There must be blood test results showing that one of these problems exists.

2. Once the diagnosis is proven, either Part (a)(1) or Part (a)(2) must be fulfilled, but not both.

3. Part (a)(1) is fulfilled if recurrent and severe infections have occurred. Minor infections would not qualify. Such infections would have to be severe enough to require treatment in a hospital. How often "recurrent" means is not defined. How many such infections there must be is a matter of judgement by the person in S. S. Disability evaluating the case. This would take into account the type of infections involved, how long they last, their effect on the claimant, and how effectively they could be treated.

4. Part (a)(2) is fulfilled, if there are diseases present, in addition to the claimant's immune deficiency disease. Some exam-

ples are given by the Listing, such as "growth retardation", "chronic lung disease", "collagen disorders", or "tumors". However, other diseases could also qualify, if they make the claimant's immune deficiency disease worse.

B. Part (b)

1. Part (b) is fulfilled, if there is one of the "thymic dysplastic syndromes" present.

2. The thymus is a gland in the neck that plays a very important part in the development of the immune system of the body necessary to fight disease. In thymic dysplastic syndromes, the thymus doesn't grow or function properly. Examples are given as the "Swiss" or "diGeorge" syndromes.

§ 3.12 Neurological

Listing 111.02

Major motor seizure disorder:

(a) *Major motor seizures.* In a child with an established seizure disorder, the occurrence of more than one major motor seizure per month despite at least three months of prescribed treatment. With:

(1) Diurnal episodes (loss of consciousness and convulsive seizures); OR

(2) Nocturnal episodes manifesting residuals which interfere with activity during the day.

(b) *Major motor seizures.* In a child with an established seizure disorder, the occurrence of at least one major motor seizure in the year prior to application despite at least three months of prescribed treatment. And ONE of the following:

(1) I.Q. of 69 or less; OR

(2) Significant interference with communication due to speech, hearing, or visual defect; OR

(3) Significant emotional disorder; OR

(4) Where significant adverse effects of medication interfere with major daily activities.

I. General Considerations

A. This Listing deals with seizure disorders of a major kind, such as grand-mal epilepsy. Some forms of temporal lobe epilepsy could also qualify.

B. There must be a detailed description of at least one typical seizure, preferably by a medical doctor.

C. There should be an EEG report. An EEG is a tracing of the electrical activity of the brain, obtained by attaching small electrodes to the scalp. Sometimes an EEG shows abnormalities which would be expected with a seizure disorder, but it is *not* necessary to have an abnormal EEG to qualify under this Listing. However, it is necessary that an EEG has been done and the results available to S. S. Disability, in order to qualify under this Listing.

D. Since seizure disorders involve the nervous system, it is preferable to have at least one neurological examination available. It is best that such exam come from a specialist in disease of the nervous system (a neurologist), but this is not absolutely necessary.

E. The frequency of epileptic seizures must be documented. S. S. Disability will ask the treating doctor how often the claimant has seizures. The claimant's own statement about how often he has seizures would not be accepted.

F. The claimant *must* be under treatment. Most epilepsy can be effectively treated, and only claimant for whom treatment has failed can qualify. However, if the claimant is receiving inadequate treatment in the opinion of S. S. Disability, then that would have no influence on evaluation of the case. Whether treatment is adequate or not is between a claimant and his doctor and no-one else. On the other hand, the claimant must be actively participating with his doctor in an effort to bring his seizures under control. Claimants who have not seen a doctor for several years, even if they are taking anti-seizure drugs, are not making reasonable effort to have their seizures controlled and might not qualify under this Listing. There is more to being under treatment than merely having a prescription filled year after year, without any other contact with the treating doctor. Losing personal contact with the treating doctor prevents changes in therapy that might control seizures.

G. If the treating doctor's medical records show that the claimant has been negligent in taking his medicine, he will not qualify under this Listing. Blood levels of drugs used for epilepsy can be easily measured and are measured in all cases prior to allowance under this Listing. If the test shows a *zero* or unexplained low level of a drug that the claimant is supposed to be taking, S. S. Disability may assume that the claimant is not cooperating with the prescribed therapy of his doctor, and cannot qualify under this Listing. The only exceptions would be claimants so mentally retarded or mentally ill that failure to take their drugs is understandable.

H. Part (a) or (b) must be fulfilled, but not both.

II. Specific Requirements

A. Part (a)

1. The claimant must have been receiving treatment for seizures for at least 3 months.

2. Despite receiving treatment, there must be at least an average of one seizure per month. These must be spread out over a reasonable amount of time. For example, if a claimant had 12 seizures in one month, but none in the other 11 months of a year, then that would not qualify.

3. Part (a)(1) or (a)(2) must be fulfilled, but not both. Part (a)(1) deals with seizures that occur during the daytime ("diurnal seizures"). There must be loss of consciousness and convulsions (uncontrollable jerking movements of body muscles). Part (a)(2) deals with seizures that occur during the night time ("nocturnal episodes"). These nighttime seizures must be severe enough to leave residual effects mentally or physically that interfere significantly with the claimant's activities the next day. Of course, this must be interpreted in terms of the claimant's age and what a child that age would normally be doing during the day.

B. Part (b)

1. Part (b) only requires at least one major seizure during the year prior to application for disability, despite at least 3 months of treatment.

2. In addition, Part (b)(1), (b)(2), (b)(3), or (b)(4) must be fulfilled. It is only necessary to fulfill one of these.

3. Part (b)(1) is fulfilled, if the claimant has an I.Q. score of no higher than 69 on an acceptable type of I.Q. test such as W.I. S.C. (Wechsler Intelligence Scale for Children). It is important to note that if the I.Q. test is one in which there is more than one final score, S. S. Disability must take the *lowest* score. This is clearly to the advantage of the claimant.

4. Part (b)(2) can be fulfilled, if there is a "significant" problem with speech, hearing, or seeing. These problems would only have to be severe enough to be more than a "slight", or minor problem.

5. Part (b)(3) can be fulfilled, if there is a "significant" emotional disorder. This emotional disorder would only have to be severe enough to be more than a "slight", or minor problem.

6. Part (b)(4) can be fulfilled, if the drugs taken for the control of seizure produce problems significant enough to interfere with the claimant's normal daily activities, as expected for his age. There must be data clearly showing what drug side-effects are present and how this interferes with the claimant's ability to engage in normal activities for his age. There must be "significant" side-effects, not just minor ones. For example, a side-effect that made a claimant so sleepy that he fell behind in his school work would be a major side-effect. On the other hand, the mere complaint of a little sleepiness would not qualify.

Listing 111.03

Minor motor seizure disorder. In a child with an established seizure disorder, the occurrence of more than one minor motor seizure per week, with alteration of awareness or loss of consciousness, despite at least three months of prescribed treatment.

I. General Considerations

A. This Listing deals with forms of epilepsy called "minor motor seizures". In children, this is usually a form of epilepsy called "petit-mal" epilepsy.

B. These "minor" seizures are usually not as severe and do not last as long as the "major" seizures considered in Listing 111.02. For example, a seizure caused by petit-mal epilepsy might only last a few seconds and not even be noticed by anyone but an observant, trained person.

C. Other general considerations discussed under Listing 111.02 also apply to this Listing.

II. Specific Requirements

A. The claimant must have been receiving treatment for at least 3 months, at the time of application for disability.

B. The seizure must occur *more often* than once a week.

C. The seizures must cause either loss of consciousness or at least a change in awareness on the part of the claimant suffering it.

Listing 111.05

Brain tumors:

(a) Malignant gliomas (astrocytoma—grades III and IV, glioblastoma multiforme), medulloblastoma, ependymoblastoma, primary sarcoma, or brain stem gliomas; OR

(b) Evaluate other brain tumors under the criteria for the resulting neurological impairment.

I. General Considerations

A. This Listing deals with brain tumors.

B. Part (a) or (b) must be fulfilled, but not both.

II. Specific Requirements

A. Part (a)

1. Part (a) lists various types of brain tumors that can qualify.

2. If a claimant has any one of the given types of tumors, Part (a) is automatically fulfilled. These are very serious tumors that often result in death, and proof that the claimant has one is all that is necessary to fulfill Part (a).

B. Part (b)

1. Part (b) deals with brain tumors that are usually not as serious as those given in Part (a). Any type of tumor not listed in Part (a) is evaluated under Part (b).

2. No *specific* evaluation is done under Part (b). The mere existence of a brain tumor is not enough to fulfill Part (b). The brain tumor must produce effects serious enough to cause a severe impairment. Depending on the kind of problem that the brain tumor is causing, the claimant must fulfill the requirements of whatever Listing deals with that kind of problem. For example, if the brain tumor is producing epileptic seizures, the case would be evaluated according to the requirements of Listing 111.02 or 111.03. Or if it produced difficulty in walking, the case would be evaluated under Listing 111.06, etc.

Listing 111.06

Motor dysfunction (due to any neurological disorder). Persistent disorganization or deficit of motor function for age involving two extremeties, which (despite prescribed therapy) interferes with age-appropriate major daily activities and results in disruption of:

(a) Fine and gross movements; OR

(b) Gait and station.

I. General Considerations

A. This Listing deals with "motor dysfunction" caused by *any type* of disease of the nervous system.

B. Motor dysfunction mainly refers to the ability to use the hands, arms, and legs normally.

C. The abnormality must be such that it is not likely to improve ("persistent").

D. The claimant must have at least two extremities involved, despite being under treatment. This means both legs, both arms, or one leg and one arm.

E. The degree of impairment is evaluated in terms of what a normal person of the same age as the claimant would be expected to be able to do. What is normal ability to walk and stand or use the arms and hand is not the same for a 12 year old child as one 3 years old.

F. The impairment must be severe enough that it prevents the claimant from doing the major types of things that a normal child of the same age would do.

G. Part (a) or (b) must be fulfilled, but not both.

II. Specific Requirements

A. Part (a)

1. Part (a) can be fulfilled, if there is inability to do "fine and gross movements".

2. Such abnormalities refer to problems using the hands and arms—for example, reaching and picking up objects without knocking them over or dropping them would be a gross movement. The ability to write or button clothes would be examples of fine movements. But these are only examples, and must be interpreted in terms of the claimant's age. It would be impossible here to discuss the numerous possibilities that could apply to every claimant.

B. Part (b)

1. Part (b) deals with problems involving "gait and station".

2. This would apply to problems using the legs, namely walking and standing. Problems walking and standing must be

interpreted in light of the claimant's age and what he would normally be expected to be able to do.

Listing 111.07

Cerebral palsy. With:

(a) Motor dysfunction meeting the requirements of Listings 111.06 or 101.03; OR

(b) Less severe motor dysfunction (but more than slight) and ONE of the following:

(1) IQ of 69 or less; OR

(2) Seizure disorder, with at least one major motor seizure in the year prior to application; OR

(3) Significant interference with communication due to speech, hearing, or visual defect; OR

(4) Significant emotional disorder.

I. General Considerations

A. This Listing specifically deals with "cerebral palsy".

B. Cerebral palsy is not really a specific disease itself, but refers to the effects of brain damage from the time of birth. It may be very mild, or very severe.

C. Part (a), or (b) must be fulfilled, but not both.

II. Specific Requirements

A. Part (a)

1. Part (a) deals with "motor dysfunction" due to cerebral palsy. This means problems standing and walking, or using the hands and arms.

2. No actual evaluation is done under Part (a). If this type of problem is present, the case would be evaluated under either Listing 101.03 or Listing 111.06. The specific requirements of one of those Listings would have to be fulfilled. Further details can be found under the discussion of Listings 101.03 or 111.06.

B. Part (b)

1. Part (b) deals with motor dysfunction that is not quite as severe as that required in Part (a). However, it must be more than a minor problem.

2. In addition, Parts (b)(1), (b)(2), (b)(3), or (b)(4) must be fulfilled. It is necessary to qualify only under one of these, not all four.

3. Part (b)(1) can be fulfilled, if the claimant has an I.Q. score of no higher than 69 on an acceptable type of I.Q. test, such as the W.I.S.C. (Wechsler Intelligence Scale for Children). It is important to note that if the I.Q. test is one in which there is more than one final score, S. S. Disability must take the *lowest* score. This is clearly to the advantage of the claimant.

4. Part (b)(2) can be fulfilled, if the claimant has seizure disorder in addition to cerebral palsy. One major seizure in the year prior to application for disability is sufficient.

5. Part (b)(3) can be fulfilled, if there is a "significant" problem with speech, hearing, or vision. These problems would only have to be more than a "slight", or minor problem.

6. Part (b)(4) can be fulfilled if a "significant" emotional disorder is present. Such an emotional disorder must be more than minor, but need not be so severe as to fulfill the specific requirements of one of the Listings dealing with mental disorders alone.

Listing 111.08

Meningomyelocele (and related disorders). With ONE of the following despite prescribed treatment.

(a) Motor dysfunction meeting the requirements of Listing 111.06 or Listing 101.03; OR

(b) Less severe motor dysfunction (but more than slight), AND

(1) Urinary or fecal incontinence when inappropriate for age; OR

(2) IQ of 69 or less; OR

(c) Four extremity involvement; OR

(d) Noncompensated hydrocephalus producing interference with mental or motor developmental progression.

I. General Considerations

A. This Listing deals with a disorder called a "meningomyelocele" (and similar disorders).

B. "Meningo-" refers to a membrane covering the spinal cord and brain called "meninges". "Myelo-" refers to the spinal cord. "-Cele" refers to a cavity, or space. So a meningomyelocele is a sack-like defect involving the meninges covering the spinal cord and the spinal cord itself. It occurs during development before birth, with some part of the spinal cord not forming the way it should. (The unfortunately popular term "hunchback" refers to someone with a meningomyelocele). It may be so mild that it is hardly noticeable and produces no problems. It can be so severe that the claimant has a big sack of fluid and abnormal spinal cord tissue on their back. It may be anywhere up or down the spinal cord, or even involve the brain. Since the spinal cord is involved, there may be various kinds of paralysis, or other problems involving the nervous system.

C. Part (a), (b), (c), or (d) must be fulfilled, but not all four.

II. Specific Requirements

A. Part (a)

1. Part (a) deals with motor dysfunction, such as problems using the arms and hands, or legs.

2. No actual evaluation is done under Part (a). If such a problem is present, evaluation would be done under Listings 101.03 or 111.06. In either case, the specific requirements of Listings 101.03 or 111.06 would have to be fulfilled. Further details can be found under the discussions of those Listings.

B. Part (b)

1. Part (b) deals with motor dysfunction not quite as severe as that required in Part (a). However, it must be more than a minor problem.

2. In addition, Part (b)(1) or (b)(2) must be fulfilled. It is only necessary to fulfill one of these, not both.

3. Part (b)(1) is fulfilled, if there is "urinary or fecal incontinence". This means inability to control urination or bowel movements. "Inappropriate for age" means that the claimant must be old enough that he would normally be expected to have such control.

4. Part (b)(2) can be fulfilled, if the claimant has an I.Q. score of no higher than 69 on an acceptable type of I.Q. test, such as the W.I.S.C. (Wechsler Intelligence Scale for Children). It is important to note that if the I.Q. test is one in which there is more than one final score, S. S. Disability must take the *lowest* score. This is to the advantage of the claimant.

C. Part (c)

1. Part (c) is fulfilled, if there is "four extremity involvement".

2. Four extremity involvement means that use of both arms and legs is affected by the meningomyelocele.

D. Part (d)

1. Part (d) deals with "noncompensated hydrocephalus". Normally, the brain and spinal cord float in a fluid called cerebrospinal fluid. This fluid circulates smoothly in the brain and covers the spinal cord. A meningomyelocele can block this flow of cerebrospinal fluid, causing abnormal pressures to build up inside the brain called hydrocephalus (literally "waterhead"). Sometimes this pressure can be relieved with special surgery. If that is not possible, the hydrocephalus is "noncompensated".

2. The increased fluid pressure from hydrocephalus can damage brain tissue, and if severe enough can slow down normal mental and or physical development. If this happens, then Part (d) is fulfilled.

Listing 111.09

Communication impairment, associated with documented neurological disorder. And ONE of the following:

(a) Documented speech deficit which significantly affects the clarity and content of the speech; OR

(b) Documented comprehension deficit resulting in ineffective verbal communication for age; OR

(c) Impairment of hearing as described under the criteria in Listing 102.08.

I. General Considerations

A. This Listing deals with the inability to communicate normally with other people.

B. This must be due to some disease of the nervous system, not mental disorder.

C. Parts (a), (b), or (c) must be fulfilled, but not all three.

II. Specific Requirements

A. Part (a)

1. Part (a) deals with problems speaking of a "significant" kind.

2. The problem is evaluated in terms of the "clarity and content" of the claimant's speech. This often requires testing by a person qualified to evaluate such speech disorders. The clarity of speech refers to how clearly words can be spoken. The content of speech refers to how meaningful the words are to other people. This must be interpreted in terms of the claimant's age.

B. Part (b)

1. Part (b) deals with problems the claimant might have in comprehending (understanding) words spoken to him by other people.

2. This often requires testing by a person qualified to evaluate such disorders, and would have to be severe enough to prevent the claimant from communicating with people effectively through speech. This must be interpreted in terms of the claimant's age.

C. Part (c)

1. Part (c) deals with problems communicating with other people, due to difficulty in hearing.

2. No actual evaluation is done under Part (c). If there is a hearing problem, it is evaluated under Listing 102.08, which specifically deals with hearing impairments, and the requirements of that Listing must be fulfilled. Further details can be found under the discussion of Listing 102.08.

§ 3.13 Mental and Emotional Disorders

Listing 112.02

Chronic brain syndrome. With arrest of developmental progression for at least six months or loss of previously acquired abilities.

I. General Considerations

A. This Listing deals with so called "chronic brain syndromes". This refers to any type of organic damage to the brain with effects severe enough to be noticeable.

B. "Chronic" means a problem that is not likely to improve.

C. The brain damage associated with a chronic brain syndrome could be due to any cause that produces brain damage. For example, it could result from infection of the brain, trauma to the brain, or other diseases affecting the nervous system.

II. Specific Requirements

A. The claimant's mental development may have stopped at some point ("arrested") less than that expected of a normal child of the same age. This would fulfill the Listing.

B. The Listing would also be fulfilled, if the claimant started to lose mental abilities that he had once attained.

C. The use of this Listing requires a great deal of information about the claimant's mental development. This necessitates test results measuring development. Various forms of such tests can be used, but they must always have been given by a person qualified to do so. For example, S. S. Disability is interested in what parents have to say about their children applying for disability, but such opinions would not be considered sufficient to reach a decision. If necessary, S. S. Disability would request that the claimant be evaluated professionally by someone who can properly administer the needed tests. This would usually be a psychologist, pediatrician, or psychiatrist.

Listing 112.03

Psychosis of infancy and childhood. Documented by psychiatric evaluation and supported, if necessary, by the results of appropriate standardized psychological tests and manifested by marked restriction in the performance of daily age-appropriate activities; constriction of age-appropriate interests; deficiency of age-appropriate self-care skills; and impaired ability to relate to others; together with persistence of one (or more) of the following:

(a) Significant withdrawal or detachment; OR

(b) Impaired sense of reality; OR

(c) Bizarre behavior patterns; OR

(d) Strong need for maintenance of sameness, with intense anxiety, fear, or anger when change is introduced; OR

(e) Panic at threat of separation from parent.

I. General Considerations

A. This Listing deals with psychotic mental disorders, such as childhood schizophrenia.

B. The results of expert psychiatric evaluation must be available to S. S. Disability. If necessary, the claimant would be sent to a psychiatrist or psychologist for evaluation.

C. The psychotic mental illness must be severe enough to produce *all* of the following problems:

1. Inability to engage in the daily activities of a normal child of the same age.

2. Decreased interest in activities of a normal child of the same age.

3. Decreased self-care skills (such as bathing, dressing, washing, etc.) compared to a normal child the same age.

4. Decreased ability to relate to other people, compared to a normal child the same age.

D. In addition to the above requirements, Part (a), (b), (c), (d), or (e) must be fulfilled, but not all five.

II. Specific Requirements

A. Part (a)

1. Part (a) is fulfilled, if there is "significant withdrawal or detachment".

2. This means that the claimant essentially keeps to himself, with little interest in the "outside" world of things and other people.

B. Part (b)

1. Part (b) is fulfilled, if there is an "impaired sense of reality".

2. It is characteristic of psychotic mental disorders that there is a problem telling what is "real" from what is "unreal". Normal people have the same problem, but not to the same degree.

C. Part (c)

1. Part (c) is fulfilled, if the claimant shows "bizarre behavior patterns".

2. This means any kind of strange behavior that is extremely unusual, and not to be expected of a normal person. For example, repeatedly banging the head against a wall would be such a bizarre behavior, but there are many other possibilities.

D. Part (d)

1. Part (d) is fulfilled, if there is a strong need in the claimant to keep his life from changing, as shown by nervousness, fear, or anger when something does change.

2. Part (d) refers to very severe problems, such as wanting to be in exactly the same place and surrounded by exactly the same objects (bed, toys, etc.) *all of the time.*

E. Part (e)

1. Part (e) is fulfilled, if the claimant suffers a panic reaction at any attempt to separate him from a parent for even a short period of time.

2. Part (e) is similar to Part (d), except that a person is involved instead of objects.

Listing 112.04

Functional nonpsychotic disorders. Documented by psychiatric evaluation and supported, if necessary, by the results of appropriate standardized psychological tests and manifested by marked restriction in the performance of daily age-appropriate activities; constriction of age-appropriate interests; deficiency of age-appropriate self-care skills; and impaired ability to relate to others; together with persistence of one (or more) of the following:

(a) Psychophysiological disorder (e.g., diarrhea, asthma); OR

(b) Anxiety; OR

(c) Depression; OR

(d) Phobic, obsessive, or compulsive behavior; OR

(e) Hypochondriasis; OR

(f) Hysteria; OR

(g) Asocial or antisocial behavior.

I. General Considerations

A. This Listing deals with mental disorders in which psychosis is not involved. There is less difficulty in telling what is "real" from what is "unreal" than with psychotic mental disorders, but such impairments can still be very severe in other ways.

B. The general considerations are the same as those for Listing 112.03.

C. In addition, Part (a), (b), (c), (d), (e), (f), or (g) must be fulfilled, but not all seven.

II. Specific Requirements

A. Part (a)

1. Part (a) is fulfilled, if there is "psychophysiological" disorder present.

2. A psychophysiological disorder is one in which the mind creates a physical problem (unconsciously). There are many possibilities, and examples are given as "diarrhea" and "asthma". The term "diarrhea" refers to severe, difficult to treat diarrhea that is not due to any detectable physical disease, but which is apparently related to mental illness. Asthma is not necessarily caused by a mental disorder. Part (a) refers to asth-

ma in which mental illness plays an important part in causing asthmatic attacks.

B. Part (b)

1. Part (b) is fulfilled, if the claimant suffers from "anxiety".

2. Even normal people suffer some anxiety (nervousness). Part (b) refers to cases in which the anxiety is abnormally severe.

C. Part (c)

1. Part (c) is fulfilled, if the claimant suffers from "depression".

2. Even normal people feel depressed at times. Part (c) refers only to abnormally severe depression.

D. Part (d)

1. Part (d) is fulfilled, if the claimant shows "phobic, obsessive, or compulsive behavior".

2. Phobias are abnormal fears, usually of particular places or things. Obsessive-compulsive behavior refers to activities that are abnormally repeated over and over again without any good reason would be a form of obsessive-compulsive behavior, but there are many possibilities.

E. Part (e)

1. Part (e) is fulfilled, if "hypochondriasis" is present.

2. Hypochondriasis refers to extremely abnormal worry about physical illness that does not exist.

F. Part (f)

1. Part (f) is fulfilled, if the claimant suffers from "hysteria".

2. Hysteria is a form of neurosis, for which it is difficult to even give a simple definition, and none is offered here.

G. Part (g)

1. Part (g) is fulfilled, if the claimant shows significant "antisocial" or "asocial" behavior.

2. Asocial behavior refers to an abnormal tendency to engage in activities that avoid other people or society in general. Antisocial behavior refers to abnormally destructive acts directed toward other people, or society in general. For example, a hermit is showing asocial behavior and a person who engages in vandalism is showing antisocial behavior.

Listing 112.05

Mental retardation:

(a) Achievement of only those developmental milestones generally acquired by children no more than one-half the child's chronological age, OR

(b) IQ of 59 or less; OR

(c) IQ of 60–69, inclusive, and a physical or other mental impairment imposing additional and significant restriction of function or developmental progression.

I. General Considerations

A. This Listing deals with mental retardation (due to any cause).

B. Parts (a), (b), or (c) must be fulfilled, but not all three.

II. Specific Requirements

A. Part (a)

1. Part (a) is usually used to evaluate claimants who are too young for I.Q. testing, or who are so retarded that an I.Q. score cannot be obtained, or who have special handicaps in seeing or hearing which prevent I.Q. testing.

2. Part (a) requires that the claimant has developed mentally no further than a normal child half of his age. This can be determined by special tests used to measure development. These tests must be given by a person qualified and trained to give them. Under no circumstances is the testimony of parents alone sufficient to qualify under Part (a).

B. Part (b)

1. Part (b) is fulfilled if the claimant's I.Q. is 59 or less (on an acceptable I.Q. test, such as the W.I.S.C. or Standard-Binet).

2. It should be noted that some I.Q. tests have more than one final score. If this is the case, S. S. Disability must use the *lowest* I.Q. score. This is advantageous to the claimant.

3. IQ's less than 60 reflect a level of intellectual functioning below 99.5% of the general population. IQ tests most acceptable to S. S. Disability are the Wechsler series (WAIS–R, WISC, WISC–R, and WPPSI), the Revised Stanford-Binet Scale, and the Raven Progressive Matrices. Which test is best for a particular claimant depends on his age and any physical and/or mental impairments that must be taken into account. For example, the Revised Stanford-Binet is almost exclusively verbal. A child with a language disorder would be more appropriately tested

with a non-verbal scale such as the Raven Progressive Matrices, or other non-verbal scale. A WAIS scale is used for adults, but would also be preferred for older children as appropriate. A WISC or WISC–R might be more appropriate for children under age 15, but there are no hard and fast rules about which test to use. It is an area of judgment by the person reviewing the claimant's case. Tests should be administered by a psychologist or psychiatrist trained in that area. Test results obtained at younger ages are not as reliable and valid as those obtained at older ages. Below age 6, results are not as accurate. The test results should be consistent with the child's behavior and daily activities as reflected by various records available in the case evaluation. By age 16, IQ test scores tend to become more reliable and valid. Test scores obtained at age 16 or older will be considered valid indefinitely by S. S. Disability for purposes of allowance, provided they are compatible with the claimant's behavior. For example, a claimant who just completed college is not likely to have an IQ under 60, no matter what the IQ test scores say. In evaluating children under 16, both the child's age at the time of testing and the test results themselves must be taken into consideration in determining if the results are current enough to use. The following table applies as a general guideline:

	IQ Obtained Before Age 7	IQ Obtained at Age 7 or Older
IQ less than 40	Current for 2 years	Current for 4 years
IQ 40 or above	Current for 1 year	Current for 2 years

Where appropriate, S. S. Disability may use the more detailed subtest scores as well as the final scores in determining how the test results should be used in a particular case.

C. Part (c)

1. Part (c) requires an I.Q. score no higher than 69.

2. In addition, there must be some other kind of impairment which significantly affects the claimant mentally or physically. This second impairment could be many things, but it must be more than minor.

§ 3.14 Neoplastic Diseases, Malignant

Listing 113.02

Lymphoreticular malignant neoplasms. Consider under a disability:

(a) For 2½ years from the time of initial diagnosis; OR

(b) For 2½ years from the time of recurrence of active disease.

I. *General Considerations*

A. This Listing deals with forms of cancer called "lymphoreticular malignant neoplasms".

B. Included are a number of different types of cancer affecting lymph nodes. Leukemias would also be considered under this Listing.

C. It must be pointed out that S. S. Disability must have sufficient data to show that the claimant has cancer of some particular kind. With few exceptions, this proof must be in the form of a pathology report. Such a report contains the detailed results of examination (especially under a microscope) of supposedly cancerous tissue. If this has not been done, the diagnosis of cancer is not certain.

D. Part (a) or (b) must be fulfilled, but not both.

II. *Specific Requirements*

A. Part (a)

1. Part (a) states that the claimant gets disability for 2½ years from the time the diagnosis is made with certainty (by a pathology report).

2. Nothing else is required. The fact that the claimant may be receiving treatment does not change the ability to qualify under this Listing.

3. After 2½ years from the time of diagnosis, the claimant's case would again be evaluated by S. S. Disability. If there has been no evidence of the cancer for 2½ years, then the claimant would be removed from disability under this Listing.

B. Part (b)

1. Part (b) states that if the claimant was successfully treated for cancer, but it came back, then 2½ years from the time the cancer returned is automatically granted.

2. Nothing else is required. Nothing (including treatment) alters the claimant's right to $2^1/_2$ years of disability from the time the cancer is proven to have returned.

3. After $2^1/_2$ years, the claimant's case would again be evaluated by S. S. Disability. If there has been no evidence of cancer for at least $2^1/_2$ years, then the claimant would be removed from disability under this Listing.

Listing 113.03

Malignant solid tumors. Consider under a disability:

(a) For 2 years from the time of initial diagnosis; OR

(b) For 2 years from the time of recurrence of active disease.

I. General Considerations

A. This Listing deals with any form of cancer that involves solid tumors. There are many possible types of such tumors.

B. It must be pointed out that S. S. Disability must have sufficient data to show that the claimant has cancer of some particular kind. With few exceptions, this proof must be in the form of a pathology report. Such a report contains the detailed results of examination (especially under a microscope) of supposedly cancerous tissue. If this has not been done, the diagnosis of cancer is not certain.

C. Part (a) or (b) must be fulfilled, but not both.

II. Specific Requirements

A. Part (a)

1. Part (a) states that the claimant gets disability for 2 years from the time the diagnosis is made with certainty (by a pathology report).

2. Nothing else is required. The fact that the claimant may be receiving treatment does not change the ability to qualify under this Listing.

3. After 2 years from the time of diagnosis, the claimant's case would again be evaluated by S. S. Disability. If there has been no evidence of the cancer for 2 years, then the claimant would be removed from the disability under this Listing.

B. Part (b)

1. Part (b) states that if the claimant was successfully treated for cancer, but it came back, then 2 years from the time the cancer returned is automatically granted.

2. Nothing else is required. Nothing (including treatment) alters the claimant's right to 2 years of disability from the time the cancer is proven to have returned.

3. After 2 years, the claimant's case would again be evaluated by S. S. Disability. If there has been no evidence of cancer for at least 2 years, then the claimant would be removed from disability under this Listing.

Listing 113.04

Neuroblastoma. With ONE of the following:

(a) Extension across the midline; OR

(b) Distance metastasis; OR

(c) Recurrence; OR

(d) Onset at age 1 year or older.

I. General Considerations

A. This Listing deals only with a form of cancer called a "neuroblastoma".

B. A neuroblastoma is a frequent form of childhood cancer.

C. Part (a), (b), (c), or (d) must be fulfilled, but not all four.

D. A pathology report is necessary to prove the diagnosis.

II. Specific Requirements

A. Part (a)

1. Part (a) is fulfilled, if there is "extension across the midline".

2. Extension across the midline means the tumor has spread to the other side of the body from where it started.

B. Part (b)

1. Part (b) is fulfilled, if there is evidence that distant metastasis has occurred.

2. If any amount of cancer has spread anywhere in the body so far that surgical removal of the cancer is impossible, then distant metastasis is present.

C. Part (c)

1. Part (c) is fulfilled, if there is "recurrence" of the cancer.

2. Recurrence means that the cancer has come back, after having been successfully treated.

D. Part (d)

1. Part (d) is fulfilled, if a neuroblastoma is detected at age 1 year, or older.

2. Nothing else is required.

Listing 113.05

Retinoblastoma. With ONE of the following:

(a) Bilateral involvement; OR

(b) Metastasis; OR

(c) Extension beyond the orbit; OR

(d) Recurrence.

I. General Considerations

A. This Listing deals with a malignant tumor called a "retinoblastoma", which affects the eyes.

B. Part (a), (b), (c), or (d) must be fulfilled, but not all four.

II. Specific Requirements

A. Part (a)

1. Part (a) is fulfilled, if there is "bilateral involvement".

2. Bilateral involvement means both eyes are affected.

B. Part (b)

1. Part (b) is fulfilled if there are "metastasis".

2. Metastasis means that the cancer has spread to some other part of the body.

C. Part (c)

1. Part (c) is fulfilled, if there is "extension beyond the orbit".

2. Extension beyond the orbit means that the tumor has grown in size beyond the eye socket.

D. Part (d)

1. Part (d) is fulfilled, if there is "recurrence" of the cancer.

2. Recurrence means that the tumor has returned, after having been successfully treated for some period of time. It doesn't matter how much time has passed from the time the reti-

noblastoma was originally diagnosed to the time it came back. Nor does it matter whether or not the claimant is receiving treatment for the recurrence. If the cancer comes back, the claimant qualifies under Part (d). Nothing else is required.

CHAPTER 4

VOCATIONAL DISABILITY RULES

Table of Sections

§ 4.1 Introduction

If a claimant's impairment does not Meet or Equal one of the Listings, then S. S. Disability tries to determine what the claimant is still capable of doing physically and/or mentally. This rating is called a *residual functional capacity* (RFC). After the RFC is written, then S. S. Disability next analyzes this in light of the claimant's age, education, and work experience by applying what are called *vocational rules*. Claimants may be allowed benefits under the vocational rules when their impairment limits their ability to stand, walk, bend, sit, reach, lift, etc. to the degree that they cannot return to the usual type of work they have done in the 15 years before the onset of their illness, or any other type of work. Restrictions on mental capacity or other special factors may also be taken into account.

Allowance of benefits based on vocational considerations usually applies only to adults—claimants at least 18 years old. Children usually cannot be allowed benefits vocationally; if a child claimant does not Meet or Equal a Listing, his claim would usually be denied at that point. There are exceptions, but involve administrative issues beyond the scope of this book. It is important to note that although in theory anyone over 18 years old can be allowed benefits vocationally, this is not often true in actual practice. In reality, it is *unusual* for a claimant under the age of 50 to be allowed benefits for vocational reasons. In effect, S. S. Disability wastes a great deal of its own time doing vocational analyses on claimants under age 50, because such cases are almost never going to be allowed benefits. The only important exceptions are claimants who cannot read or write (illiterate), and who have very few work skills. However, for claimants over 50 years old who don't Meet or Equal a Listing, vocational allowance is a frequent way benefits are obtained. It should be pointed out that while many cases which don't fit one of the vocational rules are denied benefits, this isn't necessarily true in every case—some of these cases are still allowed when further evaluation is done by a *vocational analyst,* who is trained to deal with cases that are unusually complicated vocationally.

§ 4.2 Vocational Report (Form 3369)

If a claimant's case is being evaluated for possible allowance based on vocational factors, he will probably be asked to fill out a form about his vocational background. This form is called Vocational Report 3369, and a sample form can be found in Appendix III. In addition, a few suggestions about completing Form 3369 are as follows:

A. *Name of applicant.* Only the name of the claimant should appear here.

B. *Social Security number.* The claimant should write only his Social Security number in this space, and make sure that it is *correct.*

C. *Telephone number where you can be reached.* The claimant should write his telephone number here. If he doesn't have a telephone, he may use one belonging to someone else, in order to receive messages. In this case, "Message Telephone" should be noted, and only a reliable friend or relative should be used. Claimants have had their cases denied, because S. S. Disability was unable to contact them.

Part I. Information About Your Work History

1. *List the job or jobs you have had in the last 15 years before you stopped working.* The claimant should list his most recent job first. He should write down his job title, the type of business involved, the dates he started and stopped working, the number of days worked each week, and the wages received. This should be done for all jobs held during the past 15 years. If exact dates or wages cannot be remembered, the claimant should try to be as accurate as he can, trying not to leave any blank items or long periods of time that are not explained. All of this is important information to S. S. Disability. If not filled out correctly, then processing of the claim will be delayed, until the needed information is

obtained. If the claimant has a 6th grade education or less, and has done only heavy unskilled labor for at least 35 years, then it is very important to write this down; it will help the claimant's case.

Part II. Information About Your Job Duties

The purpose of Part II is to gain more detailed information about the jobs listed in Part I of the form.

2. *Job title.* This should be the same as that given in Part I.

A. *In your job, did you.* In this section, simply give "Yes" or "No" answers to job duties involving the following things:

- Use of machines, tools, or equipment of any kind
- Use of any technical knowledge of skills
- Writing, record-keeping, or filing reports
- Any supervisory responsibilities

B. *Describe your basic duties (explain what you did and how you did it) below.* A full, detailed description of the claimant's job duties is required here. Note that if "Yes" was answered for any of the Items in Part A, full details must be given here. The more experience a claimant has with special skills, knowledge, and machines, then the wider his job opportunities are and he is less likely to receive disability benefits. The same thing applies to supervisory experience and experience involving paperwork, such as reports, etc. In short, the greater a claimant's abilities and experience, the less chance he has of getting benefits on a vocational basis.

C. *Describe the kind and amount of physical activity this job involved during a typical day in terms of.* Here the claimant is asked to tell how much time in a typical work day he spent walking, standing, sitting, bending and reaching. The more time the claimant spent doing these things, the less likely it is that he could return to his past work, and the greater his chances of qualifying for benefits vocationally—assuming that he could not return to some other type of work. For example, suppose that a claimant had arthritis in his left knee, so that he couldn't stand for more than 3 hours a day, but his job required him to stand 8 hours a day. If he also was not qualified to do any other type of less strenuous work, his inability to stand very long would weigh in his favor for obtaining disability benefits. On the other hand, if the same claimant had been required to stand no more than 2 hours a day for his job his chances of getting benefits would be decreased, since he might be able to return to his job.

Item C also asks how much weight the claimant had to lift and carry on his job, the type of material, how far it had to be carried, and how often he had to lift such weights. The heavier the physical labor the claimant had to do, the less likely it is that S. S. Disability would consider him able to return to his usual job. This would weigh in favor of him obtaining benefits, assuming that he also is not qualified to do some other type of less strenuous work. On the other hand, if a claimant spent most of his day doing paperwork, or other things not requiring much physical effort, the greater the chances that S. S. Disability would consider him capable of going back to his job, or some other type of work. This would weigh against him obtaining benefits based on vocational considerations.

Part III. Remarks

The claimant can make any comments he wants in this space. However, he should restrict these comments to things that he really feels have an influence on his ability to work. Logical arguments are much better than emotional ones. Like all other forms, the claimant must sign and date the Vocational Report. Note that it is a federal crime to falsify information on this form.

§ 4.3 Important Evaluation Considerations

When evaluating a disability claim for possible allowance based on vocational factors, there are several areas that S. S. Disability considers very important:

1. *Age*. There are four general age groups:

a. Younger Individuals (under 50 years).

b. Closely Approaching Advanced Age (50–54 years).

c. Advanced Age (55–59 years).

d. Closely Approaching Retirement Age (60 years or older). The older a claimant is, the better his chances of being allowed benefits vocationally. It is assumed that older claimants who can't return to their usual work would have a more difficult time learning new skills and adjusting to new work environments than younger claimants. However, age is only one factor taken into consideration. Age might carry very little weight for an older claimant with highly specialized skills, such as a scientist or business executive. Also, it was previously pointed out that age alone can weigh very heavily *against* a claimant, if he is under 50 years old.

2. *Education.* In some cases, education is the least important of the vocational factors. The disadvantages of a limited education can be offset by experience, and an extensive formal education may be of little use, if it was acquired many years in the past and never applied in any practical sense by the claimant. In other cases, education can play a major role in allowance of denial of benefits vocationally. Some important definitions related to education that S. S. Disability uses are as follows:

a. *Illiteracy* refers to the inability to read or write. Such claimants have little or no formal schooling. They may be able to sign their name, but they cannot read or write simple communications, such as inventory lists.

b. *Marginal education* refers to an education that has not exceeded the 6th grade level. Such a claimant usually has reasoning, arithmetic, and language skills adequate to perform simple, unskilled jobs.

c. *Limited education* refers to grades 7 through 11. Such a claimant has more ability than someone with a marginal education, but is still probably not capable of performing the more complex job duties of skilled or semi-skilled jobs. However a person with a limited education could be considered capable of higher performance, if he has received on-the-job training, or other forms of special education which increase his abilities.

d. *High school, vocational, and college education* refers to education equivalent to the 12th grade or higher. Such claimants are considered to have the reasoning, arithmetic, and language skills required for the performance of semi-skilled and skilled work, in the areas for which they have been trained. Of course, such education would be of less value in finding meaningful work, if it was completed in the remote past (for example, 20 or 30 years ago), and never used by the claimant. Special training is looked at in the same way by S. S. Disability. For example, a claimant with special training in aviation electronics 15 years ago and never used it, would not necessarily be considered capable of such work; he probably has forgotten much of what he once knew, and the knowledge may be outdated. So higher educational levels don't always work against a claimant.

3. *Work experience.* Usually, any work experience that a claimant had more than 15 years in the past is not considered by S. S. Disability, *unless* it is similar to more recent work experience. S. S. Disability uses the *Dictionary of Occupational Titles* (U.S. Department of Labor; copies may be obtained from the Superintendent of Documents, U.S. Printing Office, Washington, D.C. 20402.) to help determine if work is unskilled, semi-skilled, or skilled. This is far too extensive a document to include in this book, but a few examples in each category follow.

If a claimant's work was *unskilled,* then it required little or no judgement. Such a job involves only the performance of simple duties, and could probably be learned in no more than 30 days. Considerable physical strength may or may not be required for such a job. Most unskilled jobs involve working only with physical objects, rather than working with other people or with data such as paperwork. Since most unskilled jobs don't require special work experience, such experience is of little importance in evaluating the cases of claimants who fall into this category. There are thousands of unskilled jobs. A few examples follow, though it should be noted that some of these might also involve semi-skilled work:

- Wire worker
- Garbage man
- Janitorial work
- Maid
- Chicken catcher, debeaker, or gizzard snipper
- Delivery man
- Farmhand
- Some forms of assembly work
- Lamp tester inspector (electrical industry)
- Trimmer (electrical industry)

Semi-skilled work requires some job skills, but more complex work functions are still not required. Semi-skilled work may involve alertness and close attention to watching machine processes or inspection, testing, or otherwise detecting irregularities in materials or processes. It may involve tending or guarding equipment, property, materials, or persons against loss, damage, or injury. Coordination and dexterity in use of the hands or feet may be required. There are thousands of semi-skilled jobs. A few examples follow, though it should be noted that some of these might also involve skilled work:

- Night watchman
- Truck driver
- Secretary
- Security guard
- Quality control inspector
- Merchant seaman
- Receptionist
- Typist
- Some forms of assembly line work
- Carbon cutter

Skilled work requires independent judgement in controlling machines, and manual operations necessary in obtaining the proper form, quality, or quantity of material to be produced. Skilled work may require that the claimant do layout work, estimate quality, suitability and needed quantity of materials; it may involve reading blueprints or specifications; it may involve making computations or mechanical adjustments to control or regulate processes. In addition, skilled work may require dealing with personnel, data, or abstract ideas at a high level of complexity. There are many thousands of skilled jobs. A few examples are as follows:

- Doctor
- Lawyer
- Accountant
- Machinist
- Cabinet-maker
- Architect
- Tool and Die maker
- Many types of assembly line work

- Computer programmer
- Chemist or other scientist

4. *Residual functional capacity.* Claimants with the most severe impairments Meet or Equal one of the Listings. These cases are automatically allowed, without further evaluation. Claimants with minor impairments that don't significantly affect their ability to work are said to have "non-severe" or "slight" impairments. These cases are denied benefits without further evaluation. All other adult claimants are said to have a significant impairment that is more than slight, but not severe enough to Meet or Equal a Listing. All such claimants receive a rating called a *residual functional capacity* (RFC), which is S. S. Disability's opinion about what a claimant is still capable of doing physically and/or mentally, using objective medical evidence as a guide. A residual functional capacity can be written in many ways by the disability examiner, sometimes with a DDS medical consultant's help, taking into account a particular claimant's special problems. However, physical restrictions on standing, walking, and the amount of weight that can be lifted are often put into one of the following categories:

1. *SEDENTARY WORK* would include the following:

   Prolonged sitting, usually a total of 6 hours or more in an 8 hour day and lifting a 10 lb. maximum, with occasional lifting and/or carrying of articles such as ledgers, small tools, etc., and the good use of both hands.

2. *LIGHT WORK* would include the following:

   Lifting a maximum of 20 lbs.

   Frequent lifting and carrying of objects weighing up to 10 lbs.

   Walking and standing to a significant degree, usually 6 hours in an 8 hour day. Or sitting most of the time operating arm and leg controls.

3. *MEDIUM WORK* would include the following:

   Lifting a 50 lb. maximum, with frequent lifting and carrying up to 25 lbs. Medium work usually implies the ability to walk at least 6 hours of an 8 hour day.

4. *HEAVY WORK* would include the following:

   Lifting 100 lbs. maximum, with frequent lifting and carrying up to 50 lbs. Heavy work usually means the ability to also walk 6–8 hours in an 8 hour day. The functional capacity to perform heavy work implies the functional capacity for work at all the lesser exertional levels (medium, light, and sedentary work).

5. *LESS THAN A FULL RANGE OF SEDENTARY WORK* is a special RFC level below sedentary work which is rarely used. A claimant with an RFC with sedentary work may have reduced even lower because of:

Restrictions on prolonged sitting.

Restrictions on manipulating with the hands.

Objective medical evidence which establishes the necessity to use a cane or crutch for even minimal ambulation (walking).

§ 4.4 Vocational Disability Rules

So far the actual vocational disability rules have not been considered. The following tables contain these rules, and appear almost exactly the way they appear in federal documents used by S. S. Disability. These vocational disability rules are used to decide whether most claimants can receive benefits on a vocational basis. These rules are applied after taking into account the major vocational factors of age, education, work experience, and residual functional capacity. By looking at these tables, the reader can get a general idea if S. S. Disability would consider him disabled for vocational reasons, after failing to Meet or Equal a Listing. However, it should be remembered that some cases are too complicated to fall into one of these "pidgeon-holes", and require special evaluation by a vocational analyst.

The most difficult problem the reader can encounter in trying to use these tables is uncertainty concerning what RFC rating he has. He can generally have a pretty good idea of how S. S. Disability will regard his age, education, and work experience from material that has already been discussed. If the claimant has an actual case before S. S. Disability on which a final decision has been reached, then he can go to his District Office and read the residual functional capacity rating that he has been given; in fact, he can read his entire file if he wants. If the case has been denied, then there is what is called a "denial rationale" in the front of the case file which contains the reasoning behind denial of the case. The residual functional capacity rating can be found in the denial rationale, except in cases in which S. S. Disability feels that the claimant has only a slight or non-severe impairment. In these cases, no RFC is written. Nevertheless, reading the denial rationale can be of benefit to the claimant, if he doesn't agree with its reasoning and wishes to appeal his case to a higher level, such as a hearing before an Administrative Law Judge.

However, the reader might wish to get an idea of whether he could vocationally qualify for disability, before making an application. To do this by applying the vocational disability rules requires the reader to make an educated "guess" what RFC rating S. S. Disability is likely to give in his case. Unfortunately, RFC ratings may depend on complex medical factors that can't be fully understood by most claimants. Administrative regulations also influence the way medical data is used by S. S. Disability. On the other hand, there are standard policies which generally control what RFC rating will be given for the more common impairments that S. S. Disability frequently sees. These common residual functional capacity ratings can be found in Chapter 5 of this book, and are taken from federal documents almost exactly as printed. By referring to Chapter 5 and the vocational disability rules, the reader may get a general idea what S. S. Disability itself would decide about qualification for benefits on a vocational basis.

It should be pointed out that S. S. Disability looks for jobs that are supposed to be available somewhere in the national economy. There is a book called the "Dictionary of Occupational Titles", and there are also supplements put out by the Department of Labor. These documents describe most known jobs, including how much physical exertion, education, and skill is required for any particular job. The supplements may contain information showing jobs the claimant can do, even if he can't return to his usual type of work. If such jobs can be found, the claimant's case may be denied. S. S. Disability does not have to find the exact location of such jobs, nor does it have to necessarily refer to jobs nearby the claimant's residence. Also, S. S. Disability is forbidden *by regulations* from taking employment practices into consideration. In other words, S. S. Disability only determines what the claimant can do, given the opportunity. It does not take into account the decisions, prejudices, or attitudes of particular employers. S. S. Disability confines itself to the *medical* problems influencing the ability to work; to do otherwise would result in such a complex entanglement of bureaucratic and legal problems that it would be difficult to decide a single case, much less the millions of cases that the system must handle. The tables of actual vocational disability rules follow.

Table No. 1. Residual Functional Capacity Maximum Sustained Work Capability Limited to Sedentary Work as a Result of Severe Medically Determinable Impairment(s)

Rule	Age	Education	Previous Work Experience	Decision
201.01	Advanced Age	Limited or Less	Unskilled or None	DISABLED
201.02	Advanced Age	Limited or Less	Skilled or Semi-skilled—Skills Not transferable	DISABLED
201.03	Advanced Age	Limited or Less	Skilled or Semi-skilled—Skills transferable	NOT DISABLED
201.04	Advanced Age	High School Graduate or More—does not provide for direct entry into skilled works	Unskilled or None	DISABLED
201.05	Advanced Age	High School Graduate or More—provides for direct entry into skilled works	Unskilled or None	NOT DISABLED
201.06	Advanced Age	High School Graduate or More—does not provide for direct entry into skilled works	Skilled or Semi-skilled—Skills Not transferable	DISABLED
201.07	Advanced Age	High School Graduate or More—does not provide for direct entry into skilled works	Skilled or Semi-skilled—Skills transferable	NOT DISABLED
201.08	Advanced Age	High School Graduate or More—provides for direct entry into skilled works	Skilled or Semi-skilled—Skills Not transferable	NOT DISABLED
201.09	Closely Approaching Advanced Age	Limited or Less	Unskilled or None	DISABLED
201.10	Closely Approaching Advanced Age	Limited or Less	Skilled or Semi-skilled—Skills Not transferable	DISABLED
201.11	Closely Approaching Advanced Age	Limited or Less	Skilled or Semi-skilled—Skills transferable	NOT DISABLED
201.12	Closely Approaching Advanced Age	High School Graduate or More—does not provide for direct entry into skilled works	Unskilled or None	DISABLED
201.13	Closely Approaching Advanced Age	High School Graduate or More—provides for direct entry into skilled works	Unskilled or None	NOT DISABLED
201.14	Closely Approaching Advanced Age	High School Graduate or More—does not provide for direct entry into skilled works	Skilled or Semi-skilled—Skills Not transferable	DISABLED

Rule	Age	Education	Previous Work Experience	Decision
201.15	Closely Approaching Advanced Age	High School Graduate or More—does not provide for direct entry into skilled works	Skilled or Semiskilled—Skills transferable	NOT DISABLED
201.16	Closely Approaching Advanced Age	High School Graduate or More—provides for direct entry into skilled works	Skilled or Semiskilled—Skills Not transferable	NOT DISABLED
201.17	Younger Individual Age 45–49	Illiterate or unable to communicate in English	Unskilled or None	DISABLED
201.18	Younger Individual Age 45–49	Limited or Less—At least literate and able to communicate in English	Unskilled or None	NOT DISABLED
201.19	Younger Individual Age 45–49	Limited or Less	Skilled or Semiskilled—Skills Not transferable	NOT DISABLED
201.20	Younger Individual Age 45–49	Limited or Less	Skilled or Semiskilled—Skills transferable	NOT DISABLED
201.21	Younger Individual Age 45–49	High School Graduate or More	Skilled or Semiskilled—Skills Not transferable	NOT DISABLED
201.22	Younger Individual Age 45–49	High School Graduate or More	Skilled or Semiskilled—Skills transferable	NOT DISABLED
201.23	Younger Individual Age 18–44	Illiterate or unable to communicate in English	Unskilled or None	NOT DISABLED
201.24	Younger Individual Age 18–44	Limited or Less—At least literate and able to communicate in English	Unskilled or None	NOT DISABLED
201.25	Younger Individual Age 18–44	Limited or Less	Skilled or Semiskilled—Skills Not transferable	NOT DISABLED
201.26	Younger Individual Age 18–44	Limited or Less	Skilled or Semiskilled—Skills transferable	NOT DISABLED
201.27	Younger Individual Age 18–44	High School Graduate or More	Unskilled or None	NOT DISABLED
201.28	Younger Individual Age 18–44	High School Graduate or More	Skilled or Semiskilled—Skills Not transferable	NOT DISABLED
201.29	Younger Individual Age 18–44	High School Graduate or More	Skilled or Semiskilled—Skills transferable	NOT DISABLED

Table No. 2. Residual Functional Capacity Maximum Sustained Work Capacity Limited to Light Work as a Result of Severe Medically Determinable Impairment(s)

Rule	Age	Education	Previous Work Experience	Decision
202.01	Advanced Age	Limited or Less	Unskilled or None	DISABLED
202.02	Advanced Age	Limited or Less	Skilled or Semi-skilled—Skills Not transferable	DISABLED
202.03	Advanced Age	Limited or Less	Skilled or Semi-skilled—Skills transferable	NOT DISABLED
202.04	Advanced Age	High School Graduate or More—does not provide for direct entry into skilled works	Unskilled or None	DISABLED
202.05	Advanced Age	High School Graduate or More—provides for direct entry into skilled works	Unskilled or None	NOT DISABLED
202.06	Advanced Age	High School Graduate or More—does not provide for direct entry into skilled works	Skilled or Semi-skilled—Skills Not transferable	DISABLED
202.07	Advanced Age	High School Graduate or More—does not provide for direct entry into skilled works	Skilled or Semi-skilled—Skills transferable	NOT DISABLED
202.08	Advanced Age	High School Graduate or More—provides for direct entry into skilled works	Skilled or Semi-skilled—Skills Not transferable	NOT DISABLED
202.09	Closely Approaching Advanced Age	Illiterate or unable to communicate in English	Unskilled or None	DISABLED
202.10	Closely Approaching Advanced Age	Limited or Less—At least literate and able to communicate in English	Unskilled or None	NOT DISABLED
202.11	Closely Approaching Advanced Age	Limited or Less	Skilled or Semi-skilled—Skills Not transferable	NOT DISABLED
202.12	Closely Approaching Advanced Age	Limited or Less	Skilled or Semi-skilled—Skills transferable	NOT DISABLED
202.13	Closely Approaching Advanced Age	High School Graduate or More	Unskilled or None	NOT DISABLED
202.14	Closely Approaching Advanced Age	High School Graduate or More	Skilled or Semi-skilled—Skills Not transferable	NOT DISABLED

Rule	Age	Education	Previous Work Experience	Decision
202.15	Closely Approaching Advanced Age	High School Graduate or More	Skilled or Semi-skilled—Skills transferable	NOT DISABLED
202.16	Younger Individual	Illiterate or unable to communicate in English	Unskilled or None	NOT DISABLED
202.17	Younger Individual	Limited or Less—At least literate and able to communicate in English	Unskilled or None	NOT DISABLED
202.18	Younger Individual	Limited or Less	Skilled or Semi-skilled—Skills Not transferable	NOT DISABLED
202.19	Younger Individual	Limited or Less	Skilled or Semi-skilled—Skills transferable	NOT DISABLED
202.20	Younger Individual	High School Graduate or More	Unskilled or None	NOT DISABLED
202.21	Younger Individual	High School Graduate or More	Skilled or Semi-skilled—Skills Not transferable	NOT DISABLED
202.22	Younger Individual	High School Graduate or More	Skilled or Semi-skilled—Skills transferable	NOT DISABLED

Table No. 3. Residual Functional Capacity Maximum Sustained Work Capacity Limited to Medium Work as a Result of Severe Medically Determinable Impairment(s)

Rule	Age	Education	Previous Work Experience	Decision
203.01	Closely Approaching Retirement Age	Marginal or None	Unskilled or None	DISABLED
203.02	Closely Approaching Retirement Age	Limited or Less	None	DISABLED
203.03	Closely Approaching Retirement Age	Limited	Unskilled	NOT DISABLED
203.04	Closely Approaching Retirement Age	Limited or Less	Skilled or Semi-skilled—Skills Not transferable	NOT DISABLED
203.05	Closely Approaching Retirement Age	Limited or Less	Skilled or Semi-skilled—Skills transferable	NOT DISABLED
203.06	Closely Approaching Retirement Age	High School Graduate or More	Unskilled or None	NOT DISABLED

Rule	Age	Education	Previous Work Experience	Decision
203.07	Closely Approaching Retirement Age	High School Graduate or More—does not provide for direct entry into skilled works	Skilled or Semiskilled—Skills Not transferable	NOT DISABLED
203.08	Closely Approaching Retirement Age	High School Graduate or More—does not provide for direct entry into skilled works	Skilled or Semiskilled—Skills transferable	NOT DISABLED
203.09	Closely Approaching Retirement Age	High School Graduate or More—provides for direct entry into skilled works	Skilled or Semiskilled—Skills Not transferable	NOT DISABLED
203.10	Advanced Age	Limited or Less	None	DISABLED
203.11	Advanced Age	Limited or Less	Unskilled	NOT DISABLED
203.12	Advanced Age	Limited or Less	Skilled or Semiskilled—Skills Not transferable	NOT DISABLED
203.13	Advanced Age	Limited or Less	Skilled or Semiskilled—Skills Transferable	NOT DISABLED
203.14	Advanced Age	High School Graduate or More	Unskilled or None	NOT DISABLED
203.15	Advanced Age	High School Graduate or More—does not provide for direct entry into skilled works	Skilled or Semiskilled—Skills Not transferable	NOT DISABLED
203.16	Advanced Age	High School Graduate or More—does not provide for direct entry into skilled works	Skilled or Semiskilled—Skills transferable	NOT DISABLED
203.17	Advanced Age	High School Graduate or More—provides for direct entry into skilled works	Skilled or Semiskilled—Skills Not transferable	NOT DISABLED
203.18	Closely Approaching Advanced Age	Limited or Less	Unskilled or None	NOT DISABLED
203.19	Closely Approaching Advanced Age	Limited or Less	Skilled or Semiskilled—Skills Not transferable	NOT DISABLED
203.20	Closely Approaching Advanced Age	Limited or Less	Skilled or Semiskilled—Skills transferable	NOT DISABLED
203.21	Closely Approaching Advanced Age	High School Graduate or More	Unskilled or None	NOT DISABLED
203.22	Closely Approaching Advanced Age	High School Graduate or More—does not provide for direct entry into skilled works	Skilled or Semiskilled—Skills Not transferable	NOT DISABLED

Rule	Age	Education	Previous Work Experience	Decision
203.23	Closely Approaching Advanced Age	High School Graduate or More—does not provide for direct entry into skilled works	Skilled or Semi-skilled—Skills transferable	NOT DISABLED
203.24	Closely Approaching Advanced Age	High School Graduate or More—provides for direct entry into skilled works	Skilled or Semi-skilled—Skills not transferable	NOT DISABLED
203.25	Younger Individual	Limited or Less	Unskilled or None	NOT DISABLED
203.26	Younger Individual	Limited or Less	Skilled or Semi-skilled—Skills Not transferable	NOT DISABLED
203.27	Younger Individual	Limited or Less	Skilled or Semi-skilled—Skills transferable	NOT DISABLED
203.28	Younger Individual	High School Graduate or More	Unskilled or None	NOT DISABLED
203.29	Younger Individual	High School Graduate or More—does not provide for direct entry into skilled works	Skilled or Semi-skilled—Skills Not transferable	NOT DISABLED
203.30	Younger Individual	High School Graduate or More—does not provide for direct entry into skilled works	Skilled or Semi-skilled—Skills transferable	NOT DISABLED
203.31	Younger Individual	High School Graduate or More—provides for direct entry into skilled works	Skilled or Semi-skilled—Skills Not transferable	NOT DISABLED

CHAPTER 5

COMMON RESIDUAL FUNCTIONAL CAPACITY RATINGS

Table of Sections

---

§ 5.1 Introduction

This chapter contains some common residual functional capacity (RFC) ratings for adult claimants that are not severe enough to Meet or Equal a Listing. Considering the great number of possible impairments, there can be no complete list of RFC's for every situation. However, the following examples cover some of the more common impairments that affect claimants and are verbatim from federal documents used by S. S. Disability.

NONSEVERE IMPAIRMENTS—OFFICIAL EXAMPLES

A. Musculoskeletal

1. Osteoarthritis corroborated by X-ray findings, with symptoms of pain and stiffness of lumbar or cervical spine or major joints, and minimal abnormal findings on physical examination.

2. Traumatic fracture of a vertebral body, in the absence of metabolic bone disease, with loss of less than 50 percent of height of the vertebra without significant physical findings or neurologic abnormalities.

3. Status postsurgery for excision of lumbar disc without ongoing significant motor abnormalities or significant objective abnormal physical findings.

B. Special Senses

1. Retention of best corrected visual acuity of 20/40 in the better eye (phakic) without significant restriction of visual fields.

> [*Author's note*: "phakic" means the eye has not had its lens removed]

2. Retention of visual field in better eye of a radius of 45 degrees or better (visual field efficiency of approximately 70 percent).

C. Respiratory

1. Obstructive airway disease where the FEV_1 or MVV is greater than values in POMS DI 2201, and there is no clinical evidence of impairment of gas exchange.

> [*Author's note*: POMS DI 2201 is a federal document that contains the following table:
>
> **Table A**
>
> | Height[1] (Inches) | MVV (MBC) Equal to or Less Than | AND | FEV_1 Equal to or Less Than |
> |---|---|---|---|
> | 60 or less | 56 L./Min. | | 1.4 L. |
> | 61–63 | 60 | | 1.5 |
> | 64–65 | 64 | | 1.6 |
> | 66–67 | 68 | | 1.7 |
> | 68–69 | 72 | | 1.8 |
> | 70–71 | 76 | | 1.9 |
> | 72 or more | 80 | | 2.0 |
>
> 1. Height without shoes.
>
> If the claimant's FEV_1 *or* MVV is higher than the values in the above table, then the impaiment is considered nonsevere. If both the FEV_1 *and* MVV are equal to or less than the values in the table, then a significant impairment is present. This would be either medium or light work, depending on the judgement of S. S. Disability as to just how severe the obstructive lung disease is. Sedentary RFC's are not given on the basis of pulmonary function tests.]

2. Diffuse pulmonary fibrosis where the arterial blood gas values do not meet the requirements of Listing 3.04, table III, at an exercise level of 25 ml.O_2/kg./min., or work equivalent.

> [*Author's note*: This refers to the claimant's ability to maintain adequate oxygenation of blood at a given level of work. Such tests are currently not frequently purchased by S. S. Disability, though their use may increase in the future.]

D. Cardiovascular

1. Hypertension without significant organ damage, current or past.

2. History of chest pain without specific ischemic findings on EKG (rest and exercise), less than 50 percent narrowing on angiography, and without significant cardiomegaly.

3. Status postsurgery for peripheral arterial disease with palpable pulses below the femoral level and no intermittent claudication.

E. Digestive

1. Colostomy, uncomplicated, with proper function of the stoma and nutrition is adequately maintained.

2. Peptic ulcer, uncomplicated or with recovery from complications.

3. Chronic liver disease, in the absence of ascites, with total bilirubin less than 1.5 mg. per deciliter and serum albumin 3.5 gm. per deciliter or greater.

4. Inflammatory bowel disease (regional enteritis, ulcerative colitis) in clinical remission for 12 months prior to adjudication.

F. Genito-Urinary

1. Nephrotic syndrome, in remission, with persistent mild edema in which urinary protein excretion is less than 500 mg. per 24 hours and serum albumin is 3.5 gm. per deciliter or greater.

2. Chronic renal disease (other than nephrotic syndrome) in which the serum creatinine is persistently less than 3.0 mg. per deciliter (100 ml.), in the absence of clinical complications.

G. Endocrine

Diabetes mellitus, adult onset, controlled on prescribed therapy, without significant end-organ damage or recent episodes of acidosis.

H. Neurological

1. Epilepsy with no major motor seizures for 12 months prior to adjudication.

[*Author's note*: A single seizure in the year prior to adjudication constitutes a significant work-related impairment, provided that the claimant is undergoing active therapy for attempted seizure control, and is compliant with that therapy.]

2. Peripheral neuropathy or neuritis, due to any cause, with no significant motor or sensory loss.

I. Mental Disorders

IQ of 80 or greater in all major areas of intellectual functioning.

§ 5.2 Additional Examples of RFC's—Official

A. Musculoskeletal System

1. Rheumatoid arthritis with clinical evidence of continued activity corroborated by laboratory tests without significant restriction of function of the affected joints. Heavy work activity would be precluded. The distinction between the capacity to perform medium and light work activity requires consideration of the joints involved, the extent of involvement, any residual abnormality of these joints, and the status of associated muscles. Consideration of limitation of walking or standing may be pertinent if major joints of the lower extremities are involved. Fine and gross manipulation may be limited if there is involvement of the fingers, hands, or wrists. The complications from, or the side effects of, large doses of medication must be considered.

2. Osteoarthritis of major joints of the lower extremities (hip, knee, ankle) with pain and abnormal findings on physical examination demonstrating significant interference with function of one or more joints and abnormal findings on X-ray. Heavy work activity would be precluded. The distinction between the capacity to perform medium and light work activity requires consideration of the joints involved, the extent of involvement (particularly of limitation of motion), and evidence of atrophy of muscles moving that joint. There must be consideration of whether the impairment imposes a significant limitation on walking or standing or more specific activities such as repeated operation of foot controls or climbing stairs.

3. Osteoarthritis of major joints of the upper extremities (shoulder, elbow, wrist-hand) with pain and abnormal findings on physical examination demonstrating significant interference with function of one or more joints and abnormal findings on X-

ray. Heavy work activity would be precluded. The distinction between the capacity to perform medium and light work activity requires consideration of the joints involved. Consideration must be given as to whether involvement of the shoulder or elbow significantly restricts the individual's reach.

4. Amputation of lower extremity above the knee, with ability to use prosthesis effectively. The impairment is considered to impose a significant limitation on walking, standing, and climbing stairs. The individual would be limited to sedentary work activity. (Note: These criteria do not apply to amputations due to peripheral arterial disease or diabetic necrosis. See Listing 4.13C or 9.08C.)

5. Amputation of lower extremity at or above the tarsal region, but below the knee, with ability to use prosthesis effectively. Heavy work activity would be precluded. Usually there is no significant restriction in the ability to walk or stand unless there is a complication of the amputation site. There would be a limitation on excessive climbing of stairs and walking on grossly uneven terrain and operating foot controls with the affected extremity. (Note: These criteria do not apply to amputations due to peripheral arterial disease or diabetic necrosis. See Listing 4.13C or 9.08C.)

6. Amputation of upper extremity above the elbow. The individual would be limited to light work activity with additional limitations because of loss of bimanual manipulation and difficulty or inability to handle bulky objects. The limitation on fine manipulation even with the remaining hand would depend upon which was the dominant extremity, the time since loss of the extremity, and subsequent acquisition of any fine manipulative abilities by the remaining nondominant extremity.

7. Amputation of upper extremity below the elbow. Heavy work activity would be precluded. The distinction between the capacity to perform medium and light work activity requires consideration of the extent and condition of the remaining stump and the ability to use a prosthesis. There would be a loss of bilateral fine manipulation and some limitation of gross manipulation. The limitation on fine manipulation even with the remaining hand would depend upon which was the dominant extremity, the extent and condition of the remaining stump, the time since loss of the extremity, and subsequent acquisition of any fine manipulative abilities by the remaining, nondominant extremity.

8. Replacement of hip or knee. Heavy and medium work activity would be precluded, but the individual is not automati-

cally restricted to sedentary work activity. Function returning after full recovery from surgery must be evaluated to determine the capacity for light work activity. In the evaluation, limitation of walking is a more important consideration than limitation of standing. Consideration must be given to range of motion of the joint, integrity of the associated musculature, evidence of loosening of the prosthesis, and evidence of significant arthritis in other major joints.

9. Status postsurgery for excision of lumbar disc with significant abnormal physical findings short of meeting the Listings. Heavy work activity would be precluded and bending and stooping would be limited. The distinction between the capacity to perform medium and light work activity requires consideration of the severity of the underlying orthopedic impairment and any residual neurological abnormalities. Further limitation on ability to walk, stand, or operate foot controls would have to be considered if warranted by the severity of the impairment.

10. Stable fusion of lumbar vertebrae without neurological complications. Heavy work activity would be precluded, but ability to engage in medium work activity ordinarily would be retained. Bending and stooping would be limited. Significant limitation in walking and standing is not expected.

B. Cardiovascular System

1. Ischemic heart disease with angina, treadmill exercise test "negative" at 5 METs, but "positive" at 7 METs or less. Medium work activity would be precluded, but ability to engage in light work activity would be retained unless restricted by other cardiac impairments such as congestive heart failure. (The terms "negative" and "positive" are defined in Listing 4.04A.)

2. Ischemic heart disease with angina, treadmill exercise test "negative" at 7 METs, but "positive" at 10 METs or less. Heavy work activity would be precluded, but ability to engage in medium work activity would be retained unless restricted by other cardiac impairments such as congestive heart failure. (The terms "negative" and "positive" are defined in Listing 4.04A.)

3. Postmyocardial infarction or coronary artery bypass graft, without angina, congestive heart failure, or significant arrhythmias. Heavy work activity would be precluded unless specific exercise testing establishes the ability to engage in heavy work activity. The distinction between the capacity to perform medium and light work activity requires consideration of the medical evidence describing the individual's clinical condition.

4. Previous congestive heart failure because of "chronic" heart disease, currently compensated and with electrocardiographic and X-ray abnormalities not currently meeting the requirements of Listing 4.02. Heavy work activity would be precluded. The distinction between the capacity to perform medium and light work activity requires consideration of the underlying heart disease and the residual impairment.

5. Hypertension without previous congestive heart failure, but with electrocardiographic evidence of left ventricular strain pattern as shown in Listing 4.02.B.2. Heavy work activity would be precluded. The distinction between the capacity to perform medium and light work activity requires the consideration of the medical evidence describing the individual's clinical condition, including the extent of cardiac abnormality and any adverse effects of medication.

6. Replacement of heart valve. Heavy work activity would be precluded. The distinction between the capacity to perform medium and light work activity requires consideration of the underlying heart disease, the type of surgery performed, and the residual impairment.

In addition to the above examples several more relevant policies are to be noted:

1. Someone who is of advanced age, has a limited education, has no relevant work experience, and has more than a nonsevere mental impairment will generally be found disabled.

2. Acquired Immune Deficiency Syndrome (AIDS) may result in serious systemic infection by viruses, fungi, bacteria, or parasites that would otherwise rarely affect a normal person. The cause of AIDS is unknown, but may itself be a virus.

Serious pulmonary or dessiminated infections arising because of the immune deficiency caused by AIDS will be allowed as an Equal by virtue of that part of the legal definition of disability which states ". . . inability to do any substantial gainful activity by reason of any medically determinable physical or mental impairment which can be expected to result in death." This doesn't mean that everyone with AIDS will die, but the mortality is high if serious infection develops. Cases allowed will be reevaluated in one year.

"Unofficial Examples of RFC's"

The previously given examples of RFC's represent current official policy. In contrast, the examples that follow do *not* represent official policy. At one time they represented RFC guidelines from one of the Regional Offices, but have subsequently been withdrawn. The author feels that they would still be of some value to the reader, as long as they are interpreted with caution. Under no circumstances should the following RFC examples be taken as official medical policy within S. S. Disability. They are included here because they were not replaced with new guidelines, yet may still be somewhat relevant in certain cases.

§ 5.3 "Non-Severe" Impairments—Unofficial

A. Musculoskeletal

1. Osteoarthritis of the thoracic or lumbar spine with no encroachment on neural foramina.

2. Lumbar strain, with no demonstrable X-ray changes.

3. Traumatic fracture, in the absence of metabolic bone disease involving a vertebral body with less than 50% compression in height, no neurologic signs.

4. Post-laminectomy without significant residuals.

> [*Author's note*: a "laminectomy" is a common back operation in which part of a bony vertebral body is removed along with a herniated disk.]

B. Special Senses

1. Hearing threshold (average of bone and air conduction, both ears) of pure tones at 500, 1000, and 2000 Hz of less than 70 dB.

2. Blindness in one eye with vision in the remaining eye (phakic) of 20/40 or better, without significant visual field restriction.

C. Respiration

1. Obstructive airway disease where FEV_1 or MVV are greater than those in Table A.

2. Diffuse pulmonary fibrosis with FVC greater than 65% of predicted normal for age, sex, and height.

3. Other restrictive lung disease—where FVC is 50% or greater of the predicted normal for age, sex, and height.

D. Cardiovascular System

1. Hypertension with no end organ damage.

2. Angina with negative exercise ECG evidence or negative angiogram (less than 50% narrowing) and with normal cardiac size.

3. Symptoms of congestive heart failure in the absence of cardiomegaly, and in the absence of a recognized clinical syndrome in which lack of cardiomegaly is expected despite congestive symptoms and signs (e.g., cor pulmonale, constrictive pericarditis, acute MI with acute left ventricular failure).

> [*Author's note*: "constrictive pericarditis" means inflammation of the pericardial sac surrounding the heart. "Acute left ventricular failure" refers to heart failure that has developed too quickly for there to be obvious findings of heart failure or heart enlargement.]

4. Status post-surgery for intermittent claudication with palpable pulses below femoral level and no claudication.

5. Claudication with good pulses at all levels, and no gangrenous ischemic changes on physical exam.

6. Absent or reduced pulses in the lower extremities in the absence of claudication or gangrenous ischemic changes.

E. Digestive

1. Peptic ulcer, uncomplicated (no evidence of bleeding, obstructive, recurrence, weight loss or fistula formation).

2. Cirrhosis of the liver, in the absence of ascites, with currently-normal bilirubin and serum albumin.

3. Fatty infiltration of the liver.

4. Acute alcoholic hepatitis without clinical (or biopsy, if available) evidence of cirrhosis, with evidence of resolution of liver function abnormalities.

5. Inflammatory bowel disease (regional enteritis, ulcerative colitis) in complete clinical remission for the past 12 months prior to application for disability.

F. Genito-Urinary

1. Urinary tract infection (excluding tuberculosis).

G. Hemic

1. Anemia, the cause for which cannot be established by standard evaluation techniques, in which hemoglobin is greater than 11 grams % or Hematocrit is greater than 33%.

2. Readily treatable anemias in the absence of systemic complication (e.g., simple Fe deficiency, Folate or B_{12} deficiency anemias).

> [*Author's note*: "simple Fe deficiency" refers to anemia due to lack of iron, it is usually easily treatable and by far the most common cause of anemia. Folate and B_{12} are vitamins, and anemia caused by their deficiency can usually be treated.]

H. Endocrine

1. Diabetes mellitus, adult onset, under good control, and with no end organ damage, or recent episodes of acidosis.

> [*Author's note*: "no end organ damage" means no damage to eyes, kidneys, arteries, heart, or nervous system.]

2. *Hypo*thyroidism, controlled with replacement therapy.

> [*Author's note*: "replacement therapy" means artificial hormones.]

3. *Hyper*thyroidism, controlled with medical or surgical therapy.

4. Adrenal insufficiency, controlled with replacement therapy.

5. Diabetes insipidus, controlled with replacement therapy.

I. Mental Disorders

1. I.Q. of 80 or greater in all major areas of intellectual functioning.

J. Multiple Body Systems

1. Obesity with no functional limitations.

> [*Author's note*: "functional limitations" means problems standing, walking, bending, reaching, breathing, etc.]

K. Neurologic

1. Epilepsy—major motor seizures—occurring less than once per year (with or without therapy).

2. Epilepsy—minor motor seizures—occurring less than once per month (with or without therapy).

3. **Peripheral neuropathies.** With normal gait in the absence of assistive devices and no trophic changes (if involving upper extremity, ability to grasp objects must be intact).

> [*Author's note*: "trophic changes" means obvious tissue damage caused by the neuropathy.]

4. Brain tumor, benign, encapsulated, with complete removal and no sensory or motor deficits.

> [*Author's note*: "encapsulated" means the tumor was in a capsule of connective tissue, making it easier to remove surgically.]

5. Status post cerebrovascular accident with no residual motor weakness, aphasia, or ataxia.

L. Neoplastic

1. Stage I Hodgkin's disease.

> [*Author's note*: "stage I" refers to early Hodgkin's disease (a form of lymphatic cancer) that has not spread far from where it started.]

2. All primary, resectable tumors without local extension, recurrence or metastases beyond the regional lymph nodes and in which there are no post-therapeutic residuals that limit function. Exceptions to this are oat cell carcinoma of lung, testicular choriocarcinoma, pancreatic adenocarcinoma, hepatic, bileduct and gallbladder carcinoma and sarcoma of skin and soft parts.

§ 5.4 "Moderate" Impairments—Unofficial

A. Musculoskeletal

1. Rheumatoid arthritis with elevated sedimentation rate, and either positive rheumatoid factor, or positive anti-nuclear antibody test with recurrent acute attacks lasting less than 2 months, occurring at least once but less than three times during the year prior to adjudication.

2. Osteoarthritis of major joints with pain and abnormal findings on physical examination such as limited motion, enlargement of effusion in the affected joints, but without gross anatomical deformity such as subluxation, bony or fibrous ankylosis.

3. Status post cervical or lumbar fusion, involving two adjacent vertebrae, with solid fusion, and complete relief of symptoms, no neurologic signs.

> [*Author's note*: "fusion" refers to the fusion of two or more bony vertebral bodies by surgery.]

4. Traumatic compression fracture (in the absence of generalized osteoporosis) with loss of at least 50% height of a vertebral body, no neurologic signs, other than sensory changes.

> [*Author's note*: "generalized osteoporosis" means thinning of bone affecting the entire body. This could actually meet a Listing and would be worse than a moderate impairment.]

5. Amputation below the knee, with ability to use prothesis effectively.

B. Special Senses

1. Blindness in one eye and remaining vision in the other eye between 20/40 and 20/100 after best correction.

2. Hearing loss (bilateral) with average pure tone detection thresholds (average of air and bone conduction at 500, 1000 and 2000 Hz, both ears) between 70 and 79 dB.

3. Meniere's Disease with attacks of vertigo occurring at least once every two months, no cerebellar signs, and hearing loss no greater than in 2 above.

> [*Author's note*: "Meniere's Disease" is a fairly uncommon disorder of the inner ear producing progressive vertigo and deafness. "Cerebellar signs" refers to the abnormalities caused by disease of the cerebellum of the brain.]

4. Visual field efficiency between 35% and 70% with no loss of central acuity.

C. Respiratory

1. Chronic obstructive pulmonary disease, with MVV and FEV_1 less than values in Table A.

[*Author's note*: It is a matter of judgement by the reviewer whether a rating of "moderate" or "moderately severe" would be given.]

2. Diffuse pulmonary fibrosis, with FVC 55% or greater but less than 65% of normal predicted values.

3. Other restrictive lung disease where FVC is 40% or greater but less than 50% of normal predicted values.

D. Cardiovascular System

1. Venous insufficiency of a leg with moderate edema despite supportive hose (No ulcerations, with or without pigmentation).

[*Author's note*: pigmentation refers to abnormal change in skin color caused by disease of veins.]

2. Venous insufficiency of a lower extremity with healed ulcerations and minimal current edema (with or without pigmentation).

3. Cardiomegaly of less than 55% C/T ratio, currently compensated, with previous episode of congestive heart failure.

[*Author's note*: "currently compensated" means treated and not in heart failure at the time of application for disability.]

4. Cardiomegaly due to established heart disease but without objective findings of congestive heart failure at any time.

[*Author's note*: "cardiomegaly" usually means a C/T ratio of at least 55%. The established heart disease refers to any kind of heart disease.]

[*Author's note*: "reduced pulses" means weak pulses in the major arteries of the legs.]

5. Status post myocardial infarction, without current angina or congestive heart failure.

6. Status post coronary bypass surgery without current angina or congestive heart failure.

7. Coronary angiographic findings of significant obstruction of a proximal coronary artery (more than 50%) but in the absence of typical angina pectoris.

8. Positive (ischemic) exercise electro-cardiogram in the absence of typical angina pectoris.

9. Status post replacement of heart valve without current angina or congestive heart failure:

E. Digestive

1. Chronic liver disease in the absence of ascites with persistent elevation of serum bilirubin between 1.5 mg % and 2.5 mg % or serum albumin persistently below 3.5 grams %.

[*Author's note*: "ascites" means an abnormal accumulation of fluid in the abdominal cavity.]

2. Ulcerative colitis or regional enteritis with acute attacks occurring at least every 3 months without abscess, fistula formation, intestinal obstruction, or systemic complications.

F. Genito-Urinary

1. Nephrotic syndrome, with persistent findings of proteinuria greater than 500 mg/24 hours but less than 2.5 grams/24 hours, and serum albumin less than 3.5 grams % but greater than 3.0 grams %.

G. Endocrine

1. Diabetes mellitus requiring insulin therapy with episodes of ketoacidosis occurring at least twice in the year prior to adjudication.

[*Author's note*: "adjudication" refers to the time of application for disability.]

H. Mental

1. I.Q. of 70–79.

I. Neurological

1. Epilepsy—major motor seizures—with episodes occurring at least once but no greater than four times yearly, despite prescribed treatment.

2. Epilepsy—minor motor seizures—with seizure frequently of 1–2 per month in spite of prescribed treatment.

3. Status post CVA (3 months or longer) with demonstrable mild weakness in two extremities, mild or intermittent aphasia, mild ataxia, or a moderate motor deficit involving only upper extremity.

[*Author's note*: "CVA" means cerebrovascular accident, or stroke.]

4. Multiple Sclerosis, Cerebral Palsy, or residuals of surgical or non-surgical traumas, with mild but demonstrable neuro-

logic deficits involving vision, speech, gait, gross coordination or fine movement.

[*Author's note*: "neurologic deficits" means abnormalities due to disorder of the nervous system.]

J. Neoplastic

1. Carcinoma of the breast, post radical mastectomy, with persistent lymphedema and restricted range of motion in the affected extremity.

[*Author's note*: "lymphedema" means swelling from lymph fluid. "Affected extremity" refers to one of the arms.]

2. Other neoplastic disease in which there has been complete excision, no distant metastases, but with significant post-therapeutic residuals which affect function.

[*Author's note*: "neoplastic disease" literally means any new abnormal growth, but here it refers only to cancer.]

3. Malignant lymphoma, prostatic carcinoma or testicular carcinoma (except choriocarcinoma) with extension beyond the primary site treated with radiotherapy or chemotherapy with good control of symptoms, but with evidence of residual metastatic disease.

[*Author's note*: "malignant" means cancerous.]

§ 5.5 "Moderately Severe" Impairments—Unofficial

A. Musculoskeletal

1. Rheumatoid arthritis, with diagnosis confirmed as listed above, manifested by repeated acute flares with pain, joint swelling and limitation of motion, with no single episode lasting beyond two months and occurring at least three times yearly.

[*Author's note*: "as listed above" means the diagnosis must be proven, just as it must be in the Listing dealing with rheumatoid arthritis.]

2. Rheumatoid arthritis, diagnosis confirmed as listed above, with persistent pain, joint swelling or enlargement and limitation of motion in more than one major joint, but without gross anatomic deformity, such as subluxation, bony or fibrous ankylosis.

3. Degenerative arthritis, with pain, swelling, limitation of motion and X-ray changes of joint space narrowing or osteophytosis and:

a. Involvement of both shoulders with limitation in abduction of one limited to less than 90 degrees.

[*Author's note*: "osteophytosis" means bony spurs due to degenerative arthritis, which is the same as osteoarthritis. "Abduction" means moving the arm straight out sideways.]

b. Involvement of both elbows with ankylosis of more than 40 degrees of flexion in one.

c. Persistent pain or swelling or limitation of motion in at least two weight bearing joints, but without gross anatomic deformity such as subluxation, bony or fibrous ankylosis.

4. Status post surgical fusion of two or more adjacent vertebrae of the cervical, or lumbar spine, with flexion limited to no greater than 60 degrees in the lumbar spine, or 15 degrees in the cervical spine.

[*Author's note*: "flexion" refers to forward bending of the neck.]

B. Special Senses

1. Visual field efficiency between 20–35% with no loss of central acuity.

C. Respiratory

1. Chronic obstructive pulmonary disease with either MVV or FEV_1 less than the value in Table A.

[*Author's note*: It is a matter of judgment by the reviewer whether a rating of "moderate" or "moderately severe" would be given.]

2. Diffuse interstitial fibrosis with FVC at least 45% but less than 55% of predicted normal values.

3. Other restrictive pulmonary disorders with FVC at least 30% but less than 40% of predicted normal values.

D. Cardiovascular System

1. Venous insufficiency of a lower extremity with severe edema, without ulceration or with healing ulceration, but no history of previous ulcerations, with persistent edema despite supportive hose.

[*Author's note*: "supportive hose" refers to special support stockings for the leg.]

2. More than one episode of congestive heart failure in past with current cardiomegaly of less than 55% C/T ratio despite therapy.

3. Status post myocardial infarction with significant ventricular arrythmias occurring despite therapy.

[*Author's note*: "ventricular arrythmias" refers to very abnormal heart rhythm from the ventricular chambers of the heart.]

4. Typical angina pectoris with angiographic findings of greater than 50% narrowing but less than 70% narrowing in a single proximal coronary artery.

E. Digestive

1. Chronic liver disease not meeting any Listing but with a past history of ascites and persistent abnormal liver function studies since onset comparable to total bilirubin between 1.5 mg% and 2.5 mg% or serum albumin of 3.0 grams% or less.

F. Genito-Urinary

1. Nephrotic syndrome, with persistent findings of proteinuria of at least 2.5 grams (24 hours) but less than 3.5 grams (24 hours) or persistent of serum albumin below 3.0 grams% with a 24 hour urine protein of less than 3.5 grams/24 hours.

G. Neurologic

1. Epilepsy—major motor seizures—with 5 to 12 seizures per year (not all of which occur in one 90 day period) in spite of prescribed treatment.

2. Epilepsy—minor motor seizures—with 3–4 seizures per month despite prescribed treatment.

3. Status post CVA with residual moderate motor deficit involving a lower extremity.

4. Cerebral Palsy or Multiple Sclerosis with a moderate motor deficit in a lower extremity.

5. Residuals of surgical or non-surgical cerebral trauma with moderate motor deficit in a lower extremity.

APPENDICES

Appendix

I. Impairments Unlikely to Qualify for Disability.
II. Disability Report.
III. Vocational Report.
IV. Report of Continuing Disability Interview.
V. Reconsideration Disability Report.
VI. Work Despite Severe Impairment.
VII. Evaluation of Pain.
VIII. Substantial Gainful Activity.
IX. Medical Records.
X. Request for Hearing.
XI. Request for Review of Hearing Decision/Order.
XII. Medical History and Disability Report—Widow, Widower, Surviving Divorced Wife, or Disabled Child.
XIII. Predicted Normal FEV, MVV, and FVC Values For Men and Women.

APPENDIX I

IMPAIRMENTS UNLIKELY TO QUALIFY FOR DISABILITY

The following is a list of impairments not likely to qualify for disability. These would probably be coded "nonsevere" by S. S. Disability. Unlike the official examples of "nonsevere" impairments given in Chapter 5, the following list is based on the author's personal experience, and is merely meant to be supplementary to the official examples. The exception is *Crime,* the treatment of which is fixed in Social Security regulations.

1. *Hypertension.* High blood pressure itself is rarely the basis for disability. It is important only in cases where there has been significant damage to some important part of the body, such as the heart, eyes, kidneys, brain, etc.

2. *"Nervous".* Many claimants allege that they are unable to work, because of "nerves". That is, they feel they are too anxious or nervous to work. However, nervousness must be associated with a severe mental disorder to qualify.

3. *Headaches.* With very rare exceptions, disability is not granted for headaches of any kind.

4. *Pregnancy.* Regardless of the problems a claimant may be having with a pregnancy, the minimum duration for disability requires an illness of at least 12 months. No pregnancy ever lasts that long.

5. *"Tiredness".* Feeling "tired" never gets anyone disability, unless it is related to some severe disease that can be identified. Claimants who feel "tired" for no apparent reason will not qualify.

6. *"Weakness".* Feeling "weak" never gets anyone disability, unless it is related to some severe disease that can be identified. Claimants who feel "weak" for no apparent reason will not qualify for disability.

7. *Bladder infections.* Bladder infections have very little to do with a claimant's ability to work. The author has never seen a case allowed, because of a bladder infection, which is a common minor problem affecting millions of people. It should also be pointed out that infections of the kidneys are extremely unlikely to result in allowance of disability benefits, unless the infections have resulted in kidney failure.

8. *Hysterectomy.* Simple hysterectomies (removal of the uterus) are done on many thousands of women yearly. A hys-

terectomy has absolutely no effect on the ability of a claimant to work.

9. *"Dizziness".* Unless "dizziness" is related to a severe medical problem that can be identified (such as severe disease of the brain or inner ear), it will not result in allowance of benefits. "Dizziness" severe enough to qualify is extremely rare.

10. *Hypotension.* Low blood pressure is almost never a basis for disability. Exceptions are very rare, and associated with some severe and unusual disorders such as uncontrolled Addison's Disease with blood pressure falling to shock levels.

11. *"Poor Vision".* Poor vision that can be corrected with glasses, or which affects only one eye is never a basis for disability.

12. *"Poor Hearing".* Poor hearing that can be corrected with a hearing aid, or which affects only one ear is never a basis for disability.

13. *Bursitis.*

14. *Cosmetic deformity.* With extremely rare exceptions involving very severe deformity of the face, this is not a basis for disability. The last case the author remembers being allowed because of cosmetic deformity involved such destruction of the face that the brain could be seen pulsating through one of his eye sockets. [An Equal code was used.]

15. *Insomnia.* The author is not aware of any case ever being allowed, because of insomnia alone. It would have to be associated with a severe mental disorder, and most cases of insomnia are not.

16. *Allergies.* Unless associated with severe asthma, the author is not aware of any claimant getting disability because of allergies.

17. *Noncancerous tumors.* Unless a brain tumor is involved, very few noncancerous tumors result in allowance of disability benefits.

18. *"Skin rashes".* Minor rashes of the skin never result in allowance of benefits.

19. *Sinusitis.*

20. *Hemorrhoids.*

21. *Poor dental hygiene.*

22. *Age.* Age alone is never the basis for receiving disability.

23. *Gallbladder disease.*

24. *Crime.* The previous items on this list are based on the author's experience. However, impairments associated with crime involve specific laws beginning on or after October 1, 1980. The following comments are exactly as they appear in federal documents affecting the way S. S. Disability handles such cases ["Legislative Report" No. 10, 1–14–81]:

Benefits to Certain Prisoners

Suspension of Benefits to Certain Prisoners. Requires suspension (effective beginning with benefits for October 1980) of social security childhood disability benefits or disabled workers' benefits for any period during which the beneficiary is incarcerated in a penal or correctional institution due to the conviction of a felony, unless he or she is participating in a court-approved rehabilitation program that is expected to result in the prisoner being able to engage in substantial gainful activity upon release from prison and within a reasonable time. The suspension of a prisoner's benefits does not affect payments to others who are entitled to benefits on the basis of the same earnings record as the prisoner.

[*Author's note*: such as a disabled spouse.]

Restrictions on Entitlement of People Convicted of a Felony. Restricts entitlement to benefits for certain people who are convicted of a felony that is committed after October 19, 1980 (enactment):

Such a person cannot be entitled to benefits based on full-time school attendance while incarcerated because of the conviction.

Such a person cannot have an impairment that arose in the commission of the felony considered for determining entitlement to disability benefits. (And an impairment that was aggravated during the commission of the felony must be disregarded to the extent that it was so aggravated.)

Such a person cannot, during his or her incarceration for the felony, have an impairment that arises while incarcerated considered for determining entitlement to disability benefits. (And the extent of any aggravation, during the incarceration, of a preexisting impairment must also be disregarded.)

The above list of items by no means includes all of the minor things for which claimants allege disability, but for which the DDS is not likely to grant disability benefits. Allegations of disability based on minor medical problems constitute a large number of disability applications, at an average cost of several hundred dollars apiece, even when the decision is one of denial of benefits. (Such cost, of course, is to the government and not the applicant.)

APPENDIX II

DISABILITY REPORT

DEPARTMENT OF HEALTH AND HUMAN SERVICES
Social Security Administration

Form Approved
OMB No 0960-0141

DISABILITY REPORT

PLEASE PRINT, TYPE, OR WRITE CLEARLY AND ANSWER ALL ITEMS TO THE BEST OF YOUR ABILITY. If you are filing on behalf of someone else, enter his or her name and social security number in the space provided and answer all questions. COMPLETE ANSWERS WILL AID IN PROCESSING THE CLAIM.

PRIVACY ACT NOTICE: The information requested on this form is authorized by Title 20 CFR 404.1512 and Title 20 CFR 416.912. The information provided will be used in making a decision on your claim. While completion of this form is voluntary, failure to provide all or part of the requested information could prevent an accurate or timely decision on your claim and could result in the loss of some benefits. Information you furnish on this form may be disclosed by the Social Security Administration to another person or governmental agency only with respect to social security programs and to comply with Federal laws requiring the exchange of information between Social Security and another agency.

A. NAME OF CLAIMANT	B. SOCIAL SECURITY NUMBER ___ / __ / ____	C. TELEPHONE NUMBER where you can be reached (include area code)

D. WHAT IS YOUR DISABLING CONDITION? *(Briefly explain the injury or illness that stops you from working.)*

PART I — INFORMATION ABOUT YOUR CONDITION

1. When did your condition first bother you:	MONTH	DAY	YEAR

2A. Did you work after the date shown in item 1? *(If "no", go on to items 3A and 3B.)*	☐ YES ☐ NO
2B. If you did work since the date in item 1, did your condition cause you to change —	
Your job or job duties?	☐ YES ☐ NO
Your hours of work?	☐ YES ☐ NO
Your attendance?	☐ YES ☐ NO
Anything else about your work?	☐ YES ☐ NO

(If you answered "no" to all of these, go to items 3A and 3B.)

2C. If you answered "yes" to **any** item in 2B, explain below what the changes in your work circumstances were, the dates they occurred, and how your condition made these changes necessary.

3A. When did your condition finally make you stop working?	MONTH	DAY	YEAR

3B. Explain how your condition now keeps you from working.

FORM **SSA-3368-F8** (3-82) DESTROY PRIOR EDITIONS

(C7756)

APPENDIX II

PART II — INFORMATION ABOUT YOUR MEDICAL RECORDS

4. List the name, address and telephone number of the doctor who has the latest medical records about your disabling condition.		If you have **no** doctor check ☐
NAME	ADDRESS	
TELEPHONE NUMBER (include area code)		
HOW OFTEN DO YOU SEE THIS DOCTOR?	DATE YOU **FIRST** SAW THIS DOCTOR	DATE YOU **LAST** SAW THIS DOCTOR

REASONS FOR VISITS *(show illness or injury for which you had an examination or treatment)*

TYPE OF TREATMENT OR MEDICINES RECEIVED (such as surgery, chemotherapy, radiation, and the medicines you take for your illness or injury, if known. If no treatment or medicines, show "NONE".)

5A. Have you seen any other doctors since your disabling condition began? *If "yes", show the following:*		☐ YES ☐ NO
NAME	ADDRESS	
TELEPHONE NUMBER (include area code)		
HOW OFTEN DO YOU SEE THIS DOCTOR?	DATE YOU **FIRST** SAW THIS DOCTOR	DATE YOU **LAST** SAW THIS DOCTOR

REASONS FOR VISITS *(show illness or injury for which you had an examination or treatment)*

TYPE OF TREATMENT OR MEDICINES RECEIVED (such as surgery, chemotherapy, radiation, and the medicines you take for your illness or injury, if known. If no treatment or medicines, show "NONE".)

5B. Identify below any other doctor you have seen since your illness or injury began.

NAME	ADDRESS	
TELEPHONE NUMBER (include area code)		
HOW OFTEN DO YOU SEE THIS DOCTOR?	DATE YOU **FIRST** SAW THIS DOCTOR	DATE YOU **LAST** SAW THIS DOCTOR

REASONS FOR VISITS *(show illness or injury for which you had an examination or treatment)*

TYPE OF TREATMENT OR MEDICINES RECEIVED (such as surgery, chemotherapy, radiation, and the medicines you take for your illness or injury, if known. If no treatment or medicines, show "NONE".)

FORM **SSA-3368-F8** (3-82)

[C7757]

DISABILITY REPORT

6A. Have you been hospitalized or treated at a clinic for your disabling condition? ☐ YES ☐ NO
If "yes," show the following:

NAME OF HOSPITAL OR CLINIC | ADDRESS

PATIENT OR CLINIC NUMBER

WERE YOU AN INPATIENT? (stayed at least overnight?) ☐ NO ☐ YES *(If "yes", show.)*

WERE YOU AN OUTPATIENT? ☐ NO ☐ YES *(If "yes", show.)*

DATES OF ADMISSIONS	DATES OF DISCHARGES	DATES OF VISITS

REASON FOR HOSPITALIZATION OR CLINIC VISITS *(show illness or injury for which you had an examination or treatment.)*

TYPE OF TREATMENT OR MEDICINES RECEIVED (such as surgery, chemotherapy, radiation, and the medicines you take for your illness or injury, if known. If no treatment or medicines, show "NONE".)

6B. If you have been in other hospital or clinic for your illness or injury, identify it below

NAME OF HOSPITAL OR CLINIC | ADDRESS

PATIENT OR CLINIC NUMBER

WERE YOU AN INPATIENT? (stayed at least overnight?) ☐ NO ☐ YES *(If "yes", show.)*

WERE YOU AN OUTPATIENT? ☐ NO ☐ YES *(If "yes", show.)*

DATES OF ADMISSIONS	DATES OF DISCHARGES	DATES OF VISITS

REASON FOR HOSPITALIZATION OR CLINIC VISITS *(show illness or injury for which you had an examination or treatment.)*

TYPE OF TREATMENT OR MEDICINES RECEIVED (such as surgery, chemotherapy, radiation, and the medicines you take for your illness or injury, if known. If no treatment or medicines, show "NONE".)

If you have been in other hospitals or clinics for your illness or injury, list the names, addresses, patient or clinic numbers, dates and reasons for hospitalization or clinic visits in Part VI.

7. Have you been seen by other agencies for your disabling condition? (VA, Workmen's Compensation, Vocational Rehabilitation, Welfare, etc.) ☐ YES ☐ NO
(If "yes," show the following:)

NAME OF AGENCY | ADDRESS

YOUR CLAIM NUMBER

DATE OF VISITS

TYPE OF TREATMENT, EXAMINATION OR MEDICINES RECEIVED (such as surgery, chemotherapy, radiation, and the medicines you take for your illness or injury, if known. If no treatment or medicines, show "NONE".)

If more space is needed, list the other agencies, their addresses, your claim numbers, dates, and treatment received in Part VI.

FORM **SSA-3368-F8** (3-82)

(C7758)

APPENDIX II

8. **Have you had any of the following tests in the last year?**

TEST	CHECK APPROPRIATE BLOCK OR BLOCKS	IF "YES" SHOW	
		WHERE DONE	WHEN DONE
Electrocardiogram	☐ NO ☐ YES		
Chest X-Ray	☐ NO ☐ YES		
Other X-Ray (name body part here) ______	☐ NO ☐ YES		
Breathing Tests	☐ NO ☐ YES		
Blood Tests	☐ NO ☐ YES		
Other (Specify)	☐ NO ☐ YES		

9. If you have a medicaid card, what is your number (some hospitals and clinics file your records by your medicaid number.)

PART III — INFORMATION ABOUT YOUR ACTIVITIES

10. **Has your doctor told you to cut back or limit your activities in any way?** ☐ YES ☐ NO
If "yes", give the name of the doctor below and tell what he or she told you about cutting back or limiting your activities.

11. Describe your daily activities in the following areas and state what and how much you do of each and how often you do it:

- **Household maintenance** (including cooking, cleaning, shopping, and odd jobs around the house as well as any other similar activities):

- **Recreational activities and hobbies** (hunting, fishing, bowling, hiking, musical instruments, etc.):

- **Social contacts** (visits with friends, relatives, neighbors):

- **Other** (drive car, motorcycle, ride bus, etc.)

FORM **SSA-3368-F8** (3-82)

[C7759]

DISABILITY REPORT

PART IV — INFORMATION ABOUT YOUR EDUCATION

12. What is the highest grade of school that you completed and when?

13. Have you gone to trade or vocational school or had any type of special training? *If "yes", show:* ☐ YES ☐ NO

- The type of trade or vocational school or training:
- Approximate dates you attended:
- How this schooling or training was used in any work you did:

PART V — INFORMATION ABOUT THE WORK YOU DID

14. List all jobs you have had in the last 15 years before you stopped working, beginning with your usual job. Normally, this will be the kind of work you did the longest. (If you have a 6th grade education or less, AND did only heavy unskilled labor for 35 years or more, list all of the jobs you have had since you began to work. If you need more space, use Part VI.)

JOB TITLE (Be sure to begin with your usual job)	TYPE OF BUSINESS	DATES WORKED (Month and Year)		DAYS PER WEEK	RATE OF PAY (Per hour, day, week, month or year)
		FROM	TO		

15A. Provide the following information for your usual job shown in item 14, line 1.

In your job did you:
- Use machines, tools, or equipment of any kind? ☐ Yes ☐ No
- Use technical knowledge or skills? ☐ Yes ☐ No
- Do any writing, complete reports, or perform similar duties? ☐ Yes ☐ No
- Have supervisory responsibilities? ☐ Yes ☐ No

15B. Describe your basic duties (explain what you did and how you did it) below. Also, explain all "Yes" answers by giving a FULL DESCRIPTION of: the types of machines, tools, or equipment you used and the exact operation you performed; the technical knowledge or skills involved; the type of writing you did, and the nature of any reports; and the number of people you supervised and the extent of your supervision:

FORM **SSA-3368-F8** (3-82) [C7788]

15C. Describe the kind and amount of physical activity this job involved during typical day in terms of:

- **Walking** (circle the number of hours a day spent walking) — 0 1 2 3 4 5 6 7 8
- **Standing** (circle the number of hours a day spent standing) — 0 1 2 3 4 5 6 7 8
- **Sitting** (circle the number of hours a day spent sitting) — 0 1 2 3 4 5 6 7 8
- **Bending** (circle how often a day you had to bend) — Never Occasionally Frequently Constantly
- **Reaching** (circle how often a day you had to reach) — Never Occasionally Frequently Constantly
- **Lifting and Carrying**: Describe below what was lifted, and how far it was carried. Check heaviest weight lifted, and weight frequently lifted and/or carried

HEAVIEST WEIGHT LIFTED	WEIGHT FREQUENTLY LIFTED/CARRIED
☐ 10 lbs	☐ Up to 10 lbs
☐ 20 lbs	☐ Up to 25 lbs
☐ 50 lbs	☐ Up to 50 lbs
☐ 100 lbs	☐ Over 50 lbs
☐ Over 100 lbs	

PART VI — REMARKS

Use this section for additional space to answer any previous questions. Also use this space to give any additional information that you think will be helpful in making a decision in your disability claim, (such as information about other illnesses or injuries not shown in Parts I and II.) Please refer to the previous items by number

Knowing that anyone making a false statement or representation of a material fact for use in determining a right to payment under the Social Security Act commits a crime punishable under Federal law, I certify that the above statements are true.

NAME (Signature of claimant or person filing on the claimant's behalf)

SIGN HERE ▶ DATE

Witnesses are required ONLY if this statement has been signed by mark (X) above. If signed by mark (X), two witnesses to the signing who know the person making the statement must sign below, giving their full addresses.

1. Signature of Witness	2. Signature of Witness
Address (Number and street, city, state, and ZIP code)	Address (Number and street, city, state, and ZIP code)

FORM SSA-3368-F8 (3-82)

(C776)

DISABILITY REPORT

PART VII — FOR SSA USE ONLY - DO NOT WRITE BELOW THIS LINE

NAME OF CLAIMANT	SOCIAL SECURITY NUMBER
	___ ___ ___/___ ___/___ ___ ___ ___

16. Check any of the following categories which apply to this case:

PRESUMPTIVE DISABILITY CONSIDERATION
(If any of these boxes are checked, DO's (and DDS's) should be alert to the possibility of a presumptive disability determination in SSI claims per DI 00404.210 and DI 2152.5)

A. ☐ Amputation of two limbs

B. ☐ Amputation of a leg at the hip

C. ☐ Allegation of total deafness

D. ☐ Allegation of total blindness

E. ☐ Allegation of bed confinement or immobility without a wheelchair, walker, or crutches, allegedly due to a longstanding condition — exclude recent accident and recent surgery

F. ☐ Allegation of a stroke (cerebral vascular accident) more than 3 months in the past and continued marked difficulty in walking or using a hand or arm.

G. ☐ Allegation of cerebral palsy, muscular dystrophy or muscular atrophy and marked difficulty in walking (e.g., use of braces), speaking or coordination of the hands or arms.

H. ☐ Allegation of diabetes with amputation of a foot.

I. ☐ Allegation of Down's Syndrome (Mongolism).

J. ☐ An applicant filing on behalf of another individual alleges severe mental deficiency for claimant who is at least 7 years of age. The applicant alleges that the individual attends (or attended) a special school, or special classes in school, because of his mental deficiency, or is unable to attend any type of school (or if beyond school age was unable to attend), and requires care and supervision of routine daily activities.

K. ☐ Allegation of renal disease requiring dialysis on a regularly scheduled basis.

17A. Does the claimant speak English? .... ☐ Yes ☐ No
If "no," what language does he speak?

17B. Does the claimant need assistance in prosecuting his or her claim? .... ☐ Yes ☐ No
If "yes," show name, address, relationship, and telephone number of an interested party willing to assist the claimant.

NAME	ADDRESS	RELATIONSHIP	TELEPHONE NUMBER (area code)

17C. Can the claimant (or his representative) be readily reached by telephone with no communication problems due to language, speech or hearing difficulties? *If "no", DO should complete SSA-3369-F6.* ☐ Yes ☐ No

FORM **SSA-3368-F8** (3-82)

[C7762]

APPENDIX II

18A. Check each item to indicate if any difficulty was observed:

Reading	☐ Yes	☐ No	Using Hands	☐ Yes	☐ No
Writing	☐ Yes	☐ No	Breathing	☐ Yes	☐ No
Answering	☐ Yes	☐ No	Seeing	☐ Yes	☐ No
Hearing	☐ Yes	☐ No	Walking	☐ Yes	☐ No
Sitting	☐ Yes	☐ No			
Understanding	☐ Yes	☐ No	Other (Specify):		

18B. If any of the above items were checked "yes," describe the exact difficulty involved:

18C. Describe the claimant fully (e.g., general build, height, weight, behavior, any difficulties that add to or supplement those noted above, etc.):

19. Medical Development — Initiated by District or Branch Office

SOURCE	DATE REQUESTED	DATE(S) OF FOLLOW-UP	CAPABILITY DEVELOPMENT REQUESTED

20. DO or BO curtailed completion of Parts III - V per DI 00403.105 (DI 2019). ☐ YES ☐ NO

21. Is capability development by the DDS necessary? ☐ YES ☐ NO
If "yes", show "DDS capability development needed" in item 11 of the SSA-831-U5

22. Is development of work activity necessary? ☐ YES ☐ NO
If "yes", is an SSA-820-F4 or SSA-821-F4 ☐ Pending ☐ In File

23. SSA-3368-F8 taken by:
☐ Personal Interview ☐ Telephone ☐ Mail

24. Form supplemented: ☐ Yes ☐ No
If "yes" by:
☐ Personal Interview ☐ Telephone ☐ Mail

SIGNATURE OF DO OR BO INTERVIEWER OR REVIEWER	TITLE	DATE

FORM **SSA-3368-F8** (3-82)

[C7763]

COMMENT

Reference should be made to § 1.3, "How to Apply For Social Security Disability", as regards completion of this Form 3368.

APPENDIX III

VOCATIONAL REPORT

DEPARTMENT OF HEALTH AND HUMAN SERVICES
SOCIAL SECURITY ADMINISTRATION

Form Approved
OMB No. 0960-0141

VOCATIONAL REPORT

This report supplements the Disability Report (Form SSA-3368-F8) by requesting additional information about your past work experience. PLEASE PRINT, TYPE, OR WRITE CLEARLY AND ANSWER ALL ITEMS TO THE BEST OF YOUR ABILITY. If you are filing on behalf of someone else, enter his or her name and social security number in the space provided and answer all questions. COMPLETE ANSWERS WILL AID IN PROCESSING THE CLAIM.

PRIVACY ACT NOTICE: The information requested on this form is authorized by Title 20 CFR 404.1512 and Title 20 CFR 416.912. The information provided will be used in making a decision on your claim. While completion of this form is voluntary, failure to provide all or part of the requested information could prevent an accurate or timely decision on your claim and could result in the loss of some benefits. Information you furnish on this form may be disclosed by the Social Security Administration to another person or governmental agency only with respect to social security programs and to comply with Federal laws requiring the exchange of information between Social Security and another agency.

A. Name of Claimant	B. Social Security Number	C. Telephone number where you can be reached (include area code)

PART I — INFORMATION ABOUT YOUR WORK HISTORY

List all jobs you have had in the last 15 years before you stopped working, beginning with your usual job; normally, this will be the kind of work you did the longest. (If you have a 6th grade education or less, **AND** did only heavy unskilled labor for 35 years or more, list all of the jobs you have had since you began to work. If you need more space, use Part III.) If you have already given information about your usual job on the Form SSA-3368-F8 (Disability Report), begin with your other jobs.

JOB TITLE (Be sure to begin with your usual job)	TYPE OF BUSINESS	DATES WORKED (Month and Year)		DAYS PER WEEK	RATE OF PAY (Per hour, day, week, month or year)
		FROM	TO		
1					
2					
3					
4					
5					
6					
7					
8					
9					
10					
11					
12					

FORM **SSA-3369-F6** (3-82) DESTROY PRIOR EDITIONS 1 [C7853]

APPENDIX III

PART II — INFORMATION ABOUT YOUR JOB DUTIES

Provide the following information (on pages 2-5) for each of the jobs listed in Part I starting with your usual job:

Job Title (from Part I):

A. In your job did you:

- Use machines, tools, or equipment of any kind? ☐ Yes ☐ No
- Use technical knowledge or skills? ☐ Yes ☐ No
- Do any writing, complete reports, or perform similar duties? ☐ Yes ☐ No
- Have supervisory responsibilities? ☐ Yes ☐ No

B. Describe your basic duties (explain what you did and how you did it) below. Also, explain all "Yes" answers by giving a FULL DESCRIPTION of: the types of machines, tools, or equipment you used and the exact operation you performed; the technical knowledge or skills involved; the type of writing you did, and the nature of any reports; and the number of people you supervised and the extent of your supervision:

C. Describe the kind and amount of physical activity this job involved during a typical day in terms of:

- **Walking** (circle the number of hours a day spent walking) — 0 1 2 3 4 5 6 7 8
- **Standing** (circle the number of hours a day spent standing) — 0 1 2 3 4 5 6 7 8
- **Sitting** (circle the number of hours a day spent sitting) — 0 1 2 3 4 5 6 7 8
- **Bending** (circle how often a day you had to bend) — Never · Occasionally · Frequently · Constantly
- **Lifting and Carrying:** Describe what was lifted, and how far it was carried. Check below heaviest weight lifted, and weight frequently lifted and/or carried.

Heaviest weight lifted	Weight frequently lifted/carried
☐ 10 lbs.	☐ Up to 10 lbs.
☐ 20 lbs.	☐ Up to 25 lbs.
☐ 50 lbs.	☐ Up to 50 lbs.
☐ 100 lbs.	☐ Over 50 lbs.
☐ Over 100 lbs.	

FORM SSA-3369-F6 (3-82) 2 IC7854

VOCATIONAL REPORT

Job Title (from Part I):

A. In your job did you:

- Use machines, tools, or equipment of any kind? ☐ Yes ☐ No
- Use technical knowledge or skills? ☐ Yes ☐ No
- Do any writing, complete reports, or perform similar duties? ☐ Yes ☐ No
- Have supervisory responsibilities? ☐ Yes ☐ No

B. Describe your basic duties (explain what you did and how you did it) below. Also, explain all "Yes" answers by giving a FULL DESCRIPTION of: the types of machines, tools, or equipment you used and the exact operation you performed; the technical knowledge or skills involved; the type of writing you did, and the nature of any reports; and the number of people you supervised and the extent of your supervision:

C. Describe the kind and amount of physical activity this job involved during a typical day in terms of:

- **Walking** (circle the number of hours a day spent walking) — 0 1 2 3 4 5 6 7 8
- **Standing** (circle the number of hours a day spent standing) — 0 1 2 3 4 5 6 7 8
- **Sitting** (circle the number of hours a day spent sitting) — 0 1 2 3 4 5 6 7 8
- **Bending** (circle how often a day you had to bend) — Never - Occasionally - Frequently - Constantly
- **Lifting and Carrying:** Describe what was lifted, and how far it was carried. Check below heaviest weight lifted, and weight frequently lifted and/or carried.

Heaviest weight lifted	Weight frequently lifted/carried
☐ 10 lbs.	☐ Up to 10 lbs.
☐ 20 lbs.	☐ Up to 25 lbs.
☐ 50 lbs.	☐ Up to 50 lbs.
☐ 100 lbs.	☐ Over 50 lbs.
☐ Over 100 lbs.	

FORM SSA-3369-F6 (3-82) 3 [C7856]

APPENDIX III

Job Title (from Part I):

A. In your job did you:

- Use machines, tools, or equipment of any kind? ☐ Yes ☐ No
- Use technical knowledge or skills? ☐ Yes ☐ No
- Do any writing, complete reports, or perform similar duties? ☐ Yes ☐ No
- Have supervisory responsibilities? ☐ Yes ☐ No

B. Describe your basic duties (explain what you did and how you did it) below. Also, explain all "Yes" answers by giving a FULL DESCRIPTION of: the types of machines, tools, or equipment you used and the exact operation you performed; the technical knowledge or skills involved; the type of writing you did, and the nature of any reports; and the number of people you supervised and the extent of your supervision:

C. Describe the kind and amount of physical activity this job involved during a typical day in terms of:

- **Walking** (circle the number of hours a day spent walking) — 0 1 2 3 4 5 6 7 8
- **Standing** (circle the number of hours a day spent standing) — 0 1 2 3 4 5 6 7 8
- **Sitting** (circle the number of hours a day spent sitting) — 0 1 2 3 4 5 6 7 8
- **Bending** (circle how often a day you had to bend) — Never · Occasionally · Frequently · Constantly
- **Lifting and Carrying:** Describe what was lifted, and how far it was carried. Check below heaviest weight lifted, and weight frequently lifted and/or carried.

Heaviest weight lifted	Weight frequently lifted/carried
☐ 10 lbs.	☐ Up to 10 lbs.
☐ 20 lbs.	☐ Up to 25 lbs.
☐ 50 lbs.	☐ Up to 50 lbs.
☐ 100 lbs.	☐ Over 50 lbs.
☐ Over 100 lbs.	

FORM **SSA-3369-F6** (3-82) 4 [C7858]

VOCATIONAL REPORT

Job Title (from Part I):

A. In your job did you:

● Use machines, tools, or equipment of any kind?	☐ Yes	☐ No
● Use technical knowledge or skills?	☐ Yes	☐ No
● Do any writing, complete reports, or perform similar duties?	☐ Yes	☐ No
● Have supervisory responsibilities?	☐ Yes	☐ No

B. Describe your basic duties (explain what you did and how you did it) below. Also, explain all "Yes" answers by giving a FULL DESCRIPTION of: the types of machines, tools, or equipment you used and the exact operation you performed; the technical knowledge or skills involved; the type of writing you did, and the nature of any reports; and the number of people you supervised and the extent of your supervision:

C. Describe the kind and amount of physical activity this job involved during a typical day in terms of:

- **Walking** (circle the number of hours a day spent walking) — 0 1 2 3 4 5 6 7 8
- **Standing** (circle the number of hours a day spent standing) — 0 1 2 3 4 5 6 7 8
- **Sitting** (circle the number of hours a day spent sitting) — 0 1 2 3 4 5 6 7 8
- **Bending** (circle how often a day you had to bend) — Never · Occasionally · Frequently · Constantly
- **Lifting and Carrying:** Describe what was lifted, and how far it was carried. Check below heaviest weight lifted, and weight frequently lifted and/or carried.

Heaviest weight lifted	Weight frequently lifted/carried
☐ 10 lbs.	☐ Up to 10 lbs.
☐ 20 lbs.	☐ Up to 25 lbs.
☐ 50 lbs.	☐ Up to 50 lbs.
☐ 100 lbs.	☐ Over 50 lbs.
☐ Over 100 lbs.	

IF YOU NEED ADDITIONAL SPACE TO PROVIDE INFORMATION ABOUT OTHER JOBS LISTED IN PART I OF THIS FORM, USE PART III OR ASK THE SOCIAL SECURITY OFFICE FOR ADDITIONAL COPIES OF THIS FORM.

APPENDIX III

PART III — REMARKS

Use this section for any other information you may want to give about your work history, or to provide any other remarks you may want to make to support your disability claim:

(If you need more space, use separate sheets of paper.)

Knowing that anyone making a false statement or representation of a material fact for use in determining a right to payment under the Social Security Act commits a crime punishable under Federal law, I certify that the above statements are true.

NAME (Signature of Claimant or Person Filing on the Claimant's Behalf)

SIGN HERE ▶ DATE

Witnesses are required ONLY if this statement has been signed by mark (X) above. If signed by mark (X), two witnesses to the signing who know the person making the statement must sign below, giving their full addresses.

1. Signature of Witness	2. Signature of Witness
Address (Number and street, city, state, and ZIP code)	Address (Number and street, city, state, and ZIP code)

Do not write below this line

SSA-3369-F6 taken by: ☐ PERSONAL INTERVIEW ☐ TELEPHONE ☐ MAIL	FORM SUPPLEMENTED: ☐ YES ☐ NO If "Yes," by ☐ PERSONAL INTERVIEW ☐ TELEPHONE ☐ MAIL	
SIGNATURE OF INTERVIEWER OR REVIEWER	TITLE (also check office) ☐ DDS ☐ DO ☐ BO	DATE

FORM SSA-3369-F6 (3-82) 6

[C7855] ✩ U.S. Government Printing Office: 1982— 381-189/2020

COMMENT

Reference is made to § 4.2, supra, with respect to completion of Form 3369.

APPENDIX IV

REPORT OF CONTINUING DISABILITY INTERVIEW

DEPARTMENT OF HEALTH AND HUMAN SERVICES
SOCIAL SECURITY ADMINISTRATION

Form Approved
OMB No. 0960-0072

REPORT OF CONTINUING DISABILITY INTERVIEW (Write Legibly)	OFFICE	DATE
	REPORT MADE ☐ IN PERSON ☐ TELEPHONE	PLACE OF REPORT ☐ DO ☐ CONTACT STATION ☐ HOME ☐ OTHER

SOCIAL SECURITY NUMBER	WAGE EARNER	BENEFICIARY'S NAME IF NOT WAGE EARNER

PERSON REPORTING

☐ BENEFICIARY ☐ OTHER PERSON (Show name, address, relationship, and why beneficiary is not reporting.)

NAME AND RELATIONSHIP	ADDRESS	WHY BENEFICIARY IS NOT REPORTING

PRIVACY ACT/PAPERWORK ACT NOTICE: The information requested on this form is authorized by the Social Security Act, Sections 205(a) and 1631(e)(A) and (B), and Title 20 CFR 404.1589 and 416.989. The information provided will be used to further document your claim and permit a determination about your continuing disability. Information requested on this form is voluntary. However, if you do not provide the required information, a decision based on the evidence in your file can result in a determination that your period of disability is ceased. While the information you furnish on this form would almost never be used for any purpose other than making a determination about your disability, such information may be disclosed by SSA for the following purposes: (1) To assist SSA in determining the right to Social Security benefits for yourself or another person; (2) To facilitate statistical research and audit activities necessary to assure the integrity and improvement of programs administered by the Social Security Administration, and (3) to comply with laws and regulations requiring the exchange of information between the Social Security Administration and another agency.

Please use this form to describe your disabling condition since (date disability began or, if later, date of prior investigation.)	DATE

NOTE: All information (except Part II) must reflect the beneficiary's (or his/her representative's) statements regarding the disabling condition since the last interview, i.e., the initial disability application or continuing disability investigation. This report will be one of the criteria in verifying continuing eligibility to disability benefits. If, after completion of the investigation, it is determined that there no longer is a disabling condition, benefits will be terminated.

PART I INFORMATION ABOUT YOUR CONDITION

1. a. What is your disabling condition? (Describe all injuries or illnesses and tell how they prevent you from working.)

   b. Has there been any change (for better or worse) in your disabling condition since you first reported such information to us?
   ☐ Yes ☐ No
   If "yes," describe any changes.

   c. Do you have any new injuries or illnesses?
   ☐ Yes ☐ No
   If "yes," describe any changes.

2. a. Do you feel you are able to return to work?
   ☐ Yes (If yes, explain and describe any limitations in Part VI) ☐ No (If no, explain in part VI)

   b. Has your doctor told you that you are able to return to work?
   ☐ Yes (If yes, answer items c, d and e below) ☐ No ☐ Did not say

FORM SSA-454 BK (12-82) Destroy prior editions (C7770)

APPENDIX IV

2. (continued)

c. List the name and address of the doctor(s) who told you to return to work.

NAME

ADDRESS

d. What date did your doctor tell you that you could return to work? (month, day, year)	e. Did the doctor restrict you to limited or part-time work? ☐ Yes (If yes, explain in Part VI) ☐ No

PART II – INFORMATION ABOUT YOUR MEDICAL RECORDS

NOTE: When completing Part II provide a summary of all medical examinations and treatments which you have received in the last 12 months.

3. List the name, address and telephone number of the doctor who has your latest medical records. — If you have seen no doctor check ☐

NAME	ADDRESS	
TELEPHONE NUMBER (Include area code)		
How often do you see this doctor?	Date you first saw this doctor (mo., day, yr.)	Date you last saw this doctor (mo., day, yr.)

Reasons for visits (show illness or injury for which you had an examination or treatment)

Type of treatment received or medicines received (such as surgery, chemotherapy, radiation and the medicines you take for your illness or injury, if known. If no treatment or medicines show "NONE")

a. Have you seen any other doctors in the last 12 months? If "yes," show the following: ☐ Yes ☐ No

NAME	ADDRESS	
TELEPHONE NUMBER (Include area code)		
How often do you see this doctor?	Date you first saw this doctor (mo., day, yr.)	Date you last saw doctor (mo., day, yr.)

Reasons for visits (show illness or injury for which you had an examination or treatment)

Type of treatment received or medicines received (such as surgery, chemotherapy, radiation and the medicines you take for your illness or injury, if known. If no treatment or medicines show "NONE")

NAME	ADDRESS	
TELEPHONE NUMBER (Include area code)		
How often do you see this doctor?	Date you first saw this doctor (mo., day, yr.)	Date you last saw this doctor (mo., day, yr.)

Reasons for visits (show illness or injury for which you had an examination or treatment)

Type of treatment received or medicines received (such as surgery, chemotherapy, radiation and the medicines you take for your illness or injury, if known. If no treatment or medicine show "NONE")

FORM **SSA-454 BK** (12-82) Destroy prior editions [C7771]

REPORT OF CONTINUING DISABILITY INTERVIEW

3. continued

NAME

ADDRESS

TELEPHONE NUMBER (Include area code)

How often do you see this doctor?

Date you first saw this doctor (mo., day, yr.)

Date you last saw this doctor (mo., day., yr.)

Reasons for visits (show illness or injury for which you had an examination or treatment)

Type of treatment or medicines received (such as surgery, chemotherapy, radiation and the medicines you take for your illness or injury, if known. If no treatment or medicines show "NONE")

4. Have you been hospitalized or treated at a clinic for your disabling condition in the last 12 months. If "yes," show the following: ☐ Yes ☐ No

NAME OF HOSPITAL OR CLINIC

ADDRESS

PATIENT OR CLINIC NUMBER

Were you an inpatient (Stayed at least overnight) ☐ Yes (If "yes," show) ☐ No

Were you an outpatient ☐ Yes (If "yes," show) ☐ No

DATES OF ADMISSIONS	DATES OF DISCHARGE	DATES OF VISITS

Reason for hospitalization or clinic visits (show illness or injury for which you had an examination or treatment)

Type of treatment or medicine received (such as surgery, chemotherapy, radiation and the medicines you take for your illness or injury, if known. If no treatment or medicines show "NONE")

NAME OF HOSPITAL OR CLINIC

ADDRESS

PATIENT OR CLINIC NUMBER

Were you an inpatient (stayed at least overnight) ☐ Yes (If "yes," show) ☐ No

Were you an outpatient ☐ Yes (If "yes," show) ☐ No

DATES OF ADMISSIONS	DATES OF DISCHARGE	DATES OF VISITS

Reason for hospitalization or clinic visits (show illness or injury for which you had an examination or treatment)

Type of treatment or medicines received (such as surgery, chemotherapy, radiation and the medicines you take for your illness or injury, if known. If no treatment or medicines show "NONE")

If you have seen other doctors or if you have been in other hospitals or clinics for your illness or injury, list the names, addresses, patient or clinic numbers, dates and reasons for hospitalization or clinic visits in Part VI.

FORM **SSA-454 BK** (12-82) Destroy prior editions

(C7772)

APPENDIX IV

5. Have you been seen by other agencies for your injury or illness? (VA workmen's compensation, vocational rehabilitation, welfare, etc.)
If "yes," show the following: ☐ Yes ☐ No

NAME OF AGENCY	ADDRESS OF AGENCY
YOUR CLAIM NUMBER	
DATES OF VISITS (mo., day, yr.)	TYPES OF TREATMENTS OR EXAMINATION RECEIVED

If more space is needed, list the other agencies, their addresses, your claim numbers, dates, and treatment received in Part VI.

6. Have you had any of the following tests in the past 12 months?

TEST	Check appropriate block(s)		IF "YES" SHOW	
	YES	NO	WHERE DONE	WHEN DONE
EKG—Resting	☐	☐		
EKG—Treadmill	☐	☐		
Chest x-ray	☐	☐		
Other x-ray (specify)	☐	☐		
Breathing tests	☐	☐		
Blood tests	☐	☐		
Other (specify)	☐	☐		
Other	☐	☐		
Other	☐	☐		
Other	☐	☐		

PART III – INFORMATION ABOUT YOUR ACTIVITIES

7. Has any doctor told you to cut back or limit your activities in any way since the date shown on page one?
If "yes," give the name of the doctor below and tell what he or she told you about cutting back or limiting your activities: ☐ Yes ☐ No

8. Describe your daily activities in the following areas and state what and how much you do of each, how often you do it and any assistance you require.

PERSONAL MOBILITY (walking, moving about, exercising your legs, etc.)

PERSONAL NEEDS AND GROOMING (dressing, bathing, etc.):

FORM **SSA-454 BK** (12-82) Destroy prior editions (C7773)

REPORT OF CONTINUING DISABILITY INTERVIEW

8. continued HOUSEHOLD MAINTENANCE (including cooking, cleaning, shopping, and odd jobs around the house as well as any other similar activities):

RECREATIONAL ACTIVITIES AND HOBBIES (TV, radio, newspapers, or books, fishing, bowling, musical instruments, etc.):

SOCIAL CONTACTS (visits with friends, relatives, neighbors, church, social clubs):

OTHER (drive car, motorcycle, ride bus or subway, etc.):

9. Have you attended (trade, vocational or academic) school or had any other type of vocational training since you began receiving disability benefits?

☐ Yes ☐ No

If "yes," explain

10. Are you attending school?

NAME OF SCHOOL	ADDRESS OF SCHOOL (Number and Street, City, State and Zip Code)	CURRENT GRADE

PART IV – INFORMATION ABOUT THE WORK YOU DID

When completing Part IV provide information since date you became disabled.

11. Since you became disabled, have you done any work? ☐ Yes ☐ No

If "yes," complete the following for each work attempt, no matter how short it was.

JOB TITLE (Be sure to begin with your usual job)	TYPE OF BUSINESS	DATES WORKED (month/year) FROM	TO	DAYS PER WEEK	RATE OF PAY (per hour, day, week, month or year)

FORM **SSA-454 BK** (12-82) Destroy prior editions

[C7774]

APPENDIX IV

12. Describe your basic duties (explain what you did and how you did it) below. Also, explain why you stopped working for each work attempt listed in item 11.

PART V – INFORMATION ABOUT REHABILITATION SERVICES

13. VOCATIONAL REHABILITATION — IMPORTANT: Even if it is determined that you are not disabled, you may be eligible for continued payments if you are in an approved State vocational rehabilitation program and meet other requirements of the law.

a. Are you receiving help, such as services, training or counseling from the state vocational rehabilitation agency?
If "yes," complete the following: ☐ Yes ☐ No

b. What kind of help have you been receiving?

c. Do you expect to receive any type of training? ☐ Yes (If "yes," when?) ☐ No

d. What is the name, address and phone number of your VR counselor?

NAME	ADDRESS	TELEPHONE NO. (Include area code)

PART VI – REMARKS

14. Use this section for additional space to answer any previous questions. Also, use space to give any additional information that you think will be helpful in the review of the continuing entitlement to social security disability benefits. (If you need more space, use a separate sheet of paper. Also, if you wish, you may attach any evidence that shows your current condition.)

FORM **SSA-454 BK** (12-82) Destroy prior editions [C7775]

REPORT OF CONTINUING DISABILITY INTERVIEW

14. continued | Remarks

FORM **SSA-454 BK** (12-82) Destroy prior editions [C7776]

APPENDIX IV

PART VII – AUTHORIZATION AND NOTIFICATION STATEMENTS

I understand that this report will be used to determine whether to continue or to stop my disability benefits. I also understand that if I am receiving Social Security disability benefits and supplemental security income payments, this questionnaire is applicable to both claims.

- Copies of medical records may be provided to a physician or medical institution prior to my appearance for an independent medical examination if an examination is necessary.
- Results of any such independent examination may be provided to my personal physician.
- Medical information may be furnished to any contractor for transcription, typing, record copying, or other related clerical or administrative service performed for the State Disability Determination Service.
- The State Vocational Rehabilitation Agency may review any medical evidence for determining my eligbility for rehabilitative services.
- I agree to notify the Social Security Administration if my medical condition improves or I go to work.
- I know that anyone who makes a false statement or representation of a material fact in an application or for use in determining a right to payment under the Social Security Act commits a crime punishable under Federal Law. I affirm that the above statements are true.

SIGNATURE OF CLAIMANT OR PERSON FILING ON THE CLAIMANT'S BEHALF	DATE (Mo., Day, Yr.)
	TELEPHONE NUMBER

MAILING ADDRESS (Number and Street, Apt. No., P.O. Box or Rural Route)

CITY AND STATE	ZIP CODE	ENTER NAME OF COUNTY (In which you now live)

Witnesses are required ONLY if this statement has been signed by mark (X) above. If signed by mark (X) two witnesses to the signing who know the person making the statement must sign below giving their full addresses.

1. SIGNATURE OF WITNESS	2. SIGNATURE OF WITNESS
ADDRESS (Number & street, city, state and zip code)	ADDRESS (Number & street, city, state and zip code)

FORM **SSA-454 BK** (12-82) Destroy prior editions [C7777]

REPORT OF CONTINUING DISABILITY INTERVIEW

PART VIII – FOR SSA USE ONLY – DO NOT WRITE BELOW THIS LINE

NAME OF CLAIMANT	SOCIAL SECURITY NUMBER

15. a. Check each item to indicate if any difficulty was observed:

	Yes	No		Yes	No
Breathing	☐	☐	Use of hands and arms	☐	☐
Sight	☐	☐	Writing	☐	☐
Speaking	☐	☐	Reading	☐	☐
Hearing	☐	☐	Comprehending	☐	☐
Sitting	☐	☐	Responding	☐	☐
Walking	☐	☐	Relating to people	☐	☐
Standing	☐	☐	Other (specify)	☐	☐

b. If any of the above items were checked "yes," describe the exact difficulty involved.

c. Describe the claimant fully (e.g., general build, height, weight, behavior, any difficulties that add to or supplement those noted above). Indicate any other noticeable physical/mental limitations/impairments. Also, indicate any unusual circumstances surrounding the interview, e.g., how claimant came to the DO/BO for the interview, lack of difficulty where it might be expected.

FORM **SSA-454 BK** (12-82) Destroy prior editions (C7778)

APPENDIX IV

16. Does the claimant need assistance in processing his or her claim?

☐ Yes ☐ No

If "yes," show name, address, relationship, and telephone number of an interested party willing to assist the claimant.

NAME	ADDRESS
RELATIONSHIP	TELEPHONE NUMBER (Include area code)

17. Does the claimant speak English?

☐ Yes ☐ No

If "no," what language does he/she speak?

18. Is work in the past 15 years documented in file?

☐ Yes ☐ No

If "no," secure SSA-3369-F6

19. Is capability development by the DDS necessary?

☐ Yes ☐ No

20. Is development of work activity necessary?

☐ Yes ☐ No

If "yes," is an SSA-820-F4 or SSA-821-F4 in file?

☐ Yes ☐ No

If "no," explain why below.

SIGNATURE OF DO or BO INTERVIEWER OR REVIEWER	TITLE	DATE

FORM SSA-454 BK (12-82) Destroy prior editions

U.S. GOVERNMENT PRINTING OFFICE: 1983-381-185/1156 [C7779]

COMMENT

Reference should be made to § 1.10, supra, with respect to completion of the above "Report of Continuing Disability Interview".

APPENDIX V

RECONSIDERATION DISABILITY REPORT

DEPARTMENT OF HEALTH, EDUCATION, AND WELFARE
SOCIAL SECURITY ADMINISTRATION

Form Approved
OMB No.72-R1047

For SSA Use Only - Do NOT Complete This Item.	
Name of Wage Earner	Social Security Number
Name of Claimant	Social Security Number
Type of Claim:	
Title II — ☐ Freeze ☐ DIB ☐ DWB ☐ CDB	Title XVI — ☐ Disability ☐ Blind ☐ Child

RECONSIDERATION DISABILITY REPORT

PLEASE PRINT, TYPE, OR WRITE CLEARLY AND ANSWER ALL ITEMS TO THE BEST OF YOUR ABILITY. If you are filing on behalf of someone else, answer all questions. COMPLETE ANSWERS WILL AID IN PROCESSING THE CLAIM.

Privacy Act Notice: The information requested on this form is authorized by Title 20 CFR 404.1523 and Title 20 CFR 416.923. The information provided will be used to further document your claim. Information requested on this form is voluntary, but failure to provide all or any part of the requested information may affect the determination of your claim. Information you furnish on this form may be disclosed by the Social Security Administration to another person or governmental agency only with respect to social security programs and to comply with Federal laws requiring the exchange of information between the Social Security Administration and another agency.

PART I — INFORMATION ABOUT YOUR CONDITION

1. Has there been any change (for better or worse) in your illness or injury since you filed your claim? .... ☐ Yes ☐ No
   If "Yes," describe any changes in your symptoms.

2. Describe any physical or mental limitations you have as a result of your condition.

3. Have any restrictions been placed on you by a physician? .... ☐ Yes ☐ No
   If "Yes," give name, address, and telephone number of the physician and show what kinds of restrictions have been imposed.

4. Do you have any additional illness or injury that isn't recorded in the file? .... ☐ Yes ☐ No
   If "Yes," describe the kind of illness or injury and the date that it occurred.

Form **SSA-3441 F6** (9-78) [C5393]

APPENDIX V

PART II — INFORMATION ABOUT YOUR MEDICAL RECORDS

5. Have you seen any physician since you filed your claim? .... ☐ Yes ☐ No
   If "Yes," provide the following about the physician you last visited:

NAME	ADDRESS *(Include ZIP Code)*
AREA CODE AND TELEPHONE NUMBER	
HOW OFTEN DO YOU SEE THIS PHYSICIAN	DATES YOU SAW THIS PHYSICIAN
REASONS FOR VISITS	
TYPE OF TREATMENT RECEIVED *(Include drugs, surgery, tests)*	

6. Have you seen any other physician since you filed your claim? .... ☐ Yes ☐ No
   If "Yes," show the following:

NAME	ADDRESS *(Include ZIP Code)*
AREA CODE AND TELEPHONE NUMBER	
HOW OFTEN DO YOU SEE THIS PHYSICIAN?	DATES YOU SAW THIS PHYSICIAN
REASONS FOR VISITS	
TYPE OF TREATMENT RECEIVED *(Include drugs, surgery, tests)*	

If you have seen other physicians since you filed your claim, list their names, addresses, dates and reasons for visits in Part V.

7. Have you been hospitalized, or treated at a clinic or confined in a nursing home or extended care facility for your illness or injury since you filed your claim? .... ☐ Yes ☐ No
   If "Yes," show the following:

NAME OF FACILITY	ADDRESS OF AGENCY (Include ZIP Code)
PATIENT OR CLINIC NUMBER	
WERE YOU AN INPATIENT? *(Stayed at least overnight)* ☐ Yes ☐ No IF "YES," SHOW →	DATES OF ADMISSIONS AND DISCHARGES
WERE YOU AN OUTPATIENT? ☐ Yes ☐ No IF "YES," SHOW →	DATES OF VISITS
REASON FOR HOSPITALIZATION, CLINIC VISITS, OR CONFINEMENT	
TYPE OF TREATMENT RECEIVED *(Include drugs, surgery, tests)*	

If you have been in other hospitals, clinics, nursing homes, or extended care facilities for your illness or injury, list the names, addresses, patient or clinic numbers, dates and reasons for hospitalization, clinic visits, or confinement in Part V.

8. Have you been seen by other agencies for your injury or illness? .... ☐ Yes ☐ No
   (VA, Workmen's Compensation, Vocational Rehabilitation, Welfare, Special Schools, Unions, etc.)
   If "Yes," show the following:

NAME OF AGENCY	ADDRESS OF AGENCY *(Including ZIP Code)*
YOUR CLAIM NUMBER	
DATES OF VISITS	NAME OF COUNSELOR, SOCIAL WORKER, ETC.
TYPE OF TREATMENT OR EXAMINATION RECEIVED *(Include drugs, surgery, tests)*	

If more space is needed, list the other agencies, their addresses, your claim numbers, dates, and treatment received in Part V.

Form **SSA-3441 F6** (9-78) [C5394]

RECONSIDERATION DISABILITY REPORT

PART III — INFORMATION ABOUT WORK

9. Have you worked since you filed your claim? .... ☐ Yes ☐ No

If "Yes," you will be asked to give details on a separate form.

PART IV — INFORMATION ABOUT YOUR ACTIVITIES

10. How does your illness or injury affect your ability to care for your personal needs?

11. What changes have occurred in your daily activities since you filed your claim? (If none, show, "None")

PART V — REMARKS AND AUTHORIZATIONS

12.(a) READ CAREFULLY: I authorize the Social Security Administration to release information from my records, as necessary to process my claim, as follows:

Copies of my medical records may be furnished to a physician or a medical institution for background information if it is necessary for me to have a medical examination by that physician or medical institution. The results of any such examination may be given to my personal physician.

Information from my records may also be furnished, if necessary, to any company providing clerical and administrative services for the purposes of transcribing, typing, copying or otherwise clerically servicing such information. The State Vocational Rehabilitation Agency may also have access to information in my records to determine my eligibility for rehabilitative services.

I understand and concur with the statement and authorizations given above, except as follows (If there are no exceptions, write "None" in the space below. If you do not concur with any part of the above statement, state your objections clearly):

12. (b)	**Telephone number where you can be reached:**	**Best time to reach you:**

Form **SSA-3441 F6** (9-78) [C3395]

APPENDIX V

12(b) Use this section to continue information required by prior sections. Identify the section for which the information is provided.

Note: This section may also be used for any special or additional information which you wish to be recorded

Knowing that anyone making a false statement or representation of a material fact for use in determining a right to payment under the Social Security Act commits a crime punishable under Federal Law, I certify that the above statements are true.

NAME (SIGNATURE OF CLAIMANT OR PERSON FILING ON THE CLAIMANT'S BEHALF)

SIGN HERE

DATE

Form **SSA-3441 F6** (9-78)

[C5396]

RECONSIDERATION DISABILITY REPORT

PART VI — FOR SSA USE ONLY — DO NOT WRITE BELOW THIS LINE

Name of Wage Earner	Social Security Number
Name of Claimant	Social Security Number

13. Check each item to indicate whether or not any difficulty was observed:
(Explain all items checked "Yes," in Item 14 below)

Reading:	☐ Yes	☐ No	Using Hands:	☐ Yes	☐ No
Writing:	☐ Yes	☐ No	Breathing:	☐ Yes	☐ No
Answering:	☐ Yes	☐ No	Seeing:	☐ Yes	☐ No
Hearing:	☐ Yes	☐ No	Walking:	☐ Yes	☐ No
Speaking:	☐ Yes	☐ No	Sitting	☐ Yes	☐ No
Understanding:	☐ Yes	☐ No	Assistive Devices:	☐ Yes	☐ No

Other *(Specify)*: ________________

14. If any of the above items were checked "Yes," describe the observed difficulty:

15. Describe fully: General appearance, behavior, any unusual observed difficulties not noted elsewhere, any unusual circumstances surrounding the interviews.

Form **SSA-3441 F6** (9-78)

16. Claimant requires assistance .... ☐ Yes ☐ No
If "Yes," show name, address, phone number, and relationship of interested person.
Also show why claimant requires assistance (foreign-speaking, unable to ambulate, etc.)

17. Capability development appears needed .... ☐ Yes ☐ No
If "Yes," indicate whether DO will undertake development because it is also developing medical evidence from a special arrangement source. (Show name and address of source.)

18. Is development of work activity necessary? .... ☐ Yes ☐ No

If "Yes," is an SSA-821 or SSA-821B ☐ Pending ☐ In File

19. SSA-3441 Taken By:
☐ Personal Interview
☐ DO/BO ☐ Home ☐ Other ______
☐ Telephone
☐ Mail

Signature of Interviewer or Reviewer	Title	DO, BO, or TSC	Date

Form **SSA-3441 F6** (9-78) [C5398]

COMMENT

Reference should be made to § 1.11, supra, with respect to completion of above Form 3441.

APPENDIX VI

WORK DESPITE SEVERE IMPAIRMENT

Sometimes a claimant has a medical condition severe enough to Meet or Equal a Listing, or to be an allowance vocationally before applying for S. S. Disability, but who continues to work rather than applying for benefits. These are people who really love their work, or do not wish to take money from the government. However, this may cause them problems when they finally stop working and apply for disability, even though their impairment technically is severe enough to qualify, if the work is considered substantial gainful activity. S. S. Disability might be forced to deny such claimants benefits, due to the fact that they have proven they are capable of work. Fortunately, there are several ways the claimant can still qualify for benefits, under special circumstances. This involves demonstrating to S. S. Disability that the claimant didn't really do the normal job he appeared to be engaged in—that he was given *special considerations* by his employer which made the work easier than it normally is, *and* those special considerations were removed. Examples of such special considerations are as follows:

1. The claimant required and received special assistance on the job.

2. The claimant was allowed to work irregular hours and/or take frequent rest periods.

3. The claimant was provided with special equipment because his impairment, or assigned work specially designed to accommodate his impairment.

4. The claimant was able to work only within a framework of specially arranged circumstances, such as requiring the help of others in getting to work and returning home.

5. The claimant was permitted to perform at lower standards of productivity or efficiency than other employees doing similar work.

6. Work was made available to the claimant despite his impairment, because of family relationships, past association with the company, or other reasons secondary to the kindness of the employer.

The claimant's employer can be contacted by S. S. Disability, in regard to the above information.

APPENDIX VI

In addition to the special considerations given, a claimant who has worked despite a severe impairment might still be allowed benefits, if the medical evidence clearly shows that he had to stop work due to worsening of his medical condition to even greater severity, or because he developed another impairment that made his over-all condition worse. Also, he might be allowed if work simply became unavailable to him.

In practice, S. S. Disability tries very hard to help claimants who have worked despite a severe impairment to qualify for disability benefits. However, the pride and determination that keeps some claimants temporarily working despite severe impairments can ruin their chances for benefits when they finally do stop working.

APPENDIX VII

EVALUATION OF PAIN

Applicants for S. S. Disability benefits frequently complain of pain. Unfortunately, pain is a completely subjective experience which cannot be directly measured by any known medical technique. It is well known in medicine that two people with exactly the same type of illness or injury may still express very different levels of pain. Because of this difficulty, it is not easy for S. S. Disability to evaluate complaints of pain. If S. S. Disability literally accepted claimants' pain complaints at face value, almost all applicants would be allowed benefits—until the system was rapidly plunged into bankruptcy, at which time no money would remain for anyone.

S. S. Disability has only one reasonable course to follow in evaluating the influence of pain, and that is to look at the claimant's pain in terms of the type and severity of his physical impairment. S. S. Disability will believe only that level of pain which is reasonably expected from a given illness or injury.

In most cases, pain doesn't represent a special problem in evaluating cases, because people with the same disorders are generally assumed to have the same amount of pain. In cases which involve the claimant alleging unusually severe pain, it is necessary for S. S. Disability to acquire a large amount of very detailed information about the claimant, in order to justify that his complaints are valid. The following things would be very closely analyzed:

1. The exact nature and extent of the claimant's physical impairment. This requires extremely detailed medical records. The impairment must be reasonably capable of producing severe pain in most people.

2. Observations by any social security representative about the claimant's behavior which might indicate the presence of pain, or the absence of pain.

3. The claimant's interests and activities in his everyday life may be evaluated. A claimant's daily activities give a very revealing insight into how limiting his pain really is. S. S. Disability isn't very impressed with a claimant who says he has unbearable back pain, yet manages to play tennis, 18 holes of golf, or go deer hunting. S. S. Disability may not only ask the claimant and his family for details about his daily activities, but also his treating doctor.

4. What the treating doctor says about a claimant's pain is carefully evaluated, including his medical records about the claimant. Does the doctor think the claimant exaggerates his pain complaints? How often does the claimant go to his doctor complaining of pain? What types of drugs are given for pain, if any? Do the drugs control the pain? How often does the claimant have to take such drugs? How long has he taken them? Do the drugs cause any severe side-effects? Has the claimant been through any type of special pain control program? Did the claimant cooperate in such a program, if he did take it? How effective was the program in relieving the claimant's pain? Do medical records, including any psychological tests that may have been done, indicate that the claimant's complaints of pain come from an emotional disorder, rather from a physical impairment? These are some of the questions that S. S. Disability might ask.

In summary, everything known about the claimant must support the viewpoint that he has severe pain that is due to a reasonable medical cause, if this is to be taken into account in evaluating the case. S. S. Disability looks very suspiciously at pain, and will give such complaints weight only when backed up by objective evidence. But this applies only to the DDS level of evaluation. Administrative Law Judges are much more likely to accept a claimant's pain complaints at face value, and such complaints can play a major role in determining the judge's decision.

APPENDIX VIII

SUBSTANTIAL GAINFUL ACTIVITY

The S. S. District Office usually has the responsibility for deciding if work activity is "substantial gainful activity" (SGA). In most cases, the claimant's ability to perform SGA will prevent them from qualifying for disability benefits. An eligible claimant for benefits must be *unable* to perform SGA.

SGA means the performance of significant duties over a reasonable period of time in work for wages or profit, *or* in work of a type that is generally performed for wages or profit. Significant duties implies not only that the duties are useful in the accomplishment of a job or the operation of a business, but also that they have a degree of economic value. Work performed in self-care of one's household, hobbies, institutional therapy or training, school attendance, clubs, and other types of such special programs usually does not count as SGA. If someone is actively engaging in SGA, this is usually proof in itself that they are capable of such work (See Appendix VI, "Work Despite Severe Impairment").

Under current law, earnings averaging more than $300.00 per month are considered SGA for both Title II and Title XVI claims. However, it is important to know that a claimant who earns *more* than $300.00 per month can still qualify for benefits. For example, if a claimant's employer paid him a salary in excess of $300.00 per month, but he was allowed to work less than normal employees, S. S. Disability might not count the excess over $300.00 per month as true earnings. The excess could be considered a "gift" from the employer, and not count toward SGA. This is clearly to the advantage of the claimant.

In determining if a claimant is doing SGA, there is another important concept called the *secondary level.* The secondary level refers to earnings in the $190–300 range. A claimant earning money in this range could still be considered capable of SGA, even though he is not making more than $300.00 per month, *if* that same job normally pays more than $300.00 per month. In other words, the fact that a claimant may work for a stingy employer is no argument that he is incapable of SGA. Of course, claimants receiving "special considerations" would not face this difficulty. Earnings less than $190.00 per month usually cannot be considered SGA by the concept of secondary level.

Special rules regarding SGA apply to statutorily (legally) blind claimants. A statutorily blind claimant for S. S. Disability is one with vision so poor that it Meets Listing 2.02 or 2.03. Such a claimant is not said to be performing SGA, until his earnings exceed $550.00 per month. In 1984, this will rise to about $600.00 per month. Therefore, blind claimants have an advantage over other claimants.

A self-employed person is considered engaged in SGA under any of the following circumstances:

1. Hours of work, skills, energy output, efficiency, duties and responsibilities are comparable to that of unimpaired individuals in the same community engaged in similar businesses as a means of livelihood.

2. The work activity is worth over $300.00 per month, considered in terms of its effect on business, or when compared to the salary an owner would pay an employee for such duties in that business setting.

3. The services rendered in any year are significant to the operation of the business or the person receives from it a substantial income. Aside from statutorily blind claimants, this would mean that the person receives income that averages more than $300.00 per month, *or* the livelihood derived from work activity is either comparable to that before onset of their impairment or comparable to that of unimpaired self-employed individuals in the community engaged in the same or similar businesses. In determining the net income produced by a self-employed person in any year, it is necessary to deduct business expenses from gross income. Such expenses would be any legitimate overhead in running a business, such as rent, utilities, equipment, repairs, etc.

The amount of wages or other income shown by a claimant may not reflect the amount actually earned. For example, a claimant may have extra expenses in connection with his work activity because of his impairment, work may be in a military service work therapy program with continuation of full salary, but the work worth less than that; wages may include a subsidy from the employer which the claimant could not really earn; or the employer may pay expenses that the claimant would otherwise have to pay himself. All of these things can help a claimant lower his true income below the SGA level, and S. S. Disability attempts to help the claimant identify such factors. Usually, this is done at the District Office when application for disability is made by the claimant.

Another factor in determining if a person is doing SGA is called an *unsuccessful work attempt.* This means that the claimant attempted to work, but because of his impairment could not sustain work over a long enough period of time. A claimant who adequately performs such seasonal jobs as "crop harvester" or "lifeguard" loses work because of the nature of the business, and such jobs do not qualify as unsuccessful work attempts. Work usually has to stop due to a claimant's impairment preventing him from continuing it. An unsuccessful work attempt is present, if the claimant worked 3 months or less, and had to stop due to conditions related to his impairment, or removal by his employer of special conditions necessary for him to be able to do the work, such as special assistance by other employees. If a claimant worked more than 3 months, but less than 6 months, he can still qualify for an unsuccessful work attempt, if his employer removed special conditions necessary for him to be able to do his job, or he had to quit because of his impairment, if one of the following is also true:

1. The claimant had frequent absences from work, due to his impairment.

2. The claimant's work was unsatisfactory, because of his impairment.

3. The work was done under special conditions, such as having help not received by normal employees.

4. The work was done during a temporary remission (improvement) of the impairment. In other words, the claimant had some type of disease that could and did temporarily improve, but which then became worse again.

5. The work was not SGA.

In summary, the ability to perform SGA is one of the first things evaluated by the District Office when someone applies for disability. Except in certain blind cases, the fact that a claimant is performing SGA will usually stop processing of the application at that point. It should be pointed out that a person can receive money from investments (such as the interest from savings accounts, income from stocks, bonds, etc.) without it being considered income counting as SGA. An exception, of course, would be someone who actively engages in such activity as a means of livelihood, such as a stock broker.

It is important to know that the above brief discussion of substantial gainful activity is over-simplified. It is impossible to discuss in this book all of the regulations and rules that might apply to every individual case. However, if the reader wants exactly accurate information about whether his work is SGA, he can easily find this out by contacting his nearest District Office; it is their job as public servants to provide such help.

APPENDIX IX

MEDICAL RECORDS

Nothing can be more important to a claimant's case than adequate medical records. S. S. Disability must have adequate medical information about a claimant's impairments to reach any kind of accurate decision. Medical records may be obtained by S. S. Disability from doctors, hospitals, clinics, or other federal or state agencies. Records are sought from whatever sources the claimant gives, and for which the claimant is willing to sign a legal consent for release of information. S. S. Disability files often contain medical information from many different sources.

The reader should be aware that it may be much more difficult for S. S. Disability to obtain a claimant's medical records than he realizes, and even when successful it often takes a great deal of time. Medical records present a serious problem for S. S. Disability for a number of reasons. Few claimants are really aware of these problems, although they can seriously affect the ultimate decision in his case. Some problem areas are as follows:

1. *Hospitals.* Medical records are often sought from hospitals, and generally they cooperate. Usually, privately-run hospitals are more cooperative and respond more quickly than hospitals operating under States or the federal government.

Also, private hospitals are less likely to lose important medical records. It is sometimes extremely difficult to find a claimant's medical records in a federal or state-funded institution, even if S. S. Disability sends a personal representative to try to find them. It is not uncommon for S. S. Disability to ask such an institution for pathology reports, which are necessary to prove the existence of cancer, only to find that such important documents can't be found. It is also a fairly serious problem with private hospitals. This is one of the most frustrating things that a disability examiner has to face in evaluating cancer cases, yet hospitals are notorious for losing such documents. This is not a blanket criticism of all hospitals, but it is frequently true.

2. *Doctors.* Most doctors are highly cooperative with S. S. Disability, because they want to help their patients. This is true, even though doctors are usually under intense time pressures in treating their other patients, and constantly flooded with mountains of paperwork from many different sources.

However, there are some doctors that refuse to provide any information to S. S. Disability whatsoever. In other cases, they will give the information that they want to give, and not what S. S. Disability must have. There are many reasons that a doctor might not be cooperative with S. S. Disability, but these are beyond the scope of this discussion, and probably different for each doctor. The important point is that if a claimant has an uncooperative doctor, there is nothing S. S. Disability can do to force that doctor to provide the needed information. That problem is between the claimant and his doctor. However, the claimant may never be aware that he has a doctor who won't give any information to S. S. Disability, or that he has a doctor who won't provide the right kind of information.

Another common problem that S. S. Disability has with claimants' treating doctors is the fact that most doctors know very little about the kind of information S. S. Disability must have. They are used to writing letters to other agencies, or private insurance companies, which will accept their statements at face value, concerning their patient's impairments and ability to work. Such statements from a treating doctor are virtually useless to S. S. Disability. S. S. Disability operates under laws which require extremely detailed *objective* information that will justify a finding that a claimant is disabled, such as *specific* physical findings on examination of the claimant, X-rays, and laboratory reports. In mental disorders, thorough psychiatric evaluation is required. S. S. Disability cannot legally use opinions and diagnoses from a doctor, unless supported by enough facts to prove they are correct. Some doctors find it extremely irritating that S. S. Disability won't "take their word" concerning the claimant's problems. However, S. S. Disability cannot possibly be consistent and equally fair in decisions, if it accepts anything other than hard facts. Also, most treating doctors in supplying information to S. S. Disability will write that their patient is "totally and permanently disabled"—almost always using these exact words. They often will write that in a letter and sign it, regardless of how sick the claimant really is. Sometimes the treating doctor really believes this to be true, but often it is obviously meant to protect the doctor against the fact that their patient might blame them for failure to get disability benefits, in the opinion of the author. However, it should be pointed out in all fairness that a *few* doctors will write what they really think. If S. S. Disability let treating doctors decide who would get disability, almost everyone who applied would succeed in getting benefits—until the money ran out. There are a few doctors who have made an effort to understand S. S. Disability and cooperate with its requirements. A claimant who has such a doctor is lucky, and the doctor saves himself a great deal of time and frustration. Lastly, it should be noted that a doctor can no more "pressure" S. S. Disability than a claimant can do so. S. S. Disability will not violate legal requirements, no matter how powerful a doctor thinks he is, or should be.

3. *Consultative examinations.* Because of S. S. Disability's requirements for very detailed medical information, it is sometimes necessary to request that a claimant be examined by a doctor on a panel of consultants used for that purpose. Such doctors are *not* employees of S. S. Disability. They are doctors in private practice, who agree to examine claimants for a fee. This fee is paid by S. S. Disability. Often, X-rays and other kinds of laboratory tests are also purchased by S. S. Disability.

Consultative examinations are necessary when the claimant has no treating doctor, when the treating doctor refuses to provide needed information, or when the treating doctor's medical records do not contain enough information to evaluate the claimant's impairments. Specialists in all fields of medicine are used for these examinations.

S. S. Disability spends many millions of dollars a month purchasing consultative examinations, in order to obtain the high quality of data required for a fair decision. In doing so, one of the most vast sources of medical information in the world is created. Much of it is information based on examination of claimants by specialists in every medical field, from arthritis to heart disease. Often, claimants have never had such examinations or tests performed, because it was beyond their financial means, or because they were never referred to a specialist by their treating doctor. Such data would be of great social benefit, not to speak of benefit to the claimant, if it were routinely released to the claimant's regular treating doctor. S. S. Disability will do this, if the claimant signs a release of information consent requesting that it be done. Unfortunately, the claimant often doesn't notice this consent among the documents sent to him, or mistakenly doesn't think it important in his medical care. But it is very important that records of consultative examinations be transferred to the claimant's treating doctor. One possible example among many can illustrate this. It often happens that a claimant's treating doctor has told him that he has heart disease. This has a very serious effect on any patient; this diagnosis may produce painful psychological effects, such as fear of doing much physically to avoid having a "heart attack" and dying. It has social consequences in obtaining health insurance, life insurance, and employment, and increased anxiety among family members. All of this may be unavoidable, if the claimant does indeed have serious heart disease. On the other hand, S. S. Disability very frequently sees claimants who have been told they have serious heart disease and are being treated for it, but the treating doctor is unable to provide firm objective evidence that heart disease is in fact present. In that case, the claimant may be sent to a heart specialist (cardiologist), or internal medicine specialist. He will be examined by these specialists carefully, and a number of tests attempting to show the presence of heart disease may be done. The opinion and findings of this specialist will then be given to S. S. Disability for its evaluation. It is not at all unusual that no objective evidence of heart disease is found! The author bases this statement on the evaluation of many thousands of claims alleging disability because of heart disease, although exact statistics to prove this viewpoint have been impossible to keep. Obviously, when S. S. Disability gets such information it will tell the claimant that he has no objective signs of heart disease of significance and deny him disability benefits. Such a claimant is not likely to believe S. S. Disability, instead of his treating doctor. He is more likely to continue to believe that he is a cardiac cripple. The treating doctor is also likely to consider S. S. Disability ignorant and/or incompetent. But if that treating doctor could read the evaluation and findings of a heart specialist, would he not re-consider his own diagnosis? Or would he reject the specialist's negative findings, unwilling to admit that he may be wrong? The author can't answer these questions, but many doctors are men and women of integrity and might welcome the findings of another doctor from a consultative examination. And in cases where the heart specialist agrees with the treating doctor that heart disease is present, his findings can still be of great value to the treating doctor.

S. S. Disability rarely makes any active effort to get claimants to release the results of consultative examinations to their treating doctors. An added negative effect of this is that not knowing what the doctor doing the consultative exam found, there is no way the treating doctor can as effectively argue for the claimant that the doctor doing the consultative exam for S. S. Disability is wrong, if that is what he believes. In the opinion of the author, the failure of the results of consultative examinations to be routinely sent to treating doctors is an inexcusable waste of valuable medical information in an era of burdensome medical costs.

MEDICAL RECORDS

In regard to S. S. Disability being able to obtain medical records from the claimant's treating doctors or hospitals, the reader should be aware that only the claimant has the power to demand that those records be found and released. He has certain legal rights in this regard, and in applying for disability he should *not* simply assume that S. S. Disability will be able to obtain the needed information, or that he will necessarily be informed of the failure to do so. The fact that S. S. Disability sends a signed consent for release of information to a claimant's treating doctor and/or hospital does *not* mean the doctor and/or hospital will adequately respond to S. S. Disability. A wise claimant will take a personal interest in this himself, if he wants to make sure that S. S. Disability gets his records.

The above comments about medical records are based on the author's experience, and are firmly believed to be true. They are also felt to be based on fairly common experience by people actively engaged in evaluating disability claims at the level of a DDS. However, it should be emphasized that such comments are made only with constructive intent, and are not to be interpreted as alleging negligence or incompetence on the part of any claimant, doctor, or medical facility.

APPENDIX X

REQUEST FOR HEARING

DEPARTMENT OF HEALTH, EDUCATION, AND WELFARE
SOCIAL SECURITY ADMINISTRATION
OFFICE OF HEARINGS AND APPEALS

REQUEST FOR HEARING

Take or Mail original and all copies to your local Social Security Office.

CLAIMANT

WAGE EARNER *(Leave blank if same as above)*

SOCIAL SECURITY NUMBER

SPOUSE'S NAME AND SOCIAL SECURITY NUMBER
(Complete ONLY in Supplemental Security Income Case)

(Check One)
Initial Entitlement ☐ Termination or other Post-Entitlement Action ☐

Type Claim (Check ONE)

Retirement or Survivors.................Only ☐ (RSI)
Disability, Worker or Child.................Only ☐ (DIWC)
Disability, Widow or Widower.................Only ☐ (DIWW)

SSI, Aged.........Only ☐ (SSIA) With Title II Claim ☐ (SSAC)
SSI, Blind.........Only ☐ (SSIB) With Title II Claim ☐ (SSBC)
SSI, Disability...Only ☐ (SSID) With Title II Claim ☐ (SSDC)
Other (Specify)________

I disagree with the determination made on the above claim and request a hearing. My reasons for disagreement are:

Check one of the following:

☐ I have additional evidence to submit (Attach such evidence to this form or forward to the Social Security Office within 10 days.)

☐ I have no additional evidence to submit.

Check ONLY ONE of the statements below:

☐ I wish to appear in person.

☐ I do not wish to appear at a hearing. I request that a decision be made on the basis of the evidence in my case.

Signed by: (Either the claimant or representative should sign. Enter addresses for both. If claimant's representative is not an attorney, complete Form SSA-1696.)

SIGNATURE OR NAME OF CLAIMANT'S REPRESENTATIVE

☐ ATTORNEY ☐ NON ATTORNEY

CLAIMANT'S SIGNATURE

ADDRESS

ADDRESS

CITY, STATE, AND ZIP CODE

CITY, STATE, AND ZIP CODE

TELEPHONE NUMBER

DATE

TELEPHONE NUMBER

(Claimant should not fill in below this line)

TO BE COMPLETED BY SOCIAL SECURITY ADMINISTRATION

Is this request timely filed? ☐ YES ☐ NO

If "No" is checked: (1) Attach claimant's explanation for delay. (2) Attach any pertinent letter, material, or information in the Social Security Office.

Interpreter Needed ________ (Language)

ACKNOWLEDGMENT OF REQUEST FOR HEARING

This request for hearing was filed on________at________

The Administrative Law Judge will notify you of the time and place of the hearing at least 10 days in advance of the hearing.

HEARING OFFICE COPY

TO:

☐ Hearing Office________ (Location)

☐ ________ (Location) (Claims Involving SSI or combined SSI RSDI)

☐ Supplemental Security Income File Attached

CLAIM FILE COPY

TO:

☐ Hearing Office

☐ Claim File(s) Requested by Teletype to________ (Location)

☐ ACB (BDP)

For the Social Security Administration:

By:________ (Signature)

________ (Title)

________ (Street Address)

________ (City, State, and Zip Code)

Servicing Social Security Office Code________

Form HA-501 U5 (7-79) (C5399)

CLAIM FILE

APPENDIX XI

REQUEST FOR REVIEW OF HEARING DECISION/ORDER

DEPARTMENT OF HEALTH, EDUCATION, AND WELFARE
SOCIAL SECURITY ADMINISTRATION
OFFICE OF HEARINGS AND APPEALS

REQUEST FOR REVIEW OF HEARING DECISION/ORDER

Take or mail original and all copies to your local social security office.

CLAIMANT	(Check One) Initial Entitlement ☐ Termination or other Post-Entitlement Action ☐
WAGE EARNER (Leave blank if same as above)	Type Claim (Check ONE)
SOCIAL SECURITY NUMBER	Retirement or Survivors .... Only ☐ (RSI) Disability, Worker or Child .... Only ☐ (DIWC) Disability, Widow, or Widower .... Only ☐ (DIWW) Health Insurance, Part A .... Only ☐ (HIA)
SPOUSE'S NAME AND SOCIAL SECURITY NUMBER (Complete ONLY in Supplemental Security Income Case)	SSI, Aged ...... Only ☐ (SSIA) With Title II Claim ☐ (SSAC) SSI, Blind ...... Only ☐ (SSIB) With Title II Claim ☐ (SSBC) SSI, Disability ...... Only ☐ (SSID) With Title II Claim ☐ (SSDC) Other (Specify)________

I disagree with the action taken on the above claim and request review of such action by the Appeals Council, of the Office of Hearings and Appeals. My reasons for disagreement are:

____

____

ADDITIONAL EVIDENCE

Any additional evidence which you wish to submit must be either attached to this form or forwarded within 15 days to the Appeals Council at the address shown below. Where the evidence is not submitted within 15 days of this date, or within any extension of time granted by the Appeals Council, the Council will proceed to take its action based on the evidence of record.

Signed by: (Either the claimant or representative should sign - Enter addresses for both)

SIGNATURE OR NAME OF CLAIMANT'S REPRESENTATIVE ☐ ATTORNEY ☐ NON-ATTORNEY		CLAIMANT'S SIGNATURE
STREET ADDRESS		STREET ADDRESS
CITY, STATE, AND ZIP CODE		CITY, STATE, AND ZIP CODE
TELEPHONE NUMBER	DATE Claimant should not fill in below this line	TELEPHONE NUMBER

TO BE COMPLETED BY SOCIAL SECURITY ADMINISTRATION

Is this request filed timely? ☐ Yes ☐ No If "No" is checked: (1) attach claimant's explanation for delay; (2) attach any pertinent letter, material or information in Social Security Office.

ACKNOWLEDGMENT OF REQUEST FOR REVIEW OF HEARING DECISION/ORDER

Request for Review of Hearing Decision/Order in this case was filed on ______________ at ______________

The APPEALS COUNCIL will notify you of its action on your request.

For The Social Security Administration

BY (Signature)

(Title)

(Street Address)

(City) (State) (ZIP Code)

Appeals Council
Office of Hearings and Appeals, SSA
P.O.Box 2518
Washington, D.C. 20013

(C5400)

APPEALS COUNCIL — FILE
IN CLAIM FILE

FORM HA-520 U6 (3-79) DESTROY ALL STOCK DATED EARLIER THAN 7/78

APPENDIX XII

MEDICAL HISTORY AND DISABILITY REPORT—WIDOW, WIDOWER, SURVIVING DIVORCED WIFE, OR DISABLED CHILD

DEPARTMENT OF HEALTH AND HUMAN SERVICES
Social Security Administration

Form Approved
OMB No. 0960-014?

MEDICAL HISTORY AND DISABILITY REPORT
WIDOW, WIDOWER, SURVIVING DIVORCED WIFE, OR DISABLED CHILD

PLEASE PRINT, TYPE, OR WRITE CLEARLY AND ANSWER ALL ITEMS TO THE BEST OF YOUR ABILITY. If you are filing on behalf of someone else, enter his or her name and social security number in the space provided and answer all questions. COMPLETE ANSWERS WILL AID IN PROCESSING THE CLAIM. If a particular question or item does not apply to your claim show "N/A" (not applicable) in the space provided for the answer.

PRIVACY ACT NOTICE: The information requested on this form is authorized by Title 20 CFR 404.1512 and Title 20 CFR 416.912. The information provided will be used in making a decision on your claim. While completion of this form is voluntary, failure to provide all or part of the requested information could prevent an accurate or timely decision on your claim and could result in the loss of some benefits. Information you furnish on this form may be disclosed by the Social Security Administration to another person or governmental agency only with respect to social security programs and to comply with Federal laws requiring the exchange of information between Social Security and another agency.

PART I — IDENTIFYING INFORMATION

1. Print name of person on whose social security record this claim is being filed (*First name, middle initial, last name*)	Enter his or her Social Security Number _ _ _ / _ _ / _ _ _ _
2. Print your name (*disabled person*) (*First name, middle initial, last name*)	Enter your Social Security Number _ _ _ / _ _ / _ _ _ _

PART II — INFORMATION ABOUT YOUR CONDITION AND TREATMENT

3A. What is your disabling condition? (*Briefly describe the disabling illness or injury.*)

3B. When did you become disabled? →	MONTH	DAY	YEAR

4A. Have you worked since you became disabled? ☐ YES ☐ NO

4B. If "yes," show the dates you worked and the amount of money you earned.

DATES	AMOUNTS

5. If you are no longer disabled, show the date you believe your disability ended →	MONTH	DAY	YEAR

FORM SSA-3820-F6 (3-82) DESTROY PRIOR EDITIONS [C7764]

If more space is needed, list the other agencies, their addresses, your claim numbers, dates, and treatment received in Part III.

6. List the name, address and telephone number of the doctor who has the latest medical records about your disabling condition. — If you have no doctor, check here ☐

NAME

ADDRESS

TELEPHONE NUMBER (include area code)

HOW OFTEN DO YOU SEE THIS DOCTOR? | DATE YOU **FIRST** SAW THIS DOCTOR | DATE YOU **LAST** SAW THIS DOCTOR

REASONS FOR VISITS *(show illness or injury for which you had an examination or treatment.)*

TYPE OF TREATMENT OR MEDICINES RECEIVED (such as surgery, chemotherapy, radiation, and the medicines you take for your illness or injury, if known. If no treatment or medicines, show "NONE".)

7. Have you seen any other doctors since your disabling condition began? ☐ YES ☐ NO
If "yes", show the following:

NAME

ADDRESS

TELEPHONE NUMBER (include area code)

HOW OFTEN DO YOU SEE THIS DOCTOR? | DATE YOU **FIRST** SAW THIS DOCTOR | DATE YOU **LAST** SAW THIS DOCTOR

REASON FOR VISITS *(show illness or injury for which you had an examination or treatment.)*

TYPE OF TREATMENT OR MEDICINES RECEIVED (such as surgery, chemotherapy, radiation, and the medicines you take for your illness or injury, if known. If no treatment or medicines, show "NONE".)

If you have seen other doctors since your illness began, list their names, addresses, dates and reasons for visits in Part III.

8. Have you been hospitalized or treated at a clinic for your disabling condition? ☐ YES ☐ NO
If "yes", show the following:

NAME OF HOSPITAL OR CLINIC

ADDRESS

PATIENT OR CLINIC NUMBER

Were you an inpatient (Stayed at least overnight?) ☐ NO ☐ YES *If "yes", show*

Were you an outpatient? ☐ NO ☐ YES *If "yes", show:*

DATES OF ADMISSIONS	DATES OF DISCHARGES	DATE OF VISITS

REASON FOR HOSPITALIZATION OR CLINIC VISITS *(show illness or injury for which you had an examination or treatment.)*

TYPE OF TREATMENT OR MEDICINES RECEIVED (such as surgery, chemotherapy, radiation, and the medicines you take for your illness or injury, if known. If no treatment or medicines, show "NONE".)

If you have been in other hospitals or clinics for your illness or injury, list the names, addresses, patient or clinic numbers, dates and reasons for hospitalization or clinic visits in Part III.

9. Have you been seen by other agencies for your disabling condition? (VA, Workmen's Compensation, Vocational Rehabilitation, Welfare, etc.) *If "yes" show:* ☐ YES ☐ NO

NAME OF AGENCY

ADDRESS OF AGENCY

YOUR CLAIM NUMBER

DATES OF VISITS

TYPE OF TREATMENT, EXAMINATION, OR MEDICINES RECEIVED (such as surgery, chemotherapy, radiation, and the medicines you take for your illness or injury, if known. If no treatment or medicines, show "NONE".)

FORM **SSA-3820-F6** (3-87) [C7765]

HISTORY & DISABILITY REPORT

10. Have you had any of the following tests in the last year?

TEST	CHECK APPROPRIATE BLOCK OR BLOCKS	If "Yes", show: WHERE DONE	WHEN DONE
Electrocardiogram	☐ NO ☐ YES		
Chest X-Ray	☐ NO ☐ YES		
Other X-Ray (Name the body part here) ________	☐ NO ☐ YES		
Breathing Tests	☐ NO ☐ YES		
Blood Tests	☐ NO ☐ YES		
Other (Specify)	☐ NO ☐ YES		

11. If you have a Medicaid card, what is your number (some hospitals and clinics file your records by your Medicaid number)

12A. Give the name(s) and address(es) of any school(s) where you received special training or attended special classes. Also, show the dates you attended such school(s). If you did not attend any such school or classes show "None."

NAMES AND ADDRESSES OF SCHOOLS	DATES ATTENDED

12B. What is the highest grade you completed in school?	HIGHEST GRADE COMPLETED

13. Daily Activities - Describe what you do in a typical day. For example: describe your household duties, recreational activities, your social contacts with other people, etc. Also describe any help you receive from others in a typical day.

FORM SSA-3820-F6 (8-80) (C7706)

PART III — REMARKS

Use this section for additional space to answer any previous questions and to provide any additional information that you think will be helpful in making a decision on your disability claim. Please refer to the previous questions by number.

PART IV — AUTHORIZATION AND NOTIFICATION STATEMENTS

I authorize any physician, hospital, agency, or other organization to disclose to the Social Security Administration or to the State Agency that may review my claim or continuing disability, any medical records or other information about my disability.

I agree to notify the Social Security Administration if my medical condition improves or I go to work.

I know that anyone who makes a false statement or representation of a material fact in an application or for use in determining a right to payment under the Social Security Act commits a crime punishable under Federal Law. I affirm that the above statements are true.

SIGNATURE OF CLAIMANT OR PERSON FILING ON THE CLAIMANT'S BEHALF *(First name, middle initial, last name)*	DATE *(Month, Day, Year)*
	TELEPHONE NUMBER(S) at which you may be contacted during the day *(include area code)*

MAILING ADDRESS *(Number and Street, Apt. No., P. O. Box, or Rural Route)*

CITY AND STATE	ZIP CODE	ENTER NAME OF COUNTY *(if any)* IN WHICH YOU NOW LIVE

Witnesses are required ONLY if this statement has been signed by mark (X) above. If signed by mark (X), two witnesses to the signing who know the person making the statement must sign below, giving their full addresses.

1. SIGNATURE OF WITNESS	2. SIGNATURE OF WITNESS
ADDRESS *(Number and Street, City, State, and Zip Code)*	ADDRESS *(Number and Street, City, State, and Zip Code)*

FORM **SSA-3820-F6** (3-82)

☆ U.S. Government Printing Office: 1982—381-189/2024
[C7767]

HISTORY & DISABILITY REPORT

DETACH THIS PAGE →

PART V — FOR SSA USE ONLY — DO NOT WRITE BELOW THIS LINE

NAME OF CLAIMANT	CLAIM NUMBER

14A. Was claimant ever or is now entitled to any type of monthly social security benefits?

☐ YES (If "yes", answer B, C, D and E) ☐ NO (If "no", go on to item 15.)

14B. ENTER NAME OF PERSON ON WHOSE SOCIAL SECURITY RECORD CLAIMANT FILED OTHER APPLICATION.	14C. ENTER SOCIAL SECURITY NUMBER OF PERSON NAMED IN B (If unknown so indicate)

14D. WHAT KIND OF BENEFITS DID OR DOES CLAIMANT RECEIVE? (For example, widows, mother's, disabled child's)	14E. ENTER MONTH AND YEAR BENEFITS ENDED OR WILL END.	
	MONTH	YEAR

15. **Check any of the following categories which apply to this case:**

Presumptive Disability or Blindness Considerations
(If any of these boxes are checked, DO's (and DDS's) should be alert to the possibility of a presumptive disability or blindness decision in SSI claims per DI 00404.210 and DI 2152.5)

A ☐ Amputation of two limbs

B ☐ Amputation of a leg at the hip

C ☐ Allegation of total deafness

D ☐ Allegation of total blindness

E ☐ Allegation of bed confinement or immobility without a wheelchair, walker, or crutches, allegedly due to a longstanding condition (excluding [illegible]ent accident and recent surgery

F ☐ Allegation of a stroke (cerebral vascular accident) more than 3 months in the past and continued marked difficulty in walking or using a [illegible] and or arm

G ☐ Allegation of cerebral palsy, muscular dystrophy or muscular atrophy and marked difficulty in walking (e.g., use of braces), speaking or coordination of the hands or arms

H ☐ Allegation of diabetes with amputation of a foot

I. ☐ **Allegation of Down's Syndrome (Mongolism).**

J. ☐ An applicant filing on behalf of another individual alleges severe mental deficiency for claimant who is at least 7 years of age. The applicant alleges that the individual attends (or attended) a special school, or special classes in school, because of his mental deficiency, or is unable to attend any type of school (or if beyond school age was unable to attend), and requires care and supervision of routine daily activities

K. ☐ Allegation of renal disease requiring dialysis on a regularly scheduled basis

16. Does the claimant speak English? ☐ YES ☐ NO **(If "no", what language does he or she speak?)**	LANGUAGE(S)

17. Does the claimant need assistance in prosecuting his or her claim? (If "yes", show name, address, relationship and telephone number of interested party willing to assist claimant.) ☐ YES ☐ NO

NAME	ADDRESS	RELATIONSHIP	TELEPHONE NUMBER (area code)

18. Is capability development by the DDS necessary? (If "yes", show "DDS Capability Development needed" in item 11 of the **SSA-831-U5.**) ☐ YES ☐ NO

FORM **SSA-3820-F6** (3-82) (C7768)

APPENDIX XII

19A. Check each item to indicate if any difficulty was observed:

Reading	☐ Yes	☐ No	Using Hands	☐ Yes	☐ No
Writing	☐ Yes	☐ No	Breathing	☐ Yes	☐ No
Answering	☐ Yes	☐ No	Seeing	☐ Yes	☐ No
Hearing	☐ Yes	☐ No	Walking	☐ Yes	☐ No
Sitting	☐ Yes	☐ No			
Understanding	☐ Yes	☐ No	Other *(Specify)*:		

19B. If any of the above items were checked "yes," describe the exact difficulty involved:

PRESCRIBED PERIOD — COMPLETE IN ALL CASES EXCEPT DISABLED CHILD CASES.

20A. Beginning date *(fill in all applicable dates, check latest)*	MONTH
☐ W/E's death	
☐ Last month of previous entitlement to Disabled Widow(er) benefits	
☐ Last month of entitlement to Mother's benefits	
20B. Ending date *(fill in dates, check earliest)*	**MONTH**
☐ If filing for monthly benefits, the month before the month widow(er) attains age 60	
☐ If filing for Medicare only, the month before the month widow(er) attains age 65	
☐ Eighty-four months (7 years) following the beginning date checked in 20A.	

21. Controlling date for development of medical evidence — DWB case ⟶	MONTH	DAY	YEAR

22. Medical Development — Initiated by District or Branch office

SOURCE	DATE REQUESTED	DATE(S) OF FOLLOW-UP	CAPABILITY DEVELOPMENT REQUESTED

23. DO curtailed completion of items 12 and 13 per DI 00403.105 (DI 2019). ☐ Yes ☐ No

24. Is development of work activity necessary? ☐ Yes ☐ No
If "yes", is an SSA-820-F4 or SSA-821-F4 ☐ Pending ☐ In File

25. SSA-3820-F6 taken by:
☐ Personal Interview ☐ Telephone ☐ Mail

26. Form supplemented ☐ Yes ☐ No
If "yes" by:
☐ Personal Interview ☐ Telephone ☐ Mail

Signature of DO or BO Interviewer or Reviewer	TITLE	DATE

FORM **SSA-3820-F6** (3-82) [C7769]

APPENDIX XIII

PREDICTED NORMAL FEV, MVV, AND FVC VALUES FOR MEN AND WOMEN

The following tables (2–7) contain the predicted normal values for FEV_1, MVV, and FVC for men and women. This data is from "Guides to the Evaluation of Permanent Impairment", *The Respiratory System,* Journal of the American Medical Association, 1965. These are re-printed by courtesy of the A.M.A.

The information given in tables 2–7 does not necessarily represent the most current data regarding normal breathing capacities, but for all practical purposes will give the reader some idea of what is normal.

APPENDIX XIII

Table 2.—Predicted Normal $FEV_{1.0}$ Values for Men (ATPS)

Age	59	60	61	62	63	64	65	66	67	68	69	70	71	72	73	74	75	76	77	78	79
20	3.14	3.23	3.32	3.40	3.49	3.58	3.66	3.75	3.84	3.92	4.01	4.10	4.18	4.27	4.36	4.45	4.53	4.62	4.7[illegible]	4.79	4.88
21	3.11	3.20	3.29	3.38	3.46	3.55	3.64	3.72	3.81	3.90	3.98	4.07	4.16	4.25	4.33	4.42	4.51	4.59	4.[illegible]	4.77	4.85
22	3.09	3.18	3.26	3.35	3.44	3.52	3.61	3.70	3.79	3.87	3.96	4.05	4.13	4.22	4.31	4.39	4.48	4.57	4.6[illegible]	4.74	4.83
23	3.06	3.15	3.24	3.32	3.41	3.50	3.59	3.67	3.76	3.85	3.93	4.02	4.11	4.19	4.28	4.37	4.45	4.54	4.6[illegible]	4.72	4.80
24	3.04	3.12	3.21	3.30	3.39	3.47	3.56	3.65	3.73	3.82	3.91	3.99	4.08	4.17	4.26	4.34	4.43	4.52	4.6[illegible]	4.69	4.78
25	3.01	3.10	3.19	3.27	3.36	3.45	3.53	3.62	3.71	3.79	3.88	3.97	4.06	4.14	4.23	4.32	4.40	4.49	4.5[illegible]	4.66	4.75
26	2.99	3.07	3.16	3.25	3.33	3.42	3.51	3.59	3.68	3.77	3.86	3.94	4.03	4.12	4.20	4.29	4.38	4.46	4.5[illegible]	4.64	4.72
27	2.96	3.05	3.13	3.22	3.31	3.39	3.48	3.57	3.66	3.74	3.83	3.92	4.00	4.09	4.18	4.26	4.35	4.44	4.5[illegible]	4.61	4.70
28	2.93	3.02	3.11	3.19	3.28	3.37	3.46	3.54	3.63	3.72	3.80	3.89	3.98	4.06	4.15	4.24	4.33	4.41	4.5[illegible]	4.59	4.67
29	2.91	3.00	3.08	3.17	3.26	3.34	3.43	3.52	3.60	3.69	3.78	3.86	3.95	4.04	4.13	4.21	4.30	4.39	4.4[illegible]	4.56	4.64
30	2.88	2.97	3.06	3.14	3.23	3.32	3.40	3.49	3.58	3.66	3.75	3.84	3.93	4.01	4.10	4.19	4.27	4.36	4.45	4.53	4.62
31	2.86	2.94	3.03	3.12	3.20	3.29	3.38	3.47	3.55	3.64	3.73	3.81	3.90	3.98	4.07	4.16	4.25	4.33	4.42	4.51	4.60
32	2.83	2.92	3.00	3.09	3.18	3.27	3.35	3.44	3.53	3.61	3.70	3.79	3.87	3.96	4.05	4.13	4.22	4.31	4.40	4.48	4.57
33	2.80	2.89	2.98	3.07	3.15	3.24	3.33	3.41	3.50	3.59	3.67	3.76	3.85	3.93	4.02	4.11	4.20	4.28	4.37	4.46	4.54
34	2.78	2.87	2.95	3.04	3.13	3.21	3.30	3.39	3.47	3.56	3.65	3.74	3.82	3.91	4.00	4.08	4.17	4.26	4.34	4.43	4.52
35	2.75	2.84	2.93	3.01	3.10	3.19	3.27	3.36	3.45	3.54	3.62	3.71	3.80	3.88	3.97	4.06	4.14	4.23	4.32	4.40	4.49
36	2.73	2.81	2.90	2.99	3.07	3.16	3.25	3.34	3.42	3.51	3.60	3.68	3.77	3.86	3.94	4.03	4.12	4.21	4.29	4.38	4.47
37	2.70	2.79	2.87	2.96	3.05	3.14	3.22	3.31	3.40	3.48	3.57	3.66	3.74	3.83	3.92	4.01	4.09	4.18	4.27	4.35	4.44
38	2.68	2.76	2.85	2.94	3.02	3.11	3.20	3.28	3.37	3.46	3.54	3.63	3.72	3.81	3.89	3.98	4.07	4.15	4.24	4.33	4.41
39	2.65	2.74	2.82	2.91	3.00	3.08	3.17	3.26	3.34	3.43	3.52	3.61	3.69	3.78	3.87	3.95	4.04	4.13	4.21	4.30	4.39
40	2.62	2.71	2.80	2.88	2.97	3.06	3.15	3.23	3.32	3.41	3.49	3.58	3.67	3.75	3.84	3.93	4.01	4.10	4.19	4.28	4.36
41	2.60	2.68	2.77	2.86	2.95	3.03	3.12	3.21	3.29	3.38	3.47	3.55	3.64	3.73	3.81	3.90	3.99	4.08	4.16	4.25	4.34
42	2.57	2.66	2.75	2.83	2.92	3.01	3.09	3.18	3.27	3.35	3.44	3.53	3.61	3.70	3.79	3.88	3.96	4.05	4.14	4.22	4.31
43	2.55	2.63	2.72	2.81	2.89	2.98	3.07	3.15	3.24	3.33	3.42	3.50	3.59	3.68	3.76	3.85	3.94	4.02	4.11	4.20	4.28
44	2.52	2.61	2.69	2.78	2.87	2.95	3.04	3.13	3.22	3.30	3.39	3.48	3.56	3.65	3.74	3.82	3.91	4.00	4.08	4.17	4.26
45	2.49	2.58	2.67	2.75	2.84	2.93	3.02	3.10	3.19	3.28	3.36	3.45	3.54	3.62	3.71	3.80	3.89	3.97	4.06	4.15	4.23
46	2.47	2.55	2.64	2.73	2.82	2.90	2.99	3.08	3.16	3.25	3.34	3.42	3.51	3.60	3.69	3.77	3.86	3.95	4.03	4.12	4.21
47	2.44	2.53	2.62	2.70	2.79	2.88	2.96	3.05	3.14	3.22	3.31	3.40	3.49	3.57	3.66	3.75	3.83	3.92	4.01	4.09	4.18
48	2.42	2.50	2.59	2.68	2.76	2.85	2.94	3.02	3.11	3.20	3.29	3.37	3.46	3.55	3.63	3.72	3.81	3.89	3.98	4.07	4.16
49	2.39	2.48	2.56	2.65	2.74	2.82	2.91	3.00	3.09	3.17	3.26	3.35	3.43	3.52	3.61	3.69	3.78	3.87	3.96	4.04	4.13
50	2.36	2.45	2.54	2.63	2.71	2.80	2.89	2.97	3.06	3.15	3.23	3.32	3.40	3.49	3.58	3.67	3.76	3.84	3.93	4.02	4.10
51	2.34	2.43	2.51	2.60	2.69	2.77	2.86	2.95	3.03	3.12	3.21	3.29	3.38	3.47	3.56	3.64	3.73	3.82	3.90	3.99	4.08
52	2.31	2.40	2.49	2.57	2.66	2.75	2.83	2.92	3.01	3.10	3.18	3.27	3.36	3.44	3.53	3.62	3.70	3.79	3.88	3.96	4.05
53	2.29	2.37	2.46	2.55	2.63	2.72	2.81	2.90	2.98	3.07	3.16	3.24	3.33	3.42	3.50	3.59	3.68	3.76	3.85	3.94	4.03
54	2.26	2.35	2.43	2.52	2.61	2.70	2.78	2.87	2.96	3.04	3.13	3.22	3.30	3.39	3.48	3.56	3.65	3.74	3.83	3.91	4.00
55	2.23	2.32	2.41	2.50	2.58	2.67	2.76	2.84	2.93	3.02	3.10	3.19	3.28	3.37	3.45	3.54	3.63	3.71	3.80	3.89	3.97
56	2.21	2.30	2.38	2.47	2.56	2.64	2.73	2.82	2.90	2.99	3.08	3.17	3.25	3.34	3.43	3.51	3.60	3.69	3.77	3.86	3.95
57	2.18	2.27	2.36	2.44	2.53	2.62	2.70	2.79	2.88	2.97	3.05	3.14	3.23	3.31	3.40	3.49	3.57	3.66	3.75	3.84	3.92
58	2.16	2.24	2.33	2.42	2.50	2.59	2.68	2.77	2.85	2.94	3.03	3.11	3.20	3.29	3.37	3.46	3.55	3.64	3.72	3.81	3.90
59	2.13	2.22	2.31	2.39	2.48	2.57	2.65	2.74	2.83	2.91	3.00	3.09	3.17	3.26	3.35	3.44	3.52	3.61	3.70	[illegible].78	3.87
60	2.11	2.19	2.28	2.37	2.45	2.54	2.63	2.71	2.80	2.89	2.97	3.06	3.15	3.24	3.32	3.41	3.50	3.58	3.67	[illegible].76	3.84
61	2.08	2.17	2.25	2.34	2.43	2.51	2.60	2.69	2.78	2.86	2.95	3.04	3.12	3.21	3.30	3.38	3.47	3.56	3.64	[illegible].73	3.82
62	2.05	2.14	2.23	2.31	2.40	2.49	2.58	2.66	2.75	2.84	2.92	3.01	3.10	3.18	3.27	3.36	3.44	3.53	3.62	3.71	3.79
63	2.03	2.11	2.20	2.29	2.38	2.46	2.55	2.64	2.72	2.81	2.90	2.98	3.07	3.16	3.24	3.33	3.42	3.51	3.59	3.68	3.77
64	2.00	2.09	2.18	2.26	2.35	2.44	2.52	2.61	2.70	2.78	2.87	2.96	3.04	3.13	3.22	3.31	3.39	3.48	3.57	3.65	3.74
65	1.98	2.06	2.15	2.24	2.32	2.41	2.50	2.58	2.67	2.76	2.85	2.93	3.02	3.11	3.19	3.28	3.37	3.45	3.54	3.63	3.71
66	1.95	2.04	2.12	2.21	2.30	2.38	2.47	2.56	2.65	2.73	2.82	2.91	2.99	3.08	3.17	3.25	3.34	3.43	3.52	3.60	3.69
67	1.92	2.01	2.10	2.18	2.27	2.36	2.45	2.53	2.62	2.71	2.79	2.88	2.97	3.05	3.14	3.23	3.32	3.40	3.49	3.58	3.66
68	1.90	1.99	2.07	2.16	2.25	2.33	2.42	2.51	2.59	2.68	2.77	2.85	2.94	3.03	3.12	3.20	3.29	3.38	3.46	3.55	3.64
69	1.87	1.96	2.05	2.13	2.22	2.31	2.39	2.48	2.57	2.65	2.74	2.83	2.92	3.00	3.09	3.18	3.26	3.35	3.44	3.52	3.61
70	1.85	1.93	2.02	2.11	2.19	2.28	2.37	2.45	2.54	2.63	2.72	2.80	2.89	2.98	3.06	3.15	3.24	3.32	3.41	3.50	3.59
	59	**60**	**61**	**62**	**63**	**64**	**65**	**66**	**67**	**68**	**69**	**70**	**71**	**72**	**73**	**74**	**75**	**76**	**77**	**78**	**79**

Height (in inches)

$FEV_{1.0}$ in liters[*] $=0.087H-0.026A-1.471$; SEE = 0.52 liters.

$FEV_{1.0}$=one-second forced expiratory volume; H=height in inches, A=age in years; SEE=standard error of estimate; ATPS—ambient temperature and pressure saturated with water vapor. The values in this table have been adapted for use at a room temperature of approximately 77 °F (25 C).

The axes of the table are age (in years) at the side and height (in inches) at the bottom. The predicted normal $FEV_{1.0}$ in liters for the male patient is found at the intersection of the row for his age and the column for his height.

[*]Adapted from VA-Army Cooperative Study, Kory, Callahan, Boren, and Snyder, *Amer J Med* **30**:243-258 (Feb) 1961.

[C7796]

APPENDIX XIII

Table 3.—Predicted Normal FVC Values for Men (ATPS)

Age	59	60	61	62	63	64	65	66	67	68	69	70	71	72	73	74	75	76	77	78	79
20	3.52	3.64	3.77	3.89	4.01	4.14	4.26	4.38	4.51	4.63	4.75	4.87	5.00	5.12	5.24	5.37	5.49	5.61	5.74	5.86	5.98
21	3.50	3.62	3.75	3.87	3.99	4.12	4.24	4.36	4.49	4.61	4.73	4.85	4.98	5.10	5.22	5.35	5.47	5.59	5.72	5.84	5.96
22	3.48	3.60	3.73	3.85	3.97	4.10	4.22	4.34	4.46	4.59	4.71	4.83	4.96	5.08	5.20	5.33	5.45	5.57	5.70	5.82	5.94
23	3.46	3.58	3.71	3.83	3.95	4.08	4.20	4.32	4.44	4.57	4.69	4.81	4.94	5.06	5.18	5.31	5.43	5.55	5.67	5.80	5.92
24	3.44	3.56	3.69	3.81	3.93	4.06	4.18	4.30	4.42	4.55	4.67	4.79	4.92	5.04	5.16	5.29	5.41	5.53	5.65	5.78	5.90
25	3.42	3.54	3.67	3.79	3.91	4.03	4.16	4.28	4.40	4.53	4.65	4.77	4.90	5.02	5.14	5.27	5.39	5.51	5.63	5.76	5.88
26	3.40	3.52	3.65	3.77	3.89	4.01	4.14	4.26	4.38	4.51	4.63	4.75	4.88	5.00	5.12	5.24	5.37	5.49	5.61	5.74	5.86
27	3.38	3.50	3.63	3.75	3.87	3.99	4.12	4.24	4.36	4.49	4.61	4.73	4.86	4.98	5.10	5.22	5.35	5.47	5.59	5.72	5.84
28	3.36	3.48	3.60	3.73	3.85	3.97	4.10	4.22	4.34	4.47	4.59	4.71	4.83	4.96	5.08	5.20	5.33	5.45	5.57	5.70	5.82
29	3.34	3.46	3.58	3.71	3.83	3.95	4.08	4.20	4.32	4.45	4.57	4.69	4.81	4.94	5.06	5.18	5.31	5.43	5.55	5.68	5.80
30	3.32	3.44	3.56	3.69	3.81	3.93	4.06	4.18	4.30	4.43	4.55	4.67	4.79	4.92	5.04	5.16	5.29	5.41	5.53	5.66	5.78
31	3.30	3.42	3.54	3.67	3.79	3.91	4.04	4.16	4.28	4.40	4.53	4.65	4.77	4.90	5.02	5.14	5.27	5.39	5.51	5.64	5.76
32	3.28	3.40	3.52	3.65	3.77	3.89	4.02	4.14	4.26	4.38	4.51	4.63	4.75	4.88	5.00	5.12	5.25	5.37	5.49	5.61	5.74
33	3.26	3.38	3.50	3.63	3.75	3.87	4.00	4.12	4.24	4.36	4.49	4.61	4.73	4.86	4.98	5.10	5.23	5.35	5.47	5.59	5.72
34	3.24	3.36	3.48	3.61	3.73	3.85	3.97	4.10	4.22	4.34	4.47	4.59	4.71	4.84	4.96	5.08	5.20	5.33	5.45	5.57	5.70
35	3.22	3.34	3.46	3.59	3.71	3.83	3.95	4.08	4.20	4.32	4.45	4.57	4.69	4.82	4.94	5.06	5.18	5.31	5.43	5.55	5.68
36	3.20	3.32	3.44	3.56	3.69	3.81	3.93	4.06	4.18	4.30	4.43	4.55	4.67	4.80	4.92	5.04	5.16	5.29	5.41	5.53	5.66
37	3.18	3.30	3.42	3.54	3.67	3.79	3.91	4.04	4.16	4.28	4.41	4.53	4.65	4.77	4.90	5.02	5.14	5.27	5.39	5.51	5.64
38	3.16	3.28	3.40	3.52	3.65	3.77	3.89	4.02	4.14	4.26	4.39	4.51	4.63	4.75	4.88	5.00	5.12	5.25	5.37	5.49	5.62
39	3.13	3.26	3.38	3.50	3.63	3.75	3.87	4.00	4.12	4.24	4.37	4.49	4.61	4.73	4.86	4.98	5.10	5.23	5.35	5.47	5.60
40	3.11	3.24	3.36	3.48	3.61	3.73	3.85	3.98	4.10	4.22	4.34	4.47	4.59	4.71	4.84	4.96	5.08	5.21	5.33	5.45	5.57
41	3.09	3.22	3.34	3.46	3.59	3.71	3.83	3.96	4.08	4.20	4.32	4.45	4.57	4.69	4.82	4.94	5.06	5.19	5.31	5.43	5.55
42	3.07	3.20	3.32	3.44	3.57	3.69	3.81	3.93	4.06	4.18	4.30	4.43	4.55	4.67	4.80	4.92	5.04	5.17	5.29	5.41	5.53
43	3.05	3.18	3.30	3.42	3.55	3.67	3.79	3.91	4.04	4.16	4.28	4.41	4.53	4.65	4.78	4.90	5.02	5.14	5.27	5.39	5.51
44	3.03	3.16	3.28	3.40	3.53	3.65	3.77	3.89	4.02	4.14	4.26	4.39	4.51	4.63	4.76	4.88	5.00	5.12	5.25	5.37	5.49
45	3.01	3.14	3.26	3.38	3.50	3.63	3.75	3.87	4.00	4.12	4.24	4.37	4.49	4.61	4.74	4.86	4.98	5.10	5.23	5.35	5.47
46	2.99	3.12	3.24	3.36	3.48	3.61	3.73	3.85	3.98	4.10	4.22	4.35	4.47	4.59	4.71	4.84	4.96	5.08	5.21	5.33	5.45
47	2.97	3.10	3.22	3.34	3.46	3.59	3.71	3.83	3.96	4.08	4.20	4.33	4.45	4.57	4.69	4.82	4.94	5.06	5.19	5.31	5.43
48	2.95	3.07	3.20	3.32	3.44	3.57	3.69	3.81	3.94	4.06	4.18	4.30	4.43	4.55	4.67	4.80	4.92	5.04	5.17	5.29	5.41
49	2.93	3.05	3.18	3.30	3.42	3.55	3.67	3.79	3.92	4.04	4.16	4.28	4.41	4.53	4.65	4.78	4.90	5.02	5.15	5.27	5.39
50	2.91	3.03	3.16	3.28	3.40	3.53	3.65	3.77	3.90	4.02	4.14	4.26	4.39	4.51	4.63	4.76	4.88	5.00	4.13	5.25	5.37
51	2.89	3.01	3.14	3.26	3.38	3.51	3.63	3.75	3.87	4.00	4.12	4.24	4.37	4.49	4.61	4.74	4.86	4.98	5.11	5.23	5.35
52	2.87	2.99	3.12	3.24	3.36	3.49	3.61	3.73	3.85	3.98	4.10	4.22	4.35	4.47	4.59	4.72	4.84	4.96	5.08	5.21	5.33
53	2.85	2.97	3.10	3.22	3.34	3.47	3.59	3.71	3.83	3.96	4.08	4.20	4.33	4.45	4.57	4.70	4.82	4.94	5.06	5.19	5.31
54	2.83	2.95	3.08	3.20	3.32	3.44	3.57	3.69	3.81	3.94	4.06	4.18	4.31	4.43	4.55	4.67	4.80	4.92	5.04	5.17	5.29
55	2.81	2.93	3.06	3.18	3.30	3.42	3.55	3.67	3.79	3.92	4.04	4.16	4.29	4.41	4.53	4.65	4.78	4.90	5.02	5.15	5.27
56	2.79	2.91	3.03	3.16	3.28	3.40	3.53	3.65	3.77	3.90	4.02	4.14	4.27	4.39	4.51	4.63	4.76	4.88	5.00	5.13	5.25
57	2.77	2.89	3.01	3.14	3.26	3.38	3.51	3.63	3.75	3.88	4.00	4.12	4.24	4.37	4.49	4.61	4.74	4.86	4.98	5.11	5.23
58	2.75	2.87	2.99	3.12	3.24	3.36	3.49	3.61	3.73	3.86	3.98	4.10	4.22	4.35	4.47	4.59	4.72	4.84	4.96	5.09	5.21
59	2.73	2.85	2.97	3.10	3.22	3.34	3.47	3.59	3.71	3.84	3.96	4.08	4.20	4.33	4.45	4.57	4.70	4.82	4.94	5.07	5.19
60	2.71	2.83	2.95	3.08	3.20	3.32	3.45	3.57	3.69	3.81	3.94	4.06	4.18	4.31	4.43	4.55	4.68	4.80	4.92	5.04	5.17
61	2.69	2.81	2.93	3.06	3.18	3.30	3.43	3.55	3.67	3.79	3.92	4.04	4.16	4.29	4.41	4.53	4.66	4.78	4.90	5.02	5.15
62	2.67	2.79	2.91	3.04	3.16	3.28	3.40	3.53	3.65	3.77	3.90	4.02	4.14	4.27	4.39	4.51	4.64	4.76	4.88	5.00	5.13
63	2.65	2.77	2.89	3.02	3.14	3.26	3.38	3.51	3.63	3.75	3.88	4.00	4.12	4.25	4.37	4.49	4.61	4.74	4.86	4.98	5.11
64	2.63	2.75	2.87	3.00	3.12	3.24	3.36	3.49	3.61	3.73	3.86	3.98	4.10	4.23	4.35	4.47	4.59	4.72	4.84	4.96	5.09
65	2.61	2.73	2.85	2.97	3.10	3.22	3.34	3.47	3.59	3.71	3.84	3.96	4.08	4.21	4.33	4.45	4.57	4.70	4.82	4.94	5.07
66	2.59	2.71	2.83	2.95	3.08	3.20	3.32	3.45	3.57	3.69	3.82	3.94	4.06	4.18	4.31	4.43	4.55	4.68	4.80	4.92	5.05
67	2.57	2.69	2.81	2.93	3.06	3.18	3.30	3.43	3.55	3.67	3.80	3.92	4.04	4.16	4.29	4.41	4.53	4.66	4.78	4.90	5.03
68	2.54	2.67	2.79	2.91	3.04	3.16	3.28	3.41	3.53	3.65	3.77	3.90	4.02	4.14	4.27	4.39	4.51	4.64	4.76	4.88	5.01
69	2.52	2.65	2.77	2.89	3.02	3.14	3.26	3.39	3.51	3.63	3.75	3.88	4.00	4.12	4.25	4.37	4.49	4.62	4.74	4.86	4.98
70	2.50	2.63	2.75	2.87	3.00	3.12	3.24	3.37	3.49	3.61	3.73	3.86	3.98	4.10	4.23	4.35	4.47	4.60	4.72	4.84	4.96

Height (in inches)

FVC in liters* = 0.123H−0.0204A−3.33; SEE = 0.58 liters.

FVC = forced vital capacity; H = height in inches; A = age in years; SEE = standard error of estimate; ATPS = ambient temperature and pressure saturated with water vapor. The values in this table have been adapted for use at a room temperature of approximately 77 F (25 C).

The axes of the table are age (in years) at the side and height (in inches) at the bottom. The predicted normal FVC in liters for the male patient is found at the intersection of the row for his age and the column for his height.

*Adapted from VA-Army Cooperative Study, Kory, Callahan, Boren, and Snyder, *Amer J. Med* 30:243-258 (Feb) 1961.

[C7797]

APPENDIX XIII

Table 4.—Predicted Normal $FEV_{1.0}$ Values for Women (ATPS)

Age	55	56	57	58	59	60	61	62	63	64	65	66	67	68	69	70	71	72
20	2.43	2.49	2.55	2.62	2.69	2.76	2.82	2.89	2.95	3.02	3.09	3.15	3.22	3.28	3.35	[illegible]	3.48	3.55
21	2.41	2.47	2.54	2.61	2.67	2.74	2.80	2.87	2.93	3.00	3.07	3.13	3.20	3.26	3.33	[illegible]	3.46	3.53
22	2.39	2.45	2.52	2.59	2.65	2.72	2.78	2.85	2.92	2.98	3.05	3.11	3.18	3.24	3.31	3.38	3.44	3.51
23	2.37	2.44	2.50	2.57	2.63	2.70	2.76	2.83	2.90	2.96	3.03	3.09	3.16	3.22	3.29	3.36	3.42	3.49
24	2.35	2.42	2.48	2.55	2.61	2.68	2.74	2.81	2.88	2.94	3.01	3.07	3.14	3.21	3.27	3.34	3.40	3.47
25	2.33	2.40	2.46	2.53	2.59	2.66	2.73	2.79	2.86	2.92	2.99	3.05	3.12	3.19	3.25	3.32	3.38	3.45
26	2.31	2.38	2.44	2.51	2.57	2.64	2.71	2.77	2.84	2.90	2.97	3.03	3.10	3.17	3.23	3.30	3.36	3.43
27	2.29	2.36	2.42	2.49	2.55	2.62	2.69	2.75	2.82	2.88	2.95	3.02	3.08	3.15	3.21	3.28	3.34	3.41
28	2.27	2.34	2.40	2.47	2.54	2.60	2.67	2.73	2.80	2.86	2.93	3.00	3.06	3.13	3.19	3.26	3.32	3.39
29	2.25	2.32	2.38	2.45	2.52	2.58	2.65	2.71	2.78	2.85	2.91	2.98	3.04	3.11	3.17	3.24	3.31	3.37
30	2.23	2.30	2.37	2.43	2.50	2.56	2.63	2.69	2.76	2.83	2.89	2.96	3.02	3.09	3.15	3.22	3.29	3.35
31	2.21	2.28	2.35	2.41	2.48	2.54	2.61	2.67	2.74	2.81	2.87	2.94	3.00	3.07	3.14	[illegible]	3.27	3.33
32	2.19	2.26	2.33	2.39	2.46	2.52	2.59	2.66	2.72	2.79	2.85	2.92	2.98	3.05	3.12	[illegible]	3.25	3.31
33	2.17	2.24	2.31	2.37	2.44	2.50	2.57	2.64	2.70	2.77	2.83	2.90	2.96	3.03	3.10	[illegible]	3.23	3.29
34	2.16	2.22	2.29	2.35	2.42	2.48	2.55	2.62	2.68	2.75	2.81	2.88	2.95	3.01	3.08	[illegible]	3.21	3.27
35	2.14	2.20	2.27	2.33	2.40	2.47	2.53	2.60	2.66	2.73	2.79	2.86	2.93	2.99	3.06	[illegible]	3.19	3.25
36	2.12	2.18	2.25	2.31	2.38	2.45	2.51	2.58	2.64	2.71	2.77	2.84	2.91	2.97	3.04	[illegible]	3.17	3.24
37	2.10	2.16	2.23	2.29	2.36	2.43	2.49	2.56	2.62	2.69	2.76	2.82	2.89	2.95	3.02	3.08	3.15	3.22
38	2.08	2.14	2.21	2.28	2.34	2.41	2.47	2.54	2.60	2.67	2.74	2.80	2.87	2.93	3.00	3.06	3.13	3.20
39	2.06	2.12	2.19	2.26	2.32	2.39	2.45	2.52	2.58	2.65	2.72	2.78	2.85	2.91	2.98	3.05	3.11	3.18
40	2.04	2.11	2.17	2.24	2.30	2.37	2.43	2.50	2.57	2.63	2.70	2.76	2.83	2.89	2.96	3.03	3.09	3.16
41	2.02	2.09	2.15	2.22	2.28	2.35	2.41	2.48	2.55	2.61	2.68	2.74	2.81	2.88	2.94	3.01	3.07	3.14
42	2.00	2.07	2.13	2.20	2.26	2.33	2.40	2.46	2.53	2.59	2.66	2.72	2.79	2.86	2.92	2.99	3.05	3.12
43	1.98	2.05	2.11	2.18	2.24	2.31	2.38	2.44	2.51	2.57	2.64	2.70	2.77	2.84	2.90	2.97	3.03	3.10
44	1.96	2.03	2.09	2.16	2.22	2.29	2.36	2.42	2.49	2.55	2.62	2.69	2.75	2.82	2.88	2.95	3.01	3.08
45	1.94	2.01	2.07	2.14	2.21	2.27	2.34	2.40	2.47	2.53	2.60	2.67	2.73	2.80	2.86	2.93	2.99	3.06
46	1.92	1.99	2.05	2.12	2.19	2.25	2.32	2.38	2.45	2.51	2.58	2.65	2.71	2.78	2.84	2.91	2.98	3.04
47	1.90	1.97	2.03	2.10	2.17	2.23	2.30	2.36	2.43	2.50	2.56	2.63	2.69	2.76	2.82	2.89	2.96	3.02
48	1.88	1.95	2.02	2.08	2.15	2.21	2.28	2.34	2.41	2.48	2.54	2.61	2.67	2.74	2.80	2.87	2.94	3.00
49	1.86	1.93	2.00	2.06	2.13	2.19	2.26	2.32	2.39	2.46	2.52	2.59	2.65	2.72	2.79	2.85	2.92	2.98
50	1.85	1.91	1.98	2.04	2.11	2.17	2.24	2.31	2.37	2.44	2.50	2.57	2.63	2.70	2.77	2.83	2.90	2.96
51	1.83	1.89	1.96	2.02	2.09	2.15	2.22	2.29	2.35	2.42	2.48	2.55	2.62	2.68	2.75	2.81	2.88	2.94
52	1.81	1.87	1.94	2.00	2.07	2.14	2.20	2.27	2.33	2.40	2.46	2.53	2.60	2.66	2.73	2.79	2.86	2.92
53	1.79	1.85	1.92	1.98	2.05	2.12	2.18	2.25	2.31	2.38	2.44	2.51	2.58	2.64	2.71	2.77	2.84	2.91
54	1.77	1.83	1.90	1.96	2.03	2.10	2.16	2.23	2.29	2.36	2.43	2.49	2.56	2.62	2.69	2.75	2.82	2.89
55	1.75	1.81	1.88	1.95	2.01	2.08	2.14	2.21	2.27	2.34	2.41	2.47	2.54	2.60	2.67	2.73	2.80	2.87
56	1.73	1.79	1.86	1.93	1.99	2.06	2.12	2.19	2.25	2.32	2.39	2.45	2.52	2.58	2.65	2.72	2.78	2.85
57	1.71	1.77	1.84	1.91	1.97	2.04	2.10	2.17	2.24	2.30	2.37	2.43	2.50	2.56	2.63	2.70	2.76	2.83
58	1.69	1.76	1.82	1.89	1.95	2.02	2.08	2.15	2.22	2.28	2.35	2.41	2.48	2.54	2.61	2.68	2.74	2.81
59	1.67	1.74	1.80	1.87	1.93	2.00	2.06	2.13	2.20	2.26	2.33	2.39	2.46	2.53	2.59	2.66	2.72	2.79
60	1.65	1.72	1.78	1.85	1.91	1.98	2.05	2.11	2.18	2.24	2.31	2.37	2.44	2.51	2.57	2.64	2.70	2.77
61	1.63	1.70	1.76	1.83	1.89	1.96	2.03	2.09	2.16	2.22	2.29	2.35	2.42	2.49	2.55	2.62	2.68	2.75
62	1.61	1.68	1.74	1.81	1.88	1.94	2.01	2.07	2.14	2.20	2.27	2.34	2.40	2.47	2.53	2.60	2.66	2.73
63	1.59	1.66	1.72	1.79	1.86	1.92	1.99	2.05	2.12	2.18	2.25	2.32	2.38	2.45	2.51	2.58	2.65	2.71
64	1.57	1.64	1.70	1.77	1.84	1.90	1.97	2.03	2.10	2.17	2.23	2.30	2.36	2.43	2.49	2.56	2.63	2.69
65	1.55	1.62	1.69	1.75	1.82	1.88	1.95	2.01	2.08	2.15	2.21	2.28	2.34	2.41	2.47	2.54	2.61	2.67
66	1.53	1.60	1.67	1.73	1.80	1.86	1.93	1.99	2.06	2.13	2.19	2.26	2.32	2.39	2.46	2.52	2.59	2.65
67	1.51	1.58	1.65	1.71	1.78	1.84	1.91	1.98	2.04	2.11	2.17	2.24	2.30	2.37	2.44	2.50	2.57	2.63
68	1.50	1.56	1.63	1.69	1.76	1.82	1.89	1.96	2.02	2.09	2.15	2.22	2.28	2.35	2.42	2.48	2.55	2.61
69	1.48	1.54	1.61	1.67	1.74	1.80	1.87	1.94	2.00	2.07	2.13	2.20	2.27	2.33	2.40	2.46	2.53	2.59
70	1.46	1.52	1.59	1.65	1.72	1.79	1.85	1.92	1.98	2.05	2.11	2.18	2.25	2.31	2.38	2.44	2.51	2.57

Height (in inches)

$FEV_{1.0}$ in liters = 0.0658H−0.0194A−0.802; SEE = 0.33 liters.

$FEV_{1.0}$ = one-second forced expiratory volume; H = height in inches; A = age in years; SEE = standard error of estimate; ATPS = ambient temperature and pressure saturated with water vapor. The values in this table have been adapted for use at a room temperature of approximately 77 F (25 C).

The axes of the table are age (in years) at the side and height (in inches) at bottom. The predicted normal $FEV_{1.0}$ in liters for the female patient is found at the intersection of the row for her age and the column for her height.

[C7798]

APPENDIX XIII

Table 5.—Predicted Normal FVC Values for Women (ATPS

Age	55	56	57	58	59	60	61	62	63	64	65	66	67	68	69	70	71	72
20	2.48	2.57	2.67	2.77	2.86	2.96	3.06	3.15	3.25	3.34	3.44	3.54	3.63	3.73	3.83	3.92	4.02	4.12
21	2.46	2.55	2.65	2.75	2.85	2.94	3.04	3.14	3.23	3.33	3.42	3.52	3.62	3.71	3.81	3.91	4.00	4.10
22	2.44	2.54	2.64	2.73	2.83	2.93	3.02	3.12	3.22	3.31	3.41	3.50	3.60	3.70	3.79	3.89	3.99	4.08
23	2.43	2.52	2.62	2.72	2.81	2.91	3.01	3.10	3.20	3.29	3.39	3.49	3.58	3.68	3.78	3.87	3.97	4.07
24	2.41	2.51	2.60	2.70	2.80	2.89	2.99	3.09	3.18	3.28	3.37	3.47	3.57	3.66	3.76	3.86	3.95	4.05
25	2.39	2.49	2.59	2.68	2.78	2.88	2.97	3.07	3.17	3.26	3.36	3.45	3.55	3.65	3.74	3.84	3.94	4.03
26	2.38	2.47	2.57	2.67	2.76	2.86	2.96	3.05	3.15	3.24	3.34	3.44	3.53	3.63	3.73	3.82	3.92	4.02
27	2.36	2.46	2.55	2.65	2.75	2.84	2.94	3.04	3.13	3.23	3.32	3.42	3.52	3.61	3.71	3.81	3.90	4.00
28	2.34	2.44	2.54	2.63	2.73	2.83	2.92	3.02	3.12	3.21	3.31	3.40	3.50	3.60	3.69	3.79	3.89	3.98
29	2.33	2.42	2.52	2.62	2.71	2.81	2.91	3.00	3.10	3.19	3.29	3.39	3.48	3.58	3.68	3.77	3.87	3.97
30	2.31	2.41	2.50	2.60	2.70	2.79	2.89	2.99	3.08	3.18	3.27	3.37	3.47	3.56	3.66	3.76	3.85	3.95
31	2.29	2.39	2.49	2.58	2.68	2.78	2.87	2.97	3.07	3.16	3.26	3.35	3.45	3.55	3.64	3.74	3.84	3.93
32	2.28	2.37	2.47	2.57	2.66	2.76	2.86	2.95	3.05	3.14	3.24	3.34	3.43	3.53	3.63	3.72	3.82	3.92
33	2.26	2.36	2.45	2.55	2.65	2.74	2.84	2.94	3.03	3.13	3.22	3.32	3.42	3.51	3.61	3.71	3.80	3.90
34	2.24	2.34	2.44	2.53	2.63	2.73	2.82	2.92	3.02	3.11	3.21	3.30	3.40	3.50	3.59	3.69	3.79	3.88
35	2.23	2.32	2.42	2.52	2.61	2.71	2.81	2.90	3.00	3.09	3.19	3.29	3.38	3.48	3.58	3.67	3.77	3.87
36	2.21	2.31	2.40	2.50	2.60	2.69	2.79	2.89	2.98	3.08	2.17	3.27	3.37	3.46	3.56	3.66	3.75	3.85
37	2.19	2.29	2.39	2.48	2.58	2.68	2.77	2.87	2.97	3.06	3.16	3.25	3.35	3.45	3.54	3.64	3.74	3.83
38	2.18	2.27	2.37	2.47	2.56	2.66	2.76	2.85	2.95	3.05	3.14	3.24	3.33	3.43	3.53	3.62	3.72	3.82
39	2.16	2.26	2.35	2.45	2.55	2.64	2.74	2.84	2.93	3.03	3.12	3.22	3.32	3.41	3.51	3.61	3.70	3.80
40	2.14	2.24	2.34	2.43	2.53	2.63	2.72	2.82	2.92	3.01	3.11	3.20	3.30	3.40	3.49	3.59	3.69	3.78
41	2.13	2.22	2.32	2.42	2.51	2.61	2.71	2.80	2.90	3.00	3.09	3.19	3.28	3.38	3.48	3.57	3.67	3.77
42	2.11	2.21	2.30	2.40	2.50	2.59	2.69	2.79	2.88	2.98	3.07	3.17	3.27	3.36	3.46	3.56	3.65	3.75
43	2.09	2.19	2.29	2.38	2.48	2.58	2.67	2.77	2.87	2.96	3.06	3.15	3.25	3.35	3.44	3.54	3.64	3.73
44	2.08	2.17	2.27	2.37	2.46	2.56	2.66	2.75	2.85	2.95	3.04	3.14	3.23	3.33	3.43	3.52	3.62	3.72
45	2.06	2.16	2.25	2.35	2.45	2.54	2.64	2.74	2.83	2.93	3.02	3.12	3.22	3.31	3.41	3.51	3.60	3.70
46	2.04	2.14	2.24	2.33	2.43	2.53	2.62	2.72	2.82	2.91	3.01	3.10	3.20	3.30	3.39	3.49	3.59	3.68
47	2.03	2.12	2.22	2.32	2.41	2.51	2.61	2.70	2.80	2.90	2.99	3.09	3.18	3.28	3.38	3.47	3.57	3.67
48	2.01	2.11	2.20	2.30	2.40	2.49	2.59	2.69	2.78	2.88	2.97	3.07	3.17	3.26	3.36	3.46	3.55	3.65
49	1.99	2.09	2.19	2.28	2.38	2.48	2.57	2.67	2.77	2.86	2.96	3.05	3.15	3.25	3.34	3.44	3.54	3.63
50	1.98	2.07	2.17	2.27	2.36	2.46	2.56	2.65	2.75	2.85	2.94	3.04	3.13	3.23	3.33	3.42	3.52	3.62
51	1.96	2.06	2.15	2.25	2.35	2.44	2.54	2.64	2.73	2.83	2.92	3.02	3.12	3.21	3.31	3.41	3.50	3.60
52	1.94	2.04	2.14	2.23	2.33	2.43	2.52	2.62	2.72	2.81	2.91	3.00	3.10	3.20	3.29	3.39	3.49	3.58
53	1.93	2.02	2.12	2.22	2.31	2.41	2.51	2.60	2.70	2.80	2.89	2.99	3.08	3.18	3.28	3.37	3.47	3.57
54	1.91	2.01	2.10	2.20	2.30	2.39	2.49	2.59	2.68	2.78	2.87	2.97	3.07	3.16	3.26	3.36	3.45	3.55
55	1.90	1.99	2.09	2.18	2.28	2.38	2.47	2.57	2.67	2.76	2.86	2.95	3.05	3.15	3.24	3.34	3.44	3.53
56	1.88	1.97	2.07	2.17	2.26	2.36	2.46	2.55	2.65	2.75	2.84	2.94	3.03	3.13	3.23	3.32	3.42	3.52
57	1.86	1.96	2.05	2.15	2.25	2.34	2.44	2.54	2.63	2.73	2.82	2.92	3.02	3.11	3.21	3.31	3.40	3.50
58	1.85	1.94	2.04	2.13	2.23	2.33	2.42	2.52	2.62	2.71	2.81	2.90	3.00	3.10	3.19	3.29	3.39	3.48
59	1.83	1.92	2.02	2.12	2.21	2.31	2.41	2.50	2.60	2.70	2.79	2.89	2.98	3.08	3.18	3.27	3.37	3.47
60	1.81	1.91	2.00	2.10	2.20	2.29	2.39	2.49	2.58	2.68	2.78	2.87	2.97	3.06	3.16	3.26	3.35	3.45
61	1.80	1.89	1.99	2.08	2.18	2.28	2.37	2.47	2.57	2.66	2.76	2.85	2.95	3.05	3.14	3.24	3.34	3.43
62	1.78	1.87	1.97	2.07	2.16	2.26	2.36	2.45	2.55	2.65	2.74	2.84	2.93	3.03	3.13	3.22	3.32	3.42
63	1.76	1.86	1.95	2.05	2.15	2.24	2.34	2.44	2.53	2.63	2.73	2.82	2.92	3.01	3.11	3.21	3.30	3.40
64	1.75	1.84	1.94	2.03	2.13	2.23	2.32	2.42	2.52	2.61	2.71	2.80	2.90	3.00	3.09	3.19	3.29	3.38
65	1.73	1.82	1.92	2.02	2.11	2.21	2.31	2.40	2.50	2.60	2.69	2.79	2.88	2.98	3.08	3.17	3.27	3.37
66	1.71	1.81	1.90	2.00	2.10	2.19	2.29	2.39	2.48	2.58	2.68	2.77	2.87	2.96	3.06	3.16	3.25	3.35
67	1.70	1.79	1.89	1.98	2.08	2.18	2.27	2.37	2.47	2.56	2.66	2.75	2.85	2.95	3.04	3.14	3.24	3.33
68	1.68	1.77	1.87	1.97	2.06	2.16	2.26	2.35	2.45	2.55	2.64	2.74	2.83	2.93	3.03	3.12	3.22	3.32
69	1.66	1.76	1.85	1.95	2.05	2.14	2.24	2.34	2.43	2.53	2.63	2.72	2.82	2.91	3.01	3.11	3.20	3.30
70	1.65	1.74	1.84	1.93	2.03	2.13	2.22	2.32	2.42	2.51	2.61	2.70	2.80	2.90	2.99	3.09	3.19	3.28

Height (in inches)

FVC in liters = 0.0963H−0.0166A−2.487; SEE = 0.371 liters.

FVC = forced vital capacity; H = height in inches; A = age in years; SEE = standard error of estimate; ATPS = ambient temperature and pressure saturated with water vapor. The values in this table have been adapted for use at a room temperature of approximately 77 F (25 C).

The axes of the table are age (in years) at the side and height (in inches) at the bottom. The predicted normal FVC in liters for the female patient is found at the intersection of the row for her age and the column for her height.

[C7799]

APPENDIX XIII

Table 6.—Predicted Normal MVV Values for Men (BTPS)

Age	59	60	61	62	63	64	65	66	67	68	69	70	71	72	73	74	75	76	77	78	79
20	153	157	160	164	167	170	174	177	181	184	187	191	194	198	201	204	208	211	[illegible]	218	221
21	152	156	159	162	166	169	173	176	179	183	186	189	193	197	200	203	206	210	[illegible]	217	220
22	151	154	158	161	165	168	171	175	178	181	185	188	192	195	198	202	205	209	[illegible]	215	219
23	150	153	156	160	163	167	170	173	177	180	184	187	190	194	197	201	204	207	[illegible]	214	218
24	148	152	155	159	162	165	169	172	176	179	182	186	189	192	196	199	203	206	[illegible]	213	216
25	147	151	154	157	161	164	168	171	174	178	181	184	188	191	195	198	201	205	[illegible]	212	215
26	146	149	153	156	159	163	166	170	173	176	180	183	187	190	193	197	200	204	[illegible]	210	214
27	145	148	151	155	158	162	165	168	172	175	179	182	185	189	192	195	199	202	[illegible]	209	212
28	143	147	150	154	157	160	164	167	171	174	177	181	184	187	191	194	198	201	204	208	211
29	142	146	149	152	156	159	162	166	169	173	176	179	183	186	190	193	196	200	203	207	210
30	141	144	148	151	154	158	161	165	168	171	175	178	182	185	188	192	195	198	202	205	209
31	140	143	146	150	153	157	160	163	167	170	174	177	180	184	187	190	194	197	[illegible]	204	207
32	138	142	145	149	152	155	159	162	165	169	172	176	179	182	186	189	193	196	[illegible]	203	206
33	137	140	144	147	151	154	157	161	164	168	171	174	178	181	185	188	191	195	[illegible]	201	205
34	136	139	143	146	149	153	156	160	163	166	170	173	177	180	183	187	190	193	[illegible]	200	204
35	135	138	141	145	148	152	155	158	162	165	168	172	175	179	182	185	189	192	[illegible]	199	202
36	133	137	140	143	147	150	154	157	160	164	167	171	174	177	181	184	188	191	[illegible]	198	201
37	132	135	139	142	146	149	152	156	159	163	166	169	173	176	180	183	186	190	[illegible]	196	200
38	131	134	138	141	144	148	151	155	158	161	165	168	171	175	178	182	185	188	[illegible]	195	199
39	130	133	136	140	143	146	150	153	157	160	163	167	170	174	177	180	184	187	[illegible]	194	197
40	128	132	135	138	142	145	149	152	155	159	162	166	169	172	176	179	183	186	189	193	196
41	127	130	134	137	141	144	147	151	154	158	161	164	168	171	174	178	181	185	188	191	195
42	126	129	133	136	139	143	146	149	153	156	160	163	166	170	173	177	180	183	187	190	194
43	124	128	131	135	138	141	145	148	152	155	158	162	165	169	172	175	179	182	186	189	192
44	123	127	130	133	137	140	144	147	150	154	157	161	164	167	171	174	177	181	184	188	191
45	122	125	129	132	136	139	142	146	149	152	156	159	163	166	169	173	176	180	183	186	190
46	121	124	127	131	134	138	141	144	148	151	155	158	161	165	168	172	175	178	182	185	189
47	119	123	126	130	133	136	140	143	147	150	153	157	160	164	167	170	174	177	180	184	187
48	118	122	125	128	132	135	139	142	145	149	152	155	159	162	166	169	172	176	179	183	186
49	117	120	124	127	130	134	137	141	144	147	151	154	158	161	164	168	171	175	178	181	185
50	116	119	122	126	129	133	136	139	143	146	150	153	156	160	163	167	170	173	177	180	183
51	114	118	121	125	128	131	135	138	142	145	148	152	155	158	162	165	169	172	175	179	182
52	113	117	120	123	127	130	133	137	140	144	147	150	154	157	161	164	167	171	174	178	181
53	112	115	119	122	125	129	132	136	139	142	146	149	153	156	159	163	166	170	173	176	180
54	111	114	117	121	124	128	131	134	138	141	145	148	151	155	158	161	165	168	172	175	178
55	109	113	116	120	123	126	130	133	136	140	143	147	150	153	157	160	164	167	170	174	177
56	108	111	115	118	122	125	128	132	135	139	142	145	149	152	156	159	162	166	169	173	176
57	107	110	114	117	120	124	127	131	134	137	141	144	148	151	154	158	161	164	168	171	175
58	106	109	112	116	119	123	126	129	133	136	139	143	146	150	153	156	160	163	167	170	173
59	104	108	111	114	118	121	125	128	131	135	138	142	145	148	152	155	159	162	165	169	172
60	103	106	110	113	117	120	123	127	130	134	137	140	144	147	151	154	157	161	164	167	171
61	102	105	109	112	115	119	122	126	129	132	136	139	142	146	149	153	156	159	163	166	170
62	101	104	107	111	114	117	121	124	128	131	134	138	141	145	148	151	155	158	162	165	168
63	99	103	106	109	113	116	120	123	126	130	133	137	140	143	147	150	154	157	160	164	167
64	98	101	105	108	112	115	118	122	125	129	132	135	139	142	145	149	152	156	159	162	166
65	97	100	104	107	110	114	117	120	124	127	131	134	137	141	144	148	151	154	158	161	165
66	96	99	102	106	109	112	116	119	123	126	129	133	136	140	143	146	150	153	157	160	163
67	94	98	101	104	108	111	115	118	121	125	128	132	135	138	142	145	148	152	155	159	162
68	93	96	100	103	107	110	113	117	120	123	127	130	134	137	140	144	147	151	154	157	161
69	92	95	99	102	105	109	112	115	119	122	126	129	132	136	139	143	146	149	153	156	160
70	90	94	97	101	104	107	111	114	118	121	124	128	131	135	138	141	145	148	151	155	158
	59	**60**	**61**	**62**	**63**	**64**	**65**	**66**	**67**	**68**	**69**	**70**	**71**	**72**	**73**	**74**	**75**	**76**	**77**	**78**	**79**

Height (in inches)

MVV in liters per minute* = 3.39H−1.26A−21.4; SEE = 29 liters/min.

MVV = maximal voluntary ventilation; H = height in inches; A = age in years; SEE = standard error of estimate; BTPS = body temperature and pressure saturated with water vapor. Correction for temperature is necessary for use of these values with spirometer data.

The axes of the table are age (in years) at the side and height (in inches) at the bottom. The predicted normal MVV in liters per minute for the male patient is found at the intersection of the row for his age and the column for his height.

*From VA-Army Cooperative Study, Kory, Callahan, Boren and Snyder, *Amer J Med* **30**:243-258 (Feb) 1961.

[C7800]

APPENDIX XIII

Table 7.—Predicted Normal MVV Values for Women (BTPS)

Age	55	56	57	58	59	60	61	62	63	64	65	66	67	68	69	70	71	72
20	112	114	116	119	122	124	127	130	133	135	138	141	143	146	149	152	154	157
21	111	113	115	118	121	123	126	129	132	134	137	140	142	145	148	151	153	156
22	110	112	114	117	120	122	125	128	131	133	136	139	141	144	147	150	152	155
23	109	111	113	116	119	121	124	127	130	132	135	138	140	143	146	149	151	154
24	108	110	112	115	118	120	123	126	129	131	134	137	139	142	145	148	150	153
25	107	109	111	114	117	119	122	125	128	130	133	136	138	141	144	147	149	152
26	106	108	110	113	116	118	121	124	127	129	132	135	137	140	143	146	148	151
27	105	107	109	112	115	117	120	123	126	128	131	134	136	139	142	144	147	150
28	104	106	108	111	114	116	119	122	125	127	130	133	135	138	141	143	146	149
29	103	105	107	110	113	115	118	121	123	126	129	132	134	137	140	142	145	148
30	102	104	106	109	112	114	117	120	122	125	128	131	133	136	139	141	144	147
31	101	102	105	108	111	113	116	119	121	124	127	130	132	135	138	140	143	146
32	100	101	104	107	110	112	115	118	120	123	126	129	131	134	137	139	142	145
33	99	100	103	106	109	111	114	117	119	122	125	128	130	133	136	138	141	144
34	98	99	102	105	108	110	113	116	118	121	124	127	129	132	135	137	140	143
35	97	98	101	104	107	109	112	115	117	120	123	126	128	131	134	136	139	142
36	96	97	100	103	106	108	111	114	116	119	122	125	127	130	133	135	138	141
37	95	96	99	102	105	107	110	113	115	118	121	124	126	129	132	134	137	140
38	94	95	98	101	104	106	109	112	114	117	120	123	125	128	131	133	136	139
39	93	94	97	100	103	105	108	111	113	116	119	122	124	127	130	132	135	138
40	92	93	96	99	102	104	107	110	112	115	118	121	123	126	129	131	134	137
41	91	92	95	98	101	103	106	109	111	114	117	120	122	125	128	130	133	136
42	90	91	94	97	100	102	105	108	110	113	116	119	121	124	127	129	132	135
43	89	90	93	96	99	101	104	107	109	112	115	118	120	123	126	128	131	134
44	88	89	92	95	98	100	103	106	108	111	114	117	119	122	125	127	130	133
45	87	88	91	94	97	99	102	105	107	110	113	116	118	121	124	126	129	132
46	85	87	90	93	96	98	101	104	106	109	112	114	117	120	123	125	128	131
47	84	86	89	92	95	97	100	103	105	108	111	113	116	119	122	124	127	130
48	83	85	88	91	93	96	99	102	104	107	110	112	115	118	121	123	126	129
49	82	84	87	90	92	95	98	101	103	106	109	111	114	117	120	122	125	128
50	81	83	86	89	91	94	97	100	102	105	108	110	113	116	119	121	124	127
51	80	82	85	88	90	93	96	99	101	104	107	109	112	115	118	120	123	126
52	79	81	84	87	89	92	95	98	100	103	106	108	111	114	117	119	122	125
53	78	80	83	86	88	91	94	97	99	102	105	107	110	113	116	118	121	124
54	77	79	82	85	87	90	93	96	98	101	104	106	109	112	115	117	120	123
55	76	78	81	84	86	89	92	95	97	100	103	105	108	111	114	116	119	122
56	75	77	80	83	85	88	91	94	96	99	102	104	107	110	113	115	118	121
57	74	76	79	82	84	87	90	93	95	98	101	103	106	109	112	114	117	120
58	73	75	78	81	83	86	89	92	94	97	100	102	105	108	111	113	116	119
59	72	74	77	80	82	85	88	91	93	96	99	101	104	107	110	112	115	118
60	71	73	76	79	81	84	87	90	92	95	98	100	103	106	109	111	114	117
61	70	72	75	78	80	83	86	89	91	94	97	99	102	105	108	110	113	116
62	69	71	74	77	79	82	85	88	90	93	96	98	101	104	107	109	112	115
63	68	70	73	76	78	81	84	87	89	92	95	97	100	103	105	108	111	114
64	67	69	72	75	77	80	83	86	88	91	94	96	99	102	104	107	110	113
65	66	68	71	74	76	79	82	84	87	90	93	95	98	101	103	106	109	112
66	65	67	70	73	75	78	81	83	86	89	92	94	97	100	102	105	108	111
67	63	66	69	72	74	77	80	82	85	88	91	93	96	99	101	104	107	110
68	62	65	68	71	73	76	79	81	84	87	90	92	95	98	100	103	106	109
69	61	64	67	70	72	75	78	80	83	86	89	91	94	97	99	102	105	108
70	60	63	66	69	71	74	77	79	82	85	88	90	93	96	98	101	104	107

Height (in inches)

MVV in liters per minute° = 2.712H−1.008A−17.2; SEE = 29 liters/min.

MVV = maximal voluntary ventilation; H = height in inches; A = age in years; SEE = standard error of estimate; BTPS = body temperature and pressure saturated with water vapor. Correction for temperature is necessary for use of these values with spirometer data.

The axes of the table are age (in years) at the side and height (in inches) at the bottom. The predicted normal MVV in liters per minute for the female patient is found at the intersection of the row for her age and the column for her height.

°The Committee has set the values for MVV for women 20% lower than the values used for men (Table 6).

[C7843]

GLOSSARY

OF

MEDICAL TERMS

Table of Glossaries

Introduction to the Glossaries

It is said that learning the nomenclature of medicine is equivalent to mastering a second language, in addition to that of everyday English. Indeed, the very large number of technical terms in medicine puts the layman at a disadvantage in understanding medical data. In order to assist the reader in overcoming this problem, the glossaries that follow are offered.

These glossaries are especially helpful in the non-physician's evaluation of disability cases, because the terms defined and discussed are precisely those most relevant to the requirements of the Listings of impairments. The glossaries reprinted here are from federal documents; more specifically, they are from the "Instructor's Manuals" used in the training of disability examiners.

GLOSSARY OF MEDICAL TERMS

To facilitate ease of use, the glossaries are divided into the principal body systems corresponding to the Listings. There may also be more than one glossary under each body system.

In addition, the Listings most pertinent to a given glossary are listed, in order to help the reader find what he desires most quickly. More than one glossary may contain information relevant to a given Listing, and there is some degree of over-lap among these glossaries which may further save time when searching for information.

MUSCULOSKELETAL SYSTEM

Glossary 1

General Terms

Adult Listings— 1.02, 1.03, 1.04, 1.05, 1.08, 1.09

Child Listings— 101.02, 101.03, 101.05, 101.08

Abduction—Moving away from the midline of the body.

Acute—Having a short and relatively severe course.

Adduction—Moving toward the midline of the body.

Adhesion—A fibrous band or structure by which parts abnormally adhere.

Agglutination—Clumping of cells distributed in fluid.

Anesthesia—Partial or complete loss of sensation. Numbness.

Ankylosis—Bony fusion and fixation of a joint.

Apophyseal—Pertaining to a bony process or outgrowth that has never been entirely separated from the bone of which it forms a part.

Arthritis—Inflammation of a joint.

Arthrodesis—Surgical fixation of a joint.

Arthropathy—Any joint disease.

Arthroplasty—Plastic repair of a joint.

Articulation—The place of union or junction between two or more bones.

Aspiration—The removal of fluid.

Atrophy—Wasting away of tissue.

Biopsy—The removal and examination, usually microscopic, of tissue or other material from the body for purposes of diagnosis.

Bursa—Soft tissue sac located between parts that move upon one another; often lying between bones and muscles.

Bursitis—Inflammation of a bursa.

Calcaneus—The heel bone.

Carpus—The wrist.

Cartilage—Elastic substance attached to articular bone surface, and forming certain parts of the skeleton.

Cervical—Pertaining to the neck.

Charcot Joint—Diseased, unstable joint due to infection (usually syphilis), trauma, or faulty innervation.

Chronic—Of long duration; not acute.

Circumduction—Circular movement.

Clavicle—The collar bone.

Connective Tissue—Tissue which supports and binds together various structures of the body.

Contracture—The permanent shortening of a muscle, tendon, or structure so that it cannot be straightened, flexed, or extended. Scar tissue often results in contractures.

Contralateral—Situated on the other side.

Coccyx—The last bone in the vertebral column.

Coxae—Innominate bone, or hip bone; composed of three bones: (1) ilium, (2) ischium, and (3) pubis.

Crepitation—Crackling noise, often heard in arthritic joints on movement.

Decalcification—Loss of calcium from bone.

Disarticulation—Amputation or separation at a joint.

Disc—See Nucleus Pulposus.

Discectomy—Excision of an intervertebral disc.

Distal—Farthest away from trunk. (The fingernail is at the distal portion of the finger.)

Dorsolumbar—Referring to middle and low back.

Eburnation—State of being highly polished.

Effusion—The escape of fluid into a part or tissue.

Exacerbation—Increase in the severity of any symptoms or disease.

Exotosis—A bony growth projecting outward from the surface of a bone.

Extension—Straightening.

Femur—The thigh bone.

Fibrosis—The formation of scar tissue, composed of or containing fibers.

Fibula—The slender bone at the outer part of the lower leg.

Fixation—The condition of being held in a fixed position.

Foramen—The opening in a bone for transmissions of vessels, nerves, etc.

Flail—Showing abnormal mobility.

Flexion—The act of bending.

Fusion—The abnormal coherence of adjacent parts of bodies (may be surgically induced).

Hematocrit—A reading (by laboratory test) describing the volume of red cells per unit of circulating blood.

Hemipelvectomy—Amputation of a lower limb through the sacroiliac joint.

Histologic—Pertaining to tissue.

Humerus—The bone extending from the shoulder to the elbow.

Hyperextension—Straightening beyond 180 degrees.

Hypertrophy—Morbid cellular overgrowth or enlargement.

Innominate Bone—See Coxae.

Innervation—The supply of nerves to a part.

Intervertebral Disc—See Nucleus Pulposus.

Intramedullary—Within the bone marrow canal.

Ischemia—Deficiency of blood in a part.

Kyphosis—Hunchback; outward curvature of thoracic (dorsal) spine.

Laminectomy—The excision of the posterior arch of a vertebra for inspection and exploration of the spinal cord and its nerve roots. This procedure is often followed by the removal of an intervertebral disc and/or a fusion.

Ligaments—Fibrous, connective tissue bands uniting articular ends of bones.

Lordosis—Hollow-back; inward curvature of lower spine.

Metatarsus—The forefoot, between the tarsus and the toes.

Modality—A specific sensory entity, i.e., pain, heat or touch.

Myelogram—An X-ray of the spine involving the injection of opaque dye.

Myositis—Inflammation of a muscle.

Neurogenic—Originating in the nervous system.

Nucleus Pulposus—Semi-elastic cartilage; disc between the vertebrae.

Oscalcis—See Calcaneus.

Osseous—Bony.

Osteitis—Inflammation of a bone.

Osteoarthritis—Chronic degenerative joint disease.

Osteomalacia—Softening of bone due to increased porosity.

Osteomyelitis—Inflammation of bone caused by bacteria.

Osteophytosis—A condition characterized by formation of bony outgrowth.

Osteoporosis—A loss in bony substances producing brittleness and softness of bones.

Osteotomy—Surgical cutting of a bone.

Paravertebral—Beside the spine.

Paresthesia—A perverted sensation.

Patella—Kneecap.

Pelvis—The bony ring interposed between the vertebrae above and the lower limbs below.

Periosteum—Outer covering of long bones.

Phalanges—The bones forming the fingers and toes.

Periarticular—Around a joint.

Polymorphonuclear Leukocytosis—An increase in the number of white blood cells containing a nucleus which is lobed or constructed so as to make it look like two or more nuclei instead of one.

Prosthesis—An artificial part.

Proximal—Nearest; as opposed to distal.

Radicular—Referring to the nerves originating in the spine.

Radius—The bone on the outer or thumb side of the forearm.

Rotation—The process of turning around an axis.

Scapula—The shoulder blade.

Seriologic—Pertaining to blood.

Scoliosis—Abnormal curvature of the spine, usually lateral.

Spondylitis—Arthritis of the spine.

Spondylo- —Denoting relationship to the spine.

Spondylolisthesis—Forward displacement of one vertebra over another.

Spondylosis—Fusion of the vertebrae with one another.

Subcutaneous Nodule—A swelling or lump situated beneath the skin.

Subluxation—A partial dislocation of a bone or joint.

Synovial Fluid—Lubricating fluid in the joint encased by the synovial membrane.

Synovial Membrane—Membrane encasing synovial fluid in a joint.

Tabes—Any wasting (atrophy) of the body.

Tarsus—The instep proper, between the tibia and the metatarsus.

Tarsal—Referring to the instep.

Tendons—Cords or bands which serve to attach muscles to bones.

Tenosynovitis—Inflammation of a tendon sheath.

Tibia—Larger bone of the leg below the knee.

Trauma—An injury caused by mechanical violence, as a blow, twist, etc.

Trochanter—Either of the two processes below the neck of the femur.

Ulna—The inner and larger bone of the forearm, opposite the thumb.

Ulnar Deviation—A twisting of the hands outward at the wrist.

Vertebra—One of the bones of the spinal column.

Glossary 2

Spinal Disorders

Adult Listings— 1.05

Child Listings— 101.05

Ankylosing Spondylitis—Inflammation of the vertebrae resulting in fixation; also called Marie Strumpell Disease.

Annulus—Fibrous ring that encircles the nucleus pulposus.

Apophyseal—Pertaining to a bony outgrowth.

Calcification—Hardening.

Compression Fracture—Crush or collapsing fracture.

Conservative Treatment—Nonoperative treatment; i.e., bed rest, traction, analgesics, braces, exercises; etc.

Discectomy—Surgical removal of intervertebral disc.

Electromyography—A test designed to reveal abnormalities of the nerves in muscles.

Intervertebral Disc—Layer of fibrocartilage between the bodies of vertebrae; composed of an annulus and a nucleus pulposus.

Kyphosis—Outward curvature of thoracic spine (hunchback).

Laminectomy—Surgical removal of lamina.

Lordosis—Inward curvature of lower spine.

Myelography—X-ray of the spine obtained after the injection of a contrast medium into the spine.

Nucleus Pulposus—Semifluid mass of fiber that forms the central portion of an intervertebral disc.

Osteoporosis—Rarefaction, or thinning of bone.

Scoliosis—Lateral deviation of the spine.

Spinal Fusion—Surgical ankylosis (arthrodesis) of 2 or more vertebrae.

Spondylosis—Ankylosis of a vertebral joint.

Glossary 3

Arthritis

Adult Listings— 1.03, 1.04

Child Listings— 101.02

Abduction—Movement away from the median line of the body.

Adduction—Movement toward the median line of the body.

Ankylosis—Abnormal union of two bones at a joint.

Arthrodesis—Surgical stiffening of the joint sometimes resorted to in cases of uncontrollable pain and infection or used to give stability.

Arthropathy—Name given to any type of joint disease.

Atrophy—Wasting away of tissue or cells.

Contracture—A condition of fixed high resistance to passive stretch of a muscle.

Effusion—The escape of fluid into a part or tissue.

Erosion—Small defects in the margins of the bones near articulating surfaces caused by the rubbing of bones together.

Extension—The straightening of a part of the body at a joint.

Flexion—The bending of a part of the body at a joint.

Lipping—The development of a bony structure.

Osteophyte—A bony outgrowth.

Osteoporosis—A decrease in tissue mass in the bone or the formation of cavities in the bone.

Subluxation—An incomplete or partial dislocation of a joint.

Glossary 4

Fractures/Surgery

Adult Listings— 1.10, 1.11, 1.12, 1.13

Child Listings— 101.03

Closed Reduction—Manipulative correction of a fracture without incision.

Comminuted Fracture—One in which the bone has been broken into small fragments at the fracture site.

Compound Fracture—One in which there is an external wound leading to the fracture site (open fracture).

Full Weight Bearing—Ability of a leg to support full body weight.

Hemipelvectomy—Amputation through the sacroiliac joint.

Hip disarticulation—Amputation through the hip joint.

GLOSSARY OF MEDICAL TERMS

Ischemia—Deficiency of blood in a part of the body.

Nonunion—Failure of the ends of a fractured bone to unite.

Open Reduction—Correction of a fracture after incision into the fracture site.

Prosthesis—Artificial limb or appliance.

Simple Fracture—One in which there is no open wound leading to the site of the fracture (closed fracture).

Staged Surgical Procedures—Planned series of operations.

Tarsal Region—Instep; the area of the tarsal bones in the foot.

SPECIAL SENSES AND SPEECH

Glossary 5

Auditory System

Adult Listings— 2.07, 2.08

Child Listings— 102.08(a)(b)

Ac—Air conduction.

Acou—Pertaining to sound, or sense of hearing.

Acquired Deafness—Hearing loss developed due to outside causes, degeneration.

Air Conduction—The transmission of sound vibrations through the external auditory canal and the middle ear and into the inner ear.

Amplification—Process of increasing auditory stimulus as a means of improving its perception.

ANSI—American National Standards Institute.

ASHA—American Speech and Hearing Association.

Aud—Pertaining to auditory/hearing.

Audio—Pertaining to auditory/hearing.

Audiogram—A chart for the depiction or notation of the variations in hearing acuity for an individual, both by frequency and decibel levels for both bone and air conduction.

Audiologist—A non-medical person skilled in the science of hearing, including rehabilitation of those whose impaired hearing cannot be improved by medical or surgical means.

Audiology—The science of hearing.

Audiometer—An instrument for testing hearing acuity.

Audiometrist—A non-medical person trained to test hearing on an audiometer but not to interpret audiogram or advise therapy.

Auditory Canal (External Meatus)—The tube through which sound vibrations are conducted to the eardrum and middle ear.

Auditory Nerve—(8th cranial [acoustic] nerve)—The nerve that carries sound neural impulses from the inner ear to the hearing center of the brain.

Auri—Pertaining to the ear.

GLOSSARY OF MEDICAL TERMS

Auris—Ear.

a. dextra—right ear.

a. sinistra—left ear.

B C—Bone conduction.

Bekesy Audiometry—A hearing test that provides graphically four distinct types of hearing curves: hearing acuity by frequency and decibel level for bone and air conduction; differentiation of conductive from sensorineural dysfunction; sensorineural diagnostic differentiation such as cochlea from eighth nerve dysfunction; more severe cochlea lesions.

Bone Conduction—Transmission of sound vibrations through the mastoid process or through the skull to activate the sensory organs of the inner ear directly, without involving the transmission structures of the middle or outer ear.

CID—Central Institute for the Deaf.

CNS—Central nervous system.

Cerebro—Cerebrum.

Caloric Test—A test for labyrinthine disturbance. If the normal ear is irrigated with hot water, a rapid, rotary movement of the eye (nystagmus) develops toward the side of the irrigated ear. With cold water, nystagmus occurs in the opposite direction. With a disordered ear, nystagmus develops in the opposite direction, or no nystagmus occurs.

Cochlea—The primary organ of hearing; a closed, spirally wound tube, resembling a snail shell, housing sensory organs which convert the mechanical movement created by vibrations into neural impulses, which are transmitted to the brain.

Cps—Cycles per second.

Conductive Deafness (Transmission Deafness)—Loss of hearing due to mechanical interference with the passage of sound vibrations through the outer and middle ear.

Congenital Deafness—Hearing loss is present since birth, or early in infancy that time of onset cannot be determined.

Cranial Nerve (Eighth Nerve)—The nerve that carries sound neural impulses from the inner ear to the hearing center of the brain.

dB—Decibel.

Deaf-Mutism—The absence of both the sense of hearing and the faculty of speech.

Deafness—The loss of ability to hear, complete or partial. The loss of the power to perceive sound.

Decibel—A unit used to express the ratio of two acoustic powers. One decibel is approximately equal to the smallest difference which the human ear can detect between two volumes of a tone. Used to designate the intensity of sound.

Diplacusis—A hearing disturbance in which the same sound is heard at a different pitch in each ear causing hearing to become distorted and causing a decreased ability in speech discrimination.

Eardrum (Tympanic Membrane)—A membrane that separates the outer and middle ear where the sound wave strikes and vibrates.

Eighth Cranial Nerve—C-VIII. The auditory (acoustic) nerve.

Electronystagmography (ENG)—The electroencephalographic (EEG) recording of eye movements which provide objective documentation of induced and spontaneous nystagmus.

Enceph—Brain.

Eng—Electronystagmography.

Ent—Ear, nose, and throat.

Eustachian Tube—A passage between the nose and the middle ear through which air passes to equalize pressure in the inner ear.

Frequency—A sound wave length that determines the pitch of sound.

Hearing Aid—A mechanical device used to amplify sound.

Hearing Evaluation Specialist—A nonmedical person who uses the audiogram to measure hearing loss for the purpose of recommending hearing aid appliances.

Hertz (Hz)—A unit of frequency equal to one cycle per second (cps).

Hz—Hertz.

-iasis—Pathological state or condition.

Impulsion—The sensation of rocking or swaying associated with labyrinthine disturbance.

Inner Ear—The primary organ of hearing and equilibrium, consisting of the cochlea, the vestibule and the semicircular canals.

-itis—Inflammation.

Labyrinth The system of fluid-filled bony and membranous interconnecting canals within the inner ear. Movements of and variations in pressure of the fluid, caused by sound vibrations, stimulate nerve cells which convert the mechanical movement into nerve impulses to the centers for hearing and balance in the brain.

Labyrinthine-Vestibular Disturbance—The abnormal perceptions which arise from disorders of the inner ear. Cochlear dysfunctions range from hissing, high-pitched ringing sensations to the total absence of sound perception. Vestibular disturbances are primarily associated with position, with abnormal sensations, ranging from dizziness (falling, rocking, swaying and rotating) to the total loss of position perception, with the resulting inability to remain erect or to walk independently.

Mastoiditis—A disorder of the middle ear, with inflammation of the mastoid bone.

Meniere's Disease—A disorder of the inner ear, with symptoms ranging from sensations of ringing, buzzing, and dizziness to total deafness and loss of equilibrium.

Middle Ear—A bony cavity in the skull containing three small bony structures (incus, malleus, stapes) which serve to mechanically transmit sound vibrations from the tympanum (ear drum) to the oval window of the vestibule of the inner ear.

Mixed Hearing Loss—Conductive mechanism and neural components involved in the loss of hearing.

Neuro-otolaryngologist—A physician who specializes with that part of otology dealing especially with the portion of the nervous system related to the ear.

Nystagmus—An involuntary rapid movement of the eyeball.

Organ of Corti—The sensory organ in the inner ear with nerve endings that convert the mechanical sound wave vibrations into neural impulses.

-osis—Diseased condition or process.

Osteo—Bone

Ot—Ear. Otology.

Otitis Media—Infection or inflammation of the middle ear.

Oto—Ear. Otology.

Otol—Otology.

Otolaryngology—A medical specialty combining the knowledge of treatment of disorders of the ear (oto-) and the throat, pharynx, larynx, nasopharynx, and the tracheobronchial tree.

Otologist—A physician specializing in the diagnosis and treatment of ear disorders.

Otosclerosis—A hereditary disease in which there is the formation of spongy bone around the capsule of the inner ear.

Otoscope—A device to examine the outer ear.

Outer Ear—The outer chamber of the ear through which the external sound passes through to the eardrum.

PAL—Psycho-Acoustic Laboratories.

Paroxysm—A sudden recurrence or intensification of symptoms.

-pathy—Disease of.

Perceptive Deafness (Nerve Deafness)—Inability to perceive air-conducted or bone-conducted sound vibrations due to degeneration of dysfunction of those neural structures which either translate mechanical vibrations into neural impulses or which transmit those impulses to the brain.

Perforated—Punctured.

Peripheral Vertigo—The hallucination of movement induced by irritation of the neural impulse transmission structures other than those located in the brain, i.e., those in the semicircular canals and the vestibule of the inner ear, or, of those nerves which convey nerve impulses from the inner ear to the brain.

Positional Testing—Clinical tests to identify the presence and degree of nystagmus, past pointing, falling reactions; the major responses to labyrinthine-vestibular irritation.

Presbycusis—Progression of bilateral sensorineural hearing loss due to aging.

Proprioceptors—Sensory nerve terminals which give information concerning movements and position of the body. They occur chiefly in the muscles, tendons and the labyrinth.

Pure Tone—A sound frequency free of other tones or harmonics.

Recruitment—An abnormally rapid increase in loudness of sound.

Rinne Test—Tuning fork test for hearing. If the partially deaf ear hears longer by air conduction, the test is positive, indicative of perceptive (nerve) loss. If the sound is heard longer with the fork handle touched to the mastoid process of the partially deaf ear, the test is negative, indicating a conductive loss (mechanical or obstructive defect) which may be correctable or improvable.

Semicircular Canals—The three semicircular tubes of the inner ear which are attached to and communicate with the vestibule and which serve to detect sudden changes in movement of the head and body.

Simulated Hearing Loss—Apparent loss of hearing not due to organic disease; the result from functional (involuntary) disorder or representing malingering.

Speech Audiometer—Instrument that reproduces the spoken voice that measures speech discrimination ability.

Speech Discrimination Tests—Tests for determining the degree of ability to effectively perceive and comprehend speech; employs lists of selected words, phrases and sentences which are read to the individual being tested, with and without amplification.

Speech Reading (Lip Reading)—Ability to understand speech through observation of lip and tongue movements.

Speech Reception Tests—Test for determining the decibel level at which speech can be perceived.

SRT—Speech reception threshold.

Statokinetic System—Includes the labyrinth, eighth nerve, vestibular nuclei.

Temporal Lobe—The region in the cerebrum where sound is perceived.

Threshold—Intensity of a stimulus required to just barely elicit a sound sensation.

Tinnitus—A sensation of ringing, buzzing or clicking in the ear. These sensations may be hallucinatory due to neural irritation, or, actual physical noises such as might be caused by the bones in the middle ear.

Tympanic Membrane—A membrane that separates the outer and middle ear where the sound wave strikes and vibrates.

Utricle (Utriculus)—The major organ of the vestibular system providing perception of balance and movement of the head. It is the larger of the two divisions of the membranous labyrinth, located in the posterior segment of the vestibule.

Vertigo—Inability to maintain equilibrium; an hallucinatory sensation of the surroundings revolving, or moving forward or backward.

Vestibule (Vestibulum Auris)—The bichambered division of the inner ear, situated between the cochlea and the semicircular canals. It serves to convey sound vibrations to the cochlea and is, in combination with the semicircular canals, the organ of balance and equilibrium. The oval and round windows are located in the vestibule.

Vestibular Apparatus—The principal organ of balance, position and equilibrium, consisting of the vestibule, the utricle and the semicircular canals.

Weber Test (Lateralization Test)—A tuning fork test. The stem of a vibrating tuning fork is placed against the top of the forehead. Sound is heard better in the nonaffected ear if there is nerve damage. Sound is heard better in the affected ear if deafness is due to an obstruction of or interference with air conduction.

Glossary 6

Visual System

Adult Listings— 2.02, 2.03, 2.04, 2.05, 2.06

Child Listings— 102.02

Accommodation—The adjustment of the eye for seeing at different distances, accomplished by changing the shape of the crystalline lens through action of the ciliary muscle, thus focusing a clear image on the retina.

Amblyopia—Dimness of vision due to any cause.

Angular distance—The distance in degrees of arc that the field of vision subtends the visual angle. On a visual field chart, the sum of the two meridians in the same plane equals the angular distance.

Anterior Chamber—Space in the front of the eye, bounded in front by the cornea and behind by the iris; filled with aqueous.

Aphakia—Absence of the lens of the eye. Absence of lens in one eye is called monocular aphakia; in both eyes, binocular aphakia.

Aqueous—Clear, watery fluid which fills the anterior and posterior chambers within the front part of the eye.

Astigmatism—Refractive error which prevents the light rays from coming to a single focus on the retina because of different degrees of refraction in the various meridians of the eye.

Binocular Vision—The ability to use the two eyes simultaneously to focus on the same object and to fuse the two images into a single image.

Blepharospasm—Increased winking of the eye.

Cataract—A condition in which the crystalline lens of the eye becomes opaque.

Central Visual Efficiency—An estimate in percentages of the remaining central visual acuity. May be derived from Table 1, Listing 2.04.

Choroid—The vascular, intermediate coat which furnishes nourishment to the other parts of the eyeball.

Ciliary Body—Portion of the uveal tract between the iris and the choroid. It consists of ciliary processes and the ciliary muscle.

Concave Lens—Lens having the power to diverge rays of light; also known as diverging, reducing, negative, myopic, or minus lens, denoted by the sign (-).

Concentric Contraction—A concentric contraction of the visual fields is a contraction affecting all parts of the periphery alike. This definition excludes sector-shaped and irregular contractions.

Conjunctiva—Mucous membrane which lines the posterior aspect of the eyelids and the anterior sclera.

Convergence—The process of directing the visual axes of the two eyes to a near point, with the result that the pupils of the two eyes are closer together.

Convex Lens—Lens having power to converge rays of light and to bring them to a focus; also known as converging, magnifying, hyperopic, or plus lens, denoted by the sign (+).

Cornea—Clear, transparent portion of the outer coat of the eyeball forming the anterior wall of the aqueous chamber.

Corneal Graft—Operation to restore vision by replacing a section of opaque cornea with transparent cornea.

Crystalline Lens—A transparent, colorless body suspended in the eyeball, between the aqueous and the vitreous, the function of which is to bring the rays of light to a focus on the retina.

Cycloplegia—Chronic dilation of the pupil, due to paralysis of the ciliary muscles of the iris, resulting in loss of accommodation.

Cylindrical Lens—A segment of a cylinder, the refractive power of which varies in different meridians.

Diameter—The sum of the two radii in the same axis. (For example, the sum of the nasal and temporal radii of a visual field.)

Diopter—Unit of measurement of strength of refractive power of lenses.

Diplopia—The seeing of one object as two.

Enucleation—Complete surgical removal of the eyeball.

Exophthalmos—Abnormal protrusion of the eyeball.

Field of Vision—The entire area which can be seen without shifting the gaze.

Fixation Point—The target on which the gaze is fixed. On the visual field chart, this point is the center of the concentric circles, the point at which the radii of the circles converge.

Floaters—Small particles consisting of cells or fibrin which move in the vitreous.

Focus—The point to which rays are converged after passing through a lens; focal distance is the distance rays travel after refraction before focus is reached.

Fovea—Small depression in the retina at the back of the eye; the part of the macula adapted for most acute vision, composed of cone cells.

Fundus—The posterior layers of the eye which can be seen with an ophthalmoscope.

Fusion—The power of coordinating the images received by the two eyes into a single mental image.

Glaucoma—Increased intraocular pressure with resultant optic nerve damage; blindness may result if pressure not controlled or relieved.

Heterotropia (Strabismus)—Manifest deviation of the visual axis of an eye out of alignment with the other eye.

Homonymous Hemianopsia—Blindness of one-half the field of vision of one eye. Complete H.H. affects both eyes.

Hyperopia, Hypermetropia (Farsightedness)—A refractive error in which the point of focus for rays of light from distant objects (parallel light rays) is behind the retina.

Hypertropia—A manifest upward deviation of one eye.

Injection—Congestion of conjunctival blood vessels.

Interstitial Keratitis—Inflammation of the cornea, usually due to congenital syphilis.

Iris—Colored, circular membrane, suspended behind the cornea and immediately in front of the lens.

Jaeger Test—A test for near vision; lines of reading matter printed in a series of various sizes of type.

Keratoconus—A cone-shaped deformity of the cornea.

Lens—A refractive medium having one or both surfaces curved.

Light Adaptation—The power of the eye to adjust itself to variations in the amount of light.

Macula—The small area of the retina that surrounds the fovea and, with the fovea, comprises the most sensitive area of the retina.

Meridian—The meridian on a visual field chart is a line radiating from the point of fixation. In visual field testing, the boundaries of the visual field are usually determined by ascertaining the extent of vision every 45 degrees. These 8 radii of the visual field chart are known as the 8 *principal meridians.*

Monocular Vision—The use of only one eye.

Myopia (Nearsightedness)—A refractive error in which the point of focus for rays of light from distant objects is in front of the retina.

Near Point of Accommodation—The nearest point at which the eye can perceive print distinctly.

Near Point of Convergence—The nearest single point at which the two eyes can direct their visual lines.

Nystagmus—An involuntary rapid movement of the eyeball.

O.D.—Oculus dexter—right eye.

O.S.—Oculus sinister—left eye.

O.U.—Oculus uterque—both eyes.

Ophthalmologist—A physician who is a specialist in the diseases of the eye.

Opthalmoplegia—Paralysis of the eye muscles.

Optic Atrophy—Degeneration of the tissue of the optic nerve.

Optic Chiasm—The crossing of the fibers of the optic nerves on the lower surface of the brain.

Optic Disk—Visible portion of the optic nerve in the eyeball.

Optic Nerve—The nerve which carries visual impulses from the retina to the brain.

Optometrist—One trained in the measurement of refraction of the eye for prescription of glasses. Abbreviated OD.

Palpebral—Pertaining to the eyelid.

Perimeter—An instrument for measuring the field of vision.

Peripheral Vision—Ability to perceive the presence, motion, or color of objects outside of the direct line of vision.

Phakic—Presence of the lens of the eye.

Photophobia—Abnormal sensitivity to and discomfort from light.

Posterior Chamber—Space between the back of the iris and the front of the lens; filled with aqueous humor.

Presbyopia—A gradual lessening of the power of accommodation due to a physiologic change which becomes noticeable by virtue of blurred near vision after the age of 40.

Pterygium—A triangular fold of tissue which extends from the conjunctiva over the cornea.

Ptosis—Drooping of the eyelid.

Quadrant—One-quarter of the visual field.

Refraction—(1) deviation in the course of rays of light in passing from one transparent medium into another of different density. (2) Determination of refractive errors of the eye and corrected by glasses.

Refractive Error—A defect in the eye that prevents light rays from being brought to a single focus exactly on the retina.

Refractive Media—The transparent parts of the eye having refractive power.

Retina—Innermost coat of the eye, formed of light sensitive nerve elements.

Retinal Detachment—A separation of the retina from the choroid.

Retinitis Pigmentosa—A hereditary degeneration and atrophy of the retina.

Sclera—The white part of the eye, a tough covering which, with the cornea, forms the external protective coat of the eye.

Scotoma—A blind or partially blind area in the visual field.

Snellen Chart—Used for testing central visual acuity. It consists of lines of letters, numbers, or symbols in graded sizes drawn to Snellen measurements.

Strabismus (Squint, Heterotropia)—A manifest deviation of an eye.

Sympathetic Ophthalmia—Inflammation of one eye following inflammation in the other eye.

Tonometer—An instrument for measuring intraocular pressure.

Trachoma—A form of infectious keratoconjunctivitis caused by a specific virus which in the chronic form produces severe scarring of the eyelids and cornea.

Uvea—Entire vascular coat of the eyeball: Iris, ciliary body, and choroid.

Uveitis—Inflammation of the vascular coat of the eye.

Visual Acuity—A measurement of the ability of the eye to distinguish detail.

Visual Angle—The angle formed by two lines drawn from the extremities of the object through the nodal point of the eye.

Visual Field—The area in which objects are visible when the eye is fixed. The field of vision in a given plane includes the field measurement on either side of the point of fixation in the same plane, or the sum of the 2 radii which form the diameter of a visual field chart.

Visual Field Efficiency—An estimate in percentage of the efficiency of the remaining visual field. May be derived from Listing 2.03.

Visual Efficiency—The product of the percent of remaining central visual efficiency and the percent of remaining visual field efficiency.

Vitreous Humor—Transparent, colorless mass of soft, gelatinous material filling the eyeball behind the lens.

Vitreous (V. Humor, Corpus Vitreum)—Transparent, colorless and gelatinous substance filling the inner chamber of the eye between the lens and the retina.

Weighted Grid Scale—A technique for estimating visual field percentages, in which a standardized grid is superimposed over a standard notated visual field chart. Each of the grid squares had a dot in its center. To obtain percentages, the dots falling within the charted field boundaries are counted. This numerical count has been determined to be roughly equivalent to percentages obtained by standard calculations with established meridian values. The grid is most reliable for percentage estimates where the greater field loss is in the lower half of the visual field.

Glossary 7

Speech System

Adult Listings— 2.09

Child Listings— 102.08(c)

Aphonia—Loss of voice due to disease of the larynx.

Esophageal Speech—A substitute method for producing base tones in instances where vocal cords no longer function or are missing (laryngeal paralysis, laryngectomy). To produce the tones, air is swallowed into the stomach and forced (burped) past the partially contracted upper sphincter of the esophagus, causing vibration in the air column in the esophagus. With practice the individual can produce a variance of tone by controlling sphincter contraction. As in ordinary speech, the mouth parts modify this basic tone to produce speech.

Glottis—The two vocal folds and the space between them.

Laryngalgia—Pain or neuralgia of the larynx.

Laryngeal—Of or pertaining to the larynx.

Laryngeal Cartilages—The cartilages forming the framework of the larynx.

Laryngectomy—Excision of the larynx.

Laryngemphraxis—Closure or obstruction of the larynx.

Laryngitis—Inflammation of the larynx. It may be acute or chronic.

Laryngocentesis—Puncture of the larynx.

Laryngofissure—Surgical division of the larynx for the removal of tumors or foreign bodies.

Laryngogram—Representation of the larynx, usually radiographic.

Laryngologist—A person who specializes in laryngology.

Laryngoparalysis—Paralysis of the laryngeal muscles.

Laryngoplegia—Paralysis of one or more muscles of the larynx.

Laryngospasm—Spasmodic closure of the glottis.

Laryngostenosis—Contraction or stricture of the larynx.

Larynx—The musculocartilaginous, box-like structure at the top of the trachea in which are contained the vocal cords (the organs of sound production (see also Speech).

Otolaryngology—A medical specialty combining the knowledge of treatment of disorders of the ear (oto-) and the throat, pharynx, larynx, nasopharynx, and the tracheobronchial tree.

Palate—The roof of the mouth.

Paralytic Aphonia—Loss of the faculty for speech due to paralysis of the laryngeal muscles second to disorder of the laryngeal nerves.

Speech—Complex sound produced by the interaction and positioning of the lips, tongue, cheeks, and palate, which modify the basic tones produced by the vocal cords.

Stenosis of the Larynx—Narrowing or stricture of the larynx.

Vocal Cords—The two small opposing vanes positioned in the upper portion of the larynx, which normally are retracted to the sides of the larynx but which can be extended into the laryngeal cavity by laryngeal muscles. Air from the lungs, forced past these vanes causes them to vibrate, which creates a vibration (resonance) in the air column, producing tone. Pitch of the tone is varied by the degree of muscular contraction, varying the degree of tension of the cords (see *Speech*).

RESPIRATORY SYSTEM

Glossary 8

General Terms

Adult Listings— 3.02, 3.03, 3.04, 3.05, 3.06, 3.07, 3.08, 3.09, 3.11, 3.12

Child Listings— 103.02, 103.13

Abscissa—The coordinate representing the distance of a point from the vertical scale (y-axis) in a plane Cartesian Coordinate System (graph), measured along a line parallel to the x-axis.

Acid Fast Bacillus—A microorganism which is not readily decolorized by acids when stained for microscopic examination; a characteristic of mycobacteria stained by the Zeihl-Nelson procedure.

Acute—Having a short and relatively severe course.

Allergen—A protein or nonprotein substance capable of inducing allergy or hypersensitivity.

Allergy—A pathological condition in which the body's immune defenses overreact to a foreign agent invading or introduced into the body; ordinarily, the immune bodies produced by the body cells attack only the foreign agent (protein, toxin, etc.) which prompted their formation. Sometimes, however, these immune bodies (antibodies, antitoxins, etc.) attack the body tissue as well. This overreaction is termed an allergy. Such allergic reactions may be immediately observable on initial exposure to a particular allergen, or may be delayed, the initial exposure creating a decreased immunity that is not brought to light until there is a reexposure to the allergen.

Alveoli, Pulmonary—small, multifaceted outpouchings along the walls of the alveolar sacs, alveolar ducts and terminal bronchioles, through which gas exchange takes place between alveolar air and pulmonary capillary blood.

Anoxia—Failure to oxygenate the blood.

Anoxic Anoxia—Failure of oxygen to reach the blood of the lungs, due to (1) too little oxygen in the atmosphere, (2) air way obstruction, (3) thickening of the alveolar membranes, and (4) decreased area of the pulmonary membrane.

Anthracosilicosis—A pneumoconiosis resulting from the combined effects of the deposit of both coal dust and silica dioxide in the lungs.

Anthracosis—A usually asymptomatic form of pneumoconiosis caused by the deposition of coal dust in the lungs. Large accumulations of coal dust may result in the pneumoconiosis of coal workers, which is typically characterized by centrilobular emphysema.

Antibody—Protein immune bodies which are formed by the body to destroy bacterial protein and which attack the entire body of the bacterium. (Immune bodies formed against *toxins* are called anti-*toxins*.)

Antigen—That part of a foreign protein or toxin which causes the cells of the body to form protective immune bodies to neutralize the toxin.

A-P—Abbreviation for anterior-posterior.

Arterial Blood Gas Studies—Laboratory test procedure for determining the relative concentrations of gases in the blood, particularly oxygen and carbon dioxide.

Aspiration—(1) The act of inhaling. (2) The removal of fluids or gases from a cavity through the application of suction.

Asthma—A condition marked by recurrent attacks of intensified shortness of breath, with wheezing, due to spasmodic contraction of the bronchi, resulting from a variety of causes, including such as allergies, particulate inhalation, emotional disorders, infection, etc.

Asthmatic Bronchitis (Bronchitic Asthma)—Asthma complicated by bronchial inflammation; in asthmatic individuals, bronchitis presents a special hazard. The intrabronchial exudate and the swelling of the lining of the bronchi often further occlude the already narrowed air passages and precipitate attacks of severe dyspnea.

Atelectasis—Collapse of the adult lung.

Atypical Mycobacterium—See Mycobacterium.

Atopic Bronchial Asthma—Bronchial asthma arising from a hereditary predisposition to hypersensitivity. (See Asthma).

Auscultation—The act of listening for sounds within the body, chiefly for ascertaining the condition of the lungs, heart, pleura, etc.

Barrel Chest—A rounded, bulging chest with abnormal increase in the anteroposterior diameter, showing little or no movement on respiration; seen in emphysema and kyphosis.

GLOSSARY OF MEDICAL TERMS

Berylliosis—Beryllium poisoning. A disease producing condition, usually of the lungs, more rarely of the skin, lymph nodes, liver and other structures, resulting from exposure to the fumes and dusts of beryllium salts and alloys. The acute form presents findings and symptoms of bilateral diffuse pneumonitis. The chronic form is characterized by marked emphysema and bilateral diffuse granular or nodular infiltration.

Biopsy—The removal and examination, usually microscopic, of tissue from the living body, performed to establish precise diagnosis; of various types: exploratory b., needle b., punch b., sternal b., etc.

Black Lung Disease—A term applied to a form of pneumoconiosis developed by persons working with coal and resulting from the permanent deposition of fine particles of coal in the lungs. (See Anthracosis and Anthracosilicosis.)

Bleb, Pulmonary—A large, flaccid, fluid-filled vesicle (sac), usually at least one cm. in diameter, observed in the emphysematous lung and resulting from the distention and breakdown of multiple alveoli, forming a single cavity. (Ref. Bulla and Radioluceucy).

Blood Gas Studies—See Arterial Blood Gas Studies.

Breathing—See Respiration and Ventilation.

Bronchial Asthma—See Asthma.

Bronchiectasis—Chronic, excessive dilation of the bronchi resulting from the weakening of the walls of the bronchioles, usually as the result of repeated infections, marked by fetid breath and spasmodic coughing, with the expectoration of mucopurulent matter. It may affect the bronchus uniformly (cylindric b.) or occur in irregular pockets (sacculated b.) or the dilated tubes may have terminal enlargements (fusiform b.).

Bronchiole (Bronchiolus)—One of the finer (one mm. or less) subdivisions of the bronchial tree, differing from the bronchi in having no cartilage plates and having cuboidal epithelial cells. These subdivide into smaller *terminal* bronchioles, the last portion of the bronchial tree, the sole function of which is to conduct gases. The final branches of the bronchioles are called *respiratory bronchioles* (or alveolar b.) and have several alveolar out-croppings and divide into alveolar ducts.

Bronchiolitis—Bronchopneumonia.

Bronchitis—Inflammation of one or more of the bronchi. *Acute Bronchitis* is inflammation resulting from exposure to cold, inhaling irritants as acute infection, and marked by fever, pain in the chest (especially on coughing), dyspnea and cough. Its course is short and relatively severe. *Chronic bronchitis* is a long-continued form due to repeated attacks of acute bronchitis or chronic general diseases, and is characterized by a tendency to recurrence following periods of quiescence.

Bronchodilator—An agent which causes expansion of the air passages of the bronchi.

Bronchogram—An X-ray film picturing the bronchial tree, taken after an opaque contrast medium has been injected into the bronchi.

Broncho-Pleural Fistula—An abnormal passage or channel communicating with the thoracic pleural space and a bronchus or bronchiole; may result from trauma, infection or the rupture of an emphysematous bulla and may lead to collapse of the lung as air accumulates in the pleural space.

Bronchopneumonia—A name given to an inflammation of the lungs which usually begins in the terminal bronchioles. These become clogged with mucopurulent exudate; usually secondary in nature, following infection of the upper respiratory tract.

Bronchoscopy—Examination of the interior of the bronchi by means of a bronchoscope; the bronchoscope is an instrument containing a light source which provides illumination and a lens system which permits observation of the bronchus. It is also equipped to remove foreign objects from the bronchus.

Bronchus—Any of the larger air passages of the lungs, having an outer fibrous coat, with irregularly placed plates of cartilage, an interlacing network of smooth muscle, and a mucous membrane lining of columnar epithelial cells. The bronchi serve only to conduct respiratory gases.

Bulla, Emphysematous—Any space of more than one centimeter in diameter of distended areas in the emphysematous lung; usually formed by the destruction of multiple alveolar sacs.

Calcification—The process by which organic tissue becomes hardened by the deposit of calcium salts within its substance.

Carbon Dioxide (CO_2)—An odorless, colorless gas resulting from the oxidation of carbon. It is formed in the tissues during the metabolism of carbohydrates and is eliminated from the body by the lungs. CO_2 and its carbonates are essential to maintaining the neutrality of body tissues and fluids.

Cardiac—Pertaining to the heart.

Cardiomegaly—Hypertrophy (enlargement) of the heart; a distinction is made between a healthy *large* heart (functional hypertrophy), as is seen in individuals sustaining vigorous physical activity, and the various pathological hypertrophies which result from disease or injury.

Cardiopulmonary—Pertaining to both the heart and the lungs.

Caseation—A form of necrosis in which tissue is changed into a dry mass resembling cheese.

Cavitation—The formation of abnormal cavities in the lung through the destruction of lung tissue.

Chronic—Persisting over a long period of time.

Cilia—A minute, vibratile, hair-like process attached to the free surface of a cell; as in the air passages of the lung, which cilia serve to move mucous excretions up and out of the lungs, thereby also removing inhaled debris.

Clubbing—An increased growth of the soft tissue of the ends of the fingers or toes giving the affected digits a blunted, knob-like appearance.

CO_2—A symbol used in chemistry to represent the carbon dioxide molecule; also used as an abbreviation for carbon dioxide gas.

Coccidioidomycosis—A disease caused by the fungus coccidiodes immitis, occurring in primary and secondary forms. The *primary form* is an acute, benign respiratory infection due to inhalation of spores and varying in severity of symptoms from those of the common cold to those accompanying severe influenza. The *secondary form,* caused by reinfection or reactivation of primary disease, is a virulent, chronic progressive granulomatous disease involving not only the lungs, but the skin and body tissues, organs and nervous system, as well.

Congestive Heart Failure—An impairment resulting from heart disease, characterized by shortness of breath and abnormal sodium and water retention resulting in edema. The congestion (abnormal accumulation of blood) may occur in the lungs or in the peripheral circulation, or both, depending upon whether the heart failure is right-sided, left-sided, or generalized; in *left-sided failure,* the left ventricle is unable to move the blood into the systemic circulation. The resulting accumulation of blood increases the pressure in all the pulmonary vessels and fluid leakage from the capillaries into the lung tissues takes place, resulting in *pulmonary* edema. In severe cases, fluid may leak into the air spaces of the lung, resulting in hypostatic pneumonia. Many patients who die of heart failure, die because of the failure of water soaked lungs to aerate the blood; in *right-sided failure,* the blood attempting to return to the heart is dammed in the peripheral circulation and is accompanied by venous distention and engorgement of the liver and spleen. Increased venous pressure causes fluid leak with resulting tissue edema.

An additional complication of left-sided failure is decreased arterial pressure, decreasing the amount of urine formed by the kidneys, causing excessive water retention. Also, decreased blood flow causes the adrenal cortex to secrete hormones which cause further water and salt retention, increasing extra-cellular fluid volume, resulting in extreme generalized edema.

Conglomerative Fibrosis—See Pulmonary Fibrosis.

Cor Pulmonale—Right-sided heart failure resulting from obstruction of the pulmonary capillary bed, due to chronic pulmonary disease.

Culture—A laboratory procedure by which suspected micro-organisms are induced to grow in prepared mediums for purposes of identification and for determining whether the organism is pathogenically viable. Inactive or dead micro-organisms do not grow in a culture medium.

Cyanosis—A bluish tint to the skin, particularly noticeable in the mucous membranes and nail beds, due to excessive concentration of insufficiently oxygenated hemoglobin.

Diaphragm—The musculomembranous partition separating the thoracic and abdominal cavities and which, by contracting, draws air into the lungs.

Diffuse—(1) not definitely limited or localized, widely distributed, (2) to pass through or spread widely through a tissue or structure.

Diffusion—(1) the process of becoming diffused, or widely spread; it requires no addition of energy to the system, (2) dialysis through a membrane.

Disseminated Fibrosis—See Pulmonary Fibrosis.

Dyspnea—Difficult or labored breathing. Common term—shortness of breath (SOB).

Edema—The presence of abnormally large amounts of fluid in the intercellular tissue spaces of the body; usually applied to demonstrable accumulation of excessive fluid in the subcutaneous tissues.

Effusion—The escape into and accumulation of body fluid in a potential space or body part; *pleural effusion*—the accumulation in the potential space between the pleura of the lungs and chest wall; *peritoneal effusion*—accumulation of body fluid in the potential spaces in the abdomen, ordinarily referred to as *ascites*.

Embolism—The sudden blocking of an artery by a clot or foreign material (embolus) which has been brought by the blood from another vessel and forced into a smaller one, thus obstructing circulation.

Emphysema—A pathological accumulation of air in tissues or organs; applied especially to such a condition of the lungs. (See Pulmonary Emphysema).

Exacerbation—Increase in the severity of a disease or of any of its symptoms.

Excision—Removal, as of an organ, by cutting.

Expectorant—An agent that promotes the ejection of mucus or exudate from the lungs, bronchi, and trachea.

Expectorate—To cough up and spit out materials from the lungs, bronchi and trachea.

Expiration—The act of breathing out or expelling air from the lungs.

FEV—Abbreviation for Forced Expiratory Volume.

Fibrosis—The formation of fibrous tissue. (See Pulmonary Fibrosis).

Fluoroscopy—Examination of internal body structures by means of a fluoroscope, a device which directs X-rays through the body onto a fluorescent screen, rather than a photographic plate, thus permitting observation of the deep structures in movement.

Focal Fibrosis—See Pulmonary Fibrosis.

Forced Expiratory Volume (FEV)—In ventilatory testing, a timed, fractional measurement of forced vital capacity: following several resting, normal respirations, the individual rapidly takes as deep a breath as possible, then immediately breathes out as quickly and completely as possible. Ordinarily in healthy individuals this will be accomplished in three seconds. Measurement of liters or cubic centimeters of air expired, as well as measurement of the timed rate of exhalation can be diagnostic of both restrictive and obstructive ventilatory disorders.

Forced Vital Capacity (FVC)—The vital capacity obtained during spirometry and demonstrating the largest volume of air which can be exhaled as forcefully and rapidly as possible, following the deepest possible inspiration. (Formerly called "timed vital capacity")

Friction Rub—An auscultatory sound caused by the rubbing together of two serous surfaces, as in pericardial rub.

Gastric Washings (G. Aspirate)—Fluid removed from the stomach by suction.

Guinea Pig Inoculation—An infrequently used laboratory testing procedure for determining activity or viability of micro-organisms through the injection of preparations containing the micro-organism into a guinea pig.

Hammon-Rich Syndrome (Diffuse Interstitial Pulmonary Fibrosis)—Acute, rapidly fatal, progressive fibrosis of the pulmonary alveolar walls, with steadily progressive dyspnea, resulting finally in death from lack of oxygen, or right-sided heart failure.

Heart Failure—Failure of the heart to pump all of the blood attempting to return to it from the veins. Most frequently, damage to the heart by disease or trauma impairs its pumping efficiency, with the result that blood would be dammed up in the veins. Since the heart is two separate pumps, it is possible for one side of the heart to fail independent of the other; i.e., the left ventricle might fail, damming blood in the systemic circulation.

Hemoptysis—The expectoration of blood or blood-stained sputum.

Hemorrhage—The escape of blood from the vessels; bleeding. Small hemorrhages are classified by size as petechial (very small), purpura (up to 1 cm), and ecchymoses (larger). The massive accumulation of blood within a tissue is called a hematoma.

Hilus, Pulmonary—The depression on the mediastinal surface of the lung where the bronchus, blood vessels and nerves enter.

Histoplasmosis—Infection resulting from inhalation of spores of the fungus Histoplasma Capsulatum. In most cases infection is asymptomatic, but in 1–5 percent, it causes acute pneumonia or reticuloendothelial hyperplasia, with liver and spleen enlargement and anemia, or an influenza-like illness with joint effusion and erythema nodosum.

Hypertrophy—Enlargement or overgrowth of an organ or part due to an increase in size of its constituent parts; *adaptive h.*—the increase in size in response to changed conditions; e.g., increased thickness of the walls of a hollow organ when the outflow is obstructed; *compensatory h.*—that which results from increased workload due to some physical defect, as of the left ventricle of the heart, due to hypertension.

Functional h.—hypertrophy of an organ or part due to its increased activity.

Hyperventilation—Rapid and deep-breathing (tachypnea) increasing the amount of air entering the alveoli, resulting in reduced carbon dioxide tension (pCO_2) and eventually leading to alkylosis.

Hypoxia—Low oxygen content or tension (PO_2); deficiency in oxygen of the inspired air. *Anemic H.*—Hypoxia due to reduction of the oxygen-carrying capacity of the blood as a result of a decrease in the total hemoglobin or an alteration of the hemoglobin constituents.

Idiopathic—Spontaneously developing, or of unknown etiology.

Infiltration—The diffusion or accumulation in a tissue of substances not normal to it.

Inspiration—The act of drawing air into the lungs.

Intercostal—Situated between the ribs.

Interstitial—Situated between the cellular elements of a structure or part.

Kyphoscoliosis—Foreward and lateral curvature of the spine.

Kyphosis—Abnormally increased forward curvature of the spine; hunch back.

Laminagram—An X-ray film of a selected layer of tissue at a selected depth. Usually multiple layers (lamina) are filmed. (See Planigram).

Lesion—Any pathological or traumatic disruption of tissue or loss of function of a part.

Lobe—A division of the lung. The lungs are divided into five lobes; on the right, the superior, middle, and inferior lobes and on the left, the superior and inferior lobes.

Lobectomy—The surgical excision of a lobe of a lung.

Match Test—A rough screening test of expiration in which a lighted match is held 3 inches from the subject's wide open mouth while attempts are made to blow it out. Failure after six full-effort attempts indicates a maximum breathing capacity below 40 liters/minute, and a maximum mid-expiratory flow rate below 0.6 liters/second.

Maximum Breathing Capacity (MBC)—Older term for the currently preferred expression, maximum voluntary ventilation.

Maximum Voluntary Ventilation (MVV)—Formerly termed maximum breathing capacity: The greatest volume of air which can be breathed per minute by voluntary effort. Obtained during spirometry by having the subject inhale and exhale as deeply and as rapidly as possible for 15 seconds.

Mechanical (Breathing) Restriction—See Restriction.

Mediastinum—The mass of tissues and organs separating the lungs, bounded in front by the sternum and to the rear by the vertebral column. It contains the heart and its large vessels, the trachea, the esophagus, the thymus, lymph nodes, and other structures and tissues.

MVV—Abbreviation for Maximum Voluntary Ventilation.

Mycobacterium—A genus of micro-organisms occuring as gram-positive slender rods and distinguished by acid fast staining. *M. Tuberculosis*—the causative agent of tuberculosis in man, most commonly pulmonary; also called *"M. tuberculosis var. hominis"* and "tubercle bacillus". *Atypical mycobacteria, Group I–IV mycobacteria, anonymous mycobacteria*—Acid fast bacteria resembling the tubercle bacilli, found in pulmonary infections, usually of a chronic nature, in man, and for which species names have not been established. They are divided into chromogens and nonchromogens, the former including photochromogens (Group I) which produce yellow pigment in the presence of light and scotochromogens (Group II) which produce orange pigment independent of light. The nonchromogens are subdivided into filamentous groups (Group III) and rapid growers (Group IV).

Pathogenic—Causing disease or morbid symptoms.

Pathogenic Atypical Mycobacteria—See Mycobacteria.

pCO_2—Symbol for the partial pressure of carbon dioxide; that amount of presure which carbon dioxide exerts as part of the total pressure exerted by a gas mixture, in air or in solution.

Percussion—The act of striking or tapping a part of the body with short, sharp blows as an aid in diagnosing the condition of the underlying parts by the sound obtained.

pH—Symbol representing hydrogen ion concentration or activity in a solution, as with the blood and interstitial fluids. A pH of 7 is neutral; above 7, alkalinity increases and below 7, acidity increases.

Phrenic Nerve—Originating the cervical plexus, C4–C5 innervating the pleura, pericardium, diaphragm, peritoneum,and sympathetic plexuses; in tuberculosis, the phrenic nerve has sometimes been cut or a portion extracted to paralyze the corresponding side of the diaphragm in order to secure the rest of the lung.

Planigram—X-ray film obtained by a special radiographic tech nique in which detailed X-ray images of structures lying in a pre-determined plane out of focus. Other such body section

X-ray techniques are: laminagraphy, radiotomy, stratigraphy, tomography and vertigraphy.

Pleura—The continuous serous membrane investing one lung (visceral pleura) and lining one-half of the thoracic cavity (parietal pleura), completely enclosing a potential space called the pleural cavity. There are two pleural cavities, right and left, entirely distinct from each other. The pleurae are moistened by a serous secretion, serving as a lubricant and facilitating the movement of the lungs within the thoracic cavity.

Pleural Cavity—The potential space between that portion of the continuous pleura which lines one-half of the thoracic cavity (parietal pleura) and that portion which covers one lung (visceral pleura). There are two pleural cavities, right and left.

Pleurisy (Pleuritis)—Inflammation of the pleura, with exudation into its cavity and upon its surface. In acute pleurisy, the pleura becomes reddened, then covered with an exudate of lymph, fibrin and cellular elements (the dry stage); the disease may progress to the second stage in which copious exudation of serum occurs (liquid effusion) and accumulates in the pleural space. The inflamed surfaces of the pleura tend to become united by adhesions, which are usually permanent.

Pneumoconiosis—A generic term comprising all of the chronic fibrous reactions which arise in the lung as a result of the *prolonged* inhalation of excessive quantities of *injurious* mineral dusts, such as those of sand, granite, flint and asbestos. Many of the pneumoconioses are scarcely to be considered as diseases, since they may be present without producing symptoms or impairing physical efficiency, as in the case of anthracosis, chalicosis, siderosis, etc. On the other hand, dusts containing high concentrations of finely divided silica produce serious forms of pulmonary fibrosis (silicosis). Admixtures of alumina, carbon, gypsum, and hematite with silica in dust result in a modification of the reaction to silica, retarding or inhibiting its noxious effects. Symptoms and pathological findings depend on both the causative agent and the duration and concentration of exposure.

Pneumonectomy—Excision of lung tissue, especially of an entire lung. *Total p.*—surgical excision of an entire lung.

Pneumonia—An infectious lung disease which causes the walls of the alveoli and distal bronchioles to become inflamed and edematous and the alveoli to become filled with fluid and white blood cells. This results in anoxia for two reasons:

first, exudate prevents seration of the alveoli; and second, because the walls of the alveoli are thickened by edema, although they are aerated, oxygen cannot diffuse easily.

Pneumonitis—Inflammation of the lungs.

Pneumothorax—An accumulation of air or gas in the pleural space, which may occur spontaneously or as the result of trauma or a pathological process, or may be induced deliberately (artificial p.) to collapse the lung during treatment.

pO_2—Symbol for the partial pressure of oxygen; that amount of pressure which oxygen exerts as part of the total pressure exerted by a gas mixture, in air or in solution.

Polycythemia—An increase in the red blood cell values (hemoglobin, hematocrit, erythrocyte count) above normal. Polycythemia (or erythrocytosis) is not a disease, rather it is a manifestation of an underlying disorder. Not all etiologies are pathological. For example, heavy tobacco smoking can cause an elevated red blood cell count (RBC), since the carbon monoxide, produced by the burning tobacco, combines *permanently* with the blood hemoglobin, reducing the RBC oxygen carrying capacity. The body therefore manufactures more RBC's than normal to compensate for the oxygen transport loss.

Potential Cavity—Those areas of nonadherent contact of the serous membranes which line the body cavity and cover the viscera, which, normally, are devoid of appreciable fluids or gases, but which can become actual spaces when expanded by abnormal accumulations (or the intentional introduction of) fluids, gases or other substances between the membrane surfaces.

Pulmonary—Pertaining to the lungs.

Pulmonary Edema—Generalized pulmonary edema is usually caused by failure of the left heart to pump blood from the pulmonary circulation into the systemic circulation. This can result from heart muscle or valve damage. Increased pulmonary circulatory pressure results and fluid flows from the capillaries into the alveoli and interstitial spaces of the lungs, impairing oxygen diffusion.

Pulmonary Embolism—The sudden blocking of a pulmonary artery by a blood clot or other substance, such as fat, cholesterol plaque (embolus) from a distinct source in the body. Seriousness of impairment depends upon how many and how large the emboli are.

Pulmonary Emphysema—A condition of the lung resulting from abnormal distention of the respiratory elements of the lung (alveoli, respiratory bronchioles) due to restriction and obstruction of the outflow of inspired air. Chronic distention and associated inflammatory processes cause degeneration and destruction of alveolar walls, which rupture or collapse. Distended and ruptured alveoli become filled with fluid, others trap air which cannot be expelled rapidly. Impairment to respiratory function is due to both reduced ventilation (movement of air in and out of the alveoli) and reduced respiration (exchange of gases). Air trapping further reduces ventilation by restricting the total volume of air which can be breathed. Pulmonary hypertension usually accompanies advanced emphysema, for as alveolar walls are destroyed, so are the associated capillaries, increasing circulatory resistance in the lungs and elevating arterial pressure. Consequently, respiratory function may then be further complicated by edema, impairing the function of the otherwise uninvolved alveoli.

Pulmonary Fibrosis—The development of fibroid tissue infiltrating or replacing pulmonary tissue; the nature and extent of pulmonary fibrosis depends upon the causative agent or disorder involved. Fibrosis is the result of the body's effort to replace tissue damaged by inflammation, trauma, or undetermined cellular degeneration. It may be localized, in multiple discrete areas or disseminated or generalized throughout the lungs. Fibrotic structure may take the defined form of nodules or bands, or may uniformly infiltrate or surround pulmonary structures, without definite consolidation; *Impairment* arises from both (1) restriction of ventilation due to the loss of lung expansion and constriction and blockage of air ways and (2) diffusion restriction caused by the fibrotic thickening of the alveolar walls.

Pulmonary Insufficiency—Failure of the lungs to efficiently oxygenate the blood due to obstructive and/or restrictive ventilatory disorder, respiratory diffusion disorder, or reduced pulmonary circulation.

Pulmonary Resection—Excision of a portion of the lung.

Pulmonary Reserve—That additional volume of air which can be moved in and out of the lungs beyond that moved during normal resting ventilation; *Inspiratory reserve volume (IRV)*—The additional volume of air which can be inspired above that of resting inspiration; *Expiratory reserve volume*—that additional volume of air which can be exhaled above that of normal resting expiration.

Pulmonary Ventilation—(See Ventilation).

RESPIRATORY SYSTEM

Pulmonary Ventilation Testing (Ventilatory Studies)—A laboratory procedure to obtain a timed measurement of the volumes of air inhaled and exhaled during resting and exertional ventilation of the lungs. Results are recorded by a breath-activated apparatus (spirometer) onto a chart which is scaled both for volume of air and for time; also known as *Pulmonary Function Studies (PFS),* a misleading title, since pulmonary *function* involves *respiration* as well as ventilation and ventilatory studies measure only ventilation.

Radiolucency (Radiolucent Area)—The dark portions of an X-ray film, representing the less dense structures of the body; in X-ray films of the lung, dark "spots" may represent cavities or bullae, and streaks fibrosis.

Radiopaque Materials—Substances, such as barium sulfate, which block the passage of radiant energy, such as X-rays, the representative areas appearing light or white on the exposed film; also called *contrast media.*

Rales—An abnormal breath sound heard in auscultation; distinguished as dry or moist, according to the absence or presence of fluid in the air passages; classified according to site of origin as bronchial, cavernous, laryngeal, pleural, tracheal and vesicular (crepitant).

Regression—A return to a former or earlier stage; a subsidence of symptoms or of a disease process.

Remission—A diminution or abatement of the symptoms of a disease; also the period during which such diminution occurs.

Resection—Excision of a portion of an organ or structure; *Wedge r.*—removal of a triangular wedge of tissue.

Respiration—The exchange of gases (primarily oxygen and carbon dioxide) between the atmosphere and the cells of the body. The process includes ventilation (inspiration and expiration), the diffusion of oxygen through the alveoli into the blood and of carbon dioxide from the blood into the alveolar spaces (alveolar r.) and the transport of oxygen to and carbon dioxide from body cells (cellular r.).

Restrictive Disorder—Pulmonary disorders which are characterized by their limitation or reduction of the volume of air which can be moved in and out of the lungs. *Fibrotic restriction*—loss of ventilatory volume due to fibrosis of the lung tissue, bronchioles and alveoli, reducing the lungs capacity to expand and contract. *Mechanical restriction*—loss of ventilatory volume due to disruption of the anatomical mechanisms of ventilation; e.g., fixation of the rib cage, paralysis of the diaphragm, compression of the lungs by thoracic skeletal abnormalities, such as kyphosis and scoliosis.

Rhonchi—Coarse, dry abnormal breath sounds due to partial obstruction of the bronchial tubes.

Roentgenogram—An X-ray film.

Rub—An auscultory sound caused by the rubbing together of two serous surfaces; associated with inflammation, as in pleural rub.

Sarcoidosis—A chronic, progressive, abnormal increase in cells derived from granular endoplastic reticulum, which can involve almost any organ or tissue of the body; characterized by the formation of nodules and fibrosis. In *pulmonary* involvement, X-ray may show tracheobronchial and mediastinal lymphadenopathy. The degenerative process may extend along peribronchial structures to involve the lung in increasing fibrosis, fading in the periphery. Fibrosis may also be generalized throughout the lung. Pulmonary involvement can become so extensive that right heart embarrassment may develop.

Serial X-rays—The taking of several exposures of a selected area at arbitrary intervals.

Siderosis—A pneumoconiosis resulting from the inhalation of iron particles.

Silicosis—Pneumoconiosis due to the inhalation of dust of stone, sands, or flint containing silicon dioxide, with formation of generalized nodular fibrotic changes in both lungs.

Smear—A specimen for microscopic study prepared by spreading the material across a glass slide.

Spirogram (Spirometric Tracing)—A tracing or graph of respiratory movements.

Spirometer—An apparatus for measuring the volume of air inspired and expired.

Spirometry (Spirometric Testing)—Measurement of the breathing capacity of the lungs.

Sputum—Matter ejected from the lungs, bronchi and trachea; obtained by coughing and spitting.

Status Asthmaticus—Asthmatic crisis; asthmatic shock; a sudden, intense and continuous aggravation of a state of asthma, marked by dyspnea to the point of exhaustion and collapse and not responding to usual therapeutic efforts.

Sternum—The plate of bone forming the middle of the anterior thorax, articulating above with the clavicles and along the sides with the cartilages of the first seven ribs.

Tachypnea—Excessive rapid, shallow, breathing resulting from oxygen deficiency of the blood (pathological or exertional), or from emotional stress, or a combination of both.

Thoracoplasty—Surgical removal of the ribs, allowing the chest wall to move inward and collapse a diseased lung.

Timed Vital Capacity—See Forced Expiratory Volume.

Total Vital Capacity—The volume of air which can be expelled from the lungs following maximal inspiration, with no limit to the duration of expiration; it is equal to the inspiratory capacity plus the expiratory reserve volume.

Trachea—The cartilaginous and membranous tube descending from the larynx and branching into the right and left bronchi; it is kept dilated by a series of horseshoe-shaped cartilages.

Tracheostomy—The surgical creation of an opening into the trachea through the neck; usually performed as a temporary compensation for airway obstruction above the trachea.

Trapping—The condition in which airway obstruction allows entrance of air into the alveoli but restricts its exit, ballooning the alveoli and impairing their respiratory function.

Tubercle—A small rounded nodule produced by infection with M. Tuberculosis; the characteristic lesion of tuberculosis, consisting of a gray, translucent mass encased in a fibrous covering.

Tubercle Bacillus—See Mycobacterium.

Tuberculosis—Any of the infectious diseases caused by species of mycobacterium and characterized by the formation of tubercles and caseous necrosis of the tissues.

TVC—Abbreviation for Timed Vital Capacity, currently called Forced Vital Capacity.

Ventilation—The process of exchange of air between the lungs and the atmosphere. *Pulmonary V.* (usually measured in liters or cubic centimeters per minute) refers to the total volume of exchange, whereas *Alveolar V.* refers to the exchange of air in the alveoli, in which the exchange of gases with the blood takes place.

Ventilation Studies—See Pulmonary Ventilation Studies.

Wedge Resection—Surgical excision of a wedge-shaped segment of a lobe of the lung.

Wheezing—Whistling sounds produced in breathing by the partial obstruction of the bronchi.

X-ray—(1) Roentgen ray; a form of electromagnetic radiation, similar to light rays but of shorter wave length and capable of penetrating solids and of ionizing gases. (2) Also used to refer to a roentgenogram or radiograph made by X-rays.

CARDIOVASCULAR SYSTEM

Glossary 9

General Terms

Adult Listings— 4.02, 4.04, 4.13

Child Listings— 104.02, 104.03

Abdominal Aorta—The part of the aorta that extends down into the abdomen.

Aorta—The arterial trunk which carries oxygenated blood from the left ventricle out to the body.

Aortic Arch—The part of the aorta that curves over the heart.

Aortic Valve—Heart valve between left ventricle and aorta.

Apex—The pointed tip of a structure (e.g., the apex of the heart).

Arteriole—A minute branch of an artery.

Artery—A vessel that carries blood away from the heart.

Atrial Septum—Upper part of the septum (muscular wall), between the atria.

Atrium (Plural Atria), Right and Left—An upper heart chamber, also called auricle(s).

Auricle(s)—See Atrium.

A–V Node (Atrio-Ventricular Node)—The part of the heart's conduction system that initiates contractions of the ventricles.

Bifurcation—The point where a structure divides into two branches; e.g., the bifurcation of an artery.

Blood Pressure (BP)—The pressure of blood against the walls of the arteries, highest at systole (systolic BP) and lowest at diastole (diastolic BP).

Brachial Artery—Main artery in the upper arm.

Capillaries—Microscopic blood vessels that connect arteriles and venules. By osmosis, capillaries deliver oxygen and nutrients to the cells and absorb waste products from them.

Card-, cardi-, cardio-—Prefixes referring to the heart.

Cardiovasclur—Refers to the heart and blood vessels.

Carotid Arteries—Arteries that branch into neck and head on each side.

GLOSSARY OF MEDICAL TERMS

Circulatory System—The heart and blood vessels. The functions of the circulatory system is to provide a constant supply of oxygen and nutrients to the tissues by means of the blood; and to carry away waste products from the cells, chiefly byproducts (including carbon dioxide) from the metabolism of nutrients.

Conducting System (of Heart)—Is composed of special muscle fibers that conduct electrical impulses to cause contractions of heart chambers.

Coronary Arteries, Right and Left—Arteries that supply blood to the heart muscle (myocardium).

Costal—Refers to the ribs.

Cusp—A tapering projection; e.g., the flaps or leaflets of the heart valves or venous valves.

Diastole—The momentary relaxation of the heart muscle between beats, when the chambers are filling.

Dorsalis Pedis Artery—Artery that runs along top of foot.

Electrocardiogram (EKG, ECG)—A graphic tracing of the passage of electrical impulses through the myocardium.

Endocardium—Membrane lining the inside of the myocardium.

Epicardium—Membrane lining the outside of the myocardium.

Eyeground(s)—See Retina.

Femoral Artery—Artery that extends from groin through thigh, near femurbone. (A continuation of iliac artery.)

Fundus (Plural Fundi)—See Retina.

Great Vessels—Term referring to the aorta, superior vena cava and inferior vena cava.

Iliac Arteries—Arteries that bifurcate from abdominal aorta into each side of the pelvis.

Inferior Vena Cava—Vein that carries deoxygenated blood from lower body into right atrium.

Inter—Prefix meaning between.

Intercostal Space (ICS)—Spaces between the ribs. Normally the apex of the heart is at the 5th ICS (between the 5th and 6th ribs), at the midclavicular line.

Jugular Veins—Veins in the neck.

Kidneys—Organs that filter wastes from the blood, especially those from the breakdown of proteins.

Left Bundle Branch (LBB)—Branch of the A–V node that controls contraction of the heart.

Midclavicular Line (MCL)—Imaginary line down from the center of clavicle (collarbone).

Midline—Imaginary line down the center (e.g., midline of the chest).

Mitral Valve—Heart valve between left atrium and left ventricle.

Myo- —Prefix meaning muscle.

Myocardium—The heart muscle.

Pericardium—Elastic, two-layer membranous sac which surrounds the heart and the roots of the great vessels.

Popliteal Artery—Artery that runs behind the knee (a branch off the femoral artery).

Posterior Tibial Artery—Artery behind tibial bone in lower leg, that extends inside the ankle into foot (a branch off the popliteal artery).

Pulmonary Artery—Artery that carries deoxygenated blood from right ventricle to lungs. (All other arteries carry oxygenated blood.)

Pulmonary Circulation—Circulation of blood from right ventricle, through pulmonary artery to lungs and back via pulmonary vein to left atrium.

Pulmonary Valve—Heart valve between right ventricle and pulmonary artery.

Pulmonary Vein—Vein that carries oxygenated blood from lungs into left atrium. (All other veins carry deoxygenated blood.)

Pulse—The rhythmic expansion of an artery (coinciding with heart contractions) which can be felt with the fingers at points where arteries come close to the surface. Normal resting pulse rate in an adult is 60–90 per minute.

Radial Artery—Artery from elbow through wrist on thumb side of arm.

Reflux—Backward flow (e.g., reflux of blood in a vein).

Regular Sinus Rhythm (RSR)—Normal heart rhythm.

Regurgitation—Backward flow (e.g., regurgitation of blood through a defective heart valve).

Renal Arteries—Branches off the abdominal aorta that deliver blood to the kidneys.

Retina (Plural Retinae)—The innermost layer of the eyeball, also called the fundus (plural fundi) or eyeground(s).

Right Bundle Branch (RBB)—Branch of the A–V node that controls contraction of the right ventricle.

S–A Node (Sino-Atrial Node)—The "pacemaker" of the heart's conduction system, that initiates contractions of the atria.

Saphenous Veins—Numerous veins that branch throughout the leg (branches off the "great saphenous" that extends from top of foot to top of leg).

Septum—Muscular wall dividing the heart into left and right sides.

Sinus—A cavity or widening in a vessel or chamber.

Sinus Nodes—Term for the S–A and A–V nodes.

Sternum—The breastbone.

Superior Vena Cava—Vein that carries deoxygenated blood from upper body into right atrium.

Systemic Circulation—Circulation of blood from left ventricle, out aorta, through body and back to heart.

Systole—Time at which heart muscle contracts to empty chambers.

Tricuspid Valve—Heart valve between right atrium and right ventricle.

Trunk—The large undivided base of a part; e.g., the trunk of an artery or vein.

Ulnar Artery—Artery from elbow to wrist on outside of arm.

Valve—Membranous folds of tissue that close to prevent backward flow (reflux or regurgitation) in a vessel or chamber (e.g., heart valves or venous valves).

Vas—Prefix meaning vessel or tube.

Vascular—Refers to blood vessels or blood supply.

Vasoconstrictor—A drug that constricts blood vessels, especially arterioles or arteries.

Vasodilator—A drug that dilates blood vessels, especially arterioles or arteries (e.g., nitroglycerin).

Vein—A vessel that carries blood to the heart.

Vena Cavas (Vena Cavae)—The two venous trunks draining into the heart (see inferior vena cava and superior vena cava).

Ventricle(s), Right and Left—A lower heart chamber.

Ventricular Septum—Lower Part of the septum (muscular wall), between the ventricles.

Venule—A minute branch of a vein.

Glossary 10

Hypertensive Vascular Disease

Adult Listings— 4.03

Child Listings— 104.03

CARDIOVASCULAR SYSTEM

Albumin—A protein found normally in the body. Presence of albumin in urine is an indication of problems with the kidney's filtering system.

Angina Pectoris—A condition in which the heart muscle receives an insufficient blood supply, causing pain in the chest and often in the left arm and shoulder.

Aphasia—Inability to express oneself properly through speech or loss of verbal comprehension.

Motor Aphasia—Person knows what he wants to say but can't say it. Unable to coordinate muscles controlling speech.

Sensory Aphasia—Inability to understand spoken words if auditory center involved or written words if visual word center affected.

Arteriolar Light Reflex—A phenomenon in the retina which gives an indication of the severity of arteriole wall constriction when viewed by ophthalmoscope.

Arteriolar Resistance—Resistance in the arterioles determined by the constriction or dilation of the arteriolar walls.

Arteriole/Venous Ratio—Known as AV ratio, the ratio of the diameter of arterioles to those of veins. This is used for assessing damage in the retina.

Arteriosclerosis—A group of diseases characterized by thickening and loss of elasticity of arterial walls.

Ataxia—Muscular incoordination, especially manifested when voluntary muscular movements are attempted.

Atherosclerosis—A common form of arteriosclerosis in which deposits of yellowish plaques are formed within the inner lining and the middle structure of the large and middle-sized arteries.

AV Crossing Defect—View of vein in retina compressed by arteriole indicating damage to the eye grounds.

A–V Ratio—Ratio of the diameters of the arterioles to those of the veins in the retina of the eye.

Blood Pressure—Pressure or push of blood against the walls of blood vessels.

Blood Pressure Cuff—Device called a sphygmomanometer used to measure arterial blood pressure.

Blood Pressure Gradient—The difference between blood pressures taken from two areas of the circulation system. Without the difference, circulation would not be possible.

Caliber—Opening or diameter.

GLOSSARY OF MEDICAL TERMS

Cardiac Compensation—An adjustment of size of the heart or rate of heartbeat made to counterbalance a defect in structure or function. Adequate circulation is maintained.

Cardiac Decompensation—Inability of the heart to maintain adequate circulation, usually resulting in a waterlogging of tissues.

Carotid Sinus—A slight dilation at the point where the internal carotid artery branches from the common carotid artery. The carotid sinus contains special nerve end organs which respond to a change in blood pressure by causing a change in the rate of heartbeat.

Cerebral—The brain; having to do with the brain.

Cerebral Vascular Accident—CVA—also called a stroke. Occlusion of blood vessel or hemorrhage which results in abnormal function or death of certain nerve cells with observable neurological changes.

Cerebrovascular—Pertaining to the blood vessels in the brain.

Coarctation of the Aorta—A pressing together or narrowing of the aorta which is the main trunk artery which conducts blood from the heart to the body.

Complete Blood Count—Also known as CBC, a blood study analyzing a blood sample for numbers of white (WBC) and red (RBC) blood cells as well as platelet counts and other portions of the blood.

Congestive Heart Failure—A backing up of blood in the veins leading to the heart, often accompanied by accumulation of fluid in various parts of the body. Results from the heart's inability to pump out all the blood that returns to it.

Constriction—Narrowing of the internal diameter of the blood vessels.

Copper Wire Effect—View of arteriolar light reflex in retina in which changes to the arteriole produce a broad yellow line with blood column present but not easily visible. This is part of KW Grade II eye ground changes.

Cotton Wool Patches—Exudates present in the retina have a soft and fluffy or cotton wool appearance. Therefore, the use of the term cotton wool patches indicates exudates.

Diastole—The part of the heart cycle when the heart muscle is at rest.

Diastolic Pressure—The blood pressure on the arterial walls when the heart is at rest.

Dilation—Expansion of an organ, orifice or vessel.

CARDIOVASCULAR SYSTEM

Diuretics—Drugs which have the capability to stimulate increased secretion of urine.

Edema—Excessive accumulation of fluid in the tissues causing swelling.

Electrocardiogram—(EKG, ECG) A graphic reading of the electrical impulses produced by excitation of the heart muscle.

End Organ—Those organs which are particularly perceptible to damage from hypertension. They are the heart, kidney, brain and retina of the eye.

Essential Hypertension—Elevation of blood pressures not caused by any other evident disease.

Exudate—Material such as fluid, cells or cellular debris which has escaped from blood vessels and has been deposited in tissues or on tissue surfaces.

Eyeground—The inside of the back part of the eye seen by looking through the pupil. Examining the eyeground is one means of assessing changes in the blood vessels. Also called the fundus of the eye.

Fundus of the Eye—The inside of the back part of the eye seen by looking through the pupil. Examining the fundus of the eye is used as a means of assessing changes in the blood vessels. Also called the eyeground.

Hemorrhage—The escape of blood from the vessels, bleeding.

Hypertension—An unstable or persistent elevation of blood pressure above the normal range.

Hypertensive Cardiovascular Disease—Disease manifested by hypertension and affecting either the structure or function of the heart.

Hypertensive Encephalopathy—An acute disease involving damage to the brain due to constriction of the vascular system, edema or arteriolar spasms.

Hypertensive Vascular Disease—A general term used in a sense of a disease manifested by arterial hypertension which may be accompanied by organ or vessel damage.

Hypertrophy—Increase in the size of an organ.

Hypotension—Abnormally low blood pressure.

Infarct—An area of a tissue which is damaged or dies as a result of not receiving a sufficient blood supply.

Ischemia—Local and temporary deficiency of blood, chiefly due to the contraction of a blood vessel.

Ischemic Heart Disease—Heart disease characterized by deficient blood supply to heart muscles.

Keith-Wagener-Barber—Grading system for assessing permanent damage to the eyegrounds. Severity increases from Grade I to Grade IV.

Labile Hypertension—Unstable elevation of blood pressures above the normal range. Blood pressures will fluctuate.

Left Ventricular Hypertrophy—Enlargement of the left lower portion of the heart. Also written as LVH.

Malignant Hypertension—Severe high blood pressure which can rapidly cause damage to end organs and vessels.

Myocardial Infarction—Death of heart muscle (myocardium) due to obstructed or deficient blood supply.

Necrosis—Muscle death.

Nephron—Microscopic filtering unit in the kidney.

Nitrates—A group of chemical compounds, many of which cause dilation of the small blood vessels, and thus lower blood pressure. They are vasodilators.

Nitroglycerin—A drug (one of the nitrates) which relaxes the muscles in the blood vessels. Often used to relieve attacks of angina pectoris and spasm of coronary arteries. It is one of the vasodilators.

Occlusion—Blockage of a vessel.

Ophthalmoscope—Instrument for examining interior (retina) of the eye.

Palpitations—Unduly rapid actions of the heart, which is noted by the patient.

Papilledema—Gross swelling of optic disk due to pressure of abnormally large amounts of fluid (edema).

Percussion—Tapping the body as an aid in diagnosing the condition of parts beneath by the sound obtained, much as one taps on a barrel to detect its fullness.

Point of Maximum Impulse—Point at which the strongest heart beat can be felt by percussion. Often seen written as P.M.I.

Postural Hypotension—Sudden decrease in blood pressure occurring when an individual suddenly arises from a recumbent position or from standing still. This can produce fainting spells.

Primary Hypertension—Sometimes called essential hypertension, and commonly known as high blood pressure. An elevated blood pressure not caused by kidney or other evident disease.

Pulmonary Edema—Fluid buildup in the lungs.

Renin—A protein formed in an ischemic kidney.

Retina—Innermost coat of the eye, formed of light sensitive nerve elements and containing veins and arterioles.

Retinopathy—Damage to the retina of the eye.

Secondary Hypertension—Elevated blood pressure caused by certain specific diseases or infections.

Serum Creatinine—A blood test that measures the kidney's ability to remove nitrogen waste from the blood.

Silver Wire Effect—View of arteriolar light reflex in retina in which changes to the arterioles produce a broad white line with blood column not present in the areas where the line is most prominent.

SMA Series—A series of tests performed by a special computerized machine based on a single blood sample. The machine may be calibrated to give results of 6, 12, 18 or more studies.

Symptom—Any subjective evidence of a patient's condition.

Systole—The part of heart cycle when heart is contracting.

Systolic Hypertension—Condition in which systolic pressures are increased above the normal range while the diastolic pressures remain in the normal range. Systolic hypertension is usually secondary to other disease processes.

Target Organ—Organ which may be severely affected by hypertension. Another name is end organ. The four target organs are the brain, retinae of eyes, heart and kidneys.

Urinalysis—An analysis of a urine sample.

Vasoconstrictor—The vasoconstrictor nerves are one part of the involuntary nervous system. When these nerves are stimulated they cause the muscles of the arterioles to contract, thus narrowing the arteriole passage, increasing the resistance to the flow of blood, and raising the blood pressure. Chemical substances which stimulate the muscles of the arterioles to contract are called vasoconstrictor agents or vasopressors.

Vasodilators—Drugs which dilate or expand blood vessels to reduce peripheral resistance.

Glossary 11

Ischemic Heart Disease

Adult Listings— 4.04

Child Listings— not applicable

GLOSSARY OF MEDICAL TERMS

Angina Pectoris—Pain characterized by a squeezing, crushing, burning or oppressive pain of cardiac origin relieved promptly by nitroglycerin or rest.

Angiocardiography (Arteriography)—X-ray examination of the heart and blood vessels that follows the course of a dye which has been injected into a coronary artery or specific chamber.

Arterial Blood—Oxygenated blood.

Artery—Carries blood away from the heart.

Atheroma—Fatty deposit in the inner lining of artery wall.

Atherosclerosis (Arteriosclerosis-ASHD)—Commonly called hardening of the arteries. Artery walls become thick and irregular because of yellowish plaque deposits.

Atrial Septum—Muscular wall dividing left and right upper chambers of the heart.

Atrioventricular Node (A-V Node)—Specialized muscle fibers between the upper and lower chambers of the heart that serves to conduct impulses from the rhythmic heartbeat.

Atrium (Auricle)—One of the two upper chambers of the heart.

Bradycardia—Abnormally slow heart rate.

Capillaries—Extremely narrow tubes between the arterioles and veins.

Cardiac—Pertaining to heart.

Cardiovascular—Pertaining to heart and blood vessels.

Carditis—Inflammation of the heart.

Cholesterol—A fatlike substance found in animal tissue.

Collateral Circulation—Circulation of the blood through nearby small vessels when a main vessel has been blocked.

Contractility—Ability to shorten in reaction to a stimulus.

Costochrondritis—Inflammation of a rib or its cartilage. Pain secondary to this inflammation may masquerade as angina pectoris.

Cyanosis—Blueness of skin caused by insufficient oxygen in the blood.

Dyspnea—Difficult or labored breathing.

Electrocardium (EKG)—Graphic record of the electrical currents produced by the heart.

Enzyme—Organic substance capable of speeding up specific biochemical processes in the body.

Heart Block—Interference with the conduction of the electrical impulses of the heart which can be either partial or complete.

Hypertension (Commonly Called High Blood Pressure)—An unstable or persistent elevation of blood pressure above the normal range.

Infarction—A localized or circumscribed area of ischemic tissue necrosis secondary to inadequate flow of blood.

Ischemia—Local deficiency in blood supply to an area often caused by a constriction or obstruction in the blood vessel supplying that part.

Myocardium—Muscular wall of the heart. The thickest of the three layers, it lies between the endocardium and epicardium.

Necrosis—Pathologic death of a cell or group of cells in contact with living cells.

Nitroglycerin—A vasodilator which relaxes the muscles in the blood vessels.

Pancreatitis—Inflammation of the pancreas. Pain secondary to this inflammation may masquerade as angina pectoris.

Pericarditis—Inflammation of the thin membrane sac which surrounds the heart.

Pericardium—Thin, membrane sac which surrounds the heart.

Sino-Atrial Node (S-A Node)—Specialized mass of cells in right upper chamber of heart which initiates contractions of the heart.

Subendocardial—Denotes an infarction occurring beneath the endocardium or between the endocardium and myocardium.

Tachycardia—Abnormally fast heart rate.

Transmural—(Across a wall) denotes a heart attack involving the full thickness of ventricular wall in a given location.

Glossary 12

Cardiac Arrhythmias

Adult Listings— 4.04C, 4.05

Child Listings— 104.05, 104.07

Adams-Stokes Syndrome, also *Stokes-Adams Syndrome*—Sudden attacks of unconsciousness, sometimes with convulsions, which may accompany heart block.

Arrhythmia—An abnormal rhythm of the heart beat due to a dysfunction in impulse formation or conduction.

A-V Block, Atrioventricular Block—An interruption of the impulse from the A-V node.

A-V Node, Atrioventricular Node—A small mass of special muscular fibers at the base of the wall between the two upper chambers of the heart. It receives the electrical impulse from the natural pacemaker and transmits it on to the Bundle of His.

Bradycardia—Abnormally slow heart rate, generally below 60 beats per minute.

Bundle Branch Block—A form of heart block in which the two ventricles contract independently of each other because of an obstruction of the electrical impulse along one of the bundle branches.

Bundle of His—A small mass of specialized muscular fibers which transmits the electrical impulse from the A-V node to the two bundle branches.

Conduction—The transference of the electrical impulse.

Diastole—The period of relaxation in the cardiac cycle in which the heart fills with blood.

Electrolytes—Blood salts. Refers to the capability of a substance to conduct electricity.

Fibrillation—Uncoordinated contractions of the heart muscle occurring when the individual muscle fibers take up independent irregular contractions.

Heart Block—Interference with the conduction of the electrical impulses of the heart. This can result in dissociation of the rhythms of the upper and lower heart chambers.

Left Bundle Branch—The left division of the bundle of specialized muscle fibers which runs along the septum from the Bundle of His to the bottom of the ventricle.

Mobitz I and Mobitz II—refers to a specific type of second degree A-V block.

Pacemaker—The *natural pacemaker* is the S-A node. An *artificial pacemaker* is a device which stimulates the ventricular contraction by means of electrical impulses at a present rate.

Purkinje Fibers—Specialized muscular fibers forming a network in the walls of the ventricles which are believed to be involved in conducting electrical impulses to the muscular walls of the ventricles.

Rhythm—The pattern of the heart beat.

Right Bundle Branch—The right division of the bundle of specialized muscle fibers which runs along the septum from the Bundle of His to the bottom of the ventricle.

S-A Node, Sino-Atrial Node—The natural pacemaker.

Sick Sinus Syndrome—A term which indicates a failing S-A node. The electrical impulse can be slowed, blocked, or cause alternative fast and slow heart rates such as alternating tachycardia and bradycardia.

Syncope—A feeling of weakness and dizziness, or a fainting spell which results from decreased blood flow to the brain.

Systole—The contraction phase of the cardiac cycle.

Tachycardia—An abnormally fast heart rate—generally over 100 beats per minute.

Wenchebach—A specific type of second degree A-V block.

Wolff-Parkinson-White Syndrome (WPI)—A syndrome which is characterized by the electrical impulse being directly transmitted to the ventricles without passing through the A-V node.

Glossary 13

Vascular

Adult Listings— 4.11, 4.04B7

Child Listings— not applicable

Aneurysm—Balloon-like sac formed by the dilation of the walls of an artery damaged by arteriosclerosis.

Angina Pectoris—Spasmodic chest pains usually resulting from decreased blood flow to the heart caused by atherosclerotic disease of the coronary arteries.

Aorta—The main artery carrying blood from the heart to the rest of the body. The ascending aorta is that part between the heart and the aortic arch where it turns to become the descending aorta; the aorta with the chest or thorax is known as the thoracic aorta and within the abdomen is called the abdominal aorta.

Aortic Arch—The point in the aorta at which it curves from an upward to a downward direction within the chest or thoracic cavity.

Aortic Insufficiency—An improper closing of the valve between the aorta and the ventricle admitting a back flow of blood.

Aortic Valve—The valve at the junction of the aorta and the ventricle. Formed by 3 cup-shaped membranes it allows the blood to flow from the heart into the artery and prevents a back flow.

Aortography—An X-ray of the aorta after an opaque medium has been injected into a blood vessel.

Arteriosclerosis—Disease of arteries, often referred to as hardening of the arteries. It includes and is often used synonymously with atherosclerosis.

GLOSSARY OF MEDICAL TERMS

Arteriovenous Aneurysm—Abnormal direct communications between arteries and veins through which blood flow bypasses capillary beds.

Bypass Operation—A surgical procedure in which a graft is attached to an artery above and below the site of obstruction for the purpose of providing a normal blood flow distal to the diseased vessel.

Cardiovascular Syphilis—Syphilis affects the cardiovascular system many years after the primary infection; the aortic valve ring may become dilated producing aortic insufficiency and there may be pathological changes in the wall of the aorta that may lead to aneurysm.

Carotid Arteries—The principal arteries which supply blood to the brain.

Congenital—An abnormality present at birth.

Dilation—The condition of being dilated or stretched beyond the normal dimensions.

Dissecting Aneurysm—An aneurysm which occurs when a portion of a vessel's wall gives way leaving openings between the layers through which blood enters causing splitting of the arterial wall.

Distention—The state of being thickened or enlarged.

Etiology—The study of the cause of any disease.

Femoral Artery—An artery in the upper leg.

Heart Failure—Failure of the heart to pump all of the blood attempting to return to it from the veins.

Hemiplegia—Paralysis of one side of the body caused by damage to the opposite side of the brain.

Iliac Arteries—The terminal branches of the abdominal aorta; the principle organs supplying blood to the pelvic or this region and the legs.

Infarct—An area of tissue which is damaged or dies as a result of not receiving a sufficient blood supply.

Infrarenal—Beneath the renal arteries.

Lesion—An abnormality in any structure of the body.

Myocardial Infarction—Used synonymously with heart attack or coronary thrombosis, but refers specifically to the death of part of the heart muscle or myocardium.

Paraplegia—Loss of motion and sensation in the legs and lower part of the body. This sometimes results from hemorrhage in an artery conducting blood to the spinal cord.

Poplital Artery—An artery behind the knee.

Sac—Pouch.

Subclavian Arteries—Arteries that supply blood to the upper chest, shoulders and arms.

Syncope—A fainting or swooning. One cause for syncope can be an insufficient supply of blood to the brain.

Thoracic—Pertaining to the chest.

Ventricular Aneurysm—An aneurysmal dilation of a portion of a wall of the left ventricle.

Glossary 14

Heart Failure

Adult Listings— 4.02, 4.09

Child Listings— 104.02, 104.07

Anorexia—Lack or loss of appetite.

Aortic Valve—The valve between the left ventricle and the aorta.

Ascites—Fluid accumulation in the abdominal cavity.

Auscultation—Listening for sounds in the body. It can be performed without (direct or immediate) or with (mediate) the aid of an instrument such as a stethoscope.

Cardio-Thoracic Ratio (CTR)—The percentage calculation of heart size in comparison to the size of the thoracic cavity.

Cardiomegaly—Enlargement of the heart.

Commissurotomy—A surgical procedure that involves insertion of the finger or finger knife into a stenotic valve to increase the valve opening.

Compensation (Cardiac)—The maintenance of adequate blood flow without distressing symptoms. May be accomplished by natural mechanisms (e.g., hypertrophy) or be drug induced (e.g., digitalis).

Congestion—Engorgement of tissue with blood beyond the normal supply which prevents normal function.

Congestive Heart Failure (CHF)—An impairment that results from the inability of the heart to pump enough oxygenated blood to body tissues. An accumulation of fluid in various parts of the body results from the inability of the heart to maintain adequate circulation.

Contractility—Capacity to become short in reaction to a stimulus, such as in the contraction of the ventricles.

Cor Pulmonale—Heart disease resulting from disease of the lungs or the blood vessels in the lungs due to resistance to the passage of blood through the lungs.

Decompensation—Inability of the heart to maintain adequate circulation, usually resulting in a waterlogging of tissues (edema), dyspnea, and venous distention.

Diastole—The period of a cardiac cycle when the heart relaxes. Ventricular and auricular diastole occur alternately. When speaking of arterial pressure, the term commonly applied to ventricular relaxation.

Digitalis—A drug that acts to shorten cardiac muscle fibers, producing a faster and stronger contraction with longer time between beats. It also constricts peripheral arterioles, increasing blood pressure.

Dilatation (Dilation)—A stretching of the size of a heart chamber so that it holds a larger volume of blood.

Distention—Dilation or enlargement.

Diuretic—A drug that reduces the retention of sodium and water, thus reducing edema.

Dyspnea—Difficult or labored breathing. (DOE—dyspnea on exertion.)

Edema—Swelling due to abnormally large amounts of fluid in the body.

Electrocardiogram (ECG, EKG)—A graphic representation of the electrical currents which occur during heart functioning.

Fluorscopy—Examination of a structure deep in the body by use of X-rays passed through the body and captured on a fluorescent screen.

Hepatomegaly—Enlargement of the liver.

Hypertrophy (Cardiac)—A thickening of the muscle wall of a heart chamber. An increase in cell size.

Incompetence—Inadequacy or insufficiency, for example, in a cardiac valve

Insufficiency (Valvular)—Incomplete closure of a valve which permits regurgitation, backwards flow, of the blood.

Ischemia—Deficient blood supply.

Mitral (valve)—The valve between the left atrium and ventricle.

Murmur—A sustained sound vibration of the heart during systole and/or diastole.

Necrosis—Death of tissue.

Orthopnea—A form of shortness of breath that occurs when an individual is in a recumbent position, relieved by elevating the upper body.

Outflow Tract, Right—The pulmonary arteries and the vessels of the lungs through which blood is pumped by the right ventricle. An X-ray term.

Paroxysmal Nocturnal Dyspnea—A form of shortness of breath that occurs episodically during the night, awakening the individual.

Percussion—Tapping a part of the body and noting the sound.

Pitting Edema—The imprint of a finger on the skin of the foot will remain for a period of time.

Pulmonic (Valve)—The valve between the right ventricle and the pulmonary artery (pulmonary valve).

Regurgitation—Incomplete closure of a valve (insufficiency).

Roentgenogram—An X-ray.

SOB—Shortness of breath.

Stenosis (Valvular)—A narrowing or stricture of a valve that reduces blood flow.

Systole—The period of a cardiac cycle when the heart contracts. Ventricular and auricular systole occur alternately. When speaking of arterial pressure, the term commonly applied to ventricular contraction.

Tachycardia—Abnormally fast heart rate usually considered to be a rate over 100 beats per minute.

Tricuspid (Valve)—The valve between the right atrium and ventricle.

Vasodilator—A drug that acts to dilate vessels.

Glossary 15

Peripheral Vascular

Adult Listings— 4.12, 4.13

Child Listings— not applicable

Arteriogram—X-ray picture of the opening or channel of an artery made by injecting a radiopaque substance into the blood (see radiopaque).

Arteriosclerosis—Disease of arteries, often referred to as hardening of the arteries. It includes and is often used synonomously with atherosclerosis.

GLOSSARY OF MEDICAL TERMS

Arteriosclerosis Obliterans—Arteriosclerosis in which thickening of the lining of small vessels has completely obliterated the opening of an artery.

Artery—A vessel that carries blood from the heart to the tissues of the body, ending in small branches called arterioles which in turn branch to form the capillaries.

Atherosclerosis—A form of arteriosclerosis in which there is a characteristic focal deposition of lipids initially within the intimal layer of the artery; associated with a growth of smooth muscle cells and other changes in the arterial wall; this form of arteriosclerosis causes most strokes and heart attacks.

Atrophy—A wasting or diminution in the size of a cell, tissue, organ or part.

Brawny Edema—Tough, firm, long-standing congestion with excess fluid in dependent extremities—due to poor circulation.

Buerger's Disease—Thromboangiitis obliterans.

Capillaries—Small vessels, only one cell in thickness from which blood supplies oxygen and nutrients to tissues; formed by the branching of arterioles, they combine into larger vessels called venulse.

Collateral Circulation—The development of connecting around an obstruction to blood flow through the growth of small arteries above and below the obstruction; nature's method of compensating for an obstruction in blood flow.

Communicating Veins—Veins that connect the deep veins and the superficial veins.

Coumarin—A class of chemical substances which delay clotting of the blood. An anti-coagulant.

Cyanosis—A clinical condition characterized by a bluish appearance caused by a lack of oxygen in the blood.

Deep Veins—Run inside the muscles of the leg and thigh.

Dependency—Lowering the extremities.

Dermatitis—A skin condition that results from poor blood supply.

Doppler Effect—A diagnostic technique using a Doppler ultrasound machine by which ultrasonic vibrations are introduced into a patient's arm, leg or neck. The sound vibrations bounce back.

Dorsalis Pedis Artery—The artery on the dorsum of the foot, continuance of the anterior tibial artery.

Edema—The presence of abnormally large amounts of fluid in the intercellular tissue spaces of the body.

Embolectomy—Surgical removal of an embolus from a blood vessel.

Embolism—The sudden blockage of an artery by a clot or foreign material which has been brought to the sight of obstruction by the blood stream.

Embolus—A clot or other matter which travels through the bloodstream to lodge in a small vessel and cause an obstruction to the circulation.

Etiology—The study of the cause of any disease.

Femoral—Pertaining to the femur or to the thigh.

Femoral Artery—An artery in the upper leg.

Fibrinogen—A protein found in the blood; transformed into a smaller protein called fibrin during the formation of a bloodclot.

Functional—A term used to describe disturbances of circulation caused by changes in the caliber of the blood vessels, which are not structural/organic in character. These changes are usually transient and reversible.

Gangrene—Irreversible necrosis (death) of tissue usually in considerable mass, generally associated with loss of vascular supply and followed by bacterial invasion.

Heparin—An acid occurring in various tissues, but most abundantly in the liver; when injected into the circulation it blocks blood coagulation and promotes the clearing of fat.

Iliac Arteries—The terminal branches of the abdominal aorta; the principle arteries supplying blood to the pelvic or hip region and the legs.

Incompetent—Pertaining to an organ, structure or system which cannot perform its function.

Incompetent Valve—Any valve which does not close tight and leaks blood back in the wrong direction.

Induration—State of being hard.

Infarct—Death of tissue (necrosis) due to deficiency of blood supply (ischemia).

Intermittent Claudication—A symptom of arterial occlusive disease in the legs; it is characterized by pain by walking or exercising and by relief of pain on resting.

Ischemia—An inadequate supply of arterial blood to a part of the body. The relative lack of oxygen produces pain, and the deficiency of nutrients leads to various stages of death of tissues.

Ischemic—The state in which a cell or tissue has an insufficient supply of oxygen.

itis—A word termination that denotes inflammation.

Lesion—An abnormality in any structure of the body.

Ligation—Process of tying off veins (without stripping).

Noninvasive Procedure—A procedure which does not involve injection or insertion of foreign chemical, catheters or other substances into the patient.

Occlusion—The closing off or closure of a passage; an obstruction.

Organic—An adjective used to describe disturbances of circulation caused by structural changes in the walls of the blood vessels. These changes are usually permanent.

Oscillometer—An instrument which measures the changes in magnitude of the pulsations in the arteries.

Patent—Open, unobstructed or unclosed.

Peripheral—Pertaining to or situated in that portion of a system outside the central region.

Peripheral Edema—Excess fluid buildup in the extremities.

Phlebitis—Inflammation of a vein often in the leg.

Phlebos—Greek word for vein.

Pigmentation—Discoloration.

Plaque—A well-demarcated area, raised patch or swelling on a body surface. Atheromatous plaques occur on the inner surface of an artery and have a yellowish color produced by fatty deposits.

Plethysmography—The recording of the changes in the size of a part of the body as modified by the circulation of the blood in it.

Popliteal Artery—An artery behind the knee that carries blood from the femoral artery to the lower leg.

Posterior Tibial Artery—Situated behind the ankle.

Pulmonary Embolus—A substance that is carried from a distal part of the vascular tree to the lungs where it is too large to pass through the pulmonary vessels; most frequently an embolus arises from a blood clot in a vein.

Pulse—The expansion and contraction of an artery which may be felt with the finger.

Radiopaque—The property of blocking X-rays resulting in a light or white appearance on the exposed X-ray film.

Renal Arteries—Major arteries from the abdominal aorta to the kidneys.

Rubor—Redness, one of the cardinal signs of inflammation.

Saphenous Veins—Two large superficial veins of the legs.

Stasis—A stoppage or slackening of the blood flow.

Stripping—Cutting out lengths of large veins and incompetent tributaries by subcutaneous dissection.

Subcutaneous—Beneath the skin.

Superficial Veins—Veins lying just under the skin.

Sympathectomy—An operation which interrupts some part of the sympathetic nervous system.

Tarsal Region—The instep.

Thrombo—Derived from a Greek word meaning clot.

Thromboangiitis Obliterans (Buerger's Disease)—An inflammatory and obliterative disease of the blood vessels of the extremities, primarily of the lower extremities, occurring chiefly in young men and leading to ischemia of the tissues and gangrene.

Thrombophlebitis—Inflammation and blood clotting in a vein.

Thrombosis—The formation or presence of a blood clot (Thrombus) inside a blood vessel or cavity of the heart.

Thrombus—A blood clot which forms inside a blood vessel or cavity of the heart. (See embolus)

Trophic Changes—Changes in the skin resulting from ischemia are known as trophic changes. The skin becomes cold and thickened. The color changes may vary from bluish-white to dark brownish-yellow discolorations. The nails become thickened, hard and brittle. With marked or prolonged ischemia, the skin undergoes various stages of death of tissue.

Ulceration—Loss of epithelial tissue and necrosis due to poor circulation (commonly in the extremities).

Ulcers—Sores on the legs which appear when venous insufficiency is in an advanced stage.

Varicose—Swollen, enlarged.

Varicosity—Enlarged and tortuous vein filled with pooled blood.

Vein—A vessel that transports blood from the capillaries in the tissues back to the heart.

Venous Insufficiency—Inadequacy of valves in the veins due to damage to the valves or distortion of the vein which allows blood to flow backward in the vein, i.e., away from the heart.

Glossary 16

Special Terms for Child Listings

Adult Listings— not applicable

Child Listings— 104.02, 104.04, 104.05, 104.08, 104.09

GLOSSARY OF MEDICAL TERMS

Acquired Defect—Not congenital.

Arrhythmia—An abnormal rhythm of the heart beat.

Arterial Oxygen (O_2) Saturation—The percent of oxygen-carrying capacity of the blood in arteries.

Cardiac Thrill—A low frequency vibration felt in association with a murmur when the hand is placed over the chest.

Cardiac Syncope—A feeling of weakness and dizziness, or a fainting spell which results from decreased blood flow to the brain.

Cardiomegaly—Heart enlargement.

Characteristic Squatting—A position assumed by children with congenital heart disease to relieve shortness of breath.

Clubbing (of Digits)—The fingers and toes develop a broadened, rounded tip because the small blood vessels are distended with poorly oxygenated blood.

Congenital Defect—A condition which existed prior to, or at, birth.

Congestive Heart Failure—An accumulation of fluid in the lungs which results from backing up of blood when the heart is unable to maintain satisfactory circulation.

Cyanosis—A blueness of the skin, especially about the lips and nails, caused by insufficient oxygen in the blood.

Dextroposition—Displacement to the right.

Ductus Arteriosus—A small duct which connects the aorta to the pulmonary artery in the fetus. It normally closes shortly after birth.

Dyspnea—Difficult or labored breathing. DOE—Dyspnea on exertion.

Edema—Swelling due to accumulation of fluid in the tissues. *Pulmonary edema*—Accumulation of fluid in the lung tissues.

Heart Block—Disturbance of the conducting system of the heart in which the electrical impulse is either partially or completely blocked.

Hemoptysis—The spitting up of blood or of blood-streaked sputum.

Hepatomealy—Liver enlargement.

Hypercyanosis—Extreme cyanosis.

Murmur—A gentle blowing sound perceived by listening to the chest. *Machinery murmur*—A constant, grinding sound heard in association with patent ductus arteriosus.

Palliative—Affording relief of symptoms, but not a cure.

Polycythemia—An abnormality of the blood in which there is an excessive number of blood cells.

Stenosis—A narrowing or stricture of an opening.

Subclavian Artery—An artery which branches from the aorta to supply oxygenated blood to the upper body. It lies under the clavicle.

Tachycardia—Usually a heart rate over 100 beats per minute—a fast rate.

Common Diagnostic Tools

Angiocardiography—Visualization of the heart and great vessels after intravenous injection of a contrast medium.

Arterial Blood Gas Studies (ABGS)—A special blood test from arterial blood which demonstrates the oxygen-carrying capacity of the blood.

Cardiac Catheterization—Passage of a small, flexible tubular instrument through a vein in an arm or a leg or in the neck and into the heart, to obtain blood samples, determine intracardiac pressures and to detect cardiac anomalies.

Electrocardiogram (ECG–EKG)—A graphic tracing of the electrical current produced by the excitation of the heart muscle. The excitation deflections resulting from atrial and ventricular activity.

Eight Common Cardiac Defects

Patent Ductus Arteriosus—A congenital defect in which the small duct between the aorta and the pulmonary artery fails to close after birth.

Ventricular Septal Defect—A congenital defect in which there is an abnormal opening between the two ventricles.

Atrial Septal Defect—A congenital defect in which there is an abnormal opening between the two atria.

Tetralogy of Fallot—A congenital malformation involving four distinct heart defects. Included are (1) a ventricular septal defect, (2) dextroposition of the aorta, (3) pulmonary stenosis and (4) right ventricular hypertrophy.

Transportation of Great Arteries—A congenital defect in which the aorta originates in the right ventricle, and the pulmonary artery originates in the left ventricle.

Pulmonary Stenosis—A congenital defect in which the pulmonary valve or the muscular wall above or below the valve is narrowed.

Coarctation of Aorta—A congenital defect in which some portion of the aorta is narrowed or pressed together.

Aortic Valve Stenosis—A congenital defect in which the aortic valve or the muscular wall above or below the valve is narrowed.

Glossary 17

Dysfunction

Adult Listings— as applicable

Child Listings— as applicable

Angina—A "strangling" pain.

Angina Pectoris—A "strangling" (crushing) pain in the chest, a symptom of cardiac ischemia.

Arrhythmia—Abnormal heart rhythm due to defective conduction in the heart.

Arterial Insufficiency—Arterial disease in the lower extremities, causing ischemia.

Arteriosclerosis—Hardening of the arteries; a group of diseases characterized by thickening and loss of elasticity of arterial walls.

Atherosclerosis—A type of arteriosclerosis in which the insides of the arteries are coated with fatty deposits.

Atrial Septal Defect (ASD)—A hole in the atrial septum.

Bradycardia—A slow heart rate, less than 60 per minute.

Cardiac Disability—Results from one or more of three consequences of heart disease: cardiac ischemia (with or without necrosis); congestive heart failure; and conduction defects and/or arrhythmias.

Cardiac Ischemia—Deficiency of blood to the myocardium (heart muscle).

Cardiac Shadow—The image of the heart as seen on a chest X-ray.

Cardiomegaly—Heart enlargement.

Congestive Heart Failure (CHF)—The failure of the heart as a pump so that the chambers do not empty completely at systole.

Coronary Artery Disease—Usually refers to atherosclerosis of coronary arteries.

Coronary Occlusion—See Myocardial Infarction.

Cyanosis—Blueness or duskiness of skin and mucous membranes reflecting inadequate oxygen in the blood.

Dyspnea—Difficult or labored breathing; shortness of breath.

CARDIOVASCULAR SYSTEM

Edema—The accumulation of fluid in tissue (e.g., edema of the lower extremities, which causes swelling).

End Organ Damage—Term for damage to organs caused by disease in the arteries.

End Organs—Heart, brain, eyes (retinae), kidneys.

Endocarditis—Inflammation of the endocardium.

Epicarditis—Inflammation of the epicardium.

Hyper—Prefix meaning increase.

Hypertension—High blood pressure (HBP).

Hypertrophy—Enlargement (e.g., cardiac hypertrophy).

Infarction—The death of an area of tissue due to cessation of arterial blood flow.

Ischemia—Deficiency of blood supply to a part.

-itis—Suffix meaning inflammation.

-megaly—Suffix meaning large.

Murmur—An abnormal heart sound that may be associated with a defective heart valve.

Myocardial Infarction (MI)—A "heart attack", necrosis of an area of the myocardium. Also called coronary occlusion (i.e., occlusion of coronary artery).

Myocarditis—Inflammation of the myocardium.

Necrosis—Death of tissue.

Occlusion—Blockage (e.g., occlusion of an artery).

Pectoris—Refers to the chest.

Pericarditis—Inflammation of the pericardium.

Sclerosis, Sclerotic—Hardening, hard.

Shortness of Breath (SOB)—A common symptom of heart disease, especially associated with congestive heart failure.

Stenosis, Stenotic—Narrowing, Narrowed (e.g., stenosis of an artery or heart valve).

Tachycardia—A fast heart rate, over 100 per minute.

Venous Insufficiency—Venous disease in the lower extremities (involving inadequacy of the venous valves), causing backup of blood.

Ventricular Septal Defect (VSD)—A hole in the ventricular septum.

DIGESTIVE SYSTEM

Glossary 18

General Terms

Adult Listings— 5.02, 5.03, 5.04, 5.05, 5.06, 5.07, 5.08

Child Listings— 105.03, 105.05, 105.07, 105.08

Abscess—A localized collection of pus in a cavity formed by the disintegration of tissue.

Absorption—The uptake of substances into or across tissues, as in the uptake from the intestinal lumen of fluids, solutes, proteins, fats, and other nutrients into the intestinal epithelial cells, blood, lymph, or interstitial fluids of the intestine.

Alimentary Canal—A tube that extends throughout the length of the torso; also known as the digestive tract, or gastrointestinal tract.

Anal Sphincter—The ring-like muscle which surrounds the anus.

Anastomosis—1. A communication between two vessels by collateral channels. 2. An opening created by surgical, traumatic, or pathological means between two normally distinct spaces or organs.

Anemia—A reduction below normal in the number of erythrocytes per cu.mm., in the quantity of hemoglobin, or in the volume of packed red cells per 100 ml. of blood. Anemia occurs when the equilibrium between blood loss (through bleeding or destruction) and blood production is disturbed.

Anorexia—Lack of desire for food.

Arthritis—A general term referring to a variety of inflammatory joint diseases.

Ascites—Effusion and accumulation of serous fluids in the abdominal cavity.

Assimilation—The transformation of food into living tissue.

Atresia—Absence or closure of a normal orifice or passage.

Barium (B. Sulphate)—A bulky, fine, white powder, without odor or taste, used as a contrast medium in roentgenography of the digestive tract.

Barium Studies—Visualization of the lumen of the digestive tract through the introduction of a contrast medium which can be detected by X-ray or fluoroscopy, such as barium sulfate. *B. enema*—X-ray or fluoroscopic visualization of the rectum and colon through the use of a contrast medium introduced through the rectum. *B. swallow*—Visualization of the upper gastrointestional tract, particularly of the esophagus, through the ingestion of a contract medium observed by X-ray filming or fluoroscopy.

Bile—A brownish or greenish-yellow, bitter, alkaline fluid secreted by the liver and emptied into the small intestine through the gallbladder and bile ducts; functions to neutralize the acidity of the upper small intestine and to act as a detergent, dissolving cholesterol and the products of fat digestion.

Biliary—Pertaining to the bile ducts, or the gallbladder.

Biliary cirrhosis—See Cirrhosis.

Bilirubin—A bile pigment; it is a breakdown of the iron constituent of hemoglobin, mainly formed from the degradation of red blood cells. Bilirubin normally circulates in plasma and is taken up by the liver to form bile pigment. In individuals with blockage of the flow of bile into the intestine and in certain liver disorders, bilirubin accumulates in the blood and tissues and is excreted in the urine. *Indirect b.* (unconjugated b.)—The percent volume of the lipid soluble form of bilirubin which circulates in loose association with plasma proteins. *Total serum b.*—The percent volume of bilirubin in the blood including both free bilirubin (direct b.) and indirect bilirubin.

Calcium—A critical life element found in the body as calcium carbonate (bone and teeth), in combination with plasma proteins, and in the free ion state. The proper concentration of calcium ion is essential to muscle and nerve function, to blood coagulation and to the strength of cell membranes. If calcium ion concentration falls below 50 percent of normal, tetany occurs and death results from spasm of respiratory muscles. Excessive concentration can cause severe mental and heart problems. *Serum calcium*—the concentration of calcium in the blood, usually expressed in milligrams per 100 milliliter (mg./100 ml.).

Cardiac Sphincter—The ring-like muscle surrounding the esophagus where it opens into the stomach.

Cecum—The first part of the ascending colon, forming a dilated pouch into which open the cecum, the colon ileum and the appendix.

Cholangitis—Inflammation of a bile duct.

Cholecystectomy—Surgical removal of the gallbladder.

Cholecystitis—Inflammation of the gallbladder.

Cholelithiasis—The presence or formation of gallstones.

Chronic Liver Disease—Any of a variety of liver disorders which have persisted for a long time; e.g., cirrhosis, hepatitis, with resulting interference with liver functions.

Chyme—The semifluid, homogenous, creamy or gruel-like material produced by gastric digestion of food; also called chymus.

Cirrhosis—A group of chronic diseases of the liver characterized by loss of normal lobular structure, with fibrosis and nodular regeneration, following the destruction of liver cells. *Biliary c., secondary*—Cirrhosis due to obstruction or infection of the bile ducts. *Laennec's c.*—See portal c. *Portal c.*—Cirrhosis of the liver closely associated with chronic, excessive, alcohol consumption. In early stages liver enlargement may reflect fatty infiltration of liver cells (fatty c.), with necrosis and inflammation due to acute alcohol injury. Followed later by progressive fibrosis extending from the portal area.

Colectomy—Excision of a portion of the colon (partial c.) or of the entire colon (complete or total c.).

Colitis—Inflammation of the colon. *Granulomatous c.*—Inflammation of the colon affecting the full thickness of the colon wall with the formation of small, rounded, fibrotic masses composed largely of capillaries. *Ulcerative c.*—Chronic, recurrent ulceration of the colon, chiefly of the mucosa and submucosa, or unknown cause.

Colon—That part of the large intestine which extends from the cecum to the rectum.

Colon, Ascending—Portion of the colon between the cecum and the right colic flexure.

Colon, Descending—Portion of the colon between the left colic flexure and the sigmoid colon.

Colon, Sigmoid—The part of the colon in the pelvis that extends from the descending colon to the rectum.

Colon, Transverse—The portion of the colon that runs transversely across the upper part of the abdomen from the right to the left colic flexure.

Colostomy—The surgical creation of an opening between the colon and the surface of the body; also used to refer to the opening (stoma) thus created.

Coma—A state of unconsciousness from which the patient cannot be aroused, even by powerful stimulation. *Diabetic co-*

ma—The coma of severe diabetic acidosis. *Hepatic c.*—Coma accompanying the degenerative disease of the brain associated with severe liver disease. See encephalopathy.

Contrast Medium—Substances, such as barium sulphate, which block the passage of radiant energy (X-rays), with the representative areas appearing light or white on the exposed film; also called radiopaque material.

Debility—Lack or loss of strength.

Diaphragm—Musculomembranous partition which separates the abdominal and thoracic cavities.

Diastasis Recti—Separation of the rectus muscle of the abdomen away from the median line, sometimes occurring in pregnancy.

Dilatation—The condition, as of an orifice or tubular structure, of being expanded or stretched beyond normal dimensions.

Dilation—The act of stretching or expanding an orifice, tubular structure or hollow organ.

Distention—Expansion or stretching of an organ or structure.

Diverticulum—A sac or pouch in the walls of a canal or organ, especially the colon.

Dumping Syndrome—A complex reaction probably due to excessively rapid emptying of the stomach, manifested by nausea, weakness, sweating, palpitation, varying degrees of syncope, often a sensation of warmth, and sometimes diarrhea; occurs after ingestion of food in some patients who have had partial gastrectomy and gastrojejunostomy.

Duodenal Ulcer—See ulcer.

Duodenum—The first portion of the small intestine, extending from the pylorus of the stomach to the jejunum. It is about 12 finger breadths in length.

Dysphagia—Difficulty in swallowing.

Encephalopathy—Any degenerative disease of the brain. *Hepatic e.*—A condition usually occurring secondary to advanced disease of the liver but also seen in the course of any severe disease, or in patients with portacaval shunt. It is marked by disturbances of consciousness which may progress to deep coma (hepatic coma), psychiatric changes, and flapping tremor.

Endocrine—Secreting internally; applied to organs and structures which function to secrete hormones into the blood or lymph, having a specific effect on another organ or part.

Endoscopy—Procedure for examining the interior of a hollow organ, such as the bladder or intestine, using an endoscope.

Barium Enema—See Barium studies.

Enteritis—Inflammation of the intestine applied chiefly to the small intestine. *Regional e.*—See ileitis, regional.

Enterocolitis—Inflammation involving both the small intestine and the colon.

Enzyme—A protein capable of accelerating or producing, by catalytic action, some change in a substrate for which it is often specific.

Esophageal—Pertaining to the esophagus.

Esophagitis—Inflammation of the esophagus.

Esophagus—The musculomembranous, tubular passage extending from the pharynx to the stomach.

Fistula—An abnormal passage or communication, usually between two internal organs or leading from an internal organ to the surface of the body.

Fundus of Stomach—Enlarged portion of stomach to the left, located above the cardiac orifice.

Gallbladder—The organ which concentrates and stores bile.

Gastrectomy—Excision of the whole (total g.) or part of (subtotal g., partial g. gastric resection) the stomach.

Gastroenterostomy—The surgical construction of an opening between the stomach and small intestines.

Gastroileostomy—Surgical creation of an anastomosis between the stomach and the distal part of the small intestine.

Gastrointestinal—Pertaining to or communicating with the stomach and the intestine.

Gastroscopy—Direct visual examination of the interior of the stomach by means of a gastroscope (an endoscope).

GI—Abbreviation for gastrointestinal.

Glucose—The simple sugar most frequently found in certain foods, especially fruit and in the blood.

Glycogen—Sugar as it is stored in the liver and held ready for release for use by the body.

Guaiac Test—A blood stain treated with tincture of guaicum, and then with hydrogen dioxide, assumes a blue tint (used in testing stool for blood).

HCT—Abbreviation for hematocrit.

Hematemesis—The vomiting of blood.

Hematocrit (HCT)—The volume percentage of red blood cells in whole blood.

Hemoglobin—The oxygen carrying pigment of the red blood cells.

Hemorrhage—The escape of blood from the vessels; bleading. Small hemorrhages are classified by size as: petechiae (very small), purpura (up to one cm.), and ecchymoses (larger; bruises, black eye, etc.) Massive accumulation of blood within a tissue is called a hematoma.

Hepatic—Pertaining to the liver.

Hepatic Cirrhosis—See Cirrhosis.

Hepatic Coma—See Coma.

Hepatic Encephalopathy—See Encephalopathy.

Hernia—The protrusion of a loop or knuckle of an organ or tissue through an abnormal opening.

Hyperglycemia—Abnormally increased content of sugar in the blood.

Hypoalbuminemia—An abnormally low content of albumin in the blood.

Hypoglycemia—An abnormally low content of sugar in the blood.

Icteric—Relating to jaundice.

Icterus Index—Reading showing degree of jaundice by measuring the color of blood serum.

Ileitis—Inflammation of the ileum (the distal portion of the small intestine). *Regional i.*—A chronic inflammatory disease of unknown etiology, commonly affecting the distal portion of the ileum and characterized by scarring and thickening of the bowel wall; frequently leads to intestinal obstruction, and fistula and abscess formation.

Ileum—The distal portion of the small intestine, extending from the jejunum to the cecum.

Ileostomy—The surgical creation of an opening into the ileum, usually by establishing an ileal stoma on the abdominal wall.

Inoperable—Not suitable for the application of surgery, either because the morbid condition cannot be approached surgically due to its location, or because surgical intervention will not improve the prognosis for improvement.

Insulin—A protein hormone formed in the pancreas and secreted into the blood, where it regulates carbohydrate (sugar) metabolism.

Intractable—Resistant to cure, relief, or control.

Iritis—Inflammation of the iris, usually marked by pain, congestion of the ciliary region, photobia, contraction of the pupil, and discoloration of the iris.

Jaundice—A syndrome characterized by deposition of bile pigment in the skin and mucous membranes with resulting yellow appearance of the patient.

Jejunum—That portion of the small intestine which extends from the duodenum to the ileum.

Ketosis—Abnormally elevated concentration of ketone bodies, such as acetone and acetoacetic acid, which are the product of the metabolism of lipids (fatty acids, neutral fats, waxes, steroids, and phosphatides): it is a complication of diabetes mellitus and starvation.

Lesion—Any pathological or traumatic discontinuity of tissue or loss of function of an anatomical part.

Lipid—A group of organic substances which serve as a source of fuel to the cells of the body and which are an important constituent of cell structure. The term embraces fatty acids, neutral fats, waxes, steroids, and phosphatides.

Liver—The body's largest organ. It is located under the diaphragm and has multiple functions in production, storage, and detoxification.

Malabsorption—Imperfect absorption of nutritive material.

Malassimilation—Impairment of the body's cells ability to transform food into living tissue and energy.

Malnutrition—Any disorder of nutrition; it may be due to unbalanced or insufficient diet or to defective assimilation or utilization of food.

Melena—1. The passing of dark, pitchy, and clotted stools, stained with blood pigments or with altered blood. 2. Black vomit.

Nausea—An unpleasant sensation, vaguely referred to the epigastrium and abdomen, often culminating in vomiting.

Necrosis—Death of tissue, usually as individual cells or in small, localized areas.

Necrotic—Pertaining to or characterized by death of tissue.

Nutrition—The sum of the processes involved in the body's taking in nourishment and assimilating and utilizing it.

Obstruction—1. The act of blocking or clogging; 2. The state of being blocked or clogged.

Operable—Subject to surgical treatment with a reasonable degree of safety.

Pancreas—A large gland situated behind the stomach and between the spleen and the duodenum. The pancreas secretes digestive enzymes which are ducted into the duodenum, and secretes insulin directly into the blood.

Pancreatitis—Inflammation of the pancreas.

Parancentesis—Surgical puncture of a cavity in order to aspirate fluid.

Peptic—Pertaining to (pepsin) or to digestion; related to the action of gastric juice.

Peptic Ulcer—See ulcer.

Peristalsis—The serial contraction of the muscles of the digestive tract, each contraction following the other in a wave action that moves the food mass forward.

Pharynx—A cavity which serves as a common passageway for both the respiratory and digestive tracts.

Portal—Pertaining to an entrance, particularly to the hepatic portal, the transverse fissure on the surface of the liver at the portal vein and the hepatic ducts exit.

Prothrombin—Coagulation factor II; A protein present in the blood plasma, which, in the presence of other factors, converts to thrombin, which converts fibrinogen to fibrin, which forms the essential portion of a blood clot.

Pyloroplasty—A plastic operation to relieve pyloris obstruction or to accelerate gastric emptying.

Pylorus—The distal opening of the stomach, surrounded by a strong band of muscle, through which the stomach contents are emptied into the duodenum.

Regional Enteritis—See Ileitis, regional.

Resection—Excision of a portion of an organ or other structure. *Gastric r.*—partial gastectomy. *Wedge r.*—removal of a triangular wedge of tissue.

Roentgenogram—A photographic film produced through exposure to radiant energy such as Roentgen rays (X-rays).

Serum Blood—The clear liquid which separates from the clot and the corpuscles in the clotting or centrifuging of blood.

Serum Bilirubin—See Bilirubin, serum.

Serum Calcium—See Calcium, serum.

Serum Enzymes—See Enzymes, serum.

Shunt, Portacaval—Surgical creation of an anastamosis between the portal vein and the vena cava, performed in patients with esophageal varices secondary to portal hypertension.

Sigmoidoscopy—Inspection of the sigmoid flexure with a tubular speculum (sigmoidoscope).

Sphincter—A series of muscles capable of contracting or expanding to close or allow a passageway to open.

Stenosis—Narrowing or stricture of a duct or canal.

Stoma—A mouth or opening entrance into an organ or structure, particularly one surgically created in the abdominal wall by colostomy, ileostomy, etc.; also the opening between two portions of the intestine in an anastamosis.

Stricture—Decrease in the caliber of a canal, duct or other passage, as a result of scar contraction or the deposit of abnormal tissue.

Subtotal Gastrectomy—See Gastrectomy.

Surgery—The treatment of disease, injury or deformity through manual or operative methods.

Systemic Manifestations—Those signs, symptoms, and findings which indicate that a disease or disorder is affecting the body as a whole.

Ulcer—A local defect or excavation of the surface of an organ or tissue, which is produced by the sloughing of inflammatory necrotic tissue. *Duodenal u.*—An ulcer of the duodenum caused by the corrosive action of the gastric digestive juice pepsin; may be the result of excessive acid secretion or insufficient bile secretion. *Gastric u.*—Ulcer of the stomach lining. *Jejunal u.*—An ulcer of the jejunum. *Peptic u.*—An ulceration of the lining of the esophagus, stomach, or duodenum, caused by the action of the acid gastric juice, pepsin. *Perforating u.*—An ulcer involving the full thickness of an organ, such as the stomach or intestine, creating an opening on both sides. *Trophic u.*—An ulcer due to imperfect nutrition of the part.

Ulcerative Colitis—Chronic ulceration of the colon.

Upper GI Study—Reg. Barium studies.

Vagotomy, Complete—Transection of all vagal secretory fibers, sufficient to prevent increased flow or acidity of gastric secretion in insulin hypoglycemia.

Varices (plural of varix)—Enlarged and tortuous veins, arteries, or lymphatic vessels. *Esophageal v.*—Varicosities of the vein which joins with tributaries of the portal vein in the lower esophagus, occurring in patients with portal hypertension.

Viscus—Any large interior organ in any one of the three great cavities of the body, especially in the abdomen.

Wilson's Disease—Hepatolenticular degeneration; a hereditary disease characterized by degenerative changes in the brain and cirrhosis of the liver. *X-ray*—See Roentgenogram.

Genitourinary

Glossary 19

General Terms

Adult Listings— 6.02, 6.06

Child Listings— 106.02, 106.06

Albuminuria—The presence in the urine of serum albumin, the chief protein constituent of human blood plasma.

Anasarca—Generalized massive edema.

Dialysis—The removal of toxic metabolic byproducts from the blood by diffusion in an artificial kidney machine.

Edema—Collection of fluid in the tissues.

Glomerulonephritis—A common allergic kidney disease in which the glomerular tuft (Bowman's capsule) becomes inflamed. The glomerular membranes become extremely porous, allowing both protein and blood cells to flow freely into the nephron tubules. Occasionally, episodes of acute glomerulonephritis permanently destroy nephron capsules. Repeated small bouts may destroy more and more nephrons, causing *Chronic Glomerulonephronitis.*

Hematuria—Blood in the urine.

Hydroarthrosis—Swelling of a joint due to accumulation of water.

Hydronephrosis—A disorder of the kidney in which the ureter becomes obstructed (kidney stone, inflammation, fibrosis, etc.) causing the kidney to become distended by the accumulated urine. Prolonged distention can cause atrophy of nephrons, with residual reduction or loss of kidney function.

Immunosuppressive Agents—Agents which block the body's efforts to reject foreign bodies or tissues; used especially in organ transplants.

Nephrolithiasis—A condition marked by the presence of renal calculi in the kidney or its excretory tributaries.

Nephrosclerosis—Sclerosis (hardening) of the vascular arteries, arterioles, and, sometimes, the capillaries of the kidney; the form of "end-organ" damage due to hypertension.

Polycystic Kidney Disease—A hereditary, congenital condition characterized by multiple cysts of both kidneys.

Proteinuria—The presence of protein in the urine.

Pyelonephritis—A kidney inflammation primarily affecting the tubules and supportive tissues.

Renal Failure—Severe renal insufficiency, generally accompanied by signs and symptoms or uremia.

Renal Insufficiency—Abnormal (decreased) kidney function, ranging from mild to severe.

Renal Osteodystrophy—Demineralization of bone, caused by chronic renal insufficiency.

Uremia—The retention in the blood of excessive byproducts of protein metabolism, which produces a toxic condition marked by nausea, vomiting, headache, vertigo, dimness of vision, coma or convulsions and a fetid odor of the breath; result of nephron failure to adequately excrete urea and other protein byproducts.

Glossary 20

Specific Terms

Adult Listings— 6.02, 6.06

Child Listings— 106.02, 106.06

Albuminuria—The presence in the urine of serum albumin, the chief protein constituent of human blood plasma.

Anasarca—Generalized massive edema.

Anorexia—Lack of or loss of appetite for food.

Anuria (Anuresis)—Absence of excretion of urine from the body.

Azotemia—An excess of urea or other nitrogenous substances in the blood (elevated BUN) generally due to abnormal kidney function.

Blood Urea Nitrogen (BUN)—One of the nonprotein nitrogenous constituents of blood plasma.

Bowman's Capsule—(See Glomerulus.)

Corticosteroid—Any of the steroids produced by the adrenal cortex, including cortisol, corticosterone, aldosterone and their synthetic equivalents.

Creatinine—A normal product of muscle metabolism; level of which in blood is an index of level of kidney function.

Creatinine Clearance Test—A test for renal function based on the rate at which creatinine is excreted by the kidney.

Cutaneous Ureterostomy—Surgical procedure in which the ureter is brought to the surface of the abdomen through an incision in the iliac region, to conduct urine outside the body; usually preceded and necessitated by surgical removal of the bladder. (See Urinary diversion).

Cylindruria—Presence of casts in urine.

Cystectomy—Partial or complete surgical removal of the urinary bladder.

Cysto—Referring to the urinary bladder.

Cystoscope—A tube-like instrument containing lenses for viewing the interior of the bladder, entering through the urethra.

Dialysis—(See Hemodialysis and Peritoneal Dialysis.)

Diuresis—Increased secretion of urine.

Dysuria—Painful or difficult urination.

Edema—Collection of fluid in the tissues; swelling.

Glomerulonephritis—A common allergic kidney disease in which the glomerular tuft (Bowman's capsule) becomes inflamed. The glomerular membranes become extremely porous, allowing both protein and blood cells to flow freely into the nephron tubules. Occasionally, episodes of acute glomerulonephritis permanently destroy nephron capsules. Repeated small bouts may destroy more and more nephrons, causing CHRONIC GLOMERULONEPHRITIS.

Glomerulus (of Kidney)—A small tuft or cluster of capillaries enclosed within a bulb-shaped dilation (Bowman's capsule) the beginning of nephron tubule within the kidney. It is from the glomerulus that fluid filters from the blood system into the renal collection system.

Hematocrit—Volume percentage of red blood cells (erythrocytes) in whole blood.

Hematuria—Blood in the urine.

Hemodialysis—The removal of toxic metabolic byproducts from the blood by diffusion of an artificial kidney machine (hemodialyzer).

Hemodialyzer (Artificial Kidney Machine)—An apparatus which forces the affected individual's blood through semipermeable tubes immersed in fluid. Urea and other metabolic byproducts diffuse from the blood into the surrounding fluid; performs limited kidney function. Blood must be anticoagulated during dialysis.

Hydrarthrosis—Swelling of a joint due to accumulation of water.

Hydronephrosis—A disorder of the kidney in which the ureter becomes obstructed (kidney stone, inflammation, fibrosis, etc.) causing the kidney to become distended by the accumulated urine. Prolonged distention can cause atrophy of nephrons, with residual reduction or loss of kidney function.

Hyperlipidemia—Abnormally high concentration of lipids (usually fats) in the blood.

Immunosuppressive Agents—Agents which block the body's efforts to reject foreign bodies or tissues; used especially in organ transplants.

Kidney—Either of the two organs in the lumbar region which filter the blood of toxic metabolic byproducts, excreted as urine; also regulate the concentration of electrolytes (hydrogen, sodium, phosphorus, potassium, etc.) in the blood.

Kidney Stone—See Renal Calculus.

Nephrectomy—Surgical removal of a kidney.

Nephritis—Inflammation of the kidney; may be localized or diffuse and may involve the glomeruli, tubules, or the interstitial renal tissue.

Nephrolithiasis—A condition marked by the presence of renal calculi in the kidney or its excretory tributaries.

Nephron—The functioning filtering unit of the kidney, consisting of the glomerulus (Bowman's capsule) and uriniferous tubule. The two kidneys contain approximately two million nephrons and approximately 3/4 of these nephrons can be destroyed before blood composition becomes excessively abnormal.

Nephrosclerosis—Sclerosis (hardening) of the vascular arteries, arterioles and, sometimes, the capillaries of the kidney; the form of "end-organ" damage due to hypertension.

Nephrosis—A generic term for any disease of the kidney characterized by degenerative lesions of the renal tubules and/or glomeruli; generally used synonymously with the term, "nephrotic syndrome."

Nephrostomy, Cutaneous—The surgical construction of a permanent fistula from the surface of the skin (usually lumbar) directly into the pelvis of the kidney; usually compensatory for the loss of both the ureter and the bladder.

Nephrotic Syndrome—A condition characterized by edema, proteinuria, hypoalbuminemia, hyperlipidemia.

Nocturia—Excessive frequency of urination at night.

Obstruction (Urinary Tract)—Blockage of the outflow of urine from the kidneys at any level of the urinary tract.

Peritoneal Dialysis—The removal of toxic metabolic byproducts from the blood by diffusion (via a dialyzing solution) which takes place inside the abdominal cavity. The dialyzing solution is infused into, and removed from, the abdominal cavity on either a continuous or intermittent basis.

Polycystic Disease—A hereditary, congenital condition characterized by multiple cysts of both kidneys.

Polydipsia—Excessive thirst, persisting for long periods of time.

Polyuria—Excessive discharge of urine.

Proteinuria—The presence of protein in the urine.

Pruritus—Generalized itching.

Pyelography (IVP)—X-ray of the kidney and ureter using a contrast medium.

Pyelonephritis—A kidney inflammation primarily affecting the tubules and supportive tissues.

Pyuria—The presence of pus in the urine.

Rejection Crisis—Severe immune reaction of the body against grafted tissue, in which the body's defense mechanisms (antibodies, white blood cells, platelets, fibrin, etc.) attack the foreign tissue and cause failure of the graft; usually accompanied by pain and swelling.

Renal Calculus (Kidney Stone)—A solidified deposit developing in the kidney, usually composed of mineral salts (calcium, oxalates, uric acid, ammonium magnesium, phosphates, cholesteral) and occurring in a variety of sizes and shapes; may be singular or multiple.

Renal Failure—Severe renal insufficiency, generally accompanied by signs and symptoms of uremia.

Renal Insufficiency—Abnormal (decreased) kidney function, ranging from mild to severe.

Renal Osteodystrophy—Demineralization of bone, caused by chronic renal insufficiency.

Stricture (Ureteral, Urethral)—Abnormal narrowing (of the urethra or the ureter) due to fibrosis or the deposit of abnormal tissue.

Suprapubic cystostomy—The surgical construction of a fistula of combined skin and bladder flap to enable the collection of urine in a reservoir without using a cystotomy tube.

Urea—The chief nitrogenous constituent of urine and the chief nitrogenous end-product of the metabolism of proteins. It is formed in the liver from amino acids and compounds of ammonia.

Uremia—The retention in the blood of excessive byproducts of protein metabolism, which produces a toxic condition marked by nausea, vomiting, headache, vertigo, dimness of vision, coma or convulsions and a fetid odor of the breath; result of nephron failure to adequately excrete urea and other protein byproducts.

Ureter—The bilateral membranous canals conducting urine from the kidneys to the bladder.

Uretero-enterostomy—Surgical procedure to graft the ureter to an incision in the intestine to divert urinary flow into the intestine. Has higher potential of infection than other urinary diversion procedures because of high bacteria count in the intestine.

Ureterostomy, Cutaneous—See Cutaneous Ureterostomy.

Urethra—The membranes canal conducting urine from the bladder outside the body.

-uria—A suffix denoting a characteristic or constituent of the urine.

Urinary Diversion—Any of the surgical procedures (cystostomy, ureterointestinal diversion, cutaneous ureterostomy, cutaneous nephrostomy) undertaken to compensate for the loss of part of the urinary tract (ureter, bladder, urethra) by creating a substitute orifice to conduct urine outside the body.

Urinary Tract—Those organs and ducts which participate in the secretion and elimination of urine; i.e., the kidneys, ureters, bladder, and urethra.

Urine—The fluid excreted by the kidneys, stored in the bladder, and discharged by the urethra.

HEMIC AND LYMPHATIC SYSTEM

Glossary 21

General Terms

Adult Listings— 7.02, 7.05, 7.06, 7.07, 7.08, 7.09, 7.10, 7.11, 7.12, 7.13, 7.14, 7.15, 7.16

Child Listings— 107.03, 107.05, 107.06, 107.08, 107.11

AHF—Antihemophilic Factor, a coagulation factor absent in hemophiliacs.

AHG—Abbreviation for antihemophilic globulin; blood coagulation factor VIII.

Anemia—Reduction below normal in the number of red blood cells (RBC) per cu. mm., or in the quantity of hemoglobin, or in the volume of packed RBC's per 100 ml. of blood; anemia results when the equilibrium between blood loss (through bleeding or RBC destruction) and blood production is disturbed. *Aplastic a.*—A form of anemia, not readily responsive to treatment, in which the bone marrow fails to produce sufficient blood elements, even though there may be no demonstrated cellular abnormality of the marrow. Hemolytic (acquired) a.—Anemia due to factors other than heredity, such as poison, infection, or physical agents, in which red blood cells are prematurely destroyed faster than they can be produced. *Herric a.* (See Sickle Cell Anemia.) *Hypochromic a.*—The disproportionate reduction in the amount of hemoglobin compared to the volume of packed red cells; generally, the RBC's are also reduced in size. *Normocytic a.*—Anemia in which hemoglobin content, the volume of packed RBC's, and the number of RBC's per cu. mm. are all proportionately decreased. *Sickle cell a.*—Hereditary, genetically predetermined anemia, occuring almost exclusively in Negroes, characterized by joint pain, acute attacks of abdominal pain, ulceration of the lower extremities, sickle-shaped RBC's in the blood, and the presence of S hemoglobin in the RBC's, as defined by electrophoresis.

Anisocytosis—Variation of size of red blood cells.

Biopsy—The removal and examination, usually microscopic, of tissue from the living body, performed to establish precise diagnosis.

Blast—An immature or precursor cell form.

Bone Marrow—The soft material filling the cavities of the bones, made up of a meshwork of connective tissue, the meshes being filled with marrow cells, which consist variously of fat cells, large nucleated cells (myelocytes) and giant cells (megakaryocytes). *Yellow b.m.*—Ordinary bone marrow of the kind in which the fat cells predominates. *Red bone marrow*—Marrow of the cell developing bones (ribs, vertebrae, and many small bones) which is the producing site of red blood cells and granular white cells.

Calcium—A critical life element found in the body as calcium carbonate (bone and teeth) in combination with plasma proteins and in the free ion state. It is found in nearly all organized tissues and has been called coagulation factor IV because of its role in multiple phases of blood coagulation. *Serum c.*—The concentration of calcium in the blood, usually expressed in milligrams per 100 milliliter (mg./100 ml.).

CBC—Abbreviation for complete blood count.

Cerebrospinal Fluid—The fluid contained in the ventricles of the brain, the center of the spinal cord and surrounding both the brain and the cord, which serves to cushion the central nervous system from shock.

Coagulation (Blood)—The sequential process in which the multiple coagulation factors interact, ultimately resulting in the formation of an insoluble fibrin clot. *Coagulation deficit*—Any disorder of any stage of the cycle of coagulation, such as a deficiency of prothrombin, of thrombin, or of fibrin.

Coagulation Mechanism—As blood platelets flow through the vessels, they are normally repelled by the endothelial cells of the vessel walls which carry the same negative charge as do the platelets. When a vessel ruptures, the endothelial cell loses its negative charge and the platelets immediately adhere to the broken edges of the vessel and:

1. Rupture, releasing thromboplastin.
2. Thromboplastin and calcium and prothrombin and factor V and other factors produce thrombin.
3. Thrombin and fibrinogen form fibrin.
4. Fibrin threads entrap red blood cells and form a clot.

Complete Blood Count (CBC)—An estimate of the total number of the formed elements of the blood inferred from the representative number of these elements appearing in the microscopic examination of a blood sample. The elements counted are: lymphocytes, monocytes, neutrophils (young and mature), eosinophils, basophils, erythrocytes, leukocytes, platelets, and reticulocytes.

-cyte, cyto- —Combining forms indicating "cell."

Cytologic—Pertaining to the study of cells, their origin, structure, formation, and pathology.

Electrophoresis—The movement of charged particles suspended in a liquid under the influence of an applied electric field.

Erthrocyte (Red Blood Cell or Corpuscle)—One of the formed elements found in the peripheral blood. Normally, the mature form is a non-nucleated, yellowish biconcave disc, adapted by virtue of its hemoglobin content to transport oxygen and carbon dioxide.

Erythrocytosis—Abnormally elevated numbers of red blood cells (erythrocytes).

Fibrosis—The formation of fibrous tissue; fibroid or fibrous degeneration into scar tissue.

Fracture (Bone)—A breaking or rupture of a bone. *Pathologic f.*—Fracture occurring from mild injury, due to pre-existing bone involvement with tumor, cyst, infection, etc.

Globulin—Any of a group of proteins which are found in the blood and other body tissues. They include antibodies.

HCT—Abbreviation for hematocrit.

Hemarthrosis—Bleeding into joint spaces. The blood seriously damages the joint and may eventually destroy it.

Hematocrit—The proportion of red blood cells in a volume of blood.

Hemic—Pertaining to the blood.

Hemo—Combining form denoting relationship to blood.

Hemoglobin—The oxygen carrying iron-compound pigment of the red blood cells (erythrocytes). It carries oxygen to the cells and carbon dioxide from the cells to the lungs. There are many kinds of hemoglobin. *Hemoglobin C*—A form of hemoglobin the abnormal molecular structure of which produces moderate hemolytic anemia. *Hemoglobin S (Sickle Cell h.)*—A form of hemoglobin created by a single amino acid substitution in its molecular structure; one form causes sickle cell trait, the other sickle cell anemia.

Hemolysis—Release of hemoglobin into the blood plasma as the result of the destruction of red blood cells.

Hemophilia—A hereditary hemorrhagic tendency due to a coagulation factor deficiency and characterized by spontaneous or traumatic hemorrhage. Due to the coagulation deficiency bleeding may be both prolonged and profuse.

Hemorrhage—The escape of blood from the vessels; small hemorrhages are classified by size as petechiae (very small), purpura (up to 1 cm.), and ecchymoses (larger). The massive accumulation of blood within a tissue is called a hematoma. *Spontaneous h.*—Hemorrhage occurring without overt provocation.

Hodgkins Disease—A lymphoma manifested by progressive enlargement and matting of lymph nodes. This process spreads throughout the body until vital organs are compromised and death results.

Hypercalcemia—An excess of calcium in the blood. Excessive calcium can cause mental symptoms, affect heart performance, interfere with coagulation of the blood and can precipitate in the kidney, causing renal problems.

Infarction—The formation of an area of coagulation necrosis in a tissue due to the local deprivation of oxygen and nutriment, resulting from an obstruction of blood circulation to the area, most commonly by a blood clot.

Infection—Invasion and multiplication of a micro-organism in body tissues, resulting in local cellular injury.

Intracranial—Situated within the upper part of the head (cranium) lodging the brain.

Leukemia—A progressive malignant disease of the blood forming organs producing an excess of white blood cells (leukocytes) in the circulation. Leukemias arising from the bone marrow are called *myelogenous,* those from the lymphoid tissue, *lymphocytic.* Leukemias have all degrees of severity. In *acute leukemia,* the malignancy progresses extremely rapidly and the cells released into the blood are usually very early forms—in the case of *myelogenous* leukemia, myeloblasts, and in the case of *lymphocytic leukemia,* lymphocytes. In *chronic leukemia,* development is slower and the cells released into the system may be almost entirely normal.

Leukocyte—White blood cell. The varieties of leukocytes are classed into two main groups: *granular* (having abundant granules in the cytoplasm) and *agranular* (having no specific granules in their cytoplasm—also called lymphoid leukocytes).

Leukocytosis—A transient increase in the number of leukocytes in the blood resulting from various causes, as hemorrhage, fever, infection, inflammation, etc.

Lymph—A transparent, slightly yellow liquid found in the lymphatic vessels and derived from the tissue fluids. It occasionally contains red blood cells and often contains particles of fat. It consists of a liquid portion and of cells, mostly lymphocytes and is collected from all parts of the body to be returned to the blood via the lymphatic system.

Lymphatic—Pertaining to lymph or to a lymph vessel. In the plural (lymphatics), the term is used to designate the lymphatic system.

Lymph Node—Any of the accumulations of lymphoid tissue organized as definite lymphatic organs, varying from 1 to 22 mm. in diameter situated along the course of lymphatic vessels. The lymph nodes are the main source of lymphocytes in the peripheral blood and serve as a defense mechanism by removing noxious agents such as bacteria and toxins. May also play a role in antibody production.

Lymphocyte—A white cell with one nucleus, which is the only white cell not produced in the bone marrow. Lymphocytes are produced instead by lymphoid tissue in the lymph nodes, spleen, thymus gland and in the submucosa of the GI and respiratory tracts. As with other white cells, lymphocytes can pass into cell tissue spaces through the small pores in the capillaries. They participate in immune reactions and are usually destroyed in the performance of their immune defense of the body.

Lymphoma—A malignancy of the lymphatic tissue.

Macroglobulinemia—The pathologic production of variant globulins by disordered immature lymph and plasma cells which displace normal cells. The result is failure to produce normal cells and normal antibodies, with resultant anemia, coagulation defects, susceptibility to infections, and renal damage due to the abnormal globulins.

Myelocyte—An immature form or early developmental stage of any of the white cells (neutrophils, basophils, monocytes and the precursor of platelets, megakaryocytes) developed in the bone marrow.

Myelofibrosis—Replacement of the bone marrow by fibrous tissue, occurring in association with proliferation of bone marrow constituents secondary to unrelated conditions. Also called myelosclerosis.

Myeloma—A tumor composed of cells normally found in the bone marrow.

Neutrophil—A granular, amoeba-like leukocyte having a nucleus with 3 to 5 lobes connected by a filament, a cytoplasm containing five granules. These are the most important of the leukocytes in the protection of the body against acute infection by bacteria. They can pass through the pores of the capillaries and into the tissue spaces to attack, envelop, and digest any agent causing tissue damage.

Osmosis—The movement of molecules in solution through a permeable or semipermeable membrane.

Osteosclerosis—Hardening or abnormal density of the bone in which bone cells are replaced by deposits of calcium and phosphorus salts.

Pathology—That branch of medicine which addresses the essential nature of disease, especially of the structure and functional changes in tissues and body organs which cause or are caused by disease.

Plasma—Plasma suspends the blood cells and particulate components of blood, including nutriments, and is to be distinguished from *serum,* which is the cell-free portion of the blood from which fibrinogen has been separated in the process of clotting.

Phagocyte—Any granular leukocyte which ingests and devours bacteria and foreign substances.

Plasma Cells—Spherical or ellipsoidal cells which are functionally involved in the synthesis of immunoglobulins or antibodies.

Platelet—A disc-shaped structure found in the blood, approximately $^1/_7$ the diameter of a white cell, which is formed by the fragmentation of megakaryocytes (a leukocyte produced by the bone marrow) and chiefly known for its role in blood coagulation.

Poikilocytosis—Variation of normal shape of red cells.

Polycythemia Vera—A disorder of undetermined etiology, in which the rate of red blood cell production becomes far greater than normal, with no apparent physiological basis, and normal regulatory mechanisms fail to stop this production. Tremendous amounts of red cells are poured into the system. The viscosity of the blood increases as much as five times normal, impeding circulation. Often cells clump together and block vessels, further impeding circulation. In some cases, arterial pressures rise, overloading the heart and resulting in heart failure; frequently there is associated splenomegaly, leukocytosis and thrombocytopenia.

Prophylactic—Pertaining to treatment or measures undertaken to prevent disease.

Purpura—Hemorrhage under or into the skin or mucous membranes.

Radiology—The science of radiant energy and radiant substances (X-rays, radioactive isotopes), especially the branch of medicine which deals with the use of radiant energy in the diagnosis and treatment of disease.

RBC—Abbreviation for red blood cell. (See Erythrocyte) or red blood count.

Reticulocyte—An immature form of red blood cell.

Serum (Blood)—Blood plasma from which fibrinogen has been removed.

Serum Protein—Proteins in the serum component of the blood, including immunoglobulins, albumin, clotting factors, and enzymes.

Sickle Cell-Thalassemia Disease—A hereditary anemia involving two genetically predetermined hemoglobin abnormalities: the S-type hemoglobin of sickle cell disease and one of the hemoglobinopathies of thalassemia.

Spleen—A large gland-like but ductless organ situated in the upper left abdomen near the stomach. Of its known functions, a major function is to cleanse the blood of foreign debris. Reticuloendothelial cells line its highly vascular structure and envelope and digest foreign protein. The spleen also disintegrates fragile or old red blood cells, releasing the hemoglobin to be converted by the liver into bilirubin. Another major function is as a reservoir for concentrations of red blood cells.

Splenomegaly—Enlargement of the spleen.

Telangiectasia—A vascular lesion formed by the dilation of a group of small blood vessels, the basis for a variety of angiomas. *Hereditary hemorrhagic t.*—A hereditary disorder characterized by multiple small angiomas of the skin and mucous membranes, often with nose bleed or GI bleeding and sometimes with pulmonary or hepatic arteriovenous fistula.

Thalassemia—A hereditary group of anemias involving red blood cell disruption.

Thrombocyte—Blood platelet.

Thrombocytopenia, Chronic—A persisting decrease in the number of blood platelets, a factor which impairs blood clotting.

Thrombocytosis—Increased number of blood platelets in the blood.

Thrombosis—The formation, development, or presence of a blood clot (thrombus). A thrombus may occlude a blood vessel, interrupting blood flow to tissue, which, deprived of oxygen nutriments, may die.

Thrombotic Crisis—A symptom complex in sickle sell anemia, characterized by episodes of acute pain in the limbs or abdomen, accompanied by fever, indicative of infarctions of organs and tissue due to the occlusion of blood vessels.

Thrombus—An aggregation of blood factors, primarily platelets and fibrin, with entrapment of cellular element, frequently causing vascular obstruction at the point of its formation; an intravascular blood clot.

Vaco-occlusive—Pertaining to the obstruction of blood vessels.

Venesection—Surgical blood letting to thin the blood.

Viscera—(Plural of viscus) the large interior organs in any one of the three great cavities of the body (thoracic, abdominal, or pelvic).

SKIN

Glossary 22

Definitions of Skin Lesions

Adult Listings— 8.02, 8.03, 8.04, 8.05, 8.06

Child Listings— not applicable

Macule—A discolored spot on the skin that is not elevated above the surface.

Papule—A small, circumscribed solid elevation of the skin.

Nodule—A small rounded bump or node which is solid and can be detected by touch.

Wheal—A smooth, slightly elevated area which is redder or paler than the surrounding skin.

Polyp—A protruding growth from a mucous membrane.

Pustule—A small elevation of the epidermis filled with pus.

Ulcer—A loss of substance of cutaneous or mucous surface, causing gradual necrosis of the tissues.

Cyst—A sac which contains liquid or semi-solid material.

Fissure—A cleft or groove.

Glossary 23

Specific Terms/Diseases

Adult Listings— as above

Child Listings— not applicable

Acne Conglobata—A form of acne characterized by numerous blackheads, marked pus formation, infected cysts and sinuses, resulting in severe scarring.

Acrosclerosis—A form of systemic or generalized scleroderma, combining the features of Raynaud's disease with scleroderma of the distal parts of the extremities and of the neck and face.

Apocrine Gland—Large, branched, specialized sweat glands which empty into the upper portion of a hair follicle rather than directly onto the skin surface and which are found only in certain areas of the body, such as the axilla and perineum.

Atopic Dermatitis—A chronic skin condition of unknown etiology occurring in adolescents and adults, marked by roughening, cracking, and crusting of the skin, accompanied by intense itching.

Axilla (-ae)—Essentially, the armpit, but including also the nerves, vessels, lymph nodes, and tissue structures therein.

Bulla (-ae)—A large vesicle (blister) usually 2 cm. or larger, containing fluid.

Bullous Pemphigoid—A chronic, generalized eruption of bullae (blisters) over the skin, resembling but distinguished from pemphigus; usually seen in elderly adults.

Comedo (-ones)—A plug in an excretory duct of the skin; a blackhead.

Contracture—High resistance to passive stretch of a muscle, resulting from fibrosis of the tissues supporting the muscles or joints, or from disorders of the muscle fibers; can cause joint deformity.

Cutaneous—Pertaining to the skin.

Cyst—A closed cavity lined by epithelium containing liquid or semisolid material.

Dermatitis—Any inflammation of the skin.

Dermatitis Herpetiformis—A chronic dermatitis presenting successively appearing crops of grouped symmetrical lesions involving varied combinations of erythema, papules, eczema, vesicles, and bullae.

Desquamation—Shedding of the outer layer of the skin in small sheets and scales, similar to that seen after a bad sunburn.

Diffuse Scleroderma—See Systemic Scleroderma.

Disseminated (Systemic) Lupus Erythematosus—Progressive, systemic disease involving multiple organs and body tissues, in which skin lesions are but a superficial manifestation of severe underlying vascular and tissue lesions. (See Disseminated L. E. in Multiple Body System glossary).

Dyshidrosis—Any disorder of the eccrine sweat glands. (See Eccrine gland).

Ecchymosis—Large hemorrhages under the surface of the skin; "black and blue" marks, bruises, "black eye."

Eccrine Gland—Any exocrine gland, but specifically referring to the ordinary sweat glands, which are unbranched, coiled, tubular glands distributed over almost all of the body surface and promote cooling of the body through evaporation of their secretion.

Eczema—A superficial inflammation primarily of the epidermis, characterized in the early stages by redness, itching, minute papules and vesicles, weeping, oozing and crusting; later by scaling, lichenification, and pigmentation.

Epidermolytic Hyperkeratosis (Bullous Ichthyosiform Erythroderma)—A hereditary disease characterized by thickening and scaling of the skin, erythema, and blisters. The scales shed, leaving a raw surface on which scales reform.

Erythema—Redness of the skin produced by congestion of surface capillaries; resulting from a variety of causes.

Erythema Multiform Bullosum—A symptom complex characterized by vivid erythematous, primarily bullous, lesions but also presenting urticarial and purpuric lesions; appears suddenly in symmetrical distribution, usually on the face, neck, forearms, legs and the dorsal surfaces of the hands and feet.

Erythroderma—Abnormal redness of the skin, usually widespread over the body; a phase of exfoliative dermatitis.

Erythroderma, Ichthyosiform—A condition recognized as two distinct congenital diseases: *Bullous form* (See Epidermolytic hyperkeratosis) and the *nonbullous* (See Lamellar Ichthyosis); also called erythroderma ichthyosiforme congenitum.

Excoriation—Any superficial loss of skin substance, such as that produced on the skin by scratching or abrasion.

Exfoliation—A shedding of the skin in scales or layers.

Exfoliative Dermatitis—A skin disorder evolving from any of several preceding skin disorders, such as psoriasis or drug reaction, and characterized by erythema covering virtually the entire body, with itching, scaling, desquamation, and loss of hair.

Extensor Surface—The aspect of a joint or limb (such as the knee or elbow) on the side toward which extension is directed.

Fissure—A crack or split in the superficial tissue around an opening.

Flexsor Surface—The aspect of a joint or limb (such as the knee or elbow) on the side toward which flexion is directed.

Fungate—To produce fungus-like growths; to grow rapidly as does a fungus.

Hidradenitis, Suppurative (Hydradenitis, s.)—A disease of the apocrine sweat glands (located in the axilla and perineum), marked by the development of shot-like cutaneous nodules which gradually enlarge, undergo softening, and produce and drain pus.

Hydradenitis, Suppurative—See Hidradenitis, s.

Ichthyosiform Erythroderma—See Erythroderma, ichthyosiform.

Ichthyosis—Any of several generalized skin disorders characterized by dryness, roughness, and scaling, due to thickening of the horny, outer layer of the skin.

Lamellar Ichthyosis—A hereditary disease characterized by diffuse erythema and large grayish-brown scales; may be associated with small stature, oligophrenia, spastic paralysis and shortened life span.

Lesion—Any injury, damage, or abnormal change to a tissue or organ.

Lichenification—Thickening of the skin with exaggeration of its normal markings so that the striae form a criss-cross pattern, enclosing flat-topped shiny, smooth, quadrilateral facets; caused by scratching and rubbing in excess of that which the normal pain threshold would permit.

Lupus—See Disseminated (Systemic) Lupus Erythematosus.

Lymph—A yellowish, transparent liquid found in the lymphatic vessels and in various tissues and organs. Lymph has the consistency and function of modified blood.

Macule (Macula)—Discolored area of skin, not elevated above surrounding area.

Mycotic Infection—Any disease caused by a fungus.

Neoplastic Skin Lesions—Any disorganization of skin tissue due to malignant or nonmalignant growths, including warts.

Papule—A small circumscribed, superficial, solid elevation of the skin.

Pemphigus—Term for a group of skin diseases characterized by successive crops of bullae (blisters), the specific type indicated by a modifying term; frequently used alone to designate pemphigus vulgaris.

Perineum—Area of the pelvic floor bounded by the pubis, the upper thighs and the coccyx; the crotch.

Petechia—A pinpoint, nonraised, perfectly round, purplish-red spot caused by hemorrhage within the skin or mucous membrane.

Plaque—Any patch or flat area.

Pompholyx—Skin eruption of the sides of the fingers or toes, or on the palms or soles, consisting of small round blisters (vesicles), accompanied by intense itching.

Pruritus—Itching; also the term applied to various conditions causing intense itching.

Purpura—A group of skin disorders characterized by purplish or brownish-red discoloration, easily visible through the epidermis, caused by hemorrhage into the tissue. (See Petechia and Ecchymosis).

Purulent—Consisting of or containing pus; associated with the formation of or caused by pus.

Psoriasis—A chronic, hereditary, recurrent skin disorder, the distinctive lesions of which are vivid red macules, papules or plaques covered by silvery scales; usually involves the scalp and extensor surfaces of the limbs, especially of the elbows, knees, and shins.

Scleroderma—Chronic hardening and shrinking of the connective tissues of any part of the body; skin may be thickened, hard, rigid with pigmented patches; may be generalized (systemic or diffuse s.) or localized to the distal parts of the extremities and the face (acrosclerosis) or to the digits (sclerodactyly).

Sebaceous Gland—A gland secreting a thick oily substance (sebum) consisting of fat and cellular debris from the gland; secretion serves to lubricate the skin.

Sinus—An abnormal channel or fistula permitting the escape of pus.

Subcutaneous—Under the skin.

Sudoriferous Glands—Sweat glands (See Apocrine g. and Eccrine g.).

Suppuration—The formation of pus; the act of becoming converted into and discharging pus.

Supperative Hidradenitis (S. Hydradenitis)—(See Hidradenitis, Supperative).

Systemic Disease—A disease affecting a number of body tissues and organs.

Systemic Erythematosus—(See Disseminated Erythematosus).

Systemic Scleroderma—A form of scleroderma involving large areas of the body surface and internal organs (including the heart, lungs, esophagus and kidneys), marked by increase and swelling of the collagen fibers of connective tissue, loss or fragmentation of elastic elements, atrophy of the junction of dermal and epidermal skin layers, deposition of melanin in the basal skin cells, and the retention of calcium.

Sweat glands—Sudoriferous Gland (See Apocrine g. and Eccrine g.).

Ulcerate—To form an ulcer, localized excavation of the surface of an organ or tissue, produced by the sloughing of inflammatory necrotic tissue.

Urticaria—A vascular reaction of the skin marked by the transient appearance of smooth, slightly elevated patches (wheals) which are redder or paler than the surrounding skin and accompanied by severe itching.

Vesicle—A small (less than 1 cm.) blister; a small elevation of the skin, containing a serous fluid. (See also bulla).

Wheal—A smooth, slightly elevated arc on the skin, redder or paler than the surrounding skin; often accompanied by intense itching; usually changing its size or shape, or even disappearing within a few hours. It is the typical lesion of urticaria and the dermal evidence of allergy.

ENDOCRINE

Glossary 24

General Terms

Adult Listings— 9.02, 9.03, 9.04, 9.05, 9.06, 9.08

Child Listings— 109.03, 109.04, 109.05, 109.06, 109.08, 109.09, 109.10

Acidosis—A pathological accumulation of acids; can occur in severe diabetes mellitus (also called ketoacidosis).

Acromegaly—Postpuberty overgrowth of body tissues.

Addison's Disease—Characterized by bronzelike skin pigmentation, severe prostration, low blood pressure and digestive disturbance; also called adrenal cortical insufficiency (hypopituitarism).

Adrenal Gland—Endocrine gland situated in the retroperitoneal tissues above each kidney; consists of an outer portion (cortex) and inner portion (medulla).

Coma (Diabetic)—Unconsciousness resulting from accumulation of toxins in severe acidosis.

Cretinism—Severe lack of thyroid activity (hypothyroidism) in infants and children with a resulting failure of physical growth and mental development.

Cushing's Syndrome—A condition due to hyperfunctioning of the adrenal cortex characterized by rounding of the face, neck and trunk, kyphosis due to softening of the spine, dusky complexion with purple markings and hypertension.

Diabetes Insipidus—A disorder caused by hypofunction of the pituitary gland characterized by great thirst and the passage of a large amount of urine with no excess of sugar.

Diabetes Mellitus—A disorder resulting from failure of the pancreas to produce sufficient insulin. Excess sugars build up in the blood (hyperglycemia) with resulting sugar in the urine. Symptoms include increased thirst, urinary frequency and shortness of breath.

Dwarfism—Underdevelopment of the body due to hypopituitarism.

Exophthalmos—Protruding eyeballs caused by thyroid dysfunction (usually hyperthyroidism).

Exudates—Material such as fluid, cells or cellular debris which has escaped from blood vessels; seen in severe retinopathy; also referred to as cotton wool patches.

Gigantism—Abnormal overgrowth caused by hyperpituitarism.

Glucose—The most common of the body sugars.

Goiter—Enlargement of the thyroid gland, causing swelling in the front of the neck.

Gonads—Sex glands.

Graves' Disease—Hyperthyroidism.

Hemorrhage—Escaping blood; i.e., as seen in retinopathy.

Hirsutism—Abnormal hairiness, especially in women.

Hormone—A chemical substance that stimulates certain body activities.

Hyper—Prefix indicating excessive.

Hypo—Prefix indicating deficient.

Insulin—A hormone produced in the pancreas that regulates sugar in metabolism.

Ketosis—The presence of excess ketones (organic acids) in the blood.

Metabolism—The sum of all the physical and chemical processes by which living organized substance is produced and maintained; also the transformation by which energy is made available for the uses of the organism.

Myxedema—A condition in adults due to hypothyroidism characterized by a puffy face, physical sluggishness and slowed mental activity.

Neuropathy—Any functional disturbance and/or pathological changes in the peripheral nervous system.

Osteitis Fibrosa Cystica—A condition due to hyperfunction of the parathyroid gland characterized by skeletal deformities, loss of muscle tone and difficulty of movement.

Ovaries—Female sex glands.

Pancreas—The gland that produces insulin, (it also produces digestive juices); it is situated behind the stomach.

Parathyroid Glands—Four small glands located near the thyroid whose major function is the regulation of the metabolism of calcium and phosphorous.

Pituitary Gland—An endocrine gland divided into 2 lobes (anterior and posterior) located at the base of the brain; often called the governing endocrine gland of the body.

Poly—Combining form meaning many or much.

Polydipsia—Excessive thirst.

ENDOCRINE

Polyphagia—Excessive or voracious eating.

Polyuria—Passage of an abnormally large volume of urine.

Retinitis Proliferans—Formation of fibrous tissue bands extending from the retina; retinal detachment can result.

Retinopathy—Any noninflammatory disease of the retina; diabetes mellitus may cause retinal changes (diabetic retinopathy).

Testes—Male sex glands.

Tetany—A syndrome manifested by sharp flexion of the wrist and ankle joints, muscle twitchings, cramps and convulsions.

Thyroid Gland—An endocrine gland situated in the lower front of the neck which regulates metabolism.

Virilism—Development of male secondary characteristics in a female.

MULTIPLE BODY SYSTEMS

Glossary 25

General Terms for Adult Listings

Adult Listings— 10.02, 10.03, 10.04, 10.05, 10.10

Child Listings— not applicable

ANA (Anti-nuclear Antibody)—A blood test for disseminated (systemic) lupus erythematosus.

Autoimmune Disease—A disease in which the body inexplicably produces antibodies against its own tissue.

Biopsy—Removal and examination of tissue or bone from a living body for diagnostic purposes.

"Butterfly Rash"—A rash over the bridge of the nose and under the eyes typical of lupus erythematosus.

Collagen Disease—Collective term for a disorder of the connective tissue of the body; collagen disease may affect any part of the body.

Connective Tissue—Tissue that binds together and supports the various structures of the body.

Corticosteroids—Drugs used in the treatment of collagen disorders.

Diffuse—Generalized.

Discoid (Cutaneous) Lupus Erythematosus—Inflammatory tissue disorder which is limited to the skin and does not involve the internal organs.

Disseminated—Spread of disease process over large areas of the body.

Disseminated Lupus Erythematosus—Collagen disorder characterized by inflammatory tissue damage.

Endogenous—Originating in the body—as in endogenous obesity.

Erythema—Redness of the skin produced by congestion of the capillaries.

Exogenous—Originating outside of the body or entering the body from the outside—as in exogenous obesity.

Hansen's Disease (Leprosy)—Chronic infectious disease producing lesions of skin, mucous membranes and pheripheral nervous system.

Immunosuppressive Drugs—Drugs which chemically suppress the body's natural tendency to protect itself from foreign substances.

LE Prep—A blood test for lupus erythematosus.

Leprosarium—An institution for the treatment of Hansen's Disease (Leprosy).

Lesion—An injury, damage, or abnormal change in a portion of tissue.

Miliary Tuberculosis—Tubercular infection spread through the blood stream to multiple organs of the body.

Mucous Membranes—A thin, moist layer of tissues which line those body cavities which have an external opening on the body (e.g.—nose, mouth, bronchial tubes, etc.)

Mycobacterium Leprae—Bacteria causing Hansen's Disease (Leprosy).

Obesity—Excess accumulation of fat in the body beyond the limits of physical and skeletal requirements.

Periarteritis Nodosa (Polyarteritis)—A collagen disease characterized by inflammation of small and medium arteries causing functional impairment to tissues supplied by the affected blood vessels.

Sclerodactylia—A condition marked by thickening and hardening of the skin of the fingers.

Scleroderma—Collagen disorder characterized by hardening and shrinking of connective tissue.

Sclerosis—Hardening of a tissue or organ; often seen in diseases of connective tissue.

Tubercle Bacilli—Bacteria causing pulmonary and miliary tuberculosis.

Visceral—Pertaining to the larger internal organs of the body.

Visceral Manifestations—Changes in the structure or function of a major internal body organ.

Glossary 26

General Terms for Child Listings

Adult Listings— not applicable

Child Listings— 110.08, 110.09

Anencephaly—A congenital defect in which the bones of the skull and the brain tissue are either absent or poorly developed.

GLOSSARY OF MEDICAL TERMS

Antibody—A productive or defensive material produced by the body in response to the introduction of a foreign substance into the tissues.

Catastrophic Congenital Abnormalities—Birth defects which are so severe that the infant will not survive for more than a short period of time.

Cerebellum—The part of the brain which coordinates muscular movement.

Cerebrum—The main part of the brain situated in the upper part of the skull. It consists of two equal parts known as hemispheres. Regulates voluntary and conscious activities.

Chromosome—The part of a cell which carries hereditary material (genes).

Congenital—Present or existing at the time of birth.

Congenital Anomaly—A malformation present at birth.

Cranium (The Skull)—Bony sphere of the skull. The part which contains the brain.

Cri du Chat Syndrome—A birth defect with a complex of physical and mental abnormalities that result from a defect in the chromosomes.

Cyclopia—A birth defect in which the two eye sockets are fused into one eye.

Dysgammaglobulinemia—A disease in which there is an abnormality in the structure of the gamma globulin.

Dysplasia—Abnormal growth or development of a tissue or organ.

Gamma Globulin—A part of the blood plasms containing antibodies which help protect the body against bacteria and viruses.

Hypogammaglobulinemia—A disease in which there is an abnormally low level of gamma globulin in the blood.

Lymphocyte—A type of white blood cell which is produced by lymph tissue. These cells help protect the body against infection.

Tay-Sachs Disease—A hereditary condition which causes progressive mental and physical deterioration.

Thymic Dysplastic Syndromes—Disorders resulting from abnormal function of the thymus gland.

Trisomy——An abnormal condition in which the individual has an extra chromosome.

NEUROLOGICAL

Glossary

General Terms

Adult Listings— 11.02, 11.03, 11.04, 11.05, 11.06, 11.07, 11.09, 11.10, 11.11, 11.12, 11.13, 11.14, 11.15, 11.16, 11.17, 11.18, 11.19

Child Listings— 111.02, 111.03, 111.05, 111.06, 111.07, 111.08, 111.09

Aphasia—Defect or loss of the power of expression by speech, writing, or signs, or of comprehending spoken or written language (sensory aphasia, motor aphasia). Aphasias are due to organic brain disorder.

Ataxia—Loss of muscular coordination; and irregularity of muscular action. *Cerebellar ataxia*—Muscular incoordination, usually unilateral, associated with infection, tumor, or trauma of the cerebellum, resulting in marked loss of muscle tone and coordination on the affected side, with assumption of a characteristic posture. *Friedreich's ataxia*—An inherited disease, with sclerosis of the dorsal and lateral columns of the spinal cord, attended by ataxia, speech impairment, lateral curvature of the spine, with peculiar swaying and irregular movement and paralysis, especially of the muscles of the lower extremities. *Sensory ataxia*—Ataxia due to loss of joint position sensation, resulting in poorly judged movements, the incoordination becoming more pronounced when the eyes are closed.

Athetoid Movement—See Athetosis.

Athetosis—A derangement marked by involuntary continuous slow, sinuous, writhing movements, especially severe in the hands.

Atrophy—A decrease in size or wasting away of a body part or tissue.

Aura—A subjective sensation or muscular action which precedes and marks the beginning of an epileptic seizure, such as a peculiar odor or taste, or sensation of dizziness.

Autonomic Nervous System—The section of the nervous system which regulates the internal organs; consists primarily of ganglia connecting with the brain stem and with the spinal cord and may be divided into the sympathetic and parasympathetic systems.

Axon—The part of a neuron or nerve cell that conducts impulses away from the nerve cell.

Brain Syndrome—Complex of symptoms resulting from impairments of brain tissue function. *Acute*—Those symptoms occurring in the acute state. *Chronic*—Residual.

Bradykinesia—Abnormal slowness of movement; sluggishness of mental and physical responses.

Broadbased Gait—See Gait.

Bulbar Signs—Symptoms of degeneration of the motor neuron pathways of the medulla (brain stem) reflected by hoarseness; difficulties in speaking (progressing from slightly indistinct to total loss). Difficulty in swallowing and facial weakness are later manifestations. There is no sensory disturbance.

Cataplexy—Sudden paralysis resulting in loss of muscle tone and collapse of the whole body.

Central Nervous System—The part of the nervous system consisting of the brain and spinal cord.

Cerebellar Signs—Symptoms of degeneration of motor neuron pathways and motor areas of the cerebrum, such as ataxia, double vision or inability to control range of movement in muscular action.

Cerebellum—That part of the brain concerned in coordination of movements, located beneath the cerebrum.

Cerebrum—The main upper portion of the brain concerned with, among other functions, memory, reasoning, emotions, and will.

Cerebral Palsy—Disease of the central nervous system with onset before birth or in early life. Common symptoms are spastic weakness of extremities, disturbed speech and/or vision and mental retardation.

Choreiform Movements—Ceaseless occurrence of a wide variety of rapid jerky movements which appear to be well-coordinated but are performed involuntarily.

Clonus—A series of rapid alternating contractions and relaxations of a muscle or of a group of muscles.

Coma—Complete unconsciousness.

Convulsion—A violent, uncontrolled muscle spasm or a series of them, sometimes repeated at rapid intervals. Some convulsions are accompanied by unconsciousness.

Dendrite—That which comprises most of the receptive surface of a neuron.

Diplegia—Paralysis of similar parts on each side of the body, such as both arms.

Diplopia—A condition in which single objects are seen double.

Dysarthria—Imperfect articulation in speech.

Dysphagia—Painful and difficult swallowing.

Dysrhythmia—Disturbance of rhythm.

Effector—A nerve end organ which serves to distribute impulses which activate muscle contraction and gland secretion.

Epilepsy—Brain disorder accompanied by periodic convulsions.

Episodic—Recurring separate exacerbations of a disorder following periods of remission.

Exacerbation—A sudden recurrence or intensification of the symptoms of a disorder.

Gait—Manner or style of walking.

Ganglion—A mass of nerve tissue transmitting nerve impulses. Located outside of central nervous system.

Grand Mal Seizure—See Major Motor Seizure.

Hematoma—A swelling containing effused blood. Intracerebral hematomas are common in severe head injuries. If there is blockage of blood vessels to nervous tissue neurological damage may occur such as hemiplegia or mental changes.

Hemiplegia—Paralysis of one lateral half of the body.

Intention Tremor—A tremor which is not apparent at rest but which develops on attempting voluntary motion.

Involuntary Movement—As opposed to a voluntary movement this occurs independent of conscious intent.

Lesion—A change in tissue structure due to injury or disease. Ulcers, tumors, abscesses, etc. may all be referred to as lesions.

Major Motor Seizure—A sudden convulsion as seen in grand mal epilepsy, characterized by loss of consciousness and general convulsive movements of most or all of the body. Frequently preceded by an aura.

Medulla (M. Oblongata)—That portion of the brain stem located between the pons and the beginning of the spinal cord; it contains ascending and descending neural tracts, and important collections of nerve cells which deal with such vital functions as respiration, circulation, and special senses.

Minor Motor Seizure Disorder—Slight epileptic attacks consisting of brief impairment of or loss of consciousness, or localized motor or sensory symptoms, as in petit mal epilepsy and psychomotor epilepsy

Monoplegia—Paralysis of a single extremity or muscle group.

Motor Aphasia—Expressive aphasia; aphasia in which there is impairment of the ability to speak (and write) due to a lesion of the cortical center. The patient understands written and spoken words and knows what he wants to say but cannot utter the words.

Motor Deficit—A deficiency of, or an interference with, impulse transmission along a motor pathway, resulting in diminished contraction of a voluntary muscle; reflected by muscle weakness and reflex changes. Measurable through electromyography.

Motor Disorganization—Inability to properly control the extremities due to disruption of nerve pathways. Usual manifestations are interference in locomotion or control of hands and arms.

Motor Function—Effecting or producing movement through the innervated contraction of voluntary skeletal muscles.

Multiple Sclerosis—A chronic central nervous system disease. Some manifestations are visual and speech disturbances, partial paralysis of extremities and emotional problems. General course of disease is characterized by frequent remissions and recurring exacerbations.

Myelopathy—Functional disturbance and/or pathological changes in the spinal cord.

Neuron—Any of the impulse conducting cells of the nervous system; also called nerve cell.

Palsy—Paralysis.

Paralysis—Loss or impairment of motor function in a part, due to lesion of the neural or muscular mechanism.

Parasthesia—Abnormal sensation as burning, prickling, pain, etc.

Parkinsons Syndrome—Slowly progressive central nervous system disorder with diffuse effects such as muscular rigidity, involuntary tremors and slowed incoordinated voluntary motions. Occurs in middle aged and elderly.

Paraplegia—Paralysis of the legs and lower part of the body.

Paresis—Slight or incomplete paralysis.

Pathologic—Due to disease.

Pathology—That branch of medicine which deals with the origin, nature and course of diseases; also, the conditions and processes of a disease.

Peripheral Neuropathy—Functional disturbance and/or pathological changes in nervous system, exclusive of the brain and spinal cord. Cf., Encephalopathy and myelopathy.

Petit Mal Seizure—See Minor Motor Seizure Disorder.

Posterior Column Signs—Pathological abnormalities of sensation or perception of movement associated with damage to the posterior sensory nerve tracts of the spinal cord and of the posterior nerve roots. These include sensations of severe pain and other associated sensory phenomena such as parethesia, numbness, coldness, warmth and tingling. Ataxia may develop due to loss of fiber in the posterior column and roots. Sphincter control of bladder and rectum may be affected and trophic disturbances such as charcot joint and perforating ulcer may later evolve. Symptoms usually involve lower extremities but may involve the arms and hands if the lesion is high on the spinal column.

Postictal Manifestations—Residuals which often follow major motor seizure activity; e.g., heavy sleep, drowsiness, vomiting, muscular soreness, confusion, depression of spirits. There are no postictal residuals following minor motor seizure attacks.

Proprioceptive Disturbance—Impairment of the effective transmission of or of the perception of impulses arising in proprioceptors. Proprioceptors are the sensory nerve terminals which give information concerning the movement and position of the body; they occur chiefly in the muscles, tendons and in the labyrinth.

Prosthesis—An artificial substitute for a missing body part, such as an arm, leg, eye, or tooth, used for functional or cosmetic reasons, or both.

Psychomotor Seizures—Type of seizure disorder characterized by automatic movements repeated over and over again or staring spells, dizziness or sudden changes in temperment expressed by fear or rage.

Quadriplegia—Paralysis of all four extremities.

Receptor—Ending of an afferent sensory nerve which receives impulses.

Reflex—An involuntary muscular or glandular response resulting from the stimulation of receptor; e.g., knee jerk on tapping patellar tendon; secretion of saliva on olfactory, visual, or gustatory stimulus of food.

Remission—A diminution or abatement of the symptoms of a disease; also the period during which such diminution is present.

Rigidity—Stiffness or inflexibility, chiefly that which is abnormal or pathological.

Seizure—A sudden attack of a condition such as a convulsion in epilepsy.

Sensory Aphasia (Receptive A.)—Inability to understand written, spoken or tactile speech symbols due to disease of the auditory and visual work centers of the brain, as in word blindness.

Sequela (AE)—Any lesion or affection following or caused by an attack of disease.

Sleep Record (EEG)—EEG tracing recorded while the patient is asleep.

Spastic—Increased muscle action of nerve origin characterized by spasms, i.e., sudden, involuntary contractions of a muscle or group of muscles.

Station—The position assumed in standing, the manner of standing.

Sympathectomy—The cutting of a portion of the sympathetic nerve pathways.

Synapse—The gap between one nerve cell and another over which the impulses travel.

Tremor—An involuntary trembling or quivering.

MENTAL DISORDERS

Glossary 28

Definitions

Adult Listings— 12.02, 12.03, 12.04, 12.05

Child Listings— 112.02, 112.03, 112.04, 112.05

Abberation—Marked deviation from the usual.

Abreaction—Expression of or release of pent-up emotions.

Acting-out—Manifesting conflicts through overt behavior rather than controlling them through suppression or other defenses. A common characteristic of "antisocial personalities."

Acute Brain Disorder (Syndrome)—Temporary, reversible, diffuse impairment of brain tissue function; orientation and intellectual functions impaired; transient delusions and hallucinations common. Acute syndromes include those associated with intracranial or systemic infection, alcohol, drug or poison intoxication, brain trauma, circulatory disturbance, convulsive disorder, metabolic disturbance, intracranial neoplasm, as well as those of undetermined origin.

Acute Situational Reaction—Superficial maladjustment to newly experienced life situations which are especially difficult or trying.

Adequacy—Feeling of ability to cope with one's problems.

Adjustment—The effectiveness of the individual's efforts to meet personal needs and adapt to environment.

Affect—Any experience of emotion or feeling.

Agitation—Abnormally disturbed, profoundly troubled, accompanied by marked restlessness and psychomotor excitement.

Alzheimer's Disease—A presenile dementia second to cerebral arteriosclerosis and resolving into psychosis.

Ambivalence—Coexisting, contradictory emotional attitudes toward the same person; e.g., love and hate.

Antisocial Personality—Diagnostic classification which includes individuals who chronically engage in behaviors which are legally and/or morally unacceptable; e.g., murder, robbery, theft, drug peddling, sexual assault, prostitution.

Anxiety—A state of emotional tension characterized by apprehension and fearfulness.

Anxiety Reaction (Anxiety Neurosis, Anxiety Hysteria)—A functional nonpsychotic disorder characterized by persisting abnormal apprehension and fear, often punctuated by acute attacks of intensified anxiety.

Apathy—Marked diminution or absence of feeling and emotion (affect) in situations which usually elecits such reactions.

Aphonia—Loss of or marked impairment of the ability to speak resulting from organic or emotional cause.

Asthenic Reaction (More Current Term for Neurasthenia)—A functional nonpsychotic disorder characterized by feelings of listlessness, lack of enthusiasm and mental and physical fatigue.

Ataxia—Muscular incoordination, particularly in the legs and arms. (See Locomotor ataxia.)

Athetosis—Recurring, involuntary, tentaclelike movements of the hands and feet, usually associated with brain pathology.

Atrophy—A wasting away or shrinking of a functional body part.

Attitude—Mental predisposition or "set" associated with referential patterns, established by training or experience.

Autistic Thinking—Imaginary gratification of desires through fantasy, as contrasted with realistic attempts to gratify them. Self-centered thinking.

Autochthonous Idea—Idea which appears independent of the individual's train of thought and which is usually regarded as foreign and thrust upon him.

Autonomic Nervous System—The section of the nervous system which regulates the internal organs; consists primarily of ganglia connected to the brain stem and spinal cord and made up of *two* separate parallel systems: *parasympathetic*, which excites function and *sympathetic* which suppresses function.

Behavior—The manner in which an organism reacts to stimulation or stress.

Bender Visual—Motor Gestalt Test—A projective visual motor test which assesses personality conflicts, ego function and structure, and organic brain damage. The patient has to reproduce geometric figures.

Bizarre Behavior—Odd or eccentric behavior; reactions which are strikingly unsuitable to the situation or inconsistent with the stimulus.

MENTAL DISORDERS

Blocking—Involuntary inhibition of recall, ideation, or communication (including sudden stoppage of speech).

Catatonia (Schizophrenia, Catatonic Type)—Characterized by alternation between stupor and excitement.

Character and Behavior Disorder—Characterized by developmental defects of a pathological type, rather than disorganization or decompensation resulting from stress.

Chronic Brain Disorders (Syndrome)—Resulting from relatively permanent, diffuse impairment of brain tissue function. Neurotic, psychotic, or personality disorder reactions may be superimposed. Chronic brain syndromes include those associated with congenital but nonhereditary defect, central nervous system infection, toxic agent poisoning as with lead and carbon monoxide, permanent residuals of brain trauma, cerebral arteriosclerosis, and other circulatory disturbances, convulsive disorder, senile brain degeneration metabolic disturbance, intracranial neoplasm, as well as those resulting from undetermined causes.

Circumstantial Speech—The introduction of many irrelevant details into conversation.

Compensation—Ego defense mechanism whereby an undesirable trait is covered up through the exaggeration of a desirable trait.

Compulsion—The irresistible tendency to perform some act, even though the individual realizes it to be irrational and may not want to do it.

Confabulation—The filling in of memory gaps with false and often irrelevant details.

Conversion Reaction (Hysteria)—The ego defensive process by which emotional conflicts are "converted" into physical-illness symptoms; a psychoneurotic reaction.

Cyclothymic Personality—Characterized by frequently alternating moods of elation and sadness seemingly initiated by internal rather than external stimuli.

Decompensation—Ego or personality disorganization under excessive stress.

Defense Mechanism—Behaviors, beliefs and attitudes maintained to protect, compensate for, or conceal an established self-image. The individual may be unaware of either the behavior or the motivating stimulus.

Delusion—A logical but false belief which is maintained despite experience and evidence to the contrary.

Denial of Reality—A defense mechanism where the individual protects against unpleasant aspects of reality by refusing to perceive them.

Depersonalization—Loss of sense of personal identity; often with the feeling of being someone else.

Depressive Affect—Emotional state characterized by dejection, gloomy preoccupations, feelings of worthlessness and guilt, and usually, apprehension.

Dereistic Thinking—Thought (including fantasy) in which the individual ignores reality and logical organization. Often applied to "irrational" schizophrenic fantasies.

Deterioration of Personal Habits—A breaking up of the individual's customary patterns of dress, personal hygiene, grooming.

Deviant Logic—Thought sequences often found in psychotic behavior in which conclusions are drawn which are not compatible with the premise or the evidence.

Disorientation—The loss of appreciation of time, place, or personal identity.

Dissociation—Separation or "isolation" of mental processes in such a way that they become split off from the main personality or lose their normal thought/effect relationship.

Dissociative Reaction—Neurotic reaction characterized by amnesia, fugue, somnambulism, or multiple personality.

Down's Syndrome—Mongolism, a condition characterized by a small, flattened skull, short, flat-bridged nose and other physical abnormalities with moderate to severe mental retardation, and associated with a chromosomal abnormality.

Ego Structure—The self and environmental attitudes, typical defense mechanisms, and other aspects of the ego or self, as the integrating core of the personality.

Egocentric—Self-centered, inclined to view everything in relation to self interest.

Elation—Intense feeling of well-being. Elevated or exalted mood.

Emotional Immaturity—Failure to develop normal degrees of adult independence and self-reliance, with consequent use of immature adjustive patterns and inability to maintain equilibrium under stresses which most people can meet satisfactorily.

Ethical Attitudes (Dimensions)—Attitudes which relate to the individual's concepts of "right" and "wrong," variously referred to as "conscience" or "superego."

Euphoria—Exaggerated feeling of well-being and contentment.

Fabrication—Relating imaginary events as if they were true, without intent to deceive; confabulation.

Festinating Gait—Incoordinated, hurried, uncertain walk, as in paralysis agitans.

Fixation—Unreasonable or exaggerated attachment to some person, or arrestment of emotional development on a childhood or adolescent level.

Flight of Ideas—Rapid succession of ideas, without logical association or continuity.

Free Floating Anxiety—Anxiety not referable to any specifically identifiable cause or situation.

Frustration—The thwarting of a need or desire.

Fugue—A type of dissociative reaction in which the individual leaves his current life situation and establishes a somewhat different mode of life in another locale. Although amnesic for past life, other performance and memory functions are unimpaired and the individual appears "normal" to those around him.

Functional Disorder—Having no demonstrable organic basis or etiology; psychogenic.

Guilt—Unpleasant feeling of sinfulness arising from behavior or desires contrary to one's ethical principles. Involves both self-devaluation and apprehension, growing out of fear of punishment.

Hallucination—A sensory perception distortion in which the individual hears, sees, smells, tastes, or feels the presence of a stimulus which is not actually present. (See "Illusion").

Hostility—The overt verbal or physical demonstration of antagonistic, threatening, or aggressive behavior directed at persons or things which are interpreted as a source of frustration or threat.

Hysteria—Older term used to include conversion and dissociative reactions. It involves the simulation of symptoms of organic illness in the absence of any related organic pathology.

Illusion—A false or distorted interpretation of a real sensory impression.

Impulse—Drive or tendency toward action.

Inaccessible—Patient so disturbed or withdrawn that it is impossible to elicit attention, cooperation, or conversation

Inadequate Personality—Individuals who are neither physically nor mentally grossly deficient, but who manifest inadequate responses to intellectual, emotional, social, and physical demands; e.g., ineptness, poor judgment, lack of adaptability.

Inappropriate Affect—Experiencing emotions or feelings which are inconsistent with or out of proportion to the situation.

Incompetent—Legal designation of individual as incapable of managing personal affairs with ordinary prudence because of mental illness or deficiency.

Inferiority Complex—Strong feelings of inadequacy and insecurity which color the individual's entire adjustive efforts.

Inhibition—Conscious restraint of impulse or desire.

Insane—Legal term for mental disorder, implying lack of responsibility for one's acts and the inability to manage one's affairs.

Insight—Clinically, the individual's understanding of his illness or of the motivations underlying his behavior; in general psychology, the sudden grasp of understanding of meaningful relationships in a situation.

Intellectualization—An ego defense mechanism by which the individual achieves some measure of insulation from emotional hurt by cutting off or distorting the emotional charge which normally accompanies hurtful situations.

Intropunitive—Tendency to direct hostility aroused by a stress situation toward self; blaming self for difficulties.

Introvert—Personality type characterized by direction of interests toward oneself and one's inner world of expression.

Involutional Melancholia (Psychosis)—A psychotic-depressive reaction characterized by depression, agitation and apprehension.

Isolation—An ego defense mechanism through which contradictory attitudes, as well as the feelings which normally accompany particular attitudes, are kept apart, thus preventing conflict or hurt.

Jacksonian Epilepsy—Muscle spasm usually restricted to a small group of muscles or to one-half of the body, although occasionally the entire body may become affected. Consciousness is usually retained.

Judgment—The process of choosing from among alternatives that behavior response which will best satisfy the desires of the individual and is most consistent with his self-interest.

Korsakoff's Psychosis—Psychosis usually associated with chronic alcoholism and characterized by disorientation, gross memory defects confabulation, and multiple areas of nerve inflammation (polyneuritis).

Labile—Unstable, particularly with regard to the experiencing of emotion or feeling.

Locomotor Ataxia—Muscular incoordination, usually resulting from syphilitic infection damage to the spinal cord pathways.

Maladjustment—Lack of harmony with self or environment; inadequate or poor adjustment.

Malinger—To fake illness or impairment symptoms consciously.

Mania—Suffix denoting a compulsive or morbid preoccupation with some impulse or activity; e.g., compulsive stealing is called klepto*mania*.

Manic-Depressive Reaction—A group of psychotic reactions characterized by prolonged periods of excitement and overactivity (manic), or by periods of depression and underactivity (depressive), or by alternation or mixture of the two.

Mannerism—A recurring, stereotyped gesture, posture, or movement.

Meninges—The membranes which envelope the brain and spinal cord.

Mental Deficiency (Primary)—Mental retardation since birth, without known organic brain pathology; usually considered to be of hereditary origin.

Mental Retardation (Secondary)—Mental retardation resulting from organic damage to the brain, whether congenital or acquired.

Minnesota Multiphasic Personality Inventory (MMPI)—A nonprojective test typically using questionnaire, inventory, and rating-scale techniques of measurement, covering topics from physical condition to moral and social attitudes. The individual indicates the attitudes or conditions presented which most apply to him. The number of items that the individual checks in the same way as a schizophrenic, manic, or other type of patient would answer them, indicates that individual's tendency in that diagnostic direction.

Mongolism—A condition characterized by a small, anteroposteriorly flattened skull, short, flat-bridged nose, almond shaped eyes, short fingers and toes, and widened spaces between the first and second digits of the hands and feet, with moderate to severe mental retardation, and associated with a chromosomal abnormality.

Morbid—Unhealthy, typical or reflective of an abnormal condition or of illnesss (pathological).

Myxedema—A condition associated with hypothyroidism characterized by edema and mental dullness. The edema is nonpitting and the facial characteristics are strikingly distinctive, with swollen lips and a thickened nose.

Need—A biological or physical condition for which gratification is necessary to maintain homeostasis or for self-actualization.

Negativism—A form of aggressive withdrawal, involving the refusal to cooperate or obey commands, or doing the exact opposite of what has been requested.

Nervous Breakdown—Popular term denoting neurotic or psychotic levels of personality decompensation, particularly those characterized by anxiety, irritability, restlessness, depression and inability to concentrate.

Neurosis (Psychoneurosis)—A nonpsychotic functional personality disorder in which there is no gross personality disorganization and for which the patient ordinarily does not require hospitalization.

Obsession—A persistent idea or thought which the individual recognizes as irrational but which persists despite the efforts to ignore or forget it.

Organic Psychosis—A psychosis associated with brain pathology resulting from neural destruction, due to infection, neoplasm, circulation disturbance, toxins and other lesion producing conditions.

Orientation—Individual's ability to comprehend the environment relative to time, place, and person.

Panic—Severe personality disorganization involving intense anxiety and, usually, paralyzed immobility or blind flight.

Paranoia—A type of disorder characterized by slowly developing, logical, well-systemized delusions of persecution and/or grandeur.

Paranoid Personality—Category applied to individuals showing abortive paranoid reaction characterized by the use of projection as a defense mechanism, suspiciousness, envy, jealousy, and stubbornness.

Paranoid State—A type of disorder characterized by transient, delusions of persecution and/or grandeur, which are not well systemized.

Passive-Aggressive Reaction—Immaturity reaction in which aggressiveness is expressed by such passive measures as pouting, stubbornness, procrastination, inefficiency, and passive destruction.

Passive-Dependency Reaction—Immaturity reaction characterized by helplessness, indecisiveness, and a tendency to cling to others for protection and support.

Pathological Personality Types—Individuals who are neither neurotic nor psychotic, but maintain a borderline adjustment which might be likened to an abortive stage in the development of a more severe mental disorder.

Pathology—The field of science dealing with the abnormal changes in structure and function which occur in physical and mental disorders.

Perserveration—The persistent continuation of a line of thought or activity once it is under way. Clinically, inappropriate repetition.

Phantasy—See Fantasy.

Phobia—A persistent fear of some object or situation which presents no actual danger to the individual, or is magnified out of all proportion to its actual seriousness. In phobic reactions, this fear is intense and interferes with the individual's daily activities.

Phobic Ruminations—Preoccupation with a phobia which is disruptive to other thought patterns.

Pick's Disease—A form of presenile dementia.

Predisposition—A tendency toward the development of a particular disorder if placed under excessive stress.

Prodromal—Symptoms preceding and heralding the appearance of a disease.

Prognosis—Prediction as to the probable course and outcome of a disorder.

Projection—An ego defense mechanism in which the individual places the blame for his difficulties upon others or attributes to them his own unethical desires or impulses.

Psychomotor Disturbances—Nonorganic disturbance of muscle function, including hypo- and hyperactivity, mannerisms and stereotypes, such as: impulsive hitting, screaming; chanting; sterotyped use of words, phrases or movement; stilted talking and walking; imitative repetition of words or motion; grimacing; spitting; whirling; tense and strained behavior; restless overactivity; jerking; and smearing with feces or other untidiness.

Psychopathic Personality—Older term used to refer to a variety of immature and pathological personality types, now included under the general heading of "character and behavior disorders."

Psychopathology—The field of science dealing with the causes and the nature of abnormal behavior.

Psychophysiological Disorder (Psychosomatic Disorder)—Physical disorders which have no organic basis and which arise from emotional disturbances to mental disorders. The brain can produce physical disorders in three general ways. (1) by transmission of signals through the autonomic nervous system, (2) by transmission of signals to the muscles through motor-neuron pathways, and (3) by control of the endocrine glands.

Psychosis—Severe personality disorder involving loss of contact with reality and usually characterized by delusions and/or hallucinations. Hospitalization is usually required.

Psychosomatic Disorder—See Psychophysiological Disorder.

Rationalization—An ego defense mechanism in which the individual thinks up "good" reasons to justify what he has done, is doing, or intends to do.

Reaction Formation—An ego defense mechanism in which dangerous desires or impulses are prevented from entering consciousness or from being carried out in action by the fostering of opposed types of behavior and attitudes.

Reactive Depression (Neurotic Depressive Reaction)—A mild depression in the face of loss or environmental setbacks.

Reality—The world as it actually is (relatively speaking) as distinct from the world of daydreams and fantasy.

Reality Testing—The individual's behavior aimed at testing or exploring the nature of his social and physical environment; often used more specifically to refer to the testing of the limits of permissiveness of his social environment.

Regression—An ego defense mechanism in which there is a retreat to the use of less mature responses in the attempt to cope with stress and to maintain ego integrity.

Remission—Marked improvement or recovery appearing in the course of mental illness; may not be permanent.

Resistance—The tendency to maintain symptoms and to resist treatment or the uncovering of repressed material.

Retrograde Amnesia—Loss of memory for events preceding an accident or injury.

Ritualistic Behavior—The compulsive performance of an act or pattern of behaviors which assume a ceremonial character and which function for the individual as a defense mechanism. Ordinarily, interference with or prevention of the completion of the ceremony will precipitate an escalation of personality disintegration.

Romberg Sign—Tendency to sway when eyes are closed and the feet are placed close together; diagnostic sign in locomotor ataxia.

Rorschach Test—A projective test of general personality structure, consisting of often symmetrical ink blots to which the individual responds in succession. With each ink blot presentation, the individual is asked to report what he sees in the blot. The test is revealing of the manners in which the individual deals with inner drives, introvert or extrovert tendencies, as well as pathological emotional disorders.

Rumination (Phobic, Obsessive, Etc.)—Prolonged preoccupation with or consideration of an idea, a situation, an object; etc.; recurrent thoughts which are pondered or repeatedly considered.

Schizoid Personality—An abortive schizophrenic reaction characterized by unsociability, seclusiveness, serious-mindedness, and often eccentricity.

Schizophrenia—A major psychotic disorder characterized by emotional blunting and distortion, disturbances in thought processes, and a withdrawal from reality. Classification includes six subtypes: Latent, Simple, Hebephrenic, Catatonic, Paranoid, Unclassified.

Self (Ego)—The integrating core of the personality which mediates between needs and reality.

Shock Reaction—Transient personality decompensation in the face of acute stress.

Somatic—Pertaining to the body; organic as distinct from psychological.

Somatization Reaction (See Psychophysiological Reaction)—Psychoneurotic reaction in which the stress-aroused anxiety is channeled through the visceral organs, resulting in various physical symptoms.

Spasm—An intense, usually painful contraction of a muscle or group of muscles.

Spasticity—Marked hypertonicity of muscles, causing stiffness, awkwardness, and motor incoordination.

Stanford-Binet—An intelligence test which assesses intellectual functioning ages 2 to adult. Patient performs problem solving and developmental tasks.

Stress Tolerance (Frustration Tolerance)—The nature, degree and duration of stress which an individual can withstand without undergoing serious personality disintegration.

Superego—Conscience; ethical or moral dimensions (attitudes) of personality.

Suppression—The conscious forcing of desires or thoughts out of awareness; conscious inhibition of desires or impulses.

Syndrome—A group or pattern of symptoms which occur together in a disorder and represent the typical picture of the disorder.

Tension—The condition arising out of the mobilization of psychobiological resources to meet a threat; physically, involves an increase in muscle tonus and other emergency changes; psychologically, is characterized by feeling of strain, uneasiness and anxiety.

Thematic Apperception Test (TAT)—A projective test of imagination and creativity, in which the individual is shown a picture and requested to construct the events leading to the situation depicted and to offer conclusions as to what will occur; elicits information about the individual's conflicts, attitudes, levels of aspiration and related aspects of personality.

Threat—Danger to need gratification.

Tic—Intermittent twitching or jerking, usually of facial muscles.

Tonic—Pertaining to muscle tension or contraction; muscle tone.

Toxic Psychosis—Psychosis resulting from or associated with a poisonous agent.

Tremor—A continuous, involuntary muscular trembling or spasm, limited to a small area.

Unconscious—Lack of awareness; that portion of the mind which is the storehouse of repressed or forgotten memories and desires which are not directly accessable to consciousness.

Vasomotor—Pertaining to the muscles within the walls of the blood vessels.

Vegetative—Withdrawn or deteriorated to the point that the individual leads an isolated and passive life, with activity limited to little more than eating, sleeping, and existing.

Vertigo—Dizziness, loss of equilibrium.

Wechsler Adult Intelligence Scale (WAIS)—An intellectual capacity test, encompassing both verbal and performance materials, measuring: general information, general comprehension, and detail differentiation.

Wechsler Intelligence Scale for Children (WISC)—An intelligence test which assesses intellectual functioning, thought processes, and ego functioning of children, ages 5 to 15 years.

Withdrawal—Intellectual, emotional or physical retreat.

Worry—Persistent, undue concern about past behavior or about anticipated dangers in the present or future.

Glossary 29

List of Functional Psychotic Disorders

Adult Listings— 12.03, 12.04

Child Listings— 112.03, 112.04

I. Mood Disorders

A. *Involutional Melancholia*—This disorder occurs during the period of life when the endocrine and reproductive glands begin to decrease in functional activity; called the involutional period. This reaction occurs for women during the 40's and for men during the 50's.

It is characterized by worry, anxiety, agitation, and severe insomnia. The individual also exhibits thought disturbances typified by preoccupation with physical complaints, guilt, sin, and despair. Sometimes they also show feelings of persecution (paranoid ideation).

B. *Manic-Depressive.* This disorder is characterized by severe mood swings from the manic phase of elation, irritability and increased motor activity to the depressed phase of sadness, guilt, loss of interest and a slowed motor activity. More commonly seen is a recurrence of the depressive episodes (unipolar) rather than the two phases of elation then depression (bipolar). Tendency to remission and recurrence.

C. *Psychotic Depressive Reaction.* The symptoms seen here are similar to those found in the depressive stage of the manic-depressive except that there is an absence of history of repeated depression or of mood cycles. In addition, with psychotic depressive reactions, precipitating factors in the environment are present, such as a divorce or death of a loved one.

II. Schizophrenia—Major Types

A. *Acute Schizophrenia*—A condition characterized by the acute onset of schizophrenia, involving a wide variety of symptoms, including confusion of thinking, emotional turmoil, and ideas of reference. (The person incorrectly believes that he is the object of special attention by those around him.) In some cases the patient recovers within weeks, but sometimes his disorganization becomes progressive. In time it may take on the characteristics of other types of schizophrenia.

B. *Catatonic Schizophrenia*—In this type the symptoms are phases of stupor or of excitement. Catatonia more frequently has a somewhat acute onset and appears to be precipitated by an emotionally disturbing experience. The prognosis for recovery is more favorable than in other types.

C. *Childhood Schizophrenia*—Schizophrenia appearing before puberty. It is frequently manifested by autism and withdrawn behavior; failure to develop an identity separate from the mother's and gross immaturity.

D. *Chronic Undifferentiated Schizophrenia*—A condition manifested by disturbance of thought, affect, and behavior that is mixed and cannot be classified into one of the other types of schizophrenia.

E. *Hebephrenic Schizophrenia*—A disorder characterized by silliness, giggling, inappropriate smiling and laughing. Delusions and hallucinations are usually bizarre and not well organized.

F. *Latent Schizophrenia*—A condition manifested by clear symptoms of schizophrenia but no history of psychotic schizophrenic episodes. Sometimes referred to as "borderline schizophrenia".

G. *Paranoid Schizophrenia*—A schizophrenic disorder characterized by delusions, hallucinations, and suspiciousness. Delusions of persecution are the most prominent and are often presented in a grandiose framework.

H. *Schizophrenia, Schizo-Affective Type*—Mixture of schizophrenic symptoms and pronounced elation or depression.

I. *Schizophrenia, Simple Type*—Slow and insidious and progressive reduction of external attachments and interests and apathy and indifference leading to impoverishment of interpersonal relations, mental deterioration. In general, is less dramatically psychotic than catatonic, hebephrenic or paranoid types.

List of Functional Non-Psychotic Disorders

I. *Psychophysiological Disorders*—The individual's anxiety is expressed as physical complaints referred to an organ of the involuntary nervous system, e.g., heart, stomach. These disorders are usually named and classified according to the organ system involved.

II. Psychoneurotic Disorders

Anxiety Neurosis—Anxious overconcern occasionally progressing to panic and frequently associated with functional symptoms.

Depersonalization Neurosis—Feeling of unreality and estrangement from self, body, and environment.

Depressive Neurosis—Excessive depression due to an internal conflict or to some event such as loss of a cherished person or object.

Hypochondriacal Neurosis—Preoccupation with body and presumed diseases. Fears are not delusional.

Hysterical Neurosis—Psychogenic loss or disturbance of function in response to emotional stress. There are two subtypes to this condition.

Conversion Type—Disturbance of functioning of the special senses (seeing, hearing) or of the voluntary nervous system, e.g., blindness, pain, paralysis. The individual may be indifferent to the systems because they provide sympathy or relieve him of unpleasant responsibilities (secondary gain).

Dissociative Type—This is manifested by changes in the individual's consciousness or identity (self-awareness). The dissociation may defer or postpone experiencing some emotional impact. Symptoms include amnesia, fugue, multiple personality.

Neurasthenic Neurosis (Neurasthenia)—A neurosis characterized by complaints of chronic weakness, easy fatigability, and exhaustion.

Obsessive Compulsive Neurosis—A neurosis characterized by persistent intrusion of unwanted thoughts or actions. The thoughts may range from a single word to a train of thought; the actions may be simple or involve complex rituals.

Phobic Neurosis—An intense fear of an object or situation that the individual *consciously* recognizes as harmless.

III. Personality Disorders

Anti-social Personality—Characterized by a basic lack of socialization and behavior patterns in which the individual has repeated conflicts with society. This individual is rude, crude, and irresponsible.

Asthenic Personality—Oversensitiveness to physical and emotional stress with low energy level, fatigability, lack of enthusiasm, and marked incapacity for enjoyment.

Cyclothymic Personality (Affective Personality)—Changes in personality alternating periods of depression and elation—not attributable to external sources.

Explosive Personality—Outbursts of rage or of verbal or physical aggressiveness. The outbursts are strikingly different from the individual's usual behavior.

Hysterical Personality (Histrionic Personality)—Characterized by excitability, emotional instability, and self-dramatization that is attention-seeking. The individual may not be aware of its purpose.

Inadequate Personality—Ineffectual response to emotional, social, intellectual, and physical demands—a general ineptness with poor judgment.

Obsessive Compulsive Personality (Anancastic Personality)—Excessive concern with conformity and adherence to standards of conscience.

Paranoid Personality—A tendency to blame others and ascribe evil motives to them with unwarranted suspicion, jealousy, and envy.

Passive-Aggressive Personality—Aggressive behavior manifested in a passive manner, e.g., stubbornness, pouting. The aggressiveness often comes about because the individual is not satisfied with a relationship, the object of which he is overly dependent upon.

Schizoid Personality—Characterized by shyness, seclusiveness, oversensitiveness, and avoidance of close relationships. The individual reacts to disturbing experiences with detachment.

NEOPLASTIC DISEASES—MALIGNANT

Glossary 30

Specific Terms and Definitions

Adult Listings— 11.05, 13.02, 13.03, 13.04, 13.05, 13.06, 13.07, 13.08, 13.09, 13.10, 13.11, 13.12, 13.13, 13.14, 13.15, 13.16, 13.17, 13.18, 13.19, 13.20, 13.21, 13.22, 13.23, 13.24, 13.25, 13.26, 13.27, 13.28

Child Listings— 113.02, 113.03, 113.05

Adamantinoma; Adamantoma—Older terms for the more current ameloblastoma (See Ameloblastoma).

Adenocarcinoma—A malignant neoplasm which has microscopic cellular arrangement and structure similar to that normally seen in glandular tissue.

Adjacent Lesions—Neighboring or bordering lesions which are not physically connected (see satellite lesions).

Adrenal Glands—Paired ductless glands, adjacent to the upper lobe of the kidneys, which produce adrenalin. Commonly called suprarenal glands.

Alveolar Cell Carcinoma—A malignant neoplasm which microscopically resembles pulmonary alveolar cells (pneumonocytes), the characteristic cell of the lung.

Ameloblastoma (Adamantinoma)—A true epithelial tissue neoplasm with microscopic characteristics of the type of cells which produce tooth enamel (ameloblasts). In the neoplastic state, the ameloblasts do not fully develop into enamel.

Anal Canal—The terminal position of the alimentary canal, extending from the rectum to the anus.

Anaplasia—A condition in neoplasms in which the constitutent cells lose normal differentiation, organization and specific function.

Angiosarcoma—A neoplasm made up of tissue resembling embryonic connective tissue, with close packed cells embedded in fibrillar or homogeneous substance and containing an extensive network of finc blood vessels; often highly malignant.

Anorexia—Lack of appetite for food.

GLOSSARY OF MEDICAL TERMS

Antrum (of Highmore; sinus Maxillaris)—One of the paired paranasal sinuses (air cavities) located on either side and communicating with (opening into) the middle meatus of the nasal cavity on the same side.

Ascites—The escape and accumulation of body fluids into the abdominal pleural space (ref. pleural effusion).

Astrocytoma—A tumor primarily of the brain composed of star-shaped cells known as astrocytes.

Basal Cell Carcinoma—An epithelial neoplasm microscopically similar to cells of the deep layers of the skin. Seldom metastisizes but has potential for local invasion and extension.

Benign—Mild, not malignant, not recurrent.

Biopsy—The removal and examination (usually microscopic) of tissue or other material from the body for purposes of diagnosis. Ordinarily identified by the method used to obtain the sample; e.g., needle, punch, aspirated, surface or scrape, and necessary to the identification of malignancy.

Cachexia—The weak and emaciated condition observed in cases of advanced malignancy and in other severe diseases.

Carcinoid Tumor—A yellow, circumscribed tumor occurring in the small intestine, appendix or stomach.

Carcinogen—An agent capable of producing a tumor.

Carcinoma—A malignant neoplasm made up of epithelial cells, tending to invade or infiltrate adjacent tissues and structures, and to metastasize.

Carcinomatosis—A condition in which cancer has invaded, infiltrated and metastasized widely throughout the body.

Cellular Sarcoma Retroperitoneal—Cancerous condition of the cells behind the peritoneum.

Cervix (Uteri)—The lower portion (neck) of the uterus opening into the vagina.

Chemotherapy—A form of cancer treatment which uses toxic drugs to destroy malignant cells.

Choriocarcinoma (Chorio-Epithelioma)—An epithelial neoplasm formed by malignant proliferation of the chorionic villi and including chorioadenoma, choriosarcoma and syncytioma.

Corpus—The main body of the uterus.

Cystectomy—Surgical removal of the entire urinary bladder.

Definitive Irradiation—Treatment by X–ray or other radioactive substance, such as radium, radioactive gold, cobalt. Definition of the specific type of irradiation is determined by the nature of the neoplasm. Not all neoplasms are sensitive or responsive to irradiation therapy.

Differentiation (Cellular)—The development or acquisition of specific physical and functional cellular characteristics.

Diffuse Involvement—Widely distributed throughout the body and involving multiple organs.

Distant Metastasis (Neoplastic)—Metastasis which establishes itself beyond the lymph drainage channels common to the organ, structure, or region in which the primary malignancy is located. As applied in the SSDI Program, distant metastasis further qualified as being situated beyond the structures ordinarily removed in the radical en bloc surgical procedure (ref. Radical en bloc Resection).

Eosinophilic Granuloma—A benign condition characterized by lesions confined to bone which is one of a triad of conditions known as histiocytosis.

Ependymoblastoma—A malignant tumor arising from primitive cells from the lining membrane of the ventricles of the brain and spinal cord.

Epidermis—The outermost, nonvascular layer of the skin, made up of five strata or layers: corneum (horny), lucidum, granulosum, spinosum and basal (basal cell layer).

Epidermoid Carcinoma—A malignant neoplasm of epidermoid tissue which tends to differentiate in the same manner as the cells of the epidermis do.

Embryonal—Pertaining to an embryo, also to marked immaturity.

Embryonal Carcinoma (Seminoma, Dysgerminoma)—A neoplasm of the testes arising from the cells which produce spermatozoa, but which have not differentiated into cells of either male or female type. Usually highly malignant.

Esophagus—The muscular tube which conveys food from the throat to the stomach.

Ethmoid Sinus—An air cavity in one of the bones (ethmoid) forming the walls and septum of the nasal cavity.

Ewing's Tumor—A malignant neoplasm of the bone, always arising in medullary tissue. Occurs more often in cylindrical bones, with pain, fever and leucocytosis as prominent symptoms.

Excise—To cut out, remove by surgery.

Exenteration—Surgical removal of interior organs.

Extension (Neoplastic)—The spread of a neoplasm through one tissue or part to or into another adjacent to it (ref. invasion).

Extralymphatic Organs—Any structure or tissue outside of the lymphatic collecting and filtering structures.

Fallopian Tubes—The paired tubes which conduct the ova from the ovaries into the uterus; attached to and communicating with the upper portion of the uterus immediately below the fundus.

Ganglioneuroma—A benign neoplasm consisting mostly of nerve fibers and mature nerve cells. When malignant, nerve cells are immature or embryonic and the neoplasm is termed nephroblastoma.

Giant Follicular Lymphoblastoma—A malignant neoplasm of lymph tissue microscopically characterized by multiple, proliferative, immature multinucleated follicle-like cells.

Glioma—A term which includes all primary intrinsic neoplasms of the brain and spinal cord.

Glioblastoma Multiforme—An astrocytoma of Grade III and IV which is rapidly growing and usually confined to the cerebral hemisphere.

Grading—A method used in determining the aggressiveness of a tumor based on a determination of the number of dividing cancer cells.

Gross Tissue Examination—Nonmicroscopic examination of tissue, describing physical characteristic of size, shape, texture, color, etc.

Hilar—Pertaining to hilus.

Hilus (Thoracic)—Point at which nerves, blood vessels and other organs enter the thoracic mediastinum.

Histiocytosis X—A generic term embracing eosinophilic granuloma, Letterer-Siwe disease and Hand-Schuller-Christian disease.

Histiocytosis—A condition marked by the appearance of histiocytes (macrophages) in the blood.

Histogenesis—The formation and development of tissue.

Histopathology—The study of the minute structure, composition, and function of tissues and the changes and disruptions which cause or are caused by disease.

Hodgkin's Disease—A disease of the lymph nodes and nonnodal lymphatic tissue; reticulum cells are more specifically affected than lymphocytes. Lymph node enlargement is usually initially painless but involvement becomes more generalized with secondary effects from pressure, obstruction or infiltration.

Hormone-Dependent Tumors—Neoplasms which develop and grow only in the presence of specific hormones. Suppression or removal of the hormone causes neoplastic regression.

Hormone—Chemical substances secreted by endocrine glands which act to increase or decrease activities of other body cells. Some hormone producing organs are: the thyroid and parathyroid glands, the ovaries and testes and the pancreas and adrenals.

Hysterectomy—Surgical removal of the uterus. In subtotal hysterectomy, the cervix is left in place.

Ileocecal Valve—Folds of tissue at the junction of the small and large intestine which serve to prevent flow back into the small intestine.

Immunotherapy—Using nonspecific stimulus or vaccine made from inactivated tumor cells; is under investigation by many surgeons and has been effective in some patients with melanoma and soft tissue sarcoma.

Incomplete Excision—The partial surgical removal of a tissue, structure or organ.

Inoperable Condition—A condition for which surgery offers no therapeutic benefit, in terms either of improvement or of alteration of a terminal course (See nonresectable).

In Situ—In the natural or normal place; confined to the site of origin without invasion of neighboring tissues.

Intracranial—Situated within the bones of the head, excluding the bones of the face and mandible.

Invasion—In terms of neoplasms, the direct growth or extension of a neoplasm from one organ or structure into another adjacent organ or structure.

Irradiation—(See Definitive Irradiation).

Islet Cell Carcinoma—Neoplasm of the pancreas evolving from the irregular clusters of cells (islets of Langerhans), which secrete insulin.

Isotope Sensitive Metastasis—Neoplastic metastasis which may be brought under control by the use of radioactive substances, such as metastatic thyoma, which can respond to radioactive iodine.

Lesion—Any pathological discontinuity or loss of function of a tissue, structure or organ.

Leukemia—A progressive, malignant disease of the bloodforming organs, characterized by a marked increase in the number of formed and immature white blood cells (leukocytes), together with enlargement and proliferation of the lymphoid tissue of the spleen, lymphatic glands and bone marrow.

Local (or Regional) Recurrence—The development of another neoplastic growth of the same type as that previously removed or resolved, and located within the same organ, structure of lymph drainage channels common to the organ, structure or region as the previous neoplasm.

Lymph Nodes—Nodulelike organs appearing at intervals along the lymphatic vessels, which filter cellular debris, bacteria and other large particles. Reticuloendothelial cells lining the nodes digest "foreign" particles, breaking them down into components not harmful to the body.

Lymphaden—A lymph node.

Lymphangiography—Visualization of lymphatic vessels following the injection of a contrast medium which can be observed by X-ray.

Lymphatic Organs (System)—The accessory circulatory system serving to return fluids, cellular wastes and unused nutrients from the tissue spaces back to the blood circulatory system; consists of lymphatic capillaries, lymphatic vessels and lymph nodes.

Lymphoepithelioma—A poorly differentiated, transitional cell carcinoma arising from the epithelia tissue lining the nose and throat.

Lymphoma—Any tumor made up of lymphoid tissue.

Lymphoreticular Tumors—Proliferation of reticuloendothelial cells of the lymph glands.

Lymphosarcoma—A type of malignant neoplasm arising in lymphatic tissue.

Malignant Melanoma—A malignant neoplasm usually developing from a pigmented nevus and consisting of masses of black cells which have a marked tendency to metastasize.

Mandible—The horseshoe shaped bone forming the lower jaw.

Malignant Neoplasm—Any new or abnormal growth of tissue, which is progressive and uncontrolled. Such neoplasms have the properties of invading and infiltrating adjacent structures or organs and of metastasis.

Maxilla—One of the paired bones forming the upper jaw and lodging the teeth. The mandibles also assist in forming the palate, the nasal cavity and the orbit.

Mediastinum—That body area bounded on the sides by the lungs, in the front by the sterum, behind by the spinal column, above by the thoracic inlet and below by the diaphragm, containing the heart and its large vessels, the trachea, the esophagus, the thymus, lymph nodes and vessels and other structures and tissues.

Medulloblastoma—Tumor of the cerebellum of the brain.

Melanoma—A neoplasm made up of cells pigmented with melanin. These black tumors have a strong tendency to become malignant (See malignant melanoma).

Meningeal—Pertaining to the three membranes which envelope the brain and spinal cord; the duramater, the piamater and the arachnoid.

Mesothelioma—A neoplasm arising from the squamous-celled layer of the epithelium which covers the surface of all true serous membrances (peritonem, pericardium, pleura).

Metastasis—In neoplasms, the separation and transfer of cells of a primary or initial neoplasm to a part of the body different from the original location. This "seeding" is accomplished by the migration of neoplastic cells through lymph or blood vessels, or through body spaces or such natural passages as the digestive tract or pulmonary air passages.

Midline—An artificial reference point represented by a plane which would divide the body into a right and left half.

Mycosis Fungoides—A rare, chronic, malignant neoplasm of the skin arising from the reticular cells of the lymph nodes. In later stages there is involvement of the lymph nodes and the viscera, with the development of painful ulcerating tumors. The disease is usually terminal after a number of years.

Myelogenous Leukemia—Leukemia of bone marrow origin.

Myeloma—A neoplasm composed of cells of a type ordinarily found in the bone marrow.

Multiple Myeloma (Diffuse Myeloma)—A malignant neoplasm of plasma cells, usually arising in the bone marrow, manifested by bone pain, pathological fractures and skeletal destruction, and by the presence of anomalous circulating immunoglobulins, protein urea and anemia.

Neoplasm—Literally "new formation." A new or abnormal development of cells or tissue.

Nephroblastoma—A malignant solid tumor of the kidney.

Neuroblastoma—A highly malignant solid tumor arising from sympathetic nerve tissue, frequently affecting the adrenal glands.

Nonresectable Neoplasm—A neoplastic growth which cannot be surgically removed because of its location or because critical structures or organs are involved.

Oat Cell Carcinoma—An anaplastic, small-celled carcinoma, usually bronchogenic and highly malignant.

Omentum—A fold of peritoneum extending from the stomach to adjacent organs in the abdominal cavity.

Orbit—The bony cavity which contains the eyeball.

Osteogenic Sarcoma—A primary malignant bone tumor composed of immature connective tissue, bone cells and/or cartilage cells.

Ovaries—Paired female gonads, located to each side of the uterus.

Palliative—Affording relief but not altering the course of the disorder.

Pancreas—A large elongated gland situated behind the stomach, extending from the spleen to the duodenum.

Pathology—The branch of medicine which addresses the essential nature of disease, especially the structural and functional changes in tissues and organs which cause or are caused by disease. Also used in reference to those changes.

Pelvic Exenteration, Total—The surgical removal en mass of the bladder, lower ureters, vagina, uterus, adnexa, the pelvic and lower sigmoid colon, the pelvic lymph nodes and the entire pelvic peritoneum.

Peritoneum—The serous membrane covering the abdominal and pelvic walls and all of the organs. In the male, it forms a closed sack; in the female it is continuous with the mucous membrane of the uterine tubes.

Pharynx—The area behind the tongue, below the nasal passages and above the epiglottis; commonly called the throat.

Pleura—The serous membrane which forms a continuous lining of the lungs and thoracic cavity. There are two pleura, right and left.

Pleural Effusion—The escape and accumulation of body fluids into a thoracic pleural space (Ref. ascites).

Posttherapeutic—The period following the completion of treatment.

Primary Malignancy—The principle malignancy; the first to develop.

Prostate—A gland which, in the male, surrounds the neck of the bladder and the urethra.

Pyriform Sinus (Pyriform Recess)—An elongated depression in the wall of the lower pharynx between the base of the tongue and the epiglottis.

Radical En Bloc Resection—Surgical procedure intended to remove in one mass all of the regional tissue, muscle and lymphatics which could potentially harbor metastatic or infiltrated malignancy.

Rathke's Pouch (Craniobuccal P.; Neurobuccal P.)—In the embryo, a sacklike extension of the mouth cavity from which the anterior lobe of the pituitary gland develops. In adults, residuals of this pouch persist as colloid filled cysts and clefts adjacent to the pituitary gland.

Recurrence—Recurrence of a neoplasm after it has been resected.

Resection—Excision of a considerable portion of an organ or structure.

Reticulum Cell Sarcoma (Malignant Lymphoma)—A malignant neoplasm arising from the networklike cells of lymphatic tissue. Cellular development may be undifferentiated or may be histocytic, depending upon the degree of maturity of the malignant cells.

Retinoblastoma—A malignant solid tumor of the eye.

Rhabdomyosarcoma—A malignant solid tumor involving smooth muscles.

Salivary Glands—The glands opening into the mouth which produce saliva.

Sarcoma—A neoplasm composed of close packed cells embedded in fibrous or homogeneous substance, resembling embryonic connective tissue; often highly malignant.

Satellite Lesions (Neoplastic)—Small neoplasms located adjacent to the primary neoplasm; in melanomas. Their appearance indicates that the neoplasm has begun to metastasize.

Seminoma—A neoplasm arising from the tissue which produces sperm cells, but which has not undergone differentiation into male or female cells. This type of tumor and, in its malignant form, its metastases, are very responsive to irradiation therapy.

Soft Parts—All tissues of the body, excluding bones, teeth, and nails.

Sphenoid Sinus—An air space in the bony structure which forms the base of the cranium, located above the soft palate and behind the nasal passages.

Squamous Cell Carcinoma—A malignant neoplasm arising from tissues which form the external and internal covering of the surfaces of the body appearing as thin platelike cells.

Staging—A method of determining the extent of spread of a tumor which aids in the decision about the treatment regimen.

Suprarenal Glands—See Adrenal Glands.

Synchronous—In neoplasm, the simultaneous appearance of identical neoplastic growths in different locations.

Temporal Fossa—The bony depressions on each side of the skull immediately behind the eyes; commonly called the temples.

Teratocarcinoma—A malignant neoplasm having cellular characteristics of a teratoma.

Teratoma—A true neoplasm consisting of a number of different cells, none of which is native to the area in which it occurs; most common to the ovaries and testes.

Teratoma, Embryonic—A malignant teratoma noted for early metastasis; and resistance to irradiation; may form growths resembling rudimentary fetuses.

Testes (Testicles)—The paired, egg shaped male reproductive organs which produce sperm cells and male hormones, principally testosterone.

Thymoma—A neoplasm arising from the epithelial or lymphoid elements of the thymus.

Thymus—A ductless, glandlike organ located in the anterior mediastinal cavity below the thyroid.

Thyroid—A shield shaped gland which is attached to and envelops the front and sides of the trachea below the larynx, which produces principally the hormone thyroxin.

Tumor—A mass of new tissue which persists, growing independent of its surrounding structures and which has no physiological use.

Undifferentiated Carcinoma—A malignant epithelial neoplasm, the cells of which have not developed into discretely identifiable cellular or tissue structure.

Unresectable—Surgical excision cannot be accomplished because of the site or extent of involvement.

Ureter—The paired fibromuscular tubes which conduct urine from the kidneys to the bladder.

Urethra—The fibromuscular tube which conducts urine from the bladder to the exterior of the body.

Urinary Diversion—The surgical grafting of the ureters through the abdominal wall (ureterocutaneostomy) or into the colon (ureterocolostomy).

Glossary 31

General Terms

Adult Listings— as above

Child Listings— as above

NEOPLASTIC DISEASES—MALIGNANT

Anaplasia—A condition in neoplasms in which the constituent cells lose normal differentiation, organization, and specific function.

Benign—A tumor which remains localized at the site of origin.

Carcinoma—A malignant tumor originating in the skin or mucous membrane.

Distant Metastasis—Neoplastic spread beyond the regional lymph nodes.

Histogenesis—Maturation of cells from an embryonic stage to fully developed cells whose function is determined by the organ or part of the body that the cells are associated with.

Lymphoma—A primary tumor of a lymph node.

Malignant—A tumor which spreads beyond the site of origin.

Metastasis—Spread of neoplastic cells from the site of origin to other parts of the body with continued growth and reproduction.

Neoplasm—New, abnormal growth of tissue resulting in nonfunctional mass of tissue.

Primary site—Original site of development of neoplasm.

Regional Lymph Nodes—Lymph nodes which serve as a filtering system for a particular region.

Regional Metastasis—Neoplastic spread into the regional lymph nodes.

Sarcoma—A tumor derived from connective tissue or bone.

Tumor—A neoplasm.

Undifferentiated—Neoplastic cells which are so disorganized that the type of tissue histogensis cannot be determined.

Well Differentiated—Neoplastic cells which maintain enough histogenic characteristics to be able to identify which organ or part of the body is involved.

Glossary 32

Some General Tests and Procedures

Adult Listings— as above

Child Listings— as above

Angiogram—An X-ray diagnostic procedure which fills the blood vessels with X-ray opaque materials in order to photograph abnormalities.

Cachexia—The weak and emaciated condition observed in cases of advanced malignancy and in other severe diseases.

Chordotomy—Surgical division of the anterolateral tracts of the spinal cord for relief of severe pain.

Cytotoxin—A toxin or antibody which has a specific toxic or poisonous action upon cells of special organs. Cytotoxins are named according to the special variety of cell for which they are specific, as, nephrotoxin.

Gross Examination—A review of a surgical specimen which describes the size, shape, weight, color, texture and variations from portion to portion of the specimen and the area from which the portion was taken.

Hodgkin's Disease—A malignant disease of the lymph nodes and non-nodal lymph tissue.

Lymphedema—Swelling of the subcutaneous tissues due to presence of excessive lymph fluid.

Microscopic Examination—Review of microscopic slide prepared from a section of a surgical specimen to study the morphological appearance or arrangement of abnormal cells and the surrounding zone of normal tissue in order to establish a histologic diagnosis as to type of tumor and in some cases the degree of malignant transformation.

Neutropenia—A decrease in the number of a particular type of leukocyte in the blood.

Rhizotomy—Surgical interruption of the roots of the spinal nerves within the spinal cord.

Scan—A diagnostic X-ray technique which gives a two-dimensional representation of the gamma rays emitted by a radioisotope revealing its particular concentration in a specific body tissue.

Skeletal Survey—A diagnostic X-ray technique to review the entire skeleton to determine the presence of a malignancy.

Tomograph—An X-ray machine which makes a roentgenogram of a layer of tissue at any depth.

Tomogram—A roentgenogram of a selected layer of the body made by tomography.

Glossary 33

Specific Neoplasms

Adult Listings— 13.03, 13.05, 13.06, 13.11, 13.13, 13.14, 13.20

Child Listings— 113.03

Adamantinoma—Older term for the current ameloblastoma which is a true epithelial tissue neoplasm with microscopic characteristics of the type of cells which produce tooth enamel.

Angiosarcoma—A neoplasm made up of tissue resembling embryonic connective tissue with close packed cells embedded in fibrillar or homogenous substance and containing an extensive network of fine blood vessels often highly malignant.

Antrum—One of the paired paranasal sinuses located on either side and communicating with the middle meatus of the nasal cavity on the same side.

Choriocarcinoma—An epithelial neoplasm formed by malignant proliferation of the chorionic villi and including chorioadenoma, choriosarcoma, and syncytioma.

Epidermoid Carcinoma—A malignant neoplasm of epidermoid tissue which tends to differentiate in the same manner as the cells of the epidermis do.

Ethmoid Sinus—An air cavity in one of the bones (ethmoid) forming the walls and septum of the nasal cavity.

Islet Cell—An irregular cluster of cells within the pancreas (islets of Langerhans) which secrete insulin.

Melanoma—A neoplasm made up of cells pigmented with melanin. These black tumors have a strong tendency to become malignant.

Mesothelioma—A neoplasm arising from the squamous-celled layer of the epithelium which covers all true serous membranes (peritoneum, pericardium, pleura).

Mycosis Fungoides—A rare, chronic malignant neoplasm of the skin arising from the reticular cells of the lymph nodes. In later stages, there is involvement of the lymph nodes and viscera, with the development of painful ulcerating tumors. The disease usually terminates in death after a number of years.

Oat Cell Carcinoma—An anaplastic small-celled carcinoma, usually bronchogenic and highly malignant.

Pyriform Sinus—An elongated depression in the wall of the lower pharynx between the base of the tongue and the epiglottis.

Rathke's Pouch—In the embryo, a saclike extension of the mouth cavity from which the anterior lobe of the pituitary gland develops. In adults, residuals of the pouch persist as colloid-filled cysts and clefts adjacent to the pituitary gland.

Satellite Lesions—Small neoplasms located adjacent to the primary neoplasm in melanomas. Their appearance indicates that the neoplasm has begun to metastasize.

Sphenoid Sinus—An air space in the bony structure which forms the base of the cranium, located above the soft palate and behind the nasal passages.

Glossary 34

Specific Neoplasms

Adult Listings— 11.05, 13.10, 13.11, 13.24B

Child Listings— 111.05, 113.03, 113.04, 113.05

Cerebellar Astrocytoma—A tumor of the brain composed of star-shaped cells known as astrocytes.

Embryonal Tumor—A neoplasm of the testes arising from germinal or reproductive cells but which remain in a poorly differentiated state.

Immune System—An intercellular system within the body which acts to attack and destroy foreign substances.

Neuroblastoma—A highly malignant solid tumor arising from sympathetic nerve tissue, frequently affecting the adrenal glands.

Occult Malignancy—A tumor which is concealed from observation and discovery.

Osteogenic Sarcoma—A primary malignant bone tumor composed of immature connective tissue, bone cells and/or cartilage cells.

Retinoblastoma—A malignant solid tumor of the eye.

Rhabdomyosarcoma—A malignant solid tumor involving skeletal or striated muscle. Often occurs in the area of the head, neck and orbit of the eye.

Wilm's Tumor—A malignant solid tumor of the kidney.

GENERAL INDEX

Indices

GENERAL INDEX

INDEX TO ADULT LISTINGS

INDEX TO ADULT LISTINGS

INDEX TO ADULT LISTINGS

*

INDEX TO CHILDHOOD LISTINGS

INDEX TO CHILDHOOD LISTINGS

INDEX TO CHILDHOOD LISTINGS

INDEX TO CHILDHOOD LISTINGS

INDEX TO CHILDHOOD LISTINGS

INDEX TO CHILDHOOD LISTINGS

†